Course	Retail Marketing
Course Number	**4250**

University of Missouri
Trulaske College of Business

Marketing Department

http://create.mheducation.com

ISBN-10: 1308485239   ISBN-13: 9781308485232

Contents

Credits

Chapters

Introduction to the World of Retailing

When I was a senior in college, I had a revelation about my life and the direction in which I was heading. I immediately called my parents and told them that I was not going to marry my high school boyfriend and go to law school like I had planned. I was going to follow my passion and head to New York to work in the fashion industry. Needless to say, they were surprised.

When I received my first VP position at 26, my parents finally stopped asking when I was going to go back and get my law degree. I've been on an exciting ride since then and have been fortunate enough to hold esteemed positions at great companies, such as the SVP of menswear at Warnaco, VP of new business development at Polo Ralph Lauren, president of Chaps Ralph Lauren, president and CEO of Polo Jeans Company, and global VP for Nike.

Then I received a call one day to meet with Barry Diller, who was the president of IAC, which owned HSN at the time. After discussing my ideas with him, I discovered I had the ability to make an impact on this company and transform HSN into a lifestyle network. My friends and colleagues were shocked when I announced that I was leaving Nike and going to HSN. They had gone through eight CEOs in 10 years and I would be the first female CEO of the company. I saw the company's potential and was excited to take on the challenge.

Over the last seven years, we have transformed HSN into a dynamic, interactive, multichannel retailer that offers a curated assortment of exclusive products from top lifestyle brands and engages our customers wherever and whenever they would like to shop. As a matter fact, close to 40 percent of our HSN sales come from our digital platform—online, tablet, mobile, and social media.

Our product offering is diverse with 79,000 unique products, 70 percent of which are proprietary to HSN. Widely respected celebrities and designers, such as Queen Latifah, India Hicks, Badgley Mischka, Naeem Khan, and New York fashion icon, Iris Apfel, have come to our campus in St. Petersburg, Florida to promote their products. We also have had Mary J. Blige, Mariah Carey, and P. Diddy sell their fragrances on HSN.

CHAPTER 1

LEARNING OBJECTIVES

LO1 Identify retailing activities.

LO2 Realize the importance of retailing in the U.S. and world economies.

LO3 Analyze the changing retail industry.

LO4 Recognize the opportunities in retailing for you.

LO5 Understand the strategic retail management decision process.

Our ability to entertain and inspire versus just selling a product is really how retail is evolving. We bring content, community, and commerce to life through our strategic partnerships with the entertainment community across film, music, and live events. We were Universal's partner for the launch of *Snow White and the Huntsman* and our 24-hour event featured 25 designers and brands that created over 220 unique products inspired by the film, including the launch of Oscar-winning costume designer Colleen Atwood's first consumer collection. Our HSN Live concert series provides our customers with a live music experience featuring some of the music industry's biggest stars. Lionel Richie held a concert at HSN's studios to kick off the release of *Tuskegee,* his first best-selling album in more than 25 years. The power of appearing on HSN is unparalleled.

When I met with Lady Gaga about potentially developing a line for HSN, she said, "You have the coolest job." Think of all the amazing things she has done in her career, and here she was telling me I had a cool job. And you know what? She's absolutely right.

Retailing is such a common part of our everyday lives that we often take it for granted. For most people, retailers simply are places to buy things. At a very young age, children know what stores have the things they want, and they expect to find the products they want when they visit a store or website. Sometimes consumers talk to a sales associate when they visit a store, and other times the only retail employees they interact with are cashiers collecting the money for purchases. Some college students work part-time or over the holidays for retailers and have a somewhat deeper insight into what retailers do. But these limited exposures to retailing are just the tip of the iceberg. Behind the stores, website, sales associates, and cashiers are an army of managers responsible for making sure that the products and services that people want are available when

EXHIBIT 1–1
Quiz on What You
Know about Retailing

1. Which of the following companies is *not* a retailer:
   (a) McDonald's
   (b) Holiday Inn
   (c) Macy's
   (d) eBay
   (e) All are retailers

2. What is the annual compensation (salary plus bonus) of a typical Walmart Supercenter 30-something store manager?
   (a) Under $49,999
   (b) $50,000 to $89,999
   (c) $90,000 to $149,999
   (d) over $150,000

3. Which of the following products/concepts was initiated or developed by retailer buyers?
   (a) tea bags
   (b) panty hose
   (c) Rudolph the Red-Nosed Reindeer
   (d) establishing Thanksgiving on the third Thursday of November
   (e) All of these products/concepts were developed/initiated by retailers.

4. What is the largest company in the world in terms of number of employees?
   (a) Walmart
   (b) General Electric
   (c) IBM
   (d) ExxonMobil
   (e) Mitsubishi

5. Which of the following retailers is owned by a company headquartered outside the United States?
   (a) Food Lion
   (b) Ben & Jerry's Ice Cream
   (c) 7-Eleven
   (d) A&P supermarkets
   (e) All of these are owned by foreign companies.

6. What country has the most efficient retail structure (lowest cost to move merchandise from a manufacturer's factory to a retail stores)?
   (a) Japan
   (b) United States
   (c) South Korea
   (d) France
   (e) Germany

7. What percentage of total retailer sales in the United States are made over the Internet?
   (a) 30 percent
   (b) 20 percent
   (c) 14 percent
   (d) 8 percent
   (e) 3 percent

8. What percent of the U.S. workforce is employed by retailers or firms selling products or providing services to retailers?
   (a) 10 percent
   (b) 17 percent
   (c) 25 percent
   (d) 43 percent
   (e) 62 percent

they want them, where they want them, and at a fair price. Take the quiz in Exhibit 1–1 to check out the accuracy of your views about the retail industry and career opportunities the industry offers. The answers are at the end of the chapter.

To illustrate what is below the tip of the iceberg, consider Macy's. Macy's stocks and sells more than 100,000 different sizes, colors, and brands of products. Managers at Macy's need to determine what subset of these 100,000 items they are going to offer from the millions of potential products Macy's could sell. Then managers negotiate with more than 3,000 suppliers the price they will pay the supplier for the products and the prices they will charge their customers. Managers decide which of the 100,000 products will be sold at each of Macy's 840 stores and how they will be displayed. Managers select, train, and motivate the 150,000 store employees to make sure the merchandise is attractively displayed and customers get the service they expect. And, perhaps most importantly, Macy's managers develop strategies to guide these decisions and provide a good return to its stock-holders while facing intense competition.[1]

Working in this highly competitive, rapidly changing retail environment is both challenging and exciting, and it offers significant financial rewards. This book describes the world of retailing and offers key principles for effectively managing retail businesses. Knowledge of retailing principles and practices will help you develop management skills for many business contexts. For example, retailers are the customers for most business-to-consumer (B-to-C) companies such as Procter & Gamble and Hewlett-Packard. Thus, brand managers in B-to-C companies need to have a thorough understanding of how retailers operate and make money so that they can encourage retailers to offer and promote their products. Financial and health care institutions use retail principles to develop their offerings; improve customer service; and provide convenient, easy access to their customers. Thus, any student interested in professional B-to-C selling, marketing management, or finance should find this book useful.

WHAT IS RETAILING?

Retailing is the set of business activities that adds value to products and services sold to consumers for their personal or family use. Often, people think of retailing only as the sale of products in stores, but retailing also involves the sale of services such as overnight lodging in a motel, a doctor's exam, a haircut, or a home-delivered pizza. Not all retailing is done in stores. Examples of nonstore retailing include ordering a T-shirt on your mobile phone app, buying cosmetics from an Avon salesperson, ordering hiking boots from an L.L. Bean catalog, and renting a Blu-Ray from a Redbox kiosk.

LO1
Identify retailing activities.

REFACT
The word *retail* is derived from the French word *retailer,* meaning to cut a piece off or break bulk.[2]

The Retailer's Role in a Supply Chain

A **retailer** is a business that sells products and/or services to consumers for their personal or family use. Retailers are a key component in a supply chain that links manufacturers to consumers. A **supply chain** is a set of firms that make and deliver goods and services to consumers. Exhibit 1–2 shows the retailer's position within a supply chain.

Retailers typically buy products from wholesalers and/or manufacturers and resell them to consumers. Why are retailers needed? Wouldn't it be easier and cheaper for consumers to cut out the middlemen, the wholesalers and retailers, and buy directly from manufacturers? The answer, generally, is no, because retailers add value and are more efficient at adding this value than manufacturers or wholesalers.

Retailers Create Value

The value-creating activities undertaken by retailers include (1) providing an assortment of products and services, (2) breaking bulk, (3) holding inventory, and (4) providing services.

EXHIBIT 1–2
Example of a Supply Chain

Retailers add value by providing an assortment of products that customers can buy at one location when they want them.

Providing Assortments Conventional supermarkets typically carry about 30,000 different items made by more than 500 companies. Offering an assortment enables their customers to choose from a wide selection of products, brands, sizes, and prices at one location. Manufacturers specialize in producing specific types of products. For example, Frito-Lay makes snacks, Yoplait makes yogurt, Skippy makes peanut butter, and Heinz makes ketchup. If each of these manufacturers had its own stores that sold only its own products, consumers would have to go to many different stores to buy the groceries needed to prepare a single meal.

Breaking Bulk To reduce transportation costs, manufacturers and wholesalers typically ship cases of frozen dinners or cartons of blouses to retailers. Retailers then offer the products in smaller quantities tailored to individual consumers' and households' consumption patterns—an activity called **breaking bulk**. Breaking bulk is important to both manufacturers and consumers. It allows manufacturers to efficiently make and ship merchandise in larger quantities at one time and enables consumers to purchase merchandise in smaller, more useful quantities.

Holding Inventory A major value-providing activity performed by retailers is **holding inventory** so that products will be available when consumers want them. Thus, consumers can keep a smaller inventory of products at home because they know local retailers will have the products available when they need more. This activity is particularly important to consumers with limited storage space, such as families living in small apartments.

Providing Services Retailers provide services that make it easier for customers to buy and use products. For example, retailers offer credit so that consumers can have a product now and pay for it later. They display products so that consumers can see and test them before buying. Some retailers employ salespeople in stores or maintain Web sites to answer questions and provide additional information about the products they sell.

Costs of Channel Activities

While the value-creating activities undertaken by channel members provide benefits to customers, they also increase the cost of products and services. Exhibit 1–3 illustrates the supply chain costs of getting a T-shirt from the manufacturer to the consumer. In this example, it costs the T-shirt manufacturer $10.00 to make and market the T-shirt. These costs include the design, raw materials, labor, production equipment, transportation to the wholesaler, and so on. The manufacturer sells the T-shirt to the wholesaler for $11.00 and makes $1.00 profit. The wholesaler incurs $2.00 to handle and store the T-shirt and transport it to the retailers. The wholesaler sells the T-shirt to the retailers for $14.00, making a $1.00 profit.

Channel Member			Profit as a Percentage of Sales
Manufacturer	Cost	$10.00	
	Profit	$1.00	9.10%
	Selling price to wholesaler	$11.00	
Wholesaler	Price paid to manufacturer	$11.00	
	Cost to add value	$2.00	
	Profit	$1.00	8.00%
	Selling price to retailer	$14.00	
Retailer	Price paid to distributor	$14.00	
	Cost to add value	$4.00	
	Profit	$1.95	
	Selling price to customer	$19.95	9.77%

EXHIBIT 1–3
Costs Incurred to Undertake Value-Added Activities in the Distribution Channel for a T-Shirt

The retailer then incurs costs to fold the shirt, put price tags on it, store it, employ sales associates, light and air condition the store, and so on. The retailer sells the shirt to a customer for $19.95, making a profit of $1.95.

Note that the costs in the supply chain, $8.95 ($19.95 − $11.00), are almost as much as the cost to make the product. These costs are justified by the considerable value added by the wholesaler and retailers to the product. By providing assortments, breaking bulk, holding inventory, and providing services, retailers increase the benefits that consumers receive from their products and services.

Consider a T-shirt in a shipping crate in an Iowa manufacturer's warehouse. The T-shirt will not satisfy the needs of a student who wants to have something to wear at the basketball game tonight. The student finds the T-shirt more valuable and will pay more for it if it is available from a nearby department store that also sells pants, belts, and other items complementing the T-shirt and provides sales associates who can help the student find what he likes. If retailers did not provide these benefits, wholesalers or manufacturers would have to provide them, and they would typically not be as efficient as retailers in providing these benefits.

Retailers Perform Wholesaling and Production Activities

Wholesalers buy and store merchandise in large quantities from manufacturers and then resell the merchandise (usually in smaller quantities) to retailers. When manufacturers like Apple and Nike sell directly to consumers, they are performing the production, wholesaling, and retail business activities. Some large retailers, like Costco and Home Depot, function as both retailers and wholesalers: They perform retailing activities when they sell to consumers, but they engage in wholesaling activities when they sell to other businesses, such as restaurants or building contractors.

In some supply chains, the manufacturing, wholesaling, and retailing activities are performed by independent firms, but most supply chains feature some vertical integration. **Vertical integration** means that a firm performs more than one set of activities in the channel, as occurs when a retailer engages in wholesaling activities by operating its own distribution centers to supply its stores. **Backward integration** arises when a retailer performs some wholesaling and manufacturing activities, such as operating warehouses or designing private-label merchandise. **Forward integration** occurs when a manufacturer undertakes retailing and wholesaling activities, such as Apple operating its own retail stores.

Most large retailers such as Safeway, Walmart, and Lowe's manage their own distribution centers and perform activities undertaken by wholesalers. They buy directly from manufacturers, have merchandise shipped to their warehouses, and then distribute the merchandise to their stores. Other retailers, such as J. Crew and Victoria's Secret, are even more vertically integrated. They design the merchandise they sell and then contract with manufacturers to produce it exclusively for them.

Apple is a vertically integrated company because it performs the manufacturing, distribution, and retailing activities in its supply chain.

Differences in Distribution Channels around the World

Some critical differences among the retailing and distribution systems in the United States, European Union, China, and India are summarized in Exhibit 1–4. As this exhibit suggests, the U.S. retail industry has the greatest retail density (retail stores per person) and concentration of large retail firms. Real estate in the United States is relatively inexpensive, and most consumers own automobiles. Thus, retailers often operate large stores in lightly populated areas. Many U.S. retailers have stores with more than 20,000 square feet. Due to their size, they have the scale economies to operate their own warehouses, eliminating the need for wholesalers. This combination of large stores and large firms in the United States results in a very efficient distribution system.

In contrast, the Indian distribution system is characterized by small stores operated by relatively small firms and a large independent wholesale industry. To make the daily deliveries to these small retailers efficiently, the merchandise often passes through several different wholesalers. In addition, the infrastructure to support modern retailing, especially the transportation and communication systems, is not as well developed in India as it is in more developed economies. These efficiency

EXHIBIT 1–4   Comparison of Retailing and Distribution across the World

	United States	Northern Europe	India	China
Concentration (percent of sales made by large retailers)	Highest	High	Lowest	Low
Retail density (square feet of retail space per person)	Highest	Modest	Lowest	Low
Average store size	Highest	Modest	Lowest	Modest
Role of wholesalers	Minimal	Modest	Extensive	Extensive
Infrastructure supporting efficient supply chain	Best	Good	Weakest	Weak
Restrictions on retail locations, store size, and ownership	Minimal	Extensive	Extensive	Modest

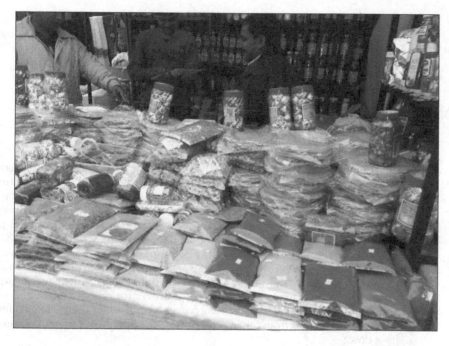

The retail industry in India is
dominated by small, local
retailers with few modern
national chains.

differences mean that a much larger percentage of the Indian labor force is employed in distribution and retailing than is the case in the United States, and the supply chain costs in India are higher.[3]

China's retail industry is highly fragmented like the retail industry in India. It is composed of many small and medium-sized firms. The number of national and even regional chains is limited. However, China's retail distribution system is going through a period of rapid development. This development is spurred by the government's shifting interest from focusing on exports and satisfying basic consumer needs that provide a higher quality of life. In China, the government removed most restrictions on direct foreign investments, and global retailers flocked to this huge and growing market. Now, Walmart operates 370 stores in China, and Carrefour, the second largest retailer in the world, operates 204. However, there is great disparity between the distribution system in the first-tier, eastern coastal cities—Beijing, Shanghai, and Guangdong—and the smaller western cities. The retail offering in the first-tier cities is very similar to the urban retail environment in U.S. cities such as New York and Chicago. In contrast, retailing in the smaller western cities is more similar to retailing in India.[4]

The European distribution system falls between the American and Indian systems on this continuum of efficiency and scale. In northern Europe, retailing is similar to that in the United States, with high concentration levels in some national markets. For example, 80 percent or more of sales in sectors such as food and home improvements are made by five or fewer firms. Southern European retailing is more fragmented across all sectors. For example, traditional farmers' market retailing remains important in some sectors, operating alongside large "big-box" formats.[5]

Social and political objectives have created some of these differences in distribution systems in countries. An important priority of the Indian and European economic policies is to reduce unemployment by protecting small businesses such as independent neighborhood retailers.[6] Some countries have passed laws prohibiting large stores, as well as strict zoning laws to preserve green spaces, protect town centers, and inhibit the development of large-scale retailing in the suburbs.

Finally, retail productivity is reduced when countries restrict the hours that stores can operate. For example, in France, many stores close at 7 p.m. on weeknights. Labor unions in France and elsewhere in Europe are opposed to U.S.-style 24/7 shopping because of the strains it could put on store employees.[7]

SOCIAL AND ECONOMIC SIGNIFICANCE OF RETAILING

Role in Developed Economies

LO2

Realize the importance of retailing in the U.S. and world economies.

Retail sales (excluding automobile and automotive parts sales) in 2011 were $4.3 trillion. More than 8 percent of the total U.S. gross domestic product comes from retailing, almost as much as the contribution of the entire U.S. manufacturing industry sector.[8] But this sales level underestimates the impact of retailing on the U.S. economy because it does not include the sales and employment of many firms providing consumer services such as entertainment, home repairs, and health care.

Consumer spending plays a critical role in the economies of the United States and other developed countries. When consumers spend more money buying goods and services from retailers, a country's economy flourishes. Merchandise flies off the shelves, and retailers place orders for replacement merchandise. Manufacturers hire more employees, place orders for raw materials, and make more products. However, if consumers feel uncertain about their financial future and decide to refrain from buying new refrigerators or blue jeans, the economy slows down.

The retail sector plays a key role in developed economies, not only because consumer demand is an indication of a vibrant financial system, but also because retailers are large employers. More than 14 million people were employed in retailing in 2012—approximately 11 percent of the U.S. workforce—and an additional 15 percent work for companies that either provide services to and/or sell products through retailers.[9]

Corporate Social Responsibility

In addition to providing the benefit to their customers outlined in the previous section and a fair return for their stockholders, most retailers engage in socially responsible activities. **Corporate social responsibility (CSR)** involves an organization voluntarily engaging in business practices that meet or exceed the ethical and legal expectations of its stakeholders—its employees, customers, community, and society in general.

Many retailers now go the extra mile to support their communities, environment, and social causes. Examples include reducing their use of energy, supporting local schools, and working with national organizations such as the American Red Cross and Habitat for Humanity. These corporate social responsibility activities promote a positive image to customers, build employee morale, and save money—a win–win scenario for both the companies and their stakeholders.[10]

For example, community philanthropy is the cornerstone of Target's CSR activities. Store managers have a budget for donations they can make to local events. Since 1946, Target has given 5 percent of its income to support local activities in the communities in which it has stores, such as company-sponsored youth leagues or a special exhibit at the local zoo. Target has been innovative in using social media to support its CSR program. Target's "Bullseye Gives" program asked its million Facebook fans to vote on how the company should allocate $3 million among 10 nonprofits.[11]

Many retailers are building LEED-certified stores. The Leadership in Energy and Environmental Design (LEED) certification is based on an assessment of the store's impact on human and environmental health, sustainable site development, water savings, energy efficiency, materials selection, and indoor environmental

REFACT

Shoppers in the United Kingdom are more likely to buy goods on the basis of environmental, animal welfare, or fair trade claims than their counterparts in continental Europe. About 41 percent of British consumers have bought ethically produced products, compared with 34 percent in Germany, 31 percent in France, and 12 percent in Spain.[12]

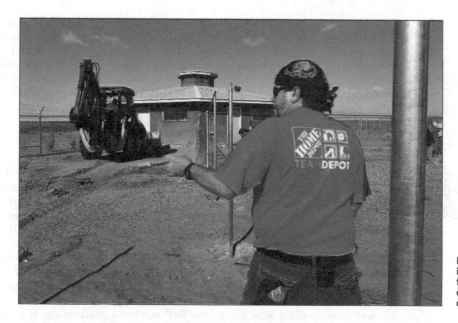

Home Depot employees' involvement with Habitat for Humanity helps the local community and builds company morale.

quality. Some features in a prototype LEED-certified McDonald's restaurant are its permeable pavement that cleans rainwater; a cistern buried behind the restaurant that collects rainwater, which is used to water the landscaping; a roof garden that insulates the restaurant; the use of less-toxic cleaners and of paints and resins that do not emit chemical odors; and the installation of low-flow toilets and urinals that use less water than standard low-flow toilets. Walmart's new stores have fuel cells that supply half of the electricity. Holes are punched in the roof for skylights that provide 70 percent of the store's lighting needs during the day. To help keep the scorching sun at bay and cool the building naturally, roofs are painted white.[13]

The production of apparel has adverse effects on the environment because it involves the use of dyes, solvents, and huge amounts of water and petroleum for transportation. An industry group called the Sustainable Apparel Coalition has developed an index to rate the relative sustainability of apparel. Some members of the coalition are Walmart, Target, Kohl's, Nordstrom, and Patagonia. Environmentalists anticipate that the index will be used by consumers when selecting products and by retail buyers when they select the assortments of products to offer. The index considers the entire life of a product—from raw materials to disposal. Brands can get higher scores by asking consumers to wash items in cold, rather than hot, water. Some buyers are rewarded for the design of products with high index levels. A new Nike "Flyknit" running shoe worn by U.S., Kenyan, and other marathoners at the London Olympics was designed based on the index. The shoe is knit from polyester, eliminating the waste of shoes sewn from cut textiles.[14]

Companies typically go through several stages before they fully integrate CSR into their strategy. Companies in the first stage engage only in CSR activities required by law. In this stage, companies are not actually convinced of the importance of CSR actions. In the second stage, companies go beyond activities required by law to engage in CSR activities that also provide a short-term financial benefit to the

The Nike Flyknit receives a high Sustainable Apparel Coalition index because its construction reduces waste by an average of 80 percent when compared to typical Nike running footwear.

company. For example, a retailer might reduce the energy consumption of its stores just because doing so reduces its costs. In the third stage, companies operate responsibly because they believe this is the "right thing" to do. Companies in the fourth and final stage engage in socially and environmentally responsible actions because they believe these activities must be done for the "well-being" of everyone. These companies have truly incorporated the concept of CSR into their business strategy.[15]

Role in Developing Economies— The Bottom of the Pyramid

Retailers need to also focus on opportunities available by serving the needs of the 4 billion people (25 percent of the world's population) at the lowest end of the income distribution. Serving these customers also provides an important social benefit: reducing worldwide poverty.[16] Consumers in this low income consumer segment, referred to as the **base of the pyramid** or **bottom of the pyramid (BoP)**, have a potential spending power of more than $5 trillion. The sheer size and growth of the BoP markets, especially in the countries with emerging economies such as China, India, and Brazil, and maturation of consumer goods and retail markets in developed economies is motivating firms to enter the BoP market.

Undertaking retailing activities to the BoP market is challenging. It is difficult to communicate and complete transactions with people in the BoP market because they are more likely to lack access to mass media, the Internet, mobile phones, or credit cards than more affluent markets. Most people in BoP markets live in rural areas—remote villages that are not connected to the outside world through adequate roads. Limited local demand combined with the high cost of transporting goods to and from remote villages results in higher costs and prices for consumer goods. Thus, engagement at the BoP markets requires innovative approaches for doing business. Retrofitting business models used in the more developed markets will not work.[17] Retailing View 1.1 describes how Grupo Elektra has improved the lifestyle of Latin America's working poor.

THE GROWING IMPORTANCE OF RETAILING AND RETAILERS

Evolution of the Retail Industry

LO3

Analyze the changing retail industry.

REFACT

James Cash Penney opened the first JCPenney store, called Golden Rule, in Kemmerer, Wyoming, in 1902.[18]

From a consumer's perspective, retailers are local businesses. Even though many consumers collect information and make purchases using the Internet or a mobile device, more than 90 percent of all retail sales are made in stores—usually stores that are less than a 15-minute drive from the consumer's home or workplace. Thus, retail stores predominately compete against other stores that are located nearby.

There has been a dramatic change in the structure of the retail industry over the past 50 years. Fifty years ago, Sears and JCPenney were the only retail firms that had chains of stores across the United States. The retail industry consisted of the small, independent, local retailers competing against other small, independent retailers in the same community. Walmart, Home Depot, Staples, and Best Buy did not exist or were small companies with a few stores. Now, the retail industry is dominated by large, national, and even international retail firms. While there are more than 1 million retailers in the United States, over 40 percent of U.S. retail sales are made by companies with more than 10,000 employees. Home improvement centers are the most concentrated sector in the retail industry, with the four largest firms accounting for 92.7 percent of U.S. annual sales in the sector. The top four department store chains account for 73.2 percent of annual U.S. sales in that sector, and the top four drug store chains account for 63.0 percent in that sector. On the other hand, the least concentrated sectors are food service and drinking, where only 5.8 percent of sales are represented by the top four firms in the sector, and furniture stores where only 13.9 percent of sales are represented by the top four firms in the sector.[19]

The largest retailers in the world are shown in Exhibit 1–5. Nine of the top 20 retailers are headquartered in the United States; while Germany has five. Of these top 20 retailers, the U.S. retailers have fewer global operations than the non-U.S. based retailers. The average number of countries that these U.S.-based retailers operate in is five, compared to the non-U.S.-headquartered retailers, who operate in an average of 16 countries. Five of the largest U.S.-based retailers operate in only one or two countries. Only four of the 11 non-U.S-based retailers operate stores in the United States, the largest retail market in the world.

The development of information systems is one the forces facilitating the growth of large retail firms—the shift from an industry dominated by small, local retailers to large multinational chains. Prior to the development of these systems, it was difficult for someone other than the local store manager to track

REFACT

Walmart's annual sales are five times greater than the sales of Procter & Gamble, the largest consumer product producer.[20]

RETAILING VIEW   Grupo Elektra Improves the Lifestyle of Latin America's Working Poor

1.1

Grupo Elektra, with headquarters in Mexico City, owns and operates more than 2,600 specialty stores in Mexico, Brazil, Argentina, Guatemala, El Salvador, Honduras, Panama, and Peru. Its stores sell consumer electronics and appliances to Latin America's working poor. It is quite a challenge to sell consumer durable goods to families earning less than $400 per month and spend 90 percent of their income on basic necessities, such as food and housing. In addition, these BoP consumers often do not have formal jobs or bank accounts. But Grupo Elektra, and its banking affiliate, Banco Azteca, have been increasing sales and profits during one of the worst economic recessions in decades by servicing these low-income consumers. For the past five years, revenues and operating profits have grown at a double-digit rate.

Rather than wait for low-income consumers to open their own bank accounts so they can afford to buy its products, Elektra launched its own banks inside its network of specialty retail shops. These banks make small "micro-loans" to Elektra's customers so they can afford to buy its appliances. It determines how much money its new customers can really afford to borrow—and then pay back. Within 24 hours, the bank approves or denies a client's loan application using the information gathered by the credit officer at the branch. The officer visits the customers' houses to determine their income and expenses. The bank then establishes weekly installment payments that match the borrowing capacity of each customer. More than 5,000 loan officers travel by motorcycles to the applicants' homes to assess their creditworthiness and, when necessary, to collect payments from customers. Usually, however, cash payments are made once a week at an Electra store.

This approach has enabled thousands of low-income consumers to acquire durables that have long been inaccessible to them because they lacked the opportunity to use credit. Traditionally, these low-income people—the taxi drivers, mango vendors, and cleaning ladies of Latin

Grupo Elektra has developed a successful strategy for selling products and providing micro-loans to its customers at the base of the pyramid.

America—put their money in a cookie jar or below their mattresses. Now, they can establish a bank account for a minimum of only US $5 and have access to a debit card.

Sources: Erin Carlyle, "Billionaire Ricardo Salinas: Mexico's Credit Card," *Forbes*, May 7, 2012, p.100; Erin Carlyle, "Mexican Billionaire Buys Advance America, Largest Payday Lender In U.S.," *Forbes*, April 23, 2012, p. 102; and "Grupo Elektra: Will Selling in Brazil Prove to Be the Retailer's Next 'Growth Moment?" *Knowledge @ Wharton*, April 07, 2010.

DISCUSSION QUESTION

The typical interest rate charged by Grupo Elektra is 50 percent, a rate that would be illegal in most U.S. states. Is Elektra providing a benefit to its customers or taking advantage of its customers' lack of knowledge about these financial contracts?

EXHIBIT 1–5   The 20 Largest Retailers in the World

Rank	Name	Headquarters Location	Number of Countries	Stores in U.S.	Sales ($ millions)	Primary Format
1	Walmart	U.S.	16	Yes	418,993	Supercenter
2	Carrefour	France	33	No	119,652	Supercenter
3	Tesco	UK	13	Yes	92,171	Supercenter
4	Metro	Germany	33	No	86,931	Warehouse club
5	Kroger	U.S.	1	Yes	82,189	Supermarket
6	Schwarz Untematmens Trauhard	Germany	26	No	79,119	Discount store
7	Costco	U.S.	9	Yes	76,225	Warehouse club
8	Home Depot	U.S.	5	Yes	67,997	Home improvement
9	Walgreens	U.S.	2	Yes	67,420	Drug store
10	Aldi Einkauf	Germany	18	Yes	67,112	Discount store
11	Target	U.S.	1	Yes	65,786	Discount store
12	Rewe	Germany	13	No	61,134	Supermarket
13	CVS	U.S.	2	Yes	57,345	Drug store
14	Seven & Holding	Japan	18	Yes	57,055	Convenience store
15	Groupe Auchan	France	13	No	55,212	Supercenter
16	Edeka Zentrale	Germany	1	No	54,074	Supermarket
17	Aeon	Japan	8	No	53,458	Supercenter
18	Woolworth	Australia	2	No	51,171	Supermarket
19	Best Buy	U.S.	15	Yes	50,272	Electronics category specialist
20	Lowe's	U.S.	3	Yes	48,815	Home improvement

Source: "2011 Global 250 Retailers," *Stores Magazine,* January 2012.

REFACT

Walmart processes more than 100 million transactions per hour through its POS terminals in stores around the world.[21]

REFACT

Walmart has a data warehouse with more than 2.5 petabytes (2,500 terrabytes) of information—the equivalent of 167 times more than all of the books in America's Library of Congress.[22]

how the merchandise in the store was selling—whether it was selling above plan and needed to be reordered or was selling below plan and needed to have its price reduced. It was also difficult to collect and consolidate the plans from a number of different stores so that a buyer could place large orders with vendors to get price discounts. Thus, before the availability of modern information systems, it was difficult for retailers to lower costs through scale economies, and larger retailers had limited advantages over small local or regional retailers.

Most consumers shopping in their local stores don't realize the sophisticated information systems used by retailers today to manage these large, complex supply chain systems. To illustrate the complexity of these systems, consider the following example. You go to Best Buy and find a tablet you are going to buy. When you decide to buy a tablet in a store, the point-of-sale (POS) terminal transmits data about the transaction to the retailer's distribution center and then on to the manufacturer. Data about your purchase are incorporated into a sophisticated inventory management system. When the in-store inventory level drops below a prespecified level, an electronic notice is automatically transmitted, authorizing the shipment of more units to the retailer's distribution center and then to the store. The retail buyer or a computer program analyzes the sales data to determine how many and which tablet models will be stocked in the retailer's stores and what price will be charged.

To add even another layer of complexity, most large retailers contract with factories around the world to have merchandise made for them. Thus, for example, nearly 1,500 employees, working in both quality-control and full-service buying centers, help Target ensure that any factory worldwide that produces products with the Target name meet Target's own standards for product quality, without violating ethical labor standards.[23]

Role of Information Systems

Now, retailers are inundated with data about the thousands of transactions that take place each day. The challenge for retailers is to convert this raw data into information that managers can use to make better decisions. Many retailers now use the data they have on their customers to identify their best customers and target customized promotions to them, place products close to each other when they find that many customers are buying the same products at the same time, and tailor the assortment of products in each store to better match the needs of the store's local market.

In addition to playing an important role in society in general, retailing provides personal opportunities to work for a company in an exciting, challenging environment or to start an entrepreneurial venture. These opportunities are discussed in the next section.

Sophisticated supply chains have facilitated the economies of scale that large retailers have been able to achieve.

MANAGEMENT AND ENTREPRENEURIAL OPPORTUNITIES

Management Opportunities

To exploit these new technologies and systems and gain advantage in a highly competitive and challenging environment, retailers need to hire and promote the best and brightest. Sherry Hollack, a former vice president of talent development at Macy's, emphasized this point: "One of the biggest challenges facing Macy's, and most other retail chains, is hiring and retaining managers to lead our company in the coming years. The changing demographics are working against us. Over the next ten years, a lot of our senior managers, members of the Baby Boomer generation, will be retiring. So we are going to be competing with other retailers and firms in other industries for a smaller pool of available managers in the generations behind the Boomers. In addition, retailing is becoming a much more sophisticated business. Our managers need to be comfortable with new technologies, information and supply chain management systems, and international business as well as managing a diverse workforce and buying merchandise."[24]

Students often view retailing as part of marketing because managing distribution (place) is one of the 4 Ps of marketing. But retailers are businesses and, like manufacturers, undertake all the traditional business activities. Retailers raise capital from financial institutions; purchase goods and services; use accounting and

LO4

Recognize the opportunities in retailing for you.

management information systems to control their operations; manage warehouses and distribution systems; design and develop new products; and undertake marketing activities such as advertising, promotion, sales force management, and market research. Thus, retailers employ people with expertise and interests in finance, accounting, human resource management, supply chain management, and computer systems, as well as management and marketing.

Retail managers are often given considerable responsibility early in their careers. Retail management is also financially rewarding. Starting salaries are typically between $35,000 and $65,000 for college graduates entering management trainee positions. After completing a management training program, retail managers can

1.2   RETAILING VIEW   Sam Walton, Founder of Walmart (1918–1992)

Like Henry Ford with his Model T, Sam Walton revolutionized the retail industry. After graduating from the University of Missouri in 1940, Walton began working at a JCPenney store in Des Moines, Iowa. He served in the army during World War II and then purchased a Ben Franklin variety store franchise in Newport, Arkansas. He

REFACT

With 2.2 million employees, Walmart is the largest company in the world in terms of number of employees.[25]

boosted sales by finding suppliers that would sell him merchandise at lower prices than his cost to buy from Ben Franklin.

Walton lost his store, however, in 1950 when the landlord refused to renew his lease. He then moved to Bentonville, Arkansas, where he and a younger brother franchised an-

other Ben Franklin store. Walton employed a new self-service system that he had discovered at two Ben Franklin stores in Minnesota. He placed the checkout registers and clerks at the front of the store rather than scattering them throughout. By 1960, Walton had 15 stores in Arkansas and Missouri that laid the foundation for Walmart.

By the early 1960s, some retailers in large, urban, eastern cities had developed the discount store concept, incorporating self-service, shallow but broad assortments, low overhead costs, and large parking lots. In 1962, Walton brought this format to small southern towns, opening his first Walmart Discount City in Rogers, Arkansas.

Walton often visited his stores, dropping in unannounced to check the merchandise presentation or financial performance and talk to his "associates." He prided himself on a profit-sharing program and a friendly, open, supportive atmosphere—business practices he had learned when working for JCPenney. He often led his workers in the Walmart cheer: "Give me a W! Give me an A! Give me an L! Give me a Squiggly! (Here, everybody sort of does the twist. As part of Walmart's campaign to modernize its image, in 1998, it dropped the squiggly from its trademark.) Give me an M! Give me an A! Give me an R! Give me a T! What's that spell? Walmart! What's that spell? Walmart! Who's number one? THE CUSTOMER!"

He offered his own formula for how a large company should operate: "Think one store at a time. That sounds easy enough, but it's something we've constantly had to

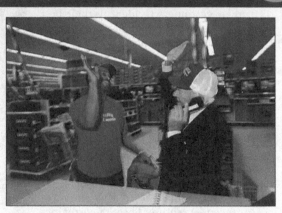

Sam Walton believed in "management by walking around."

stay on top of. Communicate, communicate, communicate: What good is figuring out a better way to sell beach towels if you aren't going to tell everybody in your company about it? Keep your ear to the ground: A computer is not—and will never be—a substitute for getting out in your stores and learning what's going on."

In 1991, due to the success of his concept and management practices, Walton became America's wealthiest person; however, he maintained his simple, unassuming lifestyle. Whenever he traveled on business, he rented the same compact economy cars and stayed in the same inexpensive hotels as his employees did. He died of leukemia in 1992. Walmart is now the world's largest corporation.

Sources: Michael Bergdahl, *The Retail Revolution: How Wal-Mart Created a Brave New World of Business* (New York: Metropolitan Books, 2009); and Michael Bergdahl, *The 10 Rules of Sam Walton: Success Secrets for Remarkable Results* (Hoboken, NJ: Wiley, 2006).

DISCUSSION QUESTION

What were the key factors that led to Walmart's phenomenal growth and dominance of the retail industry?

double their starting salary in three to five years if they perform well. Senior buyers and others in higher managerial positions and store managers make between $120,000 and $300,000. (See Appendix 1A at the end of this chapter.)

Entrepreneurial Opportunities

Retailing also provides opportunities for people who wish to start their own business. Some of the world's most successful people are retailing entrepreneurs. Many are well known because their names appear over stores' doors; others you may not recognize. Retailing View 1.2 examines the life of one of the world's greatest entrepreneurs, Sam Walton. Some other innovative retail entrepreneurs include Jeff Bezos, Do Won and Jin Sook Chang, Ingvar Kamprad, and Howard Schultz. These entrepreneurs came from humble backgrounds and changed the way retailing is done.

Jeff Bezos (Amazon.com)   After his research uncovered that Internet usage was growing at a 2,300 percent annual rate in 1994, Jeffrey Bezos, the 30-year-old son of a Cuban refugee, quit his job on Wall Street and left behind a hefty bonus to start an Internet business. While his wife MacKenzie was driving their car across country, Jeff pecked out his business plan on a laptop computer. By the time they reached Seattle, he had rounded up the investment capital to launch the first Internet book retailer. The company, Amazon.com, is named after the river that carries the greatest amount of water, symbolizing Bezos's objective of achieving the greatest volume of Internet sales. Under his leadership, Amazon developed technologies to make shopping on the Internet faster, easier, and more personal than shopping in stores by offering personalized recommendations and home pages. Amazon.com has become more than a bookstore. It is now the largest online retailer, with annual sales greater than $48 billion. Amazon also provides virtual stores and fulfillment services for many other retailers.[26]

Do Won and Jin Sook Chang (Forever 21)   Do Won and Jin Sook Chang are self-made billionaires. In 1984, they cofounded the "fast fashion" retail chain Forever 21. The pair emigrated from South Korea in 1981 and became naturalized

Forever 21 founder Do Won and his daughter Linda Chang (senior marketing manager) visiting their flagship store in Times Square.

American citizens. The couple opened their first store in 1984, focused on trendy, exciting clothing options. That year, sales grew from $35,000 to $700,000. Forever 21 has continued to experience explosive growth, as evidenced by recent store openings, like a flagship Las Vegas attraction with 127,000 square feet, a massive 45,000-square-foot store in Los Angeles, and two new megastores in New York of 86,000 and 91,000 square feet. Today, it operates more than 500 stores worldwide with more than 35,000 employees and projected sales of greater than $3.5 billion. Forever 21 is a family operation with Do Won at the helm, Jin Sook in charge of merchandising, eldest daughter Linda running marketing, and daughter Esther managing visuals.[27]

REFACT

The acronym IKEA is made up of the initials of the founder's name (Ingvar Kamprad) plus those of Elmtaryd, his family farm, and the nearby village Agunnaryd.[28]

Ingvar Kamprad (IKEA)   Ingvar Kamprad, the founder of the Swedish-based home furnishing retailer chain IKEA, was always an entrepreneur. His first business was selling matches to neighbors from his bicycle. He discovered he could make a good profit by buying matches in bulk and selling them individually at a low price. He then expanded to selling fish, Christmas tree decorations, seeds, ballpoint pens, and pencils. By the time he was 17 years of age, he had earned a reward for succeeding in school. His father gave him the money to establish what is now IKEA. Like Sam Walton, the founder of Walmart, Kamprad is known for his frugality. He drives an old Volvo, flies economy class, and encourages IKEA employees to write on both sides of a sheet of paper. This thriftiness has translated into a corporate philosophy of cost cutting throughout IKEA so that the chain can offer quality furniture with innovative designs at low prices. According to *Forbes* magazine, Kamprad is the richest person in Europe and the fourth-richest person in the world, with an estimated net worth of around $33 billion.[29]

REFACT

At $300 million, Starbucks spends more on health care insurance for its employees than on coffee beans.[30]

Howard Schulz (Starbucks)   In 1982, Howard Schultz, a salesperson for a plastic manufacturer, was hired as the new head of marketing for Starbucks, a coffee roaster with six cafés. Shortly after he was hired, he went Verona, Italy, to attend an international housewares show. He had his first latte in Verona, but he saw something more important than the coffee. The café patrons were enjoying themselves while sipping their coffees in the elegant surroundings. He had a vision of recreating the Old World magic and romance behind the Italian coffee bar. The owner wanted to focus on his plan to sell roasted whole beans, and eventually Schultz acquired Starbucks and began the company's march across the world. Schultz's father struggled at low-paying jobs with little to show for it when he died. "He was beaten down, he wasn't respected," Schultz said. "He had no health insurance, and he had no workers' compensation when he got hurt on the job." So with Starbucks, Schultz "wanted to build the kind of company that my father never got a chance to work for, in which people were respected." Due to this childhood experience, Schultz initiated practices at Starbucks that are still uncommon in retailing, such as providing comprehensive health care for all employees working at least 20 hours a week, including coverage for unmarried spouses, and offering an employee stock-option plan. In 2012, Starbucks' sales were greater than $11 billion from the 17,000 stores it operates in 40 countries.[31]

In the next section, we discuss the decisions that retailers make to design and implement their retail strategy. This book is organized around this strategic decision-making process.

THE RETAIL MANAGEMENT DECISION PROCESS

LO5

Understand the strategic retail management decision process.

This book is organized around the management decisions that retailers make to provide value to their customers and develop an advantage over their competitors. Exhibit 1–6 identifies the chapters in this book associated with each type of decision.

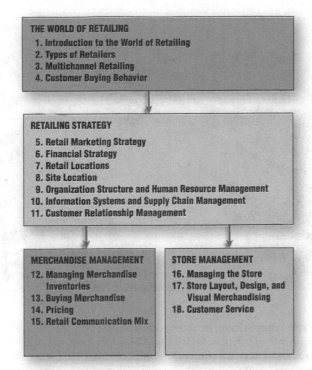

EXHIBIT 1–6
Retail Management
Decision Process

Understanding the World of Retailing—Section I

The first step in the retail management decision process, as Exhibit 1–6 shows, is understanding the world of retailing. Retail managers need to know the environment in which they operate before they can develop and implement effective strategies. The first section of this book therefore provides a general overview of the retailing industry and its customers.

The critical environmental factors in the world of retailing are (1) the macroenvironment and (2) the microenvironment. The impacts of the macroenvironment—including technological, social, and ethical/legal/political factors—on retailing are discussed throughout this book. For example, the influence of technology on the rise of multichannel retailing is reviewed in Chapter 3, the use of new information and supply chain technologies are examined in Chapter 10, customer relationship management systems are reviewed in Chapter 11, and new communication technologies are discussed in Chapter 15.

Competitors   The retailer's microenvironment focuses specifically on its competitors and customers. At first glance, identifying competitors appears easy: A retailer's primary competitors are other retailers that use the same retail approach. Thus, department stores compete against other department stores, and supermarkets compete with other supermarkets. This competition between the same type of retailers is called **intratype competition**.

Yet to appeal to a broader group of consumers, many retailers are increasing the variety of merchandise they offer. By offering greater variety, retailers satisfy the needs of customers seeking a one-stop shopping experience. For example, Walgreens has added jewelry, accessories, and apparel to its already extensive health and beauty categories to meet the lifestyle needs of its customers. Amazon seems to offer any product you might ever want to buy or rent. When retailers offer merchandise not typically associated with their type of store, such as clothing in a drugstore, the result is **scrambled merchandising**. Scrambled merchandising increases

Scrambled merchandise
increases the level of
intertype competition.

intertype competition, or competition among retailers that sell similar merchandise using different types of retail outlets, such as drug and department stores.

Increasing intertype competition makes it harder for retailers to identify and monitor their competition. In one sense, all retailers compete against one another for the dollars that consumers spend on goods and services. But the intensity of competition is greatest among retailers whose offerings are viewed as very similar.

Management's view of competition also may differ depending on the manager's position within the retail firm. For example, the manager of the Saks Fifth Avenue women's sportswear department in Bergen County, New Jersey, views the other women's sportswear specialty stores in the Riverside Square mall as her major competitors. But the Saks store manager views the Bloomingdale's store in a nearby mall as her strongest competitor. These differences in perspective arise because the department sales manager is primarily concerned with customers for a specific category of merchandise, whereas the store manager is concerned with customers seeking the entire selection of all merchandise and services offered by a department store. The chief executive officer (CEO) of a retail chain, in contrast, views competition from a much broader perspective. For example, Nordstrom might identify its strongest competitor as Saks, Neiman Marcus, Bloomingdale's, and even Bluefly.com.

Chapter 2 discusses various types of retailers and their competitive strategies, and Chapter 3 concentrates on different types of channels that retailers use to complete transactions with their customers.

Customers   The second factor in the microenvironment is customers. Retailers must respond to broad demographic and lifestyle trends in our society, such as the growth in the senior and minority segments of the U.S. population or the importance of shopping convenience to the increasing number of two-income families. To develop and implement an effective strategy, retailers must understand why customers shop, how they select a store, and how they select among that store's merchandise—the information found in Chapter 4.

Developing a Retail Strategy—Section II

The next stages in the retail management decision-making process, formulating and implementing a retail strategy, are based on an understanding of the macro- and microenvironments developed in the first section of this book. Section II

Toys R Us focuses on toys and apparel for children, while Walmart's strategic focus is much broader.

focuses on decisions related to developing a retail strategy, whereas Sections III and IV pertain to decisions surrounding the implementation of the strategy and building a long-term competitive advantage. The decisions discussed in Sections III and IV are more tactical.

Retail Strategy   The **retail strategy** identifies (1) the target market, or markets, toward which the retailer will direct its efforts; (2) the nature of the merchandise and services the retailer will offer to satisfy the needs of the target market; and (3) how the retailer will develop unique assets that enable it to achieve long-term advantage over its competitors.

The nature of a retail strategy can be illustrated by comparing the strategies of Walmart and Toys R Us. Initially, Walmart identified its target market as small towns (fewer than 35,000 in population) in Arkansas, Texas, and Oklahoma. It offered name-brand merchandise at low prices in a broad array of categories, ranging from laundry detergent to girls' dresses, but offerings in each category were limited. Today, even as Walmart stores have expanded across the world, the selection in each category remains limited. A Walmart store might have only 3 models of flat-screen television sets, while an electronic category specialist like Best Buy might carry 30 models.

In contrast to Walmart, Toys R Us defines its primary target as consumers living in suburban areas of large cities. Rather than carrying many merchandise categories, Toys R Us stores specialize in toys and children's apparel and carry most types and brands currently available in the market. Walmart emphasizes self-service: Customers select their merchandise, bring it to the checkout line, and then carry it to their cars. But Toys R Us provides more customer service. It has salespeople to assist customers with certain types of merchandise.

Because Walmart and Toys R Us both emphasize competitive prices, they have made strategic decisions to sustain their low prices by developing a cost advantage over their competitors. Both firms have sophisticated distribution and management information systems to manage inventory. Their strong relationships with their suppliers enable them to buy merchandise at low prices.

Strategic Decision Areas   The key strategic decisions a retailer makes are defining its target market and its financial objectives. Chapter 5 discusses how the selection of a retail market strategy requires analyzing the environment and the firm's strengths and weaknesses. When major environmental changes occur, the current strategy and the reasoning behind it must be reexamined. The retailer then decides what, if any, strategy changes are needed to take advantage of new opportunities or avoid new threats in the environment. The retailer's market strategy must be consistent with the firm's financial objectives. Chapter 6 reviews how financial variables, such as return on investment, inventory turnover, and profit margin, can be used to evaluate the market strategy and its implementation.

The next set of strategic decisions involves the development of critical assets that enable retailers to build strategic advantages. These strategic assets are location, human resource, information and supply chain systems, supply chain organization, and customer loyalty.

Decisions regarding location (reviewed in Chapters 7 and 8) are important because location is typically consumers' top consideration when selecting a store. Generally, consumers buy gas at the closest service station and patronize the shopping mall that's most convenient to their home or office. In addition, location offers an opportunity to gain a long-term advantage over the competition. When a retailer has the best location, a competing retailer must settle for the second-best location.

Retailing is a very labor-intensive industry. Employees play a critical role in providing the services customers seek when patronizing a retailer. Chapter 9 outlines how retailers coordinate the activities of buyers, store managers, and sales associates in the implementation of the retailing strategy.

Retail information and supply chain management systems also offer a significant opportunity for retailers to gain strategic advantage. Chapter 10 reviews how retailers are developing sophisticated computer and distribution technologies to monitor flows of information and merchandise from vendors to retail distribution centers to retail stores. These technologies are part of an overall inventory management system that enables retailers to (1) make sure desired merchandise is available when customers want it and (2) minimize the retailer's inventory investment.

Retailers, like most businesses, want to develop repeat purchases and loyalty in their best customers. Chapter 11 examines the process that retailers use to identify, design programs for, increase the share of wallet of, provide more value to, and build loyalty among their best customers. The implementation decisions are discussed in the next two sections.

Implementing the Retail Strategy—Sections III and IV

To implement a retail strategy, retailers develop a retail mix that satisfies the needs of its target market better than that of its competitors. The **retail mix** is a set of decisions retailers make to satisfy customer needs and influence their purchase decisions. Elements in the retail mix (Exhibit 1–7) include the types of merchandise and services offered, merchandise pricing, advertising and promotional

EXHIBIT 1–7
The Retail Mix

programs, store design, merchandise display, assistance to customers provided by salespeople, and convenience of the store's location. Section III reviews the implementation decisions made by buyers, and Section IV focuses on decisions made by store managers.

Managers in the merchandise management area decide how much and what types of merchandise to buy (Chapter 12), what vendors to use and how to interact with them (Chapter 13), the retail prices to set (Chapter 14), and how to advertise and promote merchandise (Chapter 15). Store managers must determine how to recruit, select, and motivate sales associates (Chapter 16); where and how merchandise will be displayed (Chapter 17); and the nature of services to provide for customers (Chapter 18). Whole Foods Market is one of the fastest growing and most profitable supermarket chains. In the next section, we illustrate the strategic and more tactical decisions Whole Foods has made and continues to make to achieve and sustain its success. The background of its founder and CEO, John Mackey, is described in Retailing View 1.3.

Whole Foods Market: An Organic and Natural Food Supermarket Chain

Retail Strategy   In the 1960s, natural, organic foods were available only in farmers' markets or small specialty stores catering to counterculture consumers. Consumers who patronized these health food stores felt that eating organic food would liberate them from the grasp of big agribusiness and food processors that were destroying the land with chemical pesticides, mistreating migrant farmworkers, and encouraging people to consume unhealthy processed foods. Whole Foods' strategy is to target health-conscious, environmentally conscious, middle-class consumers by using a modern supermarket format, rather than small, specialty health food stores. Its mission is to promote the vitality and well-being of all individuals by supplying the highest quality, most wholesome foods available.

Strategic Advantages   Some of the strategic assets Whole Foods has developed over the years to provide long-term advantages are a strong brand image that builds customer loyalty; committed employees who provide excellent customer service; good relationships with organic food suppliers that ensures a supply of organic food, even as demand for organic food grows faster than supply; an efficient supply chain connecting local growers to a national store network; and extensive information about its customers that it uses to develop assortments and target promotions.

Merchandise Management   In terms of merchandise, Whole Foods stores offer the array of food categories typically found in a supermarket. However, the assortment emphasizes organic and natural products that are fresh, nutritious, and safe to eat. Products are free of artificial preservatives, colors, flavors, and sweeteners, as well as hydrogenated fats and other unacceptable ingredients. In addition, Whole Foods seeks out and supports local producers whose fruits and vegetables meet its standards, particularly those who farm organically and are dedicated to environmentally friendly, sustainable agriculture.

Whole Foods offers seven lines of private-label products. Buyers work with artisan food producers and organic farmers to attain products sold under the super-premium Authentic Food Artisan brand. Its core private brands are called Whole Brands (department-specific products), Whole Foods (premium products), and Whole Kids Organic (organic products for children). The 365 Day Everyday Value and 365 Day Organic Everyday Value line provide natural products at value prices.

Whole Foods communicates the benefits of its offering through its website and social media. Its website has extensive information about natural and organic

1.3   RETAILING VIEW   Whole Foods: The Birth of the Organic Supermarket

John Mackey had a relatively conventional, middle-class, suburban upbringing. But it was the 1970s, so Mackey quit college and embraced an alternative lifestyle (e.g., long beard, wild hair). After having worked for a time in a vegetarian collective, he solicited money from family and friends so that he could open a new sort of co-op in 1978: organic food store on the first floor, restaurant on the second floor, and living quarters on the top of the old Victorian house he had found.

REFACT

Whole Foods has a rule that no employee can have a salary greater than 19 times the average salary of store employees. On average, a U.S. CEO makes 319 times the compensation of a production worker in their companies.[32]

A couple of years later, Mackey went further and opened the first Whole Foods store in a 10,000-square-foot space that had once been a nightclub. In keeping with its history, Mackey made sure his natural food store was no stodgy, boring site with just granola. He stocked beer, meat, and wine, and he "loved it. I loved retail. I loved being around food. I loved natural foods. I loved organic foods. I loved the whole idea of it. And a thought entered into my mind that maybe this is what I could do."

But being a grocer was not a particularly popular aspiration with his family. His mother, a former teacher, strongly discouraged his interest in Whole Foods. According to Mackey's account, on her deathbed in 1987, she asked him to promise to return to school to get his college degree; when he demurred, she complained, "I wish you'd just give up that stupid health-food store. Your father and I gave you a fine mind, and you're wasting it being a grocer."

He never did give up on his "stupid" store, though. Instead, as the concept spread across the United States, Mackey adopted and adapted his ideas to fit local tastes. Through decentralized decision-making units, Whole Foods stores could choose to stock items specific to the preferences of the local markets, like live lobsters in Portland, Maine, or a kombucha bar in Venice, California. Through acquisitions, Whole Foods gained additional knowledge, too. In buying Wellspring Grocery, it learned about private-label options. The purchase of Mrs. Gooch's provided Whole Foods with insights into diet supplements. When it purchased

Whole Foods founder and CEO, John Mackey

Bread & Circus, it gained access to the Boston chain's famed seafood procurement expertise.

Sources: www.wholefoodsmarket.com/company-info/whole-foods-market-history; and Nick Paumgarten, "Food Fighter," *New Yorker*, January 4, 2010.

DISCUSSION QUESTION

What factors in Whole Foods' macro- and microenvironment contributed to its success?

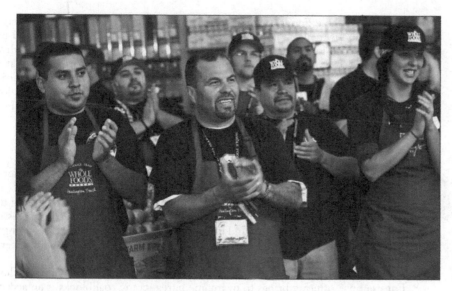

Employees at Whole Foods participate in decision making through self-managed teams.

foods. Its iPhone app provides not just the location information about the nearest Whole Foods store (by zip code) but also approximately 2,000 recipes, searchable by various criteria, including diet restrictions, ingredients, budgets, or family appeal. The "On Hand" option allows users to input the items on their pantry shelves and receive recommendations for some meal options. Moreover, the app offers special deals for each store, right next to a map that shows customers how to get there.[33]

Whole Foods also uses social media extensively. A global manager and community manager assigned at every store are responsible for customer engagement. A single Global Online Community Manager runs the company's central Twitter link, @Whole Foods. Most of the tweets in this realm come from individual customers with questions, complaints, or suggestions. The manager makes sure to respond almost immediately, to ensure that no customers get the sense Whole Foods is uninterested or ignoring their concerns. Then, in each community, another manager attends to local needs, including special deal postings, charity opportunities, and upcoming events. A Los Angeles store located on Third Street owns the Twitter handle @WholeFoods3rdSt; a Mount Washington location, near Baltimore, tweets from the @WholeFoodsMTW account.[34]

Store Management   All Whole Foods employees are organized into self-managed teams that meet regularly to discuss issues and solve problems. Almost all team members have stock options in the firm. They also receive a 20 percent discount in stores. Their personal wellness accounts help them cover health care expenses, both for themselves and their domestic partners. To select the benefits package, the entire company takes a vote every three years. Whole Foods thus has been on *Fortune* magazine's "100 Best Companies to Work For" list for 13 consecutive years.[35]

Whole Foods' decisions on visual merchandising and store design reinforce its strategy.[36] Its stores are designed to make grocery shopping fun—to transform a supermarket into an interactive theater with corporate staff serving as the producer and store management as the director. Sections of its newer stores are designed with self-contained architecture that curves inward, creating a feeling of intimacy that encourages shoppers to linger. The warm feeling of the store is enhanced by signs made of an eco-friendly, woodlike material rather than plastic. Art gallery–type lighting focuses attention on produce.

Finally, Whole Foods' store management provides excellent customer service. Curious about the life of a chicken in the display case? It comes with a 16-page booklet and an invitation to visit the live chickens at the company's Pennsylvania farm. Want to know the name of the farmer who grew those organic tomatoes? That information, along with some personal details, is readily available. Curious about the fish you're getting dressed at the free filleting station? The employee can offer not just ideas for cooking it but also the identity of the Whole Foods boat and the captain who caught it for you.[37]

Ethical and Legal Considerations

When making the decisions discussed previously, managers need to consider the ethical and legal implications of their decisions, in addition to the effects that those decisions have on the profitability of their firms and the satisfaction of their customers. **Ethics** are the principles governing individuals and companies that establish appropriate behavior and indicate what is right and wrong. Defining the term is easy, but determining what the principles are is difficult. What one person thinks is ethical, another may consider unethical.

What is ethical can vary from country to country and from industry to industry. For example, offering bribes to overcome bureaucratic roadblocks is an accepted practice in Middle Eastern countries but is considered unethical, and even illegal, in the United States. Ethical principles also can change over time. For example, some years ago, doctors and lawyers who advertised their services were considered unethical. Today, such advertising is accepted as common practice.

Examples of difficult situations that retail managers face include the following:

- Should a retailer sell merchandise that it suspects was made using child labor?
- Should a retailer advertise that its prices are the lowest available in the market, even though some are not?
- Should a retail buyer accept an expensive gift from a vendor?
- Should a retailer charge a supplier a fee for getting a new item in its store?
- Should retail salespeople use a high-pressure sales approach when they know the product is not the best for the customer's needs?
- Should a retailer disclose product information that may affect whether or not it is purchased?
- Should a retailer promote a product as being "on sale" if it never sold at a higher, nonsale price?
- Should a retailer offer credit at a higher interest rate or sell products at higher prices in stores patronized mostly by low-income customers?

Laws dictate which activities society has deemed to be clearly wrong, those activities for which retailers and their employees will be punished through the federal or state legal systems. However, most business decisions are not regulated by laws. Often retail managers have to rely on their firms' and industries' codes of ethics and/or their own codes of ethics to determine the right thing to do.

Many companies have codes of ethics to provide guidelines for their employees in making their ethical decisions. These ethical policies provide a clear sense of right and wrong so that companies and their customers can depend on their employees when questionable situations arise. However, in many situations, retail managers need to rely on their personal code of ethics—their personal sense of what is right or wrong.

Exhibit 1–8 lists some questions you can ask yourself to determine whether a behavior or activity is unethical. The questions emphasize that ethical behavior is determined by widely accepted views of what is right and wrong. Thus, you should engage only in activities about which you would be proud to tell your family, friends, employer, and customers. If the answer to any of these questions is yes, the behavior or activity is probably unethical, and you should not do it.

1. Would I be embarrassed if a customer found out about this behavior?
2. Would my supervisor disapprove of this behavior?
3. Would most coworkers feel that this behavior is unusual?
4. Am I about to do this because I think I can get away with it?
5. Would I be upset if a company did this to me?
6. Would my family or friends think less of me if I told them about engaging in this activity?
7. Am I concerned about the possible consequences of this behavior?
8. Would I be upset if this behavior or activity was publicized in a newspaper article?
9. Would society be worse off if everyone engaged in this behavior or activity?

EXHIBIT 1–8
Checklist for Making
Ethical Decisions

Your firm can strongly affect the ethical choices you will have to make. When you view your firm's policies or requests as improper, you have three choices:

1. *Ignore your personal values, and do what your company asks you to do.* Self-respect suffers when you have to compromise your principles to please an employer. If you take this path, you will probably feel guilty and be dissatisfied with your job in the long run.

2. *Take a stand, and tell your employer what you think.* Try to influence the decisions and policies of your company and supervisors.

3. *Refuse to compromise your principles.* Taking this path may mean you will get fired or be forced to quit.

You should not take a job with a company whose products, policies, and conduct conflict with your standards. Before taking a job, investigate the company's procedures and selling approach to see whether they conflict with your personal ethical standards. Throughout this text, we will highlight the legal and ethical issues associated with the retail decisions made by managers.

SUMMARY

LO1 **Identify retailing activities.**

Retailing is defined as a set of business activities that add value to the products and services sold to consumers for their personal or family use. These value-added activities include providing assortments, breaking bulk, holding inventory, and providing services.

LO2 **Realize the importance of retailing in the U.S. and world economies.**

Retailing plays an important role in the U.S. economy. One out of four workers in the United States works for a retailer or for a company selling products to a retailer, and the U.S. retail sector accounts for about the same percentage of the U.S. GDP as the entire manufacturing sector. Retailing also plays an important role in developing economies. Some business scholars feel that there is need for modern retail methods to be used to serve consumers at the bottom of the pyramid.

LO3 **Analyze the changing retail industry.**

The retail industry has changed dramatically over the last 50 years. Many well-known national and international retailers were small startup companies 50 years ago. Now the industry is dominated by large firms. The development of information systems is one of the forces facilitating the growth of large retailers.

Before the availability of modern information systems, it was difficult for retailers to lower costs through economies of scale, and larger retailers had limited advantages over small local or regional retailers. With these information systems, retailers are able to efficiently and effectively manage millions of customer transactions with thousands of stores and suppliers across the globe.

LO4 **Recognize the opportunities in retailing for you.**

Retailing offers opportunities for exciting, challenging careers, either by working for a retail firm or starting your own business. Aspects of retail careers are discussed in Appendix 1A. Suggestions about starting your own business appear in Appendix A at the end of the book.

LO5 **Understand the strategic retail management decision process.**

The retail management decision process involves developing a strategy for creating a competitive advantage in the marketplace and then developing a retail mix to implement that strategy. The strategic decisions, discussed in the first section of this textbook, involve selecting a target market; defining the nature of the retailer's offering; and building a competitive advantage through locations, human resource management, information and supply chain management systems, and customer relationship management programs.

The merchandise and store management decisions for implementing the strategy, discussed in the second half of this textbook, involve selecting a merchandise assortment, buying merchandise, setting prices, communicating with customers, managing the store, presenting merchandise in stores, and providing customer service. Large retail chains use sophisticated information systems to analyze business opportunities and make these decisions about how to operate their businesses in multiple countries.

Answers to the Quiz in Exhibit 1–1

1. (d)	**3.** (e)	**5.** (e)	**7.** (d)
2. (d)	**4.** (a)	**6.** (b)	**8.** (b)

KEY TERMS

backward integration, *9*	forward integration, *9*	retail mix, *24*
base of the pyramid, *14*	holding inventory, *8*	retail strategy, *23*
bottom of the pyramid (BoP), *14*	intertype competition, *22*	scrambled merchandising, *21*
breaking bulk, *8*	intratype competition, *21*	supply chain, *7*
corporate social responsibility (CSR), *12*	retailer, *7*	vertical integration, *9*
ethics, *28*	retailing, *7*	wholesalers, *9*

GET OUT AND DO IT!

1. **CONTINUING CASE ASSIGNMENT** In most chapters of this textbook, there will be a GET OUT AND DO IT! assignment that will give you an opportunity to examine the strategy and tactics of one retailer. Your first assignment is to select a retailer and prepare a report on the retailer's history, including when it was founded and how it has evolved over time. To ensure that you can get information about the retailer for subsequent Continuing Case Assignments, the retailer you select should:

   - *Be a publicly held company so that you can access its financial statements and annual reports.* Do not select a retailer that is owned by another company. For example, Bath & Body Works is owned by Limited Brands, so you can get financial information about only the holding company and not the individual companies it owns, such as Victoria's Secret and White Barn Candle.
   - *Focus on one type of retailing.* For example, Abercrombie & Fitch operates just one type of specialty store and thus would be a good choice. However, Walmart operates discount stores, warehouse club stores, and supercenters and thus would not be a good choice.
   - *Be easy to visit and collect information about.* Some retailers and store managers may not allow you to interview them about the store, take pictures of the store, talk with sales associates, or analyze the merchandise assortment in the store. Try to pick a retailer with a local store manager who can help you complete the assignments.

   Some examples of retailers that meet the first two criteria are Whole Foods Market, Dress Barn, Burlington Coat Factory, Ross Stores, Ann Taylor, Cato, Finish Line, Foot Locker, Brookstone, Claire's, Walgreens, Staples, Office Depot, American Eagle Outfitter, Pacific Sunwear, Abercrombie & Fitch, Tiffany & Co., Zales, Autozone, Pep Boys, Hot Topic, Wet Seal, Best Buy, Family Dollar, Dollar General, Michaels, PetSmart, Dillard's, Pier 1 Imports, Home Depot, Lowe's, Bed Bath & Beyond, Men's Wearhouse, Kroger, Kohl's, Radio Shack, Safeway, and Target.

2. **GO SHOPPING** Visit a local retail store, and describe each of the elements in its retail mix.

3. **INTERNET EXERCISE** Data on U.S. retail sales are available at the U.S. Bureau of the Census Internet site at www.census.gov/retail/#ecommerce. Look at "Estimates of Monthly Retail and Food Services Sales by Kind of Business" for the most recent year. In which months are sales the highest? Which kinds of businesses experience the greatest fluctuations in monthly sales? List reasons that help explain your findings.

4. **INTERNET EXERCISE** Go to the home pages of Macy's, Target, Walmart, Toys R Us, and the National Retail Federation Retail Careers Center (www.nrf.com/RetailCareers/) to find information about retail careers with these organizations. Review the information about the different positions described. In which positions would you be interested? Which positions are not of interest to you? Which employer would interest you? Why?

5. **INTERNET EXERCISE** Choose one of the top 20 retailers (Exhibit 1–5). Go to the company's website, and find out how the company started and how it has changed over time.

6. **INTERNET EXERCISE** Go online and find an example of a retailer involved in corporate social responsibility. In a brief paragraph, describe how this retailer is taking steps to contribute to a social or ethical cause.

DISCUSSION QUESTIONS AND PROBLEMS

1. How do retailers add value to the products bought by consumers?

2. What is your favorite retailer? Why do you like this retailer? What would a competitive retailer have to do to get your patronage?

3. What are the benefits and limitations of purchasing a home entertainment system directly from a number of component manufacturers rather than from a retailer?

4. What retailers would be considered intratype competitors for a convenience store chain such as 7-Eleven? What firms would be intertype competitors?

5. How does Walmart contribute and/or detract from the communities in which it operates stores?

6. The same brand and style of men's suits are sold at different prices at a department store like Macy's and at a specialty store like Men's Wearhouse. Why would a customer choose to buy the suit from one store rather than the other?

7. Compare and contrast the retail mixes of department stores and full-line discount stores. Use bullet points or a table to list the similarities and differences.

8. An entrepreneur approaches you about how to sell her new writing pens to consumers. The pens have a unique benefit—they are more comfortable to use than traditional pens. The entrepreneur is concerned the retailers she has approached want to buy the pens from her at $10.00 a piece and then sell the pens in their stores at $18.00 to consumers. The entrepreneur is dismayed at the extra $8.00 the retailers are getting and has decided to sell the product directly to consumers for $10.00. She wants to know your opinion. What do you think? Why?

9. From a personal perspective, how does retailing rate as a potential career compared with others you are considering? Why?

10. In this chapter, some socially responsible activities engaged in by retailers are described. Take the perspective of a stockholder in one of these companies. What effect will these activities have on the value of its stock? Why might they have a positive or negative effect?

SUGGESTED READINGS

"2012 Global Retail Industry Trends." *Stores Magazine*, January 2012.

Ferrell, O.C., John Fraedrich, and Linda Ferrell. *Business Ethics: Ethical Decision Making & Cases*, 9th ed., Impendence, KY: Southwestern, 2012.

Fisher, Marshall L., and Ananth Raman. *The New Science of Retailing: How Analytics Are Improving Performance*. Boston: Harvard Business Press, 2010.

"Global Powers of Retailing Top 250." *Stores Magazine*, January 2012.

Lee, Min-young, Ann Fairhurst, and Scarlett Wesley. "Corporate Social Responsibility: A Review of the Top 100 US Retailers." *Corporate Reputation Review* (London) 12 (Summer 2009), pp. 140–159.

Mantrala, Murali K., and Manfred Krafft (Eds). *Retailing in the 21st Century: Current and Future Trends*, 2nd ed. Berlin: Springer, 2010.

Ortinau, David J., Barry J. Babin, and Jean-Charles Chebat, "Retailing Evolution Research: Introduction to the Special Section on Retailing Research," *Journal of Business Research*, 64, no. 6 (June 2011), pp. 541–542.

Plunkett, Jack (Ed). *Plunkett's Retail Industry Almanac 2012*. Houston: Plunkett Research, 2012.

Roberts, Bryan. *Walmart: Key Insights and Practical Lessons from the World's Largest Retailer*. Philadelphia: Kogan Page, 2012.

APPENDIX 1A   Careers in Retailing

Retailing offers exciting and challenging career opportunities. Few other industries grant as many responsibilities to young managers. When students asked Dave Fuente, former CEO of Office Depot, what they needed to become a CEO someday, he responded, "You need to have profit and loss responsibility and the experience of managing people early in your career." Entry-level retail jobs for college graduates offer both these opportunities. Most college graduates begin their retail careers as assistant buyers, merchandise planners, or department managers in stores. In these positions, they are responsible for the profitability of a line of merchandise or an area of the store, and they manage people who work for them.

Even if you work for a large company, retailing provides an opportunity for you to do your own thing and be rewarded. You can come with an idea, execute it almost immediately, and see how well it is doing by reviewing the sales data at the end of the day.

Retailing offers a variety of career paths, such as buying, store management, sales promotion and advertising, personnel, operations/distribution, real estate, loss prevention, and finance. In addition, retailing offers almost immediate accountability for talented people, so they can reach key management positions fairly quickly. Starting salaries are competitive, and the compensation of top management ranks among the highest in any industry.

CAREER OPPORTUNITIES

In retail firms, career opportunities are in merchandising/buying, store management, and corporate staff functions. Corporate positions are in accounting, finance, real estate, promotions and advertising, computer and distribution systems, and human resources.

The primary entry-level opportunities for a retailing career are in the areas of buying and store management. Buying positions are more numbers-oriented, whereas store management positions are more people-oriented. Entry-level positions on the corporate staff are limited. Retailers typically want all of their employees to understand their customers and their merchandise. Therefore, most executives and corporate staff managers begin their careers in merchandise or store management.

Store Management

Successful store managers must have the ability to lead and motivate employees. They also need to be sensitive to customers' needs by making sure that merchandise is available and neatly displayed.

Store management involves all the discipline necessary to run a successful business: sales planning and goal setting, overall store image and merchandise presentation, budgets and expense control, customer service and sales supervision, personnel administration and development, and community relations.

Because store managers work in stores, they are often at quite a distance from the home office, which means they have limited direct supervision. Their hours generally mirror those of their store and can therefore include some weekends and evenings. In addition, they spend time during nonoperating hours tending to administrative responsibilities.

The typical entry-level store management position is a department manager with responsibility for merchandise presentation, customer service, and inventory control for an area of the store. The next level is an area or group manager with responsibility for executing merchandising plans and achieving sales goals for several areas, as well as supervising, training, and developing department managers. Beyond these positions, you might be promoted to store manager, then to district manager responsible for a group of stores, and then to regional manager responsible for a group of districts.

Merchandise Management

Merchandise management attracts people with strong analytical capabilities, an ability to predict what merchandise will appeal to their target markets, and a skill for negotiating with vendors as well as store management to get things done. Many retailers have broken the merchandising management activities into two different yet parallel career paths: buying and merchandise planning.

Retail merchandise buyers are similar to financial portfolio managers. They invest in a portfolio of merchandise; monitor the performance (sales) of the merchandise; and on the basis of the sales, either decide to buy more merchandise that is selling well or get rid of (discount) merchandise that is selling poorly. Buyers are responsible for selecting the type and amount of merchandise to buy, negotiating the wholesale price and payment terms with

suppliers, setting the initial retail price for the merchandise, monitoring merchandise sales, and making appropriate retail price adjustments. Thus buyers need to have good financial planning skills, knowledge of their customers' needs and wants and competitive activities, and the ability to develop good working relationships with vendors. To develop a better understanding of their customers, buyers typically stay in contact with their stores by visiting them, talking to sales associates and managers, and monitoring the sales data available through their merchandise management systems.

Planners have an even more analytical role than buyers. Their primary responsibility is to determine the assortment of merchandise sent to each store—how many styles, colors, sizes, and individual items. Once the merchandise is in the stores, planners closely monitor sales and work with buyers on decisions such as how much additional merchandise to purchase if the merchandise is doing well or when to mark down the merchandise if sales are below expectations.

The typical entry-level position of college graduates interested in merchandise management is either assistant buyer or assistant planner in a merchandise category such as men's athletic shoes or consumer electronics. In these positions, you will do the sales analysis needed to support the decisions eventually made by the planner or buyer for whom you work. From this entry-level position, you could be promoted to buyer and then divisional merchandise manager, responsible for a number of merchandise categories. Most retailers believe that merchandise management skills are not category-specific. Thus, as you are promoted in the buying organization, you will probably work in various merchandise categories.

Corporate Staff

The corporate staff positions in retail firms involve activities and require knowledge, skills, and abilities similar to those in comparable positions in nonretail firms. Thus, many managers in these positions identify with their profession rather than the retail industry. For example, accountants in retail firms view themselves as accountant, not retailers.

Management Information Systems (MISs)   Employees in this area are involved with applications for capturing data and developing and maintaining inventory, as well as the design of store systems such as POS terminals, self-checkout systems, and in-store kiosks.

Operations/Distribution   Operations employees are responsible for operating and maintaining the store's physical plant; providing various customer services; overseeing the receipt, ticketing, warehousing, and distribution of a store's inventory; and buying and maintaining store supplies and operating equipment. Students in operations and MIS typically major in production, operations, or computer information systems.

Promotions/Advertising   Promotion's many aspects include public relations, advertising, visual merchandising, and special events. This department attempts to build the retail firm's brand image and encourage customers to visit the retailer's stores and/or website. Managers in this area typically major in marketing or mass communications.

Loss Prevention Loss prevention employees are responsible for protecting the retailer's assets. They develop systems and procedures to minimize employee theft and shoplifting. Managers in this area often major in sociology or criminology, although, as we discuss in Chapters 9 and 16, loss prevention is beginning to be viewed as a human resource management issue.

Finance/Accounting Many retailers are large businesses involved in complicated corporate structures. Most retailers also operate with a tight net profit margin. With such a fine line between success and failure, retailers continue to require financial experts. The finance/accounting division is responsible for the financial health of the company. Employees in this division prepare financial reports for all aspects of the business, including long-range forecasting and planning, economic trend analysis and budgeting, shortage control and internal audits, gross and net profit, accounts payable to vendors, and accounts receivable from charge customers. In addition, they manage the retailer's relationship with the financial community. Students interested in this area often major in finance or accounting.

Real Estate Employees in the real estate division are responsible for selecting locations for stores, negotiating leases and land purchases, and managing the leasehold costs. Students entering this area typically major in real estate or finance.

Store Design Employees working in this area are responsible for designing the store and presenting merchandise and fixtures in the store. Talented, creative students in business, architecture, art, and other related fields will have innumerable opportunities for growth in the area of retail store design.

Human Resource Management Human resource management is responsible for the effective selection, training, placement, advancement, and welfare of employees. Because there are seasonal peaks in retailing (such as Christmas, when many extra people must be hired), human resource personnel must be flexible and highly efficient.

ATTRACTIVENESS OF RETAILING CAREERS

Immediate Responsibility

Management trainees in retailing are given more responsibility more quickly than their counterparts in other industries. Buyers are responsible for choosing, promoting, pricing, distributing, and selling millions of dollars' worth of merchandise each season. The department manager, generally the first position after a training program, is often responsible for merchandising one or more departments, as well as managing 20 or more full- and part-time sales associates.

Many students and their parents think that people working in retailing have jobs as sales clerks and cashiers. They hold this view because, as customers in retail stores, they typically interact only with sales associates, not their managers. But as we have discussed in this chapter, retail firms are large, sophisticated corporations that employ managers with a wide variety of knowledge, skills, and abilities. Entry-level positions for college are typically management trainees in the buying or store organization, not sales associates.

While some employees are promoted on the basis of their retail experience, a college degree is needed for most retail management positions, ranging from store manager to CEO. More than 150 colleges and universities in the United States offer programs of study and degrees or majors in retailing.

Financial Rewards

Starting salaries for management trainees with a college degree range from $30,000 to $60,000 a year, and the compensation of top management ranks with the highest in any industry. For example, store managers with only a few years of experience can earn up to $100,000 or more, depending on their performance bonuses. A senior buyer for a department store earns from $50,000 to $90,000 or more. A big-box store manager can earn from $50,000 to $150,000; a discount store manager makes from $70,000 to $100,000 or more; and a specialty store manager earns from $35,000 to $60,000 or more.

Compensation varies according to the amount of responsibility. Specialty store managers are generally paid less than department store managers because their annual sales volume is lower. But advancements in this area can be faster. Aggressive specialty store managers often are promoted to district managers and run 8 to 15 units after a few years, so they quickly move into higher pay brackets.

Because information systems enable retailers to assess the sales and profit performance of each manager, and even each sales associate, the compensation of retail managers is closely linked to objective measures of their performance. As a result, in addition to their salaries, retail managers are generally given strong monetary incentives based on the sales they create.

A compensation package consists of more than salary alone. In retailing, the benefits package is often substantial and may include a profit-sharing plan, savings plan, stock options, medical and dental insurance, life insurance, long-term disability protection and income protection plans, and paid vacations and holidays. Two additional benefits of retailing careers are that most retailers offer employees valuable discounts on the merchandise they sell, and some buying positions include extensive foreign travel.

Opportunities for Advancement

While the growth rate of retail parallels the growth rate of the overall economy, many opportunities for rapid advancement exist simply because of the sheer size of the retail industry. With so many retail firms, there is always a large number of firms that are experiencing a high growth rate, opening many new stores, and needing store managers and support staff positions.

Types of Retailers

EXECUTIVE BRIEFING

Debbie Ferree, Vice Chairman and
Chief Merchant, DSW Inc.

Math was always my favorite subject in school and came quite naturally to me, so it was no surprise that I entered college with the goal to become a college math professor, but my passion for fashion and love for business and retail caused me to change my career aspirations and transfer to the college of business.

Before joining DSW (Designer Shoe Warehouse), I worked in senior management positions for a variety of retailers, which gave me broad experience in different channels of distribution and business models: May Company and Burdines/Federated Department Stores—department stores; Ross Dress for Less—discount stores; and Harris Company—specialty retail.

In 1997, I joined DSW, a true off-price retailer, offering customers an assortment of end-of-season, closeout merchandise at deeply discounted prices. The department store landscape was changing rapidly and dramatically, where point-of-service discounting was the norm and customers were confused about the price they paid for a product. This created an opportunity in DSW to architect a new "hybrid" business model that would provide a very different shopping experience for the customer: an assortment of current, on-trend, in-season, fashion merchandise from well-known national brands at fair, everyday value (EDV) in an open-sell, attractive environment. This would define a new direction for the future in

retail. In 2004, I was promoted to president and chief merchandising officer of DSW and we took the company public in 2005.

To implement this new concept, we developed strategic partnerships with the leading designer brands in footwear. These vendors were focused on selling their brands through the department store channel and were initially skeptical about the new business model. The new model had many advantages and financial benefits: when they sold to DSW, there would be no extra charges such as advertising allowances or vendor chargebacks, and no renegotiations on prices at the end of the season or merchandise returns. Through collaboration and the development of financial and strategic plans that would support mutually profitable growth for both parties, we aligned on a plan that today generates over $2 billion in sales revenue in over 375 stores, an e-commerce business, and provides a long-term plan for continued growth.

The pillars of our success are a breathtaking assortment of on-trend merchandise, simple convenience, and irresistible value. We are using social media to create a community of shoe lovers who are loyal to our offerings, and regularly inform their friends about the new additions to our assortment and about their shopping experience in our stores

LEARNING OBJECTIVES

LO1 List the different characteristics that define retailers.

LO2 Categorize the various types of food retailers.

LO3 Identify the various types of general merchandise retailers.

LO4 Explain the differences between service and merchandise retailers.

LO5 Illustrate the types of ownership for retail firms.

and on our website. Our fan page is a place where shoe lovers can hang out and talk about shoes. We stimulate interaction between our over two million followers by presenting what our followers think of new styles, thanking them for their suggestions, answering their questions promptly, and running fun trivia contests with free pairs of shoes as prizes.

DSW's aspiration is to become "America's Favorite Place for Shoes" and "America's Favorite Place to Work." We have a strong culture that incorporates our core values—humility, accountability, collaboration, and passion—into a fun environment that stretches talent, supports individual development, and provides a rewarding career experience!

You want to have a good cup of coffee in the morning, not instant, but you don't want to bother with grinding coffee beans, boiling water, pouring it through ground coffee in a filter, and waiting. Think of all the different retailers that could help you satisfy this need. You could get your cup of brewed coffee from the drive-through window at the local Starbucks, or you could decide to buy an automatic coffeemaker with a timer so that your coffee will be ready when you wake up. You could purchase the coffeemaker at a discount store like Walmart or Target, a department store such as Macy's, a drugstore like CVS, or a category specialist such as Best Buy. If you want to buy the coffeemaker without taking the time to visit a store, you could visit www.thefind.com, search for "coffee and espresso maker," and review the details about 83,392 products sold by 5,485 retailers, ranging from Bed Bath & Beyond to Sur La Table to Newegg.

All these retailers are competing against one another to satisfy your need for a hassle-free, good cup of coffee. Many are selling the same brands, but they offer different services, prices, environments, and convenience. For example, if you want to buy a low-priced, basic coffeemaker, you can go to a discount store. But if you are interested in a coffeemaker with more features and want to have someone explain the different features, you can visit a department store or a category specialist.

To develop and implement a retail strategy, retailers need to understand the nature of competition in the retail marketplace. This chapter describes the different types of retailers and how they compete against one another by offering different benefits to consumers. These benefits are reflected in the nature of the retail mixes used by the retailers to satisfy customer needs: the types of merchandise and services offered, the degree to which their offerings emphasize services versus merchandise, and the prices charged.

RETAILER CHARACTERISTICS

LO1

List the different characteristics that define retailers.

The 1.1 million[1] retailers in the United States range from individual street vendors selling hot dogs to multichannel retailers that offer thousands of products in their stores and through catalog and Internet channels. The different types of retailers offer unique benefits. The type of retailer a consumer chooses to patronize depends on the benefits the consumer is seeking. For example, if you are shopping for a gift, you might value the convenience of buying a shirt from a retailer's Internet channel so the retailer will ship it to a friend in another city. Alternatively, you might prefer to buy a shirt from a local store when making a purchase for yourself so that you can try it on. You might go to a discount store to buy an inexpensive shirt for a camping trip or a sporting goods specialty store to buy a shirt with the insignia of your favorite football team.

All these retailers survive and prosper because they satisfy a group of consumers' needs more effectively than their competitors, and thus consumers patronize different retail types when they have different needs. As consumer needs and competition change, new retail formats are created and existing formats evolve.

Many retailers also are broadening their assortments, which means that their offerings overlap and competition increases. At eBay Motors, for example, consumers can buy cars and motorcycles from thousands of individual sellers and established dealers. The eBay sellers compete with traditional automobile dealers that sell cars and motorcycles through conventional dealerships. In another example, office supply stores compete with warehouse clubs, supercenters, supermarkets, and convenience stores because they sell many of the same products.

The most basic characteristic used to describe the different types of retailers is their retail mix, or the elements retailers use to satisfy their customers' needs. Four elements of the retail mix are particularly useful for classifying retailers: the type of merchandise and/or services offered, the variety and assortment of merchandise offered, the level of customer service, and the price of the merchandise.

Type of Merchandise

The United States, Canada, and Mexico have developed a classification scheme, called the **North American Industry Classification System (NAICS),** to collect data on business activity in each country. Every business is assigned a hierarchical, six-digit code based on the type of products and services it sells. The first two digits identify the firm's business sector, and the remaining four digits identify various subsectors.

REFACT

Nearly 19 percent of all U.S. retail sales are for motor vehicles and parts (441); department stores (4521) account for a little more than 3 percent.[2]

The classifications for retailers selling merchandise, based largely on the type of merchandise sold, are illustrated in Exhibit 2–1. Merchandise retailers are in sectors 44 and 45. The next three digits provide a finer classification of merchandise retailers. For example, retailers selling clothing and clothing accessories are classified as 448, clothing stores as 4481, and men's clothing stores as 44811. The sixth digit, not illustrated in Exhibit 2–1, captures differences between the North American countries using the classification scheme.

NAICS Codes for Retailers   **EXHIBIT 2–1**

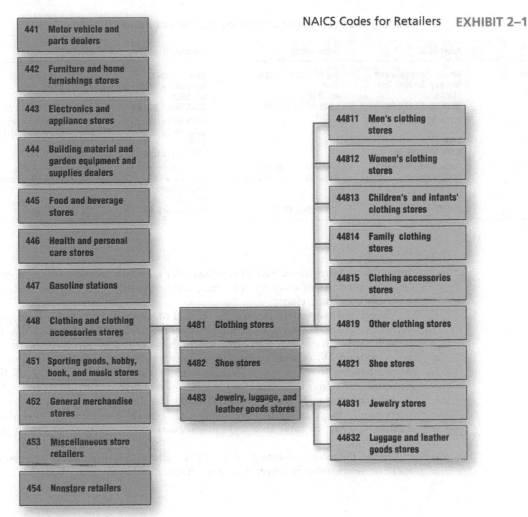

SOURCE: "North American Industry Classification System (NAICS)," U.S. Census Bureau, www.census.gov/epcd/www/naics.html.

Most services retailers are classified in sectors 71 (arts, entertainment, and recreation) and 72 (accommodation and food services). For example, food services and drinking places are in category 722, which is subdivided into full-service restaurants (7221) and limited-service eating places like fast-food restaurants (7222).

Variety and Assortment

Retailers can offer the same merchandise but differ in the variety and assortment of merchandise offered. **Variety** is the number of merchandise categories a retailer offers. **Assortment** is the number of different items offered in a merchandise category. Variety is often referred to as the **breadth of merchandise,** and assortment is referred to as the **depth of merchandise.** Each different item of merchandise is called a **stock-keeping unit (SKU).** Some examples of SKUs include an original scent, 33-ounce box of Tide laundry detergent with bleach or a blue, long-sleeve, button-down-collar Ralph Lauren shirt, size medium.

Warehouse clubs, discount stores, and toy stores all sell toys, but warehouse clubs and full-line discount stores sell many other categories of merchandise in addition to toys (i.e., they have greater variety). Stores specializing in toys stock

EXHIBIT 2–2   Variety and Assortment of Bicycles in Different Retail Outlets

	Adult Road	Adult Hybrid	Mountain	Child
Wheelworks	Bianci, Colnago, Peter Mooney, Serotta, Trek 150 SKUs $419.99–$7,999.99	Bianchi, Specialized, Trek 96 SKUs $349.99–$1,899.99	Salsa, Santa Cruz, Specialized, Trek 122 SKUs $299.99–$1,899.99	Electra, Gary Fisher, Haro, Kettler, Trek 56 SKUs $159.99–$429.99
Toys R Us	Mobo Triton Pro 3 SKUs $299.99–$359.99	—	Cycle Force, Huffy, Schwinn 4 SKUs $79.98–$135.99	Avigo, Cycle Force, Huffy, Mongoose, Pacific Cycle 228 SKUs $45.99–$499.99
Walmart	Cycle Force, Genesis, Kent, Mongoose 26 SKUs $99.97–$499.00	Cycle Force, Genesis, Schwinn, Tour de France 9 SKUs $179.00–$349.00	Havoc, Genesis, Schwinn, NEXT, Roadmaster 63 SKUs $88.00–$379.00	Huffy, Koxx, Micargi, Schwinn, Tour De France 195 SKUs $28.13–$675.00

more types of toys (more SKUs) and thus offer a greater assortment (i.e., greater depth in the form of more models, sizes, and brands) than the full-line discount stores or warehouse clubs.

Variety and assortment can also be applied to a specific merchandise category rather than an entire store. Exhibit 2–2 shows the breadth and depth of bicycles, as well as the different price points and brands carried by three very different types of stores: Wheelworks, a bicycle specialty retailer with one store in Belmont, Massachusetts; Toys R Us, a toy big-box category killer; and Walmart, a full-line discount store. Toys R Us has a large variety of merchandise besides bicycles, but its bicycle assortment is narrow. Wheelworks has the smallest variety because it carries only bicycles, parts, and accessories; but its assortment is very deep. Walmart, trying to cater to a wide target market, has a moderate variety and assortment.

One of the most interesting retailers that sells an amazing variety and assortment of merchandise is Amazon, which is highlighted in Retailing View 2.1.

How does Wheelworks' variety and assortment compare with Toys R Us and Walmart?

Why do the three retailers' assortments differ from each other?

Services Offered

Retailers also differ in the services they offer customers. Customers expect almost all retailers to provide certain services: displaying merchandise, accepting credit cards, providing parking, and being open at convenient hours. Some retailers charge customers for other services, such as home delivery and gift wrapping. However, retailers may differ on other services. For example, Wheelworks offers assistance in selecting the appropriate bicycle, as well as repairs. Walmart does not provide these services.

Prices and the Cost of Offering Breadth and Depth of Merchandise and Services

Stocking a deep and broad assortment, like the one Wheelworks offers in bicycles, is appealing to customers but costly for retailers. When a retailer offers many SKUs, its inventory investment increases because the retailer must have backup stock for each and every SKU.

Similarly, services attract customers to the retailer, but they also are costly. More staff must be paid to provide information and assist customers, alter products to meet customers' needs, and demonstrate merchandise. Child care facilities, restrooms, dressing rooms, and coat check rooms take up valuable store space that could be used to stock and display merchandise. Offering delayed billing, credit, or installment payments requires a financial investment that could be otherwise used to buy more merchandise.

To make a profit, retailers that offer broader variety, deeper assortments, and/or additional services need to charge higher prices. For example, department stores have higher prices than discount stores partially because of their higher costs. Department stores stock more fashionable merchandise and have to reduce prices when they make a mistake in guessing what the popular styles will be. They also provide more personal sales service and have more expensive mall locations. In contrast, discount stores appeal to customers who are looking for lower prices. These consumers are less interested in the costly services provided by department stores. Thus, a critical retail decision involves the trade-off between the costs and benefits of maintaining additional inventory or providing additional services. Chapters 6 and 12 address the considerations required in making this trade-off. In the next sections, we discuss the different types of food and general merchandise retailers.

2.1   RETAILING VIEW   Amazon: The Jack of All (Retail) Trades and Master of Many

When it started out in 1994, Amazon simply promised more books than anyone else. It took a few years for the online retailer to grow large enough to threaten the big names—Borders, Barnes & Noble, and so on. But today, its competitive threat spreads far beyond bookstores to take on virtually any type of retailer you might find.

Consider, for example, evidence showing that Walmart is losing sales to Amazon. Now that Amazon stocks items such as baby formula, clothing, and electronic goods,

often at lower prices than even the low-price master, people see little reason to fight with traffic or search for parking at the world's largest retailer. Instead, they sit at home and wait for the items to arrive. Won't be home during the day to receive your delivery? No problem—Amazon is testing an option to ship deliveries to local 7-Eleven convenience stores, then e-mail customers with bar codes that identify them, and their package, to the convenience store clerks.

As we know though, retail isn't simply about physical goods. It also includes services, and on that front, Amazon is also taking on a wide spread of competitors. It offers textbook rentals through its Kindle products to college students. The Kindle Lending Library allows Amazon Prime members to receive free books each month. It provides authors an easy route to self-publishing their work. Its cloud computing services are free for the first year—and its cloud offers enough storage for every person on the planet to store 82 books. With the Amazon Flow Powered app, shoppers in stores also can scan barcodes and find Amazon's (usually competitive) price immediately. And of course, for Prime customers, Amazon always offers free shipping.

But its influence is not all threat. For small-business owners, the opportunity to sell through Amazon provides unparalleled exposure. Amazon actively seeks small retailers with interesting products but insufficient resources to distribute those offerings widely. To them, Amazon is less a threat and more a golden opportunity.

Sources: Chantal Tode, "Amazon Makes Play for Greater Influence Over In-Store Shoppers," *Mobile Commerce Daily*, July 3, 2012; Brad Tuttle, "Today's Value Shopper Heads to Amazon, Not Walmart," *Time*, April 10, 2012; Greg Bensinger, "Amazon's Tough Call," *The Wall Street Journal*, July 11, 2012; Molly McHugh, "Saving Cash on College Textbooks," *Digital Trends*, July 18, 2011; Maggie Shader, "Amazon Tests After-Hours Package Pickup at 7-Eleven Locations," *Consumer Reports*, September 8, 2011; James Kendrick, "Amazon Debits Kindle Owner Lending Library," *ZDNet*, November 3, 2011; Vanchi Govind, "Amazon.com Offers Cloud Computing Services for Free," *InfoTech*, November 3, 2010; Jeffrey A. Trachtenberg, "Secret of Self-Publishing: Success," *The Wall Street Journal*, October 31, 2011; and Zoe Fox, "How Amazon Became the World's Largest Retailer," *Mashable*, November 17, 2011.

Amazon offers the largest variety and assortment of any retailer in the world.

DISCUSSION QUESTIONS

What categories is Amazon competing in? Which retailers are they competing against?

FOOD RETAILERS

LO2

Categorize the various types of food retailers.

The food retailing landscape is changing dramatically. Twenty years ago, consumers purchased food primarily at conventional supermarkets. Now conventional supermarkets only account for slightly more than 60 percent of food sales (not including restaurants).[3] Not only do full-line discount stores like Walmart and Target now offer a full assortment of grocery items in their superstores, but traditional supermarkets also are carrying more nonfood items. Many supermarkets

	Estimated Sales, 2013 ($ millions)	Estimated Sales Growth 2008–2013 (%)
Food Retailers		
Conventional supermarkets	$622,896	3.3
Supercenters	354,905	7.1
Warehouse clubs	159,075	6.7
Convenience stores	748,186	3.0
General Merchandise Retailers		
Department stores	73,291	−0.9
Apparel and accessory specialty stores	210,236	4.5
Jewelry stores	36,848	3.4
Shoe stores	29,606	1.8
Furniture stores	66,262	2.2
Home furnishing stores	59,465	2.8
Office supply stores	26,404	2.2
Sporting goods stores	49,717	5.3
Bookstores	19,101	2.1
Building material, hardware, and garden supply stores	393,254	3.6
Consumer electronics and appliance stores	141,800	4.4
Drugstores	250,172	4.2
Full-line discount stores	126,385	0.0
Extreme-value stores	52,454	3.1
Nonstore Retailers		
Nonstore retailing	340,421	9.0
E-commerce	282,055	15.0

EXHIBIT 2–3
Sales and Growth Rate for Retail Sectors

Sources: *Economic Forecast: Outlook to 2013 Food, Drug, Mass* (Columbus, OH: Retail Forward, November 2008); *Economic Forecast: Outlook to 2013 Homegoods* (Columbus, OH.: Retail Forward, November 2008); *Economic Forecast: Outlook to 2013 Softgoods* (Columbus, OH: Retail Forward, November 2008).

offer pharmacies, health care clinics, banks, and cafés. Exhibit 2–3 contains information about the size and growth rates for each of these retail sectors.

The world's largest food retailer, Walmart, attains more than $443 billion in sales of supermarket-type merchandise. On this measure, it is followed by Carrefour (France), Tesco (United Kingdom), Metro Group (Germany), Schwartz Group (Germany), and Kroger (United States).[4] In North America specifically, the largest supermarket chains in order are Walmart, Kroger, Costco, Target, Safeway, Supervalu, Loblaw, Publix, and Ahold US.[5]

Kroger is the largest supermarket chain in the United States.

EXHIBIT 2–4
Characteristics of Food
Retailers

	Conventional Supermarket	Limited-Assortment Supermarket	Supercenter	Warehouse Club	Convenience Store
Percentage food	70–80	80–90	30–40	60	90
Size (000 sq. ft.)	35–40	7–10	160–200	100–150	3–5
SKUs (000)	30–40	1–1.5	100–150	20	2–3
Variety	Average	Narrow	Broad	Broad	Narrow
Assortment	Average	Shallow	Deep	Shallow	Shallow
Ambience	Pleasant	Minimal	Average	Minimal	Average
Service	Modest	Limited	Limited	Limited	Limited
Prices	Average	Lowest	Low	Low	High
Gross margin (%)	20–22	10–12	15–18	12–15	25–30

REFACT

The first self-service grocery store was opened in 1930 by King Kullen in Jamaica, New York.[6]

Despite their similarly large sizes, most of Walmart's food sales are generated from its supercenter format, whereas Carrefour garners most of its sales using the hypermarket format that it developed. The remaining larger food retailers primarily sell through conventional supermarkets. Exhibit 2–4 shows the retail mixes for different types of food retailers.

Supermarkets

A **conventional supermarket** is a large, self-service retail food store offering groceries, meat, and produce, as well as some nonfood items, such as health and beauty aids and general merchandise.[7] Perishables, including meat, produce, baked goods, and dairy products, account for 30 percent of supermarket sales and typically have higher margins than packaged goods.[8]

REFACT

Shoppers spend an average of just under 13 minutes shopping for groceries on each trip, and half of that period is spent navigating the aisles or checking out.[9]

Whereas conventional supermarkets carry about 30,000 SKUs, **limited-assortment supermarkets,** or **extreme-value food retailers,** only stock about 1,500 SKUs.[10] The two largest limited-assortment supermarket chains in the United States are Save-A-Lot and ALDI.

Rather than carrying 20 brands of laundry detergent, limited-assortment supermarkets offer one or two brands and sizes, one of which is a store brand. Stores are designed to maximize efficiency and reduce costs. For example, merchandise is shipped in cartons on crates that can serve as displays so that no unloading is needed. Some costly services that consumers take for granted, such as free bags and paying with credit cards, are not provided. Stores are typically located in second- or third-tier shopping centers with low rents. By trimming costs, limited-assortment supermarkets can offer merchandise at prices 40 percent lower than those at conventional supermarkets.[11] These features have supported the substantial growth of such retailers, which appeal strongly to customers who are not loyal to national brands and more willing to try a store brand, especially if it means they pay lower prices.[12]

Trends in Supermarket Retailing   Although conventional supermarkets still sell the majority of food merchandise, they are under substantial competitive pressure on multiple sides: from supercenters, warehouse clubs, extreme-value retailers, convenience stores, and even drug stores.[13] All these types of retailers have increased the amount of space they devote to consumables. Family Dollar, which previously offered only discounted store brands, has expanded its assortment by about 20 percent, to include national brands such as Pepsi.[14]

Because consumers typically make three trips a week to buy food, but less than one trip a week to buy nonfood items, these competing retailers typically offer food merchandise to build the traffic in their stores and increase the sales of more profitable nonfood merchandise. They also have superior operating efficiencies and bargaining power with vendors that enable them to achieve low costs and offer low prices. These competing retailers have invested heavily in state-of-the-art supply chains, assortment planning, and pricing systems that reduce their inventories while increasing their sales and margins. These activities are discussed in more detail in Chapters 10 and 12.

To compete successfully against intrusions by other food retailing formats, conventional supermarkets are differentiating their offerings by (1) emphasizing fresh perishables, (2) targeting green and ethnic consumers, (3) providing better value with private-label merchandise, and (4) providing a better shopping experience.

Fresh Merchandise   Fresh-merchandise categories are located in the areas around the outer walls of a supermarket, known as the **"power perimeter,"** and include the dairy, bakery, meat, florist, produce, deli, and coffee bar. These departments attract consumers and are very profitable. Conventional supermarkets are building on their strength in these categories and devoting more space and attention to them. They are promoting fresh merchandise with cooking exhibitions and "action" stations, such as store-made sushi and freshly grilled meat. In response to this consumer desire for more and better fresh merchandise, food retailers such as Fresh Fare (Kroger) and Fresh Market are opening food stores focusing on the power perimeter merchandise.

Another example of the emphasis on "fresh" is the meal solutions offered to time-pressured consumers. A recent survey found that 64 percent of adult consumers have purchased ready-to-eat or heat-and-eat food from a grocery in the past month.[16] The choices in the stores are as varied as the stores themselves. Market District offers smoothies; Buehler's Fresh Food sells crab cakes and beef burgundy on a rotating "Dinner for 2" menu; Safeway's Lifestyle stores have sandwich and sushi stations. The ready-to-eat meals at a Publix store in Florida take up 4,500 square feet of space and include more than 80 entrees, such as cedar-plank salmon and Kung Pao scallops.[17]

Green Merchandise   Conventional supermarkets are offering more fair trade, natural, organic, and locally sourced foods for the growing segment of consumers who are health- and environmentally conscious. **Fair trade** is the practice of purchasing from factories that pay workers a living wage, considerably more than the prevailing minimum wage, and offer other benefits such as onsite medical treatment. Organic food purchases have jumped in recent years, with sales increasing by nearly 20 percent annually. Consumers also are buying a wider range of organic products, including staple items such as milk, eggs, and vegetables, as well as more fun options, such as ice cream and hair care products.[19]

Traditional supermarket chains also are opening smaller-format stores such as GreenWise Market (Publix) targeting health-conscious consumers who patronize Whole Foods. In a related food retailing trend, they offer locally grown products, a trend brought about in response to environmental concerns and the increasing financial costs (e.g., fuel) of transporting food long distances. The **locavore movement** focuses on reducing the carbon footprint caused by the

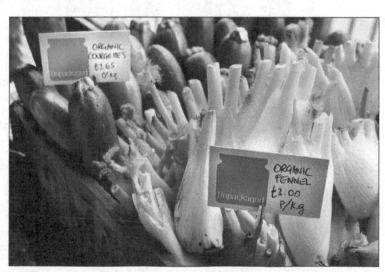

Health-conscious and environmentally conscious consumers are demanding organic and locally produced foods from food retailers.

transportation of food throughout the world. Food miles are calculated using the distance that foods travel from the farm to the plate. Many Americans appreciate the idea of supporting local businesses, but they also want the variety of products they can find everyday in their grocery store. It is difficult to maintain a balance between buying locally and maintaining such variety.

Ethnic Merchandise   Hispanics, who now constitute 15 percent of the U.S. population, have significantly different shopping and eating patterns from those of the general population.[20] They are more likely to prepare meals from scratch, spend more on groceries, prefer stores with bilingual staff and signage, and place importance on fresh food. In addition to adding more ethnic merchandise in conventional supermarkets, retailers are opening supermarkets targeting Hispanic consumers.

For example, Northgate markets in California cater to just Hispanic consumers. Their 36 stores, each approximately 50,000 square feet, feature both domestic and imported Latin American grocery items. Furthermore, they contain a dedicated tortilleria, prepared foods, and a well-stocked and staffed meat department.[21]

Supercenters offer a vast assortments under one roof.

Private-Label Merchandise   Conventional supermarket chains are leveraging their quality reputation to offer more private-label merchandise. Private-label brands (discussed in Chapter 13) benefit both customers and retailers. The benefits to customers include having more choices and finding the same ingredients and quality as in national brands at a lower price or higher quality at a similar price to the national brands. The benefits of private-label brands to retailers include increased store loyalty, the ability to differentiate themselves from the competition, lower promotional costs, and higher gross margins compared with national brands.

Improving the Shopping Experience   Creating an enjoyable shopping experience through better store ambience and customer service is another approach that supermarket chains use to differentiate themselves from low-cost, low-price competitors. Supermarkets are increasingly incorporating "food as theater" concepts, such as in-store restaurants, open-air market designs, cooking and nutrition classes, demonstrations, baby-sitting services, and food and wine tasting. To appeal to on-the-go consumers, other supermarkets are offering self-service kiosks that are both fun and convenient. Among the offerings, in place at both conventional supermarkets and limited-assortment stores, are Coinstar, a change counting machine; Redbox, a movie rental kiosk; and Starbucks kiosks selling freshly ground and brewed cups of its subbranded Seattle's Best Coffee.[22]

Supercenters

Supercenters are large stores (160,000 to 200,000 square feet) that combine a supermarket with a full-line discount store. Walmart operates more than 3,000 supercenters in the United States. Its leading competitors include Meijer, SuperTarget (Target),

Fred Meyer (Kroger), and Super Kmart Center (Sears Holding). By offering broad assortments of grocery and general merchandise products under one roof, supercenters provide a one-stop shopping experience.

General merchandise (nonfood) items are often purchased on impulse when customers' primary reason for coming to the supercenter is to buy groceries. General merchandise has higher margins, enabling the supercenters to price food items more aggressively. However, supercenters are very large, so some customers find them inconvenient because it can take a long time to find the items they want.

Hypermarkets are also large (160,000 to 200,000 square feet), combination food (60 to 70 percent) and general merchandise (30 to 40 percent) stores. The world's second-largest retailer, Carrefour, operates hypermarkets. Hypermarkets typically stock fewer SKUs than do supercenters—between 40,000 and 60,000 items, ranging from groceries, hardware, and sports equipment to furniture and appliances to computers and electronics.

Hypermarkets were created in France after World War II. By building large stores on the outskirts of metropolitan areas, French retailers could attract customers and not violate strict land-use laws. They have spread throughout Europe and become popular in some South American countries such as Argentina and Brazil.

Hypermarkets are not common in the United States, though they are similar to supercenters. Both hypermarkets and supercenters are large, carry grocery and general merchandise categories, offer self-service, and are located in warehouse-type structures with large parking facilities. However, hypermarkets carry a larger proportion of food items than do supercenters and have a greater emphasis on perishables—produce, meat, fish, and bakery items. Supercenters, in contrast, have a larger percentage of nonfood items and focus more on dry groceries, such as breakfast cereal and canned goods, instead of fresh items.

Both supercenters and hypermarkets face challenges in finding locations for new **big-box** (large, limited-service) **stores.** Although Brazil and China are promising emerging markets, many others are shrinking.[23] In Europe and Japan, land for building large stores is limited and expensive. New supercenters and hypermarkets in these areas often have to be multistory, which increases operating costs and reduces shopper convenience. Furthermore, some countries place restrictions on the size of new retail outlets. In the United States, there has been a backlash against large retail stores, particularly Walmart outlets. These opposing sentiments are based on local views that big-box stores drive local retailers out of business, offer low wages, provide nonunion jobs, have unfair labor practices, threaten U.S. workers through their purchase of imported merchandise, and cause excessive automobile and delivery truck traffic.

Warehouse Clubs

Warehouse clubs are retailers that offer a limited and irregular assortment of food and general merchandise with little service at low prices for ultimate consumers and small businesses. The largest warehouse club chains are Costco, Sam's Club (Walmart), and BJ's Wholesale Club (operating only on the East Coast of the United States). Customers are attracted to these stores because they

People go to warehouse clubs such as Costco to search for treasures like computers at prices lower than those of competitors.

can stock up on large packs of basics like paper towels, large-size packaged groceries like a quart of ketchup, best-selling books and CDs, fresh meat and produce, and an unpredictable assortment of upscale merchandise and services at low prices. For example, at Costco you can buy a 5-carat diamond ring for $99,999.99 with an appraised value of $153,450. Heavy food sampling adds to the shopping experience. Sam's Club focuses more on small businesses, providing services such as group health insurance as well as products. BJ's has beefed up its assortment of fresh meat and produce in recent years. Although package sizes are large compared to those in conventional grocery stores, BJ's provides convenient individual packaging—an attribute that is particularly appealing to its more upscale customers.

Warehouse clubs are large (100,000 to 150,000 square feet) and typically located in low-rent districts. They have simple interiors and concrete floors. Aisles are wide so that forklifts can pick up pallets of merchandise and arrange them on the selling floor. Little service is offered. Warehouse clubs can offer low prices because they use low-cost locations, have inexpensive store designs, and offer little customer service; they further keep inventory holding costs low by carrying a limited assortment of fast-selling items. In addition, they buy merchandise opportunistically. For example, if Hewlett-Packard is introducing new models of its printers, warehouse clubs will buy the inventory of the older models at a significant discount and then offer them for sale until the inventory is depleted.

Most warehouse clubs have two types of members: wholesale members who own small businesses and individual members who purchase for their own use. For example, many small restaurants are wholesale customers that buy their supplies, food ingredients, and desserts from a warehouse club rather than from food distributors. To cater to their business customers, warehouse clubs sell food items in very large containers and packages—sizes that also appeal to larger families. Typically, members pay an annual fee of around $50, which amounts to significant additional income for the chains.

Convenience Stores

Convenience stores provide a limited variety and assortment of merchandise at a convenient location in 3,000- to 5,000-square-foot stores with speedy checkout. Convenience stores enable consumers to make purchases quickly, without having to search through a large store and wait in a long checkout line. More than half the items bought are consumed within 30 minutes of purchase.

Convenience stores generally charge higher prices than supermarkets for similar products like milk, eggs, and bread. These products once represented the majority of their sales, but now the majority of sales come from lower profit products, such as gasoline and cigarettes, putting a strain on their profits.

Convenience stores also face increased competition from other formats. Supercenter and supermarket chains are attempting to appeal to customers by offering gasoline and tying gasoline sales to their frequent shopper programs. For example, shoppers who spend at least $50 and swipe their Giant Eagle Advantage Card at any

REFACT

Food service sales account for 30 percent of in-store profits for convenience stores while accounting for only 17.3 percent of sales.[24]

At convenience stores you can jump out of your car and pick up a Coke and some chewing gum while getting gas.
© BP p.l.c.

GetGo, Market District, Giant Eagle, or Giant Eagle Express location receive a 10-cent discount per gallon on their next fill-up.[25] Drugstores and full-line discount stores also have easily accessible areas of their stores filled with convenience store merchandise.

In response to these competitive pressures, convenience stores are taking steps to decrease their dependency on gasoline sales, tailor assortments to local markets, offer more fresh options, and make their stores even more convenient to shop. For example, to get gasoline customers to spend more on other merchandise and services, convenience stores are offering more food options that appeal to on-the-go consumers, especially women and young adults.[26] Finally, convenience stores are adding new services, such as financial service kiosks that give customers the opportunity to cash checks, pay bills, and buy prepaid telephone minutes, theater tickets, and gift cards.

To increase convenience, convenience stores are opening smaller stores close to where consumers shop and work. For example, 7-Eleven has stores in airports, office buildings, and schools. Easy access, storefront parking, and quick in-and-out access are key benefits offered by convenience stores. They also are exploring the use of technology to increase shopping convenience. Sheetz, a Pennsylvania-based convenience store chain, has touch-screen "Made-to-Order" kiosks at which customers can order customized deli sandwiches, wraps, salads, subs, and nachos while pumping gasoline.[28] Retailing View 2.2 describes the difference between convenience stores in the United States and Japan.

REFACT

Gasoline sales at combination gas station–convenience stores contribute 71 percent of the store's sales. Cigarette and tobacco products contribute 38 percent of in-store merchandise sales.[27]

RETAILING VIEW   Convenience Stores in Japan Are Different   2.2

Japanese corporations might own several U.S. convenience store chains (e.g., 7-Eleven, Circle K), but convenience stores (*konbinis*) in Japan and in the United States have little in common. Whereas shoppers in the United States depend heavily on their cars, most Japanese consumers commute using public transportation and work very long hours. To be convenient, the convenience stores thus locate in central business districts and train and subway stations. Rather than gasoline, *konbinis* sell a broad assortment of services, in addition to their extensive food options, including concert and amusement park tickets. Shoppers can pay their bills or make copies, as well as pick up some fashionable clothing. In turn, Japanese consumers visit convenience stores for approximately 30 percent of their food purchases, whereas in the United States, convenience stores only account for 5 to 10 percent of this market.

Part of the reason for this greater share is the quality of food available in *konbinis*. Whereas late night U.S. snackers might embrace microwaveable burritos, *konbinis* often offer pasta dishes, fresh vegetables, fruit, and prepared meals of restaurant quality. Although they traditionally catered to male customers, more Japanese women in the workforce have led the *konbinis* to adjust their assortments accordingly. A traditional bento box

REFACT

Convenience store operator 7-Eleven has replaced McDonald's as the world's largest chain in terms of number of outlets. As of July 2012, 7-Eleven had a total of 46,000 stores in 16 countries, compared with 33,510 McDonald's outlets.[29]

might contain rice with grilled fish or fatty meat—a meal not particularly appealing to female customers. Instead, today's chains prepare healthier food in nicer looking packages, such as *pho* Vietnamese-style noodles; soup in bowls; and elaborate, high-quality desserts.

With their relatively small sizes—around 300 to 600 square feet—and limited storage space, Japanese convenience stores need stellar information and supply chain management capabilities to succeed. That is, they must precisely match store-specific demand with just-in-time supply provisions. The most successful store operators gather customer information during every checkout: automatically, with a system that specifies the time of purchase, product barcode, and price, and manually, when the cashier notes the customer's approximate age and gender. An efficient data analysis system then determines when, how, and what to send to restock each *konbini*. Some stores even might receive up to seven restocking deliveries per day.

Sources: Kazuaki Nagata, "Convenience Store Chains Go With Flow, Grow," *The Japan Times*, May 8, 2012; and Stephanie Strom, "7-Eleven Shifts Focus to Healthier Food Options," *The New York Times*, December, 2012, p. B.1.

DISCUSSION QUESTION

Would Japanese-style convenience stores be successful in the United States? Why or why not?

GENERAL MERCHANDISE RETAILERS

LO3

Identify the various types of general merchandise retailers.

The major types of general merchandise retailers are department stores, full-line discount stores, specialty stores, drugstores, category specialists, extreme-value retailers, off-price retailers, and outlet stores. Exhibit 2–5 summarizes the characteristics of general merchandise retailers that sell through stores.

Department Stores

Department stores are retailers that carry a broad variety and deep assortment, offer customer services, and organize their stores into distinct departments for displaying merchandise. The largest department store chains in the United States are Sears, Macy's, Kohl's, JCPenney, Nordstrom, and Dillards.[30]

REFACT

T. Stewart was the first U.S. department store, opening in 1847 in New York.[31]

Traditionally, department stores attracted customers by offering a pleasing ambience, attentive service, and a wide variety of merchandise under one roof. They sold both **soft goods** (nondurable or consumable goods), which have a shorter lifespan such as cosmetics, clothing, and bedding) and **hard goods,** also known as **durable goods,** which are manufactured items that are expected to last several years, such as appliances, furniture, and consumer electronics. But now, most department stores focus almost exclusively on soft goods. The major departments are women's, men's, and children's apparel; home furnishings; cosmetics; kitchenware; and small appliances. Each department within the store has a specific selling space allocated to it, as well as salespeople to assist customers. The department store often resembles a collection of specialty shops.

Department store chains can be categorized into three tiers. The first tier includes upscale, high-fashion chains with exclusive designer merchandise and excellent customer service, such as Neiman Marcus, Bloomingdale's (part of Macy's Inc.), Nordstrom, and Saks Fifth Avenue (part of Saks Inc.). Macy's and Dillards are in the second tier of traditional department stores, in which retailers sell more modestly priced merchandise with less customer service. The value-oriented third tier—Sears, JCPenney, and Kohl's—caters to more price-conscious consumers.

Department stores account for some of retailing's most cherished traditions—special events and parades (Macy's Thanksgiving parade in New York City), Santa Claus lands, and holiday decorations. But many consumers question the benefits and costs of shopping at department stores. Department stores are not

EXHIBIT 2–5   Characteristics of General Merchandise Retailers

Type	Variety	Assortment	Service	Prices	Size (000 sq. ft.)	SKUs (000)	Location
Department stores	Broad	Deep to average	Average to high	Average to high	100–200	100	Regional malls
Discount stores	Broad	Average to shallow	Low	Low	60–80	30	Stand alone, power strip centers
Category specialists	Narrow	Very deep	Low to high	Low	50–100	20–40	Stand alone, power strip centers
Specialty stores	Narrow	Deep	High	High	4–12	5	Regional malls
Home improvement centers	Narrow	Very deep	Low to high	Low	80–120	20–40	Stand alone, power strip centers
Drugstores	Narrow	Very deep	Average	Average to high	3–15	10–20	Stand alone, strip centers
Off-price stores	Average	Deep but varying	Low	Low	20–30	50	Outlet malls
Extreme-value retailers	Average	Average and varying	Low	Low	7–15	3–4	Urban, strip

Macy's is a very popular department store known for great sales.

as convenient as discount stores, such as Target, because they are located in large regional malls rather than local neighborhoods. JCPenney and Sears thus are following Kohl's by opening stores in nonmall locations. Customer service has diminished in the second- and third-tier stores because of the retailers' desire to increase profits by reducing labor costs.[32]

To deal with their eroding market share, department stores are (1) increasing the amount of exclusive merchandise they sell, (2) increasing their use of private-label merchandise, (3) expanding their multichannel presence.

- *Increase exclusive merchandise.* To differentiate their merchandise offerings and strengthen their image, department stores are aggressively seeking **exclusive brands** in which national brand vendors sell them merchandise that is not available elsewhere. Jennifer Lopez has a clothing line at Kohl's. Ralph Lauren designed a line of casual apparel exclusively for JCPenney called American Living. Furthermore, clothing is not the only category with exclusive lines: Customers looking for exclusive dinnerware collections can go to Macy's and get the Rachel Bilson line or else find the Kardashian Kollection at Sears.[33]

- *Increase private-label merchandise.* Department stores are placing more emphasis on developing their own **private-label brands,** or **store brands.** These items are developed and marketed by the retailer, available only in its stores. Macy's has been very successful in developing a strong image for its brands, including Alfani (women's fashion), Hotel Collection (luxury fabrics), and Tools of the Trade (housewares).[35]

- *Expand multichannel and social media presence.* Finally, like most retailers, most department stores have become active participants in multichannel retailing. At Macy's and Nordstrom, customers can buy or reserve products online and then pick them up at the store. Customers can also return online purchases to stores. At Macy's and JCPenney, sales associates can order out-of-stock merchandise online via their point-of-sale (POS) terminals and have it delivered directly to the customer. As Retailing View 2.3 describes, Nordstrom may be one of the most connected companies in the world.

REFACT

Almost 50 percent of JCPenney sales involve exclusive lines. Kohl's sells approximately 48 percent, and Macy's level is 40 percent of total sales.[34]

2.3   RETAILING VIEW   Going Where the Customers Are

For Nordstrom, electronic offerings, such as a Facebook site or allowing customers to order online and pick up their purchases in stores, are old news. Its forward-looking, aggressive approach to social and mobile retailing has earned Nordstrom widespread recognition as a leader in terms of its connectivity—as well as a strong competitive advantage as retail continues to go virtual.

Back in 2010, Nordstrom introduced free wi-fi availability in its stores. This move exemplifies its superior recognition of how modern customers shop. Nearly all its in-store merchandise is available on its website. Furthermore, sales personnel are equipped with iPod Touch and iPad devices so that they can help a customer check out immediately, track inventory levels, and get suggestions for various departments. Staff members also are encouraged to interact with customers through social media, following Nordstrom's detailed guidelines. Such efforts reflect its goal to achieve seamless integration in its customer engagement, whether online, through mobile devices, or in stores.

Continuing its cutting-edge approach, social media for Nordstrom goes far beyond the basics of Facebook, Twitter, and YouTube. It also makes it presence felt on Pinterest, the online bulletin board; Instagram, Facebook's photo-sharing site; and the fashionista meeting place Polyvore. As a Nordstrom representative asserted, "Some people look at it as, 'If you have a Facebook site,

then you've got a social media strategy.' I think that's shortsighted."

To expand its online reach, Nordstrom has turned to an acquisitions strategy, purchasing shares in the flash sale site HauteLook, the children's clothing retailer Peek, the Sole Society shoe club, and the rapidly growing Bonobos menswear site. It also purchased advertising space in places with widespread reach, like in the massively popular Words with Friends game application.

Its efforts have paid off, not only in its image as a connected retailer, but also in the bottom line. It has attracted more than 1 million followers on Twitter. And the retailer's Internet sales grew by 30 percent in 2011. This result has prompted it to invest even more in its e-commerce efforts, up to $140 million in 2012.

Sources: David Hatch, "Nordstrom in Fashion with Social Media, Mobile Tech," *U.S. News and World Report*, May 15, 2012; Rimma Kats, "Nordstrom Put Focus on Social with New Media Initiative," *Mobile Marketer*, June 11, 2012; Sherilynn Macale, "This Retailer's Social-Powered Santa Claus Puts the Christmas Spirit Back in Gift Giving," *The Next Web*, November 25, 2011; and "Social Networking Guidelines," http://shop.nordstrom.com/c/social-networking-guidelines.

DISCUSSION QUESTION

How is social media helping Nordstrom stay connected with its customer base?

Full-Line Discount Stores

Full-line discount stores are retailers that offer a broad variety of merchandise, limited service, and low prices. Discount stores offer both private labels and national brands. The largest full-line discount store chains are Walmart, Target, and Kmart (Sears Holding). However, these full-line discount stores confront intense competition from category specialists that focus on a single category of merchandise, such as Staples, Best Buy, Bed Bath & Beyond, Sports Authority, and Lowe's.

In response, Walmart has taken a couple of routes. First, it has converted many of its discount stores into supercenters,[36] which are more efficient than traditional discount stores because of the economies of scale that result from the high traffic generated by the food offering. Second, it is expanding into more urban locations, using smaller storefronts that can be located in existing buildings, and appealing to price-oriented markets.[37]

Target has experienced considerable growth in the last decade because its stores offer fashionable merchandise at low prices in a pleasant shopping environment. It has developed an image of "cheap chic," continuously offering limited-edition exclusive apparel and cosmetic lines. In its GO International campaign, the retailer has teamed with such well-known designers as Missoni, Stefani, Harajuku Mini, Albertus Swanepoel, and Josie Natori.[38]

In contrast, Sears—and its Kmart brand—has struggled a bit in recent years and therefore is attempting an innovative and unusual solution. It will lease retail space in its stores to independent merchants. For example, in a huge Sears store in California, Western Athletic has leased approximately one-quarter of the space to insert a health club.[40]

REFACT

Hudson's Bay Company, the oldest retailer in North America, conquered the Canadian wilderness by trading furs more than 300 years ago. Today, it is one of the largest retailers in Canada, operating chains of discount, department, and home stores.[39]

Apparel/Shoe/ Accessories	Furniture	Sporting Goods	Office Supply
Mens Wearhouse	IKEA	Bass Pro Shops Outdoor World	Office Depot
DSW	Pier 1	Cabela's	Staples
	Sofa Express	Dick's Sporting Goods	Office Max
Books		L.L. Bean	**Pet Supplies**
Barnes & Noble	**Home**	Golfsmith	PetSmart
Consumer Electronics	Bed Bath & Beyond	REI	PETCO
Best Buy	The Container Store	Sports Authority	**Musical Instruments**
Crafts	World Market	**Toys**	Guitar Center
Michaels	**Home Improvement**	Toys "R" Us	
	Home Depot		
	Lowe's		

EXHIBIT 2–6
Category Specialists

Category Specialists

Category specialists are big-box stores that offer a narrow but deep assortment of merchandise. Exhibit 2–6 lists some of the largest category specialists in the United States.

Most category specialists predominantly use a self-service approach, but they offer assistance to customers in some areas of the stores. For example, Staples stores have a warehouse atmosphere, with cartons of copy paper stacked on pallets, plus equipment in boxes on shelves. But in some departments, such as computers and other high-tech products, it provides salespeople in the display area to answer questions and make suggestions. Bass Pro Shops Outdoor World is a category specialist offering merchandise for outdoor recreational activities. The stores offer everything a person needs for hunting and fishing—from 27-cent plastic bait to boats and recreational vehicles costing $45,000. Sales associates are knowledgeable outdoors people. Each is hired for a particular department that matches that person's expertise. All private-branded products are field-tested by Bass Pro Shops' professional teams: the Redhead Pro Hunting Team and Tracker Pro Fishing Team.

By offering a complete assortment in a category, category specialists can "kill" a category of merchandise for other retailers and thus are frequently called **category killers.** Using their category dominance and buying power, they buy products at low prices and are ensured of supply when items are scarce. Department stores and full-line discount stores located near category specialists often have to reduce their offerings in the category because consumers are drawn to the deep assortment and competitive prices at the category killer.

Although category specialists compete with other types of retailers, competition between them is intense. Competing category specialists such as Lowe's and Home Depot, or Staples and Office Depot, have difficulty differentiating themselves on most of the elements of their retail mixes. They all provide similar assortments because they have similar access to national brands, and they all provide a similar level of service. Primarily then, they compete on price and location. Some category specialists are also experiencing intense competition from warehouse clubs like Sam's Club and Costco.[42]

REFACT

The three office superstore chains—Staples, Office Depot, and Office Max—dominate the business with a combined $41.6 billion in annual sales, out of an estimated $100 billion market. They generally have margins of 25 to 28 percent of sales, higher than their warehouse club competition, Sam's Club and Costco.[41]

Category specialists, like Staples, offer a deep assortment of merchandise at low prices.

52 SECTION I The World of Retailing

Therefore, many of them are attempting to differentiate themselves with customer service. For example, Home Depot and Lowe's hire experienced builders as sales associates to help customers with electrical and plumbing repairs. They also provide classes to train home owners in tiling, painting, and other tasks to give shoppers the confidence to tackle their do-it-yourself (DIY) projects on their own. Home Depot offers an integrated line of Martha Stewart brand products, with different themes marked by unique icons, such that a customer can create a professional-looking decorated space simply by choosing products with matching icons.[44] Besides beefing up its sales associates' training to help customers purchase high-tech products like computers and printers, Staples has implemented "Easy Tech" in its stores to help people with computer and related problems and has installed Staples Copy and Print shops to compete with FedEx Office.

Specialty Stores

Specialty stores concentrate on a limited number of complementary merchandise categories and provide a high level of service. Exhibit 2–7 lists some of the largest specialty store chains.

Specialty stores tailor their retail strategy toward very specific market segments by offering deep but narrow assortments and sales associate expertise. Victoria's Secret is the leading specialty retailer of lingerie and beauty products in the United States. Using a multipronged location strategy that includes malls, lifestyle centers, and central business districts, the company conveys its message using supermodels and world-famous runway shows.[45]

Sephora, France's leading perfume and cosmetic chain—a division of luxury-goods conglomerate LVMH (Louis Vuitton-Moet Hennessy)—is another example of an innovative specialty store concept. Sephora provides a cosmetic and perfume specialty store offering a deep assortment in a self-service format. It also maintains separate stores-within-stores at JCPenney. The approximately 15,000 SKUs and 200 brands, including its own private-label brand, are grouped by product category instead of by brand like in department stores, with brands displayed alphabetically so customers can locate them easily. Customers are free to shop and experiment on their own. Sampling is encouraged. Knowledgeable salespeople are available to assist customers. The low-key environment results in customers' spending more time shopping.

Specialty retailers have such great appeal that they rank among the most profitable and fastest growing firms in the world. Apple stores sell a remarkable

EXHIBIT 2–7
Specialty Store
Retailers

Apparel	Electronics/Software	Jewelry	GNC
Abercrombie & Fitch	Ascend Acoustics	Blue Nile	Kiehl's
Brooks Brothers	Apple	Tiffany & Co.	M.A.C.
The Buckle	Brookstone	Zales	MakeupMania.com
Forever 21	Crutchfield		
The Gap	GameStop	**Optical**	Sephora
H&M	Newegg	1-800 Contacts	**Shoes**
Indochino.com	Radio Shack	LensCrafters	ALDO
Ralph Lauren	Tiger Direct	Pearle Vision	Allen Edmonds
J. Crew		Sunglass Hut	FootLocker
Threadless	**Housewares**		Nine West
Urban Outfitters	Crate & Barrel	**Health/Beauty**	Steve Madden
Victoria's Secret	Pottery Barn	Aveda	The Walking Company
Zara	Sur la Table	Bath & Body Works	
	Williams Sonoma	The Body Shop	Zappos

$5,647 per square foot on average, and its stock price jumped more than 25 percent in 2011. Lululemon's specialty is far less technical, involving yoga-inspired apparel and accessories, but it keeps opening its specialty stores at a remarkable rate of several per month. These stores earn an average of $1,800 per square foot.[46]

Charming Charlie stores are not quite as well known as the preceding brands, but the small company's success confirms the appeal of specialty retailers. In just seven years, the accessories and jewelry chain has grown to 178 stores, spread over 33 states. Its rapid growth is well matched by its influence: It was one of the first retailers to group merchandise by color instead of category. Furthermore, it works to maintain affordable prices ranging from less than $5 to no more than $50. That is, this specialty store specializes in helping customers update their wardrobes with new pieces, rather than forcing them to start all over again.[47]

Sephora is an innovative specialty store selling perfume and cosmetics.

REFACT

Approximately 16 to 18 percent of Americans shop at thrift resale stores.[48]

In addition, many manufacturers have opened their own specialty stores. Consider, for instance, Levi's (jeans and casual apparel), Godiva (chocolate), Cole Haan (shoes and accessories), Lacoste (apparel), Coach (purses and leather accessories), Tumi (luggage), Wolford (intimate apparel), Lucky brand (jeans and casual apparel), Samsonite (luggage), and Polo/Ralph Lauren (apparel and home). Tired of being at the mercy of retailers to purchase and merchandise their products, these manufacturers and specialty retailers can control their own destiny by operating their own stores.

Another growing specialty store sector is the resale store. Resale stores are retailers that sell secondhand or used merchandise. A special type of resale store is the **thrift store,** where merchandise is donated and proceeds go to charity. Another type of resale store is the **consignment shop,** a store that accepts used merchandise from people and pays them after it is sold. Resale stores earn national revenues of more than $13 billion. They also have enjoyed double-digit growth rates in the past few years.[49] Although the ambiance of resale stores traditionally was less appealing than that of other clothing or housewares retailers, the remarkable prices for used merchandise drew in customers.

Today, many resale stores also have increased their value by making their shopping space more pleasant and increasing levels of service.[50] With their lower expenses (in that they pay a discounted price to people selling their used apparel), resale stores are moving into storefronts in higher-end locations that have been abandoned by traditional retailers.[51]

Perhaps the best known and most widely expanded thrift shop is Goodwill Industries. In addition to its retail outlets, Goodwill runs an extensive job training and placement division, such that customers shopping at these outlets get a warm glow from knowing that their purchases help others. Unlike most other resale stores, Goodwill accepts all goods. The old stereotype of a cluttered, dark, odd-smelling Goodwill store has changed. The company has revamped and updated stores nationwide. Local stores seek to meet local needs, such that the New England–area Goodwill stores host annual bridal dress sales, and the Suncoast division in Florida maintains a catering department.[52]

Drugstores

Drugstores are specialty stores that concentrate on health and beauty care (HBC) products. Many drug stores have steadily increased the space devoted to cosmetics. Prescription pharmaceuticals often represent almost 65 percent of drugstore sales.[53]

The largest drugstore chains in the United States are Walgreens, CVS, and Rite Aid, which together run more than 36,000 stores, or 60 percent of the drug stores in the United States.[54] Much of this increased concentration has occurred through mergers and acquisitions. For instance, CVS acquired Longs, Sav-On, and Osco (as well as Caremark, which manages the prescription drug aspect for many insurance plans); Rite Aid acquired Brooks and Eckerd.

Drugstores face competition from pharmacies in discount stores and from pressure to reduce health care costs. In response, the major drugstore chains are offering a wider assortment of merchandise, including more frequently purchased food items, as well as new services, such as the convenience of drive-through windows for picking up prescriptions, in-store medical clinics, and even makeovers and spa treatments.[55]

In the Duane Reade store on Wall Street, near the New York Stock Exchange, customers find a vast array of offerings, such as $10 manicures, a hair salon staffed by a dedicated beauty consultant, a juice bar, and sushi chefs, next to typical drugstore products. Medical questions can be answered by the doctor who works there. In this store, the top sellers are now sushi, fresh juice, and bananas—though customers have not changed completely, so rounding out the top five sellers are coffee and Marlboro cigarettes.[56]

Walgreens hosts a café in its Chicago flagship store, where customers waiting to pick up a prescription can enjoy fresh coffee, breads, and pastries; munch on sushi or sandwiches; or visit the juice bar for a healthy smoothie or a nostalgic chocolate malted milkshake. But if they stop by later in the day, shoppers might prefer to browse the store's stock of 700 fine wines, artisanal cheeses, and gourmet chocolates.[57]

Although drugstores thus offer major advantages, especially in terms of convenience, they suffer from a price comparison when it comes to their grocery merchandise. A recent study indicated that the same selection of goods that cost $75.60 at a supermarket would run customers $102.94 at a nearby drug store.[58]

REFACT

Walgreens' merger/ acquisition of Alliance Boots has resulted in the largest pharmaceutical distribution network with more than 11,000 stores in 12 countries.[59]

Extreme-Value Retailers

Extreme-value retailers, also called **dollar stores,** are small discount stores that offer a broad variety but shallow assortment of household goods, health and beauty care (HBC) products, and groceries. The largest extreme-value retailers are Dollar General and Family Dollar.[60] As noted in the discussion of trends in food retailing, these stores have been expanding their assortments to include more private-label options, food, tobacco, and impulse buys such as candy, magazines, and gift cards.[61] Some extreme-value retailers, such as Dollar General, are adding refrigerated coolers and expanding their food offerings so that they can be known as the best destination store for a greater variety of household necessities. As a result, this retail model continues to attract significantly increasing numbers of shopper visits.[62]

Extreme-value retailers primarily target low-income consumers. These customers want well-known brands but cannot afford to buy the large-size packages offered by full-line discount stores or warehouse clubs. Vendors such as Procter & Gamble often create special, smaller packages for extreme-value retailers. Because these stores appeal to low-income consumers, are located where they live, and have expanded their assortments while keeping their unit prices low, they have cut into other retailers' businesses, including Walmart. Always ready for a good competitive battle, Walmart is opening smaller stores called Walmart Express in urban locations and creating smaller and less expensive packages to better compete.[63]

What you can still get for a dollar?

Despite some of these chains' names, few just sell merchandise for a dollar. The two largest—Dollar General and Family Dollar—do not employ a strict dollar limit and sell merchandise for up to $20. The names imply a good value but do not limit customers to the arbitrary dollar price point. Dollar Tree experimented with selling merchandise for more than a dollar, but it is back to being a dollar purist.[65]

REFACT

The number of visits to extreme-value retailers are increasing, while visits to large stores like Walmart are declining.[64]

Off-Price Retailers

Off-price retailers offer an inconsistent assortment of brand-name merchandise at a significant discount off the manufacturers' suggested retail price (MSRP). America's largest off-price retail chains are TJX Companies (which operates TJ Maxx, Marshalls, Winners, HomeGoods, TKMaxx, AJWright, and HomeSense), Ross Stores, Burlington Coat Factory, and Big Lots. Overstock.com and Bluefly.com are the largest Internet off-price retailers.

Off-price retailers are able to sell brand-name and even designer-label merchandise at 20 to 60 percent lower than the manufacturer's suggested retail price because of their unique buying and merchandising practices. Much of the merchandise is bought opportunistically from manufacturers that have overruns, canceled orders, forecasting mistakes causing excess inventory, closeouts, and irregulars. They also buy excess inventory from other retailers. **Closeouts** are end-of-season merchandise that will not be used in following seasons. **Irregulars** are merchandise with minor mistakes in construction. Off-price retailers can buy at low prices because they do not ask suppliers for advertising allowances, return privileges, markdown adjustments, or delayed payments. (These terms and conditions for buying merchandise are detailed in Chapter 13.)

Due to this opportunistic buying, customers cannot be confident that the same type of merchandise will be in stock each time they visit the store. Different bargains will be available on each visit. For many off-price shoppers, inconsistency is exactly why they like to go there. They enjoy hunting for hidden treasures. To improve their offerings' consistency, some off-price retailers complement their opportunistically bought merchandise with merchandise purchased at regular wholesale prices. Although not well known because few vendors to off-price retailers want to advertise their presence, the CEO of TJX asserts that the vast majority

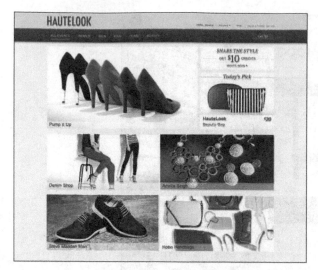

Luxury merchandise at great prices.

of merchandise in its stores is same-season items, purchased directly from manufacturers.[66] She also claims less than 5 percent of TJX merchandise is irregular.

An online twist to off-price retailing are flash-sale sights such as Gilt Groupe, Rue La La, and HauteLook. They are called **flash sales** because each day at the same time, members receive an e-mail that announces the deals available. Each deal lasts for a specific and limited time, and the sales are first-come, first-served. A shopper who misses out on a great deal is far more likely to buy the next time around. These sites often require members to register.

A special type of off-price retailer is the outlet store. **Outlet stores** are off-price retailers owned by manufacturers or retailers. Those owned by manufacturers are also referred to as **factory outlets.** Manufacturers view outlet stores as an opportunity to improve their revenues from irregulars, production overruns, and merchandise returned by retailers. Others view it as simply another channel in which to sell their merchandise. Retailers with strong brand names such as Saks Fifth Avenue (Saks Fifth Avenue's Off 5th) and Williams-Sonoma operate outlet stores too. By selling excess merchandise in outlet stores rather than at markdown prices in their primary stores, these department and specialty store chains can maintain an image of offering desirable merchandise at full price.[67] For some retailers, their outlet stores are the wave of the future. Nordstrom expects that sometime soon, it will have more Nordstrom Rack stores than regular Nordstrom department stores.[68]

Outlet stores can have an adverse effect on profits, however, because they shift sales from full-price retailers to the lower-priced outlets. Additionally, outlet stores are becoming more promotional to compete with increased activity at other outlet stores within the same mall and with traditional off-price stores.[69]

SERVICE RETAILING

LO4

Explain the differences between service and merchandise retailers.

The retail firms discussed in the previous sections sell products to consumers. However, **service retailers,** or firms that primarily sell services rather than merchandise, are a large and growing part of the retail industry. Consider a typical Saturday: After a bagel and cup of coffee at a nearby Einstein Bros. Bagels, you go to the laundromat to wash and dry your clothes, drop a suit off at a dry cleaner, leave your computer to be serviced by the Geek Squad at Best Buy, and make your way to Jiffy Lube to have your car's oil changed. In a hurry, you drive through a Taco Bell so that you can eat lunch quickly and not be late for your 1:00 p.m. haircut. By midafternoon, you're ready for a workout at your health club. After stopping at home for a change of clothes, you're off to dinner, a movie, and finally clubbing with a friend. You end your day having interacted with 10 different services retailers throughout the day.

Several trends suggest considerable future growth in service retailing. For example, the aging population will increase demand for health care services. Younger people are also spending more time and money on health and fitness. Busy parents in two-income families are willing to pay to have their homes cleaned, lawns maintained, clothes washed and pressed, and meals prepared so that they can spend more time with their families.

Exhibit 2–8 shows the wide variety of services, along with some national companies that provide these services. These companies are retailers because they sell

Type of Service	Service Retail Firms
Airlines	American, Southwest, British Airways, JetBlue
Automobile maintenance and repair	Jiffy Lube, Midas, AAMCO
Automobile rental	Hertz, Avis, Budget, Enterprise
Banks	Citi, Wachovia, Bank of America
Child care centers	Kindercare, Gymboree
Dry cleaners	Zoots
Education	Babson College, University of Florida, Princeton Review
Entertainment	Disney World, Six Flags, Chuck E. Cheese, Dave & Busters
Express package delivery	FedEx, UPS, U.S. Postal Service
Fast food	Wendy's, McDonald's, Starbucks
Financial services	Merrill Lynch, Morgan Stanley, American Express, VISA
Fitness	Jazzercise, Bally's, Gold's Gym
Health care	Humana, HCA, Kaiser
Home maintenance	Chemlawn, Mini Maid, Roto-Rooter
Hotels and motels	Hyatt, Sheraton, Marriott, Days Inn
Income tax preparation	H&R Block
Insurance	Allstate, State Farm, Geico
Internet access/electronic information	Google, Internet Explorer, Mozilla Firefox, Safari
Movie theaters	AMC, Odeon/Cineplex
QSR	Panera Bread, Red Mango, Pinkberry
Real estate	Century 21, Coldwell Banker
Restaurants	Applebees's, Cheesecake Factory
Truck rentals	U-Haul, Ryder
Weight loss	Weight Watchers, Jenny Craig, Curves
Video rental	Blockbuster
Vision centers	LensCrafters, Pearle

EXHIBIT 2–8
Services Retailers

goods and services to consumers. However, some are not just retailers. For example, airlines, banks, hotels, and insurance and express mail companies sell their services to businesses as well as consumers.

Organizations such as banks, hospitals, health spas, legal clinics, entertainment firms, and universities that offer services to consumers traditionally have not considered themselves retailers. Yet due to increased competition, these organizations are adopting retailing principles to attract customers and satisfy their needs. For example, Zoots is a dry-cleaning chain in the Boston area.[70] Founded by a former Staples executive, Zoots has adopted many retailing best practices: It has convenient locations, and it offers pickup and delivery service. Zoots stores also provide extended hours, are open on weekends, and offer a drop-off option for those who cannot get to the store during operating hours. The stores are bright and clean. Customers can check their order status, schedule a pickup, and provide special instructions using the online MY ZOOTS service. Clerks are taught to welcome customers and acknowledge their presence, especially if there is a line.

Most retailers provide both merchandise and services for their customers. However, the emphasis placed on the merchandise versus the service differs across retail formats, as Exhibit 2–9 shows. On the left side of the exhibit

Going to Zoots to pick up laundry and dry cleaning is as easy as going to an ATM machine.

EXHIBIT 2–9   Continuum of Merchandise and Services Retailers

Wholesale club | Supermarket | Category specialist | Specialty/department store | Optical center | Restaurant | Airline | Bank/University

ALL GOODS/NO SERVICES

ALL SERVICES/NO GOODS

are supermarkets and warehouse clubs. These retail formats consist of self-service stores that offer very few services, except perhaps cashing checks and assisting customers at checkout.

Moving along the continuum from left to right, department and specialty stores provide higher levels of service. In addition to providing assistance from sales associates, they offer services such as gift wrapping, bridal registries, and alterations. Optical centers and restaurants lie somewhere in the middle of the merchandise-service continuum. In addition to selling frames, eyeglasses, and contact lenses, optical centers provide important services like eye examinations and eyeglass fittings. Similarly, restaurants offer food plus a place to eat, music in the background, a pleasant ambience, and table service.

As we move to the right end of the continuum, we encounter retailers whose offerings are primarily services. However, even these retailers have some products associated with the services offered, such as a meal on an airplane or a checkbook at a bank.

Differences between Service and Merchandise Retailers

Four important differences in the nature of the offerings provided by services and merchandise retailers are (1) intangibility, (2) simultaneous production and consumption, (3) perishability, and (4) inconsistency of the offering to customers.

Intangibility   Services are less tangible than products—customers cannot see or touch them. They are performances or actions rather than objects. For example, health care services cannot be seen or touched by a patient. Intangibility introduces several challenges for services retailers. Because customers cannot touch and feel services, it is difficult for them to evaluate services before they buy them or even after they buy and consume them. Due to the intangibility of their offerings, services retailers often use tangible symbols to inform customers about the quality of their services. For example, lawyers frequently have elegant, carpeted offices with expensive antique furniture. Services retailers also have difficulty evaluating the quality of services they are providing. For example, it can be hard for a law firm to evaluate how well its lawyers are performing their jobs. To determine the quality of their offerings, services retailers often solicit customer evaluations and scrutinize complaints. In addition, online evaluation systems such as Angie's List and Yelp compile reviews from other consumers. The summary reviews give a sense of how well the service provider performs, according to people who have already purchased the service.

Simultaneous Production and Consumption   Products are typically made in a factory, stored and sold by a retailer, and then used by consumers in their homes. Service providers, however, create and deliver the service as the customer is consuming it. For example, when you eat at a restaurant, the meal is prepared and consumed almost at the same time. The simultaneity of production and consumption also creates some special problems for services retailers. First, the customers are present when the service is produced, may even have an opportunity to see it produced, and in some cases may be part of the production process. For example, customers at Build-A-Bear Workshop make their own teddy bears. Second, other customers consuming the service at the same time can affect the quality of the service provided. For example, an obnoxious passenger next to you on an airplane can make the flight very unpleasant. Third, services retailers often do not get a second chance to satisfy the needs of their customers. Whereas customers can return damaged merchandise to a store, customers who are dissatisfied with services have limited recourse. Thus, it is critical for services retailers to get it right the first time.

Because services are produced and consumed at the same time, it is difficult to reduce costs through mass production. For this reason, most services retailers are small, local firms. Some national services retailers are able to reduce costs by "industrializing" the services they offer. They make substantial investments in equipment and training to provide a uniform service.

Perishability   Services are perishable. They cannot be saved, stored, or resold. Once an airplane takes off with an empty seat, the sale is lost forever. In contrast, merchandise can be held in inventory until a customer is ready to buy it. Due to the perishability of services, services retailing must match supply and demand. Most services retailers have a capacity constraint, and their capacity cannot be changed easily. There are a fixed number of tables in a restaurant, seats in a classroom, beds in a hospital, and electricity that can be generated by a power plant. To increase capacity, services retailers need to make major investments, such as buying more airplanes or building an addition to increase the size of the hospital or restaurant. In addition, demand for service varies considerably over time. Consumers are most likely to fly on airplanes during holidays and the summer, eat in restaurants at lunch- and dinnertime, and use electricity in the evening rather than earlier in the day.

Services retailers use a variety of programs to match demand and supply. For example, airlines and hotels set lower prices on weekends, when they have excess capacity because businesspeople are not traveling. To achieve more capacity flexibility, health clinics stay open longer during flu season and tax preparation services are open on weekends during March and April. Restaurants increase staffing on weekends, may not open until dinnertime, and use a reservation system to guarantee service delivery at a specific time. Finally, services retailers attempt to make customers' waiting time more enjoyable. For example, videos and park employees entertain customers while they wait in line at Disney theme parks.

Inconsistency   Products can be produced by machines with very tight quality control, so customers are reasonably assured that all boxes of Cheerios will be identical. But because services are performances produced by people (employees and customers), no two services will be identical. For example, tax accountants can have different knowledge and skills for preparing tax returns. The waiter at the Olive Garden can be in a bad mood and make your dining experience a disaster. Thus, an important challenge for services retailers is to provide consistent high-quality services. Many factors that determine service quality are beyond the control of retailers; however, services retailers expend considerable time and effort selecting, training, managing, and motivating their service providers.

TYPES OF OWNERSHIP

LO5

Explain the types of ownership for retail firms.

Previous sections of this chapter discussed how retailers may be classified in terms of their retail mix and the merchandise and services they sell. Another way to classify retailers is by their ownership. The major classifications of retail ownership are (1) independent, single-store establishments; (2) corporate chains; and (3) franchises.

Independent, Single-Store Establishments

Retailing is one of the few sectors in most countries in which entrepreneurial activity is extensive. Many retail start-ups are owner-managed, which means management has direct contact with customers and can respond quickly to their needs. Small retailers are also very flexible and can react quickly to market changes and customer needs. They are not bound by the bureaucracies inherent in large retail organizations.[71]

For example, after more than a decade working for other UK fashion firms, Deryane Todd decided to open her own shop and, since then has expanded multiple times. The secret to the success of The Dressing Room is Todd's strong attention to determining and then providing exactly what her customers want. Despite the long hours and seven-day workweek, Todd expresses her love for her job because of the options it provides her. Todd hires her staff, trains them in her own way, determines the layout of the store, and designs the website.[72]

Whereas single-store retailers can tailor their offerings to their customers' needs, corporate chains can more effectively negotiate lower prices for merchandise and advertising because of their larger size. Corporate chains can and do invest in sophisticated analytical systems to help them buy and price merchandise. In addition, corporate chains have a broader management base, with people who specialize in specific retail activities. Single-store retailers typically must rely on their owner-managers' capabilities to make the broad range of necessary retail decisions.

To compete against corporate chains, some independent retailers join a **wholesale-sponsored voluntary cooperative group,** which is an organization operated by a wholesaler offering a merchandising program to small, independent

The secret of success to The Dressing Room in the United Kingdom is the owner's attention to understanding what her customers want.

retailers on a voluntary basis. The Independent Grocers Alliance (IGA), Tru Serv (supplier to True Value Hardware), and Ace Hardware are wholesale-sponsored voluntary cooperative groups. In addition to engaging in buying, warehousing, and distribution, these groups offer members services such as advice on store design and layout, site selection, bookkeeping and inventory management systems, and employee training programs.

Corporate Retail Chains

A **retail chain** is a company that operates multiple retail units under common ownership and usually has centralized decision making for defining and implementing its strategy. Retail chains can range in size from a drugstore with two stores to retailers with thousands of stores, such as Kroger, Walmart, Best Buy, and Macy's. Some retail chains are divisions of larger corporations or holding companies. For example, the Williams Sonoma corporation actually consists of four brands, Williams Sonoma, Pottery Barn, west elm, and Rejuvenation. Furthermore, its Pottery Barn branch features the PB teen and pottery barn kids lines. Royal Ahold owns 14 retail chains, including Stop and Shop, Giant, and Peapod in the United States and ICA and Albert Heijh in Europe.

Franchising[73]

Franchising is a contractual agreement in which the franchisor (the company) sells the rights to use its business trademark, service mark, or trade name, or another commercial symbol of the company, to the franchisee for a one-time franchise fee and an ongoing royalty fee, typically expressed as a percentage of gross monthly sales. More than 40 percent of all U.S. retail sales are made by franchisees,[74] and this type of retail ownership is growing around the world.[75]

When considering the franchise option, potential franchisees must understand the attractions and drawbacks of buying a franchise versus starting a retail business from scratch. There are many reasons to consider franchise ownership, including the success rate, which results partially from the proven business model that the franchisor offers. Success also results from the unique relationship between the franchisor and the franchisee, in which both parties benefit from the success of the franchisee. To get franchisees off to a good start, most franchisors provide off- and onsite training, location analysis assistance, advertising, and sometimes a protected territory (i.e., no other franchise may open a store within a certain radius of the first store). Some franchisors even provide financing or offer third-party financing opportunities.

There are also several drawbacks to franchise ownership. In addition to having to pay money to the franchisor, the franchisee needs financing for start-up costs, including rent or purchase price of office/retail space; modification of the space according to the guidelines of the franchisor (e.g., paint colors, flooring, lighting, layout); signage; opening inventory; and equipment. In addition to incurring the capital costs, the franchisee must adhere to the franchisor's rules and operating guidelines. In many

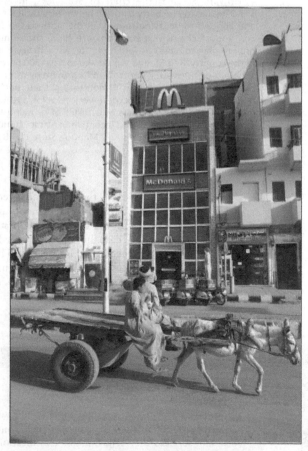

McDonald's franchises are growing all over the world.

2.4 RETAILING VIEW   Tart Frozen Yogurt—The Sweet Franchise

Frozen yogurt franchise operations Pinkberry and Red Mango both opened in the mid-2000s; they compete with old standby TCBY and some smaller regional chains. The appeal of Pinkberry and Red Mango to customers is not just the low fat of frozen yogurt but also its ability to boost people's immune system and improve calcium absorption. The tart frozen yogurt is dense with active cultures and probiotics. These health benefits, along with the great taste, has changed the way consumers think about frozen yogurt. Consumers are making multiple yogurt purchases each week, instead of buying it as an occasional nonroutine indulgence.

In addition to a limited number of exotic flavors—coconut, lychee and mango, many of which are seasonal—both Pinkberry and Red Mango offer a wide array of high-end toppings. The minimalism in the flavor choices is part of both companies' brand image, as reflected in the stark, bright store layouts. That is, these popular new chains offer consistency across their products and store images, even as it promises that customers can eat healthy, low-fat, hormone-free milk products, and still indulge in unusual yogurt flavors and interesting toppings.

Howard Schultz, the chair of Starbucks, invested $27.5 million in Pinkberry through his venture capital firm and appears to be trying to make it the Starbucks of frozen yogurt chains. Expectations are high, including a growth plan to have one Pinkberry for every 10 Starbucks in the country. Red Mango would like to have 500 units in the United States but is controlling its growth by carefully selecting its franchisees and monitoring their performance. Many franchises become very popular and ultimately fail within five years as a result of growing too large, too fast. An interesting incentive to attract franchisees by reducing their risk is Red Mango's Store Buy Back

New franchises like Red Mango appeal to customers because its frozen yogurt is low-fat, boosts people's immune systems, and improves calcium absorption.

program, in which the corporate franchise will buy back a store in the first six months if the franchisee is not satisfied.

If the frozen yogurt market becomes as competitive as the premium coffee market, then TCBY may become the Dunkin' Donuts of yogurt franchises, while Red Mango and Pinkberry will be the Starbucks.

Sources: Jaime Levy Pessin, "Yogurt Chains Give Power to the People," *The Wall Street Journal*, August 22, 2011; Yolanda Santosa, "The Making of Pinkberry," *Brand Packaging*, November 2, 2011; Blair Chancey, "Red Mango Revolution," *QSR Magazine*, October 1, 2009; and Kelly Bayliss, "Free Fro-Yo Today," *NBC Philadelphia*, September 23, 2009.

cases, the franchisee is required to purchase operating materials from the franchisor, especially in fast-food franchises that rely on standardized products across franchises for the success of the brand. The franchisor also might require the franchisee to purchase the equipment needed to offer a new product, such as fryers at a McDonald's or beds at a Holiday Inn. The hours of operation and days of the year that the business is allowed to close also may be dictated by the franchisor.

Retailing View 2.4 describes the sweet and tart world of frozen-yogurt franchises.

SUMMARY

LO1 List the different characteristics that define retailers.

To collect statistics about retailing, the federal government classifies retailers by the type of merchandise and services they sell. But this classification method may not be useful to determine a retailer's major competitors. A more useful approach for understanding the retail marketplace is to classify retailers on the basis of the retail mix, merchandise variety and assortment, services, location, pricing, and promotion decisions they make to attract customers.

LO2 Categorize the various types of food retailers.

Food retailing has undergone substantial expansion. Whereas once supermarkets were nearly the only source for food shoppers, today they can choose among traditional supermarkets, hypermarkets or superstores, limited-assortment markets, warehouse clubs, and convenience stores, to name a few.

LO3 Identify the various types of general merchandise retailers.

General merchandise retailers come in various forms, each with its own offerings, benefits, and limitations. These formats include department stores, full-line discount stores, specialty stores, drugstores, category specialists, extreme-value retailers, off-price retailers, and outlet stores.

LO4 Explain the differences between service and merchandise retailers.

The inherent differences between services and merchandise result in services retailers' emphasizing training of employees, whereas merchandise retailers emphasize inventory management issues. Retail institutions have changed in response to a changing marketplace, such that there is significant crossover between these types of retailers.

LO5 Illustrate the types of ownership for retail firms.

Small, independent retailers are usually owned and managed by a single founder. In contrast, corporate retail chains involve vast organizations and operate multiple stores. Another option that allows individual entrepreneurs to enjoy the security of corporate chains is franchising, a growing type of retail organization.

KEY TERMS

assortment, *37*

big-box store, *45*

breadth of merchandise, *37*

category killer, *51*

category specialist, *51*

closeouts, *55*

consignment shop, *53*

convenience store, *46*

conventional supermarket, *42*

department store, *48*

depth of merchandise, *37*

dollar store, *54*

drugstore, *54*

durable goods, *48*

exclusive brand, *49*

extreme-value food retailer, *42*

extreme-value retailer, *54*

factory outlet, *56*

fair trade, *43*

flash sale, *56*

franchising, *61*

full-line discount store, *50*

hard goods, *48*

hypermarket, *45*

irregulars, *55*

limited-assortment supermarket, *42*

locavore movement, *43*

North American Industry Classification System (NAICS), *36*

off-price retailer, *55*

outlet store, *56*

power perimeter, *43*

private-label brand, *49*

retail chain, *61*

services retailer, *56*

soft goods, *48*

specialty store, *52*

stock-keeping unit (SKU), *37*

store brand, *49*

supercenter, *44*

thrift store, *53*

variety, *37*

warehouse club, *45*

wholesale-sponsored voluntary cooperative group, *60*

GET OUT AND DO IT!

1. **CONTINUING CASE ASSIGNMENT: GO SHOPPING** The objective of this assignment is to have you take the retailer's, rather than the consumer's, perspective and think about the different strategies that the retailer you selected and another retailer might have, as well as how these strategies result in different retail mixes. The assignment is to conduct a comparison of the retail offerings for a specific merchandise category, such as tablets, men's suits, country/western CDs, women's athletic shoes, or house paint, for two different retailers. The other retailer selected might be a direct competitor using the same format or a retailer selling similar merchandise to a different target market with a different format.

Your comparison should include the following:
- The strategy pursued by the two retailers—each retailer's target market(s) and general approach to satisfying the needs of that target market.
- The retail mixes (store location, merchandise, pricing, advertising and promotion, location of merchandise category in store, store design, customer service) used by each of the retailers.
- With respect to the merchandise category, a detailed comparison of the variety and depth of assortment. In comparing the merchandise offerings, use a table similar to that in Exhibit 2–2.

To prepare this comparison, you need to visit the stores, observe the retail mixes in the stores, and play the role of a customer to observe the service.

2. **GO SHOPPING** Go to an athletic footwear specialty store such as Foot Locker, a department store, and a discount store. Analyze their variety and assortment of athletic footwear by creating a table similar to that in Exhibit 2–2.

3. **GO SHOPPING** Keep a diary for two weeks of where you shop, what you buy, and how much you spend. Get your parents to do the same thing. Tabulate your results by type of retailer. Are your shopping habits significantly different from or are they similar to those of your parents? Do your and your parents' shopping habits coincide with the trends discussed in this chapter? Why or why not?

4. **GO SHOPPING** Describe how the supermarket where you shop is implementing organic, locally grown, ethnic, and private-label merchandise. If any of these categories of merchandise are missing, explain whether you believe it could be a potential opportunity for growth for this supermarket. Then describe any strategies or activities that you believe are providing a better shopping experience than its competition. If you believe that competing stores are providing a better shopping experience than your store, explain what they are doing, and evaluate whether or not these activities would benefit your supermarket.

5. **INTERNET EXERCISE** Data on U.S. retail sales are available from the U.S. Bureau of the Census Internet site at www.census.gov/retail/. Look at the unadjusted monthly sales by NAICS (found in the Monthly Retail Trade Report section). Which categories of retailers have the largest percentage of sales in November and December (the holiday season)? Do your findings make sense to you? Why or why not?

6. **INTERNET EXERCISE** Three large associations of retailers are the National Retail Federation (www. nrf.com), the Food Marketing Institute (www.fmi.org), and the National Association of Convenience and Petroleum Stores (www.nacsonline.com). Visit these sites, and report on the latest retail developments and issues confronting the industry.

7. **INTERNET EXERCISE** Go to Entrepreneur Magazine's Franchise Zone web page at www.entrepreneur. com/franchise500, and view the top 500 franchises for the past year. How many of the retailers in the top 10 have you patronized as a customer? Did you know that they were operated as a franchise? Look at the lists from previous years to see changes in the rankings. Finally, what is the nature of the businesses that seem to lend themselves to franchising?

8. Bed Bath & Beyond is a category specialist with about 1,000 stores throughout the United States and Ontario, Canada. It sells domestics (bed linens, bathroom and kitchen items) and home furnishings (cookware and cutlery, small household appliances, picture frames, and organizing supplies). What are the SIC and NAICS codes used by this retailer? What other retailers compete against Bed Bath & Beyond, and which store format is implemented by each competitor?

DISCUSSION QUESTIONS AND PROBLEMS

1. Distinguish between variety and assortment. Why are these important elements of the retail market structure?

2. What sorts of competitive pressures are confronting traditional grocery stores? What options do these stores have to ease the pressure?

3. What do off-price retailers need to do to compete against other formats in the future?

4. Compare and contrast the retail mixes of convenience stores, traditional supermarkets, supercenters, and warehouse stores. Can all of these food retail institutions be successful over the long run? How? Why?

5. Why is Walmart, the largest retailer in the world, facing slower growth than in the past? What can it do to accelerate its growth?

6. Why are retailers in the limited-assortment supermarket and extreme-value discount store sectors growing so rapidly? From which retailers are they getting these additional sales?

7. The same brand and model of tablet is sold by specialty computer stores, discount stores, category specialists, online retailers, and warehouse stores. Why would a customer choose one retail format over the others?

8. Choose a product category that both you and your parents purchase (e.g., business clothing, casual clothing, music, electronic equipment, shampoo). In which type of store do you typically purchase this merchandise? What about your parents? Explain why there is, or is not, a difference in your store choices.

9. At many optical stores, you can get your eyes checked *and* purchase glasses or contact lenses. How is the shopping experience different for the service as compared to the product? Design a strategy to get customers to purchase both the service and the product. In so doing, delineate specific actions that should be taken to acquire and retain optical customers.

10. There are services and products involved when buying or renting a car, and in both cases, the customer drives away in a car. But buying a car focuses more on the product, whereas renting involves the service. Explain four ways in which marketing for a rental car company differs from marketing for an automobile dealership.

SUGGESTED READINGS

Borghini, Stefania, Nina Diamond, Roberts Kozinets, Mary Ann McGrath, Albert M. Muñiz Jr., and John F. Sherry Jr. "Why Are Themed Brandstores So Powerful? Retail Brand Ideology at *American Girl Place*." *Journal of Retailing* 85, no. 3 (2009).

Cuthbertson, Christine. *Retail Strategy: The View From the Bridge*, Oxford: Elsevier, 2012.

Enrique, Badia. *Zara and Her Sisters: The Story of the World's Largest Clothing Retailer*. New York: Palgrave Macmillan, 2009.

Fishman, Charles. *The Wal-Mart Effect*. New York: Penguin, 2007.

Grewal, Dhruv, Gopalkrishnan Iyer, Rajshekhar G. Javalgi, and Lori Radulovich. "Franchise Partnership and International Expansion: A Conceptual Framework and Research Propositions." *Entrepreneurial Theory & Practice*, May 2011, pp. 533–557.

Hammond, Richard. *Smart Retail: Practical Winning Ideas and Strategies from the Most Successful Retailers in the World*, New Jersey: FT Press, 2012.

Mitchell, Stacy. *Big-Box Swindle: The True Cost of Mega-Retailers and the Fight for America's Independent Businesses*. Boston: Beacon Press, 2006.

Roberts, Bryan, and Natalie Berg. *Walmart: Key Insights and Practical Lessons from the World's Largest Retailer*. Philadelphia: Koran Page, 2012.

Spector, Robert, and Patrick McCarthy. *The Nordstrom Way to Customer Service Excellence: The Handbook For Becoming the "Nordstrom" of Your Industry*. New Jersey: John Wiley & Sons, 2012.

Spector, Robert. *The Mom & Pop Store: True Stories from the Heart of America*. New York: Walker & Company, 2009.

Thain, Greg, and John Bradley. *Store Wars: The Worldwide Battle for Mindspace and Shelfspace, Online and In-Store*. West Sussex, UK: John Wiley & Sons, 2012.

Whitaker, Jan. *Service and Style: How the American Department Store Fashioned the Middle Class*. New York: St. Martin's Press, 2006.

Multichannel Retailing

EXECUTIVE BRIEFING
Luiza Helena Trajano
President, Magazine Luiza

I am from Franca, a small city in the state of São Paulo, Brazil. As a child, I loved to give presents to friends and relatives. When I was 12 years old, my mother told me that I would have to earn money to continue my "hobby" of giving presents. So I started working during vacations at a store owned by my Uncle Pelegrino and Aunt Luiza and have been working there ever since. I went to college in Franca during the evenings, and worked during the day at the store. In 1991, I was selected as the CEO of the company.

The company's early growth came from acquisitions of small town retailers in the state of São Paulo. We catered to the needs of consumers of all social classes. While the lower-income consumers had limited incomes, they sought the same respect shown to upper-income consumers. Our stores offered them respect and credit. With annual sales of about US$ 4 billion in 2012, our company now has more than 800 stores in Brazil selling furniture, appliances, consumer electronics, and home products. Although we are now in the major metro areas of Brazil, we have tried hard to preserve our company culture characterized by respect for our customers and employees and continuous innovation. These elements are in our DNA. Our transparent management system is designed to make associates feel part of the company, and we share the profits of the company with all employees.

In 1992, almost 10 years before e-commerce was introduced in Brazil, we used a multichannel approach. Our sales associates assisted customers placing orders on the stores' computers and having products delivered to their homes.

In 2012, we were invited to present at the National Retail Federation convention, in New York, our creative and very successful "Magazine Voce" (or Your Luiza Store) system. This system allowed our "agents" to create their own virtual Luiza store on Facebook with 20 products and sell these products to their friends. We now have more than 10,000 agents affiliated with our company.

Three years ago, we hired a new CEO, and I no longer am involved in the day-to-day operations. But I maintain our Luiza company culture by holding meetings with the staff of new stores. I also maintain direct supervision of the customer relations

CHAPTER 3

LEARNING OBJECTIVES

LO1 Understand the nonstore channels offered by retailers.

LO2 Compare the benefits offered by the four major retail channels: stores, Internet, mobile, and catalogs.

LO3 Analyze the challenges facing multichannel retailers.

LO4 Consider the multichannel shopping experience in the future.

department. This gives me the opportunity to pass along our values to the new associates, demonstrate the respect we have for them and our customers, and also highlight to all in the company our passion to serve our customers. And I still like to give presents.

A retail channel is the way a retailer sells and delivers merchandise and services to its customers. The most common channel used by retailers is a store. Retailers also use a variety of nonstore channels, including the Internet, mobile, catalogs and direct mail, direct selling, television home shopping, direct-response TV, and automated retailing (vending machines) to make sales to customers. This definition makes a distinction between a channel and a medium such as TV advertising. A *channel* involves the opportunity to complete a transaction—to sell and deliver merchandise—while a *medium* is primarily used to communicate information to consumers. Retailers communicate information through channels as well as complete transactions; however, the primary objective of the channel is to complete transactions.

Multichannel retailing involves using more than one channel to sell and deliver merchandise and services to consumers.[1] Note the term **omniretailing** is frequently used when discussing multichannel retailing; it refers to a coordinated multichannel retail offering that provides a seamless customer experience when using all of the retailer's shopping channels.

The birth of multichannel retailing can be traced back to when Sears opened its first store in 1925, 33 years after it launched its catalog that offered merchandise previously unavailable to the American masses.[2] Now, almost all large retailers

Even small, single-store retailers like Harry's Fishing Supply interact with their customers through multiple channels.

that operate stores are multichannel retailers. Most have added an Internet channel that offers customers an opportunity to buy merchandise or services by accessing their website, as well as patronizing their stores.[3]

Many small, store-based retailers also use multiple channels. For example, in its 8,000-square-foot retail store near Miami's Little River district, Capt. Harry's Fishing Supply's offers more than 20,000 products, including rods and reels, as well as at least 1,000 lures and teasers in every color, designed to tempt fish onto an angler's line. The biggest lure is nearly two feet long and the smallest less than an inch. There are scented lures, mirrored lures, lures with holographic features, and ones designed to move like a frightened fish. In the early 1980s, Harry Vernon, Jr., the company president, noticed that about 40 percent of the foot traffic was from foreign customers. So, he launched a catalog and eventually Internet channels. Now, from a second-floor warehouse, pickers fill orders from nearly every U.S. state and 120 countries.[4]

In this chapter, we take a strategic perspective to examine the four primary channels through which retailers sell merchandise and services to their customers. We first briefly describe all of the nonstore retail channels; retailers typically evolve to multichannel retailers by adding a nonstore channel to their store channel. We then review the unique benefits that each of the four major channels offer to consumers and outline the retailers' benefits from providing a multichannel offering. Next, we describe the challenges multichannel retailers face when using these channels synergistically and how they provide a seamless offering for their customers. At the end of the chapter, we illustrate how integrating these channels and using new technologies will create a compelling shopping experience in the future.

Nonstore Retail Channels

LO1

Understand the nonstore channels offered by retailers.

The estimated percentage of annual retail sales (excluding motor vehicles and food services annual sales) made through each channel is shown in Exhibit 3–1. The vast majority of sales are made through the store channel, but the Internet and catalog channels also account for significant sales, while the mobile channel has the highest growth rate.

Internet Retailing Channels—Electronic and Mobile Retailing

Internet retailing is the fastest growing channel. It involves retailers interacting with consumers via the Internet, whether they use a traditional computer or a laptop, a variety of sizes of tablets or a smartphone. We refer to the channel that

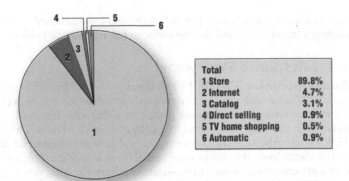

EXHIBIT 3–1
U.S. Retail Sales by
Channel

Total	
1 Store	89.8%
2 Internet	4.7%
3 Catalog	3.1%
4 Direct selling	0.9%
5 TV home shopping	0.5%
6 Automatic	0.9%

SOURCES: U.S. Census Bureau, "Estimates of Monthly Retail and Food Services Sales by Kind of Business: 2009," www.census.gov/retail/mrts/www/data/excel/mrtssales92-09.xls; personal communication with the Direct Selling Association, Direct Marketing Association, and National Automatic Merchandising Association.

*Excluding sales of motor vehicles, food services, and travel.

involves accessing the Internet through a traditional computer as the electronic channel. The mobile channel (also called **mobile retailing,** mobile commerce, or m-commerce), involves accessing the Internet using a smartphone. From a retailing perspective, smartphones differ from traditional computers in that they are more portable, have a smaller display, are location-aware, use different touch screen technology to access the Internet, and as a result of these factors produce a different interface experience with the user. Tablets retain some of the advantages and disadvantages of using a traditional computer with some of the mobility benefits and problems associated with shopping with a mobile phone.

Two decades ago, experts thought by now everyone would be doing their shopping over the Internet. These experts predicted that a new breed of high-tech, web-savvy entrepreneurs would dominate the retail industry. Stores would close due to lack of traffic, and paper catalogs would become obsolete. However, these predictions of Internet retailing transforming the retail industry have not occurred. Even though U.S. sales through Internet channels are forecasted to grow at about 10 percent annually, more than three times faster than sales growth through store channels, Internet sales are expected to only account for 11 percent of retail sales (excluding automotive and food services) by 2015, with the mobile channel accounting for 9 percent of Internet retail sales.[6]

The Internet is, therefore, a facilitating, rather than transformational, technology with respect to most sectors of the retail industry. Almost all of the traditional store-based retailers utilize Internet channels to provide a better shopping experience for their customers and now dominate these channels. Almost 75 percent of U.S. consumers use the Internet to search for information about clothes, shoes, toys, and health and beauty aids before they go to a store to buy the items. Eighty-three percent go online before buying electronics, computers, books, music, and movies in stores.[7] Just over half of all adults who own mobile phones use them to get either product reviews or pricing information while in a physical store, a process known as showrooming.[8]

Catalog Channel

The **catalog channel** is a nonstore retail channel in which the retail offering is communicated to customers through a catalog mailed to customers. About half of U.S. consumers shop through catalogs each year. The merchandise categories with the greatest catalog sales are drugs, beauty aids, computers, software, clothing, accessories, furniture, and housewares.[9] The use of catalogs has come under attack from consumer groups that believe that catalogs are an unnecessary waste of natural resources. In the United States, catalogs account for 3 percent of the roughly 80 million tons of paper products used annually. That is more than either magazines or books.[10] Further, catalogs' share of sales is declining relative to the Internet. But

REFACT

The first use of an Internet retail channel was on August 11, 1994, when a CD by Sting was sold by NetMarket over the Internet.[5]

catalogs are not going away. Their role is shifting from primarily generating sales to building a brand image and driving traffic to the Internet and physical stores.[11]

Direct-Response TV Channel

The **direct-response TV (DRTV) channel** is a retail channel in which customers watch a TV advertisement that demonstrates merchandise and then place orders for that merchandise. The orders are placed by either telephoning a phone bank of operators or accessing the Internet to use the company's website. There are two types of DRTV advertisements: a long form, referred to as an **infomercial** and typically 30 to 60 minutes long, that mixes entertainment with product demonstrations, and a short form consisting of one- to two-minute advertisements on television. Approximately $150 million in annual retail sales is made through the DRTV channel.

Unlike most TV advertising, the impact of a DRTV advertisement is precisely measureable. Within 24 hours, retailers using this channel can determine how many customers responded to each exposure to an ad. The results can be analyzed to determine the effects of location, time of week, time of day, and different scripts and creative responses.

Television Home Shopping Channel

Television home shopping is a retail channel in which customers watch a TV network with programs that demonstrate merchandise and then place orders for that merchandise, usually by telephone or via the Internet. Annual U.S. sales through TV shopping networks are approximately $20 billion. The two largest retailers using this channel are HSN and QVC, followed by ShopNBC and Jewelry Television. Although most consumers with cable or satellite television access can patronize a television shopping channel, relatively few watch on a regular basis. Furthermore, most of the purchases are made by a relatively small percentage of viewers. Like catalogs, TV home shopping networks have embraced the Internet for taking customer orders, although it is still possible to place an order by telephone and mail.

The major advantage of TV home shopping is that customers can see the merchandise demonstrated either on their television screens or through streaming videos on the Internet. In response to the increase in cooking, decorating, do-it-yourself, and other lifestyle programming, home shopping retailers have incorporated more demonstrations into their programming in an attempt to educate their potential customers.

TV home shopping retailers are also embracing social media. Today's consumer is interacting with TV home shopping channels on multiple screens. They have a smartphone, laptop computer, or tablet next to them as they view the program. The tweets that these media-savvy customers send to the network appear on live scrolls, adding user comments about various products and guests to the broadcast. At the same time, on HSN's Facebook page, they can ask questions and chat about the program as it happens; the really interesting comments and questions then get read on the air by the customers' favorite hosts.[13]

HSN's sales have more than doubled after it started selling more well-known brands.

Direct Selling Channel

Direct selling is a retail channel in which salespeople interact with customers face-to-face in a convenient location, either at the customer's home or at work. Direct salespeople demonstrate merchandise benefits and/or explain a service, take an order, and deliver the merchandise. Direct selling is a highly interactive retail channel in which considerable information is conveyed to customers through face-to-face discussions and demonstrations. However, providing this high level of personalized information, including extensive demonstrations, is costly.

Annual U.S. sales through direct selling are about $30 billion; worldwide, sales are more than $100 billion. More than 60 percent of the products sold through the direct selling channel are home/family care/home durables (cleaning products, cookware, cutlery, etc.), wellness (weight loss products, vitamins, etc.) and personal care (cosmetics, jewelry, skin care, etc.)[15]

Almost all the 15 million salespeople in the United States who work in direct sales are independent agents.[16] They are not employed by the direct sales firm but, rather, act as independent distributors, buying merchandise from the firms and then reselling it to consumers. In most cases, direct salespeople may sell their merchandise to anyone, but some companies, such as Avon, assign territories to salespeople who regularly contact households in their territory. Retailing View 3.1 describes how the direct selling channel is particularly effective in less developed countries.

RETAILING VIEW   Avon's Direct Selling Channel in Brazil   3.1

Baixada Fluminense might be one of the toughest neighborhoods in Rio de Janeiro, but that doesn't mean its residents don't worry about lipstick colors. It might even mean they worry more. Thus, Heloisa Almada Contreira visits her 80 or so customers regularly in their homes, earning weekly sales of about $930 by selling Avon products. Spending 50 reais ($27) on cosmetics might seem like a lot for many low-income consumers, but, according to Almada Contreira, "For them, it's a necessity. Brazilian women can't go without their makeup."

Her impression might be anecdotal, but the statistics back up this claim, in that Brazil constitutes the world's third largest market for beauty care products, behind only the United States and Japan. With its expansive coastline and warm climate, Brazil invites residents to visit beaches all year, though the approach of summer often finds millions of women initiating a diet and beauty regime that will enable them to live *verão sem kanga*—that is, as part of a robe-free summer on the beach. Such hot weather may be great for a beach day, but it also means that people often need at least a couple of showers. Thus, Brazilians use twice the shampoo, conditioner, and soap compared with residents of other countries. And then women need to apply their makeup a second time each day!

The constant demand for cosmetics and beauty products is no problem for Almada Contreira and her 1.1 million sales colleagues. Avon's Brazilian sales force sells door-to-door, whether their customers live in city slums, the Amazonian rainforest, or remote towns. These sorts of direct sales have long been a staple of American life, but companies such as Avon, as well as Herbalife and Amway, increasingly turn to this channel to sell to consumers in less developed countries. In these areas, direct sales can be particularly effective, because the channel does not require a sophisticated or expensive infrastructure. Instead, salespeople handle distribution on their own. These independent agents not only sell and distribute the

Avon's direct selling channel is particularly effective in developing economies such as Brazil.

products to their customers, but they also take responsibility for ordering merchandise to restock their inventory. To reach customers in the Amazon, Avon salespeople might need to hire a small boat or plane, and the product delivery might be delayed for a week or more. But for those waiting for just the right color to apply to their cheeks, a week is not too long to wait.

Sources: Christina Passariello and Emily Glazer, "Coty Knocks on Brazil's Door; Part of Avon's Allure to Fragrance Maker Is Its Sales Network in South America," *The Wall Street Journal (Online)*, April 5, 2012; Jenney Barchfield, "In Beauty-Obsessed Brazil, Clinics Offer Free Plastic Surgery to Poor," *Los Angeles Times*, March 25 2012, A.4; and Jonathan Wheatley, "Beauty Business Turns Heads in Brazil," *Investor's Choice*, January 19, 2010.

DISCUSSION QUESTION

Why is the direct sales channel so much more popular and effective in Brazil than in the United States?

Two special types of direct selling are the party plan and multilevel systems. About one-quarter of all direct sales are made using a **party plan system.** Salespeople encourage customers to act as hosts and invite friends or coworkers to a "party." The host or hostess receives a gift or commission for arranging the party. At the party, the merchandise is demonstrated and attendees place orders.

In a **multilevel system,** independent businesspeople serve as master distributors, recruiting other people to become distributors in their network. The master distributors either buy merchandise from the firm and resell it to their distributors or receive a commission on all merchandise purchased by the distributors in their network. In addition to selling merchandise themselves, the master distributors are involved in recruiting and training other distributors.

Some multilevel direct selling firms are illegal pyramid schemes. A **pyramid scheme** develops when the firm and its program are designed to sell merchandise and services to other distributors, rather than to end-users. The founders and initial distributors in pyramid schemes profit from the inventory bought by later participants, but little merchandise is sold to consumers who use it.

Automated Retailing (Vending Machines) Channel

Automated retailing is a retail channel in which merchandise or services are stored in a machine and dispensed to customers when they deposit cash or use a credit card. Automated retailing machines, also known as **vending machines,** are typically placed at convenient, high-traffic locations. About 80 percent of the automated retailing channel sales are from cold beverages, prepared food service, candy, and snacks. Annual U.S. sales in the channel were $40 billion, but between 2007 and 2010, sales declined by more than 11 percent.[17]

As a result of this decline, vending machines also are disappearing from stores and sidewalks. Unwilling to give up on this channel, some entrepreneurs are reimagining the uses of vending machines. Many of them are going high-tech, with sophisticated service offerings. Machines maintained by Minnesota-based InstyMeds Corp. appear in health clinics and dispense prescription medicines. To prevent fraud, the machines maintain an electronic link to the doctor's computer system, which allows them to confirm each patient's identity and prescription, using a unique code assigned by the doctor to each patient.[19]

Another interesting automated retailing application is taking the DVD rental business by storm. Redbox rents DVDs for $1 a day in more than 22,000 locations, including McDonald's, Walmart, Walgreens, Albertsons, and 7-Eleven Circle-K. The retailer rents more than 7.5 million movies weekly, close to the sales reported by its mail-order rival Netflix. Redbox's success, as well as its challenge, is keeping its inventory of DVDs fresh and available when customers want to rent them. Customers can check the inventory of a particular machine and reserve a copy of any title at Redbox's Internet site.[20]

REFACT

The Greek mathematician Hero invented the first vending machine in 215 B.C., selling holy water to worshippers in Egyptian temples. In the early 1880s, the first coin-operated vending machines allowed customers in London, England, to purchase postcards.[18]

RELATIVE BENEFITS OF RETAIL CHANNELS

LO2

Compare the benefits offered by the four major retail channels: stores, Internet, mobile, and catalogs.

In this section, we discuss the relative benefits and limitations of the four major retail channels: stores, catalogs, electronic, and mobile. Exhibit 3–2 summarizes these unique benefits. In the following section, we discuss how retailers provide a better customer shopping experience by integrating these channels into a true multichannel experience.

Store Channel

Stores offer several benefits to customers that they cannot get when they shop through nonstore channels such as mobile, electronic, or catalogs.

EXHIBIT 3–2
Benefits Provided by
Different Channels

Touching and Feeling Products

Perhaps the greatest benefit offered by stores is the opportunity for customers to use all five senses—touching, smelling, tasting, seeing, and hearing—when examining and evaluating products. Although new technologies such as three-dimensional and 360-degree projections can enhance representations of products on a computer or mobile phone screen, these visual improvements do not provide the same level of information customers get when they actually try on a swimsuit or smell the fragrance of a candle.

Personal Service

Although consumers are often critical of the personal service they get in stores, sales associates still have the unique ability to provide meaningful, personalized information. They can tell customers if a suit looks good on them, suggest a tie to go with a dress shirt, or answer questions customers might have about what is appropriate to wear at a business-casual event.

Risk Reduction

The physical presence of the store reduces perceived risk and increases customers' confidence that any problems with a purchase will be corrected. Customers can easily access people in the store to resolve issues concerning defective or unsuitable merchandise or get additional information on how to use a product.

Immediate Gratification

Customers can use merchandise immediately after they buy it in stores. Thus, when customers have a fever or need a last-minute gift, for example, they do not have to wait a day or two for the delivery of a prescription from Drugstore.com or of a gift from Amazon.com.

Entertainment and Social Experience

In-store shopping can be a stimulating experience for some people, providing a break in their daily routine and enabling them to interact with friends. All nonstore retail formats are limited in the degree to which they can satisfy these entertainment and social needs. Retailing View 3.2 describes how Bass Pro Shops offer an exciting and rewarding shopping experience for their customers.

Browsing

Shoppers often have only a general sense of what they want (e.g., a sweater, something for dinner, a gift) but don't know the specific item they want, so they go to a store to see what is available before they decide what to buy. Although consumers can surf the web or look through catalogs for ideas, most consumers still find it easier to browse in stores.

Cash Payment

Stores are the only channel through which consumers can make cash payments. Some customers prefer to pay with cash because it is quicker, resolves the transaction immediately, and does not result in potential interest payments or excessive debt. Other customers are concerned about security and identity theft and thus prefer to use their credit card or debit card in person rather than electronically sending the payment information via the Internet.

Catalog Channel

The catalog channel, like all nonstore channels, provides safety and convenience benefits to customers. Catalogs continue to have some unique advantages over other nonstore formats. First, consumers can look at merchandise and place an order from almost anywhere, 24/7, without needing a computer, mobile device, or Internet connection. Second, consumers can refer to the information in a catalog any time by simply picking it up from the coffee table. Finally, catalogs are easier to browse through than websites.

3.2   RETAILING VIEW   Bass Pro Shops Makes Shopping Fun

How would you like to spend your vacation? Playing in a laser arcade, rock climbing, practicing your aim in a pistol shooting range, or trying out your archery skills? If that sounds great, you're probably among the millions of people who drive for hours just to visit one of Bass Pro Shops' stores. Made to look something like hunting lodges, the stores also feature massive product displays, aided by a professional sales staff who use all the products in their own, outdoorsy lifestyles. Behind the deep product assortment, the stores' decor is enhanced by massive indoor waterfalls, aquariums, and mounted wildlife.

But a cool look isn't all there is to Bass Pro Shops. Shoppers can enjoy free activities, like making their way up the rock climbing wall or challenging their friends to a round of laser tag in the attached arcade. In soundproof rooms, surrounded by shatter-resistant glass, they can pretend to be Dirty Harry—or Katniss Everdeen, if they prefer bows and arrows. For those not quite as practiced, on-hand experts offer advice about how to sight a gun or draw a bow.

It might not be a surprise to learn that customers of Bass Pro Shops tend to be men, who otherwise proclaim just how much they hate shopping. Even a man whose wife claims that in their 35-year marriage, he'd joined her only twice on shopping trips, gets in the spirit at Bass Pro Shops, calling himself, "a kid in a candy store here."

Although these customers might drive hundreds of miles to get to them, the stores reflect their environment. In north-central Alabama, the Leeds store spreads across 120 acres, including a mile-long entryway that moves slowly through the surrounding nature park, including three bridges and a four-acre lake. But one lake isn't enough in this fish-loving area,

More than 100 million people annually visit Bass Pro Shops, compared with 60 million visitors to Disney World in Orlando. The excitement generated in a Bass Pro Shops' store cannot be equaled by other channels.

so an 18,500-gallon aquarium inside the store features fish native to Alabama, and a 3,500-gallon trout pond allows shoppers to test out the fishing equipment available in the store. Fishing too tame for you? Then how about the NASCAR ride simulator that mimics nearby Talladega Speedway? It's waiting outside the store, too.

Sources: www.bassproshop.com; Tom Bailey Jr., "Bass Pro to Open 'Newest Generation' Megastore in Little Rock," *McClatchy–Tribune Business News*, June, 15, 2012; "Outdoors Lovers Find Their 'Disneyland' in Stores Such as Bass Pro Shops," *Sacramento Bee*, September 23, 2009; "Retailer Scores by Luring Men Who Hate to Shop," *The Wall Street Journal*, December 17, 2002.

DISCUSSION QUESTION

What are the pros and cons of Bass Pro Shops' exciting store environment from the perspective of consumers? From the perspective of Bass Pro Shops?

REFACT

Bass Pro Shops' first store in Springfield, Missouri, attracts 4 million visitors a year and is the most visited tourist attraction in Missouri.

IKEA's 2013 catalog illustrates the use of a retailer's website to augment its catalog channel. IKEA dramatically improved the content and user experience with its widely distributed housewares catalog by including augmented reality. In the 2013 catalog, shoppers can place their smartphones over selected pages to get additional content from the retailer's website, such as image galleries and videos. After downloading an app, customers can interact with a series of icons in the catalog to see more information about selected products. The information ranges from how-to videos to "X-ray" photographs of the inside of storage systems. Rooms with and without textiles are shown, allowing users to build up decorative elements and explore color options.[21]

The Internet Channel

In the previous section, we detailed the relative benefits of stores from the consumers' perspective. In this section, we examine how the addition of Internet channels to traditional store-based retailers and catalogers has improved their ability to serve their customers and build a competitive advantage in several ways:

1. The addition of the Internet channels has the potential to offer a greater selection of products.
2. They allow retailers to provide more information.
3. They enable retailers to provide customers with more personalized information about products and services.
4. They offer sellers the unique opportunity to collect information about consumer shopping.
5. Internet channels provide an opportunity for retailers to enter new markets economically.
6. They provide information that they can use to improve the shopping experience across all channels.

While Internet channels offer many benefits to consumers, they also increase consumers' risks, discussed at the end of the section.

Deeper and Broader Selection   One benefit of adding the Internet channels is the vast number of alternatives retailers can make available to consumers without crowding their aisles or increasing their square footage. Stores and catalogs are limited by their size. By shopping on the Internet, consumers can easily "visit" and select merchandise from a broader array of retailers. Individual retailers' websites typically offer deeper assortments of merchandise (more colors, brands, and sizes) than are available in stores or catalogs. This expanded offering enables them to satisfy consumer demand for less popular styles, colors, or sizes. Many retailers also offer a broader assortment (more categories) on their websites. Staples.com, for instance, offers soft drinks and cleaning supplies, which are not available in stores, so that its business customers will view it as a one-stop shop.

More Information for Evaluating Merchandise   An important service offered by retailers is providing information that helps consumers make better buying decisions. Retail channels differ in terms of how much information customers can access. The amount of information available through the store channel is limited by the number and training of sales associates and the space allocated to informative signage. Similarly, the information available through a catalog channel is limited by the number of pages in the catalog. In contrast, the information provided through the Internet channels is unlimited.

The vast amount of information available through these channels enables customers using this channel to solve problems, rather than just get information about specific products. Retailing View 3.3 describes an Internet site that offers products plus information, some of which is generated by customers, that can help couples solve the problems associated with planning their wedding.

Personalization   Due to the Internet's interactive nature, the most significant potential benefit of Internet channels is their ability to economically personalize merchandise offerings and information for each customer. Customers control

---

3.3   RETAILING VIEW   Helping Couples Get Ready for the Big Day

Not only does the typical engagement and wedding today last seemingly forever (14 months) and cost a lot ($25,000), it also demands that brides, grooms, and their families make often difficult, usually emotionally charged decisions. Who gets invited? What should the invitations look like, and should they be preceded by save-the-date cards? What kind of music should be played at the reception? Wait, where should the reception be held? And just how much can a couple register for before they look greedy?

Although, at one time, the bride and her family were responsible for most of the wedding planning, modern trends—including couples who delay marriage until later, dual-income households, and transient populations who live far from their parents—mean that many of the traditional norms have gone out the window. To help these couples plan, including figuring out how to spend, Internet wedding sites such as The Knot (www.theknot.com) and WeddingChannel (www.weddingchannel.com) provide a budgeting tool. Brides enter the dollar amount they want to spend (e.g., $9,000) and the number of guests (e.g., 30). Using national averages, the website calculates how much they should spend on each feature: $540 for the bride's dress and $68 for her bouquet, in this example. As the plans progress, users enter their spending, and the tool recalculates the amounts available to be expended elsewhere.

Moving beyond the financial questions, visitors to the sites can interact with other couples, as well as etiquette experts, to get advice on how to deal with a meddling mother-in-law or where to seat divorced parents during the reception. Recommendations from other consumers seem less biased and thus more appealing than information provided by a retailer or manufacturer. Thus, shoppers turn to posted reviews of products or services.

Another planning tool sends reminders of key dates, such as the date the band needs to be reconfirmed or when the reception hall deposit is due. The sites also gather registries from various retailers, available for guests to seek out, all in one place. Bands even upload audio clips of their performances, helping bridal couples choose which one will play during their first dance. Once the reception hall and all hotels have been chosen, the website provides maps showing the best routes between

Planning Tools
from *the knot*

From keeping track of your wedding budget to managing all your to-dos, we've got the best online wedding planning tools -- and they're all free! Keep your RSVPs organized with our wedding guest list tool, spread the word with your own wedding website, and plan on the go with our iPhone wedding apps.

planning checklist
Don't miss a step with our week-by-week to-do list

wedding budgeter
Track your wedding expenses with our easy budget tool!

guest list manager
Stay on top of your guest list, RSVPs, and more

save-the-date
Give your guests a heads up with an email save-the-date

wedding websites
Share the details! Choose from 40+ stylish designs

registry central
Get our top registry picks, plus the ultimate registry checklist

my real wedding
Get inspired by other Knotties or upload your own photos

inspiration boards
Show off your wedding style with 1,000s of photos

the knot notebook
See something you like? Save gowns, articles, and more

The Knot offers information and merchandise to help couples plan their wedding.

locations, as well as online booking services for hotel reservations. And then when all is said and done, the married couple can maintain a personal site for recollections and posting wedding pictures.

Sources: www.weddingchannel.com and www.theknot.com.

DISCUSSION QUESTION

Would you use these websites to plan your wedding? Why or why not?

some of this personalization by drilling down through web pages until they have enough information to make a purchase decision. In addition, when using Internet channels, customers can format the information so that it can be effectively used when they are comparing alternatives. For example, Office Depot provides information about alternatives selected by the customer in a side-by-side comparison format. In contrast, customers in stores usually have to inspect each brand, one item at a time, and then remember the different attributes to make a comparison.

The retailer can play a more proactive role in personalizing merchandise and information through the Internet channels. For example, many retailers offer **live chats:** Customers can click a button at any time and have an instant messaging e-mail or voice conversation with a customer service representative. This technology also enables retailers to send a proactive chat invitation automatically to customers on the site. The timing of these invitations can be based on the time the visitor has spent on the site, the specific page the customer is viewing, or a product on which the customer has clicked. For example, Bluefly.com has learned that reviewing several items in a short period implies the visitor has more than a passing interest in its offerings. Therefore, the site displays a pop-up window with a friendly face offering help.[22]

The interactive nature of the Internet also provides an opportunity for retailers to personalize their offerings for each of their customers. For example, Amazon.com serves customers a personalized landing page with information about books and other products of interest based on the customer's past purchases and search behavior on the website. Amazon also sends interested customers customized e-mail messages that notify them that their favorite author or recording artist has published a new book or released a new CD. Amazon further personalizes customers' shopping experience by recommending complementary merchandise.

The Internet channels are particularly effective at making personalized recommendations.

Just as a well-trained salesperson would make recommendations to customers before checkout, an interactive web page can make suggestions to shoppers about additional items that they might like to consider.

Some multichannel retailers are able to personalize promotions and Internet homepages on the basis of several attributes tied to the shopper's current or previous web sessions, such as the time of day, time zone as determined by a computer's Internet address, and assumed gender.[23] However, some consumers worry about this ability to collect information about purchase histories, personal information, and search behavior on the Internet. How will this information be used in the future? Will it be sold to other firms, or will the consumer receive unwanted promotional materials online or in the mail?

Expand Market Presence   The market for customers who shop in stores is typically limited to consumers living in proximity those stores. The market for catalogs is limited by the high cost of printing and mailing them and increasing consumer interest in environmentally friendly practices. By adding the Internet channel, retailers can expand their market without having to build new stores or incur the high cost of additional catalogs. Adding an Internet channel is particularly attractive to retailers with strong brand names but limited locations and distribution. For example, retailers such as Neiman Marcus, REI, IKEA, and L.L. Bean are widely known for offering unique, high-quality merchandise. If these retailers only had a store, customers would have to travel vast distances to buy the merchandise they carry.

Provide Information to Improve Shopping Experience Across Channels
It is difficult for most store-based retailers to develop extensive purchase histories of their customers because the retailers are unable to link transactions to customers who pay cash or use third-party credit cards. In contrast, all transactions through the Internet have the customer identification information needed to send the product to the customer as well as their search behavior. This information can be used to provide valuable insights into how and why customers shop and are dissatisfied or satisfied with their experiences.[24]

Collecting data on how customers navigate through a website is quite easy. By placing a cookie (a small computer program that collects information about computer usage) on a customer's hard drive, the retailer can monitor each mouse click. The click-stream data provides insights into what characteristics of products customers considered and what products customers looked at but did not buy.[25] To collect this information from store shoppers would be quite difficult; someone would have to follow them around the store.

This information is useful to retailers in several ways. First, it helps them design stores or websites. By knowing how people shop, a retailer can determine, for instance, whether a store or website should be laid out by brands, size, color, or price point. It can also help the retailer give suggestions about what items a customer might be interested in purchasing. For example, after a customer purchases a book, Amazon recommends additional books that might be of interest to the customer based on purchases made by other customers who have bought that book. Finally, based on what customers clicked on or what they purchased in the past, retailers can provide unique promotions to individual customers.

Perceived Risks in Internet Shopping   Some consumers are concerned about buying products through an Internet channel. Specifically, some believe that the security of credit card transactions is greater than in stores and that there are potential privacy violations.

Although many consumers remain concerned about credit card security, extensive security problems have been rare. Almost all retailers use sophisticated technologies to encrypt communications. Also, all major credit card companies provide some consumer protection for retail transactions. Typically, customers are not liable for more than $50 as long as they report the unauthorized use in a timely manner. The consequences of security breaches can be far worse for the retailer from which the card number was stolen. Security breaches can ruin a retailer's reputation and possibly expose it to legal liability.[26]

Consumers also are concerned about the ability of retailers to collect information about their purchase history, personal information, and search behavior on the Internet without their knowledge.[27] They are worried about how this information will be used in the future. Will it be sold to other retailers, or will the consumer receive unwanted promotional materials online or in the mail? Issues related to privacy are discussed in more detail in Chapters 11 and 15.

Comparison of Electronic and Mobile Phone Internet Channels

Due to the rapid growth of domestic and international broadband access through handheld devices, such as tablets and mobile phones, retailers are very interested in developing this channel's potential. While the mobile Internet channel retains the same benefits over stores as the computer-based electronic Internet channel, it has its own unique benefits and limitations. In particular, customers can easily carry the device in their purses or pockets, and access the retailer's website from any place they are, as long as there is a mobile phone connection available.

Another advantage of a mobile channel is that customer–retailer interactions can be location-sensitive. For example, a retailer can determine where a customer is located and send location-relevant information to the customer, such as promotions, to encourage customers to buy other products nearby the store or go to another area of the store.

The major disadvantage of a mobile channel, compared to a computer-based Internet channel, is the mobile device's smaller screen and slower download speeds. To accommodate the smaller screen size, the software interface for interacting with mobile devices and computers is different. When using mobile channels, customers typically navigate using a touch screen with side scrolling, while a mouse is used with an electronic channel. The smaller screen size and touch screen navigation means that consumers using a mobile channel have to go through many more screens when browsing or trying to locate information.[29]

Apps   To provide their customers with a better shopping experience when using their mobile channels, many retailers have developed mobile shopping apps. **Apps** are software applications designed to improve the consumers' shopping experiences when using smartphones and tablets. Apps developed by retailers are typically used to easily perform some specific functions available on the retailer's website but do not provide access to all of the functions available on the website. The Amazon Mobile app offers product price comparisons with thousands of retailers. Its Snap It feature lets consumers take a photo of a product to search for it, and access to Amazon's one-click purchasing is available. Target's Shop Target makes it easy for consumers to scan barcodes and find daily and weekly deals. Users can also check product availability, search for nearby stores, and set up text alerts for discounts.

The use of tablets may provide the best trade-off between the portability of mobile phones and the navigation ease of websites accessed by computers. Most retailers serve the firm's website, rather a specially designed mobile website when a customer accesses an Internet channel. But now, some retailers are designing websites and apps for tablets. On Anthropologie's app, for example, consumers can not only browse items but also clip pictures of the most appealing options to add to their social networks, as well as check out detailed, thumbnail views of the offerings. The collage option allows them to put together outfits, including accessories

REFACT

Most online consumers express concerns that thieves might intercept the credit card data they enter; among those who have shopped the web recently, more than half indicate their worry that the online site will sell their information to other merchants.[28]

REFACT

Convenience/ease of use (39 percent), additional features (21 percent), and navigation (10 percent) are the primary reasons mobile owners prefer going to a retailer's website rather than using an app when shopping.[30]

REFACT

Even if nearly half of all smartphone users have downloaded a retail app, only about 14 percent of them have used such apps to purchase items.[31]

Anthropologie's app improves the usability of mobile devices.

and jewelry, to buy as a set. The percentage of shoppers accessing Anthropologie's website through tablets has tripled, to 6 percent, since the introduction of the app; the retailer expects that number to jump to 20 percent within about a year.[32]

CHALLENGES FACING MULTICHANNEL RETAILERS

LO3

Analyze the challenges facing multichannel retailers.

In the previous section, we outlined the benefits offered by the different retail channels. In this section, we describe how retailers are using multiple channels to improve their offerings to their customers and build a competitive advantage. The typical examples of the evolution toward multichannel retailing are when store-based retailers and catalogers add Internet channels. But retailers that focus on direct selling and TV home shopping network channels have also added Internet channels. Amazon, a retailer using only Internet channels, is even considering establishing a physical presence by having lockers in which customers can access merchandise they purchased online and/or actual stores to overcome some of the limitations of their Internet channel.[33]

Regardless of how they come to find a multichannel retailer, consumers want a seamless experience: Whether they solicit a sales associate for help, seek out an in-store kiosk, call in to the call center, or log on to the website, they also like to be recognized. Once recognized, they also need the retailer to facilitate their ability to find and pick up their purchases, even if they want to buy online and then pick up in the store, or vice versa. In addition, the various channels need to be consistent in the information they provide.

Retailers also benefit by using multiple channels synergistically. Multichannel retailers can use one channel to promote the services offered by other channels. For example, the URL of a store's website can be advertised on in-store signs, shopping bags, credit card billing statements, point-of-sale (POS) receipts, and the print or broadcast advertising used to promote the store. The physical stores and catalogs are also advertisements for a retailer's other channels. The retailer's channels can be used to stimulate store visits by announcing special store events and promotions.

Multichannel retailers can leverage their stores to lower the cost of fulfilling orders and processing returned merchandise. They can use their stores as "warehouses" for gathering merchandise for delivery to customers. Customers also can be offered the opportunity to pick up and return merchandise at the retailer's stores rather than pay shipping charges. Many retailers will waive shipping charges when orders are placed online or through the catalog if the customer physically comes into the store.

Offering customers the opportunity to buy online and pick up merchandise in a store is an example of the seamless interface customers are seeking.

However, as illustrated in Exhibit 3–3, most multichannel retailers have yet to provide these seamless customer-facing processes. This apparent lack of progress should not be interpreted as a lack of interest. The results of a recent survey indicate that cross-channel coordination is extremely important to retailers, even if they have yet to reach their full potential.[34]

In the next section, several challenges and trade-off decisions confronting multichannel retailers are discussed, including multichannel supply chain and information system issues, centralized versus decentralized multichannel retailing, maintaining a consistent brand image across channels, merchandise assortment trade-offs, pricing issues, and the challenge surrounding channel migration and showrooming.

Multichannel Supply Chains and Information Systems

Multichannel retailers still struggle to provide an integrated shopping experience because the various channels demand various skills, as well as unique resources.[35] When retail distribution centers (DCs) support a store channel, they move merchandise, packed in cartons, off the suppliers' trucks, into the DC inventory, and then onto new trucks heading to retail stores. When retailers get efficient enough, merchandise sits in the DC only briefly, often for less than a day. But DCs that supply catalog and Internet channels have other roles to fulfill as well: receive merchandise packed in cartons, then separate out the individual items to be repacked and shipped to individual end-customers. Handling individual items, rather than cartons, and shipping them to individual consumers, instead of retailers, requires unique packaging, different transportation systems, and new intermediaries.

Cross-Channel Fulfillment Activities	High-Performance Retailers	Others
Buy online, return in store	70%	59%
Buy in store, fulfill through online	70	41
Buy online, pick up in store	50	52
Buy via mobile	35	48
Buy via social media source	30	11
Buy online, fulfill through any stop	30	30

Source: *Omni-Channel 2012: Cross-Channel Comes of Age, 2012 Benchmark*, RSR, June 2012.

EXHIBIT 3–3
Percentage of Multichannel Retailers Offering Cross-Channel Fulfillment

Due to these operational differences, many store-based retailers have a separate organization to manage their Internet and catalog operations. But as the multi-channel operation matures, retailers tend to integrate all operations under one organization. Both Walmart and JCPenney initially had separate organizations for their Internet channel but subsequently integrated them with stores and catalogs.

Centralized versus Decentralized Multichannel Retailing

Because each of the channels offer a unique set of benefits, the profiles of a retailer's customers who use the different channels are not the same. Thus, a critical decision facing multichannel retailers is the degree to which they should integrate the operations of the channels or have different organizations for each channel. At one extreme of this continuum is complete integration—selling the same products at the same prices through the same distribution system for all channels. At the other extreme is having different organizations manage each channel so that the channels are tailored to different target markets. However, few retailers actually take the extreme route to pursue a strategy at one end of the continuum or the other.

Consistent Brand Image across Channels

Retailers need to provide a consistent brand image of themselves and their private-label merchandise across all channels. For example, Patagonia reinforces its image of selling high-quality, environmentally friendly sports equipment in its stores, catalogs, and website. Each of these channels emphasizes function, not fashion, in the descriptions of Patagonia's products. Patagonia's concerns about the environment are communicated by carefully lighting its stores and using recycled polyester in many of its clothes, as well as only organic, rather than pesticide-intensive, cotton. Its weblog, www.thecleanestline.com, is dedicated to essays and other features on environmental activism, innovative design, and sports. Retailing View 3.4 describes how Build-A-Bear Workshop uses multiple channels to build and reinforce its image.

Merchandise Assortment

Typically, different assortments are often appropriate for each of the channels. For example, multichannel retailers offer a broader and deeper merchandise assortment through their Internet channel than through their store channel. Because the Internet channel can have a much larger assortment, it can satisfy the needs of a larger variety of customer groups. For instance, multichannel apparel retailers can carry fringe sizes on their Internet channel, but it would be too expensive and space constricting to do so in their store channel.

The channels also differ in terms of their effectiveness in generating sales for different types of merchandise. For example, the store channel is better suited for selling products with important "touch-and-feel" attributes such as the fit of a shirt, the taste of an ice cream flavor, or the smell of a perfume. On the other hand, an Internet channel might be just as effective as a store channel for selling products with important "look-and-see" attributes such as price, color, and grams of fat. Evaluating these products does not require senses beyond sight. Because of the problems of providing touch-and-feel information, apparel retailers experience return rates of more than 20 percent on purchases made through Internet channels, but only 5 percent on purchases made in stores.

Pricing

Pricing represents another difficult decision for a multichannel retailer. Many customers expect prices to be the same across channels (excluding shipping charges). However, in some cases, retailers need to adjust their pricing strategy because of the competition they face in different channels. For example, BarnesandNoble.com offers lower prices through its Internet channels than through its stores to compete effectively against Amazon.com.

Retailers with stores in multiple markets often set different prices for the same merchandise to deal with differences in local competition. They can do so because most customers don't know about these price differences because they are exposed only to the prices in their local markets. However, multichannel retailers may have difficulties sustaining regional price differences when customers can easily check prices on the Internet.

Reduction of Channel Migration

An Internet channel helps customers search for information about products and prices. The most common multichannel usage involves an initial search online, followed by a purchase in stores. Whereas approximately 78 percent of U.S. consumers adopt this pattern of consumption, only 8 percent browse through

RETAILING VIEW   The Build-A-Bear Workshop Uses Multiple Channels to Enhance Its Image   **3.4**

The Build-A-Bear Workshop website reinforces the brand image generated by its stores.

On Bearville.com, stuffed animal fans of all ages and backgounds can enjoy the entertaining content provided by Build-A-Bear Workshop. The content includes online games, access to fun merit "certificates" and thank-you cards, and options for organizing a party. The site thus is closely integrated with the Build-A-Bear Workshop stores, as well as the company's mobile app—and of course, the cuddly products.

Just as youthful customers can name their furry friends, players of the online Bearville game can personalize their characters and purchase virtual outfits for them, then play with other global customers. These visitors spend approximately 25 million hours on the site, playing its free online games. With this Internet channel, Build-A-Bear thus hopes not only to improve its brand image, but also to keep children interested and interacting with the retailer, leading them to beg to make yet another visit to the local store.

Build-A-Bear also promises a safe and useful site. The Find-A-Bear identification program helps users find lost bears. As soon as children register, the company sends an e-mail to their parents, with a link that allows them to determine the level of communications the company will initiate, depending on their children's age, maturity, and comfort level. Furthermore, Build-A-Bear monitors the site to ensure all socialization is appropriate; as the founder of the company notes, "We're conscious of the issues of cyber-bullying, for example."

Sources: www.bearville.com, accessed September 1, 2012; "Build-a-Bear Workshop: The Bear Necessities," *Retail Week*, January 13, 2012; and "Build-A-Bear Workshop Creates Entertainment Destination," *Internet Wire*, February 9, 2011.

DISCUSSION QUESTION

Are these Internet channel activities consistent with its in-store brand?

stores first, then make their purchases via the Internet.[36] As long as the store and the Internet channel represent the same retailer, the firm is happy. But if customers gather information from one of its channels, then buy from a channel hosted by a competitor, the retailer suffers from the frustrating problem of **channel migration**.[37] Modern technologies, including those that allow customers to gather information and buy online or through their mobile devices, also make channel migration really easy. Thus, retaining customers remains a constant challenge for multichannel retailers.

As mentioned earlier in the chapter, a particularly concerning form of channel migration is called showrooming. **Showrooming** occurs when a consumer goes into a store to learn about different brands and products and then searches the Internet for the same product sold at a lower price. Three approaches that multichannel retailers can use to reduce showrooming are (1) providing better customer service, (2) offering uniquely relevant information based on proprietary data the retailer has collected about the customers, and (3) promoting private-label merchandise that can be purchased only from the retailer. These approaches are discussed in more detail in Chapter 5.[38]

MULTICHANNEL SHOPPING IN THE FUTURE

LO4

Consider the multichannel shopping experience in the future.

The following hypothetical scenario illustrates the technologies and seamless interface across channels that customers in the future may experience.

Shopping Experience Scenario

It's Tuesday morning, and Judy Jamison is eating breakfast thinking about buying a new dress for the party she'll be attending this Friday night at the new club downtown. She sends a tweet to her friends about her plans to go shopping after work today and asks for suggestions of retailers she might visit. She gets some suggestions from friends and then decides to do some research on the Internet. She logs on to her tablet, accesses her personal shopper program called FRED, and has the following interactive dialog:

> **FRED:** Do you wish to browse, go to a specific store, or buy a specific item?
>
> **Judy:** Specific item.
>
> **FRED:** What is the item? [Menu appears and Judy selects.]
>
> **Judy:** Dress.
>
> **FRED:** Occasion? [Menu appears and Judy selects.]
>
> **Judy:** Cocktail.
>
> **FRED:** Price range? [Menu appears.]
>
> **Judy:** $175–$200.
>
> [Now FRED goes out and literally shops the world electronically, visiting the servers for companies selling cocktail dresses in Europe, Asia, Africa, Australia, and North and South America.]
>
> **FRED:** 1,231 items have been identified. How many do you want to review? [Menu appears.]
>
> **Judy:** Just 7
>
> [FRED selects the seven best alternatives on the basis of information it has about Judy's style preferences. The seven cocktail dresses appear on the screen with the price, brand name, and retailer listed beneath each one. Judy clicks on each dress to get more information about it. With another click, she sees a full-motion video of a woman who looks similar to Judy modeling the dress. She selects several dresses she finds most appealing.]

However, Judy decides not to buy the dress because she is not sure the dress will fit right when it arrives, and she will not have time to return it and get another size. She likes the Robert Rodriguez styles FRED found, so she goes to Brand-Habit.com, types in the designer's name and her zip code, and finds the closest store that carries his designs and has her size in stock. The site directs her to the store's website to look at more dresses. She decides to visit the store after work.

Shortly after Judy walks into the store, a chip in her credit card signals her presence and status as a frequent shopper to a mobile device held by the store sales associate responsible for preferred clients. Information about items in which Judy might be interested, including the items she viewed on the website through FRED, is downloaded from the store server to Judy's and the sales associate's devices.

A sales associate approaches Judy and says, "Hello, Ms. Jamison. My name is Joan Bradford. How can I help you?" Judy tells the associate she needs to buy a dress for a party. She has seen some dresses on the store's website and would like to look at them in the store. The sales associate takes Judy to a virtual dressing room.

In the dressing room, Judy sits in a comfortable chair and views the dresses displayed on her image, which has been drawn from a body scan stored in Judy's customer file. Information about Judy's recent visit to the retailer's website and her past purchases is used to select the dresses displayed.

Using her mobile phone, Judy shares this personalized viewing with her friend, who is still at work in California. They discuss which dress looks best on Judy. Then, using her mobile phone again, Judy drills down to find more information about the dress—the fabric, cleaning instructions, and so forth. Finally, she selects a dress that is of most interest to her and tries it on. When she tries is on, the video cameras in the room enable her to see what she looks like from all angles. She notices that from some angles the dress does not have a flattering fit. The sales associate suggests that this problem can be overcome with a minor alteration and shows Judy how she will look in the altered dress. Using information displayed on her mobile device, the sales associate Joan suggests a handbag and scarf that would complement the dress. These accessories are added to the image of Judy in the dress. Judy decides to buy the scarf but not the handbag. Judy is informed that she will get a message on her mobile when the alterations are completed, and then she can indicate whether she wants the dress delivered to her home or she will pick it up at the store.

As Judy passes through the cosmetics department on her way to her car, she sees an appealing new lipstick shade. She decides to purchase the lipstick and a 3-ounce bottle of her favorite perfume and walks out of the store. The store systems sense her departure, and the merchandise she has selected is automatically charged to her account through signals from radio-frequency identification (RFID) chips.

Supporting the Shopping Experience

This scenario illustrates the advantages of having a customer database shared by all channels and integrated across all systems. The sales associate and the store systems are able to offer superior customer service based on this database, which contains information about Judy's body scan image, her interaction with the retailer's website, and her past purchases and preferences. The technology also supports the retailer's business model, which determines how to offer customers the products and services that will provide the best shopping experience.

Before Judy went into the store, she interacted with a search engine to find where the particular brand and product she was looking for could be found. She then interacted with the retailer's website to review the available merchandise before she went to the store, check the status of her alterations, and decide about having the merchandise delivered to her home. The scenario also includes some new technologies that will exist in the store of the future, such as RFID, self-checkout, and personalized virtual reality displays.

SUMMARY

LO1 **Understand the nonstore channels offered by retailers.**

A *retail channel* is the way a retailer sells *and* delivers merchandise and services to its customers. The most common channel used by retailers is a store. Retailers also use a variety of nonstore channels including the Internet, mobile, catalogs, direct mail, direct selling, television home shopping, direct response TV, and automated retailing (vending machines) to make sales to customers. *Multichannel retailing* involves using more than one channel to enhance the customer satisfaction experience and exploit the synergies between channels. Some of the challenges facing multichannel retailers are due to the operational and organizational differences inherent in managing multiple information and supply chain systems, channel operations, pricing, branding, and assortments.

LO2 **Compare the benefits offered by the four major retail channels: stores, Internet, and catalogs**

Stores offer several benefits to customers that they cannot get when they shop through non-store channels such as Internet, or catalogs. These benefits include touching and feeling products, personal service, increased customer service, risk reduction, immediate gratification, cash payments, and entertainment and social experiences.

The catalog channel, like all non-store channels, provides safety and convenience benefits to customers. Using the catalog channel, consumers can look at merchandise and place an order from almost anywhere 24/7 without needing a computer, mobile device, or Internet connection. Second, consumers can refer to the information in a catalog anytime by simply picking it up from the coffee table. Finally, catalogs are easier to browse through than Web sites.

There are five advantages of the Internet channels. First, the addition of the Internet channels has

the potential to offer a greater selection of products. Second, they allow retailers to provide more information. Third, they enable retailers to provide customers with more personalized information about products and services. Fourth, they offer sellers the unique opportunity to collect information about consumer shopping. Fifth, the Internet channels provide an opportunity for retailers to enter new markets economically. Finally, they provide information that they can use to improve the shopping experience across all channels. Some consumers are concerned about buying products through an Internet channel.

LO3 **Understand the issues facing multichannel retailers**

Multichannel retailers are still struggling to provide an integrated shopping experience across all their channels because unique skills and resources are needed to manage each channel. A critical decision facing multichannel retailers is the degree to which they should integrate the operations of the channels or have different organizations for each channel. Since each of the channels offers a unique set of benefits, the profiles of a retailer's customers who use the different channels are not the same. Retailers need to provide a consistent brand image of themselves and their private-label merchandise across all channels. Pricing represents another difficult decision for a multichannel retailer. Finally, the availability of an Internet channel enables customers to easily search for information about products and their prices during a shopping episode.

LO4 **Consider the multichannel shopping experience in the future**

This scenario illustrates shopping in the future from an integrated multi-channel retailer.

KEY TERMS

GET OUT AND DO IT!

1. CONTINUING CASE ASSIGNMENT: GO SHOPPING Assume that you are shopping on the Internet for an item in the same merchandise category

you analyzed for the Comparison Shopping exercise in Chapter 2. Go to the retailer's website, and compare the merchandise assortment offered, the prices, and the shopping experience in the store and on the store's website. How easy was it to locate what you were looking for? What were the assortment and pricing like? What was the checkout like? What are the categories and/or sub-categories? How many SKUs were in each category and subcategory? What features of the sites did you like and dislike, such as the look and feel of the site, navigation, and special features?

2. **INTERNET EXERCISE** Go to the websites of J. Crew (www.jcrew.com), JCPenney (www.jcpenney.com), and American Eagle Outfitters (www.ae.com), and shop for a pair of khaki pants. Evaluate your shopping experience at each site. Compare and contrast the sites and your experiences on the basis of characteristics you think are important to consumers.

3. **INTERNET EXERCISE** Assume that you are getting married and planning your wedding. Compare and contrast the usefulness of www.theknot.com and www.weddingchannel.com for planning your wedding. What features of the sites do you like and dislike? Indicate the specific services offered by these sites that you would use.

4. **INTERNET AND SHOPPING EXERCISE** Pick a merchandise category like microwave ovens, power drills, digital cameras, blenders, or coffee makers. Compare a retailer's offering in its local store and on its Internet site. What are the differences in the assortments offered through its store and Internet channel? Are the prices the same or different? What has the retailer done to exploit the synergies between the channels?

5. **INTERNET AND SHOPPING EXERCISE** Access the websites of Home Depot and Macy's using your mobile phone and computer. What are the differences in the ease of navigation when looking at the presentation of merchandise using the two methods of accessing the websites?

DISCUSSION QUESTIONS AND PROBLEMS

1. Why are store-based retailers aggressively pursuing sales through Internet channels?

2. From a customer's perspective, what are the benefits and limitations of stores? Catalogs? Retailer websites?

3. Would you buy clothes on the basis of the way they look on a customized virtual model? Why or why not?

4. Why are the Internet and catalog channels so popular for gift giving?

5. Should a multichannel retailer offer the same assortment of merchandise for sale, at the same price, on its website and in its stores? Why or why not?

6. Which of the following categories of merchandise do you think could be sold most successfully through an Internet channel: jewelry; TV sets; computer software; high-fashion apparel; pharmaceuticals; health care products such as toothpaste, shampoo, and cold remedies? Why?

7. Assume you are interested in investing in a startup Internet retailer that targets people who enjoy active outdoor recreation, such as hiking, rock climbing, and kayaking. What merchandise and information would you offer on the site? What type of entity do you think would be most effective in running the site: a well-known outdoors person, a magazine targeting outdoor activity, or a retailer selling outdoor merchandise, such as Patagonia or REI? Why?

8. What are the advantages to customers of accessing the Internet through a mobile device or a computer when browsing a website? When learning special promotions?

9. When you shop online for merchandise, how much time do you spend browsing versus buying? When you shop in a store for merchandise, how much time do you spend browsing versus buying?

SUGGESTED READINGS

Avery, Jill, Thomas J. Steenburgh, John Deighton, and Mary Caravella, "Adding Bricks to Clicks: Predicting the Patterns of Cross-Channel Elasticities Over Time," *Journal of Marketing* 76(May 2012), 7, pp. 96–111.

Brynjolfsson, Erik, Hu, Yu (Jeffrey), Rahmanand Mohammad S., "Battle of the Retail Channels: How Product Selection and Geography Drive Cross-Channel Competition," *Management Science*, November 2009, Vol. 55 Issue 11, pp. 1755–1765.

Hsiao, Cheng-Chieh; Yen, Ju Rebecca Hsiu, and Eldon Y. Li, "Exploring Consumer Value of Multi-Channel Shopping: A Perspective of Means-End Theory," *Internet Research*, 22: 3, 2012, pp. 318–339.

Lee, Hyun-Hwa and Jihyun Kim (2010), "Investigating Dimensionality of Multichannel Retailer's Cross-Channel Integration Practices and Effectiveness: Shopping Orientation and Loyalty Intention," *Journal of Marketing Channels*, 17:4, 2010, pp. 281–312.

Neslin, S.A. and V. Shankar (2009), "Keys Issues in Multichannel Customer Management: Current Knowledge and Future Directions," *Journal of Interactive Marketing*, 23: 1, pp. 70–81.

Poloian, Lynda Gamans. *Retailing Principles: Global, Multichannel, and Management Viewpoints, 2nd Ed.* Fairchild Publication: New York, 2012.

Schramm-Klein, Hanna, Gerhard Wagner, Sascha Steinmann and Dirk Morschett, "Cross-Channel Integration—Is It Valued By Customers?," *The International Review of Retail, Distribution and Consumer Research*, 21: 5, 2011, pp. 501–511.

Weitz, Barton A. "Electronic Retailing," in Retailing in the 21st Century—Current and Future Trends, 2nd ed., eds. Manfred Kraft and Murali Mantrala. Berlin: Springer, 2010, pp. 309–323.

Zhang, Jie, Paul W. Farris, John W. Irvin, Tarun Kushwaha, Thomas J. Steenburgh, Barton A. Weitz, Crafting Integrated Multichannel Retailing Strategies," *Journal of Interactive Marketing*, Volume 24, Issue 2, May 2010, pp. 168–180.

Customer Buying Behavior

EXECUTIVE BRIEFING

Don Unser, Group President, Retail Business Group, The NPD Group, Inc.

The NPD Group provides information about consumer buying behavior that helps our clients, both retailers and vendors, make better, fact-based decisions. The reports provided by our system are derived from two sources: point-of-sale (POS) data and consumer panel data.

The POS data are supplied by over 900 retail clients around the world, detailing sales in over 150,000 stores. The database provides sales for products and their prices across general merchandise categories offered by a broad cross-section of retailers including department, discount, and specialty stores. Retailers share this sales data in exchange for the knowledge we provide from our analyses.

The online consumer panel consists of over 2 million people who have agreed to participate in surveys and provide information on their purchase behavior. In addition to sales by product and retailer, the database includes demographic and other information about the panel members including customer satisfaction evaluations following specific purchase occasions. This database allows sales tracking across all channels, by demographic segments. Our technology ensures survey samples are representative of the total population or a client's particular target audience.

Our systems are designed to make it easy for retailers to get the data that help them analyze market performance and make fact-based decisions. A variety of reports are available drawing on both databases. For example, an automotive parts retailer reviewed a fair-share report that compared its market share in each merchandise category to its overall market share and discovered some areas in which it was not getting its fair share—it had a market share of 8 percent in the category compared to its overall market share of 11 percent. By drilling down into the data, the buyer for the category adjusted the assortment plan, changing the emphasis placed on specific brands and SKUs. The result was an increase in annual sales of $3 million and a promotion for the buyer.

Due to the breadth and depth of data we collect and analyze, we are able to identify key consumer trends and business opportunities. The choice of food and meals by consumers in their 20s, referred to as Gen Y or millennials, differs from other generations. We find that this segment of consumers has a high degree of confidence in their judgments, heed cravings quickly, and place high value on minimal preparation time. They are more likely than consumers in other age groups to use frozen entrées

CHAPTER 4

LEARNING OBJECTIVES

LO1 Describe the process that consumers go through when making retail patronage and buying decisions.

LO2 Identify the different types of buying processes.

LO3 Summarize how the economy and social factors affect customer purchase decisions.

LO4 Determine why and how retailers group customers into market segments.

and other quick-prep items. These young adults have been among the hardest-hit by the recession and are heavy patrons of low-priced retailers. One-third of millennials shop at Walmart and other mass merchants. For food retailers and restaurants, a major opportunity—and challenge—exists in learning how to communicate effectively with this "connected" generation, as well as offering products and meal/snack solutions that fit their spontaneous, budget-conscious lifestyles.

As discussed in Chapter 1, an effective retail strategy satisfies customer needs better than do competitors' strategies. Successful retailers are customer-centric—their strategic and tactical decisions revolve around their present and potential customers. Thus, understanding customer needs and buying behavior is critical to formulating and implementing an effective retail strategy.

This chapter focuses on how customers process information and make decisions about what stores to patronize, what channels to use, and what products and services to buy.[1] It describes the stages customers go through when making purchase decisions and the factors that influence their buying process. Because typically it is not cost-efficient for retailers to develop unique offerings for individual customers, retailers target their offerings to groups of customers (market segments) with similar needs and buying processes. Thus, this chapter continues with a discussion of how market segments are formed. We use information about the buying process to discuss how retailers can identify the market segments that will be the target of their retail strategy. The appendix to this chapter examines special aspects of consumer behavior that are of concern to retailers selling fashion merchandise.

THE BUYING PROCESS

LO1

Describe the process that consumers go through when making retail patronage and buying decisions.

The following scenario illustrates the steps consumers go through when purchasing merchandise. Eva Mendoza, a student at the University of Washington, is beginning to interview for jobs. Eva planned to wear the blue suit her parents gave her several years ago to the interviews. But looking at her suit, she realizes that it's not very stylish and that the jacket is beginning to show signs of wear. Wanting to make a good first impression during her interviews, she decides to buy a new suit.

Eva surfs the Internet for tips on dressing for interviews and looks through some catalogs to see the styles and prices being offered. Eva surfs fashion blogs such as Nubry and checks what her friends are wearing on Facebook and then checks what they "Like" and what they have "pinned" on Pinterest. She goes to retailers' websites to examine and compare all their suits. She then decides to go to a store so that she can try on a suit and have it altered if necessary. She likes to shop at American Eagle Outfitters and Banana Republic, but neither sells business suits. Before going to the Northgate Mall in Seattle, she issues a status update on her Facebook page, announcing her intentions to go to the mall and inviting friends to join her. Britt responds to her Facebook posting, and they decide to meet at the mall entrance. Betsy also responds, but she has a cold and wants to rest.

Eva and Britt first go to Macy's and are approached by a salesperson in the career women's department. After asking Eva what type of suit she wants and her size, the salesperson shows her three suits. Eva talks with Britt about the suits, and they decide to get Betsy's opinion. So Eva takes photos of the suits with her mobile phone and sends them to Betsy at her apartment. Betsy likes all three, so Eva tries them on.

When Eva comes out of the dressing room, she is unsure which suit to select, but after sending Betsy some more photos, she, Britt, and the salesperson decide the second suit is the most attractive and appropriate for interviewing. Eva is happy with the color, fit, fabric, and length of the suit, but she is concerned that it will require dry cleaning. It also costs more than she had planned to spend. Eva decides to buy the suit after another customer in the store, seeing her wearing the suit, tells her she looks very professional.

As Britt and Eva are walking toward the door, they pass the shoe department. Britt tells Eva, "You need to buy shoes that go with your suit." Eva finds a pair of Steve Madden pumps that are perfect. She tries on a few pairs to get

Consumers are increasingly turning to fashionista blogs to read reviews and pick up the latest fashion tips.

EXHIBIT 4–1
Stages in the Buying
Process

the right size. Then Britt tells her that she thinks the shoes are overpriced. Eva scans the UPC code for the shoes using her mobile phone's shopping app and finds that Zappos is selling the shoes for $20 less and with no sales tax. So she orders the shoes from Zappos for delivery to her apartment the next day.

Consider Eva's shopping trip as we describe the customer buying process. The **buying process**—the steps consumers go through when buying a product or service—begins when customers recognize an unsatisfied need. Then they seek information about how to satisfy the need—what retailers, channels, and products or services might satisfy the need. Customers then evaluate the alternatives and choose a store or Internet site to visit or a catalog to review. Their encounter with a retailer provides more information and may alert customers to additional needs. After evaluating the retailer's offering, customers may make a purchase or go to another retailer to collect more information. Eventually, customers purchase a product, use the product, and then decide whether the retailer, channel, and product satisfy their needs during the postpurchase evaluation stage of the customer buying process.

Exhibit 4–1 outlines the buying process—the stages consumers go through to select a retailer and channel and to buy a specific item. The exhibit suggests that the buying process is linear, as shown by the solid lines. First, the channel and retailer are selected and then the specific items. For each of these decisions, customers go through five stages, beginning with need recognition and ending with loyalty. As we discuss the stages in the buying process, you should recognize that customers might not go through all the stages and/or might not go through the stages in the order shown in Exhibit 4–1. For example, Eva might have decided on the brand of suit she wanted before selecting a store, or she might have collected information about suits sold at Macy's and, on the basis of this information, decided to go to another store or to use another channel, such as the Internet, to buy the suit.

Retailers attempt to influence consumers as they go through the buying process to encourage consumers to buy merchandise and services from them. Each stage in the buying process is examined in the following sections.

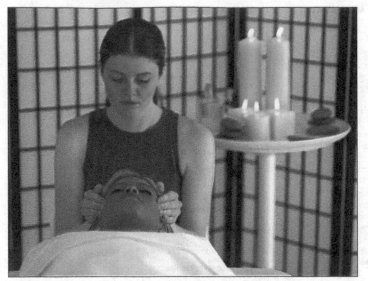

Spas make guests the center of attention and satisfy hedonic needs.

Need Recognition

The buying process is triggered when consumers recognize they have an unsatisfied need. An **unsatisfied need** arises when customers' desired level of satisfaction differs from their present level of satisfaction. For example, Eva recognized that she had a need when she was faced with the prospect of interviewing for jobs in her blue suit. She needed a suit that would make a good impression and realized her worn, outdated blue suit would not satisfy this need. Need recognition can be as straightforward as realizing you need a haircut, feeling the need for an uplifting experience after a final exam, or receiving a message about something a friend bought.

Types of Needs   The needs that motivate customers to go shopping can be classified as utilitarian or hedonic. When consumers go shopping to accomplish a specific task, such as Eva buying a suit for job interviews, they are seeking to satisfy **utilitarian needs.** When consumers go shopping for pleasure, they are seeking to satisfy their **hedonic needs**—their needs for entertaining, emotional, and recreational experiences. Thus, from the consumer's perspective, utilitarian needs are associated with work, whereas hedonic needs are associated with pleasure.[2]

Successful retailers attempt to satisfy both the utilitarian and the hedonic needs of their customers. Consumers motivated by utilitarian needs typically shop in a more deliberate and efficient manner. Thus, retailers need to provide adequate information and an effortless shopping experience for utilitarian shoppers. On the other hand, shoppers with hedonic needs desire excitement, stimulation, status and power, recreation, and adventure.[3] Examples of how retailers satisfy hedonic needs are listed next:

1. *Stimulation*. Retailers and mall managers use background music, visual displays, scents, and demonstrations in stores and malls to create a carnival-like, stimulating experience for their customers. (See Chapter 17.) Such environments encourage consumers to take a break from their everyday lives and visit stores. Retailers also attempt to stimulate customers with exciting graphics and photography in their catalogs and on their websites.

2. *Status and power*. Some people choose retailers based on the attention and respect they receive. For example, Canyon Ranch offers upscale health resorts in Tucson, Arizona, and Lenox, Massachusetts, as well as spa clubs in Las Vegas, Nevada, and on cruises, such as Oceania, Regent Seven Seas, and the Queen Mary 2. All Canyon Ranch resorts and spas make the customer the center of attention, offering spa services, medical and nutritional consultations, workshops, spiritual pursuits, and healthy gourmet cuisine.

3. *Adventure*. Often, consumers go shopping because they enjoy finding bargains, looking for sales, and finding discounts or low prices. They treat shopping as a game to be "won." Off-price retailers like Marshalls and Trader Joe's, warehouse clubs like Costco, and fast-fashion specialty retailers like Zara cater to this need by constantly changing their assortment so that customers never know what kind of treasure they will find.

Saks Fifth Avenue uses its exciting window displays to stimulate need recognition.

Conflicting Needs   Most customers have multiple needs. Moreover, these needs often conflict. For example, Eva Mendoza would like to wear a DKNY suit, which would enhance her self-image and earn her the admiration of her college friends. But satisfying these hedonic needs might conflict with her utilitarian needs—the need to stay within her budget and the need to get a job. Employers might feel that she's not responsible if she wears a suit that is too expensive for an interview for an entry-level position. Later in this chapter, we discuss a model of how customers make trade-offs between conflicting needs.

The needs and decision-making processes may differ depending on the specific situation. For example, a skier may purchase expensive Spyder goggles but wear an inexpensive snowsuit from Target. A grocery shopper might buy an inexpensive store brand of paper towels and a premium national brand of orange juice. This pattern of buying both premium and low-priced merchandise or patronizing both expensive, status-oriented retailers and price-oriented retailers is called **cross-shopping.**[4]

Stimulating Need Recognition   Customers must first recognize unsatisfied needs before they are motivated to visit a store or go online to buy merchandise. Sometimes these needs are stimulated by an event in a person's life, like Eva's impending interviews. But retailers use a variety of approaches to stimulate unmet needs. Advertising, e-mails, direct mail, publicity, and special events communicate the availability of new merchandise or special prices. Visits to SeenOn (www.SeenOn.com) can stimulate need recognition by showing products that celebrities or television characters have worn. In a social media campaign, Melrose Jewelers encouraged visitors to its Facebook page to consider a watch purchase by giving them a personality quiz that claimed to reveal which watch style best suited them.[5] Within a store, visual merchandising and salespeople can stimulate need recognition. For example, the display of shoes stimulated Eva's need for shoes to complement her new suit.

Information Search

Once customers identify a need, they typically seek information about retailers, channels, or products to help them satisfy that need. Eva's search started on the Internet and then narrowed to the three suits shown to her by the salesperson at Macy's and the opinions of her friends.[6] In other situations, Eva might have collected a lot more information by visiting several retailers and/or spending more time on the Internet getting information from fashion blogs like College Fashion, Refinery29, and FabSugar.[7]

Sources of Information   Customers have two sources of information: internal and external. **Internal sources** are information in a customer's memory, such as names, images, and past experiences with different stores. The major source of internal information is the customer's past shopping experience. Even if they remember only a small fraction of the information to which they are exposed, customers have an extensive internal information bank to draw on when deciding where to shop and what to buy.

External sources consist of information provided by a host of sources. People search for products and information using search engines such as Google, visit the websites maintained by manufacturers and retailers, acquire information from traditional media (e.g., advertising), read blogs, watch product demonstrations on YouTube, and ask friends, in person and through social media.

When customers believe that they are not well enough informed or that their internal information is inadequate, they turn to external information sources. For example, Eva asked her friends, Betsy and Britt, to help her make the purchase decision. To find out if the price of the shoes she liked was reasonable, she turned to an online shoe seller. Such external sources of information play a major role in the acceptance of fashions, as discussed in the appendix to this chapter.

Amount of Information Searched   In general, the amount of **information search** undertaken depends on the value customers believe they can gain from searching versus the cost of searching.[9] The value of the search stems from the degree to which the additional information improves the customer's purchase decision. Will the search help the customer find a lower-priced product or one that will give superior performance? The costs of the search include the customer's time and money. Traveling from store to store can cost money for gas and parking, but the major cost incurred is the customer's time.

Technology has dramatically reduced the cost of information search. For example, vast information about merchandise sold across the world is just a smartphone search away. Retailing View 4.1 describes how readily available information on the Web affects the automobile buying process.

The amount of information search is affected by (1) characteristics of the individual customer and (2) aspects of the market and buying situation in which the purchase is made.[10] Some people search more than others. Shoppers seeking hedonic benefits typically spend more time collecting information and shopping because they enjoy the process. Customers who have prior experience purchasing and using the product or service tend to search less.

Two marketplace and situational factors affecting information search are (1) the number of competing brands and retail outlets and (2) the time pressure under which the purchase must be made.[11] When competition is greater and there are more alternatives to consider, the amount of information search increases. However, the amount decreases with greater time pressures.

Reducing Information Search   The retailer's objective for customers in the information search stage is to limit the customer's search to its store or website. One measure of a retailer's performance on this objective is the **conversion rate**—the percentage of customers who enter a store or access a website and then buy a product from that same store or website.

Each element of the retailing mix can be used to increase a retailer's conversion rate. Category specialists such as Best Buy provide a very deep assortment of merchandise, everything a customer might want to consider, so that the customer can collect all the information and make the necessary comparisons between products in their stores or on their websites.

At Old Navy, the remodeled layout features a racetrack format that reduces information search by giving customers a better sense of the vast options available. It also displays more items around the checkout area.[12]

Services provided by retailers can also limit the search once at the retailer's location. By offering credit and having informed salespeople, a retailer can convince consumers that they don't need to collect additional information from other retailers. Lowe's has equipped its floor staff with iPhones to enable them to check

---

RETAILING VIEW   The Internet Has Changed the Car-Buying Process   4.1

Ten years ago, if consumers wanted to buy a car, they would visit several dealers, look at different models, test drive the cars sold by each dealer, and then negotiate price and financing with a dealer. Many consumers viewed this traditional process of buying a car as about as pleasurable as a visit to the dentist. But now the Internet has changed this experience, as well as the nature of automobile retailing.

The Internet has given consumers more control over the car-buying process. Consumers can visit websites such as www.autobytel.com, www.cars.com, or www.edmunds.com; access a wealth of information, including the dealer's costs for cars and options; compare vehicles in a side-by-side chart that lists their price, features, horsepower, mileage, legroom, and options; read multiple reviews for most models; and even take a 360-degree photo tour of car interiors that gives them an idea of what the view looks like from the driver's seat.

Through the sites' relationships with car dealers, consumers can request prices from dealers in their area. A handy calculator tells customers how much the monthly payment would be if they were to buy a car on credit. The sites also have calculators to help car buyers figure out how much they can afford to spend on a car, whether they should buy a new or used car, and whether they should lease or buy. This information enables consumers to walk into a dealership knowing as much as or more than the dealer's salespeople.

On the TrueCar website, consumers find information about recent purchases in their area. Thus, for a specific car make and model, they see a bell curve that shows them what represents a great price, what is a reasonable price, and what is simply too much to pay. The site also identifies the local dealership that will offer the lowest price, so car buyers know where to start their search.

CarFax (www.carfax.com) enables customers to access a vehicle's history report by typing in its vehicle identification number (VIN). This history describes any accidents the vehicle was in, its past ownership, odometer fraud, and any other events that might be related to the vehicle. Services such as CarFax make it much easier for customers to purchase used cars with confidence.

REFACT

Nearly three-quarters of new-vehicle buyers use the Internet during the shopping process, and 54 percent watch online videos.[13]

The Internet has dramatically reduced the time and effort needed to collect information and increased the quality of information acquired to make a decision when buying an automobile.

DISCUSSION QUESTIONS

How did you use the Internet to purchase your last car? Was your method of searching for information different than that of your parents?

Sources: Edward Niedermeyer, "TrueCar Versus Honda: Online Car Buying Challenges Hit Home," *The Truth About Cars*, December 21, 2011; Geoffrey A. Fowler, John D. Stoll, and Scott Morrison, "GM, eBay Will Let Car Buyers Dicker Online," *The Wall Street Journal*, August 11, 2009, p. B1; Thomas Pack, "Kicking the Virtual Tires: Car Research on the Web," *Information Today*, January 2009, pp. 44–45; www.cars.com; and www.carfax.com.

Lowe's uses iPhones to help customers with their shopping.

inventory levels for customers on the spot. Similarly, Pacific Sunwear gives salespeople iPads that help them create virtual outfits to show customers. Foot Locker is relying on old-fashioned training, such that employees have a better sense of how to engage customers and encourage them to buy in the store.[14]

Walmart utilizes an **everyday low pricing (EDLP) strategy** that stresses continuity of retail prices at a level somewhere between the regular nonsale price and the deep-discount sale price of its competitors. This strategy helps assure customers that they won't find a lower price for these products at a different store the next time they go shopping. In addition, many stores with everyday low prices offer money-back guarantees if a competitor offers the same merchandise at a lower price. These pricing policies tend to limit the customer information search to the retailer's offering.

Internet, Mobile, Information Search, and Price Competition   The Internet and smartphones have had a profound impact on consumers' ability to gather external information. In addition to placing their own information on their websites and smartphone apps, retailers encourage their customers to post information such as product reviews, ratings, and, in some cases, photos and videos. Consumer reviews are emerging as a prime information source for shoppers as they collect information during the buying process.[16] The Internet and new mobile apps that encourage showrooming—a practice in which consumers visit stores to gather information about the product, then buy online—enable consumers to find the best prices for any product quickly.

Retailers and manufacturers are concerned that the ease of collecting price information through the Internet increases price competition. Traditionally, store-based retailers, offering the same merchandise, experienced limited price competition because of their geographic separation. The Internet means that consumers' ability to compare prices no longer is limited by physical distance. In addition, the ease of searching for price information is facilitated by shopping sites such as mysimon.com. Or consumers can use one of the many mobile phone apps to learn about prices and availability of products at stores near where they are located.[18]

The Internet not only helps online consumers collect price information, but also gives them information about the quality and performance of products, all at a low search cost. With more information about product quality, customers might be willing to pay more for high-quality products, which would mitigate the importance of price.[20] Finally, retailers that use an Internet channel can clearly differentiate their offerings by providing better services and information.

Evaluation of Alternatives: The Multiattribute Model

The multiattribute attitude model provides a useful way to summarize how customers use the information they have collected to evaluate and select retailers, channels, and products. We discuss this model in detail because it offers a framework for developing a retailing strategy.[21]

The **multiattribute attitude model** is based on the notion that customers see a retailer, a product, or a channel as a collection of attributes or characteristics. The model is designed to predict a customer's evaluation of a product, retailer, or channel on the basis of (1) its performance on relevant attributes and (2) the importance of those attributes to the customer.

Beliefs about Performance   To illustrate this model, consider the store choice decision confronting a young, single, professional Milwaukee woman who needs groceries. She considers three alternatives: (1) a supercenter store in the next suburb, (2) her local supermarket store, or (3) a grocer that operates only an Internet channel, such as Fresh Direct. Her perception of the offerings provided by these retailers is shown in Exhibit 4–2.

The customer mentally processes the "objective" information about each grocery retailer in part A of Exhibit 4–2 and forms an impression of the benefits each one provides. Part B of Exhibit 4–2 shows her beliefs about these benefits. Notice that some benefits combine several objective characteristics. For example, the convenience benefit combines travel time, checkout time, and ease of finding products. Grocery prices and delivery cost affect her beliefs about the economy of shopping at the various retail outlets.

The degree to which each retailer provides each benefit is represented on a 10-point scale: 10 means the retailer performs very well in providing the benefit; 1 means it performs very poorly. In this example, no retailer has superior performance on all benefits. The supercenter performs well on economy and assortment

A. INFORMATION ABOUT STORES SELLING GROCERIES			
Store Characteristics	Supercenter	Supermarket	Internet Grocer
Grocery prices	20% below average	Average	10% above average
Delivery cost ($)	0	0	10
Total travel time (minutes)	30	15	0
Typical checkout time (minutes)	10	5	2
Number of products, brands, and sizes	40,000	30,000	40,000
Fresh produce	Yes	Yes	Yes
Fresh fish	Yes	Yes	No
Ease of finding products	Difficult	Easy	Easy
Ease of collecting nutritional information about products	Difficult	Difficult	Easy

B. BELIEFS ABOUT STORES' PERFORMANCE BENEFITS*			
Performance Benefits	Supercenter	Supermarket	Internet Grocer
Economy	10	8	6
Convenience	3	5	10
Assortment	9	7	5
Availability of product information	4	4	8

*10 = excellent, 1 = poor.

EXHIBIT 4–2
Characteristics of Food Retailers

but is low on convenience. The Internet grocer offers the best convenience but is weak on economy and assortment.

Importance Weights   The young woman in the preceding example forms an overall evaluation of each alternative on the basis of the importance she places on each benefit the retailers provide. The importance she places on a benefit can also be represented using a 10-point rating scale, with 10 indicating the benefit is very important to her and 1 indicating it's very unimportant. Using this rating scale, the importance of the retailers' benefits for the young woman and for a parent with four children is shown in Exhibit 4–3, along with the performance beliefs previously discussed. Notice that the single woman values convenience and the availability of product information much more than economy and assortment. But to the parent, economy is very important and assortment is moderately important, whereas convenience and product information aren't very important.

The importance of a retailer's benefits differs for each customer and also may differ for each shopping trip. For example, the parent with four children may stress economy for major shopping trips but place more importance on convenience for a fill-in trip.

In Exhibit 4–3, the single woman and parent have the same beliefs about each retailer's performance, but they differ in the importance they place on the benefits the retailers offer. In general, customers can differ in their beliefs about retailers' performances as well as in their importance weights.

Evaluating Retailers   Research has shown that a customer's overall evaluation of an alternative (in this situation, three retailers) is related to the sum of the performance beliefs multiplied by the importance weights. Thus, we calculate the young, single woman's overall evaluation or score for the supercenter as follows:

$$
\begin{aligned}
4 \times 10 &= 40 \\
10 \times 3 &= 30 \\
5 \times 9 &= 45 \\
9 \times 4 &= \underline{36} \\
&\ 151
\end{aligned}
$$

Exhibit 4–3 shows the overall evaluations of the three retailers using the importance weights of the single woman and the parent. For the single woman, the Internet grocer has the highest score, 221, and thus has the most favorable evaluation. She would probably select this retailer for most of her grocery shopping. On the other hand, the supercenter has the highest score, 192, for the parent, who'd probably buy the family's weekly groceries there.

When customers are about to select a retailer, they don't actually go through the process of listing store characteristics, evaluating retailers' performances on these

EXHIBIT 4–3
Evaluation of Retailers

Characteristic	IMPORTANCE WEIGHTS*		PERFORMANCE BELIEFS		
	Young Single Woman	Parent with Four Children	Supercenter	Supermarket	Internet Grocer
Economy	4	10	10	8	6
Convenience	10	4	3	5	10
Assortment	5	8	9	7	5
Availability of product information	9	2	4	4	8
OVERALL EVALUATION					
Young single woman			151	153	221
Parent with four children			192	164	156

*10 = very important, 1 = very unimportant.

characteristics, determining each characteristic's importance, calculating each store's overall score, and then patronizing the retailer with the highest score. The multiattribute attitude model does not reflect customers' actual decision process, but it does predict their evaluation of alternatives and their choice. In addition, the model provides useful information for designing a retail offering. For example, if the supermarket could increase its performance rating on assortment from 7 to 10 (perhaps by adding a bakery and a wide selection of prepared meals), customers like the parent might shop at the supermarket more often than at the supercenter.

The application of the multiattribute attitude model in Exhibit 4–3 deals with a customer who is evaluating and selecting a retailer. The same model can also be used to describe how a customer evaluates and selects which channel to use (store, Internet, or catalog) or what merchandise to buy from a retailer. For example, the model could be used to describe Eva Mendoza's choice among the three suits she was considering.

Implications for Retailers   In this section, we describe how a retailer can use the multiattribute attitude model to encourage customers to shop at the retailer more frequently. First, the model indicates what information customers use to decide which retailer to patronize or which channel to use. Second, it suggests tactics that retailers can undertake to influence customers' store, channel, and merchandise choices.

To develop a program for attracting customers, retailers need to do market research to collect the following information:

1. Alternative retailers that customers consider.
2. Characteristics or benefits that customers consider when evaluating and choosing a retailer.
3. Customers' ratings of each retailer's performance on the characteristics.
4. The importance weights that customers attach to the characteristics.

Armed with this information, the retailer can use several approaches to influence customers to patronize its store or Internet site.

Getting into the Consideration Set   Retailers need to be included in the customer's **consideration set,** or the set of alternatives the customer evaluates when making a choice of a retailer to patronize. To be included in the consideration set, retailers develop programs to increase the likelihood that customers will remember them when they're about to go shopping. Retailers can increase customer awareness through communication and location decisions. For example, retailers can buy placement at the top of the screen when consumers are using a search engine term for products they sell. They can develop communication programs that link categories they sell with their name. Starbucks locates several stores in the same area so that customers are exposed more frequently to the store name as they drive through the area.

After ensuring that it is in consumers' consideration set, a retailer can use three methods to increase the chances that customers will select it for a visit:

1. Increase beliefs about the store's performance.
2. Change customers' importance weights.
3. Add a new benefit.

Changing Performance Beliefs   The first approach involves altering customers' beliefs about the retailer's performance by increasing the retailer's performance rating on a characteristic. For example, the supermarket in Exhibit 4–3 would want to increase its overall rating by improving its rating on all four benefits. The supermarket could improve its rating on economy by lowering prices and its assortment rating by stocking more gourmet and ethnic foods. Retailing View 4.2 illustrates how Lowe's altered the performance beliefs of women about its stores.

Because it can get costly for a retailer to improve its performance on all benefits, retailers must focus on improving their performance on those benefits that are important to customers in their target market. For example, Best Buy knows that an important benefit for its customers is not to be without their computers for lengthy amounts of time when repairs are needed. So it maintains a 240,000-square-foot "Geek Squad City" warehouse, with more than 1,200 employees, dedicated to reducing the time it takes to repair and return a computer. Geek Squad "agents" fix more than 4,000 laptops per day.[22]

Changing Importance Weights   Altering customers' importance weights is another approach to influencing store choice. A retailer wants to increase the importance customers place on benefits for which its performance is superior and decrease the importance of benefits for which it has inferior performance.

For example, if the supermarket in Exhibit 4–3 tried to attract families who shop at supercenters, it could increase the importance of convenience for them. Typically, changing importance weights is harder than changing performance beliefs because importance weights reflect customers' personal values.

Adding a New Benefit   Finally, retailers might try to add a new benefit to the set of benefits customers consider when selecting a retailer. Senda (www.sendaathletics.com) does not just offer the typical assortment of athletic

4.2 RETAILING VIEW   Do It Herself at Lowe's

You might think that home improvement centers are a retail recreation destination mostly for men. Men visit the stores on the weekends to check out the new tools and buy material for do-it-yourself (DIY) projects. But more than 50 percent of the sales at home improvement centers actually are made to women—who make decisions about what materials to use in home improvement projects and often do much of the work themselves.

Lowe's was early to recognize the importance of female customers—though it is not the only traditionally male-oriented retailer to do so. It redesigned its stores to

REFACT

Women make more than 85 percent of all consumer purchases and purchase 50 percent or more in categories typically considered male—banking and financial services, electronics, automobiles, PCs, and many other big-ticket items. Their purchases represent more than half of the U.S. GDP.[23]

be brighter, lose the warehouse look, and feature departments more appealing to women. With wider aisles, shoppers can avoid uncomfortable, unintended contact with items on shelves—otherwise known as "butt brush." The shelves also are a bit shorter, to make it easy to reach the easy-to-find products that are well marked by aisle markers and maps.

But these changes need to be restrained, to avoid causing male customers to reject the stores as overly feminine. Moreover, women express negative views of offerings that seem condescending in their "girlie" appeals. To balance its recent findings with its long-standing performance tactics, Lowe's offers workshops to teach women about tools, rather than carrying tools specifically designed for women. One section of its website, www.lowes.com/howto, provides online clinics

Lowe's changed its store design to change women's beliefs about the pleasantness of its store environment.

and videos to help customers successfully implement their own DIY projects at home.

Sources: Tony Bingham and Pat Galagan, "Training at Lowe's: Let's Learn Something Together," T + D, November 2009, pp. 35–41; Amanda Junk, "Women Wield the Tools: Lowe's, Habitat for Humanity Teaches Them How," McClatchy-Tribune Business News, July 18, 2009; Cecile B. Corral, "Lowe's Outlines Expansion Plans," Home Textiles Today, October 5, 2009, p. 6; and Fara Warner, "Yes, Women Spend (And Saw and Sand)," The New York Times, February 29, 2004.

DISCUSSION QUESTION
Does feminizing a Lowe's make it less attractive to men?

gear; it sells unusual items such as customizable soccer balls and training vests. It believes that by providing a wider variety than its competition, its customers will find it more attractive. Other retailers attempt to add new benefits by emphasizing that their merchandise is **fair trade**—made by workers who are paid a fair wage, not just a minimum wage.[24] A fair wage means that workers are able to live relatively comfortably within the context of their local area. Offering fair trade merchandise is a benefit that is important to consumers who are concerned about the welfare of people in less developed countries.

Purchasing the Merchandise or Service

Customers don't always patronize a store or purchase a brand or item of merchandise with the highest overall evaluation. The product or service offering the greatest benefits (having the highest evaluation) may not be available from the retailer, or the customer may feel that its risks outweigh the potential benefits. Other consumers make purchase choices based on a single attribute, regardless of how well the offering performs on other characteristics. For example, Eva visited Macy's because the local store is convenient to her apartment, even though other department stores might have a wider selection of women's suits. One measure of retailers' success at converting positive evaluations to purchases is a reduction in the number of real or virtual abandoned carts in the retailer's store or website.

Retailers use various tactics to increase the chances that customers will convert their positive evaluations into purchases. First, they attempt to make it easy to purchase merchandise. More and more retailers are ensuring that their websites are mobile friendly. In their stores, they can reduce the actual wait time for buying merchandise by having more checkout lanes open and placing them conveniently in the store. In addition to reducing actual waiting time, they can reduce perceived wait times by installing digital displays to entertain customers waiting in line.[25] Many Internet retailers send reminder e-mails to visitors about items in carts they have abandoned.[26]

Second, retailers' ability to turn a positive purchase intention into a sale can also be increased by providing sufficient information that reinforces the customer's positive evaluation. For example, Eva's friend Britt, the salesperson, and another potential customer also provided Eva with positive feedback to support her purchase decision.

Third, retailers can increase the chances of making a sale by reducing the risk of making a purchase mistake. For instance, retailers can offer liberal return policies, money-back guarantees, and refunds if customers find the same merchandise available at lower prices from another retailer.

Finally, retailers often create a sense of urgency or scarcity to encourage customers to make a purchase decision. Zappos.com and Overstock.com alert customers if an item in their shopping carts is about to sell out. Flash-sale sites offer items for a specified time period; Neiman Marcus hosts two-hour online sales. The limited assortments offered by fast-fashion retailers like Zara and off-price retailers like TJX Corporation (TJ Maxx and Marshalls) have conditioned customers to buy it when they see it. Otherwise, it may be gone the next time they visit the store.

REFACT

A recent study found that one in five smartphone shoppers made a purchase via his or her smartphone in April 2012. A third of the purchases were for clothing or accessories.[27]

Postpurchase Evaluation

The buying process doesn't end when a customer purchases a product. After making a purchase, the customer uses the product and then evaluates the experience to determine whether it was satisfactory or unsatisfactory. **Satisfaction** is a postconsumption evaluation of how well a store or product meets or exceeds customer expectations. This **postpurchase evaluation** then becomes part of the customer's internal information and affects store and product evaluations and purchase decisions. Unsatisfactory experiences can motivate customers to complain to the retailer, patronize other stores, and select different brands in the future. Consistently high levels of satisfaction build store and brand loyalty, important sources of competitive advantage for retailers.[28]

To improve postpurchase assessments and satisfaction, retailers can take several steps. First, they must make sure to build realistic customer expectations, so they never let those shoppers down with their performance. Second, they should provide information about proper use and care of the items purchased. Third, as mentioned previously, guarantees and warranties reduce a negative feeling of risk, both before and after the purchase. Fourth, the best retailers make contact periodically with their customers to make sure they are satisfied, correct any problems, and remind customers of their availability. This last effort also can improve the chances that a customer puts the retailer in his or her consideration set for the next purchase occasion.

TYPES OF BUYING DECISIONS

LO2

Identify the different types of buying processes.

In some situations, customers like Eva Mendoza spend considerable time and effort selecting a retailer and evaluating alternative products—going through all the steps in the buying process described in the preceding section. In other situations, buying decisions are made automatically with little thought. This section examines three types of customer decision-making processes: extended problem solving, limited problem solving, and habitual decision making.

Extended Problem Solving

Extended problem solving is a purchase decision process in which customers devote considerable time and effort to analyze their alternatives. Customers typically engage in extended problem solving when the purchase decision involves a lot of risk and uncertainty. **Financial risks** arise when customers purchase an expensive product or service. **Physical risks** are important when customers feel that a product or service may affect their health or safety. **Social risks** arise when customers believe a product will affect how others view them. Lasik eye surgery, for instance, involves all three types of risks: It can be expensive, potentially damage the eyes, and change a person's appearance.

Consumers engage in extended problem solving when they are making a buying decision to satisfy an important need or when they have little knowledge about the product or service, as we described with car buyers in Retailing View 4.1. Due to the high risk in such situations, customers go beyond their internal knowledge to consult with friends, family members, or experts. They might also peruse online blogs; examine online reviews, both retailer-sponsored and independent review sites; and read *Consumer Reports*. They may also visit several retailers before making a purchase decision.

Retailers stimulate sales from customers engaged in extended problem solving by providing the necessary information in a readily available and easily understood manner and by offering money-back guarantees. For example, retailers that sell merchandise involving extended problem solving provide information on their websites describing the merchandise and its specifications, have informational displays in their stores (such as a sofa cut in half to show its construction), and use salespeople to demonstrate features and answer questions.

Limited Problem Solving

Limited problem solving is a purchase decision process involving a moderate amount of effort and time. Customers engage in this type of buying process when they have had some prior experience with the product or service and their risk is moderate. In such situations, customers tend to rely more on personal knowledge than on external information. They usually choose a retailer they have shopped at before and select merchandise they have bought in the past. The majority of customer purchase decisions involve limited problem solving.

Retailers attempt to reinforce this buying pattern and make it habitual when customers are buying merchandise from them. If customers are shopping elsewhere, however, retailers need to break this buying pattern by introducing new information or offering different merchandise or services. A common way to adjust the pattern is through coupons. Companies such as CVS and Walgreens often offer deep coupon discounts on commonly purchased products to get customers into their stores. Retailers are willing to give such steep discounts for two reasons. First, it breaks the established habit a customer may have of shopping elsewhere, and second, they know customers often buy many other, undiscounted items once they are in the store. After customers make these purchases, the retailers analyze their spending patterns and offer targeted coupons to encourage repatronage.[29]

Eva Mendoza's buying process illustrates both limited and extended problem solving. Her store choice decision was based on her knowledge of the merchandise in various stores she had shopped in and her search on Nubry.com. Considering this information, she felt the store choice decision was not very risky; thus, she engaged in limited problem solving when deciding to visit Macy's. But her buying process for the suit was extended. This decision was important to her; thus, she spent time acquiring information from a friend, the salesperson, and another shopper to evaluate and select a suit.

One common type of limited problem solving is **impulse buying**, or **unplanned purchasing**, which is a buying decision made by customers on the spot after seeing the merchandise.[30] Retailers encourage impulse-buying behavior by using prominent point-of-purchase (POP) or point-of-sale (POS) displays to attract customers' attention. Retailers have long recognized that the most valuable real estate in the store is at the point of purchase. An increasing number of nonfood retailers (such as Old Navy, as mentioned previously) are looking to increase impulse buys from customers by offering candy, gum, mints, and other fun, hedonic items at their cash registers. Electronic shoppers are also stimulated to purchase impulsively when Internet retailers put special merchandise on their home pages and suggest complementary merchandise just before checkout.

Habitual Decision Making

Habitual decision making is a purchase decision process involving little or no conscious effort. Today's customers have many demands on their time. One way they cope with these time pressures is by simplifying their decision-making process. When a need arises, customers may automatically respond with, "I'll buy the same thing I bought last time from the same store." Typically, this habitual decision-making process occurs when decisions aren't very important to customers and involve familiar merchandise they have bought in the past. When customers are loyal to a brand or a store, they engage in habitual decision making.

Brand loyalty means that customers like and consistently buy a specific brand in a product category. They are reluctant to switch to other brands if their favorite brand isn't available. For example, loyal Coca-Cola drinkers won't buy Pepsi, no matter what. Thus, retailers can satisfy these customers' needs only if they offer the specific brands desired.

Brand loyalty creates both opportunities and problems for retailers.[31] Customers are attracted to stores that carry popular brands, but because retailers must carry these high-loyalty brands, they may not be able to negotiate favorable terms with the suppliers of the popular national brands. If, however, the high-loyalty brands are private-label brands (i.e., brands owned by the retailer), retailer loyalty is heightened.

Retailer loyalty means that customers like and habitually visit the same retailer to purchase a type of merchandise. All retailers would like to increase their customers' loyalty, and they can do so by selecting a convenient location (see Chapters 7 and 8), offering complete assortments of national and private-label brands (Chapter 13), reducing the number of stockouts (Chapter 13), rewarding customers for frequent purchases (Chapter 11), or providing good customer service (Chapter 18).

SOCIAL FACTORS INFLUENCING THE BUYING PROCESS

LO3

Summarize how the economy and social factors affect customer purchase decisions.

Exhibit 4–4 illustrates how customer buying decisions are influenced by four influential social factors: the economy, family, reference groups, and culture.

The Economy

The state of the national and global economy has significant effects on the way people buy. In terms of the most recent global recession, the effects have lingered because consumers continue to feel a sense of uncertainty and risk.[32] At the same time, many shoppers have discovered that shopping for bargains is fun. Even if their incomes have stabilized, they see little reason to switch back to name brands when the private-label offerings they have been buying work just fine.[33]

The outcomes in terms of consumers' buying processes have been both expected and unexpected. Predictably, people have reduced their spending on luxury brands, leading retailers to revamp their offerings. For example, Neiman Marcus broadened its jewelry lines to include more funky, less expensive designs and fewer precious metals.[34] In addition, consumers make fewer shopping trips and appreciate the convenience of one-stop shopping (which also lowers gasoline expenditures) at hypermarkets or supercenters.

More surprising are the trends that suggest some buyers actually are spending a little more on higher-quality products in an effort to gain more value and make purchases last. When they do spend more lavishly, consumers tend to feel guilty. Thus, the Ritz-Carlton began avoiding its "silver tray" image in its advertising and instead encouraged visitors to consider their hotel stay a time to reconnect with family. Consumers want to splurge a little when they can; retailers have to find ways to enable them to do so without guilt.[35]

Family

Many purchase decisions involve products that the entire family will consume or use. The previous discussion of the buying process focused on how one person makes a decision. When families make purchase decisions, they often consider the needs of all family members.[36]

EXHIBIT 4–4
Social Factors
Affecting Buying
Decisions

When choosing a vacation site, for example, all family members may participate in the decision making. In other situations, one member of the family may assume the decision-making role. For example, the husband might buy the groceries, which the wife then uses to prepare their child's lunch, which the child consumes in school. In this situation, the store choice decision might be made by the husband, but the brand choice decision might be made by the wife, though it likely is greatly influenced by the child.

Children play an important role in family buying decisions. Resort hotels now realize they must satisfy children's needs as well as those of adults. The Hyatt hotel chain thus cooperates with a mail-order baby supply company, Babies Travel Lite. After parents book a room, they can order all the diapers, formula, and organic baby food they will need for the trip. The items will be ready for them when they check in, which reduces the amount of baggage and increases convenience. For older children, Hyatt offers toys, available to be checked out from the front desk. In addition, working with the famous chef Alice Waters, it has revamped the children's menus in its hotel restaurants to offer nutritious, but also fun meal options.[37]

Retailers also can attract consumers who shop with other family members by satisfying the needs of all those family members. For example, Anthropologie has enlarged its dressing rooms so families (and friends) can provide advice and try on clothes together. Macy's has added comfortable seating and televisions outside dressing rooms to keep other family members entertained.[38]

Reference Groups

A **reference group** includes one or more people whom a person uses as a basis of comparison for beliefs, feelings, and behaviors. A consumer might have a number of different reference groups, such as family, friends, celebrities, and opinion leaders. These reference groups affect buying decisions by (1) offering information, (2) providing rewards for specific purchasing behaviors, and (3) enhancing a consumer's self-image.

Reference groups provide information to consumers directly through conversation, either face-to-face or electronically, or indirectly through observation. For example, Eva received valuable information from her friend about the suits she was considering. On other occasions, Eva might look to women like soccer player Hope Solo and tennis player Caroline Wozniacki to guide her selection of athletic apparel or Demi Lovato and Katy

Shoppers look to celebrities like Katy Perry for fashion tips.

Perry for casual fashion advice. The role of reference groups in creating fashion is discussed in the appendix to this chapter.

By identifying and affiliating with reference groups, consumers create, enhance, and maintain their self-image. Customers who want to be seen as members of an elite social class may shop at prestige retailers, whereas others who want to create the image of an outdoor enthusiast might buy merchandise from the L.L. Bean website.

Retailers are particularly interested in identifying and reaching out to those in a reference group who act as store advocates and actively influence others in the group. **Store advocates** are customers who like a store so much that they actively share their positive experiences with friends and family. Retailing View 4.3 details how social media sites such as Pinterest and Facebook make sharing ideas, reviews, and "likes" even easier. Consumers see so much advertising that they have become suspicious of the claims being made. Thus, they are relying more on their own social networks for information about stores to patronize and merchandise to buy.

Culture

Culture is the meaning, beliefs, morals, and values shared by most members of a society. As the basis of the social factors that influence people's buying decisions, the culture or cultures in which each consumer participates often align with his or her reference groups. For example, Eva's cultural groups include her Latino heritage and the Pacific Northwest culture in which she lives. These cultural influences affect her consumer behavior. Because the culture at Eva's college is rather

4.3   RETAILING VIEW   Pinning Consumption Choices on Online Reference Groups

With a simple logo—a thumb pointing up and the word "Like"—Facebook revamped the way people share recommendations and interests. Users can show their approval of other users' posts and pictures. But they also can click the nearly ubiquitous Like button on retailers' sites to show their Facebook friends which retailer, merchandise item, or service they consider worthy of their approval.

The "Like" generation relies heavily on such social media recommendations. A recent study indicated that 62 percent of social media users read their friends' "social sharing" about items to purchase. Of these, 75 percent click on the link. And of the people who click, 53 percent of them actually buy the shared product. Of course, after they buy, they also share their purchase with their social network, starting the virtuous cycle (for retailers) all over again.

But purchasing is not the only promising outcome of social sharing. On Pinterest, a sort of online scrapbook for users' interests, the predominantly female (68 percent) members create pin boards that reflect their interests in their favorite retailers and the merchandise they carry. Then they post pictures to reflect those interests, which others can check to find their own inspiration. Retailers are using pin boards to enhance brand awareness among consumers who might buy later. American Eagle Outfitters (http://pinterest.com/americaneagle/) has 51 pin boards with 2,020 pins, listing images such as "Fall Shoes from AE" or "Best Gifts to Give." Saks Fifth Avenue has 52 pin boards focusing on topics like decorative fabrics, printed pants, and saturated lip colors.[40]

The increasing popularity of Pinterest seems to reflect the old adage that a picture is worth a thousand words. It also represents a new trend: Everyone is a voyeur. That is, consumers today feel as if they must know what their reference groups are doing, wearing, or buying. Retailers embrace the notion. When a retailer gets Liked or Pinned, the virtuous cycle of social sharing is likely to enhance its sales, profits, and chances of success.

Sources: Andy Kessler, "The Button That Made Facebook Billions," *The Wall Street Journal*, February 2, 2012; Social Labs, "Social Impact Study 2012 Infographic on Social Sharing," March 20, 2012; Tanzina Vega, "Marketers Find a Friend in Pinterest," *The New York Times*, April 17, 2012; and Sarah E. Needleman and Pui-Wing Tam, "Pinterest's Rite of Web Passage—Huge Traffic, No Revenues," *The Wall Street Journal*, February 16, 2012.

DISCUSSION QUESTION

Do you like the "like" button? If yes, why? If no, why not?

fashion conscious, she was immediately aware that her old suit was out of date and considered buying fashionable shoes a reasonable addition.

Many retailers and shopping center managers have recognized the importance of appealing to different cultures and subcultures.[41] For instance, the U.S. Hispanic population is growing faster than any other market segment, and Hispanics' purchasing power is rising faster than that of the general population. Many retailers, particularly supermarkets in areas with large Hispanic populations, have dedicated significant space to products that are indigenous to particular Spanish-speaking countries. The product mix will, however, differ depending on the region of the country. Merchandise should reflect that, for instance, Miami has a large Cuban and Latin American population, whereas Los Angeles and Texas have more people from Mexico. Bilingual employees are a critical success factor for stores catering to the Hispanic population. Some retailers with a long history of serving Hispanic

Many retailers and shopping center managers have adjusted their strategies to appeal to different cultures and subcultures.

customers even found that they needed to start adding more English to their products and marketing materials to better target their customers' children. Thus, Pizza Patrón, a Dallas-based pizza chain, has begun shifting its menu boards from purely Spanish to a combination of Spanish and English, and Curacao, a big box store in California serving Hispanics, has shifted from Spanish-only speaking employees and advertising to a similar mixed format.[42]

MARKET SEGMENTATION

LO4

Determine why and how retailers group customers into market segments.

The preceding discussion focused on (1) how individual customers evaluate and select stores, channels, and merchandise and (2) the factors affecting their decision making. To be cost-effective, retailers identify groups of these customers (market segments) and target their offerings to meet the needs of typical customers in a segment rather than the needs of a specific customer. At one time, Walmart used a "one-size-fits-all" strategy. The merchandise selection was very similar across the United States, without much regard to geographic or demographic variations. This approach worked well when most of its stores were located in rural areas in the Southeast. But as it opened stores in more diverse locations, it realized it had to develop different retail mixes for different market segments. For example, in urban locations, it has begun opening smaller Walmart Express and Market stores, in already-built storefronts, which feature more grocery items and a small selection of lawn furniture.[43]

A **retail market segment** is a group of customers who are attracted to the same retail mix because they have similar needs. For example, young, hip 20-somethings have different needs than executives on business trips. Thus, Marriott offers hotel chains with different retail mixes for each of these segments—AC Hotels by

Marriott for the young and hip and Marriott Hotels and Conference Centers for business executives and conferences.

The Internet enables retailers to target individual customers efficiently and market products to them on a one-to-one basis. This one-to-one marketing concept is discussed in Chapter 11 as it pertains to customer relationship management.

Criteria for Evaluating Market Segments

Customers can be grouped into segments in many different ways. Exhibit 4–5 shows some different methods of segmenting retail markets. There's no simple way to determine which method is best, though four criteria useful for evaluating whether a retail segment is a viable target market are as follows: actionable, identifiable, substantial, and reachable.

Actionable   The fundamental criteria for evaluating a retail market segment are that (1) customers in the segment must have similar needs, seek similar benefits, and be satisfied by a similar retail offering and (2) those customers' needs must differ from the needs of customers in other segments. **Actionable** means that the retailer should know what to do to satisfy needs for the consumers in the

EXHIBIT 4–5
Methods for
Segmenting Retail
Markets

Segmentation Descriptor	Example of Categories
GEOGRAPHIC	
Region	Pacific, Mountain, Central, South, Mid-Atlantic, Northeast
Population density	Rural, suburban, urban
Climate	Cold, warm
DEMOGRAPHIC	
Age	Under 6, 6–12, 13–19, 20–29, 30–49, 50–65, over 65
Gender	Male, female
Family life cycle	Single, married with no children, married with youngest child under 6, married with youngest child over 6, married with children no longer living at home, widowed
Family income	Under $19,999; $20,000–29,999; $30,000–49,999; $50,000–$74,999; over $75,000
Occupation	Professional, clerical, sales, craftsperson, retired, student, homemaker
Education	Some high school, high school graduate, some college, college graduate, graduate degree
Religion	Catholic, Protestant, Jewish, Muslim
Race	Caucasian, African-American, Hispanic, Asian
Nationality	American, Japanese, British, French, German, Italian, Chinese
PSYCHOSOCIAL	
Social class	Lower, middle, upper
Lifestyle	Striver, driver, devoted, intimate, altruist, fun seeker, creative
Personality	Aggressive, shy, emotional
FEELINGS AND BEHAVIORS	
Attitudes	Positive, neutral, negative
Benefit sought	Convenience, economy, prestige
Stage in decision process	Unaware, aware, informed, interested, intend to buy, bought previously
Perceived risk	High, medium, low
Innovativeness	Innovator, early adopter, early majority, late majority, laggard
Loyalty	None, some, completely
Usage rate	None, light, medium, heavy
Usage situation	Home, work, vacation, leisure
User status	Nonuser, ex-user, potential user, current user

segment. According to this criterion, it makes sense for Banana Republic to segment the apparel market on the basis of the demographic characteristic of physical size. Customers who wear petite sizes have different needs than those who wear regular or large sizes, so they are attracted to a store offering a unique merchandise mix. In the context of the multiattribute attitude model discussed previously, people who wear small sizes place more importance on fit and customer service because it is generally more difficult for them to get the appropriate fit and because they need knowledgeable sales associates who know and can cater to their specific needs.

In contrast, it wouldn't make sense for a supermarket to segment its market on the basis of customer size. Large and small men and women probably have the same needs, seek the same benefits, and go through the same buying process for groceries. This segmentation approach wouldn't be actionable for a supermarket retailer because the retailer couldn't develop unique mixes for large and small customers. However, a segmentation scheme based on geography or demographics such as household income and ethnicity would be actionable.

Identifiable   **Identifiable** means that the retailer is able to determine which customers are in the market segment. When customers are identifiable, the retailer can determine (1) the segment's size and (2) the consumers to whom the retailer needs to target its communications and promotions. For example, supermarket retailers use customer demographics to identify where they should put their stores and the merchandise that they should carry. More prepared and gourmet foods, fancy produce, and expensive cuts of meat would go into stores in neighborhoods with higher average incomes. Snack foods likely predominate in stores located near a college campus. It is equally important to ensure that the segments are distinct from one another because too much overlap between segments means that distinct marketing strategies aren't needed. If, for example, a regional grocery store chain had stores located in neighborhoods containing people with similar demographics, there would be no need to vary its merchandise selection.

Substantial   If a market is too small or its buying power insignificant (i.e., not **substantial**), it cannot generate sufficient profits to support the retailing mix activities. For example, the market for pet pharmaceuticals is probably not large enough in one local area to serve as a target market segment, but a national market could be served through the Internet channel.

Reachable   **Reachable** means that the retailer can target promotions and other elements of the retail mix to consumers in the segment. For example, AutoZone targets men who repair their automobiles themselves. Potential customers in this segment are reachable because they read car magazines, watch NASCAR on TV, and have distinct television viewing habits.

Approaches for Segmenting Markets

Exhibit 4–5 illustrates the wide variety of approaches for segmenting retail markets. No one approach is best for all retailers. Instead, they must explore various factors that affect customer buying behavior and determine which factors are most important for them.

Geographic Segmentation   **Geographic segmentation** groups customers according to where they live. A retail market can be segmented by countries (Japan, Mexico) or by areas within a country, such as states, cities, and neighborhoods.[44] Because customers typically shop at stores convenient to where they live and work, individual retail outlets usually focus on the customer segment reasonably close to the outlet.

4.4   RETAILING VIEW   Where Gender Matters—and Where It Doesn't

In the past, the demographic patterns seemed clear: Women bought personal care products, fragrances, women's clothing, and groceries. Men bought stereo equipment, video games, tires, and men's clothing—if they had to. But in modern-day retail environments, virtually all of these easy classifications are being challenged by shoppers who have little time to waste with gender stereotypes. And retailers are quickly catching on.

For example, when Urban Outfitters was redesigning its website, it stumbled on what the web designers thought was a brilliant and simple change. They would personalize the site so that female visitors immediately were directed to dresses and blouses, while male visitors saw work shirts and tough-guy jeans. The response was quick—and negative. Female visitors complained that they were the ones buying most of the clothing for the men in their lives. And on top of that, they found the gender-biased marketing offensive.

At the same time, more and more men are in the market for grooming and personal care products. The suggested reasons are many. Maybe the modern generation simply is more accustomed to shopping for themselves. Or perhaps job seekers in a tight economy need any edge they can get, and feeling confident about their personal grooming as they head to interviews might tip the scales in their favor. But regardless of the reason, the conventional wisdom that personal care and fragrance sellers could market just to women has gone out the window.

Overall, it appears that men and women actually have approximately equal influences on households' spending. In a recent survey, 85 percent of women and 84 percent of men agreed that they shared responsibility for shopping decisions.

Such equality of influence is not to say that women and men shop the same way, though. As men take on more grocery shopping tasks—a role traditionally assigned to women—some grocery retailers are experimenting with ways to appeal to them. For example, men appear to hate to ask for help, so the stores need to be efficient and clearly laid out with good signage, rather than providing an abundance of customer service.

Best Buy similarly recognized that women are a massive market for electronics, smartphones, and mobile devices. But its stores tended to attract very few female shoppers. Therefore, its recent store design revisions aim to appeal to women with household appliance sections that look more like kitchens than like industrial shipyards and hand sanitizer dispensers placed next to the video game test consoles.

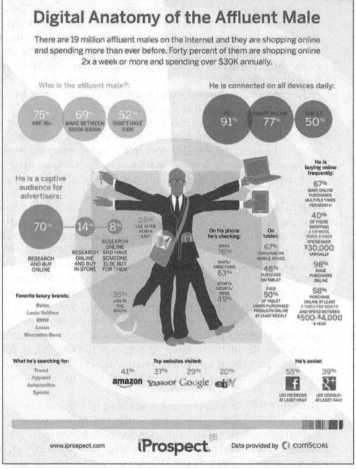

Who is the affluent male? How connected is he to his devices?

Source: www.iprospect.com/digital-affluent-male

REFACT

19 million "affluent males" shop on the Internet. They tend to be over 35 years old and make between $100,000 and $300,000 a year. They generally search for travel, apparel, automotive, and sports. Their favorite brands are Rolex, Louis Vuitton, BMW, Lexus, and Mercedes-Benz.[45]

Sources: Natasha Singer, "E-Tailer Customization: Convenient or Creepy?" *The New York Times*, June 23, 2012; "Who Makes the Call at the Mall, Men or Women?" *The Wall Street Journal*, April 23, 2011; Tom Ryan, "'His' and 'Her' Grocery Aisles," *Retail Wire*, June 6, 2011; Susan Reda, "Guess What? Men Shop, Too!" *Stores*, April 2010; and Miguel Bustillo and Mary Ellen Lloyd, "Best Buy Tests New Appeals to Women," *The Wall Street Journal*, June 16, 2010.

DISCUSSION QUESTION

How are your shopping habits different from someone you are close to of the opposite sex?

Segments based on geography can be identifiable, substantial, and reachable. It's easy to determine who lives in a geographic segment, such as the Paris metropolitan area, and then determine how many potential customers are in that area. It is also relatively simple to target communications and locate retail outlets for customers in Paris and then determine if customers are being responsive to those communications. However, when customers in different geographic segments have similar needs, it is inefficient to develop unique retail offerings by geographic markets. For example, a fast-food customer in Detroit probably seeks the same benefits as a fast-food customer in Los Angeles. Thus, it wouldn't be useful to segment the U.S. fast-food market geographically.

Demographic Segmentation   **Demographic segmentation** groups consumers on the basis of easily measured, objective characteristics such as age, gender, income, and education. Demographic variables are the most common means of defining segments, because consumers in these segments can be easily identified, their size can be determined, and the degree to which they can be reached by and are responsive to media can be easily assessed.

However, demographics may not be useful for defining segments for some retailers because the motivations for purchasing transcend simple demographics. For example, demographics are poor predictors of users of activewear, such as jogging suits and running shoes. At one time, retailers assumed that activewear would be purchased exclusively by young athletic people, but the health and fitness trend has led people of all ages to buy this merchandise. Relatively inactive consumers also find activewear to be comfortable. Several other long-held assumptions about who buys what also are being challenged in today's retail environment, as Retailing View 4.4 describes.

Geodemographic Segmentation   **Geodemographic segmentation** uses both geographic and demographic characteristics to classify consumers. This segmentation scheme is based on the principle that "birds of a feather flock together." Consumers in the same neighborhoods tend to buy the same types of cars, appliances, and apparel and shop at the same types of retailers.[46]

One widely used tool for geodemographic market segmentation is the Tapestry Segmentation system developed and marketed by Esri.[47] Tapestry Segmentation classifies all U.S. residential neighborhoods into 65 distinctive segments based on socioeconomic and demographic characteristics.[48] The information in Exhibit 4–6 describes three Tapestry segments. These neighborhoods, with their similar demographics and buying behaviors, can be any place in the United States.

Geodemographic segmentation is particularly appealing for managing the store channel because customers typically patronize stores close to their neighborhoods. Thus, retailers can use geodemographic segmentation to select locations for their stores and tailor the assortment in the stores to the preferences of the local community. In Chapter 8, we illustrate how geodemographic segmentation is used to make store location decisions.

Lifestyle Segmentation   Of the various methods of segmenting, lifestyle is the one that delves the most into how consumers describe themselves. **Lifestyle,** or **psychographics,** refers to how people live, how they spend their time and money, what activities they pursue, and their attitudes and opinions about the world in which they live. For example, a person may have a strong need for conservation. This need then motivates the person to buy products compatible with that lifestyle. Shoppers at the Austin, Texas–based, environmentally sustainable, zero-waste grocery chain in.gredients bring their own containers and purchase the organic food products they need from bulk bins.[49]

EXHIBIT 4–6
Examples of Tapestry

	Segment 01 - Top Rung	Segment 18 - *Cozy and Comfortable*	Segment 52 - *Inner City Tenants*
LifeMode Summary Group	L1 *High Society*	L2 *Upscale Avenues*	L8 *Global Roots*
Urbanization Summary Group	U3 *Metro Cities I*	U8 *Suburban Periphery II*	U4 *Metro Cities II*
Household Type	Married-Couple Families	Married-Couple Families	Mixed
Median Age	44.6	41.7	28.8
Income	High	Upper Middle	Lower Middle
Employment	Prof/Mgmt	Prof/Mgmt	Srvc/Prof/Mgmt/Skilled
Education	Bach/Grad Degree	Some College	No HS Diploma; HS; Some Coll
Residential	Single Family	Single Family	Multiunit Rentals
Race/Ethnicity	White	White	White; Black; Hispanic
Activity	Participate in public/civic activities	Dine out often at family restaurants	Play football, basketball
Financial	Own stock worth $75,000+	Have personal line of credit	Have personal education loan
Activity	Vacation overseas	Shop at Kohl's	Go dancing
Media	Listen to classical, all-news radio	Listen to sporting events on radio	Read music, baby, fashion magazines
Vehicle	Own/Lease luxury car	Own/Lease minivan	Own/Lease Honda

SOURCE: Esri, "Tapestry Segmentation: The Fabric of America's Neighborhoods."

Lifestyle segments can be identified through consumer surveys that ask respondents to indicate whether they agree or disagree with statements such as, "My idea of fun in a national park would be to stay in an expensive lodge and dress up for dinner," "I often crave excitement," or "I could not stand to skin a dead animal." Retailers today are placing more emphasis on lifestyles than on demographics to define a target segment.

One of the most widely used tools for **lifestyle segmentation** is **VALS,** by Strategic Business Insights. On the basis of responses to the VALS survey (www.strategicbusinessinsights.com/vals/presurvey.shtml), consumers are classified into the eight segments shown in Exhibit 4–7. On the horizontal dimension, the segments reflect people's primary motivation for buying, which stem from their self-image. There are three primary motivations of U.S. consumers: ideals, achievement, and self-expression. People who are primarily motivated by ideals are guided by knowledge and principles. Those who are motivated by achievement look for products and services that demonstrate success to their peers. Consumers who are primarily motivated by self-expression desire social or physical activity, variety, and risk. On the vertical dimension, the descriptions refer instead to consumers' resources, including their income, education, health, and energy level, as well as their degree of innovativeness. The segments on top have more resources and are more innovative; those on the bottom have fewer resources and are less innovative. The demographics of each group are provided in the figure.

EXHIBIT 4–7
VALS American
Lifestyle

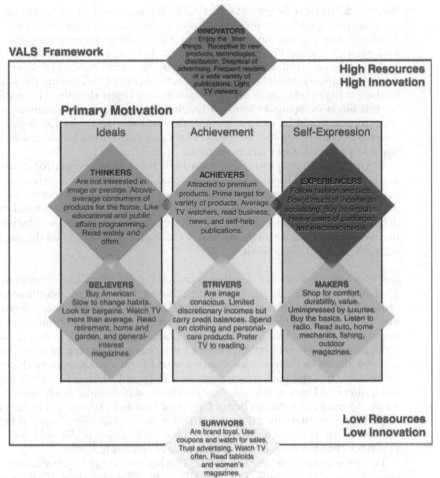

SOURCE: Strategic Business Insights (SBI) (www.strategicbusinessinsights.com/).

Firms are finding that lifestyles are often more useful for predicting consumer behavior than are demographics. In particular, VALS enables firms to identify target segments and their underlying motivations. It also reveals correlations between psychology and lifestyle choices. People who share demographics actually tend to have varying psychological traits. Two shoppers with similar demographic appearances still might have different levels of risk-taking propensity, social consciousness, or preferred benefits. College students and day laborers might earn similar incomes, but they spend that income quite differently because of their very different values and lifestyles.

There are limitations to using lifestyle segmentation, however. Lifestyles are not as objective as demographics, and it is harder to identify potential customers. With demographics, a firm like Nike can easily identify its customers as men or women and direct its marketing strategies to each group differently. For these reasons, lifestyle segmentation is often used in conjunction with other segmentation methods. In addition, psychographics are more expensive as a means to identify potential customers. To identify VALS segments, companies use the VALS questionnaire in surveys or focus groups. Then VALS provides segment description linkages with consumer product and media data, communication styles, and zip code location.

Buying Situation Segmentation   The buying behavior of customers with the same demographics or lifestyle can differ depending on their buying situation. Thus, retailers may use **buying situations,** such as fill-in versus weekly shopping, to segment a market. For example, in Exhibit 4–3, the parent with four children evaluated the supercenter more positively than the Internet grocer or supermarket for weekly grocery purchases. But if the parent ran out of milk during the week, he or she would probably go to the convenience store rather than the wholesale club for this fill-in shopping. In terms of Exhibit 4–3's multiattribute attitude model, convenience would be more important than assortment in the fill-in shopping situation. Similarly, an executive might stay at a convention hotel on a business trip and a resort during a family vacation.

Buying situation segmentation rates high among the criteria for evaluating market segments. The segments are actionable because it is relatively easy to determine what a marketer should do to satisfy the needs of a particular segment. They are identifiable and accessible because retailers or service providers can determine who the customers are on the basis of who has purchased the product or service and under what circumstances. Once they have identified the customer segment, they can assess its size.

Benefit Segmentation   Another approach for defining a target segment is to group customers seeking similar benefits; this method is called **benefit segmentation.** In the multiattribute attitude model, customers in the same benefit segment would have a similar set of importance weights for the attributes of a store or product. For example, customers who place high importance on fashion and style and low importance on price might form a fashion segment, whereas customers who place more importance on price would form a price segment. Hershey's has adopted this approach to segmentation: To appeal to hand-to-mouth munchers, it offers packages of bite-size candy versions of its popular candy bars, such as Almond Joys, Reese's Peanut Butter Cups, and Hershey's Chocolate. It also tailors its packaging in international markets to offer the key benefits demanded by consumers. When its research showed that Chinese consumers prefer gold over silver, Hershey's changed the foil that wraps its Kisses candies in China.[50]

Benefit segments are very actionable. The benefits sought by customers in the target segment clearly indicate how retailers should design their offerings to appeal to those customers. But customers in benefit segments aren't easily identified or accessed; it's hard to look at a person and determine what benefits he or she is seeking. Typically, the audience for the media used by retailers is described by demographics rather than by the benefits they seek.

Composite Segmentation Approaches

No segmentation approach meets all the criteria. For example, segmenting by demographics and geography is ideal for identifying and accessing customers, but these characteristics often are unrelated to customers' needs. Thus, these approaches may not indicate the actions necessary to attract customers in these segments. In contrast, knowing what benefits customers are seeking is useful for designing an effective retail offering; the problem is identifying which customers are seeking these benefits. For these reasons, **composite segmentation** uses multiple variables to identify customers in the target segment according to their benefits sought, lifestyles, and demographics.

CVS uses what it calls the "CVS personalities" to target three composite segments. Each of these segments, referred to by a first name, is used to develop a retail strategy for the market segment.[51] "**Caroline,**" is a segment composed of 18- to 24-year-old single or new moms who have a lower income but have the highest number of items purchased per trip. "**Vanessa**" targets a segment of 35- to 54-year-old women with children, at the peak of their income and generating the highest spending, frequency of purchases, and overall basket size. Finally, "**S**ophie" is a 55-plus empty nester woman with a median income and a health focus. These segments are useful in developing positioning messages that can be used in their ads, flyers, and displays. This information is also useful for manufacturers who sell their products through CVS. For example, for "Caroline," Dove could be positioned as a convenient reenergizer. For "Vanessa," it could be positioned as an escape. Finally, for "Sophie," it could be touted as beneficial to health.

SUMMARY

LO1 **Describe the process that consumers go through when making retail patronage and buying decisions.**

Consumers go through several stages when making a purchase decision: need recognition, information search, evaluation of alternatives, choice of alternatives, purchase, and postpurchase evaluation. It is important for retailers to understand how they can nudge their customers closer to a buying decision at each step of their buying process

LO2 **Identify the different types of buying processes.**

The importance of the stages depends on the nature of the customer's decision. When decisions are important and risky, the buying process is longer because customers spend more time and effort on the information search and evaluation of alternatives. When buying decisions are less important to customers, they spend little time in the buying process, and their buying behavior may become habitual.

LO3 **Summarize how the economy and social factors affect customer purchase decisions.**

The buying process of consumers is influenced by their personal beliefs, attitudes, and values, as well as by their social environment. The primary social influences are provided by the economy, consumers' families, their reference groups, and culture.

LO4 **Determine why and how retailers group customers into market segments.**

To develop cost-effective retail programs, retailers group customers into segments. Some approaches for segmenting markets are based on geography, demographics, geodemographics, lifestyle, usage situations, and benefits sought. Because each approach has its advantages and disadvantages, retailers typically define their target segment by several characteristics.

KEY TERMS

actionable, *108*
benefit segmentation, *114*
brand loyalty, *103*
buying process, *91*
buying situation, *114*
compatibility, *119*
complexity, *119*
composite segmentation, *114*
consideration set, *99*
conversion rate, *94*
cross-shopping, *93*
culture, *106*
demographic segmentation, *111*
everyday low pricing (EDLP) strategy, *96*
extended problem solving, *102*
external sources, *94*
fair trade, *101*
fashion, *117*

fashion leader, *118*
financial risks, *102*
geodemographic segmentation, *111*
geographic segmentation, *109*
habitual decision making, *103*
hedonic needs, *92*
identifiable, *109*
impulse buying, *103*
information search, *94*
innovator, *118*
internal sources, *94*
knockoff, *118*
lifestyle, *111*
lifestyle segmentation, *112*
limited problem solving, *102*
mass-market theory, *119*
multiattribute attitude model, *97*
observability, *119*
physical risks, *102*

postpurchase evaluation, *101*
psychographics, *111*
reachable, *109*
reference group, *105*
retailer loyalty, *103*
retail market segment, *107*
satisfaction, *101*
social risks, *102*
store advocate, *106*
subculture theory, *119*
substantial, *109*
trend setter, *118*
trialability, *119*
trickle-down theory, *118*
unplanned purchasing, *103*
unsatisfied need, *92*
utilitarian needs, *92*
VALS, *112*

GET OUT AND DO IT!

1. **CONTINUING CASE ASSIGNMENT: GO SHOPPING** Visit the retail store operated by the target firm for your continuing assignment. Determine all the things that the store does to try to stimulate customers to buy merchandise at each stage of the buying process. In which types of buying decisions are most customers involved? Based on your observations and what you know about the target firm, what type(s) of market segmentation strategies are they involved in? Do you believe these are the best strategies for this firm?

2. **GO SHOPPING** Go to a supermarket, and watch people selecting products to put in their shopping carts. How much time do they spend selecting products? Do some people spend more time than others? Why is this the case? Does consumer behavior vary in the store perimeter versus in the aisles? Explain your observations.

3. **OLC EXERCISE** Go to the student side of the book's website to develop a multiattribute attitude model describing your evaluation of and decision about some relatively expensive product you bought recently, such as a car or a consumer electronics product. Open the multiattribute model exercise. List the attributes you considered in the left-hand column. List the alternatives you considered in the top row. Fill in the importance weights for each attribute in the second column (10 = very important, 1 = very unimportant); then fill in your evaluation of each product on each attribute (10 = excellent performance, 1 = poor performance). Based on your importance weights and performance beliefs, the evaluation of each product appears in the bottom row. Did you buy the product with the highest evaluation?

4. **INTERNET EXERCISE** To better understand the segmentation classification of consumers, Strategic Business Insights has developed the VALS tool, which uses psychology to segment people according to their distinct personality traits. Go to the firm's home page at www.strategicbusinessinsights.com/vals/presurvey.shtml, and take the survey to identify your VALS profile according to your values, attitudes, and lifestyle. According to the results, what is your VALS profile type? Do you agree with your consumer profile? Why or why not? How can retailers effectively use the results of this survey when planning and implementing their business strategies?

5. **INTERNET EXERCISE** Retailers want to segment the market on the basis of the geographic classification of customers to select the best sites for their businesses. Go to the Esri Business Information Solutions home page at www.esri.com/data/esri_data/tapestry, type in the zip code for your hometown or your campus, and read the results. How would a retailer, such as a local restaurant, use the information in this report when making a decision about whether to open a location in this zip code?

6. **INTERNET EXERCISE** Go to the following Internet sites offering information about the latest fashions: *New York Magazine's* The Cut at http://nymag.com/thecut/, *New York Times*' Fashion & Style at www.nytimes.com/pages/fashion/index.html, and the U.K. *Telegraph* at fashion.telegraph.co.uk, Write a brief report describing the latest apparel fashions that are being shown by designers. Which of these fashion trends do you think will be popular with college students? Why?

DISCUSSION QUESTIONS AND PROBLEMS

1. Does the customer buying process end when a customer buys some merchandise? Explain your answer.

2. Describe how service retailers, such as hotels, provide information to potential customers to answer questions about rates, services offered, and other amenities.

3. Considering the steps in the consumer buying process (Exhibit 4–1), describe how you (and your family) used this process to select your college or university. How many schools did you consider? How much time did you invest in this purchase decision? When you were deciding on which college to attend, what objective and subjective criteria did you use in the alternative evaluation portion of the consumer buying process?

4. In Exhibit 4–6, The Inner City Tenant is described. How should banks, restaurants, drugstores, and car dealers alter their retail mixes to meet the needs of this segment compared to the Top Rung segment?

5. Any retailer's goal is to get customers in its store so that they can find the merchandise that they are looking for and make a purchase at this location. How could a sporting goods retailer ensure that the customer buys athletic equipment at its outlet?

6. A family-owned used-book store across the street from a major university campus wants to identify the various segments in its market. What approaches might the store owner use to segment this market? List two potential target market segments based on this segmentation approach. Then contrast the retail mix that would be most appropriate for the two potential target segments.

7. How does the buying decision process differ when consumers are shopping on the Internet or mobile device compared with shopping in a store in terms of locations or sites visited, time spent, and brands examined?

8. Using the multiattribute attitude model, identify the probable choice of a local car dealer for a young, single woman and for a retired couple with limited income (see the accompanying table). What can the national retail chain do to increase the chances of the retired couple patronizing its dealership? You can use the multiattribute model template on the student side of the book's website to analyze this information.

	IMPORTANCE WEIGHTS		PERFORMANCE BELIEFS		
Performance Attributes	**Young, Single Woman**	**Retired Couple**	**Local Gas Station**	**National Service Chain**	**Local Car Dealer**
Price	2	10	9	10	3
Time to complete repair	8	5	5	9	7
Reliability	2	9	2	7	10
Convenience	8	3	3	6	5

9. Think of a recent purchase that you made, and describe how economic and social environmental factors (e.g., reference group, family, and culture) influenced your buying decision. How are retailers using social media to affect your buying decisions?

10. Think about the merchandise sold at Office Depot, Staples, and Office Max, and list three to four types of merchandise that fall into extended problem solving, limited problem solving, and habitual decision making for college students. Explain how the categories of merchandise would change for each type of buying decision if the customer was the owner of a medium-size business.

SUGGESTED READINGS

Arnold, Mark J., and Kristy E. Reynolds. "Approach and Avoidance Motivation: Investigating Hedonic Consumption in a Retail Setting." *Journal of Retailing* 88, no. 3 (September 2012), pp. 399–411.

Dahl, Darren W., Jennifer J. Argo, and Andrea C. Morales. "Social Information in the Retail Environment: The Importance of Consumption Alignment, Referent Identity, and Self-Esteem." *Journal of Consumer Research*, February 2012, pp. 860–71.

Gauri, Kulkarni, Brian Ratchford, and P. K. Kannan. "The Impact of Online and Offline Information Sources on Automobile Choice Behavior." *Journal of Interactive Marketing* 26, no. 3 (2012), pp. 167–75.

Hawkins, Delbert, David L. Mothersbaugh, and Roger J. Best. *Consumer Behavior: Building Marketing Strategy*, 12th ed. New York: McGraw-Hill/Irwin, 2012.

Iverson, Annemarie. *In Fashion: From Retail to the Runway, Everything You Need to Know to Break into the Fashion Industry*. New York: Clarkson Potter, 2010.

Ma, Yu, Kusum L Ailawadi, Dinesh K Gauri, and Dhruv Grewal, "An Empirical Investigation of the Impact of Gasoline Prices on Grocery Shopping Behavior." *Journal of Marketing* 75, no. 2 (2011), pp. 18–35.

Solomon, Michael. *Consumer Behavior: Buying, Having, and Being*, 10th ed. Englewood Cliffs, NJ: Prentice Hall, 2012.

Sorensen, Herb. *Inside the Mind of the Shopper*. Philadelphia: Wharton School, 2009.

Underhill, Paco. *Why We Buy: The Science of Shopping*, updated and revised. New York: Simon & Schuster, 2008.

APPENDIX 4A   Customer Buying Behavior and Fashion

Many retailers sell fashionable merchandise. To sell this type of merchandise profitably, retailers need to (1) understand how fashions develop and diffuse throughout the marketplace and (2) use operating systems that enable them to match supply and demand for this seasonal merchandise. This appendix reviews the consumer behavior aspects of fashion; the operating systems for matching supply of and demand for fashion merchandise are discussed in Chapter 12.

Fashion is a type of product or a way of behaving that is temporarily adopted by a large number of consumers because the product, service, or behavior is considered socially appropriate for the time and place.[52] For example, in some social groups, it is or has been fashionable to have brightly colored hair or tattoos, wear a coat made from animal fur, or have a beard. Even though a wide range of activities and products go in and out of fashion, in many retail environments the term *fashion* is associated with apparel and accessories.

CUSTOMER NEEDS SATISFIED BY FASHION

Fashion gives people an opportunity to satisfy many emotional and practical needs. Through fashions, people develop their own identity. They also can use fashions to manage their appearance, express their self-image and feelings, enhance their egos, and make an impression on others. Through the years, fashions have become associated with specific lifestyles or the roles people play. You wear different clothing styles when you are attending class, going out on a date, or interviewing for a job.

People use fashions to both develop their own identity and gain acceptance from others. These two benefits of fashion can be opposing forces. If you choose to wear something radically different, you will achieve recognition for your individuality but might not be accepted by your peers. To satisfy these conflicting needs, manufacturers and retailers offer customers designs that are fashionable but that still enable consumers to express their individuality.

Consumers also adopt fashions to overcome boredom. People get tired of wearing the same clothing and seeing the same furniture in their living rooms. They seek changes in their lifestyles by buying new clothes or redecorating their houses to meet their changing tastes, preferences, and income.

HOW DO FASHIONS DEVELOP AND SPREAD?

Fashions are not universal. A fashion might be accepted in one geographic region, country, or age group and not in another. Consider how your idea of "fashionable" differs from that of your parents. Many of you might have a hard time imagining them dressed in distressed, hip-hugging jeans and a tight T-shirt. Well, they might have just as much trouble picturing you in a double-breasted business suit. One interesting sports fashion trend has been the uniforms for college and NBA basketball players. Forty years ago, they sported long hair and wore tight, short shorts and Converse shoes. Now they have short hair and wear baggy shorts and Nike shoes (see www.nba.com/photostore/).

The stages in the fashion life cycle are shown in Exhibit 4–8. The cycle begins with the creation of a new design or style. Then some consumers recognized as fashion leaders or innovators adopt the fashion and start a trend in their social group. The fashion spreads from the leaders to others and is accepted widely as a fashion. Eventually, the fashion is accepted by most people in the social group and can become overused. Saturation and overuse set the stage for that fashion's decline in popularity and the creation of new fashions. The time span of a fashion life cycle varies depending on the type of product and the market. The cycle for apparel fashions for young teenagers is measured in months or even weeks, whereas the fashion cycle for home furnishings may last several years.

Creation

New fashions arise from a number of sources. Fashion designers are one source of creative inspirations, but fashions are also developed by creative consumers, celebrities, and even retailers. When high-profile actors, performers, and athletes wear the latest styles in television shows and movies, on stage, or on the red carpet, consumers interested in fashion often adopt and follow these trends.

Adoption by Fashion Leaders

The fashion life cycle really starts when the fashion is adopted by leading consumers. These initial adopters of a new fashion are called **fashion leaders, innovators,** or **trendsetters,** and they are the first people to display the new fashion in their social group or write about them in social media, like fashion blogs. If the fashion is too innovative or very different from currently accepted fashion, it might not be accepted by the social group, thereby prematurely ending its life cycle.

Three theories have been proposed to explain how fashion spreads within a society. The **trickle-down theory** suggests that fashion leaders are consumers with the highest social status—wealthy, well-educated consumers. After they adopt a fashion, the fashion trickles down to consumers in lower social classes. When the fashion is accepted in the lowest social class, it is no longer acceptable to the fashion leaders in the highest social class.

Manufacturers and retailers stimulate this trickle-down process by copying the latest styles displayed at designer fashion shows and sold in exclusive specialty stores. These copies, referred to as **knockoffs,** are sold at lower prices through retailers targeting a broader market. For example, designers at retailers like Forever 21 view fashion shows and interpret the designs for their market.[53] If the designers in Paris and Milan are showing turtlenecks, the

REFACT

The bikini was designed by a former civil engineer, Louis Reard, in 1947.[54]

EXHIBIT 4–8
Stages in the Fashion Life Cycle

Forever 21 designers determine what aspects of that fashion will appeal to their broader market and then have their designs manufactured in Asia. It is likely that the knockoff turtlenecks will be on the shelves at Forever 21 well before the higher-priced originals get to the high-end specialty and department stores.

The second theory, the **mass-market theory,** suggests that fashions spread across different peer groups. Each group has its own fashion leaders who play key roles in their own social networks. Fashion information trickles across groups rather than down from the upper classes to the lower classes. Spain-based fast-fashion retailer Zara solicits new fashion advice from its store management all over the world. These managers funnel information to the corporate offices in Spain about fashion requests from its customers, what they are wearing, and how they are interpreting and changing off-the-rack apparel to adapt to their unique fashion senses. Zara's fashion designers synthesize the information and reinterpret this information into their own new fashions.

The third theory, the **subculture theory,** is based on the development of recent fashions. Subcultures of mostly young and less affluent consumers, such as urban youth, started fashions for such things as colorful fabrics, T-shirts, sneakers, jeans, black leather jackets, and surplus military clothing. Many times, fashions are started unintentionally by people in lower-income consumer groups and trickle up to mainstream consumer classes. For example, workers wear blue jeans that have holes in them and are distressed from manual labor, their T-shirts are faded from working in the sun, and people who paint houses are covered in splashes of paint. These looks have been adapted by manufacturers and sold to many different consumer groups. The more distress, the more people are willing to pay.

These theories of fashion development indicate that fashion leaders can come from many different places and social groups. In our diverse society, many types of consumers have the opportunity to be the leaders in setting fashion trends.

Spread to Large Consumer Groups

During this stage, the fashion is accepted by a wider group of consumers referred to as early adopters. The fashion becomes increasingly visible, receives greater publicity and media attention, and is readily available in retail stores. The relative advantage, compatibility, complexity, trialability, and observability of a fashion affect the time it takes for that fashion to spread through a social group. New fashions that provide more benefits have a higher relative advantage compared with existing fashions, and these new fashions spread faster. Fashions are often adopted by consumers because they make people feel special. Thus, more exclusive fashions like expensive clothing are adopted more quickly in an affluent target market. On a more utilitarian level, clothing that is easy to maintain, such as wrinkle-free pants, will diffuse quickly in the general population.

Compatibility is the degree to which the fashion is consistent with existing norms, values, and behaviors. When new fashions aren't consistent with existing norms, the number of adopters and the speed of adoption are lower. Head-to-toe leather apparel is only compatible with a relatively small percentage of the public. Although this look may be moderately successful for a season or two, it will never achieve widespread acceptance.

Complexity refers to how easy it is to understand and use the new fashion. Consumers have to learn how to incorporate a new fashion into their lifestyles. For example, a platform, 6-inch, stiletto-heeled pump is difficult to walk in unless you are only taking a quick strut down the runway.

Trialability refers to the costs and commitment required to adopt the fashion initially. For example, consumers buying fashions through Internet channels or catalogs cannot examine the garments or try them on before making a purchase commitment—the trialability is low compared to shopping in stores. New size-matching machines are being used in several shopping centers around the United States. The machines take consumers' measurements and match them with specifications provided by clothing manufacturers, thus providing a proper fit and increasing trialability by reducing the risk associated with buying apparel that has not been tried on.[55]

Observability is the degree to which the new fashion is visible and easily communicated to others in the social group. Clothing fashions are very observable compared with fashions for the home, such as sheets and towels. It is, therefore, likely that a fashion in clothing will spread more quickly than a new color scheme or style for the bedroom.

Fashion retailers engage in many activities to increase the adoption and spread of a new fashion throughout their target market. Compatibility is increased and complexity is decreased by showing consumers how to coordinate a new article of fashion clothing with other items the consumer already owns. Trialability is increased by providing actual or virtual dressing rooms so that customers can try on clothing and see how it looks on them. Providing opportunities for customers to return merchandise also increases trialability because it reduces purchase risk. Retailers increase observability by displaying fashion merchandise in their stores, advertising it in the media, and facilitating coverage through social media like YouTube and fashion blogs.

Saturation

In this stage, the fashion achieves its highest level of social acceptance. Almost all consumers in the target market are aware of the fashion and have decided to either accept or reject it. At this point, the fashion has become old and boring to many people.

Decline in Acceptance and Obsolescence

When fashions reach saturation, they have become less appealing to consumers. Because most people have already adopted the fashion, it no longer provides an opportunity for people to express their individuality. Fashion creators and leaders thus are beginning to experiment with new fashions. The introduction of a new fashion speeds the decline of the preceding fashion.

Retail Market Strategy

EXECUTIVE BRIEFING

David Berg, President and CEO of Outback Steakhouse International LLC

My career path in retailing is somewhat unusual. After graduating from Emory University with a degree in economics, I went to law school at the University of Florida. During law school, I was attracted to corporate law, which was a good fit with my undergraduate training in economics. I took a position in the corporate counsel's office at Nordic-Track. At the time, NordicTrack was best known for its cross-country ski simulator, which dominated the home fitness market in the late 1980s.

As the U.S. market for the NordicTrack's simulator matured, the company became interested in expanding internationally. I volunteered to set up a network of international distributors. While I did not have a lot of retail experience, in law school, I had learned how to be an effective negotiator and how to logically analyze situations—skills that were very valuable in developing a worldwide distribution network.

After NordicTrack, I went to work for Best Buy and eventually was promoted to COO of Best Buy International, responsible for the operations of all of Best Buy's brands and businesses outside of the United States. I was deeply involved in the sale of Best Buy's Musicland subsidiary; its acquisition of a majority interest in Jiangsu Five Star Appliance in China; its

expansion into Mexico and Turkey; and the creation of its joint venture with The Carphone Warehouse, which provided an opportunity to introduce the Best Buy brand in Europe.

My present position is challenging and exciting. Our corporation owns and operates more than 400 restaurants under the brands names of Outback Steakhouse, Carrabba's Italian Grill, Bonefish Grill, Roy's, and Fleming's Prime Steakhouse & Wine Bar. While we have more than 200 Outback Steakhouses in 19 countries, our potential for international expansion is tremendous.

The dining experience for our international customers is similar to our domestic experience. Our international restaurants tend to follow U.S. design guidelines with some modifications to account for local needs and customs. Most restaurants are in shopping centers or office buildings; very few are free standing. In Asian cities, where space is at a particular premium, many restaurants are located above the ground floor and sometimes split in two separate floors.

The international menu is also similar to the U.S. menu, with some changes made to meet local taste preferences. For example, we feature local beef cuts

CHAPTER 5

LEARNING OBJECTIVES

LO1 Define the retail strategy.

LO2 Illustrate how retailers build a sustainable competitive advantage.

LO3 Classify the different strategic growth opportunities retailers pursue.

LO4 Identify issues that arise as domestic retailers become global retailers.

LO5 Know the steps retailers go through to develop a strategic plan.

such as Picanha in Brazil or Neobiani in Korea, in addition to the traditional Outback Special sirloin. Product and ingredient availability in a region also drive specific menu offerings. For example, our iconic Bloomin' Onion is replaced by the Typhoon Bloom in Southeast Asia because the exact onion needed for the Bloomin' Onion is not readily available there.

Going global with retail services, particularly restaurants, is more challenging than the international expansion of product-focused retailing. Tastes in food vary significantly from country to country and even within countries, but preferences for products is pretty homogenous across the globe—shopping for flat-panel TVs is pretty universal. While we need a great deal of local input as we expand internationally, we have found that direct foreign investment is more than three times more profitable than franchising.

Retailers need to focus on long-term strategic planning to cope effectively with the growing intensity of retail competition as well as the emergence of new channels, technologies, and globalization. The retail strategy indicates how a retailer will deal effectively with its environment, customers, and competitors.[1] As the retail management decision-making process (discussed in Chapter 1) indicates, the retail strategy (Section II) is the bridge between understanding the world of retailing (Section I) and the more tactical merchandise management and store operations activities (Sections III and IV) undertaken to implement the retail strategy.

The first part of this chapter defines the term *retail strategy* and discusses three important elements of retail strategy: (1) the target market segment, (2) the retail format, and (3) the retailer's bases of sustainable competitive advantage. Then we outline approaches retailers use to build a sustainable competitive advantage. After reviewing the various growth opportunities, specifically international expansion, that retailers can pursue, the chapter concludes with a discussion of the strategic retail planning process.

WHAT IS A RETAIL STRATEGY?

LO1

Define the retail strategy.

REFACT

The word *strategy* comes from the Greek word meaning the "art of the general."[2]

The term *strategy* is frequently used in retailing. For example, retailers talk about their merchandise strategy, promotion strategy, location strategy, channel strategy, or branding strategy. The term is used so commonly that it might appear that all retailing decisions are strategic decisions, but retail strategy isn't just another expression for retail management.

Definition of Retail Market Strategy

A **retail strategy** is a statement identifying (1) the retailer's target market, (2) the format and resources the retailer plans to use to satisfy the target market's needs, and (3) the bases on which the retailer plans to build a sustainable competitive advantage.[3] The **target market** is the market segment(s) toward which the retailer plans to focus its resources and retail mix. A **retail format** describes the nature of the retailer's operations—its retail mix (type of merchandise and services offered, pricing policy, advertising and promotion programs, store design and visual merchandising, typical locations, and customer services)—that it will use to satisfy the needs of its target market. A **sustainable competitive advantage** is an advantage the retailer has over its competition that is not easily copied by competitors and thus can be maintained over a long period of time. The following are Founder's name is Ells. a few examples of retail strategies:

REFACT

Chipotle is by far the largest purchaser of natural meat in the United States.[5]

- *Chipotle Mexican Grill.* Steve Ells, founder and co-chair of Chipotle Mexican Grill, is changing the way America eats, one burrito at a time. The first store of this fast, casual restaurant chain was opened in Denver in 1993 and has grown to 1,200 locations with annual sales of more than $2 billion. Its menu consists of only four items: burritos, burrito bowls, tacos, and salads. When asked about expanding the menu, Steve Ells said, "[I]t's important to keep the menu focused, because if you just do a few things, you can ensure that you do them better than anybody else." Its mission statement, Food With Integrity, highlights its efforts to increase the use of naturally raised meat, organic produce, and dairy without added hormones. This philosophy goes beyond using fresh ingredients to understanding how the animals are raised. The majority of food is prepared in each restaurant. None of the restaurants have freezers, microwave ovens, or can openers.[4]

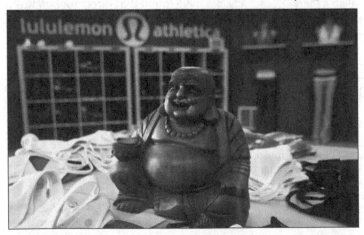

Lululemon's retail strategy is selling merchandise that appeals to consumers seeking spiritual enrichment through yoga.

- *Lululemon Athletica.* Lululemon is a Canadian specialty store chain selling apparel and accessories that support the practice of yoga. The products it sells include headbands, bamboo blocks, and yoga mats printed with encouraging healthy-living slogans like "Drink fresh water." The signature Lulu item is the Groove Pant, cut with special gussets and flat seams to create a feeling of a drop of water free from gravity. Lululemon's apparel is made with special materials, Silverescent and Luon, enabling customers to engage in vigorous yoga exercises and still look attractive. Lululemon stores are a community hub where people can learn about and discuss the physical aspects of healthy living, from yoga and diet to running and cycling, as well as the spiritual aspects of life. To create this community, the company recruits local ambassadors before opening a store. These ambassadors, usually popular yoga teachers, are featured on Lululemon's website and on bulletin boards in the store.[6]

- *Chico's.* Chico's is a specialty apparel chain serving the lifestyle needs of fashion-savvy women over 30 years old with a household income of $50,000 to $100,000. Its apparel uses easy-to-care-for fabrics; distinctive, fashionable designs; and a comfortable, relaxed fit. Accessories, such as handbags, belts, scarves, earrings, necklaces, and bracelets, are designed to coordinate with the assortment of clothing, allowing customers to easily personalize their wardrobes. All of the merchandise offered is private label, so Chico's designers and buyers specify the patterns, prints, construction, designs, fabrics, finishes, and colors. The distinctive nature of Chico's clothing is carried through to its sizing. Chico's uses sizes of 0, 1, 2, 3, rather than the more commonly used sizes of 1 to 16 so women are less sensitive to large sizes. The relaxed styles of the clothing allow Chico's to utilize a reduced number of sizes and still offer a wide selection of clothing without having to invest in a large number of different sizes within a single style.[7]

- *Save-A-Lot.* From a single store in 1977, Save-A-Lot, a wholly owned subsidiary of SuperValu, has grown to more than 1,300 stores, making it the nation's 13th-largest U.S. supermarket chain. Save-A-Lot stores offer a limited assortment of 1,250 SKUs compared to 20,000 to 30,000 SKUs in a conventional supermarket. By offering only the most popular items in each category, most of which are private-label merchandise, Save-A-Lot reduces its costs and is able to price its merchandise 40 percent lower than prices at conventional supermarkets. Due to its buying power, Save-A-Lot is able to develop customized product specifications that provide high-quality, private-label merchandise at low prices. Because the stores generally do not feature grocery store–style shelving, items instead are available in specially printed, cut-out shipping containers. Finally, most customers bring their own bags; the stores charge those customers who forget their own and need to obtain bags from the retailer.[8]

CENTRAL CONCEPTS IN A RETAIL MARKET STRATEGY

Each of these retail strategies described in the preceding section involves (1) the selection of target market segment(s), (2) the selection of a retail format (the elements in the retailer's retail mix), and (3) the development of a sustainable competitive advantage that enables the retailer to reduce the level of competition it faces. Now let's examine these central concepts of a retail strategy.

LO2

Illustrate how retailers build a sustainable competitive advantage.

Target Market and Retail Format

A **retail market** is a group of consumers with similar needs and a group of retailers that satisfy those needs using a similar retail channels and format.[9] Exhibit 5–1 illustrates a set of retail market segments for women's clothing. It lists various retail formats in the left-hand column. Each format offers a different retail mix to its customers. Market segments are listed in the exhibit's top row. As mentioned in Chapter 4, these segments could be defined in terms of the customers' geographic location, demographics, lifestyle, buying situation, or benefits sought. In this exhibit, we divide the market into three fashion-related

126   SECTION II   Retailing Strategy

EXHIBIT 5–1   Retail Market Segments for Apparel

segments: (1) conservative—consumers who place little importance on fashion; (2) traditional—those who want classic styles; and (3) fashion-forward—those who want the latest fashions.

Each square of the matrix in Exhibit 5–1 describes a potential retail market in which retailers compete for consumers with similar needs. For example, Walmart and Kmart stores in the same geographic area compete with each other using a full-line discount store format to target conservative customers. Bloomingdale's and Neiman Marcus compete against each other using a department store format targeting the fashion-forward segment.

Exhibit 5–1's matrix describes the battlefields on which women's apparel retailers compete. The position in each battlefield (cell in the matrix) indicates the first two elements of a retailer's strategy: the fashion segment (the *x*-axis) and the retail format (the *y*-axis).

Consider the situation confronting Target as it refines its retail strategy for the women's clothing market. Should Target compete in all 15 retail markets shown in Exhibit 5–1, or should it focus on a limited set of markets? If Target decides to focus on a limited set of markets, which should it pursue? Target's answers to these questions define its retail strategy and indicate how it will focus its resources.

The women's clothing market in Exhibit 5–1 is just one of several representations that we could have used. Retail formats might be expanded to include off-price stores and category specialists. Although Exhibit 5–1 isn't the only way to describe the women's retail apparel market segments, it does illustrate how retail market segments can be defined in terms of retail format and customer market segments.

Building a Sustainable Competitive Advantage

After selecting a target market and a retail mix, the final element in a retail strategy is the retailer's approach to building a sustainable competitive advantage.[10] Establishing a competitive advantage means that the retailer, in effect, builds a wall around its position in a retail market, that is, around its present and potential

	SUSTAINABILITY OF ADVANTAGE	
Sources of Advantage	Less Sustainable	More Sustainable
Customer loyalty (Chapters 11 and 16)	Habitual repeat purchasing because of limited competition in the local area	Building a brand image with an emotional connection with customers; using databases to develop and utilize a deeper understanding of customers
Location (Chapters 7 and 8)		Convenient locations
Human resource management (Chapter 9)	More employees	Committed, knowledgeable employees
Distribution and information systems (Chapter 10)	Bigger warehouses; automated warehouses	Shared systems with vendors
Unique merchandise (Chapters 12 and 13)	More merchandise; greater assortment; lower price; higher advertising budgets; more sales promotions	Exclusive merchandise
Vendor relations (Chapter 13)	Repeat purchases from vendor due to limited alternatives	Coordination of procurement efforts; ability to get scarce merchandise
Customer service (Chapter 18)	Hours of operation	Knowledgeable and helpful salespeople

EXHIBIT 5–2
Approaches for Developing a Sustainable Competitive Advantage

customers and its competitors. When the wall is high, it will be hard for competitors outside the wall (i.e., retailers operating in other markets or entrepreneurs) to enter the market and compete for the retailer's target customers.

Any business activity that a retailer engages in can be the basis for a competitive advantage. But some advantages are sustainable over a long period of time, while others can be duplicated by competitors almost immediately. For example, it would be hard for Peets Coffee & Tea to establish a long-term advantage over Starbucks by simply offering the same coffee specialties at lower prices. If Peets' lower prices were successful in attracting a significant number of customers, Starbucks would soon realize that Peets had lowered its prices and would quickly match the price reduction. This might lead to a price war that Starbucks is likely to win because it has lower costs due to its larger size. Similarly, it's hard for retailers to develop a long-term advantage by offering broader or deeper assortments of national brands. If the broader and deeper assortment attracts a lot of customers, competitors will simply go out and buy the same branded merchandise. Exhibit 5–2 indicates which aspects of these potential sources of advantage are more and less sustainable.

Over time, all advantages erode due to competitive forces, but by building high walls, retailers can sustain their advantage for a longer time. Thus, establishing a sustainable competitive advantage is the key to long-term financial performance.

Three approaches for developing a sustainable competitive advantage are (1) building strong relationships with customers, (2) building strong relationships with suppliers, and (3) achieving efficient internal operations. Each of these approaches involves developing an asset—loyal customers, strong vendor relationships, committed effective human resources, efficient systems, and attractive locations—that is not easily duplicated by competitors. Let's look at each of these approaches.

Relationships with Customers—Customer Loyalty

Customer loyalty means that customers are committed to buying merchandise and services from a particular retailer. Loyalty is more than simply liking one retailer over another. Loyalty means that customers will be reluctant to switch and patronize a competitive retailer. For example, loyal customers will continue to have their car serviced at Jiffy Lube, even if a competitor opens a store nearby and charges

REFACT

Approximately half of food and beverage shoppers and nearly 60 percent of consumers of health/beauty and household goods would purchase their preferred brands, even if a less expensive alternative were to become available.[11]

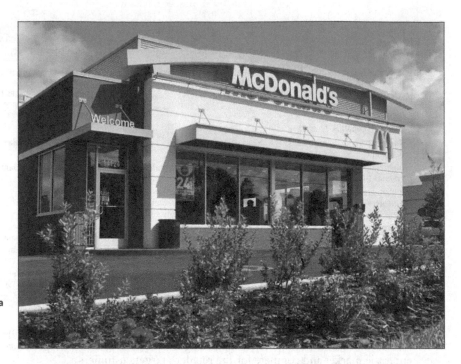

McDonald's has developed a competitive advantage by projecting an image of fast service, consistent quality, and clean restrooms.

REFACT

Brooks Brothers, a men's specialty store chain, sold the rights to the Polo brand name to Ralph Lauren.[12]

REFACT

Because brands build loyalty, they are very valuable. The five most valuable U.S. retail brands are Walmart (worth $142 billion), Target ($32 billion), Home Depot ($20 billion), Best Buy ($19 billion), and CVS ($17 billion).[13]

slightly lower prices. Approaches for developing loyalty discussed in this section are building a strong brand image, creating a unique positioning in the target market, offering unique merchandise, providing excellent customer service, implementing a customer relationship management program, and building a retail community.

Brand Image   Retailers build customer loyalty by developing a well-known, attractive image of their brands and of the name over their doors. For example, when most consumers think about fast food or hamburgers or French fries, they immediately think of McDonald's. Their image of McDonald's includes many favorable beliefs such as fast service, consistent quality, and clean restrooms.

Strong brand images facilitate customer loyalty because they reduce the customers' risks associated with purchases. They assure customers that they will receive a consistent level of quality and satisfaction from the retailer. The retailer's image can also create an emotional tie with a customer that leads the customer to trust the retailer. The steps retailers take to develop a strong brand image are discussed in Chapter 15.

Positioning   A retailer's brand image reflects its positioning strategy. **Positioning** is the design and implementation of a retail mix to create an image of the retailer in the customer's mind relative to its competitors. A **perceptual map** is frequently used to represent the customer's image and preferences for retailers.

Exhibit 5–3 offers a hypothetical perceptual map of retailers selling women's clothing. The two dimensions in this map, fashion and service, represent two important characteristics that consumers in this example use in forming their images of retailers.

Perceptual maps are developed in a way so that the distance between two retailers' positions on the map indicates how similar the stores appear to consumers. For example, Neiman Marcus and Saks Fifth Avenue are very close to each other on the map because consumers in this illustration see them as offering similar services and fashion. In contrast, Nordstrom and Marshalls are far apart, indicating consumers think they're quite different. Note that stores close to each other compete vigorously because consumers feel they provide similar benefits and have similar images.

Hypothetical Perceptual Map of Women's Apparel Market   **EXHIBIT 5–3**

In this example, Macy's has an image of offering moderately priced, fashionable women's clothing with good service. TJ Maxx offers slightly less fashionable clothing with considerably less service. Sears is viewed as a retailer offering women's clothing that is not very fashionable with moderate customer service.

The ideal points (marked by red dots on the map) indicate the characteristics of an ideal retailer for consumers in different market segments. For example, consumers in segment 3 prefer a retailer that offers high-fashion merchandise with low service, while consumers in segment 1 want more traditional apparel and aren't concerned about service. The ideal points are located so that the distance between the needs of customers in the segment (marked with a blue "x"), and the perception of the retailer's offering (marked with a red dot) indicates the consumer's probability the consumers in the segment with patronize the retailer.

Retailers that are closer to an ideal point are evaluated more favorably by the consumers in the segment than are retailers located farther away. Thus, consumers in segment 6 prefer Forever 21 and Bebe to Neiman Marcus because these retailers are more fashion-forward and their target customers do not require such high service levels. Retailers strive to develop an image desired by customers in their target segment and thus develop loyalty with those customers.

Unique Merchandise   It is difficult for a retailer to develop customer loyalty through its merchandise offerings because most competitors can purchase and sell the same popular national brands. But many retailers build customer loyalty by developing **private-label brands** (also called **store brands** or **own brands**)—products developed and marketed by a retailer and available only from that retailer.[14] For example, Costco's highly regarded private-label brand, Kirkland Signature, engenders strong brand loyalty and consequently generates considerable loyalty toward Costco. The quality image of its private-label products makes a significant contribution to the image of Costco. Retailing View 5.1 describes how IKEA builds customer loyalty through its unique merchandise. Issues pertaining to the development of store-brand merchandise are discussed in Chapter 13.

Customer Service   Retailers also can develop customer loyalty by offering excellent customer service.[15] Consistently offering good service is difficult because customer service is provided by retail employees who are less consistent than machines. Machines can be programmed to make every box of Cheerios identical, but employees do not provide a consistent level of service because they vary in their training, motivation, and mood.

REFACT

The Ritz-Carlton is the only hotel chain and the first service company to win the annual Malcolm Baldrige National Quality Award. It has won the award twice.[16]

5.1   RETAILING VIEW   The IKEA Way

IKEA, a global retailer headquartered in Sweden, offers a wide range of well-designed, functional home furnishing products at low prices. It's easy to make high-quality products and sell them at a high price or make low-quality products to sell at a low price. But IKEA has to be cost-effective and innovative to sell quality products at low prices.

Creating IKEA's unique merchandise starts on the factory floor. IKEA product developers and designers work closely with suppliers to efficiently use production equipment and raw materials and keep waste to a minimum. For example, an IKEA product developer learned about board-on-frame construction touring a door factory. This technique is cost-effective and environmentally friendly because sheets of wood are layered over a honeycomb core to provide a strong, lightweight structure with a minimal wood content. This type of construction is used in many IKEA products, such as its LACK tables.

Many items IKEA sells are shipped and sold disassembled in flat packs to reduce transportation costs and make it easier for customers to take them home. However, some products like lamps take up a lot of space even when disassembled. The LAMPAN illustrates the IKEA way of offering extremely low price with beautiful design and high quality. This was achieved by developing a new packing method in which the lamp shade could be used as a bucket for the lamp base.

IKEA reduces labor costs in its stores by providing signage with extensive information about its products and their quality, presenting its products in room settings, and prominently displaying price tags. These features enable customers to serve themselves and reduce IKEA's labor costs.

REFACT

Annually 600 million customers visit IKEA's stores, eat two billion of those meatballs, and carry off 168 million catalogues.[17]

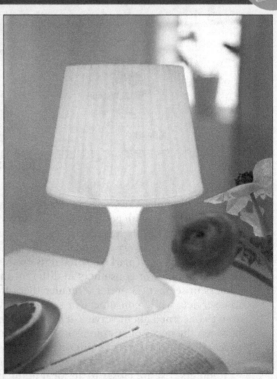

The **LACK** table and **LAMPAN** are classic IKEA designs only available at IKEA's stores and website.

Sources: www.IKEA.com; Deniz Caglar, Marco Kesteloo, and Artt Kleiner, "How Ikea Reassembled Its Growth Strategy," *Strategy+Business*, May 2012; "The Man Who Named the Furniture," *Financial Times*, January 16, 2010, p. 30; and Yongquan Hu and Huifang Jiang, "Innovation Strategy of Retailers: From the View of Global Value Chains," *6th International Conference on Service Systems and Service Management*, 2009, pp. 340–345.

DISCUSSION QUESTION

Why does IKEA's private-label furniture create a sustainable competitive advantage?

It takes considerable time and effort to build a tradition and reputation for customer service. But once a retailer has earned a service reputation, it can sustain this advantage for a long time because it's hard for a competitor to develop a comparable reputation. For example, Ritz-Carlton hotels are world-renowned for providing outstanding customer service. Employees gather daily for a 15-minute staff meeting, during which they share accounts of how they or their peers have gone above and beyond the call for conventional customer service, also known as "WOW stories." A great example involved a chef in a Balinese

Ritz-Carlton who learned that a guest had extensive food allergies and responded by having special eggs and milk flown in from a small grocery store, located in another country. Such WOW stories help maintain employees' focus on customer service and gives them recognitions for the efforts they make.[18] Chapter 18 discusses how retailers develop a customer service advantage.

Ritz Carlton's outstanding service builds customer loyalty.

Customer Relationship Management Programs   **Customer relationship management (CRM) programs,** also called **loyalty** or **frequent shopper programs,** are activities that focus on identifying and building loyalty with a retailer's most valued customers.[19] These programs typically involve offering customers rewards based on the amount of services or merchandise they purchase. For example, airlines offer free tickets to travelers who have flown a prescribed number of miles, and Subway gives customers a free sandwich for each 10 they purchase.

The discounts offered by these programs may not create loyalty. Customers may join loyalty programs of competing retailers and continue to patronize multiple retailers. However, the data collected about customer shopping behavior by these programs can provide insights that enable retailers to build and maintain loyalty. For instance, CVS Caremark's CRM program enables the retailer to collect extensive information about each of its customers and use this information to increase sales. For example, if customers shop relatively infrequently, e.g., once a month for prescriptions, CVS Caremark may provide incentives that expire in a week to encourage more frequent visits. Alternatively, if customers buy frequently, but buy less than $20 per visit, CVS Caremark offers incentives to increase each visit's purchases to, say, $25. It may provide incentives to get customers who are purchasing only national brands to purchase more private-label merchandise. CVS also uses the loyalty data to determine if a household is purchasing less of a category than it should based on usage in similar households, and therefore provide it with a "buy one, get one free" coupon. Thus, the data developed through the loyalty program enable a retailer to develop a personal relationship with customers that builds loyalty. CRM programs are discussed in detail in Chapter 11.

Building a Retail Community Using Social Media   Retailers are beginning to use their websites and social media to develop retail communities. A **retail community** is a group of consumers who have a shared involvement with a retailer. The members of the community share information with respect to the retailer's activities. The involvement in the community can range from simply becoming a fan of a retailer's Facebook page to meeting face-to-face with community members to share experiences. Increased involvement in the community by its members leads to a greater emotional feeling and loyalty toward the retailer.[20]

REFACT

Starbucks, with 29 million fans, ranks second after Coca-Cola on Facebook and ranks third after Facebook and Whole-Foods on Twitter.[21]

Starbucks builds customer loyalty by developing a community of customers who offer suggestions for improving Starbucks' offering.

Starbucks started building a community in 2008 when it launched My Starbucks Ideas (http://mystarbucksidea.force.com). The website was initially a hub for Starbucks customers to share their ideas, suggestions, and even frustrations on this mini social network. As Starbucks customers started enjoying their time interacting with other customers, the website evolved into a community. Now, the online community gives customers the ability to see what others are suggesting, vote on ideas, and check out the results. Starbucks actually implements the most popular ideas, resulting in customers feeling that they have a say on what their favorite coffee does.[22] Starbucks has extended its online efforts into the social media space. Its Facebook page (www.facebook.com/Starbucks) has more than 32 million likes.

Relationships with Suppliers

A second approach for developing a competitive advantage is to develop strong relationships with companies that provide merchandise and services to the retailer, such as real estate developers, advertising agencies, and transportation companies. Of these relationships with suppliers, the most important are relationships with vendors. For example, the relationship between Walmart and Procter & Gamble initially focused on improving supply chain efficiencies. Today, the partners in this relationship share sensitive information with each other so that Walmart is better able to plan for the introduction of new P&G products and even develop some unique packaging for P&G's national brands exclusively available at Walmart. Walmart shares its sales data with P&G so that P&G can better plan its production and use a just-in-time inventory management system to reduce the level of inventory in the system. By strengthening relationships with each other, both retailers and vendors can develop mutually beneficial assets and programs that give the retailer–vendor pair an advantage over competing pairs.[23]

Relationships with vendors, like relationships with customers, are developed over a long time and may not be easily offset by a competitor.[25] Chapter 13

examines how retailers work with their vendors to build mutually beneficial, long-term relationships.

Efficiency of Internal Operations

In addition to strong relationships with external parties, customers, and suppliers, retailers can develop competitive advantages by having more efficient internal operations. Efficient internal operations enable retailers to have a cost advantage over competitors or offer customers more benefits than competitors at the same cost.

Larger companies typically have greater internal operations efficiency. Larger retailers can invest in developing sophisticated systems and spread the fixed cost of these systems over more sales. In addition to size, other approaches for improving internal operating efficiencies are human resource management and information and supply chain management systems.

Human Resource Management   Retailing is a labor-intensive business, in which employees play a major role providing services to customers and building customer loyalty.[26] Some retailers view employees as an expense that needs to be reduced over the long run. But research has found that highly successful retail chains such as Costco invest heavily in store employees, but still have low prices, solid financial performance, and better customer service than their competitors. They recognize that under-investing in their employees makes their operations more inefficient and, therefore, much less profitable. Knowledgeable and skilled employees committed to the retailer's objectives are critical assets that support the success of these retailers. The retail landscape is increasingly dominated by retailers such as Wegman's and Costco that have adapted to this new reality.[27]

Chapter 9 examines how retailers build their human resource assets by developing programs to motivate and coordinate employee efforts, provide appropriate incentives, foster a strong and positive organizational culture and environment, and manage diversity. In Chapter 16, additional information is presented on increasing employee productivity and retention through recruiting, training, and leadership.

Distribution and Information Systems   The use of sophisticated distribution and information systems offers an opportunity for retailers to reduce operating costs—the costs associated with running the business—and make sure that the right merchandise is available at the right time and place.[28] Information flows seamlessly from Walmart to its vendors to facilitate quick and efficient merchandise replenishment and reduce stockouts. Walmart's distribution and information systems have enabled it to have a cost advantage that its competitors cannot overcome. This component of competitive advantage is discussed in Chapter 10.

In addition to using information systems to improve supply chain efficiency, the customers' purchase data collected by information systems provide an opportunity for retailers to tailor store merchandise assortments to the market served by each of its stores and to tailor promotion to the specific needs of individual customers. These data about its customers' buying behavior are a valuable asset offering an advantage that is not easily duplicated by competitors. These applications of information systems are discussed in more detail in Chapter 11.

Location

While committed relationships with customers and vendors and efficient internal operations are important sources of advantage, location is a pervasive source of advantage in retailing. The classic response to the question, "What are the three most important things in retailing?" is "Location, location, location." Location is a critical opportunity for developing competitive advantage for two reasons: (1) Location is the most important factor determining which store a consumer patronizes. For example, most people shop at the supermarket closest to where they live. (2) Location is a sustainable competitive advantage because it is not easily duplicated. Once Walgreens has put a store at the best location at an

REFACT

Seventy-four percent of U.S. consumers said that shopping locations should be located no more than a 15-minute travel time from their homes.[29]

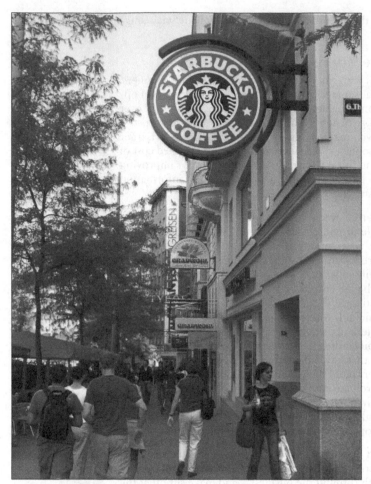

Starbucks creates a competitive advantage by saturating an area with stores, which makes it difficult for competitors to find good locations.

intersection, CVS is relegated to the second-best location.

Starbucks has developed a strong competitive advantage with its locations. As it expanded across the United States, it saturated each market before entering a new market. For example, there were more than 100 Starbucks outlets in the Seattle area before the company expanded to a new region. Starbucks frequently opens several stores close to one another. It has two stores on two corners of the intersection of Robson and Thurlow in Vancouver. By having such a high density of stores, Starbucks makes it very difficult for a competitor to enter a market and find good locations. Approaches for evaluating and selecting locations are discussed in Chapters 7 and 8.

Multiple Sources of Advantage

To build an advantage that is sustainable for a long period of time, retailers typically cannot rely on a single approach, such as good locations or excellent customer service. Instead, they use multiple approaches to build as high a wall around their position as possible.[30] For example, McDonald's long-term success is based on providing customers with a good value that meets their expectations, having efficient customer service, possessing a strong brand name, and offering convenient locations. By building strategic assets in all of these areas, McDonald's has developed a strong competitive position in the quick-service restaurant market.[31]

In addition to its unique products and associated customer loyalty, IKEA has a large group of loyal customers due to its strong brand image and the stimulating shopping experience it provides its customers. Walmart complements its size advantage with strong vendor relationships and the clear positioning of a retailer that offers superior value. Starbucks combines its location advantage with unique products, committed employees, a strong brand name, and strong relationships with coffee growers to build an overall advantage that is very difficult for competitors to erode. Retailing View 5.2 describes The Container Store, a retailer that has also built multiple bases of sustainable competitive advantages through unique merchandise, excellent customer service, and strong customer and vendor relationships.

GROWTH STRATEGIES

LO3

Classify the different strategic growth opportunities retailers pursue.

In the preceding sections, we have focused on a retailer's strategy, its target market and retail format, and the approaches that retailers take to build a sustainable competitive advantage and defend their position from competitive attacks. When retailers develop these competitive advantages, they have valuable assets. In this section, we discuss how retailers leverage these assets to expand their businesses.

Growth Opportunities

Four types of growth opportunities that retailers may pursue—market penetration, market expansion, retail format development, and diversification—are shown in Exhibit 5–4.[32] The vertical axis indicates the synergies between the retailer's present markets and the growth opportunity—whether the opportunity involves markets the retailer is presently pursuing or new markets. The horizontal axis indicates the synergies between the retailer's present retail mix and the retail mix of the growth opportunity—whether the opportunity exploits the retailer's skills and knowledge in operating its present format or requires new capabilities to operate a new format.

Market Penetration   A **market penetration growth opportunity** is a growth opportunity directed toward existing customers using the retailer's present retailing format. Such opportunities involve either attracting new consumers from the retailer's current target market who don't patronize the retailer currently or devising approaches that get current customers to visit the retailer more often and/or buy more merchandise on each visit.

Market penetration approaches include opening more stores in the target market and/or keeping existing stores open for longer hours. Other approaches involve displaying merchandise to increase impulse purchases and training salespeople to

RETAILING VIEW   The Container Store—Building a Competitive Advantage by Selling Products That Make Life Simpler   **5.2**

The Container Store sells products to help customers solve problems, or challenges, as the company likes to call them, in organizing their lives. It offers more than 10,000 innovative products, including multipurpose shelving and garment bags to organize closets; portable file cabinets and magazine holders to create order in home offices; backpacks, modular shelving, and DVD holders to make dorm rooms less cluttered; and recipe holders, bottles, jars, and recycling bins to bring harmony to kitchens. More than 1,500 new products are added to its assortment every year.

Over the years, the company has developed strong vendor relationships. Most of its vendors' primary focus was to manufacture products for industrial use. Yet, over time, the company has worked closely with its vendors to develop products that are appropriate for the home.

The Container Store's sales associates provide outstanding customer service. The company actively recruits customers who are intrigued with helping people organize. It spends considerable time educating sales associates about the merchandise (240 hours versus the typical 12 hours for new retail employees) and then empowering them to use their own intuition and creativity to solve customer challenges.

Employees are very committed to the company; as a result, its turnover rate is among the lowest in the retail industry. The Container Store also has appeared on *Fortune*'s list of the "100 Best Companies to Work For" in each of the last 11 years.

The Container Store has multiple sources of competitive advantage, including unique merchandise, excellent customer service, strong vendor relationships, and committed employees.

and Angela Ellis, "Inside the Container Store: Secrets of America's Favorite Stores," *ABC News*, March 30, 2010; and "Three Good Hires? He'll Pay More for One Who's Great," *The New York Times*, March 14, 2010.

DISCUSSION QUESTION

How does the Container Store maintain its competitive advantage?

Sources: Steven R. Thompson, "Container Store Uses Personal Approach in New Strategy," *Dallas Business Journal*, April 27, 2012; Bianna Golodryga

EXHIBIT 5–4
Growth Opportunities

cross-sell. **Cross-selling** means that sales associates in one department attempt to sell complementary merchandise from other departments to their customers. For example, a sales associate who has just sold a Blu-Ray player to a customer will take the customer to the accessories department to sell special cables to improve the performance of the player.

Market Expansion   A **market expansion growth opportunity** involves using the retailer's existing retail format in new market segments. For example, Dunkin' Donuts has been opening new stores outside its traditional target market in the northeastern United States.[33] When Chico's acquired White House Black Market, it engaged in a market expansion growth opportunity. Chico's and White House Black Market have similar retail formats. They are both mall-based specialty apparel stores. But Chico's targets women over 30 years old, while White House Black Market targets a younger age segment. In contrast, Chico's acquisition of Soma, a mall-based specialty store chain offering lingerie for women between 35 and 55, was a market penetration opportunity—same market and similar operations; however, Chico's and Soma offer different products.

Retail Format Development   A **retail format development growth opportunity** is an opportunity in which a retailer develops a new retail format—a format with a different retail mix—for the same target market. The U.K.-based retailer Tesco has employed a retail format development growth strategy by operating several different food store formats that all cater to essentially the same target market. The smallest is Tesco Express, up to 3,000 square feet. These stores are located close to where customers live and work. Tesco Metro stores are 7,000 to 15,000 square feet, bring convenience to city center locations, and specialize in offering a wide range of ready-to-eat meals. Tesco Superstores, up to 50,000 square feet, are the oldest format. In recent years, the company has added nonfood products, such as Blu-Rays and books, to improve customer satisfaction. Finally, Tesco Extra stores, more than 60,000 square feet, are designed to be a one-stop destination, with the widest range of food and nonfood products, from housewares and clothing to garden furniture.[34]

Diversification   A **diversification growth opportunity** is one in which a retailer introduces a new retail format directed toward a market segment that's not currently served by the retailer. Diversification opportunities are either related or unrelated.

Related versus Unrelated Diversification In a **related diversification growth opportunity,** the retailer's present target market and retail format shares something in common with the new opportunity. This commonality might entail purchasing from the same vendors, operating in similar locations, using the same distribution or management information system, or advertising in the same newspapers to similar target markets. In contrast, an **unrelated diversification growth opportunity** has little commonality between the retailer's present business and the new growth opportunity.

Through acquisition, Home Depot built a wholesale building supply business, called HD Supply, which had generated more than $3 billion in annual sales. Management felt that this growth opportunity would be synergistic with the firm's retail business, because its stores were already selling similar merchandise to contractors. Thus, Home Depot viewed this growth opportunity as a related diversification, because the targeted customers (i.e., contractors) would be similar, and the new large contractor market could be served using a retail mix similar to Home Depot's present retail mix. In addition, Home Depot would realize cost savings by placing larger orders with vendors because it would be selling to both retail and wholesale large and small customers.

In hindsight, though, the HD Supply actually was an unrelated diversification. The large contractor market served by HD Supply sold primarily pipes, lumber, and concrete—products with limited sales in Home Depot's retail stores. Selling these supplies to large contractors involved competitive bidding and transporting large, bulky orders to job sites—skills that Home Depot lacked. So Home Depot sold this unrelated diversification to concentrate on its core retail, small-contractor business.[35]

Vertical Integration   **Vertical integration** describes diversification by retailers into wholesaling or manufacturing. For example, some retailers go beyond designing their private-label merchandise to owning factories that manufacture the merchandise. When retailers integrate backward and manufacture products, they are making risky investments because the requisite skills to make products are different from those associated with retailing them. In addition, retailers and manufacturers have different customers. The immediate customers for a manufacturer's products are retailers, while a retailer's customers are consumers. Thus, a manufacturer's marketing activities are very different from those of a retailer. Note that designing private-label merchandise is a related diversification because it builds on the retailer's knowledge of its customers, whereas actually making the merchandise is an unrelated diversification.

Growth Opportunities and Competitive Advantage

Typically, retailers have the greatest competitive advantage and most success when they engage in opportunities that are similar to their present retail operations and markets. Thus, market penetration growth opportunities have the greatest chances of succeeding because they build on the retailer's present bases of advantage and don't involve entering new, unfamiliar markets or operating new, unfamiliar retail formats.

When retailers pursue market expansion opportunities, they build on their advantages in operating a retail format and apply this competitive advantage in a new market. A retail format development opportunity builds on the retailer's relationships and loyalty of present customers. Even if a retailer doesn't have experience and skills in operating the new format, it hopes to attract its loyal customers to it. Retailers have the least opportunity to exploit a competitive advantage when they pursue diversification opportunities.

GLOBAL GROWTH OPPORTUNITIES

LO4

Identify issues that arise as domestic retailers become global retailers.

In this section, we provide a more detailed discussion of one type of growth opportunity—expanding operations to international markets. This growth opportunity is becoming particularly attractive to large retailers as they begin to saturate their domestic market. Of the 20 largest retailers in the world, only 3 operate in one country.[36] By expanding internationally, retailers can increase their sales, leverage their knowledge and systems across a greater sales base, and gain more bargaining power with vendors. But international expansion is risky because retailers must deal with different government regulations, cultural traditions, consumer preferences, supply chains, and languages. Retailing View 5.3 describes the substantial differences in grocery shopping in Shanghai.

We first discuss the attractiveness of different opportunities for global expansion and then the keys to success for expanding globally. Finally, we review the approaches that retailers can take to enter international markets.

Attractiveness of International Markets

Three factors that are often used to determine the attractiveness of international opportunities are (1) the potential size of the retail market in the country, (2) the degree to which the country does and can support the entry of foreign retailers engaged in modern retail practices, and (3) the risks or uncertainties in sales and profits.[37] Some indicators of these factors are shown in Exhibit 5–5. The (+) or (−) indicates whether the indicator is positively or negatively related to the factor.

Note that the importance of some country characteristics depends on the type of retailer evaluating the country for entry. For example, a retailer of video games, such as Gamestop, would find a country with a large percentage of people under 19 to be more attractive than a country with a large percentage of people over 65. High-fashion retailers that sell expensive merchandise, such as Neiman Marcus and Cartier, would find a country that has a significant percentage of the population with high incomes to be more attractive than a country that has a large percentage of people in poverty.

Most retailers considering entry into foreign markets are successful multinational retailers that use sophisticated management practices. Thus, they would find countries that have modern retailing, more advanced infrastructures, and significant urban populations to be more supportive. In addition, countries lacking strong domestic retailers but having a stable economy and political environment would be more supportive.

The factors outlined in Exhibit 5–5 are weighted to develop an index scoring each country on the attractiveness dimensions. One index ranking the 20 most

EXHIBIT 5–5   Indicators of the Potential, Support, and Risk in International Markets

Country Potential	Country Support	Country Risk
Population (+)	Market share of modern retailing (+)	Political stability (+)
Population growth rate (+)	Quality of infrastructure (roads, trains, etc.) (+)	Business-friendly laws and regulations (+)
GDP (+)	Urban population (+)	Access to bank financing (+)
GDP growth rate (+)	Market share of domestic retailers (+)	National debt (−)
GDP per capita (+)	Market share of international retailers (+)	Crime (−)
Retail sales (+)	Market share of largest retailers (+)	Violence (−)
Retail sales growth rate (+)		Corruption (−)
Retail sales per capita (+)		
Population (+)		
Income distribution (+ or −)		
Age (+ or −)		

attractive international retail markets on market potential (country potential and support) and risk is shown in Exhibit 5–6. Of the top 20 counties in this ranking, 10 are emerging economies. The emerging international markets that receive the most attention from global retailers are India, China, Russia, and Brazil, collectively referred to as "the BRIC" (Brazil, Russia, India, China) countries. However, in this analysis, Russia is not in the top 20 because of its high risk.

RETAILING VIEW　Wet Markets in Shanghai　5.3

Shanghai, with more than 23 million inhabitants, is the largest city by population in the world. It is a sophisticated international city, like New York, London, and Tokyo, with substantial influence in global commerce, culture, finance, media, fashion, technology, and transportation. It is a major financial center and the busiest container port in the world. The major international food retailers (Walmart, Carrefour, Metro, and Tesco) have now opened more than 200 Western-style hypermarkets in Shanghai. In addition, there are more than 2,000 modern supermarkets operated mostly by Chinese firms. But the majority of perishable goods (fish, meat, chicken, pork, vegetables, and fruit) sales still are made in traditional wet markets.

Wet markets are buildings divided into small stalls lined along narrow corridors with small, independent retailers selling perishables in the stalls. The retailers lease the stalls from market operators. They buy the perishables from various sources, including wholesale markets, rural merchants, and farmers' cooperatives, and then sort, clean, and package the perishables for sale to their customers. These markets are called "wet markets" because the concrete floor is constantly wet from the spraying of perishables and cleaning of live meat and fish. There are more than 900 wet markets in Shanghai.

The Chinese government would like to close all wet markets because they do not reflect the modern China and because they pose health risks due to poor hygiene. But Chinese urban consumers cross-format shop for groceries: They buy manufactured goods in supermarkets and hypermarkets but perishables in wet markets. Two factors contribute to this preference for wet markets.

First, Chinese consumers place great importance on freshness. Perishables sold at supermarkets and hypermarkets usually get to the store around eight o'clock the night before and have been shelved for at least half a day before reaching consumers. At wet markets, vendors buy their perishables around four o'clock in the morning and constantly trim, spray, clean, and sort the perishables to keep them fresh. Also, wet-market vendors do not have or use refrigerators for storage; thus, they have to replenish their inventory with fresh supplies every day. The modern-format retailers simply cannot win the freshness contest.

Even though there are many modern supermarkets and hypermarkets in Shanghai, the majority of perishable groceries are still bought at traditional wet markets.

Second, for logistical reasons, most Chinese consumers shop for groceries every day and buy just enough to prepare for that day's meals. In their small homes, the average kitchen size is about 60 square feet, leaving little room to store any items for extended periods, especially perishable foods that require refrigeration. Furthermore, though the automotive market is growing in China, many families still travel by other means. In Shanghai for example, bicycles (20 percent), buses (30 percent), and walking (40 percent) are more common means of transport for shopping trips. In these locations, the small wet markets provide far more convenient locations than larger super- or hypermarkets.

Sources: "Buying the Store," *China Economic Review*, June 14, 2012; Louise Herring, Daniel Hui, Paul Morgan, and Caroline Tufft, *Inside China's Hypermarkets: Past and Prospects* (Hong Kong: McKinsey By McKinsey, 2012); and Qian Forrest Zhang and Zi Pan, *The Transformation of Urban Vegetable Retail in China: Wet Markets, Supermarkets, and Informal Markets in Shanghai*, Research Collection School of Social Sciences, 2012.

DISCUSSION QUESTION

Given the Chinese government's disdain for wet markets, do you think they will endure?

EXHIBIT 5–6   Country Attractiveness

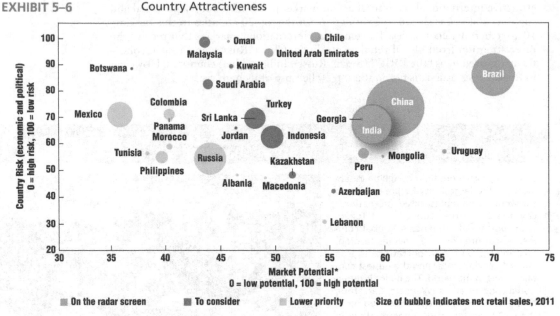

*Based on weighted score of market attractiveness, market saturation, and time pressure of top 30 countries

SOURCE: Hana Ben-Shabat, Helen Rhim, Mike Moriarity, and Fabiola Salman, *Global Retail Expansion Keeps Moving—2012* (New York: ATKearney, 2012).

India and China are by far the largest and most attractive retail markets. However, these two countries offer different opportunities and challenges for retailers contemplating entry.[38]

India   In India and most emerging economies, the retail industry is divided into organized and unorganized sectors. The **unorganized retailing** includes the small independent retailers—the local *kirana* shops, owner-operated general stores, *paan/beedi* shops, convenience stores, and handcart and street vendors. Most Indians shop in open markets and millions of independent grocery shops called *kirana*. However, India's growing, well-educated, aspirational middle class wants a more sophisticated retail environment and global brands.

REFACT

Less than 5 percent of India's retail sales are through organized retail channels.[39]

While the demand for modern (organized) retailing exists in India, entering the Indian market is challenging. As the world's largest pluralistic democracy, with myriad cultures and 22 official languages, India actually is a conglomeration of discrete markets. In addition, government regulations impede foreign investment in retailing. Retailers must comply with a myriad of regulations before opening stores and shipping merchandise. For example, there are taxes for moving goods to different states and even within states. Initially, Walmart's entry into India is a partnership with Bharti Enterprises to open wholesale outlets called Best Price Modern Wholesale. The outlets initially were allowed to

In India, most consumers shop at small, independent retail outlets.

sell only to firms that register by showing tax documents that prove they own retail outlets. The development of organized retailing is being undertaken by industrial conglomerates that have limited expertise in running retail chains.[40]

China   Government regulations of retailing are much less onerous in China than in India, and direct foreign investment is encouraged. Since the lifting of most operational restrictions on international retailers, six global food retailers (Auchan, Carrefour, Ito-Yokado, Metro, Tesco, and Walmart) have entered China, although much of this retail development has been in the large eastern coastal cities of Shanghai, Beijing, Guangzhou, and Shenzhen.[41]

China is rapidly developing the infrastructure to support modern retailing. Highway density in China is already approaching similar levels as the United States. China has a number of high-quality airports and a rapidly developing sophisticated railroad network.

However, doing business in China is still challenging. Operating costs are increasing, managerial talent is becoming more difficult to find and retain, and an underdeveloped and inefficient supply chain predominates.

Brazil   Brazil has the largest population and strongest economy in Latin America. It is a country of many poor people and a few very wealthy families. Brazilian retailers have developed some very innovative practices for retailing to low-income families, including offering credit and installment purchases. The very wealthy Brazilians provide a significant market for luxury goods and retailers. Even though they are approximately 1 percent of the population, this equates to approximately 19 million people, a market just a little smaller than all of Australia.

Russia   In Russia, the impediments to market entry are less visible but more problematic. Corruption is rampant, with various administrative authorities capable of impeding operations if payments are not made. Retailers encounter severe logistical challenges in supporting operations in Russia. There are long delays at borders and ports and a scarcity of containers. More than 70 percent of international container shipments come through the St. Petersburg port, which is very congested. Retailers often cannot rely on domestic products because the quality of products made in Russia is poor. Most major retailers offer their own credit card facility, with "signing up" booths at the entrances to their stores. Many low-income customers go from week to week paying their credit card commitments. Finally, much of the purchasing power is concentrated in Moscow, where salaries are about double those in other regions. But Moscow is already saturated with shopping centers.

REFACT

The anticorruption group Transparency International ranks Russia 143th out of 183 countries on its most recent index of the most corrupt countries.[42]

Keys to Success in Global Retailing

Four characteristics of retailers that have successfully exploited international growth opportunities are (1) a globally sustainable competitive advantage, (2) adaptability, (3) a global culture, and (4) financial resources.

Globally Sustainable Competitive Advantage   Entry into nondomestic markets is most successful when the expansion opportunity builds on the retailer's core bases of competitive advantage. For example, Walmart and ALDI have a significant cost advantage that facilitates success in international markets in which price plays an important role in consumer decision making and a distribution infrastructure is available to enable these firms to exploit their logistical capabilities. In contrast, H&M and Zara are more successful in international markets that value lower-priced, fashionable merchandise.

Some U.S. retailers have a competitive advantage in global markets because American culture is emulated in many countries, particularly by young people. Due to rising prosperity, the rapidly increasing access to broadband Internet, social media like Facebook and networks such as MTV that feature American programming, fashion trends in the United States have spread to young people in emerging countries. The global MTV generation prefers Coke to tea, Nikes to sandals, Chicken McNuggets to rice, and credit cards to cash. China's major cities have American stores and restaurants, including KFC, Pizza Hut, and McDonald's. Shanghai and Beijing have more than 100 Starbucks stores even though coffee had never been the drink of choice before Starbucks came to town. But Chinese urban dwellers go to Starbucks to impress a friend or because it's a symbol of a new kind of lifestyle. Although Western products and stores have gained a reputation for high quality and good service in China, in some ways it is the American culture that many Chinese consumers want.

Adaptability   Although successful global retailers build on their core competencies, they also recognize cultural differences and adapt their core strategy to the needs of local markets. Retailing View 5.4 illustrates how 7-Eleven changed its retail offering to be more appealing in Indonesia.

Carrefour is an expert at understanding and integrating itself into local regions. For example, it realized early on that the merchandising of fish differs for each local market. In San Francisco, fish is sold dead and filleted; in France, fish is sold

5.4   RETAILING VIEW   7-Eleven Is Trendy Hangout in Indonesia

In a local hangout in Jakarta, hipsters gather to drink iced coffee, gossip, eat nachos, listen to a live band, and text their friends. This sort of hanging out is so popular and common among young Indonesians that their language includes a word to describe sitting around, chatting, and generally doing nothing productive: *nongkrong*. For years, the most popular gathering spots were food stalls, located along the sides of roads, known as *warung*. But the *warung* are giving way to another popular *nongkrong* location: local 7-Eleven stores.

This shift is exactly the response that 7-Eleven hoped to achieve when it instituted a new strategy in Indonesia: adding seating to its existing small supermarkets and offering inexpensive, ready-to-eat meals, such as fried rice and pillow bread (i.e., small cheese- or chocolate-filled sandwiches). Jakarta is notably lacking in outdoor recreation space, so the little hangouts effectively attract social customers. And Indonesia has plenty of those, as evidenced by its massive social networking rates. In Indonesia alone, 7-Eleven has attracted nearly 60,000 Twitter followers and almost as many Facebook fans.

The strategy also means that the franchise mainly targets young customers, who constitute 65 percent of its market. These Millennials make use of the 24/7 access that 7-Eleven offers, surfing the Internet at all hours, before or after gathering with their friends. In Indonesia, one of the most electronically connected nations in the world, customers constantly update their social networks to alert them about when a band is about to start playing at the local 7-Eleven, for example. Among this generational cohort, the store appeals to a wide range of economic classes, such that the parking lots fill with Mercedes-Benzes interspersed with rusted-out motor bikes.

Despite these unique offerings, 7-Elevens are still 7-Elevens: They sell Big Gulps, flavored Slurpees, doughnuts,

7-Eleven is a trendy place for young Indonesians to hang out with their friends.

and hot coffee. But in locations in the world's most populous Muslim country, 7-Eleven only sells alcohol after conducting neighborhood surveys to obtain community approval.

Sources: Sara Schonhardt, "7-Eleven Finds a Niche by Adapting to Indonesian Ways," *The New York Times*, May 28, 2012; and Anthony Deutsch, "7-Eleven Becomes Indonesia's Trendy Hangout," *Financial Times*, September 13, 2011.

DISCUSSION QUESTION

Could 7-Eleven adapt what it has learned in Indonesia to the United States to attract young urban customers? Would it want to?

dead but whole on ice with the head still intact; and in China, fish is sold live. However, consumers in the middle and western parts of China have more confidence in frozen fish, because they are so far from the ocean.[43] Carrefour and Tesco make sure that more than 90 percent of the merchandise they sell is produced in the country in which it is sold.[44]

Peak selling seasons also vary across countries. In the United States, many stores experience a sales increase in August, when families stock up on back-to-school supplies and apparel. However, this month is one of the slowest sales periods in Europe because most people are on vacation. Back-to-school season in Japan occurs in April.

Store designs and layouts often need to be adjusted in different parts of the world. In the United States, for instance, supercenters are usually quite large and on one level, except in a few urban areas. In other parts of the world, such as Europe and parts of Asia, where space is at a premium, stores must be designed to fit smaller footprints and are often housed in multiple levels. In some cultures, social norms dictate that men's and women's clothing cannot be displayed next to each other.

Government regulations and cultural values can also affect store operations. Some differences, such as holidays, hours of operation, and regulations governing part-time employees and terminations, are easy to identify. Other factors require a deeper understanding. For example, Latin American culture is very family oriented, so traditional U.S. work schedules would need to be adjusted so that Latin American employees could have more time with their families during family meals. Boots, a U.K. drugstore chain owned by Walgreens, has the checkout clerks in its Japanese stores stand up because it discovered that Japanese shoppers found it offensive to pay money to a seated clerk, but retailers have to provide seating for checkout clerks in Germany. Retailers in Germany also must recycle packaging materials sold in their stores. Also in Germany, seasonal sales can be held only during specific weeks and apply only to specific product categories, and the amount of the discounts are limited. Spanish and French retailers work under government-controlled operating hours and must mind policies prohibiting midseason sales.

Global Culture   To be global, retailers must think globally. It is not sufficient to transplant a home-country culture and infrastructure to another country. In this regard, Carrefour is truly global. In the early years of its international expansion, it started in each country slowly, an approach that reduced the company's ethnocentrism. Further enriching its global perspective, Carrefour has always encouraged the rapid development of local management and retains few expatriates in its overseas operations. Carrefour's management ranks are truly international. One is just as likely to run across a Portuguese regional manager in Hong Kong as a French or Chinese one. Finally, Carrefour discourages the classic overseas "tour of duty" mentality often found in U.S. firms. International assignments are important in themselves, not just as stepping stones to ultimate career advancement back in France. The globalization of Carrefour's culture is perhaps most evident in the speed with which ideas flow throughout the organization. A global management structure of regional committees, which meet regularly, advances the awareness and implementation of global best practices. The proof of Carrefour's global commitment lies in the numbers: It has had more than 30 years of international experience in 30 countries, both developed and developing.[45]

Financial Resources   Expansion into international markets requires a long-term commitment and considerable up-front planning. Retailers find it very difficult to generate short-term profits when they make the transition to global retailing. Although firms such as Walmart, Carrefour, Office Depot, and Costco often initially have difficulty achieving success in new global markets, these large firms generally are in a strong financial position and therefore have the ability to keep investing in projects long enough to become successful.

Entry Strategies

Four approaches that retailers can take when entering nondomestic markets are direct investment, joint venture, strategic alliance, and franchising.[46]

Direct Investment   **Direct investment** occurs when a retail firm invests in and owns a retail operation in a foreign country. This entry strategy requires the highest level of investment and exposes the retailer to the greatest risks, but it also has the highest potential returns. A key advantage of direct investment is that the retailer has complete control of the operations. For example, McDonald's chose this entry strategy for the U.K. market, building a plant to produce buns when local suppliers could not meet its specifications.

Joint Venture   A **joint venture** is formed when the entering retailer pools its resources with a local retailer to form a new company in which ownership, control, and profits are shared. A joint-venture entry strategy reduces the entrant's risks. In addition to sharing the financial burden, the local partner provides an understanding of the market and has access to local resources, such as vendors and real estate. Many foreign countries require that foreign entrants partner with domestic firms. Problems with this entry approach can arise if the partners disagree or the government places restrictions on the repatriation of profits.

Strategic Alliance   A **strategic alliance** is a collaborative relationship between independent firms. For example, a retailer might enter an international market through direct investment but use independent firms to facilitate its local logistical and warehousing activities.

Franchising   **Franchising** offers the lowest risk and requires the least investment, but also has the lowest potential return on investment. The retailer has limited control over the retail operations in the foreign country, its potential profit is reduced, and the risk of assisting in the creation of a local domestic competitor increases. The U.K.-based Marks & Spencer, for example, has franchised stores in 30 countries.[47]

THE STRATEGIC RETAIL PLANNING PROCESS

LO5

Know the steps retailers go through to develop a strategic plan.

In the previous sections, we reviewed the elements in a strategy statement, the approaches for building a sustainable competitive advantage, the growth opportunities that retailers consider, and the factors they consider when evaluating and pursuing a global growth opportunity. In this section, we outline the process retailers use to review their present situation and decide on a strategy to pursue.

The **strategic retail planning process** is the set of steps a retailer goes through to develop a strategy and plan[48] (see Exhibit 5–7). It describes how retailers select target market segments, determine the appropriate retail format, and build sustainable competitive advantages. As indicated in Exhibit 5–7, it is not always necessary to go through the entire process each time a strategy and plan are developed (step 7). For instance, a retailer could evaluate its performance and go directly to step 2 to conduct a SWOT analysis.

The planning process can be used to formulate strategic plans at different levels within a retail corporation. For example, the corporate strategic plan of Tesco indicates how to allocate resources across the corporation's various divisions, such as Tesco, Tesco Extra, Tesco Express, Tesco Metro, Tesco Homeplus, and One Stop. Each division, in turn, develops its own strategic plan.

As we discuss the steps in the retail planning process, we will apply each step to the planning process for a hypothetical retailer owned by Kelly Bradford. Kelly owns Gifts To Go, a small, two-store chain in the Chicago area. One of her 1,000-square-foot stores is located in the downtown area; the other is in an upscale suburban mall. The target market for Gifts To Go is upper-income men and women looking for gifts in the $50 to $500 price range. The stores have an eclectic

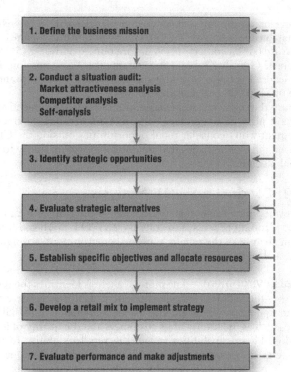

EXHIBIT 5–7
Stages in the Strategic Planning Process

selection of merchandise, including handmade jewelry and crafts, fine china and glassware, perfume, watches, writing instruments, and a variety of one-of-a-kind items. Gifts To Go also has developed a number of loyal customers who are contacted by sales associates when family anniversaries and birthdays come up. In many cases, customers have a close relationship with a sales associate and enough confidence in the associate's judgment that they tell the associate to pick out an appropriate gift. The turnover of Gifts To Go sales associates is low for the industry because Kelly treats associates as part of the family. The company pays for health insurance for all associates, and the associates share in the profits of the firm.

Step 1: Define the Business Mission

The first step in the strategic retail planning process is to define the business mission. The **mission statement** is a broad description of a retailer's objectives and the scope of activities it plans to undertake.[49] While the principle objective of a publicly held firm is to maximize its stockholders' wealth, firms also are concerned about their impact on society.

For example, Maxine Clark, founder and chief executive bear at Build-A-Bear Workshop, in discussing her goals for the company, says, "We also believe strongly that we need to give back to the communities in which we have stores. For example, as part of our on-going commitment to children's health and wellness, we introduced a series of Nicki Bears to honor Nicki Giampolo, a young girl who lost her life to cancer. A portion of the sales of each Nicki is donated to support programs that help children maintain normal lives while they struggle with difficult health issues."[50] Owners of small, privately held firms frequently have other objectives, such as achieving a specific level of income and avoiding uncertainty rather than maximizing income.

The mission statement defines the general nature of the target segments and retail formats on which the firm will focus. For example, the mission statement "Serve the customer, build value for shareholders, and create opportunities for associates," is too broad. It fails to provide a sense of strategic direction.

In developing the mission statement, managers need to answer five questions: (1) What business are we in? (2) What should our business be in the future? (3) Who are our customers? (4) What are our capabilities? (5) What do we want to accomplish? Gifts To Go's mission statement is "The mission of Gifts To Go is to be the leading retailer of higher-priced gifts in Chicago and provide a stable income of $100,000 per year for the owner."

Because the mission statement defines the retailer's objectives and the scope of activities it plans to undertake, Gifts To Go's mission statement clarifies that its management won't consider retail opportunities outside the Chicago area, selling low-priced gifts, or activities that might jeopardize its ability to generate $100,000 in annual income.

Step 2: Conduct a SWOT Analysis

After developing a mission statement and setting objectives, the next step in the strategic planning process is to conduct a **SWOT analysis.** A SWOT analysis involves an analysis of the retailer's internal environment (strengths and weaknesses) and external environment (opportunities and threats).

Internal Environment   The internal analysis identifies the retailer's *strengths and weaknesses*—the retailer's unique strategic capabilities relative to its competition. These unique capabilities are the assets, knowledge, and skills that the retailer possesses such as the loyalty of its customers and the quality of its relationships with its vendor. These capabilities reflect the retailer's ability to develop a strategic advantage as an opportunity it is considering. Exhibit 5–8 outlines some issues to consider in performing a **strengths and weaknesses analysis.**

Here is Kelly Bradford's analysis of Gifts To Go's strengths and weaknesses:

Capabilities	Gifts To Go Strength and Weaknesses
Financial resources	Good—Gifts To Go had no debt and a good relationship with a bank. Kelly has saved $255,000 that she has in liquid securities.
Customer loyalty	Good—While Gifts To Go did not achieve the sales volume in gifts done in department stores, the company has a loyal base of customers.
Locations	Excellent—Both of Gifts To Go's locations are excellent. The downtown location is convenient for office workers. The suburban mall location is at a heavily trafficked juncture.
HUMAN RESOURCES	
Merchandise management	Limited—Kelly has a flair for selecting unique gifts but has no systems to support her.
Store management	Excellent—The store managers and sales associates are excellent. They are very attentive to customers and loyal to the firm. Employee and customer theft is kept to a minimum.
Other staff and systems	Limited—An accounting firm keeps the financial records for the business.
Vendor relationships	Kelly has excellent relationships with vendors providing one-of-a-kind merchandise.
Supply chain management and information systems	Poor—While Kelly feels Gifts To Go has relatively low overhead, the company does not have a computer-based inventory control system or management and customer information systems. Her competitors (local department stores, catalog, and Internet retailers) certainly have superior systems. No skills in developing and utilizing customer databases.

EXHIBIT 5–8
Elements in a
Strengths and
Weaknesses Analysis

Financial resources	Human resources
Customer loyalty	Top managers
Strength of brand image	Store manager
Development of unique merchandise	Merchandise managers
Quality of customer service	Operation managers
Information about customers	Vendor relationships
Size and involvement of community	Supply chain management systems
Locations	Information systems

Market Factors	Competitive Factors	Environmental Dynamics
Market size	Barriers to entry	New technology
Market growth	Bargaining power of vendors	Economic conditions
Cyclicality of sales	Competitive rivalry	Changes in governmental regulations
Seasonality		Social changes

EXHIBIT 5–9
Opportunities and
Threats

External Environment   The external analysis identifies the retailer's opportunities and threats—the aspect of the environment that might positively or negatively affect the retailer's performance. These factors associated with the market, competition, and environment dynamics are typically beyond the retailer's control. Exhibit 5–9 outlines some issues to consider when doing an **opportunities and threats analysis.**

Market Factors   The attractiveness of a target market in which a retailer is involved or considering is affected by the size of the market, market growth, cyclicality of sales, and seasonality. Market size is important because it indicates a retailer's opportunity to generate revenues to cover its investment.

Growing markets are typically more attractive than mature or declining markets. For example, retail markets for limited-assortment, extreme-value retailers are growing faster than are those for department stores. Typically, the return on investment may be higher in growing markets because competition is less intense than in mature markets. Because new customers are just beginning to patronize stores in growing markets, they may not have developed strong store loyalties and thus might be easier to attract to new retail offerings.

Firms are often interested in minimizing the business cycle's impact on their sales. Thus, retail markets for merchandise that is affected by economic conditions (such as cars and major appliances) are less attractive than retail markets that are less affected by economic conditions (such as food). In general, markets with highly seasonal sales are unattractive because a lot of resources are needed to accommodate the peak season and then the resources go underutilized the rest of the year. Retailers can take steps to reduce seasonality; for instance, ski resorts can promote summer vacations.

To conduct an analysis of the market factors for Gifts To Go, Kelly Bradford went on the Internet to get information about the size, growth, and cyclical and seasonal nature of the gift market in general and, more specifically, in Chicago. On the basis of her analysis, she concluded that the market factors were attractive. The market for more expensive gifts was large, growing, and not vulnerable to business cycles. The only negative aspect was the high seasonality of gifts, with peaks at Valentine's Day, June (due to weddings), Christmas, and other holidays.

Competitive Factors   The nature of the competition in retail markets is affected by barriers to entry, the bargaining power of vendors, and competitive rivalry.[51] Retail markets are more attractive when competitive entry is costly. **Barriers to entry** are conditions in a retail market that make it difficult for other firms to enter the market. Some of these conditions are (1) scale economies, (2) customer loyalty, and (3) the availability of great locations.

Scale economies are cost advantages due to a retailer's size. Markets dominated by large competitors with scale economies are typically unattractive because the dominant firms have sustainable cost advantages. For example, an entrepreneur would view the drugstore market as unattractive because it is dominated by three large firms: Walgreens, CVS, and Rite Aid. These firms have considerable cost advantages over an entrepreneur because they have significant bargaining power over suppliers and can buy merchandise at lower prices. They have the resources to invest in the latest technology and can spread the fixed costs of such investments across more outlets.

Retail markets dominated by a well-established retailer that has developed a loyal group of customers also are unattractive. For example, Home Depot's high customer loyalty in Atlanta, where it has its corporate offices, makes it hard for a competing home improvement center like Lowe's to compete effectively in the Atlanta market.

The availability of locations may impede competitive entry. Staples, for instance, attributes part of its success over its rivals in the northeastern United States to its first-mover advantage. The Northeast has a preponderance of mature but stable retail markets, so finding new locations is more difficult there than it is in most of the rest of the United States. Because Staples started in the Northeast, it was able to open stores in the best available locations.

Entry barriers are a double-edged sword. A retail market with high entry barriers is very attractive for retailers presently competing in that market, because those barriers limit competition. However, markets with high entry barriers are unattractive for retailers not already in the market.

Another competitive factor is the **bargaining power of vendors.** Markets are less attractive when only a few vendors control the merchandise sold in the market. In such situations, vendors have the opportunity to dictate prices and other terms (like delivery dates), reducing the retailer's profits. For example, the market for retailing fashionable cosmetics is less attractive because two suppliers, Estée Lauder (Estée Lauder, Clinique, Prescriptives, Aveda, Jo Malone, Bumble and Bumble, Tommy Hilfiger, MAC, and Origins) and L'Oréal (Maybelline, Giorgio Armani, Redken, Lancôme, Garnier, and Ralph Lauren) provide most of the desirable premium brands. Because department stores need these brands to support a fashion image, the vendors have the power to sell their products to retailers at high prices.

The final competitive factor is the level of competitive rivalry in the retail market. **Competitive rivalry** is the frequency and intensity of reactions to actions undertaken by competitors. When rivalry is high, price wars erupt, retailers attempt to "steal" employees from one another, advertising and promotion expenses increase, and profit potential falls. Conditions that may lead to intense rivalry include (1) a large number of competitors that are all about the same size, (2) slow growth, (3) high fixed costs, and (4) a lack of perceived differences between competing retailers. For example, Home Depot and Lowe's have an intense rivalry in many markets.

When Kelly Bradford started to analyze the competitive factors for Gifts To Go, she realized that identifying her competitors wasn't easy. Although there were no gift stores carrying similar merchandise at the same price points in the Chicago area, there were various other retailers from which a customer could buy gifts. She identified her primary competitors as department stores, craft galleries, catalogs, and Internet retailers. Kelly felt there were some scale economies in developing customer databases to support gift retailing. The lack of large suppliers meant that vendors' bargaining power wasn't a problem, and competitive rivalry was minimal because the gift business was not a critical part of a department store's overall business. In addition, merchandise carried by the various retailers offered considerable differentiation opportunities.

Environmental Dynamics   Environmental dynamics that can affect market attractiveness include technological, economic, regulatory, and social changes. When a retail market is going through significant changes in technology, existing competitors are vulnerable to new entrants that are skilled at using the new technology. Many traditional store-based retailers were slow to develop their multichannel strategies fully. For instance, even today, many multichannel retailers do not offer customers the ability to purchase over the Internet and return merchandise to a store. Retailing View 5.5 illustrates how changes in the competitive environment forced Hot Topic to reevaluate its entire retail format.

Government regulations can reduce the attractiveness of a retail market. For example, until recently, government regulations made it difficult for retailers to open big-box stores in France and Germany.[52] Also, many local governments within the United States have tried to stop Walmart from entering their markets in an attempt to protect locally owned retailers.

Retailers need to answer three questions about each environmental factor:

1. What new developments or changes might occur, such as new technologies and regulations or different social factors and economic conditions?
2. What is the likelihood that these environmental changes will occur? What key factors affect whether these changes will occur?
3. How will these changes affect each retail market, the firm, and its competitors?

Kelly Bradford's primary concern when she did an environmental analysis was the potential growth of Internet gift retailers such as RedEnvelope. Gifts seem ideal for an electronic channel, because customers can order the item over the Internet and have it shipped directly to the gift recipient. Kelly also recognized that the electronic channel could effectively collect information about customers and then target promotions and suggestions to them when future gift-giving occasions arose.

RETAILING VIEW   Hot Topic Emphasizes Its Strength in Indie Music   5.5

Hot Topic, which started in the late 1980s, differentiated itself from other mall-based retailers targeting the Generation Y segment by offering an edgier alternative. It offered goth merchandise in its stores, which were frequented by customers and sales associates with tattoos, multiple piercings, spiked hair, and all-black clothing. Over time, Hot Topic looked like an also-ran in the crowded teen-retailer market. The tastes of fickle teens had changed. Its sales were stagnant. Mall foot traffic was down.

Hot Topic analyzed its situation and discovered that its basis of advantage among teens wasn't its goth image but its connection to the indie music scene—the small avant-garde bands it promoted with its private-label T-shirts. So it repositioned itself, reducing its emphasis on goth-look apparel and placing more emphasis on merchandise linked to cutting-edge music and entertainment.

Today, its stores feel more like campus student centers with loud music, dark walls, and bulletin boards crammed with concert flyers and staff music picks. Hot Topic began hosting free acoustic shows, called Local Static, featuring bands chosen by salespeople in its local stores. The company stresses its connection with music through its music download site, ShockHound.

It also licensed exclusively *Twilight's* four-book-and-film franchise about teen vampire love. The movie's stars did a national tour of Hot Topic stores, and the retailer supplied hot chocolate and pizza to thousands of fans.

When Hot Topic's market declined, it altered its strategic positioning to target young consumers that prefer local bands.

Sources: Schuyler Velasco, "How 'The Hunger Games' Scored a Marketing Win," *Christain Science Monitor*, March, 2012, p. 10; Nivedita Bhattacharjee, "And Hot Topic Gets Hunger Games Lift but May Not Last," *March*, March 2012: and http://community.hottopic.com/content/about-hot-topics, accessed September 6, 2012.

DISCUSSION QUESTION

Describe Hot Topic's target market. How has this changed over time?

Step 3: Identify Strategic Opportunities

After completing the SWOT analysis, the next step is to identify opportunities for increasing retail sales. Kelly Bradford presently competes in gift retailing using a specialty store format. The strategic alternatives she is considering are defined in terms of the growth opportunities in Exhibit 5–4. Note that some of these growth strategies involve a redefinition of her mission.

Step 4: Evaluate Strategic Opportunities

The fourth step in the strategic planning process is to evaluate opportunities that have been identified in the SWOT analysis. The evaluation determines the retailer's potential to establish a sustainable competitive advantage and reap long-term profits from the opportunities being evaluated. Thus, a retailer must focus on opportunities that utilize its strengths and its competitive advantage.

Both the market attractiveness and the strengths and weaknesses of the retailer need to be considered in evaluating strategic opportunities. The greatest investments should be made in market opportunities for which the retailer has a strong competitive position. Here's Kelly's informal analysis:

Growth Opportunity	Market Attractiveness	Competitive Position
Increase size of present stores and amount of merchandise in stores	Low	High
Open additional gift stores in Chicago area	Medium	Medium
Open gift stores outside the Chicago area (new geographic segment)	Medium	Low
Sell lower-priced gifts in present stores or open new stores selling low-priced gifts (new benefit segment)	Medium	Low
Sell apparel and other nongift merchandise to same customers in same or new stores	High	Medium
Sell similar gift merchandise to same market segment using the Internet	High	Low
Open apparel stores targeted at teenagers	High	Low
Open a category specialist selling low-priced gifts	High	Low

Step 5: Establish Specific Objectives and Allocate Resources

After evaluating the strategic investment opportunities, the next step in the strategic planning process is to establish a specific objective for each opportunity. The retailer's overall objective is included in the mission statement; the specific objectives are goals against which progress toward the overall objective can be measured. Thus, these specific objectives have three components: (1) the performance sought, including a numerical index against which progress may be measured; (2) a time frame within which the goal is to be achieved; and (3) the level of investment needed to achieve the objective. Typically, the performance levels are financial criteria such as return on investment, sales, or profits. Kelly's objective is to increase profits by 20 percent in each of the next five years. She expects she will need to invest an additional $25,000 in her apparel and other nongift merchandise inventory.

Step 6: Develop a Retail Mix to Implement the Strategy

The sixth step in the planning process is to develop a retail mix for each opportunity in which an investment will be made and control and evaluate performance. Decisions related to the elements in the retail mix are discussed in Sections III and IV.

Step 7: Evaluate Performance and Make Adjustments

The final step in the planning process is to evaluate the results of the strategy and implementation program. If the retailer is meeting or exceeding its objectives, changes aren't needed. But if the retailer fails to meet its objectives, reanalysis is required. Typically, this reanalysis starts with reviewing the implementation programs, but it may indicate that the strategy (or even the mission statement) needs to be reconsidered. This conclusion would result in starting a new planning process, including a new SWOT analysis.

Strategic Planning in the Real World

The planning process in Exhibit 5–7 suggests that strategic decisions are made in a sequential manner. After the business mission is defined, the SWOT analysis is performed, strategic opportunities are identified, alternatives are evaluated, objectives are set, resources are allocated, the implementation plan is developed, and, finally, performance is evaluated and adjustments are made. But actual planning processes have interactions among the steps. For example, the SWOT analysis may uncover a logical alternative for the firm to consider, even though this alternative isn't included in the mission statement. Thus, the mission statement may need to be reformulated. The development of the implementation plan might reveal that the resources allocated to a particular opportunity are insufficient to achieve the objective. In that case, the objective would need to be changed, the resources would need to be increased, or the retailer might consider not investing in the opportunity at all.

SUMMARY

LO1 Define the retail strategy.

A retail strategy is a statement that identifies (1) the retailer's target market, (2) the format and resources the retailer plans to use to satisfy the target market's needs, and (3) the bases on which the retailer plans to build a sustainable competitive advantage. The target market is the market segment(s) toward which the retailer plans to focus its resources and retail mix. A retail format describes the nature of the retailer's operations—its retail mix. A sustainable competitive advantage is an advantage the retailer has over its competition that is not easily copied by competitors and thus can be maintained over a long period of time.

LO2 Illustrate how retailers build a sustainable competitive advantage.

Three approaches for developing a sustainable competitive advantage are (1) building strong relationships with customers, (2) building strong relationships with suppliers, and (3) achieving efficient internal operations. Each of these approaches involves developing an asset—loyal customers, strong vendor relationships, committed effective human resources, efficient systems, and attractive locations—that is not easily duplicated by competitors. Three approaches for developing a sustainable competitive advantage are (1) building strong relationships with customers, (2) building strong relationships with suppliers, and (3) achieving efficient internal operations. To build an advantage that is sustainable for a long period of time, retailers typically cannot rely on a single approach, such as good locations or excellent customer service. Instead, they use multiple

approaches to build as high a wall around their position as possible.

LO3 Classify the different strategic growth opportunities retailers pursue.

Four types of growth opportunities that retailers may pursue are market penetration, market expansion, retail format development, and diversification. The success in pursuing these growth opportunities is the synergies between the retailer's present markets and the growth opportunity—whether the opportunity involves markets the retailer is presently pursuing or new markets—and the synergies between the retailer's present retail mix and the retail mix of the growth opportunity—whether the opportunity exploits the retailer's skills and knowledge in operating its present format or requires new capabilities to operate a new format.

LO4 Identify issues that arise as domestic retailers become global retailers.

By expanding internationally, retailers can increase their sales, leverage their knowledge and systems across a greater sales base, and gain more bargaining power with vendors. But international expansion is risky because retailers must deal with different government regulations, cultural traditions, consumer preferences, supply chains, and languages. The attractiveness of international opportunities is assessed by (1) the potential size of the retail market in the country, (2) the degree to which the country does and can support the entry of foreign retailers engaged in modern retail practices, and (3) the risks or uncertainties in sales and profits. The most attractive international markets are India, China, and Brazil.

152 SECTION II Retailing Strategy

LO5 **Know the steps retailers go through to develop a strategic plan.**

Strategic planning is an ongoing process. Every day, retailers audit their situations, examine consumer trends, study new technologies, and monitor competitive activities. But the retail strategy statement does not change every year or every six months; the strategy statement is reviewed and altered only when major changes in the retailer's environment or capabilities occur.

When a retailer undertakes a major reexamination of its strategy, the process for developing a new strategy statement may take a year or two.

Potential strategic directions are generated by people at all levels of the organization and then evaluated by senior executives and operating personnel to ensure that the eventual strategic direction is profitable in the long run and can be implemented.

The strategic planning process consists of a sequence of steps: (1) define the business mission, (2) conduct a SWOT analysis, (3) identify strategic opportunities, (4) evaluate the alternatives, (5) establish specific objectives and allocate resources, (6) develop a retail mix to implement the strategy, and (7) evaluate performance and make adjustments.

KEY TERMS

bargaining power of vendors, *148*

barriers to entry, *147*

competitive rivalry, *148*

cross-selling, *136*

customer loyalty, *127*

customer relationship management (CRM) program, *131*

direct investment, *144*

diversification growth opportunity, *136*

franchising, *144*

frequent shopper program, *131*

joint venture, *144*

loyalty program, *131*

market expansion growth opportunity, *136*

market penetration growth opportunity, *135*

mission statement, *145*

opportunities and threats analysis, *147*

own brand, *130*

perceptual map, *128*

positioning, *128*

private-label brand, *130*

related diversification growth opportunity, *137*

retail community, *131*

retail format, *124*

retail format development growth opportunity, *136*

retail market, *125*

retail strategy, *124*

scale economies, *147*

SWOT analysis, *146*

store brand, *130*

strategic alliance, *144*

strategic retail planning process, *144*

strengths and weaknesses analysis, *146*

sustainable competitive advantage, *124*

target market, *124*

unorganized retailing, *140*

unrelated diversification growth opportunity, *137*

vertical integration, *137*

GET OUT AND DO IT!

1. **CONTINUING CASE ASSIGNMENT** Prepare an analysis of the company you selected for the continuing assignment. Identify its direct competitors, its target market and positioning, its strategy with respect to its competitors, its retail format (the elements in its retail mix—merchandise variety and assortment, pricing, locations), and its bases for developing a competitive advantage relative to its competitors. Outline the retailer's strengths, weaknesses, opportunities, and threats relative to its competitors. Pick a specific country in which the firm does not operate, and make a recommendation about whether the retailer should enter the country and, if so, how it should do so.

2. **INTERNET EXERCISE** Visit the websites for IKEA (www.ikea.com) and Starbucks (www.starbucks.com). Are the look and feel of these Internet sites consistent with the in-store experience of these retailers?

3. **INTERNET EXERCISE** Go to the websites for Walmart (www.walmartstores.com), Carrefour

(www.carrefour.fr), Royal Ahold (www.ahold.com), and Metro AG (www.metro.de). Which chain has the most global strategy? Justify your answer.

4. **GO SHOPPING** Visit two stores that sell similar merchandise categories and cater to the same target segment(s). How are their retail formats (the elements in their retail mixes) similar? Dissimilar? On what bases do they have a sustainable competitive advantage? Explain which you believe has a stronger position.

5. **WEB OLC EXERCISE** Go to the student side of the book's website, and click on "Market Position Matrix." *Exercise 1:* This spreadsheet describes an analysis of international growth opportunities. What numbers in the matrices would have to change to make China and France more attractive opportunities? To make Brazil and Mexico less attractive opportunities? Change the numbers in the matrices, and see what effect this has on the overall position of the opportunity in the grid.

Exercise 2: The market attractiveness/competitive position matrix can also be used by a department store to evaluate its merchandise categories and determine how much it should invest in each category. Fill in the importance weights (10 = very important, 1 = not very important) and the evaluations of the merchandise categories (10 = excellent, 1 = poor), and then see what is recommended by the plot on the opportunity matrix.

Exercise 3: Think of another investment decision that a retailer might make, and analyze it using the strategic analysis matrix. List the alternatives and the characteristics of the alternatives, and then put in the importance weights for the characteristics (10 = very important, 1 = not very important) and the evaluation of each alternative on each characteristic (10 = excellent, 1 = poor).

DISCUSSION QUESTIONS AND PROBLEMS

1. For each of the four retailers discussed at the beginning of the chapter (Chipotle Mexican Grill, Lululemon, Chico's, and Save-A-Lot), describe its strategy and the basis of its competitive advantage.

2. Choose a retailer, and describe how it has developed a competitive strategic advantage.

3. Give an example of a market penetration, a retail format development, a market expansion, and a diversification growth strategy that Best Buy might use.

4. Choose your favorite retailer. Draw and explain a positioning map, like that shown in Exhibit 5–3, that includes your retailer, retailers that sell the same types of merchandise, and the target customer segments (ideal points).

5. Do a SWOT analysis for McDonald's. What is its mission? What are its strengths and weaknesses? What opportunities and environmental threats might it face over the next 10 years? How could it prepare for these threats?

6. What are Neiman Marcus's and PetSmart's bases for sustainable competitive advantage? Are they really sustainable, or are they easily copied?

7. Assume you are interested in opening a restaurant in your town. Go through the steps in the strategic planning process shown in Exhibit 5–7. Focus on conducting a SWOT analysis of the local restaurant market, identifying and evaluating alternatives, and selecting a target market and a retail mix for the restaurant.

8. The Gap owns several chains, including Old Navy, Banana Republic, Piperlime, and Athlcta. What type of growth opportunity was The Gap pursuing when it opened each of these retail concepts? Which is most synergistic with the original Gap chain?

9. Identify a store or service provider that you believe has an effective loyalty program. Explain why it is effective.

10. Choose a retailer that you believe could be, but is not yet, successful in other countries. Explain why you think it could be successful.

11. Amazon.com started as an Internet retailer selling books. Then it pursued a variety of growth opportunities, including expanding to groceries, DVDs, apparel, software, and travel services; introducing e-readers (Kindle); operating the Internet channel for other retailers; and hosting virtual stores for small, independent retailers. Evaluate these growth opportunities in terms of the probability that they will be profitable businesses for Amazon.com. What competitive advantages does Amazon.com bring to each of these businesses?

SUGGESTED READINGS

Aaker, David. *Strategic Market Management*, 6th ed. New York: Wiley, 2009.

Cao, Lanlan, and Marc Dupuis. "Strategy and Sustainable Competitive Advantage of International Retailers in China." *Journal of Asia-Pacific Business* 11, no. 1 (2010), pp. 6–27.

Cuthbertson, Christine, and Jonathan Reynolds. *Retail Strategy.* London: Routledge, 2012.

Etgar, M., and D. Rachman-Moore. "The Relationship between National Cultural Dimensions and Retail Format Strategies." *Journal of Retailing and Consumer Services* 18, no. 5 (2011), pp. 397–404.

Fox, Edward J., and Raj Sethuraman. "Retail Competition." In *Retailing in the 21st Century—Current and Future Trends,* 2nd ed., eds. Manfred Kraft and Murali Mantrala. Berlin: Springer, 2010, pp. 239–256.

Gamble, John E., Arthur A Thompson Jr., and Margaret Peteraf. *Essentials of Strategic Management: The Quest for Competitive Advantage,* 3rd ed. New York: McGraw-Hill, 2013.

Grewal, Dhruv, Ram Krishnan, Michael Levy, and Jeanne Mungar. "Retail Success and Key Drivers." In *Retailing in the 21st Century—Current and Future Trends,* 2nd ed., eds. Manfred Kraft and Murali Mantrala. Berlin: Springer, 2010, pp. 15–30.

Lehmann, Donald, and Russell Winer. *Analysis for Marketing Planning,* 8th ed. Burr Ridge, IL: McGraw-Hill/Irwin, 2010.

Ortinau, D. J., B. J. Babin and J. C. Chebat, "Retailing Evolution Research: Introduction to the Special Section on Retailing Research," *Journal of Business Research* 64, no. 6 (2011), pp. 541–542.

Rothaermel, Frank T. *Strategic Management: Concepts.* New York: McGraw-Hill, 2013.

Zentes, Joachim, Dirk Morschett, and Hanna Schramm-Klein. *Strategic Retail Management: Text And International Cases,* 2nd ed. Weisbaden: Springer, 2011.

Financial Strategy

EXECUTIVE BRIEFING

Ken Hicks, Chairman and CEO,
Foot Locker Inc.

After graduating from the U.S. Military Academy and serving six years as an artillery officer, I earned an MBA from Harvard Business School and went to work as a consultant for McKinsey. However, I realized that I wanted to develop and implement strategies, rather than just analyzing situations and making recommendations. Through my consulting experience, I recognized the exciting challenges and opportunities retailing had to offer and took a position in strategic planning for May Department Stores. Prior to becoming the chairman and CEO of Foot Locker, I had senior executive management positions at Home Shopping Network, Payless Shoes, and JCPenney.

My career path is a bit unusual for a retail executive. There aren't many jobs in the private sector for artillery officers. But, in the military, I learned how to motivate people and coordinate their activities to achieve an organization's goals, and I learned the importance of execution. These skills were particularly useful at Foot Locker when I became CEO in 1999. Foot Locker was not meeting the expectations of its customers, employees, and shareholders. Sales, comparable store sales, and earnings per share had declined significantly during the previous four years. To turn around this downward trend, the senior

management team and I developed a four-year plan that set goals and developed strategies for achieving those goals. The goals we set for 2013 were inventory turnover, 3.0; sales per square foot, $400; sales, $6 billion; net profit margin, 5 percent; and EBIT, 8 percent.

The key strategic change we made was clearly differentiating our five retail brands—Foot Locker, Footaction, Lady Foot Locker, Kids Foot Locker, and Champs Sports. The brands were operating as independent businesses, each trying to maximize their own profits and sales. Over time, the five brands lost their identities. They all offered similar assortments and stocked the most popular athletic shoes. Their stores had the same look and feel, and they competed vigorously against each other. We needed to turn the guns outward and develop a unique position for each brand, but still exploit the operational synergies among the five brands.

CHAPTER 6

LEARNING OBJECTIVES

LO1 Review the strategic objectives of a retail firm.

LO2 Contrast the two paths to financial performance using the strategic profit model.

LO3 Illustrate the use of the strategic profit model for analyzing growth opportunities.

LO4 Analyze the financial risks facing a retail firm.

LO5 Review the measures retailers use to assess their performance.

Our brands are like ice cream sundaes. They all have the same vanilla ice cream, but each specializes in different toppings for customers who like hot fudge or banana sundaes. For example, Champs focuses on customers engaged in team sports, Foot Locker on performance-oriented customers, and Footaction for fashionable shoes and apparel.

In 2011, we exceeded all of our goals two years into our four-year plan. So we adopted some more ambitious goals, which you can see at www.footlocker-inc.com/. In retailing, some performance measures are available daily or even hourly. But retailers need to balance their long-term goals with short-term measures. Foot Locker is now the leading global retailer of athletically inspired shoes and apparel. We operate more than 3,400 stores in 23 countries and have a successful Internet channel and social media program. We have more than 6 million Facebook fans and 65,000 Twitter followers.

Financial objectives and goals are an integral part of a retailer's market strategy. In Chapter 5, we examined how retailers develop their strategy and build a sustainable competitive advantage to generate a continuing stream of profits. In this chapter, we look at how financial analysis is used to assess the retailer's market strategy—to monitor the retailer's performance, assess the reasons its performance is above or below expectations, and provide insights into appropriate actions that can be taken if performance falls short of expectations.

For example, Kelly Bradford, the owner of Gifts To Go, whom we described in Chapter 5, needs to know how well she is doing because she wants to stay in business, be successful, increase the profitability of her company, and realize her goal of generating an annual income of $100,000. To assess her performance, she can add up the receipts at the end of each day. But this simple measure, sales, doesn't provide a complete assessment of how she is doing financially, and it may even be misleading. For instance, she might find that sales meet expectations and her accountant confirms that her business is profitable, but she doesn't have the cash to buy new merchandise or pay her employees. When this happens, Kelly needs to analyze her business to determine the cause of the problem and what can be done to overcome it.

In this chapter, we first review the types of objectives that retailers have. Then we introduce the strategic profit model and use it to discuss the two paths for achieving the desired financial performance. To illustrate the use of this model, we examine and compare the factors affecting the financial performance of Costco and Macy's, two very successful retailers with different retail strategies. Then we demonstrate how the model can be used to evaluate one of the growth opportunities Kelly Bradford is considering. In the last part of this chapter, we examine productivity measures that assess the performance of merchandise management and store operations decisions.

OBJECTIVES AND GOALS

LO1

Review the strategic objectives of a retail firm.

As we discussed in Chapter 5, the first step in the strategic planning process involves articulating the retailer's objectives and the scope of activities it plans to undertake. These objectives guide the development of the retailer's strategy and the specific performance goals the retailer plans to achieve. When the goals are not being achieved, the retailer knows that it must take corrective actions. Three types of objectives that a retailer might have are (1) financial, (2) societal, and (3) personal.

Financial Objectives

When assessing the financial performance of a firm, most people focus on profits: What were the retailer's profits or profit as a percentage of sales last year, and what will they be this year and into the future? But the appropriate financial performance measure is not profits but return on assets. **Return on assets (ROA)** is the profit generated by the assets possessed by the firm. A retailer might set a financial objective of making a profit of at least $1,000,000 a year, but the retailer really needs to consider the assets it needs to employ to make the desired $1,000,000. The retailer would be delighted if it made $1,000,000 and only needed $5,000,000 in assets (a 20 percent ROA) but would be disappointed if it had to use $40,000,000 in assets to make $1,000,000 profit (a 2.5 percent ROA).

Societal Objectives

Societal objectives are related to broader issues that make the world a better place to live. For example, retailers might be concerned about providing employment opportunities for people in a particular area or for minorities or for people with disabilities. Other societal objectives might include offering people unique merchandise, such as environmentally friendly products; providing an innovative service to improve personal health, such as weight reduction programs; or sponsoring community events. Retailing View 6.1 describes a retail entrepreneur offering shoes for poor families.

Compared with financial objectives, societal performance objectives are more difficult to measure. But explicit societal goals can be set, such as specific reductions in energy usage and excess packaging, increased use of renewable resources, and support for nonprofit organizations such as the United Way and Habitat for Humanity.

REFACT

In 1946, George Nelson Dayton, the son of Target Corporation's founder, established a standard of contributing 5 percent of the corporation's income to programs that serve the communities in which it has stores.[1]

Personal Objectives

Many retailers, particularly owners of small, independent businesses, have important personal objectives, including self-gratification, status, and respect. For example, the owner/operator of a bookstore may find it rewarding to interact with others who like reading and authors who visit the store for book-signing promotions. By operating a popular store, a retailer might become recognized as a well-respected business leader in the community.

While societal and personal objectives are important to some retailers, all retailers need to be concerned about financial objectives or they will fail. Therefore,

RETAILING VIEW   One for One to Achieve TOMS Shoes'
Societal Objectives   **6.1**

In 2006, after competing on the second season of *The Amazing Race*, Blake Mycoskie visited Argentina, where he was struck by the poverty—including the number of children walking around without shoes. Because the traditional Argentine alpargata shoe offers a simple, revolutionary solution for providing footwear, he set out to provide footwear for poor families by reinventing the alpargata for the U.S. market. To make the connection, Mycoskie committed to providing one new pair of shoes to a child living in poverty for every pair of shoes that consumers purchased from the One for One website. As he recounted, "I was so overwhelmed by the spirit of the South American people, especially those who had so little. And I was instantly struck with the desire—the responsibility—to do more."

The success of the initial idea pushed Mycoskie to move beyond just the Argentinean-styled classic alpargata shoes. Thus, TOMS today sells Cordones, for wear with or without laces; Botas, for both women and men; Stitchouts, which are only for men; Wedges and Wrap Boots for women; and of course, Youth and Tiny TOMS for children and toddlers. The social activist also decided that the company could increase the number of shoes provided to needy children by selling T-shirts, accessories, and hats—all of which spark the same one-to-one exchange.

This socially responsible business model appeals particularly to Millennial consumers in developed economies who want to be able to shop, socialize, and save the world, simultaneously. Wearing TOMS shoes is a

Achieving societal objectives is important to Blake Mycoskie, founder, CEO, and chief giving officer of TOMS shoes.

fashion statement that also provides a public proclamation of their own social responsibility. Through their social media networks, these TOMS afficionados, many of whom belong to the thousands of TOMS university clubs, affirm their love for TOMS and encourage others to join the movement. With annual sales estimated at greater than $100 million, by 2012, TOMS had provided more than 1 million pairs of new shoes to children in more than 25 countries—including the United States.

Sources: www.toms.com; Ricardo Lopez, "It's Doing Well by Doing Good," *Los Angeles Times*, January 25, 2012, p. B.1; and Gregory Ferenstein, "TOMS Shoes Generation Y Strategy," *Fast Company*, June 9, 2010.

DISCUSSION QUESTIONS

Does TOMS's socially responsible business model make you more likely to buy its shoes?

REFACT

Eighty percent of Millennials would be likely to switch to a brand associated with a good cause if product price and quality were comparable; 53 percent had purchased a product or service tied to a cause in the last year.[2]

the remaining sections of this chapter focus on financial objectives and the factors affecting a retailer's ability to achieve financial goals.

STRATEGIC PROFIT MODEL

LO2

Contrast the two paths to financial performance using the strategic profit model.

The **strategic profit model**, illustrated in Exhibit 6–1, is a method for summarizing the factors that affect a firm's financial performance, as measured by return on assets. Return on assets is an important performance measure for a firm and its stockholders because it measures the profits that a firm makes relative to the assets it possesses. Two retailers that each generate profits of $1 million, at first glance, might look like they have comparable performance. But the performance of the retailers looks quite different if one has $10 million in assets and the other has $25 million. The performance of the first would be higher because it needs fewer assets to earn its profit than does the other. Thus, a retailer cannot only concern itself with making a profit. It must make a profit efficiently by balancing both profit and the assets needed to make the profit.

The **operating profit margin**, also called **earnings before interest, taxes, and depreciation (EBITDA)**, is a measure of the profitability from continuing operations of a retailer and is a useful predictor of the retailer's profitability in the future. **Asset turnover** is the retailer's net sales divided by its assets. This financial measure assesses the productivity of a firm's investment in its assets. It indicates how many sales dollars are generated for each dollar of assets. Thus, if a retailer's asset turnover is 3.0, it generates $3 in sales for each dollar invested in the firm's assets.

The retailer's ROA is determined by multiplying the two components together:

$$\text{Operating profit margin percent} \times \text{Asset turnover} = \text{Return on assets (ROA)}$$

$$\frac{\text{Operating profit margin percent}}{\text{Net sales}} \times \frac{\text{Net sales}}{\text{Total assets}} = \frac{\text{Operating profit margin}}{\text{Total assets}}$$

The strategic profit model decomposes ROA into two components: (1) operating profit margin percentage and (2) asset turnover. These two components illustrate that ROA is determined by two sets of activities—profit margin management and asset turnover management—and that a high ROA can be achieved by various combinations of operating profit margins and asset turnover levels.

EXHIBIT 6–1
Strategic Profit Model

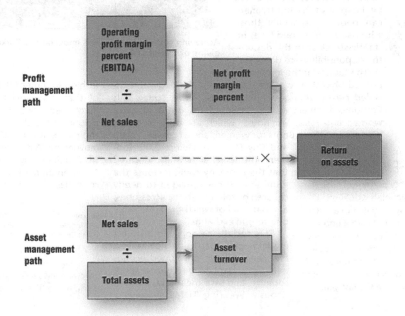

EXHIBIT 6–2
Different Approaches for Achieving an Acceptable ROA

	Net Profit Margin	×	Asset Turnover	=	Return on Assets
La Chatelaine Bakery	1%		10 times		10%
Lehring Jewelry	10%		1 time		10%

EXHIBIT 6–2
Different Approaches for Achieving an Acceptable ROA

To illustrate the different approaches for achieving a high ROA, consider the financial performance of two very different hypothetical retailers, as shown in Exhibit 6–2. La Chatelaine Bakery has a net operating profit margin percentage of only 1 percent and an asset turnover of 10, resulting in an ROA of 10 percent. Its operating profit margin percentage is low because it is in a highly competitive market with little opportunity to differentiate its offering. Consumers can buy basically the same baked goods from a wide variety of retailers, as well as from the other bakeries in the area. However, its asset turnover is relatively high because the firm has a very low level of inventory assets—it sells everything the same day it is baked.

On the other hand, Lehring Jewelry Store has a net operating profit margin percentage of 10 percent—10 times higher than that of the bakery. Even though it has a much higher operating profit margin percentage, the jewelry store has the same ROA because it has a very low asset turnover of 1. Lehring's asset turnover is low compared with the bakery's because Lehring has a high level of inventory and stocks a lot of items that take many months to sell.

In the following sections, we take a closer look at these two components of ROA. We examine the relationship between these ratios and a firm's retail strategy and describe how these financial measures can be used to assess performance with traditional accounting information. To illustrate the financial implications of different retail strategies, we compare the financial performance of Costco and Macy's. The retail strategies of these two retailers are described in Retailing View 6.2.

RETAILING VIEW   Macy's and Costco—Successful Retailers Using Different Retail Strategies

6.2

Costco (left) and Macy's (right) have very different retail strategies and financial performance measures. Costco focuses on the asset management path for achieving a high ROA, while Macy's focuses on the profit management path.

Costco

Costco pioneered the membership warehouse club format when it opened its first store in 1983. It is now the largest warehouse club chain, generating annual sales of $89 billion from its 433 locations in 40 states and Puerto Rico, as well as 162 stores in Canada, the United Kingdom, Korea, Taiwan, Japan, Australia, and Mexico. The member-oriented stores promises low prices on a limited range of around 4,000 branded and private-label products, across

(continued)

160   SECTION II   Retailing Strategy

a vast span of merchandise categories. In addition to commodity items, such as dairy products and toilet paper, the stores stock special, unique items that are always a surprise. The "treasure hunt" environment created by opportunistic buying gives the customer a sense of urgency to buy the item immediately. Some of these products with limited availability could be a four-carat diamond ring, a Louis Vuitton handbag, or a Versace china set. Costco is committed to delivering the customer a good value—low prices and high quality.

Costco's unusually high inventory turnover—combined with operating efficiencies achieved by volume purchasing, efficient distribution, and reduced handling of merchandise in no-frills, self-service warehouse facilities—enables it to operate profitably at significantly lower gross margins than traditional wholesalers, mass merchandisers, supermarkets, and supercenters. The small number of SKUs allows Costco's buyers to have a strong grasp on the movement and quality of the goods. In turn, its customers understand and appreciate its assortment better than they would if they were shopping at a supermarket or discount store that would carry many more SKUs.

Its private-labeled merchandise accounts for 20 percent of its sales. Costco is concentrating on growing its private-label, Kirkland Signature, products. It has a diverse selection of Kirkland-branded products ranging from wines and champagnes to bakery items. Its buyers make quality relationships with its vendors and can thus capitalize on a trend to develop products for the store. Many of its items are co-branded with manufacturers such as Hormel bacon, Stonyfield Farm's organic smoothies, Dannon's Activia, and Borghese upscale cosmetics. The co-branded products signal to customers that they are receiving a quality product from a trusted name at a value price.

Costco's target market is not limited to low-income customers who have to shop for the lowest prices. It has a loyal, upscale clientele who also enjoy bargains. The retailer marks products up no more than 14 percent, giving its customers true value, whether the product is a quart of ketchup or an LCD television.

Costco also is committed to carrying healthy products and being environmentally friendly. It ensures that the raw materials that are used in the products that it sells (e.g., cocoa, coffee, seafood, etc.) are all grown and produced in a fair and healthy way. It is also trying to cut down on the packaging used. The company evaluates its suppliers closely so it knows how everything is being processed. For example, Costco inspects a seafood supplier by meeting the boats when they come in to see how the products were being iced, how they are unloaded, and how they maintain the temperature from the dock to the plant. It is protocols such as this allow the company to maintain consistent quality.

Macy's

Macy's, established in 1858, is the Great American Department Store—an iconic retailing brand with more than 800 stores operating coast-to-coast and online at macys.com. It is the largest department store retailer in the United States with annual sales of more than $26 billion. Its typical store anchors an enclosed mall and includes 180,000 square feet of selling space stocking 50,000 SKUs.

Macy's primary target market is females between 25 and 54 years old who typically work outside the house, have children, and have an average family income of more than $75,000. Macy's has been particularly effective in developing private brands such as I.N.C., Charter Club, Club Room, Ideology, Jenna, Tasso Elba, Style & Co., JM Collection, Epic Threads, and First Impressions. Its store brands presently account for 20 percent of annual sales with exclusive, limited distribution brands accounting for an additional 23 percent of annual sales.

Three key strategic initiatives for Macy's are (1) My Macy's localization, (2) multichannel integration, and (3) MAGIC Selling. First, the localization initiative involves tailoring the merchandise assortment and shopping experience to the needs of the local market. Second, through multichannel integration, Macy's seeks to combine its store, Internet, and mobile operations, mainly to optimize its inventory offerings. An out-of-stock situation in a local store prompts sales associates to seek replacement merchandise from the online fulfillment centers and have the items shipped to the customer's home address; online fulfillment centers also can turn to store inventories to fill orders that originate online or through mobile devices. Third, "MAGIC Selling" refers to an acronym used in sales training that seeks to improve customers' shopping experiences: "Meet and make a connection; Ask questions and listen; Give options, give advice; Inspire to buy . . . and sell more; and Celebrate the purchase."

Together with these strategic initiatives, Macy's is experimenting with various new in-store and online technologies. For example, tablet computers located in departments throughout the store provide customers with additional information, give them the option of obtaining paperless receipts, engage them with QR code technology, link to a smartphone app with which customers can use their phones to "tap, pay, and save," and deliver special offers to them through social media (e.g., Foursquare, Shopkick, Google, Facebook).

REFACT

Macy's was the first retailer to promote a woman to an executive position and establish a fixed price for merchandise that was advertised in a newspaper. Its buyers designed and launched innovative products such as the tea bag, the Idaho baked potato, and colored bath towels.[3]

Sources: 2012 Macy's Factbook; 2011 Costco Annual Report; Karen Talley, "Three Stores, Three Scenes; Fortunes Diverge for Macy's, Penney and Kohl's," *The Wall Street Journal (Online)*, August 12, 2012; and Annie Gasparro and Timothy Martin, "What's Wrong With America's Supermarkets? Traditional Grocery Stores Are Caught in the Middle," *The Wall Street Journal (Online)*, July 12, 2012.

DISCUSSION QUESTION

What are the differences in the retailing mixes used by Costco and Macy's?

Profit Margin Management Path

The information used to examine the profit margin management path comes from the retailer's **income statement,** also called the **statement of operations.** The income statement summarizes a firm's financial performance over a period of time, typically a quarter (three months) or year. To capture all the sales, gift card purchases, and returns from the holiday season, Macy's, like many retailers, sets its fiscal year as beginning on February 1 and ending on January 31 of the following year. So its 2012 Annual Report actually focuses on 11 months in 2011 and 1 month in 2012. Costco's fiscal year begins on October 1, so most recent annual report includes 9 months in 2012 and 3 months in 2011.

Exhibit 6–3 shows income statements adapted from the annual reports of Macy's and Costco. The components in the profit margin management path portion of the strategic profit model are summarized for both retailers in Exhibit 6–4.

Components in the Profit Management Path   The four components in the profit margin management path are net sales, cost of goods sold (COGS), gross margin, and operating profit margin. **Net sales** are the total revenues received by a retailer that are related to selling merchandise during a given time period minus returns, discounts, and credits for damaged merchandise.

Sources of revenue that are not considered part of net sales are special charges to customers, membership fees, and credit card interest. For example, warehouse clubs generate revenue from annual membership fees, and retailers with frequent shopper programs may charge customers for enrolling in the program. Costco does not consider membership fees as part of its net sales because they reflect business activities unrelated to its primary activity of selling merchandise. Macy's has its own credit card on which it receives revenues from late payments, which are therefore also not part of net sales.

Some retailers have additional revenue sources related to merchandise sales, such as payments from vendors. For example, retailers often charge vendors for space in their stores known as a **slotting fee** or **slotting allowance.** Retailers may also require that vendors pay a fee, known as a **chargeback fee** when the merchandise bought from the vendor does not meet all the terms of the

	Costco Income Statement 2012	Macy's Income Statement 2012
Net sales	97,062	26,405
Membership fees	2,075	
Total revenue	99,137	26,405
Cost of goods sold (COGS)	(86,823)	(15,738)
Gross margin	12,314	10,667
Selling, general, and administrative (SG&A)	9,518	8,281
Operating profit	2,796	2,386
Other income (expenses)	(95)	25
Interest income	103	(447)
Provision for income tax		(712)
Net profit	2,720	1,252
g = + Gross margin percent	10.5%	40.4%
SG&A percent of sales	9.8%	31.4%
Operating profit percent	2.9%	9.0%
Net profit percent	2.8%	4.7%

EXHIBIT 6–3
Income Statements for Macy's and Costco

Sources: 10-K filings with the SEC.

purchase agreement, such as those regarding delivery. Such payments from vendors are typically incorporated into the income statement as a reduction in the COGS.

Cost of goods sold (COGS) is the amount a retailer pays to vendors for the merchandise the retailer sells. **Gross margin,** also called **gross profit,** is the net sales minus the cost of the goods sold. It is an important measure in retailing because it indicates how much profit the retailer is making on merchandise sold, without considering the expenses associated with operating the store and corporate overhead expenses.

$$\text{Gross margin} = \text{Net sales} - \text{Cost of goods sold}$$

Operating expenses include **selling, general, and administrative (SG&A) expenses.** SG&A expenses are overhead costs associated with normal business operations, such as salaries for sales associates and managers, advertising, utilities, office supplies, transportation from the retailer's warehouses to its stores, and rent.

Some retailers include other expenses, such as the cost of opening or closing stores and/or the cost of integrating an acquisition in their operations, as a part of their operating expenses. When estimating a retailer's operating expenses, one needs to decide whether these other expenses are related to the normal operations of the retailer or are extraordinary nonrecurring expenses that arise only during the year in which they are incurred. For example, the expenses for store openings might occur each year as a growing retailer opens new stores, while expenses related to an acquisition probably occur only in the specific year of the acquisition and may not reflect the operating income the retailer will realize in the future.

Operating profit margin, also called *earnings before interest, taxes, and depreciation (EBITDA)*, is the gross margin minus operating and extraordinary recurring expenses. Finally, **net profit margin** is the operating profit margin minus interest, taxes, and depreciation. We focus on the operating profit margin (EBITDA) because it reflects the performance of retailers' fundamental operations, not the financial decisions retailers make concerning depreciation of assets, taxes and capital structure (borrowing money versus selling stock to raise capital).

$$\text{Operating profit margin} = \text{Gross margin} - \text{Operating expenses} - \text{Extraordinary (recurring) operating expenses}$$

$$\text{Net profit margin} = \text{Operating profit margin} - \text{Extraordinary nonrecurring expenses} - \text{Interest} - \text{Taxes} - \text{Depreciation}$$

Analyzing Performance on the Profit Margin Management Path   The level of sales, gross margin, and operating profit in Exhibit 6–4 provide some useful information about the financial performance of the two retailers. However, it is difficult to compare the performance of the retailers when they differ in size. If Costco was interested in comparing its performance with Walmart, it would expect that Walmart would have a much greater gross margin and operating profit margin because it has five times greater sales than Costco. Thus, some of the differences in the income statement numbers will be due to differences in size, not in the performance of the retailers. Thus, it is useful to consider ratios with net sales in the denominator when evaluating a retailer's performance and comparing it to other retailers. Three useful ratios in the profit management path are gross margin percentage, operating profit margin percentage, and SG&A as a percentage of sales.

Gross margin percentage is gross margin divided by net sales. Retailers use this ratio to compare (1) the performance of various types of merchandise and

EXHIBIT 6–4
Profit Management
Path of Strategic Profit
Model

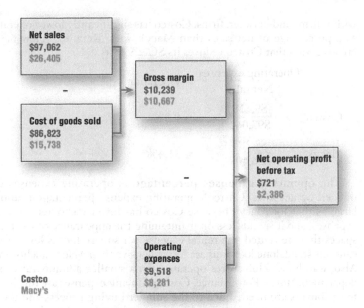

(2) their own performance with that of other retailers with higher or lower levels of sales.

$$\frac{\text{Gross margin}}{\text{Net sales}} = \text{Gross margin percent}$$

Costco: $\dfrac{\$12,314}{\$97,062}$ = 12.7%

Macy's: $\dfrac{\$10,667}{\$26,405}$ = 40.4%

Even though Costco has more than double the sales of Macy's, Macy's has a much higher gross margin percentage. This difference in gross margin percentage can be traced back to the retail strategies of the companies. Department stores generally have higher gross margin percentages than warehouse clubs because they target less-price-sensitive customers who are interested in branded fashion merchandise and personal service and are willing to pay for it. Warehouse club stores sell primarily staples, which are not as easy to differentiate as fashion apparel. That is, customers are more willing to pay a premium price for a high-fashion dress by a famous designer than for a 16-pack of kitchen towels or a quart of peanut butter. It is important for department stores to achieve a relatively high gross margin because their operating expenses are typically higher than those of some other retail formats.

Operating expenses are costs, other than the cost of merchandise, incurred in the normal course of doing business, such as salaries for sales associates and managers, advertising, utilities, office supplies, and rent. These costs are typically referred to as selling, general and administrative expenses (SG&A).

Neither Costco nor Macy's indicate other expenses or income besides the normal SG&A expenses, and all their overhead expenses are included in SG&A. However, retailers will often have other expenses. Macy's income statement shows expenses related to the acquisition of the May Company—income and expenses from inventory reevaluation, integration expenses and income from selling its **accounts receivable** (the money it is owed by customers who buy on credit), and expenses for opening new stores.

Like the gross margin, operating expenses are expressed as a percentage of net sales to facilitate comparisons across items, stores, and merchandise categories within firms and between firms. Costco has significantly lower operating expenses as a percentage of net sales than Macy's does. Retailing View 6.3 reviews the creative ways that Costco reduces its SG&A costs.

$$\frac{\text{Operating expenses}}{\text{Net sales}} = \text{Operating expenses \%}$$

$$\text{Costco:} \quad \frac{\$9,518}{\$97,062} = 9.8\%$$

$$\text{Macy's :} \quad \frac{\$8,281}{\$26,405} = 31.4\%$$

The **operating expenses percentage** is operating expenses (i.e., SG&A) divided by net sales. Costco's operating expense percentage is about a third as large as that for Macy's because Costco has lower customer service and selling expenses, and it spends less on maintaining the appearance of its stores. For store spaces that are rented, the rental expense per square foot is lower for Costco because its standalone locations are less expensive than Macy's anchor mall locations. Also, warehouse club stores operate with a smaller administrative staff than do department stores. For instance, Costco's buying expenses are much lower because fewer buyers are needed due to the simpler buying process and fewer SKUs for commodity-type merchandise, like packaged foods and fresh meat and produce,

6.3 RETAILING VIEW Cutting Costs at Costco

Costco's retail strategy focuses on offering its customer a good value—quality products at a reasonable price—on a wide merchandise assortment ranging from wheels of Parmesan cheese to 60-inch flat-screen TVs. Keeping prices low is challenging in light of increasing commodity prices, so Costco works with its vendors to control costs.

For example, Costco typically buys 70 percent of the large, premium macadamia nuts produced by Mauna Loa, a division of Hershey, leaving Mauna Loa with an inventory of small nuts. Costco buyers have worked with Mauna Loa to use smaller nuts in a new chocolate-nut cluster that will be sold exclusively at Costco. Because Mauna Loa won't have to face the uncertainty of selling those smaller nuts at a steep discount, it can afford to offer Costco better prices for its premium nuts.

Simple packaging changes can result in cost savings. For example, packaging cashews into square containers instead of traditional round ones enables Costco to increase the number of units it can stack on a pallet from 280 to 426. This relatively minor change to a product selling $100 million a year decreases the number of pallets shipped annually by 24,000 and decreases the number of truck trips by 600.

However, Costco does not scrimp on its employees. Eighty-six percent of its employees get health care and other benefits, even though half of its employees are part-timers. The average compensation of store employees is $20 an hour, more than 50 percent higher than the industry average. No Costco employees were laid off as a result of the recent recession. Costco believes that treating its employees well actually reduces labor costs in the long run. Its employee turnover is only 13 percent, among the lowest in the retail industry.

Changing this jar of nuts from a round shape to a square shape made a significant reduction in Costco's SG&A.

Sources: Zeynep Ton, "Why 'Good Jobs' Are Good for Retailers," *Harvard Business Review,* January–February 2012; Christopher Matthews, "Future of Retail: Companies That Profit by Investing in Employees," *Time,* June 18, 2012; and "Costco's Artful Discounts," *Business Week,* October 20, 2008.

DISCUSSION QUESTION

What are advantages and disadvantages of paying employees more than they can earn at comparable firms?

compared with fashion apparel. Finally, its buyers don't have to travel to fashion markets around the world like department store buyers do.

Like the gross margin and operating expenses, operating profit is often expressed as a percentage of net sales to facilitate comparisons across items, merchandise categories, and departments within and between firms. **Operating income percentage** is gross margin minus operating expenses divided by net sales.

$$\frac{\text{Gross margin} - \text{Operating expenses}}{\text{Net sales}} = \text{Operating income \%}$$

Costco: $\dfrac{\$12,314 - \$9,518}{\$97,062} = 2.9\%$

Macy's: $\dfrac{\$10,667 - \$8,281}{\$26,405} = 9.0\%$

Macy's operating profit margin percentage is more than three times greater than Costco's. Thus, this component of the strategic profit model suggests that Macy's is outperforming Costco. But the following discussion of the asset management path tells a different story.

Asset Management Path

The information used to analyze a retailer's asset management path primarily comes from the retailer's balance sheet. While the income statement summarizes financial performance over a period of time (usually a year or quarter), the balance sheet summarizes a retailer's financial position at a given point in time, typically the end of its fiscal year. Costco's and Macy's balance sheets are shown in Exhibit 6–5, and the asset management path components in the strategic profit model are shown in Exhibit 6–6.

Components in the Asset Management Path   **Assets** are economic resources (e.g., inventory, buildings, computers, store fixtures) owned or controlled by a firm. There are two types of assets, current and fixed.

Current assets are assets that can normally be converted to cash within one year. For retailers, current assets are primarily cash, accounts receivable, and merchandise inventory.

Current assets = Cash + Accounts receivable + Merchandise inventory + Other current assets

	Costco	Macy's
Cash and cash equivalents	4,009	2,827
Short-term investments	1,604	
Accounts receivable	965	368
Merchandise inventory	6,638	5,117
Other current assets	490	465
Total current assets	13,706	8,777
Property and equipment (net)	12,432	8,400
Other assets	623	4,918
Total assets	26,761	22,095
Current liabilities	12,050	6,263
Long-term debt	1,253	6,655
Other liabilities	885	2,344
Total liabilities	14,188	15,262
Stockholder equity	12,573	6,833

EXHIBIT 6–5
Balance Sheet for Macy's and Costco

Sources: 10-K reports filed with the SEC.

EXHIBIT 6–6
Asset Management
Path in Strategic
Profit Model

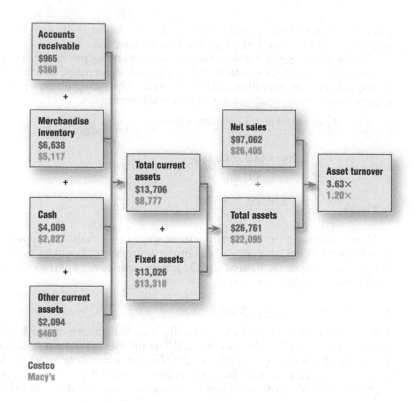

Costco
Macy's

Merchandise inventory is a critical retailer asset that provides benefits to customers. It enables customers to get the right merchandise at the right time and place. Stocking more merchandise increases sales because it increases the chances that customers will find something they want. But increasing the level of inventory also increases the amount that retailers need to invest in this asset.

Inventory turnover, which measures how effectively retailers utilize their investment in inventory, is another important ratio for assessing retail performance. **Inventory turnover** is COGS during a time period, typically a year, divided by the average level of inventory (expressed at cost) during the time period. A surrogate measure for average inventory is the inventory value at the end of the fiscal year reported on the balance sheet. Note that the inventory level reported on the balance sheet is the level on the last day of the fiscal year, not the average level. To measure the average inventory level more accurately, you would have to measure the level on each day of the year and divide by 365 or each month (see Chapter 12).

$$\frac{\text{COGS}}{\text{Average inventory at cost}} = \text{Inventory turnover}$$

$$\text{Costco:} \quad \frac{\$86,823}{6,638} = 13.08$$

$$\text{Macy's:} \quad \frac{\$15,738}{5,117} = 3.08$$

Inventory turnover is a measure of the productivity of inventory. It shows how many times, on average, inventory cycles through the store during a specific period of time (usually a year). Costco's higher inventory turnover is expected due to the nature of its retail strategy and the merchandise it sells. That is, most items in Costco are commodities and staples such as food, batteries, housewares, and basic apparel items. Unlike apparel fashions that are the mainstay for department stores like Macy's, these staples can be replenished quickly. Costco stores typically have only 4,000 SKUs in total; for example, it may only offer one brand of ketchup in two different sizes, which represents two inventory items. Department stores, on the other hand, usually stock more than 100,000 SKUs. This store format may stock 500 SKUs of just men's dress shirts (different colors, sizes, styles, and brands). Larger assortments, like those in department stores, require relatively higher inventory investments, which slows inventory turnover.

Fixed assets are assets that require more than a year to convert to cash. In retailing, the principal fixed assets are buildings (if store property is owned by the retailer rather than leased), distribution centers, fixtures (e.g., display racks), and equipment (e.g., computers, delivery trucks).

Asset turnover is net sales divided by total assets. It is a measure assessing the performance of the asset management component in the strategic profit model.

$$\frac{\text{Net sales}}{\text{Total assets}} = \text{Asset turnover}$$

$$\text{Costco:} \quad \frac{97,062}{26,761} = 3.63$$

$$\text{Macy's:} \quad \frac{26,405}{22,095} = 1.20$$

Intangible Assets   Notice that the balance sheet does not include most of the critical assets used by retailers to develop a sustainable competitive advantage (discussed in Chapter 5) such as brand image, customer loyalty, customer service, information and supply chain systems, human resources (committed, knowledgeable employees), and a database of customer buying behaviors and preferences. Due to accounting rules, the balance sheet includes only tangible assets for which there is an objective measure of value. For example, the value of a building is based on the amount the firm paid for the asset, less depreciation, not what it is worth at the end of the fiscal year.

The assets discussed in Chapter 5 are largely intangible. They cannot be objectively measured and thus are not included in the balance sheet assets. However, these intangible assets are important in generating long-term financial performance. As discussed in Retailing View 6.4, private equity firms are making significant investments in retail firms because of these intangible assets and other characteristics of the retail industry.

Analyzing the Performance of the Asset Management Path   Costco's asset turnover is more than two times greater than that of Macy's. The difference in their asset turnovers is largely due to Costco's higher inventory turnover. Typically, retailers like Costco that sell a limited assortment of commodity-type products have a higher inventory turnover than fashion apparel sold by retailers like Macy's. The sales of commodity-type products are easier to forecast accurately and thus makes it easier to control inventory levels.

Combining the Profit and Asset Management Paths

In terms of the profit management path, Macy's has a higher operating profit margin and thus performs better than Costco. But Costco has a higher asset turnover than Macy's and thus performs better on the asset management path. Although this type of performance is expected, given their overall strategy and retail formats, both retailers strive to increase their performance on these key ratios. For example, department stores like Macy's develop supply chains and buying systems that allow less merchandise to be delivered more often—more closely matching supply and demand. This lowers average inventory and, in turn, total assets, while at the same time may actually increase sales, resulting in higher inventory and asset turnovers. Warehouse club stores like Costco attempt to increase their gross margins by carrying more fresh produce, meat, and prepared foods. To further increase its margins, Costco in particular creates a treasure hunt environment by offering branded apparel and jewelry.

6.4   RETAILING VIEW   Private Equity Firms Invest in Retailers

Private equity firms make investments in retail chains such as Krispy Kreme and Neiman Marcus because retail firms typically have a high cash flow and intangible assets.

Private equity firms such as Bain Capital, the Blackstone Group, and Texas Pacific have made substantial investments in retail firms. For example, KKR teamed with several other private equity firms to buy Toys "R" Us for $6.6 billion. Some other major retailers owned by private equity firms are Neiman Marcus, Burger King, Container Store, Dollar General, Domino's, Gymboree, Hilton Hotels, Krispy Kreme, Michaels, and Sports Authority.

Rather than buying stock in companies, private equity firms buy the entire company from its stockholders, improve the efficiency of the firm (often by hiring new senior managers), and/or simply restructure the firm's financial structure, and then sell shares in the acquired company several years later. Because shares for the acquired company after the acquisition are not traded on the stock exchange, the company can take a long-term perspective toward improving the firm's operations; that is, it does not have to justify its investments to stockholders or issue the quarterly reports required by the Securities and Exchange Commission (SEC).

Private equity firms find retailers attractive investments because many of them have strong cash flows, little debt, and undervalued assets and respond quickly to efficiency improvements and changes in strategic direction. Undervalued assets include well-known store brands, leases for space in attractive locations, or the land on which their stores are located. A private equity company can sell these assets after it acquires a retailer or use the assets as collateral to get loans to finance the acquisition. For example, a private equity firm might sell the rights to use a well-known store brand like Sears' Kenmore appliances, Craftsman tools, and DieHard batteries to another company that would license the brand to other firms.

Often, private equity owners split the retail chain into an operating company that operates the stores and a property company that owns all of the chain's real estate assets. Proceeds from the sale of the real estate assets are used to repay the private equity owners for their initial investment, guaranteeing that the private equity partners will prosper regardless of whether the retail chain is successful. For example, Cerberus Capital Management LP and a group of private equity investors bought the Mervyn's chain of discount department stores from Target Corp. for $1.25 billion. The investor group structured the buyout as two separate purchases—one for the retail operations and one for the chain's valuable real-estate holdings. It earned more than $250 million in fees for managing the real estate transactions. But the retail operation was liquidated because of poor performance, eventually closing 177 stores, cutting the jobs of 18,000 employees.

Sources: Karen Talley, "Sears to License Names of Kenmore, Craftsman Brands," *The Wall Street Journal*, April 5, 2012; Dan McCrum and Stanley Pignal, "New KKR Funds to Target Retail Investors," *FT.com*, July 19, 2012; Eileen Appelbaum and Rosemary Batt, *A Primer on Private Equity at Work: Management, Employment, and Sustainability* (Washington, DC: Center for Economic and Policy Research, February 2012); Elaine Misonzhnik, "Private Equity Firms Are Hungry for Retailers, But Only the Best of Them," *Retailtraffic.com*, September 27, 2012; and Peg Brickley, "Mervyns Creditors Are Offered a Deal," *The Wall Street Journal*, October 26, 2012.

DISCUSSION QUESTION

What are the benefits to a retailer of being owned by a private equity firm?

Strategic Profit Model Ratio for Selected Retailers   **EXHIBIT 6–7**

	Sales	Operating Profit	Total Assets	Operating Profit Percentage	Asset Turnover	ROA (Operating Profit)
Department Stores						
JCPenney	17,260	1,109	11,424	6.4%	1.51	9.7%
Kohl's	18,804	2,936	14,094	15.6%	1.33	20.8%
Macy's	26,405	2,386	22,095	9.0%	1.20	10.8%
Discount Stores						
Costco	87,048	2,494	27,261	2.9%	3.19	9.1%
Walmart	443,854	26,558	193,406	6.0%	2.29	13.7%
Target	65,786	6,592	43,705	10.0%	1.51	15.1%
Specialty—Appparel						
The Gap	14,549	1,438	7,422	9.9%	1.96	19.4%
Abercrombie & Fitch	4,158	194	1,489	4.7%	2.79	13.0%
American Eagle Outfitter	3,160	393	3,048	12.4%	1.04	12.9%
Specialty—Category						
Home Depot	70,395	8,234	40,518	11.7%	1.74	20.3%
Lowe's	50,208	4,757	33,559	9.5%	1.50	14.2%
Best Buy	50,705	2,331	16,005	4.6%	3.17	14.6%
Office Depot	11,489	34	4,250	0.3%	2.70	0.8%
Staples	25,022	1,693	13,430	6.8%	1.86	12.6%
Supermarket						
Kroger	90,347	410	23,478	0.5%	3.85	1.7%
Safeway	43,630	1,134	15,074	2.6%	2.89	7.5%

Sources: SEC 10-K filings.

The two retailers' overall performance, as measured by ROA, is determined by considering the effects of both paths, that is, by multiplying the net profit margin by asset turnover:

	Asset turnover	×	Profit operating margin percent	=	Return on assets
Costco:	3.63	×	2.9%	=	10.5%
Macy's:	1.20	×	9.0%	=	10.8%

Exhibit 6–7 shows the strategic profit model ratios for a variety of retailers. The exhibit illustrates that supermarket and discount chains typically have higher asset turnovers and lower operating profit margin percentages. The apparel specialty retailers have lower asset turnovers and higher net profit margin percentages.

These differences in asset turnover and operating profit margin arise because the needs and buying behavior of customers patronizing these retailers differ, and thus, retailers targeting these customers use different approaches. Discount stores and supermarkets target more price-sensitive consumers, and they need to keep prices low. In addition, the products offered by supermarkets and discount stores are more commodity-like and face intense price competition. Thus, their profit margins are lower and they have to have higher asset turnover to provide an adequate ROA. On the other hand, specialty apparel and department stores are patronized by less-price-sensitive consumers who are looking for more customer service and deeper assortments. To satisfy these needs, inventory levels and turnover, administrative expenses, and margins are higher.

Implications for Improving Financial Performance

The profit management and asset management paths in the strategic profit model suggest different approaches for improving financial performance. Focusing on the profit management path, the operating profit margin could be increased by increasing sales or reducing COGS or operating expenses. For example, Costco could increase its sales by increasing advertising to attract more customers. The increase in sales will have a positive effect on Costco's operating profit margin percentage and its ROA as long as the increase in advertising expense generates more gross margin dollars than the advertising costs. In addition, the increase in sales will increase Costco's asset turnover because sales will increase but assets will remain the same. The net effect will have a positive impact on ROA.

Looking at the asset management path, Macy's could increase its asset turnover by decreasing the amount of inventory in its stores. However, decreasing the level of inventory could actually decrease sales because customers might not find the product they want to buy, causing them to shop elsewhere. If they tell their friends, post negative online reviews, or use social media like Twitter to voice their discontent, the lack of salable inventory could have a cascading deleterious impact on sales and profits.

The strategic profit model illustrates two important issues. First, retailers and investors should consider both operating and net profit margin and asset turnover when evaluating their financial performance. Firms can achieve high performance (high ROA) by effectively managing both profit margin and asset turnover. Second, retailers need to consider the implications of their strategic decisions on both components of the strategic profit model. For example, increasing prices might increase the gross margin and operating profit margin in the profit margin management path. However, increasing prices could also result in fewer sales, thereby having a negative impact on both gross margin and net operating profit margin. At the same time, assuming the level of assets stays the same, asset turnover will decrease. Thus, a simple change in one strategic variable, such as pricing, has multiple repercussions on the strategic profit model, all of which need to be considered when determining the impact on ROA.

EVALUATING GROWTH OPPORTUNITIES

LO3

Illustrate the use of the strategic profit model for analyzing growth opportunities.

To illustrate the use of the strategic profit model for evaluating a growth opportunity, let's look at the opportunity that Kelly Bradford, from Chapter 5, is considering. Recall that Kelly Bradford owns Gifts To Go, a two-store chain in the Chicago area. She's considering several growth options, one of which is to open an Internet channel called www.Gifts-To-Go.com. She has determined that the market size for this channel is large but very competitive. Now she needs to conduct a financial analysis for the proposed online channel, compare the projections with Gifts To Go stores, and determine the financial performance of the combined businesses. We'll first look at the profit margin management path, followed by the asset turnover management path. Exhibit 6–8 shows income statement information for Kelly's Gifts To Go stores, her estimates for Gifts-To-Go.com, and the combined businesses.

Profit Margin Management Path

Kelly thinks she can develop Gifts-To-Go.com into a business that will generate annual sales of $440,000. She anticipates some cannibalization of her store sales by the Internet channel; some customers who would have bought merchandise at Gifts To Go will no longer go into her stores to make their purchases. She also thinks the Internet channel will stimulate some store sales; customers who see gift items on her website will visit the stores and make their purchases there. Thus, she decides to perform the analysis with the assumption that her store sales will remain the same after the introduction of the Internet channel.

Gross Margin Percentage   Kelly plans to charge the same prices and sell basically the same merchandise, with an extended assortment, on Gifts-To-Go.com as

	Gifts To Go Stores	Gifts-To-Go.com (Projected)	Businesses Combined
Income Statement			
Net sales	$700,000	$440,000	$1,140,000
Less: Cost of goods sold	350,000	220,000	570,000
Gross margin	350,000	220,000	570,000
Less: Operating expenses (SG&A)	250,000	150,000	400,000
Net operating profit before tax and interest	100,000	70,000	170,000
Less: Taxes	32,200	24,500	56,700
Less: Interest	8,000	0	8,000
Net profit after taxes	24,200	24,500	48,700
Gross margin %	50%	50%	50%
Operating expenses %	36%	34%	35%
Net operating profit %	14%	16%	15%
Net operating income %	3%	6%	4%

EXHIBIT 6–8
Income Statement Information of Analysis of Gifts To Go Growth Opportunities

in her stores. Thus, she expects the gross margin percentage for store sales will be the same as the gross margin percentage for Gifts-To-Go.com sales.

$$\frac{\text{Gross margin}}{\text{Net sales}} = \text{Gross margin \%}$$

Stores: $\dfrac{350,000}{\$700,000} = 50\%$

Gifts-To-Go.com: $\dfrac{220,000}{\$440,000} = 50\%$

Operating Expenses   Initially, Kelly thought that her operating expenses as a percentage of sales would be lower for Gifts-To-Go.com because she would not need to pay rent or have highly trained salespeople. But she discovered that her operating expenses as a percentage of sales will be only slightly lower for Gifts-To-Go.com because she needs to hire a firm to maintain the website, process orders, and get orders ready for shipment. Also, Gifts To Go stores have an established clientele and highly trafficked locations with good visibility. Although some of her current customers will learn about the website from her in-store promotions, Kelly will have to invest in advertising and promotions to create awareness for her new channel and inform people who are unfamiliar with her stores.

Net Profit Margin   Because the gross margin and operating expenses as a percentage of sales for the two operations are projected to be about the same, Gifts-To-Go.com is expected to generate a slightly higher net profit margin percentage:

$$\frac{\text{Net profit}}{\text{Net sales}} = \text{Net profit \%}$$

Stores: $\dfrac{\$100,000}{\$700,000} = 14.3\%$

Gifts-To-Go.com: $\dfrac{70,000}{\$440,000} = 15.9\%$

Asset Turnover Management Path

Now let's compare the two operations using the asset turnover management path with the balance sheet information in Exhibit 6–9. Because the percentage of credit card sales is higher over the Internet channel than in stores, Kelly expects that the accounts receivable will be higher for the Internet channel than for the store channel.

EXHIBIT 6–9
Balance Sheet
Information of Analysis
of Gifts To Go Growth
Opportunities

	Gifts To Go Stores	Gifts-To-Go.com (Projected)	Businesses Combined
Accounts receivable	$140,000	$120,000	$260,000
Merchandise inventory	175,000	70,000	245,000
Cash	35,000	11,000	46,000
Total current assets	350,000	201,000	551,000
Fixed assets	30,000	10,000	40,000
Total assets	380,000	211,000	591,000
Ratios			
Inventory turnover	2.00	3.1	2.3
Asset turnover	1.84	2.09	1.93
ROA (%)	25.29%	33.25%	28.77%

Kelly estimates that Gifts-To-Go.com will have a higher inventory turnover than Gifts To Go stores because it will consolidate the inventory at one centralized distribution center that serves a large sales volume, as opposed to Gifts to Go, which has inventory sitting in several stores with relatively lower sales volumes. Additionally, Gifts-To-Go.com will have relationships with several of its vendors in which they "drop ship," or send merchandise directly from the vendor to the customer. In these situations, Gifts-to-Go.com has no inventory investment.

$$\frac{\text{Cost of goods}}{\text{Average inventory}} = \text{Inventory turnover}$$

Stores: $\dfrac{350,000}{\$175,000} = 2.0$

Gifts-To-Go.com: $\dfrac{220,000}{\$70,000} = 3.1$

Gifts To Go's store space is rented. Thus, Kelly's fixed assets consist of the fixtures, lighting, and other leasehold improvements for her stores, as well as equipment such as point-of-sale terminals. Kelly also has invested in assets that make her stores aesthetically pleasing. Gifts-To-Go.com is outsourcing the fulfillment of orders placed on its website, so it has no warehouse assets. Thus, its fixed assets are its website and order-processing computer system.

As she expects, Gifts-To-Go.com's projected asset turnover is higher than that of Gifts To Go's stores because Kelly estimates that Gifts-To-Go.com will have a higher inventory turnover, and its other assets are lower.

$$\frac{\text{Net sales}}{\text{Total assets}} = \text{Asset turnover}$$

Stores: $\dfrac{700,000}{\$380,000} = 1.84$

Gifts-To-Go.com: $\dfrac{440,000}{\$211,000} = 2.09$

Because Kelly's estimates for the net profit margin and asset turnover for Gifts-To-Go.com are higher than those for her stores, Gifts-To-Go.com achieves a higher ROA. Thus, this strategic profit model analysis indicates that Gifts-To-Go.com is a financially viable growth opportunity for Kelly.

	Net profit margin	×	Asset turnover	=	Return on assets
Stores:	14.29%	×	1.84	=	26.29%
Gifts-To-Go.com:	15.91%	×	2.09	=	33.25%

Using the Strategic Profit Model to Analyze Other Decisions

Another investment that Kelly might consider is installing a computerized inventory control system that would help her make better decisions about which merchandise to order, when to reorder merchandise, and when to lower prices on merchandise that is not being bought.

If she buys the system, her sales will increase because she will have a greater percentage of merchandise that is selling well and fewer stockouts. Her gross margin percentage will also increase because she won't have to mark down as much slow-selling merchandise.

Looking at the asset turnover management path, the purchase of the computer system will increase her fixed assets by the amount of the system, but her inventory turnover will increase and the level of inventory assets will decrease because she is able to buy more efficiently. Thus, her asset turnover will probably increase because sales will increase at a greater percentage than will total assets. Total assets may actually decrease if the additional cost of the inventory system is less than the reduction in inventory.

ANALYSIS OF FINANCIAL RISK

LO4

Analyze the financial risks facing a retail firm.

The previous sections have illustrated how the strategic profit model can be used to analyze the factors affecting some key retail performance ratios—operating profit margin percentage and asset turnover. The model provides insights into how retailers can improve their performance. However, retailing is a highly competitive industry, and thus major bankruptcies are common. Exhibit 6–10 lists some retailers of significant size that have filed for bankruptcy protection since 2000. Retailers, vendors, and investors need to assess the financial strength of a firm. Specifically, what are the chances that the retailer will continue to operate or will go bankrupt? In this section, we discuss measures used to assess the financial risk of retailers—the probability that they will go bankrupt. These measures include cash flow, debt-to-equity ratio, quick ratio, and current ratio.

Cash Flow Analysis

You might think that a retailer's profits determine its financial strength. If a retailer is profitable, there is little chance it will go bankrupt; but if it incurs losses for an extended period of time, the chances of its going bankrupt are significant. However, retailers can be forced to declare bankruptcy even when they show a profit

	Filing Year	Assets ($ billions)
Kmart	2002	14.60
Circuit City	2008	3.76
Montgomery Ward	2000	3.49
A&P	2010	2.53
Ames Department Stores	2001	2.00
Spiegel	2003	1.89
U.S. Office Products	2001	1.75
Linens 'n' Things	2008	1.74
Heilig-Meyers	2000	1.46
Borders	2011	1.28
Blockbuster	2010	1.02

EXHIBIT 6–10
Largest U.S. Retail Bankruptcies since 2000

Source: "FACTBOX—Largest U.S. Retailer Bankruptcies since 2000," *Reuters*, February 16, 2011.

on their income statements. Retailers become insolvent and declare bankruptcy when they do not have the cash needed to meet their obligations—when they cannot pay their employees, their landlords (rent), and/or their vendors.

Profits are not the same as cash flow. For example, a retailer might borrow money from a bank. The loan appears as a liability on its balance sheet. The interest on the loan, a relatively small percentage of the loan value, appears as an interest expense on the retailer's income statement and reduces the retailer's profits slightly. However, when the retailer is required to pay back the loan to the bank, the retailer must have a significant amount of cash available to pay for the entire amount of the loan.

Retailers have cash coming in from the sales of merchandise, and they use this cash to pay vendors, employees, developers, utilities, and the like. The amount of cash coming into the business, and when it comes into the business, is crucial because the availability of cash allows retailers to continue operating in the longer term.

The cash receipts and expenditures tend to be fairly stable. Employee salaries, vendor invoices, and rent, for example, are paid monthly or weekly. Sometimes, however, retailers face radical changes in the flow of cash. During the holiday season, for instance, retailers have to buy and pay for more merchandise to support the higher-than-normal level of sales. One measure of financial strength is cash flow. In addition to providing a balance sheet and income statement, firms also provide a **cash flow statement** as another indicator of the financial strength of the firm.

Debt-to-Equity Ratio

The **debt-to-equity ratio** is the retailer's short- and long-term debt divided by the value of the owners' or stockholders' equity in the firm. Owners' equity is the difference after subtracting all liabilities from assets. **Liabilities** are a company's debts, such as its accounts payable, which is the money it owes its vendors for merchandise. Owners' equity is the owners' (or stockholders') investment in the business. The debt-to-equity ratio measures how much money a company can safely borrow over long periods of time. A high ratio means the retailer faces greater risk and more potential for bankruptcy. Generally, when retailers that have a debt-to-equity ratio of more than 40 to 50 percent, they face significant risk of financial problems.

Current Ratio

The current ratio is probably the best-known and most often used measure of financial strength. The **current ratio** is short-term assets divided by short-term liabilities. It evaluates the retailer's ability to pay its short-term debt obligations, such as accounts payable (payments to suppliers) and short-term loans payable to a bank, with short-term assets such as cash, accounts receivable, and inventory.

Quick Ratio

The **quick ratio,** sometimes called the **acid-test ratio,** is short-term assets less inventory divided by short-term liabilities. It is a more stringent test of financial strength than the current ratio because it removes inventory from the short-term assets. Inventory is the short-term asset that takes the longest to convert into cash. Thus, if a retailer needs cash to pay its short-term liabilities, it cannot rely on inventory to provide an immediate source for cash.

The financial strength measures for Costco and Macy's are shown in Exhibit 6–11. These measures of financial strength indicate that Costco and Macy's are in relatively strong financial positions. Both have a significant positive cash flow. Macy's has a higher debt-to-equity ratio but strong current and quick ratios.

	Costco 8/29/2011	Macy's 1/30/2012
Net profit ($ billions)	16.1	1.25
Cash flow ($ billions)	530	1.36
Debt-to-equity	.10	.97
Current ratio	1.51	2.01
Quick ratio	1.14	1.40

EXHIBIT 6–11
Financial Risk
Measures for Costco
and Macy's

Source: Calculations from financial statements in 10-K reports filed with SEC.

SETTING AND MEASURING PERFORMANCE OBJECTIVES

LO5

Review the measures
retailers use to assess their
performance.

In the previous sections, we discussed the measures used to evaluate the overall financial performance of a retailer—ROA and its components, as well as measures for determining its financial risk. In this section, we review some measures used to assess the performance of specific assets possessed by a retailer—its employees, real estate, and merchandise inventory. Retailers use these measures to evaluate the firm's performance and set objectives.

Setting performance objectives is a necessary component of any firm's strategic management process. Performance objectives should include (1) a numerical index of the performance desired against which progress may be measured, (2) a time frame within which the objective is to be achieved, and (3) the resources needed to achieve the objective. For example, "earning reasonable profits" isn't a good objective. It doesn't provide specific goals that can be used to evaluate performance. What's reasonable? When do you want to realize the profits? A better objective would be "earning $100,000 in profit during calendar year 2014 on a $500,000 investment in inventory and building."

Top-Down versus Bottom-Up Process

Setting objectives in large retail organizations entails a combination of the top-down and bottom-up approaches to planning. **Top-down planning** means that goals get set at the top of the organization and are passed down to the lower operating levels. In a retailing organization, top-down planning involves corporate officers developing an overall retail strategy and assessing broad economic, competitive, and consumer trends. With this information, they develop performance objectives for the corporation. These overall objectives are then broken down into specific objectives for each buyer and merchandise category and for each region, store, and even department within stores and the sales associates working in those departments.

The overall strategy determines the merchandise variety, assortment, and product availability, plus the store size, location, and level of customer service. Then the merchandise vice presidents decide which types of merchandise are expected to grow, stay the same, or shrink. Next, performance goals are established for each buyer and merchandise manager. This process is reviewed in Chapter 12.

Similarly, regional store vice presidents translate the company's performance objectives into objectives for each district manager, who then develops objectives with the store managers. The process then trickles down to department managers in the stores and individual sales associates. The process of setting objectives for sales associates in stores is discussed in Chapter 16.

This top-down planning is complemented by a bottom-up planning approach. **Bottom-up planning** involves lower levels in the company developing performance objectives that are aggregated up to develop overall company objectives. Buyers and store managers estimate what they can achieve, and their estimates are transmitted up the organization to the corporate executives.

Frequently there are disagreements between the goals that have trickled down from the top and those set by lower-level employees of the organization. For example, a store manager may not be able to achieve the 10 percent sales growth set for his or her region because a major employer in the area has announced plans to lay off 2,000 employees. The differences between bottom-up and top-down plans are resolved through a negotiation process involving corporate executives and operating managers. If the operating managers aren't involved in the objective-setting process, they won't accept the objectives and thus will be less motivated to achieve them.

Who Is Accountable for Performance?

At each level of the retail organization, the business unit and its manager should be held accountable only for the revenues, expenses, cash flow, and contribution to ROA that they can control. Thus, expenses that affect several levels of the organization (e.g., labor and capital expenses associated with operating a corporate headquarters) shouldn't be arbitrarily assigned to lower levels. In the case of a store, for example, it may be appropriate to set performance objectives based on sales, sales associate productivity, store inventory shrinkage due to employee theft and shoplifting, and energy costs. If the buyer makes poor decisions and has to lower prices to get rid of merchandise and therefore profits suffer, it is not fair to assess a store manager's performance on the basis of the resulting decline in store profit.

Performance objectives and measures can be used to pinpoint problem areas. The reasons that performance may be above or below planned levels must be examined. Perhaps the managers involved in setting the objectives aren't very good at making estimates. If so, they may need to be trained in forecasting. Also, buyers may misrepresent their business unit's ability to contribute to the firm's financial goals to get a larger inventory budget than is warranted and consequently earn a higher bonus. In either case, investment funds would be misallocated.

Actual performance may differ from what the plan predicts due to circumstances beyond the manager's control. For example, there may have been a recession. Assuming the recession wasn't predicted, or was more severe or lasted longer than anticipated, there are several relevant questions: How quickly were plans adjusted? How rapidly and appropriately were pricing and promotional policies modified? In short, did the manager react to salvage an adverse situation, or did the reaction worsen the situation?

Performance Objectives and Measures

Many factors contribute to a retailer's overall performance, and this makes it hard to find a single measure to evaluate performance. For instance, sales are a global measure of a retail store's activity level. However, as illustrated by the strategic profit model, a store manager could easily increase sales by lowering prices, but the profit realized on that merchandise (gross margin) would suffer as a result. An attempt to maximize one measure may lower another. Managers must therefore understand how their actions affect multiple performance measures.

The measures used to evaluate retail operations vary depending on (1) the level of the organization at which the decision is made and (2) the resources the manager controls. For example, the principal resources controlled by store managers are space and money for operating expenses (such as wages for sales associates and utility payments to light and heat the store). Thus, store managers focus on performance measures like sales per square foot, employee costs, and energy cost as a percent of sales.

Types of Measures

Exhibit 6–12 breaks down a variety of retailers' performance measures into three types: input measures, output measures, and productivity measures. **Input measures** are the resources or money allocated by a retailer to achieve outputs, or results. For example, the amount and selection of merchandise inventory, the number of stores, the size of the stores, the employees, advertising, markdowns, store hours, and promotions all require managerial decisions on inputs.

Measure for Assessing the Performance of Retailers   **EXHIBIT 6–12**

Level of Organization	Output	Input	Productivity (Output/Input)
Corporate (measures for entire corporation)	Net sales Net profits Growth in sales, profits, comparable-store sales	Square feet of store space Number of employees Inventory Advertising expenditures	Return on assets Asset turnover Sales per employee Sales per square foot
Merchandise management (measures for a merchandise category)	Net sales Gross margin Growth in sales	Inventory level Markdowns Advertising expenses Cost of merchandise	Gross margin return on investment (GMROI) Inventory turnover Advertising as a percentage of sales* Markdown as a percentage of sales*
Store operations (measures for a store or department within a store)	Net sales Gross margin Growth in sales	Square feet of selling areas Expenses for utilities Number of sales associates	Net sales per square foot Net sales per sales associate or per selling hour Utility expenses as a percentage of sales* Inventory shrinkage*

*These productivity measures are commonly expressed as an input-output ratio.

Output measures assess the results of a retailer's investment decisions. For example, sales revenue, gross margin, and net profit margin are all output measures and ways to evaluate a retailer's input or resource allocation decisions. A **productivity measure** (the ratio of an output to an input) determines how effectively retailers use their resources—what return they get on their investments in inputs.

In general, because productivity measures are ratios of outputs to inputs, they are very useful for comparing the performance of different business units. Suppose Kelly Bradford's two stores are different sizes: One has 5,000 square feet, and the other has 10,000 square feet. It's hard to compare the stores' performances using just output or input measures because the larger store will probably generate more sales and have higher expenses. But if the larger store has lower space productivity because it generates $210 net sales per square foot and the smaller store generates $350 per square foot, Kelly knows that the smaller store is operating more efficiently, even though it's generating lower sales.

Corporate Performance   At a corporate level, retail executives have three critical resources (inputs)—merchandise inventory, store space, and employees—that they can manage to generate sales and profits (outputs). Thus, effective productivity measures of the utilization of these assets include asset and inventory turnover, sales per square foot of selling space, and sales per employee.

As we have discussed, ROA is an overall productivity measure combining the operating profit margin percentage and asset turnover. Another commonly used measure of overall performance is **comparable-store sales growth** (also called **same-store sales growth**), which compares sales growth in stores that have been open for at least one year. Growth in sales can result from increasing the sales generated per store or by increasing the number of stores. Growth in same-store sales assesses the first component in sales growth, and thus indicates how well the retailer is doing with its core business concept. New stores do not represent growth from last year's sales but, rather, new sales created where no other sales existed the year before. Thus, a decrease in same-store sales indicates that the retailer's fundamental business approach is not being well received by its customers, even if overall sales are growing because the retailer is opening more new stores.

Merchandise Management Measures   The critical resource (input) controlled by merchandise managers is merchandise inventory. Merchandise managers also have the authority to set initial prices and lower prices when merchandise is not selling (i.e., take a markdown). Finally, they negotiate with vendors over the price paid for merchandise.

Inventory turnover is a productivity measure of the management of inventory; higher turnover means greater inventory management productivity. Gross margin percentage indicates the performance of merchandise managers in negotiating with vendors and buying merchandise that can generate a profit. Discounts (markdowns) as a percentage of sales are also a measure of the quality of the merchandise buying decisions. If merchandise managers have a high percentage of markdowns, they may not be buying the right merchandise or the right quantities, because they weren't able to sell some of it at its original retail price. Note that gross margin and discount percentages are productivity measures, but they are typically expressed as an input divided by an output as opposed to the typical productivity measures that are outputs divided by inputs.

Store Operations Measures   The critical assets controlled by store managers are the use of the store space and the management of the store's employees. Thus, measures of store operations productivity include sales per square foot of selling space and sales per employee (or sales per employee per working hour, to take into account that some employees work part-time). Store management is also responsible for controlling theft by employees and customers (referred to as inventory shrinkage), store maintenance, and energy costs (lighting, heating, and air conditioning). Thus, some other productivity measures used to assess the performance of store managers are inventory shrinkage and energy costs as a percentage of sales.

Assessing Performance: The Role of Benchmarks

As we have discussed, the financial measures used to assess performance reflect the retailer's market strategy. For example, because Costco has a different business strategy than Macy's, it has a lower profit margin. But it earns an acceptable ROA because it increases its inventory and asset turnovers by stocking a more limited merchandise assortment of less fashionable, staple items. In contrast, Macy's offers a broad and deep merchandise assortment in fashionable apparel and accessories. Thus, it has lower inventory and asset turnover but achieves an acceptable ROA through its higher profit margins. In other words, the performance of a retailer cannot be assessed accurately simply by looking at isolated measures because they are affected by the retailer's strategy. To get a better assessment of a retailer's performance, we need to compare it to a benchmark. Two commonly used benchmarks are (1) the performance of the retailer over time and (2) the performance of the retailer compared with that of its competitors.

Performance over Time   One useful approach for assessing a retailer's performance compares its recent performance with its performance in the preceding months, quarters, or years. Exhibit 6–13 shows the performance measures for Costco and Macy's over a three-year period.

Over the three years, the financial performance of both Costco and Macy's has improved. ROA for both retailers has increased; however, the increases in Macy's ROA are due primarily to improvements in operating profit percentage, while Costco's ROA improvements are due to an increasing asset turnover. Costco's sales increases and comparable-store sales percentages are greater than Macy's. The gross margin percentages for both retailers have remained the same over the three years. Both retailers have reduced their SG&A and improved their labor and space productivity.

Performance Compared to Competitors   A second approach for assessing a retailer's performance involves comparing its performance with that of its competitors. Exhibit 6–14 compares the performance of Macy's with two other national department store chains, Kohl's and Nordstrom. Kohl's has the highest ROA but the lowest growth in sales and SG&A percent of sales. Macy's has the highest gross margin percent but also has the highest administrative costs. Nordstrom has the highest space and labor productivity.

Performance Measures for Costco and Macy's over Time   **EXHIBIT 6–13**

	COSTCO			MACY'S		
	2012	**2011**	**2010**	**2012**	**2011**	**2010**
Sales ($ millions)	97,062	87,048	76,255	26,405	25,003	23,489
Annual sales growth	11.5%	14.2%	9.1%	5.6%	6.4%	−5.6%
Gross margin percentage	11.3%	10.7%	10.8%	40.4%	40.7%	40.5%
SG&A percent of sales	10.5%	10.0%	10.3%	31.4%	33.0%	34.3%
Operating profit percentage	2.8%	2.9%	2.8%	9.0%	7.7%	6.2%
Net profit percentage	1.8%	2.0%	1.8%	4.7%	3.4%	1.4%
Inventory turnover	12.2	11.71	12.06	3.08	3.12	3.03
Asset turnover	3.6	3.32	3.27	1.20	1.21	1.10
ROA	10.2%	9.3%	8.8%	10.8%	9.3%	6.8%
Sales per employee	557,830	540,671	518,741	154,415	150,620	145,894
Sales per store ($ millions)	159	147	141	31	29	28
Sales per square foot	1,117	1,031	986	174	162	152
Current ratio	1.10	1.14	1.04	1.40	1.38	0.81
Debt-to-equity ratio	0.11	0.11	0.12	2.23	2.73	8.62
Quick ratio	0.58	0.59	0.54	0.58	0.43	0.27
Cash flow ($ millions)	3,057	3,198	2,780	1,363	(222)	301
Comparable-store sales	8.1	7.0	10.0	3.5	3.0	4.6

	Kohl's	Macy's	Nordstrom
Sales ($ millions)	10,497	26,405	18,804
Annual sales growth	2.2%	5.6%	12.7%
Gross margin percentage	38.2%	40.4%	37.9%
SG&A percent of sales	22.6%	31.4%	26.7%
Operating profit percentage	15.6%	9.0%	11.2%
Net profit percentage	6.2%	4.7%	6.5%
Inventory turnover	3.63	3.08	5.68
Asset turnover	1.33	1.20	1.24
ROA	20.8%	10.8%	13.8%
Sales per employee ($)	132,423	154,415	185,788
Sales per store ($ millions)	16.7	31.4	41.2
Sales per square foot ($)	229	174	424
Comparable-store sales	0.5	3.5	7.3

EXHIBIT 6–14
Financial Performance of Macy's Compared with Kohl's and Nordstrom

SUMMARY

LO1 **Review the strategic objectives of a retail firm.**

This chapter explains some basic elements of the retailing financial strategy and examines how retailing strategy affects the financial performance of a firm. The strategy undertaken by retailers is designed to achieve financial, societal, and personal objectives. However, the financial objectives are of greatest importance to large, publicly owned retailers.

LO2 **Contrast the two paths to financial performance using the strategic profit model.**

The strategic profit model is used as a vehicle for understanding the complex interrelations between financial ratios and retailing strategy. Different types of retailers have different financial operating characteristics. Specifically, department store chains like Macy's generally have higher profit margins and lower turnover ratios than warehouse club stores like Costco. Yet when margin and turnover are combined into return on assets, it is possible to achieve similar financial performance.

LO3 Illustrate the use of the strategic profit model for analyzing growth opportunities.

In addition to helping retailers understand the financial implications of the tradeoffs they face in developing a retail strategy, this chapter illustrates how the strategic profit model can be used to evaluate growth and investment opportunities.

LO4 Analyze the financial risks facing a retail firm.

In addition to assessing the performance of a retail operation, the chapter also examines measures used to assess the financial strength of a retailer—the probability of the business declaring bankruptcy. Four measures of financial strength are cash flow, debt-to-equity ratio, current ratio, and quick ratio.

LO5 Review the measures retailers use to assess their performance.

Some financial performance measures are used to evaluate different aspects of a retailing organization. Although the return-on-assets ratio in the strategic profit model is appropriate for evaluating the performance of the retail executives responsible for managing the firm, other measures are more appropriate for more specific activities. For instance, inventory turnover and gross margin are appropriate for buyers, whereas store managers should be concerned with sales or gross margin per square foot or per employee.

KEY TERMS

accounts receivable, *163*
acid-test ratio, *174*
assets, *165*
asset turnover, *158*
bottom-up planning, *175*
cash flow statement, *174*
chargeback fee, *161*
comparable-store sales growth, *177*
cost of goods sold (COGS), *162*
current assets, *165*
current ratio, *174*
debt-to-equity ratio, *174*
earnings before interest, taxes, and depreciation (EBITDA), *158*

fixed assets, *167*
gross margin, *162*
gross margin percentage, *162*
gross profit, *162*
income statement, *161*
input measures, *176*
inventory turnover, *166*
liabilities, *174*
merchandise inventory, *166*
net profit margin, *162*
net sales, *161*
operating expenses, *162*
operating expenses percentage, *164*

operating income percentage, *165*
operating profit margin, *158*
output measures, *177*
productivity measures, *177*
quick ratio, *174*
return on assets (ROA), *156*
same-store sales growth, *177*
selling, general, and administrative (SG&A) expenses, *162*
slotting allowance, *161*
slotting fee, *161*
statement of operations, *161*
strategic profit model, *158*
top-down planning, *175*

GET OUT AND DO IT!

1. **CONTINUING CASE ASSIGNMENT** Evaluate the financial performance of the retailer you have selected for the Continuing Case Assignment and of another store that sells similar merchandise categories but to a very different target market. If yours is a high-margin–low-turnover store, compare it with a low-margin–high-turnover store. You can get this information from your chosen store's latest annual report, available in the "investor relations" area of its website, at Hoovers Online, or in the Edgar files at www.sec.gov. Explain why you would expect the gross margin percentage, expense-to-sales ratio, net profit margin percentage, inventory turnover, asset turnover, and return on assets to differ between the two stores. Which retailer achieves better overall financial performance?

2. **INTERNET EXERCISE** Go to the latest annual reports, and use the financial information to update the numbers in the net profit margin management model and the asset turnover management model for Costco and Macy's. Have there been any significant changes in their financial performance? Why are the key financial ratios for these two retailers so different?

3. **GO SHOPPING** Go to your favorite store, and interview the manager. Determine how the retailer sets its performance objectives. Evaluate its procedures relative to the procedures presented in the text.

4. **WEB OLC EXERCISE** Go to the strategic profit model (SPM) on the student side of the book's website. The SPM tutorial was designed to provide a refresher course on the basic financial ratios leading to

return on assets and walks you through the process step-by-step. A calculation page is also included that will calculate all the ratios. You can type in the numbers from a firm's balance sheet and income statement to see the financial results produced with the current financial figures. You can also access an Excel spreadsheet for SPM calculations. The calculation page or the Excel spreadsheet can be used for Case 11, "Tiffany's and TJX: Comparing Financial Performance," page 563.

DISCUSSION QUESTIONS AND PROBLEMS

1. What are the key productivity ratios for measuring the retailer as a whole, its merchandise management activities, and its store operations activities? Why are these ratios appropriate for one area of the retailer's operation and inappropriate for others?

2. What are examples of the types of objectives that entrepreneurs might have for a retail business they are launching?

3. Buyers' performance is often measured by the gross margin percentage. Why is this measure more appropriate than operating or net profit percentage?

4. A supermarket retailer is considering the installation of self-checkout POS terminals. How would the replacement of cashiers with these self-checkouts affect the elements in the retailer's strategic profit model?

5. Neiman Marcus (a chain of high-service department stores) and Walmart target different customer segments. Which retailer would you expect to have a higher gross margin? Higher expense-to-sales ratio? Higher net profit margin percentage? Higher inventory turnover? Higher asset turnover? Why?

6. Why do investors place more weight on comparable-store sales than growth in sales?

7. What metrics should be used to measure the financial risk of a retailer? How is each metric used?

8. Blue Nile is a jewelry retailer than only uses an Internet channel for interacting with its customers. What differences would you expect in the strategic profit model and key productivity ratios for Blue Nile and Zales, a multichannel jewelry retailer?

9. Using the following information taken from the 2012 balance sheet and income statement for Urban Outfitters, develop a strategic profit model. (Figures are in millions of dollars.) You can access an Excel spreadsheet for SPM calculations on the student portion of the book's website.

Net sales	$2473.8
Cost of goods sold	$1316.2
Operating expenses	$ 575.8
Inventory	$ 250.1
Accounts receivable	$ 36.7
Other current assets	$ 68.9
Fixed assets	$ 690.0

10. A friend of yours is considering buying some stock in retail companies. Your friend knows that you are taking a course in retailing and ask for your opinion about Costco. Your friend is concerned that Costco is not a good firm to invest in because it has such a low net operating profit. What advice would you give your friend? Why?

SUGGESTED READINGS

Anderson, Torben Juul, and Peter Winther Schrøder. *Strategic Risk Management Practice: How to Deal Effectively with Major Corporate Exposures.* Cambridge: Cambridge University Press, 2010.

Appelbaum, E., and R. Batt. *A Primer on Private Equity at Work.* Armonk, NY: ME Sharpe, 2012.

Baud, Celine, and Cedric Durand. "Financialization, Globalization and the Making of Profits by Leading Retailers," *Socio-Economic Review* 10 (2012), pp. 241–266.

Brealey, Richard, Stewart Myers, and Alan Marcus. *Corporate Finance,* 7th ed. New York: McGraw Hill, 2012.

Farris, Paul, Neil Bendle, Phillip Pfeifer, and David Reibstein. *Marketing Metrics: The Definitive Guide to Measuring Marketing Performance,* 2nd ed. New York: Pearson Prentice-Hall, 2010.

Financial Performance Report—Profitable Growth: Driving the Demand Chain. New York: PWC, 2012.

Garrison, Ray H., Eric Noreen, and Peter C. Brewer. *Managerial Accounting,* 14th ed. New York: McGraw-Hill, 2012.

Lichtenstein, Donald, Richard G. Netemeyer, and James G. Maxham III. "The Relationships among Manager-, Employee-, and Customer-Company Identification: Implications for Retail Store Financial Performance," *Journal of Retailing* 86 (March 2010), pp. 85–93.

"Monitoring Operational and Financial Performance." In Joachim Zentes, Dirk Morschett, and Hanna Schramm-Klein, eds. *Strategic Retail Management,* pp. 383–402, New York: Springer, 2012.

Perrini, Francesco, Angelo Russo, Antonio Tencati, and Clodia Vurro. "Deconstructing the Relationship between Corporate Social and Financial Performance," *Journal of Business Ethics* 102, Suppl. 1 (2011), pp. 59–76.

Ross, Stephen, Randolph Westerfield, and Bradford Jordan. *Fundamentals of Corporate Finance,* 10th ed. New York: McGraw Hill, 2013.

Retail Locations

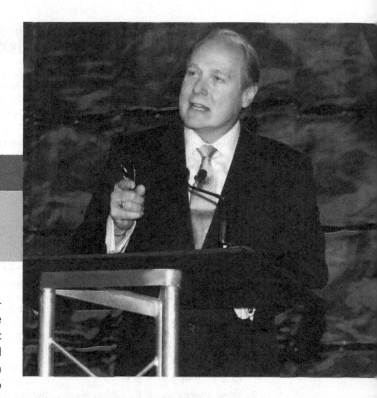

EXECUTIVE BRIEFING

Michael Kercheval, President and CEO
International Council of Shopping Centers

While I was going to college, I became very concerned about the poor quality of life in much of the world and volunteered to work on several economic development projects in Latin America sponsored by the Peace Corps and the Pan American Health Organization. From these experiences, I decided to go to medical school, become a doctor, and then return to Latin America. But pre-med chemistry did not agree with me. I discovered economics and majored in developmental economics.

After graduate school, I went to work for Equitable Life Insurance and eventually became involved in managing real estate investment activities in Latin America. I observed keenly how retail developments are a catalyst for economic development. They create a virtuous cycle: retail developments → more goods, more choices, lower prices, and greater income → more retail development. The shopping centers provided goods to people with higher quality at lower prices and greater convenience. By saving people money on necessities, they can have a higher standard of living and greater disposable income. In addition, the retail developments provided jobs that increased the incomes. Then the increased incomes spurred more retail developments.

I am president of the International Council for Shopping Centers (ICSC), which offers me a chance to serve an industry that is very involved in economic development around the world, as well as in U.S. urban and rural communities.

The retail development industry is at an interesting crossroads now. Demand for retail space across the globe is far greater than supply, and there is considerable capital available to invest in new retail developments. The primary restraint to growth is from government policymakers who are tempering new development out of concern for small retail businesses, the environment, and what they see as suburban sprawl. ICSC and its members are working on ways to meet the retail needs of consumers, stimulate economic growth, and address the concerns of policymakers.

CHAPTER 7

The oft-referenced response to the question "What are the three most important things in retailing?" is "Location, location, location." Why is store location such an important decision for a retailer? First, location is typically one of the most influential considerations in a customer's store-choice decision. For instance, when choosing where you're going to have your car washed, you usually pick the location closest to your home or work. Most consumers similarly shop at the supermarket closest to them.

Second, location decisions have strategic importance because they can be used to develop a sustainable competitive advantage. If a retailer has the best location, that is, the location that is most attractive to its customers, competitors can't copy this advantage. Competitors are relegated to occupying the second-best location.

Third, location decisions are risky. Typically, when retailers select a location, they either must make a substantial investment to buy and develop the real estate or must commit to a long-term lease with developers. Retailers often commit to leases for 5 to 15 years.

In the first part of this chapter, we discuss the types and relative advantages of three types of locations available to retailers—unplanned, planned, and nontraditional. We then examine how the location decision fits into the retailer's strategy. For example, the best locations for a 7-Eleven convenience store are not the best locations for a category specialist such as a Best Buy. We end this chapter by discussing the societal and legal considerations affecting a retailer's location decisions. In the next chapter, we discuss the issues involved in selecting areas of the country in which to locate stores and how to evaluate specific locations and negotiate leases.

TYPES OF RETAIL LOCATIONS

LO1

Describe the types of retail locations available to retailers.

Many types of locations are available for retail stores, each type with its benefits and limitations. The two basic types of location are unplanned (freestanding and urban sites) and planned (shopping centers). **Unplanned locations** do not have centralized management that determines what stores will be in a development, where the specific stores will be located, and how they will be operated. In **planned locations,** the shopping center developer and/or manager makes and enforces policies that govern store operations, such as the hours that a store must be opened. The shopping center management also maintains the common facilities such as the parking area—an arrangement referred to as **common area maintenance (CAM)**—and is responsible for providing security, parking lot lighting, outdoor signage for the center, advertising, special events to attract consumers, and so on.

In the United States, about 47 percent of the gross leasable square feet of retail space is in planned locations and the remaining in unplanned locations.[1] **Gross leasable area (GLA)** is the real estate industry's term for the total floor area designed for the retailer's occupancy and exclusive use, including any basements, mezzanines, or upper floors.

When choosing a particular location type, retailers evaluate a series of trade-offs involving the size of the trade area, the occupancy cost of the location (rent, maintenance, energy cost, etc.), the pedestrian and vehicle customer traffic associated with the location, the restrictions placed on store operations by the shopping center management, and the convenience of the location for customers. The **trade area** is the geographic area that encompasses most of the customers who would patronize a specific retail site. The following sections describe the characteristics of each type of location, as summarized in Exhibit 7–1.

EXHIBIT 7–1   Characteristics of Different Retail Locations

	Size (000 sq. ft.)	Trading Area (Miles)	Annual Occupancy Cost ($ per sq. ft.)	Shopping Convenience	Pedestrian Traffic	Vehicular Traffic	Restrictions on Operations	Typical Tenants
UNPLANNED AREAS								
Freestanding	Varies	3–7	15–30	High	Low	High	Limited	Convenience, drug stores, category specialists
Urban locations/ central business district	Varies	Varies	8–20	Low	High	Low	Limited to medium	Specialty stores
SHOPPING CENTERS								
Neighborhood and community shopping centers	30–350	3–6	8–20	High	Low	High	Medium	Supermarkets, discount stores
Power centers	250–600	5–10	10–20	Medium	Medium	Medium	Limited	Category specialists
Regional and super-regional enclosed malls	400–1,000	5–25	10–70	Low	High	Low	High	Department and specialty apparel stores
Lifestyle centers	150–800	5–15	15–35	Medium	Medium	Medium	Medium to high	Specialty apparel and home stores, restaurants
Outlet centers	50–400	25–75	8–15	Low	High	High	Limited	Off-price retailers and factory outlets
Theme/festival centers	80–250	N/A	20–70	Low	High	Low	Highest	Specialty stores and restaurants

Sources: Personal communications with industry executives; "North American Retail Highlights 2009," http://www.colliers.com/Content/Repositories/Base/Corporate/English/Market_Report_Corporate/PDFs/RetailNaHighlightsSpring2009.pdf; http://www.icsc.org/srch/lib/2009_S-C_CLASSIFICATION_May09.pdf.

UNPLANNED LOCATIONS

The three types of unplanned retail locations are freestanding sites, urban locations, and mainstreet locations.

Review the types of unplanned locations.

Freestanding Sites

Freestanding sites are retail locations for an individual, isolated store unconnected to other stores; however, they might be near other freestanding stores or near a shopping center. The advantages of freestanding locations are their convenience for customers (easy access and parking); high vehicular traffic and visibility to attract customers driving by; modest occupancy costs; and fewer restrictions on signs, hours, or merchandise that might be imposed by management of planned locations.

There are several disadvantages to freestanding sites. First, is their limited trade area. Typically, there are no other nearby retailers to attract customers interested in conveniently shopping for multiple categories of merchandise on one trip. In addition, freestanding locations typically have higher occupancy costs than shopping centers because they do not have other retailers to share the common area maintenance costs. Finally, freestanding locations generally have little pedestrian traffic, limiting the number of customers who might drop in because they are walking by.

Drugstore chains use freestanding locations for their stores with drive-through windows to make it easy for customers to pick up prescription pharmaceuticals.

Some retailers are shifting from planned locations to freestanding locations to offer their customers a better shopping experience. The three major drugstore chains (CVS, Walgreens, and Rite Aid) have shifted their emphasis from strip malls to freestanding locations because they want accessible drive-through windows for pharmacies, more floor space, and better access for receiving merchandise.

Outparcels are freestanding stores that are not connected to other stores in a shopping center, but are located on the premises of a shopping center, typically in a parking area. Some advantages of outparcels compared to other freestanding locations are that they can offer customers the convenience of a drive-through window, extensive parking, and clear visibility from the street. These locations are popular for fast-food restaurants and banks.

Urban Locations

Urban areas in large cities offer three types of locations: the central business district, inner city, and gentrified residential sites.

Central Business District   The **central business district (CBD)** is the traditional downtown financial and business area in a city or town. Due to its daily activity, it draws many people and employees into the area during business hours. There is a high level of pedestrian traffic, but shopping flow in the evening and on weekends is slow in many CBDs. Vehicular traffic is limited due to congestion in urban areas, and parking problems reduce consumer convenience. Many CBDs have a large number of residents living in nearby areas.

Risk-taking entrepreneurial developers working with forward-thinking urban planners and city leaders are slowly attracting more people to the CBD at night and during weekends. For example, coal and steel are no longer the backbone of Cleveland's economy. City leaders and local developers reinvented the CBD using an entertainment-focused strategy to redevelop East Fourth Street. Retail stores occupy about one-third of the 600,000-square-foot, $110 million, historic redevelopment project. The rest is housing. The area is spectacularly designed

Cleveland's East Fourth Street development attracts consumers to the CBD.

with art, flowers, decorative paving, planters, outdoor seating, and special overhead lighting. To increase the foot traffic, two new stadiums for the city's football and baseball teams, a new arena for its basketball team, and the Rock and Roll Hall of Fame were built. Today, city residents and suburbanites flock to East Fourth Street before and after sports and entertainment events, as well as for an interesting afternoon or evening "on the town."[2]

Inner City During the 1970s and 1980s, many U.S. and some European cities experienced urban decay. **Urban decay** is the process of a previously functioning city, or part of a city, falling into disrepair. The **inner city** is a low-income residential area within a large city. Empty lots, buildings, and condemned houses attract criminals and street gangs that make living in the inner city dangerous. One of the major causes of urban decay is when businesses relocate from the inner city to suburbs.

Some U.S. retailers avoid opening stores in the inner city because they think these stores are riskier and produce lower returns than other areas. Although income levels are lower in inner cities than in other neighborhoods, inner-city retailers often achieve a higher sales volume and higher margins, resulting in higher profits.

Inner-city residents and public policy advocates are concerned about the offerings at inner-city grocery stores. Instead of offering fresh meat and produce, they tend to feature lower-priced packaged foods that have longer shelf lives. As a result, inner-city consumers often have to travel to the suburbs using buses to shop for healthy food items. Government programs, in partnership with nonprofit organizations, are working to change the inner-city supermarket landscape. For instance, in an inner-city Philadelphia neighborhood, a new supermarket, stocked with fresh produce, a pharmacy, and various ethnic products, has opened within walking distance of most of the neighborhood. Nonprofit organizations such as Philadelphia's Food Trust lobby for loans and government subsidies to support supermarkets in lower-income areas.[3] Retailing View 7.1 describes how Magic Johnson has brought retailing to the inner city.

Retailing can play an important role in inner-city redevelopment activities by providing needed services and jobs for inner-city residents, as well as property taxes to support the redevelopment. Because of the potential of this untapped market and incentives from local governments, developers are increasing their focus on opportunities in the inner city. However, inner-city redevelopments can be controversial. Often local governments will use the right of eminent domain to buy buildings and land and then sell it to developers at an attractive price. For instance, people are concerned about the residents displaced by the development, increased traffic, and parking.

Gentrified Residential Areas Many inner-city areas are going through a process of **gentrification**—the renewal and rebuilding of offices, housing, and retailers in deteriorating areas—coupled with an influx of more affluent people that displaces the former, lower-income residents. Young professionals and retired empty-nesters are moving into these areas to enjoy the convenience of shopping, restaurants, and entertainment near where they live.

Some retailers are finding urban locations attractive, particularly in cities that are redeveloping their urban areas. Big-box retailers like Target, Walmart, Office Depot, Home Depot, and Costco, which usually locate in the suburbs, are now opening outlets in cities, typically with smaller stores.[4]

While some U.S. cities are still struggling to rekindle their business, social, cultural, and retail vitality, others like New York, Chicago, and many Canadian and European cities have not experienced significant urban decay. These cities offer very attractive markets for retailers. For example, the world's five most famous locations for high-fashion retailers are in these locations—Oxford and Regent Street in London, Fifth Avenue between 49th and 58th Streets in New York City, Rue du Faubourg Saint-Honoré in Paris, Rodeo Drive in Los Angeles, and Passeig de Gràcia in Barcelona.[5]

Retailers need to tailor their offerings to the unique characteristics of urban gentrified consumers and the restrictions associated with these locations. When selecting a store to patronize, these urban consumers, compared with suburban consumers, typically place more importance on reducing their shopping time rather than the

RETAILING VIEW   Magic Johnson Brings Retailing to the Inner City   7.1

They called him "Magic" because of the way he knew where to pass the ball without looking and his ability to make jump shots that seemingly had no hope of going in. But since retiring from the NBA and becoming one of the first public figures to announce his HIV-positive status, Earvin Johnson also has turned his magic touch to urban redevelopment and growth, creating a whole new meaning for his famous nickname.

In the mid-1990s, Magic Johnson announced a partnership with Loews Cineplex, which would seek to open more movie theaters in underserved inner-city markets. Research showed that approximately one-third of movie tickets were being purchased by lower-income, minority audiences. Yet most of these consumers had to travel long distances, often taking up to an hour, to get to a theater, because few theaters were located in urban locations. For Johnson, the natural response was to build more urban movie theaters.

Once the Magic Johnson Theaters group had built a few facilities, Johnson and his partners recognized that their success depended on attracting customers by offering complementary entertainment as well. People love to have dinner before or dessert after catching a movie, but many casual dining franchises avoided urban locations. Instead, their conventional strategies involved targeting middle-class, suburban markets, with little consideration of diverse demographics. Again weaving his magic, Johnson ultimately convinced Starbucks to enter into an exclusive joint partnership with the theater group, after which T.G.I. Fridays came on board as well.

Today, the Johnson Development Corporation (JDC) consists of four separate enterprises. In addition to Magic Johnson Theatres, it includes Urban Coffee Opportunities, Magic Johnson's T.G.I. Friday's, and the Canyon Johnson Urban Fund. Through these entitites, the JDC seeks to establish entertainment complexes, featuring theaters, coffee shops, restaurants, and retailing, in underserved U.S. markets. The 50–50 partnerships thus give JDC connections to some of the most successful names in each

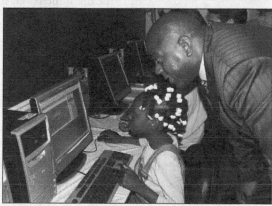

Doris Jackson, 8, left, sits at a computer as Earvin "Magic" Johnson looks over her shoulder at the Mattie Koonce Learning Center in the Overtown section in Miami, Florida. Through his foundation, Johnson has helped donate $200,000 in computer equipment to the learning center.

market, such as Loews Cineplex Entertainment, Starbucks, and T.G.I. Friday's—and they give urban consumers a fun way to spend their Saturday nights.

Sources: Roger Vincent, "Magic Johnson Built Business Empire after Court Glories Ended," *Los Angeles Times*, March 28, 2012; "Meet Magic Johnson, the Media Mogul," *CNN Money*, March 15, 2012; and Danielle Kwateng, "Decoding the Business of Earvin "Magic" Johnson," *Black Enterprise*, March 30, 2012.

DISCUSSION QUESTION

Among all of the potential retailers that could be interested in an inner-city location, why have Loews Cineplex Entertainment, Starbucks, and T.G.I. Friday's been particularly interested in working with Magic Johnson?

Rodeo Drive is an CBD location that is one the most highly regarded locations by retailers of high-fashion merchandise.

breadth and depth of the retailer's assortment. For example, Office Depot's urban stores are 5,000 square feet, about a fifth of a suburban store. The shelves are about 6 feet high, much shorter than in a suburban store, so visitors can navigate quickly. The signs above the aisles are simplified so customers do not waste time interpreting them. A suburban Office Depot store has 9,000 SKUs for sale, while its urban stores have half that number. The merchandise offered focuses on immediate-replacement items (a pen) versus stock-up items (a 25-pack of pens).

Retailers with urban locations also need to recognize the differences in consumer needs within these markets. For example, the Walgreens store in New York City's Union Square attracts commuters and tourists using the subway; the store a few blocks north draws mostly local residents. So the Union Square site carries lots of products such as umbrellas for the unprepared tourists, along with cosmetics and snacks; the other store is more heavily stocked with household-cleaning items and toothpaste.[6]

Finally, to deal with the traffic and parking problems in these gentrified residential areas, many residents use public transportation or walk when they go shopping. As a result, they are reluctant to buy bulky items like a 24-pack of toilet paper and are active users of Internet retail channels.

Main Street

Main Street refers to the traditional downtown shopping area in smaller towns and secondary shopping areas in large cities and their suburbs. Over the past 30 years, many downtowns in small U.S. towns have experienced decay similar to that of inner cities. When Walmart and other big-box retailers opened standalone stores on the outskirts of these towns, local retailers could not compete effectively with these big boxes and went out of business. In response, smaller towns are undertaking redevelopment programs to draw residents back to their downtown areas, and retailers play a major role in these efforts.

To attract consumers and retailers, these Main Street redevelopment efforts focus on providing a better shopping experience than big-box retailers do. Instead of streets, they develop pedestrian walkways. Next to major crosswalks, pedestrian shelters equipped with benches provide shady resting spots for mobile shoppers, helping them extend their visits and prolong their shopping excursions. Property owners can also receive grants if they agree to maintain and enhance their shops' appearance with necessary repairs, new signage, attractive entrances, attention-grabbing windows, and nice awnings. Furthermore, the town administrations work to improve downtown aesthetics with landscaping, which surrounds repaved sidewalks and updated (and functioning) street lights.[7]

Main Street locations share most of the characteristics of locations in gentrified urban areas, but their occupancy costs are generally lower. Main Street locations do not draw as many people as the CBD because fewer people work in the area, and the fewer stores generally mean a smaller overall draw to the area. In addition, Main Streets typically don't offer the range of entertainment and recreational activities available in the more successful primary CBDs. Finally, the planning organization for the town or redevelopment often imposes some restrictions on Main Street store operations.

SHOPPING CENTERS AND PLANNED RETAIL LOCATIONS

In this section, we discuss the different types of shopping centers—planned locations. A **shopping center** is a group of retail and other commercial establishments that are planned, developed, owned, and managed as a single property. After discussing the role of shopping center developers and management, each type of center is discussed.

By combining many stores at one location, developments attract more consumers to the shopping center than would be the case if the stores were at separate locations. The developer and shopping center management carefully select a set of retailers that are complementary to provide consumers with a comprehensive shopping experience at one, convenient location.

Lease agreements typically require that retailers in the center pay a portion of the common area maintenance (CAM) costs for the center according to the size of their store's space and/or sales volume and a retail fee based on sales. As mentioned earlier, the shopping center management group can place restrictions on the operating hours, signage, and even the type of merchandise sold in the stores.

Most shopping centers have at least one or two major retailers, referred to as **anchors,** such as Macy's, Walmart, or Kroger. These retailers are courted by the center's developer because they attract a significant number of consumers and consequently make the center more appealing for other retailers. To get these anchor retailers to locate in a center, developers frequently give them special deals, such as reduced lease costs.

These shopping centers are generally managed by a **shopping center property management firm,** which is a company that specializes in developing, owning, and/or managing shopping centers. Management of these shopping malls entails selecting and negotiating leases with retail tenants, maintaining the common areas, marketing the centers to attract consumers, and providing security. Retailing View 7.2 describes the evolution of Simon Properties—the largest retail management company in the world.

In Exhibit 7–2, the characteristics of the different types of shopping centers are outlined followed by a discussion of each type. As you can see, strip centers account for the vast majority of retail GLA. The growth rate in terms of the number of shopping centers is limited; however, the greatest growth has been lifestyle centers followed by power centers. Regional and super-regional enclosed malls have the highest sales per square foot.

LO3
Analyze the characteristics of the different types of shopping centers.

REFACT
There are 23.1 square feet of retail GLA per person in the United States.[8]

REFACT
Highland Park Shopping Village in Dallas, Texas, developed by Hugh Prather in 1931, was the first planned shopping center. Its stores were built with a unified image and managed under the control of a single owner.[9]

REFACT
There are more than 107,000 shopping centers in the United States and fewer than 7,000 in the European Union.[10]

Number, Sales per Square Foot, and Growth Rate of Shopping Centers   **EXHIBIT 7–2**

	Number	Total GLA (millions of square feet)	Percentage of Overall Shopping Center GLA	Growth in Number of Centers 2008–2011	Anchor GLA Percentage of Total Center GLA	Sales per Square Foot ($)	Growth Rate in Sales per Square Foot 2009–2011
Community, neighborhood, and convenience	101,630	4,981	67.8%	1.3%	30–60%	12.68	5.7%
Regional and super-regional enclosed malls	1,505	1,321	18.0	1.1%	40–70	21.20	1.7
Power centers	2,023	822	11.2	2.8%	N/A	10.85	4.1
Lifestyle center	396	126	1.7	6.9%	0–50	N/A	N/A
Outlet centers	334	71	1.0	1.9%	N/A	N/A	N/A
Theme/festival centers	201	27	0.4	1.2%	N/A	N/A	N/A

Source: eData, International Council of Shopping Centers.

Convenience, Neighborhood, and Community Shopping Centers

REFACT

In 1938, one of the first strip shopping centers, Silver Springs Shopping Center in Maryland, opened with a 1,000-seat movie theater, a grocery store anchor, and 19 additional stores.[11]

Convenience, neighborhood, and **community shopping centers** (also called **strip shopping centers**) are attached rows of open-air stores, with onsite parking usually located in front of the stores. The most common layouts are linear, L-shaped, and inverted U-shaped. Historically, the term *strip center* has applied to the linear configuration.

Smaller centers (convenience and neighborhood centers) are 10,000 to 60,000 square feet and are typically anchored by a supermarket. They are designed for convenience shopping. These centers typically have 10 to 15 smaller retailers such as a bakery, dollar store, dry cleaner, florist, laundry center, barber shop, and mail service. The larger centers (community centers) are typically 25,000 to

7.2   RETAILING VIEW   Simon Properties: The Largest Shopping Center Management Company in the World

Simon Properties owns, develops, and manages 326 retail real estate properties in the United States, including 151 regional malls, 58 premium outlet malls, and 66 lifestyle centers. This empire got its start in 1960, when Melvin Simon and Associates (MSA; the associates were Melvin's brothers Fred and Herbert) opened a shopping plaza in Bloomington, Indiana, followed quickly thereafter by four similar Indianapolis-area plazas. Melvin had previously established himself as a leasing agent in a local real estate firm, and MSA soon gained a reputation for managing its plazas well. Large tenants flocked to the retail centers; with big-name contracts with retailers such as Sears, Roebuck, MSA had easy access to bank financing for still more construction projects.

One of those projects was MSA's first enclosed mall, opened in the early 1960s. This format dominated its developments for years; then in the 1990s, MSA reinvented the retail real estate development market yet again by combining its malls with entertainment options. These multi-use centers attracted vast numbers of visitors, most of whom remained in the centers for hours. For example, The Forum Shops at Caesars Palace in Las Vegas sit between Caesars Palace and The Mirage, evoking an ancient Roman street. Visitors interact with animatronic statues, stop to rest at bubbling fountains, and enjoy simulated views of the awesome Mediterranean sky. In addition, MSA is responsible for perhaps the best known mall in America, that is, the Mall of America in Minnesota.

Today, the U.S. market allows for fewer new shopping centers, so Simon Properties—now led by Melvin's son David—aggressively pursues international growth and earns approximately 5.4 percent of its new operating income from international operations. In addition to investments in outlet centers in Japan, South Korea,

The Forum Shops at Caesars Palace in Las Vegas, developed and managed by Simon Properties, meld entertainment with shopping.

Malaysia, and Mexico, Simon Properties and its Paris-based Klépierre SA own nearly 300 shopping centers in 13 European countries. The global financial crisis has made Europe less attractive as a market for shopping center development; instead, Asia—particularly Shanghai, Mumbai, Dubai, and Tokyo—represent the most attractive regions with the greatest growth in rental rates.

Sources: "Buy Simon Property Group: Growth to Come from International Expansion," September 18, 2012; www.seekingalpha.com; "David Simon: Most Respected CEOs," and www.simon.com,

DISCUSSION QUESTION

What are the challenges facing Simon Properties as it pursues international growth opportunities?

50,000 square feet and are anchored by at least one big-box store such as a discount department store, an off-price retailer, or a category specialist.

The primary advantages of these centers are that they offer customers convenient locations and easy parking, and they have relatively low occupancy costs. The primary disadvantage is that smaller centers have a limited trade area due to their size, and they lack entertainment and restaurants to keep customers in the center for a longer time. In addition, there is no protection from the weather. As a result, neighborhood and community centers do not attract as many customers as do larger, enclosed malls.

National chains such as The Children's Place, Kohl's, Radio Shack, and Marshalls compete effectively against their rival mall-based retailers by offering the convenience of a neighborhood or community center. In these locations, they can offer lower prices, partly because of the lower occupancy cost, and their customers can drive right up to the door.[12]

Power Centers

Power centers are shopping centers that consist primarily of collections of big-box retail stores, such as full-line discount stores (Target), off-price stores (Marshalls), warehouse clubs (Costco), and category specialists (Lowe's, Staples, Michaels, Barnes & Noble, Best Buy, Sports Authority, and Toys "R" Us). Although these centers are open air, unlike traditional strip centers, power centers often consist of a collection of freestanding (unconnected) "anchor" stores and only a minimum number of smaller specialty store tenants. Many power centers are located near an enclosed shopping mall.

Power centers offer low occupancy costs and modest levels of consumer convenience and vehicular and pedestrian traffic. The growth in power centers reflects the growth of category specialists. Many power centers are now larger than regional malls and have trade areas as large as regional malls.

Enclosed Shopping Malls

Shopping malls are enclosed, climate-controlled, lighted shopping centers with retail stores on one or both sides of an enclosed walkway. Parking is usually provided around the perimeter of the mall. Shopping malls are classified as either **regional malls** (less than 800,000 square feet) or **super-regional malls** (more than 800,000 square feet). Super-regional centers are similar to regional centers, but because of their larger size, they have more anchors, specialty stores, and recreational opportunities and draw from a larger geographic area. They often are considered tourist attractions.

Enclosed shopping malls have several advantages over alternative locations. First, shopping malls attract many shoppers and have a large trade area because of the number of stores and the opportunity to combine shopping with an inexpensive form of entertainment. Older citizens get their exercise by walking the malls, and teenagers hang out and meet their friends, though some malls are restricting their admittance in the evenings. Thus, malls generate significant pedestrian traffic inside the mall and have sales per square foot almost twice that of power centers and strip centers. Second, customers don't have to worry about the weather, and thus malls are appealing places to shop during cold winters and hot summers. Third, mall management ensures a level of consistency that benefits all the tenants. For instance, most major malls enforce uniform hours of operation.

However, malls also have disadvantages. First, mall occupancy costs are higher than those of strip centers, freestanding sites, and most central business districts. For example, the occupancy cost (rent, common area maintenance, and taxes) for an enclosed mall is almost 140 percent greater than that for an open-air shopping center ($35.42 compared to $14.55 per square foot).[15] Second, some retailers may not like mall management's control of their operations,

REFACT

such as strict rules governing window displays and signage. Third, competition within shopping centers can be intense. Several specialty and department stores might sell very similar merchandise and be located in close proximity. Fourth, freestanding locations, strip centers, lifestyle centers, and power centers are more convenient because customers can park in front of a store, go in and buy what they want, and go about their other errands. Fifth, some malls were built more than 40 years ago and have not been subject to any significant remodeling, so they appear run-down and unappealing to shoppers. Furthermore, these older malls are often located in areas with unfavorable demographics because the population has shifted from the near suburbs to outer suburbs. Sixth, the consolidation in the department store sector has decreased the number of potential anchor tenants and diminished the drawing power of enclosed malls. Finally, the growing sales through the Internet channel is cannibalizing sales through the store channel.

For these reasons, mall traffic and sales are declining. The last new mall was opened in 2006, and it is estimated that 10 percent of the 1,500 enclosed malls will close in the next three years (see www.deadmalls.com).[17] Most malls that close are razed; however, mall managers and developers are trying to redevelop failing malls. Some redevelopment projects become mixed-used spaces, incorporating unconventional tenants like government offices, churches, medical clinics, and satellite university campuses. Others seek to turn malls into one-stop sources for various services, not just fashionable apparel. A busy working mother visiting The Westside Pavilion mall in Los Angeles can thus drop off her kids for piano lessons at Music Stars & Masters on the second floor. During their lesson, she also can send an overnight package, get a haircut, have her purse repaired, and check out some books for the kids from the public library. If the kids do well with their lessons, mom might treat them to ice cream, too.[18]

Another approach for dealing with aging malls and the changing demographics in their trade areas is to tailor the offerings to the markets that do exist today. Older shopping centers such as Northridge Mall in northern California (built in 1972) can be repositioned to appeal to immigrant populations. In recent decades, the demographics of Monterey County have changed, producing a rich Latino culture in which approximately 75 percent of the population in the mall's trade area is of Latino heritage. Thus, the courtyard at the entryway to the mall hosts mariachi bands on weekend afternoons, while clowns and dancers provide family-friendly entertainment underneath colorful piñatas that have been suspended from the ceiling. To appeal to the large Roman Catholic population, the mall also offers services with religious themes, such as celebrations on Día de los Santos Reyes and shrines to the Virgen de Guadalupe Las Posadas. The idea is that the mall can be so welcoming that the local community views it more like a weekend home than a retail destination.[19]

While the percentage of mall retail sales has declined over the past 10 years, recently malls have experienced a slight increase in market share. This increase is due to the redevelopment efforts previously described plus an influx of exciting new tenants such as Aeropostale, Forever 21, Sephora, and H&M and the improved performance of anchors such as Macy's and Nordstrom.[20]

An increasing number of malls are using exciting stores like Forever 21 to attract younger customers.

Lifestyle Centers

Lifestyle centers are shopping centers that have an open-air configuration of specialty stores, entertainment, and restaurants, with design ambience and amenities such as fountains and street furniture. Lifestyle centers resemble the main streets in small towns, where people stroll from store to store, have lunch, and sit for a while on a park bench talking to friends. Thus, they cater to the "lifestyles" of consumers in their trade areas. Lifestyle centers are particularly attractive to specialty retailers.

People are attracted to lifestyle centers not only because of their shops and restaurants but also because of their outdoor attractions such as a pop-up fountain, ice cream carts, stilt walkers, balloon artists, magicians, face painters, concerts, and other events. Because lifestyle centers have some limited auto access, customers can be dropped off right in front of a store.

Because lifestyle centers are open air, bad weather can be an impediment to traffic. But some centers, like the Easton Town Center in Columbus, Ohio, thrive despite the climate.[21] When the weather is bad, tough Ohioans simply bundle up and take a stroll.

Due to the ease of parking, lifestyle centers are very convenient for shoppers, and the occupancy costs, like those of all open-air developments, are considerably lower than those for enclosed malls. But they typically have less retail space than enclosed malls and thus may attract fewer customers than enclosed malls. Many lifestyle centers are located near higher-income areas, so the higher purchases per visit compensate for the fewer number of shoppers. Finally, many lifestyle centers are part of larger, mixed-use developments, which are described in the next section.

Mixed-Use Developments

Mixed-use developments (MXDs) combine several different uses into one complex including retail, office, residential, hotel, recreation, or other functions. They are pedestrian-oriented and therefore facilitate a live-work-play environment.[22] They appeal to people who have had enough of long commutes to work and the social fragmentation of their neighborhoods and are looking for a lifestyle that gives them more time for the things they enjoy and an opportunity to live in a genuine community. In addition, MXDs are popular with retailers because they bring additional shoppers to their stores. They are also popular with governments, urban planners, developers, and environmentalists because they provide a pleasant, pedestrian environment and are an efficient use of space. For instance, land costs the

Mizner Park in Boca Raton, Florida, combines retail, residential, and entertainment offerings in one location with unique boutiques, eateries, music, movies, and art galleries conveniently located close to ocean-front apartments and condos.

same whether a developer builds a shopping mall by itself or an office tower on top of the mall or parking structure.

The Boca Mall, a 430,000-square-foot regional shopping mall in Boca Raton, Florida, opened in 1974. Decades later, the mall was plagued by two trends: population growth occurring elsewhere and competing malls that were attracting most of its patrons. The original anchors and many of the specialty stores departed. The Boca Mall was demolished and replaced with a mixed-use development called Mizner Park. Mizner Park has commercial office space located above the ground-floor retail space on one side of the street, and residential units sit above the retail space on the opposite side of the street.[23]

Outlet Centers

Outlet centers are shopping centers that contain mostly manufacturers' and retailers' outlet stores.[24] Some outlet centers have a strong entertainment component, including movie theaters and restaurants to keep customers on the premises longer. For example, the Outlets at Orange, in Orange, California, has a multiplex theater, with an IMAX movie theater; a children's play area; and Thrill It Fun Center.[25]

In the past, outlet stores sold damaged merchandise or excess production overruns. However, retailers have improved their demand forecasting, reducing the availability of production overruns. In addition, the availability of damaged goods has been reduced because these goods are weeded out before being shipped to the United States. Thus, 82 percent of products at outlet centers are made specifically for the outlets. The quality of these made-for-outlet products is not always the same quality as the branded merchandise sold in department or specialty stores.[26]

Typically, outlet centers are in remote locations. These remote locations offer lower costs and reduce the competition between the outlet stores and department and specialty stores offering the branded merchandise at full price.

Tourism represents 50 percent of the traffic generated for many outlet centers. Thus, many are located with convenient interstate access and close to popular tourist attractions. Some center developers actually organize bus tours to bring people hundreds of miles to their malls. As a result, the primary trade area for some outlet centers is 50 miles or more.

Outlet centers are also very popular in Europe, Japan, and China. Retailing View 7.3 describes an upscale outlet center with a unique theme in China.

Theme/Festival Centers

In **theme/festival centers,** a unifying theme generally is reflected in each individual store, both in their architecture and the merchandise they sell. This seemingly simple idea was introduced relatively late in the progression of retail ideas. In the late 1970s, a private developer took Boston's historic Faneuil Hall and reconceived it as a "festival marketplace." The goal was to attract multitudes of tourists and local visitors by being more fun and interesting than a basic suburban mall. The Faneuil Hall Marketplace resonates with a colonial history theme. Subsequent applications of the idea have included Baltimore's Inner Harbor and the Grand Canal Shops at the Venetian Hotel in Las Vegas.

When they first opened, some of these festival locations were successful at drawing visitors and reinvigorating urban centers suffering from crime and an exodus of population. But now, with invented themes, generic stores, and vigorous competition from other nearby retailers, such centers are viewed by many as tourist traps and are avoided by many locals. In 1985, the themed shopping center that opened on Pier 17 in Lower Manhattan promised to reinvigorate the South Street

Seaport, but today, its owners are seeking to tear down the three-story building to replace it with a different, upscale shopping center.[27]

Larger, Multiformat Developments—Omnicenters

New shopping center developments are combining enclosed malls, lifestyle centers, and power centers. Although centers of this type do not have an official name, they may be referred to as **omnicenters.**

Omnicenters represent a response to several trends in retailing, including the desire of tenants to lower CAM charges by spreading the costs among more tenants and to function inside larger developments that generate more pedestrian traffic and longer shopping trips. In addition, they reflect the growing tendency of consumers to **cross-shop,** which is a pattern of buying both premium and low-priced merchandise or patronizing expensive, status-oriented retailers and price-oriented retailers, as occurs when a customer shops at both Walmart and Nordstrom's. Time-scarce customers are also attracted to omnicenters because they can get everything they need in one place. For example, the 1.3 million-square-foot St. John's Town Center in Jacksonville, Florida, is divided into three components: a lifestyle center with a Dillard's department store anchor, a mini-power center anchored by Dick's Sporting Goods and a Barnes & Noble bookstore, and a Main Street with Cheesecake Factory and P.F. Chang's restaurants as anchors.[28]

RETAILING VIEW   For China's High-End Fashion Consumers, "Italy"
Is Now Just a Bullet Train Away   7.3

Between Beijing and Tijanjin, you can find an Italian village—or at least a themed outlet mall that seeks to recreate one. With its luxury brand offerings, Florentia Village draws approximately 25,000 visitors daily, most of whom come to check out a sixteenth-century Italian village, with its narrow streets and piazzas. Once they have experienced a trip back in history, they can indulge in the purchase of Italian luxury brands, including Zegna, Armani, Ferragamo, Prada, Fendi, Bulgari, and Moncler. Near the "Colosseum," Tod's, Frette, Piquadro, and Brooks Brothers maintain their storefronts, whereas customers move through the "Grand Canal Promenade" to find Fendi, Gucci, and Prada.

China is both the largest source of counterfeits in the world and one of the biggest markets for luxury goods. The visitors who arrive at Florentia Village in the morning come by train. Wearing Western clothes, they are mostly young, evidently wealthy, and obviously Chinese. Later in the day, wealthy women wearing designer clothing drive their SUVs into the parking lots; they actively avoid the crowds of visitors on the weekends.

Although Chinese-owned outlet malls have existed for more than a decade, their success has been limited by their failure to attract top brands. These top brands worried about the effect of outlet sales on their brand images. The lesson learned is that an outlet mall's quality image is crucial; it must look like a location that sells luxury. Although "re-creating the Italian style has not been easy, with these kinds of projects, details make the difference. Asking Chinese workers to re-create Italian

The Florentia Village outlet center in China draws young and evidently wealthy customers from around the country.

style pink rock, pilasters, frames, and copper eaves was hard. But we did it."

Sources: Christopher Carothers, "A New Outlet for China's Consumerism," *The Wall Street Journal,* March 8, 2012; and Peter Foster, "China Builds Replica of Italian Town Called Florentia Village," *The Telegraph,* June 27, 2011.

DISCUSSION QUESTION

Why is the Florentia Village outlet center successful while Chinese-owned outlet centers have not been?

196   SECTION II   Retailing Strategy

NONTRADITONAL LOCATIONS

LO4

Discuss nontraditional retail locations.

Pop-up stores, stores within a store, kiosks, and airports are other location alternatives for many retailers. Retailing View 7.4 describes some of Subway's nontraditional locations and the accommodations it needed to make to secure those locations.

Pop-Up Stores and Other Temporary Locations

Pop-up stores are stores in temporary locations that focus on new products or a limited group of products. These "stores" have been around for centuries as individuals sold merchandise on city streets and at festivals or concerts, such as the Newport Jazz Festival, weekend crafts fairs, or farmers' markets. For instance, in New York's Columbus Circle, 100 vendors sell a variety of gifts from yogawear to handmade glass jewelry. Cities around the United States generally welcome these temporary retailers because they bring people and money to areas, creating excitement. Local retailers, who pay high rents, aren't necessarily so enthusiastic because some of the temporary retailers sell competing merchandise.

7.4   RETAILING VIEW   Subway Goes to Church

In 2011, Subway Restaurants passed McDonald's to become the largest restaurant chain in the world, in terms of number of locations. Subway has achieved this rapid growth partly by opening stores in nontraditional locations: an appliance store in Brazil, a California automobile showroom, a Goodwill store in South Carolina, a riverboat in Germany. One of the more remarkable locations is its One World Trade Center construction site in New York City, where the restaurant gets hoisted up to the next level as each floor of the 105-story building is completed. As the chain's chief development officer puts it, "We're continually looking at just about any opportunity for someone to buy a sandwich, wherever that might be. The closer we can get to the customer, the better." Noting the nearly 8,000 Subways in unusual locations, he adds, "The non-traditional is becoming traditional."

With its menu of sandwiches, Subway has an easier time opening in unusual venues because it has a simpler kitchen than traditional fast-food restaurants, which require frying and grilling equipment. Hospitals and religious facilities have a favorable attitude toward Subway because it promotes its sandwiches as a fresher, healthier alternative to traditional fast food.

Subway often has to make special accommodations when opening stores in nontraditional locations, though. For example, the first of many kosher Subway stores opened in the Jewish Community Center of Cleveland in 2006, and Subway is now the largest kosher chain in the United States. The kosher stores still have steak and cheese subs, except the cheese is a soy-based product. In observance of the Jewish Sabbath, these restaurants are closed on Friday afternoon and all day Saturday.

When a Subway opened in the True Bethel Baptist Church of Buffalo, New York, in a low-income area of town, the franchisee worked closely with church leaders. To support the congregation and create jobs, church leaders had approached several fast-food franchisers about

To maintain growth, Subway has opened outlets in nontraditional locations like this one at a Baptist church in Buffalo, New York.

opening a franchise in a corner of the church. Subway was the only chain that was flexible enough toward the space available and the operating hours to accommodate the church. The chain agreed to waive its requirement of a Subway sign on the outside of the building and created a parking pattern to keep restaurant traffic from displacing churchgoers during services.

Sources: Julie Jargon, "Unusual Store Locations Fuel Subway's Growth," *The Wall Street Journal*, March 10, 2011; and Alan J. Liddle, "10 Non-Traditional Subway Restaurants," *Nation's Restaurants*, July 26, 2011.

DISCUSSION QUESTION

What are the advantages and disadvantages to Subway's nontraditional location strategy?

Due to the recession and retail industry consolidation, shopping center vacancies have increased and occupancy costs have decreased. Retailers and manufacturers are opening pop-up stores in these vacant locations. Pop-up stores are particularly attractive to retailers with highly seasonal sales such as Toys "R" Us. Toys "R" Us has been experimenting with pop-ups for several years. In 2009, Toys "R" Us had 90 "Express" pop-up stores, and in 2010 it increased the number dramatically to 600. Opening, managing, and closing that large number of stores strained the management capabilities of the company. So, the company only opened 160 pop-ups in 2011. In 2012, it complemented its own pop-ups with pop-ups inside Macy's stores. The temporary Toys "R" Us units inside 24 Macy's stores were leased from October 15 through January 15. Each pop-up is roughly 1,500 square feet and includes items such as dolls, action figures, and puzzles.[29]

This Kate Spade pop-up store is an attractive temporary location for the high-fashion retailer/designer.

Cities have adopted the pop-up store concept to revitalizing their urban neighborhoods. In Oakland, California, the Pop-Up Hood concept grants six months' worth of rent-free space to independent retailers if they agree to test their innovative retail concepts in designated parts of the city.[30]

Store-within-a-Store

Store-within-a-store locations involve an agreement in which a retailer rents a part of the retail space in a store operated by another independent retailer. The host retailer basically "sublets" the space to the store-within retailer.[31] The store-within retailer manages the assortment, inventory, personnel, and systems and delivers a percentage of the sales or profits to the host. Grocery stores have been experimenting with the store-within-a-store concept for years with service providers such as coffee bars, banks, film processors, and medical clinics. Starbucks operates cafés in many retail stores.

Department stores in the United States have traditionally leased some space to other retailers, such as retailers of beauty salons, fine jewelry, and furs. However, most department stores in Europe, Japan, and China are a collection of store-within-a-store retailers. For example, Modern Plaza, a luxury department store in Beijing, "rents" all of the space in its store to a set of luxury brands, and the brands operate a store within Modern Plaza. Thus, Modern Plaza and European department stores perform the role of mall managers rather than retail stores.

In contrast, JCPenney's relationship with Sephora is more of a partnership. Sephora designs and develops the merchandise, and JCPenney is responsible for managing the sales associates and inventory sold in the Sephora boutique within a JCPenney store. The sales are made through JCPenney's POS system, and customers can use their JCPenney card when shopping in the Sephora boutique. The Sephora stores do not have a separate entrance, so there is some sense of creating a cohesive JCPenney experience.[32]

JCPenney has a partnership with Sephora using a store-within-a-store strategy.

Stores-within-a-store can be mutually beneficial to the store within and the host retailer. The store within gets an excellent location with high pedestrian traffic of customers in its target market. The host retailer generates increased revenue from the space and enhances its brand image. For example, JCPenney's relationship with Sephora enables it to offer a fashionable brand that it would not be able to offer normally through its channels. Similarly, Banfield Veterinarian services within PetSmart stores offers pet owners a true one-stop shop.[33] However, there are risks associated with this arrangement. Over time, the host or store within could have conflicting, rather than synergistic, target markets and/or brand images.

Merchandise Kiosks

Merchandise kiosks are small selling spaces, typically located in the walkways of enclosed malls, airports, college campuses, or office building lobbies. Some are staffed and resemble a miniature store or cart that could be easily moved. Others are twenty-first-century versions of vending machines, such as the Apple kiosks that sell iPods and other high-volume Apple products.

For mall operators, kiosks are an opportunity to generate rental income in otherwise vacant space and offer a broad assortment of merchandise for visitors. They also can generate excitement from retailers like national cell phone provider Sprint to smaller niche products like Israeli Dead Sea cosmetics, leading to additional sales for the entire mall. Moreover, mall kiosks can be changed quickly to match seasonal demand.

When planning the location of kiosks in a mall, operators are sensitive to their regular mall tenants' needs. They are careful to avoid kiosks that block any storefronts, create an incompatible image, or actually compete directly with permanent tenants by selling similar merchandise.

Airports

A high-pedestrian area that has become popular with national retail chains is airports.[34] Passengers arrive earlier for their flights than they did in the past, leaving them more time to shop. In addition, a cutback in airline food service has more people seeking sustenance in the airport. As a result, sales per square foot at airport malls are often much higher than at regular mall stores. However, rents are higher too. Also, costs can be higher—hours are longer, and because the location is often inconvenient for workers, the businesses have to pay higher wages. The best airport locations tend to be ones where there are many connecting flights (Atlanta and Frankfurt) and international flights (New York's Kennedy and London's Heathrow) because customers have downtime to browse through stores. The best-selling products are those that make good gifts, necessities, and easy-to-pack items. However, airport sales of consumer electronics accessories are increasing. The largest retailer of electronics at airports is InMotion Entertainment that rents DVD players and sells a wide variety of electronics and accessories in its 68 stores at 33 airports in the United States.

REFACT

Passengers spend an average of 136 minutes at Kennedy International Airport in New York from arrival to boarding.[35]

LOCATION AND RETAIL STRATEGY

LO5

Match the locations to the retailer's strategy.

The selection of a location type reinforces the retailer's strategy. Thus, the location-type decision is consistent with the shopping behavior and size of the target market and the retailer's positioning in its target market. Each of these factors is discussed next.

Shopping Behavior of Consumers in Retailer's Target Market

A critical factor affecting the type of location that consumers select to visit is the shopping situation in which they are involved. Three types of shopping situations are convenience shopping, comparison shopping, and specialty shopping.

Convenience Shopping When consumers are engaged in **convenience shopping** situations, they are primarily concerned with minimizing their effort to get the product or service they want. They are relatively insensitive to price and indifferent about which brands to buy. Thus, they don't spend much time evaluating different brands or retailers; they simply want to make the purchase as quickly and easily as possible. Examples of convenience shopping situations are getting a cup of coffee during a work break, buying gas for a car, or buying milk for breakfast in the morning.

Retailers targeting customers involved in convenience shopping, such as quick service restaurants, convenience stores, and gas stations, usually locate their stores close to where their customers are and make it easy for them to access the location, park, and find what they want. Thus, convenience stores, drugstores, fast-food restaurants, supermarkets, and full-line discount stores are generally located in neighborhood strip centers and freestanding locations.

Comparison Shopping Consumers involved in **comparison shopping** situations are more involved in the purchase decision. They have a general idea about the type of product or service they want, but they do not have a well-developed preference for a brand or model. Because the purchase decisions are more important to them, they seek information and are willing to expend effort to compare alternatives. Consumers typically engage in this type of shopping behavior when buying furniture, appliances, apparel, consumer electronics, and hand tools.

Furniture retailers, for instance, often locate next to one another to create a "furniture row." In New York City, a number of retailers selling houseplants and flowers are all located in Chelsea between 27th and 30th Streets on 6th Avenue, and diamond dealers are located on West 47th Street between 5th and 6th Avenues. These competing retailers locate near one another because doing so facilitates comparison shopping and thus attracts many customers to the locations.

Enclosed malls offer the same benefits to consumers interested in comparison shopping for fashionable apparel. Thus, department stores and specialty apparel retailers locate in enclosed malls for the same reason that houseplant retailers locate together on 6th Avenue in New York City. By co-locating in the same mall, they attract more potential customers interested in comparison shopping for fashionable apparel. Even though the enclosed mall might be inconvenient compared with a freestanding location, comparison shopping is easier after the customers have arrived.

Category specialists offer the same benefit of comparison shopping as a collection of co-located specialty stores like those described previously. Rather than going to a set of small hardware stores when comparison shopping for an electric drill, consumers know they can get almost anything they need to fix or build a house in either Home Depot or Lowe's. Thus, category specialists are **destination stores,** places where consumers will go even if it is inconvenient, just like enclosed malls are destination locations for fashionable-apparel comparison shopping. Category specialists locate in power centers, primarily to reduce their costs and create awareness of their location and secondarily to benefit from multiple retailers that attract more consumers and the resulting potential for cross-shopping. Basically, power centers are a collection of destination stores.

Specialty Shopping   When consumers go **specialty shopping,** they know what they want and will not accept a substitute. They are brand and/or retailer loyal and will pay a premium or expend extra effort, if necessary, to get exactly what they want. Examples of these shopping occasions include buying organic vegetables, a luxury automobile, or a high-end road or mountain bike. The retailers they patronize when specialty shopping also are destination stores. Thus, consumers engaged in specialty shopping are willing to travel to an inconvenient location. Having a convenient location is not as important for retailers selling unique merchandise or services.

Density of Target Market

A second, but closely related, factor that affects the retailer's choice of location type is the density of the retailer's target market in relation to the location. A good location has many people in the target market who are drawn to it. Thus, a convenience store located in a CBD can be sustained by customers living or working in fairly close proximity to the store. Similarly, a comparison shopping store located next to a Walmart is a potentially good location because Walmart draws lots of customers from a very large area. It is not as important to have high customer density near a store that sells specialty merchandise because people are willing to search out this type of merchandise. A Porsche dealer, for instance, need not be near other car dealers or in close proximity to its target market, because those seeking this luxury car will drive to wherever the dealer may be.

Uniqueness of Retail Offering

Finally, the convenience of their locations is less important for retailers with unique, differentiated offerings than for retailers with an offering similar to other retailers. For example, Bass Pro Shops provides a unique merchandise assortment and store atmosphere. Customers will travel to wherever the store is located, and its location will become a destination.

SOCIETAL AND LEGAL CONSIDERATIONS

LO6

Review the societal and legal considerations in selecting locations.

Societal and legal considerations often restrict where retailers can locate and operate their stores. These restrictions reflect the general concern that many communities have with urban sprawl, and more specifically with the opening of big-box retail stores in their communities. These restrictions on store location are often implemented through local zoning ordinances.

While there are relatively few restrictions on where stores can be located in the United States, location decisions are more restricted in other areas of the world. For example, western Europe and Asia have higher population densities and more people living and shopping in urban environments. Thus, less space is available for retailing, and the space that is available is costly. In addition, many western European countries restrict retailing to specific areas and then restrict the sizes of the stores that can be built.

In this section, we discuss the nature of the restrictions, reasons communities impose these restrictions, and the impact of these restrictions on society.

Urban Sprawl

Urban sprawl is the increased expansion of residential and shopping center development in suburban and rural areas outside of their respective urban centers. Before World War II, the downtown urban area was a community's commercial hub. Consumers shopped at local businesses downtown. The presence of offices, banks, and libraries guaranteed traffic in the downtown center. Downtown also

was an important part of an area's social life. On weekends, people met to
window shop, eat at restaurants, and
go to the movies.

The interstate highway system and
growth of the suburbs changed the
way Americans live and work. With
improved transportation, people could
travel longer distances to work or
shop. As a result, many downtown retailers went out of business. As customers and sales dwindled, property
values and tax revenues dropped.
Historic buildings were neglected and
storefronts boarded up, reinforcing
the decline of downtown areas.

In addition to the decline of the
downtown, some other negative consequences of urban sprawl are congestion
and air pollution due to increased auto-

Main Street locations in the U.K. and in U.S. towns face intense competition from hypermarkets located on the outskirts of the towns.

mobile travel, loss of farmland, concentrated poverty, and racial and economic seg-
regation. On the other hand, some desirable outcomes of this migration to the
suburbs are better housing opportunities, public schools, and less crime.[36]

The European Union is very concerned about urban sprawl and the effects of
big-box retailers locating outside the city limits. The EU is trying to restrain the
growth of big-box retailers, limiting their size and subsidizing the redevelopment
of inner city (called the High Street in the United Kingdom) to help local retailers
compete. Europe has greater population density and less space than the United
States, and stricter planning and greenbelt laws provide a sharp division between
town and country. Suburbs are few, thus minimizing urban sprawl. But preserving
the environment comes at a cost for Europe. The limits on out-of-town, big-box
retailing reduce competition and retailing efficiency, causing higher prices.[37]

Opposition to Big-Box Retailers

Retailers that operate big-box stores like Walmart, Target, Costco, and Home
Depot often meet with a great deal of resistance when they plan to build a store in
a community. Many people vehemently oppose big-box stores entering their
community. The opponents of the store openings argue that these retailers sell
merchandise at lower prices that drive local retailers out of business; do not provide a living wage for employees; hire part-time workers to avoid providing health
insurance benefits; and achieve their low prices by manufacturing merchandise
outside the United States, thus contributing to the decline of U.S. jobs.

Discussions between big-box stores and local communities continue to occur
throughout the United States and other countries. Some communities have allowed for the building of such stores when the retailers agree to pay employees a
set wage or fund low-cost housing for employees. Zoning, discussed in the following section, is one method used by local communities to restrict big-box retailers.

Zoning

Local governments in the United States use **zoning** to regulate land uses in specific
areas to prevent any interference with existing uses by residents or businesses, as
well as encourage the preservation of a community's sense of identity. Thus, zoning
ordinances might keep McDonald's from opening a franchise in a residential
neighborhood. In other nations, such as France and Germany, zoning regulations
and planning are enforced at national or state levels instead of locally.

EXHIBIT 7–3   Zoning Map for a Small Town

In urban areas, zoning ordinances often specify five categories of activities that are acceptable in a certain region or on a particular site: residential, commercial, mixed residential and commercial, industrial, or special. In addition, most zoning regulations include detailed density limitations, such as those indicating whether an area may host high-density high rises or instead is limited to low-density, single-family housing. Noting that exceptions can exist, most ordinances denote the conditions—usually hardship-related—that must be met for variances to be granted.

Exhibit 7–3 describes the zoning restrictions in Superior, Wisconsin. These zoning maps are typically developed by a planning commission and approved by the city council. Note that the areas dedicated for retailing shown in red are adjacent to the two major highways. Some areas (shown in green) are dedicated open spaces and residential areas are shown in yellow.

Building Codes

Building codes are legal restrictions that specify the type of building, signs, size and type of parking lot, and so forth, that can be used at a particular location. Some building codes require a certain-size parking lot or a particular architectural design. In Santa Fe, New Mexico, for instance, building codes require that buildings keep a traditional mud stucco (adobe) style.

Signs   Restrictions on the use of signs can affect a particular site's desirability. Sign sizes and styles may be restricted by building codes, zoning ordinances, or even the shopping center management group. At the Bal Harbour Shops in North Miami Beach, for example, all signs (even sale signs) must be approved by the shopping center management group before implementation by each individual retailer.

Licensing Requirements   Licensing requirements may vary in different parts of a region. For instance, some Dallas neighborhoods are dry, meaning no alcoholic beverages can be sold; in other areas, only wine and beer can be sold. Such restrictions can affect retailers other than restaurants and bars. For instance, a theme/festival shopping center that restricts the use of alcoholic beverages may find its clientele limited at night.

Legal issues such as those mentioned here can discourage a retailer from pursuing a particular site. These restrictions aren't always permanent, however. Although difficult, time consuming, and possibly expensive, lobbying efforts and court battles can change these legal restrictions.

SUMMARY

LO1 Describe the types of retail locations available to retailers.

Store location decisions are important decisions for a retailer because location is typically one of the most influential considerations in a customer's store-choice decision. Location decisions also have strategic implications because they can be used to develop a sustainable competitive advantage and location decisions are risky.

LO2 Review the types of unplanned locations.

Two basic types of location are unplanned (free-standing and urban sites) and planned (shopping centers). Unplanned locations do not have centralized management that determines what stores will be in a development, where the specific stores will be located, and how they will be operated. The three types of unplanned retail locations are freestanding sites, urban and Main Street locations. Freestanding locations are convenient for customers and have high vehicular traffic and visibility, modest occupancy costs, and few restrictions. But freestanding sites are higher in cost and have smaller trade areas. In general, urban locations have lower occupancy costs than enclosed malls; vehicular traffic is limited, and parking problems reduce consumer convenience.

LO3 Analyze the characteristics of the different types of shopping centers.

By combining many stores at one location, shopping centers attract more consumers to the center than would be the case if the stores were at separate locations. The developer and shopping center management carefully select a set of retailers that are complementary to provide consumers with a comprehensive shopping experience at one, convenient location. Each of the types of shopping centers has its advantages and disadvantages. Many central business districts, inner-city, and Main Street locations have become more viable options than they were in the past because of gentrification of the areas, tax incentives, and lack of competition. There also are a wide variety of shopping center types for retailers. They can locate in a strip or power center; an enclosed mall; or a lifestyle, theme/festival, or outlet center.

LO4 Discuss nontraditional retail locations.

Pop-up stores, stores-within-a-store, kiosks, and airports are other location alternatives for many retailers. Pop-up stores are particularly attractive to retailers with highly seasonal sales. Store-within-a-store locations involve an agreement in which a retailer rents a part of the retail space in a store operated by another independent retailer. These locations are mutually beneficial to the host and store within.

LO5 Match the locations to the retailer's strategy.

The selection of a location type reinforces the retailer's strategy. Thus, the location-type decision is consistent with the shopping behavior and size of the target market and the retailer's positioning in its target market. Different shopping locations are more appropriate for consumers engaged in three types of customer shopping situations: convenience shopping, comparison shopping, and specialty shopping.

LO6 Review the societal and legal considerations in selecting locations.

Societal and legal considerations often restrict the locations and operations of standalone stores and shopping centers. These restrictions reflect the general concern that many communities have with urban sprawl and, more specifically, with the opening of big-box retail stores in their communities. Shopping center developers and retailers often need to deal with zoning ordinances before they open stores in a community.

KEY TERMS

anchor, *189*

building codes, *202*

central business district (CBD), *185*

common area maintenance (CAM), *184*

community shopping center, *190*

comparison shopping, *199*

convenience shopping center, *190*

convenience shopping, *199*

cross-shop, *195*

destination store, *199*

freestanding site, *185*

gentrification, *186*

gross leasable area (GLA), *184*

inner city, *186*

lifestyle center, *193*

Main Street, *188*

merchandise kiosk, *198*

mixed-use development (MXD), *193*

neighborhood shopping center, *190*

omnicenter, *195*

outlet center, *194*

outparcel, *185*

planned location, *184*

pop-up store, *196*

power center, *191*

regional mall, *191*

shopping center, *189*

shopping center property management firm, *189*

shopping mall, *191*

specialty shopping, *200*

GET OUT AND DO IT!

1. **CONTINUING CASE ASSIGNMENT** Interview the manager of the shopping center that contains the retailer you selected for the Continuing Assignment. Write a report summarizing which retailers the shopping center manager thinks are his or her best tenants and why they are valued. How does the manager rate the retailer you have selected? What criteria does he or she use?

2. **INTERNET EXERCISE** Go to the web page for Faneuil Hall Marketplace at www.faneuilhallmarketplace.com and the online site for CocoWalk at www.cocowalk.net. What kinds of centers are these? List their similarities and differences. Who is the target market for each of these retail locations?

3. **GO SHOPPING** Go to your favorite shopping center, and analyze the tenant mix. Do the tenants appear to complement one another? What changes would you make in the tenant mix to increase the overall performance of the center?

4. **GO SHOPPING** Visit a lifestyle center. What tenants are found in this location? Describe the population characteristics around this center. How far would people drive to shop at this lifestyle center? What other types of retail locations does this lifestyle center compete with?

5. **INTERNET EXERCISE** Go to the home page for Simon Property Group, www.simon.com/about_simon/our_business/default.aspx, and read about the businesses that Simon is in. What is the difference between their businesses?

6. **INTERNET EXERCISE** Go to the home page of your favorite enclosed mall, and describe the mall in terms of the following characteristics: number of anchor stores, number and categories of specialty stores, number of sit-down and quick-service restaurants, and types of entertainment offered. What are the strengths and weaknesses of this assortment of retailers? What are the unique features of this particular mall?

7. **GO SHOPPING** Visit a power center that contains a Target, Staples, Sports Authority, Home Depot, or other category specialists. What other retailers are in the same location? How is this mix of stores beneficial to both shoppers and retailers?

8. **INTERNET EXERCISE** Go to www.pbs.org/itvs/storewars/. This site contains information about the Ashland town council's decision to allow Walmart to open a store in Ashland, Virginia. Summarize the pros and cons of allowing Walmart to open a store in town. Were you surprised by the town council's decision? Why or why not?

DISCUSSION QUESTIONS AND PROBLEMS

1. Why is store location such an important decision for retailers?

2. Pick your favorite store. Describe the advantages and disadvantages of its current location, given its store type and target market.

3. Home Depot typically locates in either a power center or a freestanding site. What are the strengths of each location for this home improvement retailer?

4. As a consultant to 7-Eleven convenience stores, American Eagle Outfitters, and Porsche of America, what would you say is the single most important factor in choosing a site for these three very different types of stores?

5. Retailers are locating in shopping centers and freestanding locations in central business districts that have suffered decay. As a result, these areas are rejuvenating, a process known as gentrification. Some people have questioned the ethical and social ramifications of this process. Discuss the benefits and detriments of gentrification.

6. Staples, Office Max, and Office Depot all have strong multichannel strategies. How do competition and the Internet affect their strategies for locating stores?

7. In many malls, quick-service food retailers are located together in an area known as a food court. What are the advantages and disadvantages of this location for the food retailers? What is the new trend for food retailers in the shopping environment?

8. Why would a Payless ShoeSource store locate in a neighborhood shopping center instead of a regional shopping mall?

9. How does the mall near your home or university combine the shopping and entertainment experiences?

10. Consider a big city that has invested in an urban renaissance. What components of the gentrification project attract both local residents and visiting tourists to spend time shopping, eating, and sightseeing in this location?

SUGGESTED READINGS

Brooks, Charles, Patrick J. Kaufmann, and Donald R. Lichtenstein. "Trip Chaining Behavior in Multi-Destination Shopping Trips: A Field Experiment and Laboratory Replication." *Journal of Retailing* 84, no. 1 (2008), pp. 29–38.

Curtiss, Donald L. *Operation Shopping Centers; Guidebook to Effective Management & Promotion.* Ulan Press, 2011.

Gibbs, Robert J. *Principles of Urban Retail Planning and Development.* New York: Wiley, 2012.

International Council of Shopping Centers. *Winning Shopping Center Designs,* 35th ed. New York: ICSC, 2012.

Kim, Jung-Hwan, and Rodney Runyan. "Where Did All the Benches Go? The Effects of Mall Kiosks on Perceived Retail Crowding." *International Journal of Retail & Distribution Management* 39, no. 2 (2011), pp. 130–143.

Roslin, Rosmimah, and Mohd Herwina Rosnan. "Location as a Strategic Retail Decision: The Case of the Retail Cooperative." *International Journal of Commerce and Management* 22, no. 2 (2012), pp. 152–158.

Ruoh-Nan, Yan, and Molly Eckman. "Are Lifestyle Centres Unique? Consumers' Perceptions across Locations." *International Journal of Retail & Distribution Management* 37, no. 1 (2009), pp. 24–42.

Schewel, Laura B., and Lee J. Schipper. "Shop 'Till We Drop: A Historical and Policy Analysis of Retail Goods Movement in The United States." *Environmental Science and Technology* 46, no. 18 (2012), pp. 9813–9821.

Yiu, C. Y., and Sys Xu. "A Tenant-Mix Model for Shopping Malls," *European Journal of Marketing,* 46, no. 3 (2012), pp. 234–256.

Retail Site Location

EXECUTIVE BRIEFING
Brenden O'Brien, Senior Real Estate Manager
Walgreen Co.

In May 2006, I graduated from Miami University (Oxford, Ohio). I competed on their varsity swimming and diving team while double majoring in marketing and entrepreneurship. During my senior year in college, I was fortunate to receive a job offer from Walgreens in its corporate real estate department. Growing up on the North Shore of Chicago, I never thought I would join corporate America; however, my career continues to be an exceptionally rewarding learning experience.

Our locations are critical strategic assets, and we take a long-term perspective in developing each and every store. A team comprised of market planning and research, a market VP from operations, and a real estate manager evaluate new opportunities. Accessing a vast amount of collected data in a geographic information system, the team identifies ideal target locations for our stores. Walgreens strives to lock down the best real estate deal in each neighborhood, which generally equates to the intersection with the most amount of traffic. Because we target the best locations for future stores, the real estate is not easy to put under contract nor are all locations commercially feasible. Sometimes the real estate prices are so high that the economics become cost prohibitive. To finalize each and every opportunity,

real estate managers must present them for approval to the Walgreens real estate committee. This committee is comprised of a panel of executives at corporate headquarters. Many of the highest-level executives in Walgreens are involved in the final decision, which includes the location, the economics, and a specific plan for each store. I am amazed that after only six years from college graduation, I am interacting with corporate-level executives in one of the 10 largest retail companies in the world.

Walgreens gives me the opportunity to be creative, develop new ideas, and also learn from others in the company. For example, one of my most exciting projects was developing a location directly across from SeaWorld on International Drive in Orlando, Florida. International Drive attracts a massive number of tourists who flock to the area to spend money at stores, restaurants, and attractions. Walgreens already had five successful stores on International Drive; however, I negotiated a deal to include a nontraditional store at an underserved fabulous location. We designed the exterior of the store to include unique architectural elements and designed the interior of the store to include special features

CHAPTER 8

such as a curved ceiling, in order to enhance the customer experience. The merchandise is uniquely designed for tourists with an emphasis on souvenirs, an expanded food offering, and an assortment of health and beauty aids.

To be successful in any endeavor, you need to stay ahead of the curve by continuing to learn.

Walgreens provides an atmosphere that supports my interest in developing my knowledge in real estate (my job), finance, and business in general. The company was very supportive of my efforts to complete the course work and examinations required to become a certified commercial investment member, or CCIM.

Chapter 5 emphasized the strategic importance of location decisions. Although location decisions can create strategic advantage, like all strategic decisions, they are also risky because they involve a significant commitment of resources. Opening a store at a site often involves committing to a lease of five years or more or purchasing land and building a store. If the store's performance is below expectations, the retailer may not be able to recover its investment easily by having another party move in and assume the lease or buy the building.

Chapter 7 reviewed the different types of locations available to retailers and why certain types of retailers gravitate toward particular locations. This chapter takes a closer look at how retailers choose specific sites to locate their stores.

Selecting retail locations involves the analysis of a large amount of data and the use of sophisticated statistical models. Because most retailers make these decisions infrequently, it is not economical for them to employ full-time real estate analysts with state-of-the-art skills. Thus, small retailers often use firms that provide the geographic and demographic data and consulting services needed to evaluate specific sites. However, there continues to be an element of art in making these location decisions.

This chapter reviews the steps retailers go through in selecting their store locations and negotiating leases. The first part of the chapter examines the factors retailers consider when selecting a general area for locating stores and determining the number of stores to operate in each area. Then this chapter reviews different approaches used to evaluate specific sites and estimate the expected sales if and when a store is located at that site. Finally, the chapter looks at the various terms that are negotiated when a retailer commits to leasing space for its store.

EVALUATING AREAS FOR LOCATIONS AND DETERMINING THE NUMBER OF STORES IN AN AREA

LO1

Summarize the factors considered in locating a number of stores.

The first part of this section discusses the areas retailers typically analyze when making location decisions, and the second section reviews factors retailers consider when evaluating these areas for locating stores and determining the number of stores to put in an area.

Metropolitan Statistical Area

Areas that retailers consider for locating stores might be countries, areas within a country such as a province in France or a state in the United States, particular cities, or areas within cities. In the United States, retailers often focus their analysis on a **metropolitan statistical area (MSA)** because consumers tend to shop within an MSA, and media coverage and demographic data for analyzing location opportunities often are organized by MSA.

An MSA is a core urban area containing a population of more than 50,000 inhabitants, together with adjacent communities that have a high degree of economic and social integration with the core community. For example, many people in an MSA commute to work in the central business district but live in the surrounding areas. An MSA can consist of one or several counties and usually is named after the major urban area in the MSA. For example, the Cincinnati-Middleton MSA consists of 15 counties (3 in Indiana, 7 in Kentucky, and 5 in Ohio) with a population of 2,172,191; the Missoula, Montana, MSA consists of one county with a population of 110,138.

In contrast, a **micropolitan statistical area (μSA)** is somewhat removed from larger U.S. cities, often by up to 100 miles. Although they lack big cities' pull and economic significance, these notable population centers often are responsible for substantial production capabilities and provide reasonable housing accommodations for many residents. The designation refers to the core population of a central town, so regardless of their name, a micropolitan area could be larger than a metropolitan area. The largest μSA is Seaford, Delaware, with a population of 200,330.[3]

Considerations in Evaluating Store Locations

The best areas for locating stores are those that generate the highest long-term profits for a retailer. Some factors affecting the long-term profit generated by stores that should be considered when evaluating an area include: (1) the economic conditions, (2) competition, (3) the strategic fit of the area's population with the retailer's target market, and (4) the costs of operating stores (see Exhibit 8–1). Note that these factors are similar to those that retailers consider when evaluating an investment in a new business growth opportunity or entry into a foreign market, as discussed in Chapter 5.

REFACT

California has the most shopping centers (6,379) and Wyoming has the fewest (55).[1]

REFACT

There are 366 MSAs and 576 μSAs in the United States.[2]

EXHIBIT 8–1
Factors Affecting the Attractiveness of an Area for Locating Stores

Economic Conditions   Because locations involve a commitment of resources over a long time horizon, it is important to examine an area's level and growth of population and employment. A large, fully employed population means high purchasing power and high levels of retail sales.

But population and employment growth alone aren't enough to ensure a strong retail environment in the future. Retail location analysts need to determine how long such growth will continue and how it will affect demand for merchandise sold in the stores. For instance, if growth is not diversified in various industries, the area may be unattractive because of extreme cyclical trends. The economies of some Rust Belt cities like Flint, Michigan, experience greater peaks and valleys because of their dependence on specific industries such as automobiles.

Also, it is useful to determine which areas are growing quickly and why. For instance, the east side of Seattle, Washington, has become a desirable retail location because of its proximity to Microsoft's corporate headquarters. But the performance of these retail locations is linked to the financial performance of Microsoft.

In most cases, areas where the population is large and growing are preferable to those with declining populations. However, some retailers, such as Subway, often go into new strip shopping centers with few nearby households with the anticipation that the surrounding suburban area will eventually be built up enough to support the stores.

Competition   The level of competition in an area affects the demand for a retailer's merchandise. Walmart's early success was based on a location strategy of opening stores in small towns with little competition. It offered consumers in small towns quality merchandise at low prices. Previously, rural consumers either shopped in small stores with limited assortments or drove to larger towns.

Although they once were viewed as undesirable areas, inner-city neighborhoods today host many full-service restaurant chains, including Chili's, Denny's, IHOP, and so forth. For such casual restaurants, underserved urban locations offer some strong attractions, including minimal competition levels; a large, readily accessible labor force; and, in some neighborhoods, a surrounding market of customers with high disposable incomes.

Retailing View 8.1 describes the success realized by Stage Stores targeting small towns with limited competition for fashionable apparel.

Strategic Fit   Economic conditions and competition alone don't tell the whole story. The area needs to have consumers who are in the retailer's target market— who are attracted to the retailer's offerings and interested in patronizing its stores. Thus, the area must have the right demographic and lifestyle profile. The size and composition of households in an area can be an important determinant of success. For instance, electronics, appliance, and home goods store, La Curacao, focuses on Hispanic consumers. Thus it has 11 locations in southern California and Arizona— all locations are areas with at least 250,000 Hispanics.[4] Ethnic composition of the trade area, however, is not a particularly critical issue for Toys "R" Us, which is interested in locations with heavy concentrations of families with young children.

Party City, the world's largest party supply retailer, sells celebratory merchandise for happy occasions—birthdays, holiday parties, anniversaries—through more than 600 company-owned franchised stores. Party City chooses locations that have a high density of middle-income shoppers with children.[5]

Finally, lifestyle characteristics of the population may be relevant, depending on the target market(s) that a particular retailer is pursuing. For example, areas with consumers interested in outdoor activities are attractive for REI and Bass Pro Shops.

Operating Costs   The cost of operating stores can vary across areas. For example, store rental and advertising costs in the Missoula, Montana, MSA are significantly lower than those in the Cincinnati-Middletown MSA. But, of course,

---

8.1   RETAILING VIEW   Big Payoff from Small Towns

Even though Stage Stores is a billion-dollar retail chain operating in more than 800 locations, it is relatively unknown because most of its stores are located in small towns. Being outside the big city has advantages, though. "The beauty of our business model is that we have no natural competitor," said Andy Hall, former president and CEO of Stage Stores: "Most small towns are not big enough for two stores like ours. The first one in wins." Typically, the nearest thing to competition for Stage Stores' small-town locations are regional malls 40 miles away and online sites.

Among the 801 stores, 521 are in small markets (small MSAs and larger μSAs), mostly in strip centers in towns with less than 50,000 people within a 10-mile radius. Stage Stores operates under the names Palais Royal, Bealls, Goody's, Peebles, and Stage. Of the 521 small-town Stage Store locations, 510 are near a Walmart. Customers buy their groceries and hard goods at Walmart and their apparel at Stage stores. Name brands, such as Lee, Levi's, Calvin Klein Jeans, Izod, Nike, Nautica, Dockers, Nine West, Clinique, and Estee Lauder, are 80 percent of sales.

A downside of being small-town-focused is being overlooked by many investors, according to Hall. "Most city dwellers don't understand the vibrancy of small markets. It's an amazing culture in small markets," Hall said.

Bealls, a subsidiary of Stage Stores focus on small towns where it faces little competition for its assortment of designer fashion apparel and accessories.

Sales associates and customers there are more likely to know each other, and their relationships in the stores are often warm.

Sources: David Kaplan, "Stage Stores' Strategy Pays Off Big in Small Towns," *Houston Chronicle*, August 1, 2011; www.stagestores.com.

DISCUSSION QUESTION

What are the opportunities and threats Stage Stores faces?

the potential sales and profits from stores located in the Cincinnati-Middletown MSA are substantially greater due to its larger and denser population.

Operating costs are also affected by the proximity of the area being considered to other areas in which the retailer operates stores. For example, if a store is located near other stores and the retailer's distribution centers, the cost of shipping merchandise to the store is lower, as is the cost and travel time spent by the district manager supervising the stores' operations.

The local and state legal and regulatory environment can have a significant effect on operating costs. Some retailers are reluctant to locate stores in California because they feel that the state and local governments, the political process of voter-initiated referendums, and a legal environment that fosters class-action lawsuits result in higher operating costs.[6]

Number of Stores in an Area

Having selected an area in which to locate its stores, a retailer's next decision is how many stores to operate in the area. At first glance, you might think that a retailer should choose the one best location in each MSA, but clearly, larger MSAs can support more stores than smaller MSAs. It may, therefore, be more advantageous to locate several stores in one MSA and none in others. But there is a limit to how many stores can be operated in even the largest MSAs. When making the decision about how many stores to open in an area, retailers must consider the trade-offs between lower operating costs and potential sales cannibalization from having multiple stores in an area.

Economies of Scale from Multiple Stores   Most retail chains open multiple stores in an area to lower promotion and distribution by realizing economies of scale. A retailer's total promotional costs are the same for newspaper advertising that promotes 20 stores in a MSA or only 1 store. Multiple stores in an MSA can be serviced by the same distribution center. Thus, chains like Walmart expand into areas only where they have a distribution center in place to support the stores.[7] When Kohl's entered the Florida market, it opened 14 stores in Jacksonville and Orlando on the same day. Finally, when stores are located close each other, district store managers visit each of their stores more frequently.

Cannibalization   Although retailers gain scale economies from opening multiple locations in an MSA, they also suffer diminishing returns associated with locating too many additional stores in an area. For example, suppose the first four stores opened in an MSA by a specialty store retailer generate sales of $2 million each. Because they are located far apart from one another, customers consider patronizing only the store nearest to them, and there is no cannibalization. When the retailer opens a fifth store close to one of the existing stores, it hopes for a net sales increase for the area of $2 million; the new store should generate the same sales level as the four existing stores. Instead, the increase in incremental sales might be only $1.5 million because the sales in the nearest existing store's sales drop to $1.7 million and sales from the new store are only $1.8 million because its location is only the fifth best in the area. Thus, because the new store cannibalizes sales from the closest store, it only contributes sales of $1.5 million.

Because a primary retailing objective is to maximize profits for the entire chain, retailers should continue to open stores only as long as profits continue to increase or, in economic terms, as long as the marginal revenues achieved by opening a new store are greater than the marginal costs. Exhibit 8–2 shows the location of customers that are 3 (yellow), 6 (pink), and 9 (blue) minutes from a retailer's four stores in an area. Note how there is very little overlap, thus little cannibalization except for the City East and the South East stores.

For franchise retail operations, the objectives of the franchisor and franchisee differ, and thus, disputes can arise over the number of locations in an area. The

EXHIBIT 8–2
Location of Customers
Patronizing a Retailer's
Store

franchisor is interested in maximizing the sales of all stores because it earns a royalty based on total store sales. The franchisee is interested in just the sales and profits from its store(s). Thus, the franchisor is not as concerned about cannibalization as the franchisee is. To reduce the level of conflict, most franchise agreements grant franchisees an exclusive territory to protect them from another franchisee cannibalizing their sales.[8]

CONSIDERATIONS IN EVALUATING STORE LOCATIONS

LO2

Review the characteristics
of a particular site.

Having decided to locate stores in an area, the retailer's next step is to evaluate and select a specific site. In making this decision, retailers consider three factors: (1) the characteristics of the site, (2) the characteristics of the trading area for a store at the site, and (3) the estimated potential sales that can be generated by a store at the site. The first two sets of factors are typically considered in an initial screening of potential sites. The methods used to forecast store sales, the third factor, can involve a more complex analytical approach. Each of these factors is discussed in the following sections.

Site Characteristics

Some characteristics of a site that affect store sales and thus are considered in selecting a site are (1) the traffic flow past the site and accessibility to the site, (2) parking, (3) visibility, (4) adjacent tenants, and (5) restrictions and costs.

Traffic Flow and Accessibility   One of the most important factors affecting store sales is the **traffic flow**—the number of vehicles and pedestrians that pass by the site. When the traffic is greater, more consumers are likely to stop in and shop at the store. Thus, retailers often use traffic count measures to assess a site's attractiveness. Traffic counts are particularly important for retailers offering merchandise and services bought on impulse or on frequent trips such as grocery stores, convenience, and car washes. In contrast, traffic flow is not as important for destination retailers such as The Container Store.

More traffic flow is not always better. Traffic volume counts for surrounding roadways are often used to assess the attractiveness of a retail site. But these measures can be misleading. While these measures can give a reasonable estimate of the level of activity in an area, they do not provide any indication of how much of that volume actually stops and shops at a particular retail location. Most shopping centers are located along heavily traveled roads and highways. As such, these roads are heavily traveled by drivers commuting to and from work or carrying out a number of other daily activities that don't include shopping. As such, daily traffic counts are skewed during rush hours, which creates congestion that impedes access to the stores. Also, traffic volume counts are collected over a 24-hour period, and average rates are reported, whereas retail properties are typically only open for 8 to 12 hours each day.

The **accessibility** of the site, which can be as important as traffic flow, is the ease with which customers can get into and out of the site. Accessibility is greater for sites located near major highways, on uncongested highways, and at streets with traffic lights and lanes that enable turns into the site. Retailing View 8.2 describes the importance of accessibility to a retailer's business.

Natural barriers, such as rivers or mountains, and **artificial barriers**, such as railroad tracks, divided or limited-access highways, or parks, may also affect accessibility. These barriers' impact on a particular site primarily depends on whether the merchandise or services will appeal to customers so strongly that they cross the barrier. For example, a supermarket on one side of a divided highway with no convenient crossover point will appeal only to consumers going in one direction.

A more accurate measure of traffic, which can be obtained from several specialized companies, is the number of consumers entering the shopping center, collected at store entrances within the shopping center. This measure provides a more accurate picture of the number of consumers actually patronizing the shopping center. Additionally, the measure is available for every day of the year individually, rather than the annual averages provided by firms specializing in traffic counts. This allows for more detailed and targeted analyses based on seasonal or week-to-week comparisons.

In the United States, most consumers drive to shopping centers, and thus vehicular traffic is an important consideration when evaluating a site. However, pedestrian traffic flow and access by public transportation are more important for analyzing sites in countries such as China where consumers do not drive to shop or for evaluating urban sites and sites within an enclosed mall.

Parking The amount and quality of parking facilities are critical for evaluating a shopping center. On the one hand, if there aren't enough spaces or the spaces are too far from the store, customers will be discouraged from patronizing the site and the store. On the other hand, if there are too many open spaces, the shopping center may be perceived as having unpopular stores. A standard rule of thumb is 5.5:1,000 (five and one-half spaces per thousand square feet of retail store space) for a shopping center and 10 to 15 spaces per 1,000 square feet for a supermarket.

The parking around this Best Buy store contributes to the quality of this location.

8.2   RETAILING VIEW   It Pays to Locate on the Right Side of the Road

For U.S. drivers, businesses and stores located on the right side of the road, rather than on the left, are the ones they see most readily on their commutes home from work or school. That is, if we were to measure the volume of traffic on a road, we would find that the right-hand side of the yellow lines takes up far more afternoon volume. Accordingly, for many businesses, a location on that right-hand side can be highly desirable because it is easy for customers to make a quick right turn into their properties, then an easier right turn out of the retail parking area, without having to cross many lanes of traffic.

In the morning, a right-side location might be ideal for a coffee shop or newspaper stand. But most commuters have little time to spare in the mornings, so they reserve their stops to fill up on gas, grab a gallon of milk, or perhaps sneak in an afternoon candy bar for their rides home.

For Hess gas stations and convenience stores, locating on the right-hand side for afternoon commuters is a priority. As a vertically integrated energy company, Hess is involved in oil exploration and refining, but its most familiar presence is its approximately 1,400 green-logoed retail stores, running up and down the East Coast of the United States. For its 1.3 million daily customers, "The location of our stores is critical to providing value . . . and is paramount to our success," according to Rick Lawlor, vice president of retail marketing for Hess. To generate its $6 billion in annual sales, Hess maintains

Rick Lawlor at Hess positions Hess's convenience stores on the right side of the road.

a staff that evaluates the location of stores we are considering to build or acquire. When evaluating locations, we look at all the numbers—the size and characteristics of the store's trading area, the demographics and geodemographics of the customers that drive by the location and live in the area. However, the most important factors for us are visibility and access—that is, can customers see the signage for our stores and easily make a right turn into the location on their way home? While the data on a location are useful, we never open a location without looking at it in person to assess its visibility and access.

Right turns into and out of Hess locations are particularly important for its customers, who demand a maximum of convenience from their convenience stores. For many drivers, being required to cross multiple lanes of traffic (and hold up frustrated drivers behind them) to make a left turn simply isn't worth the hassle. If they also need to make a left turn out of the parking lot to continue their commute, their quick pit stop could turn into an extended chore as they wait for gaps in the heavy rush hour traffic to enter the flow of cars.

Locations on the left-hand side of the road, from commuters' perspective, also have grown increasingly problematic with the expansion of "access control" policies by local, county, and state transportation agencies. Such controls include the installation of medians and curbing that limit left turns, as well as prohibitions on U-turns at traffic signals.

As a result of these consumer preferences and governmental policies, being on the "wrong" side of the road can result in a 5 to 20 percent decrease in customer transactions, depending on the road's specific traffic volume patterns.

The bottom line is thus that it is no longer just "location, location, location" that matters for retail sales. Location questions must be evaluated in the context of "access, access, access," especially for customers seeking convenience. Any retailer evaluating locations for stores therefore should think carefully about the traffic patterns whizzing by. Are you on the right side, or the wrong side, of the road?

Sources: "It Pays to Be on the Right Side of the Road," *TSImaster,* 2011; Rick Lawlor, personal communication.

DISCUSSION QUESTIONS

For what types of retailers is being on the right side more important during afternoon commutes? For which types of retailers is it more important during the morning commute? Are there any types of retailers for which a right-hand side location is not particularly important?

Retailers need to observe the shopping center at various times of the day, week, and season. They also must consider the availability of employee parking, the proportion of shoppers using cars, parking by non-shoppers, and the typical length of a shopping trip.

An issue closely related to the amount of available parking facilities but extended into the shopping center itself is the relative congestion of the area. **Congestion** is an excess level of traffic that results in customer delays. There is an optimal level of congestion for customers. Too much congestion can make shopping slow, irritate customers, and generally discourage sales. However, a relatively high level of activity in a shopping center creates excitement and can stimulate sales.

The location of this store is poor because the store and its signage are not visible.

Visibility   **Visibility** refers to customers' ability to see the store from the street. Good visibility is less important for stores with a well-established and loyal customer base, but most retailers still want a direct, unimpeded view of their store. In an area with a highly transient population, such as a tourist center or large city, good visibility from the road is particularly important.

Adjacent Tenants   Locations with complementary, as well as competing, adjacent retailers have the potential to build traffic. Complementary retailers target the same market segment but have a different, noncompeting merchandise offering. For example, Save-A-Lot, a limited-assortment supermarket targeting price-sensitive consumers, prefers to be co-located with other retailers targeting price-sensitive consumers, such as Big Lots, Family Dollar, or even Walmart.

Have you ever noticed that competing fast-food restaurants, automobile dealerships, antique dealers, or even shoe and apparel stores in a mall are located next to one another? Consumers looking for these types of merchandise are involved in convenience or comparison shopping situations, as we described in Chapter 7. They want to be able to make their choice easily in the case of convenience shopping, or they want to have a good assortment so that they can "shop around," in the case of shopping goods. This grouped location approach is based on the principle of **cumulative attraction,** which states that a cluster of similar and complementary retailing activities will generally have greater drawing power than isolated stores that engage in the same retailing activities.[9]

Restrictions and Costs   As we learn later in this chapter, retailers may place restrictions

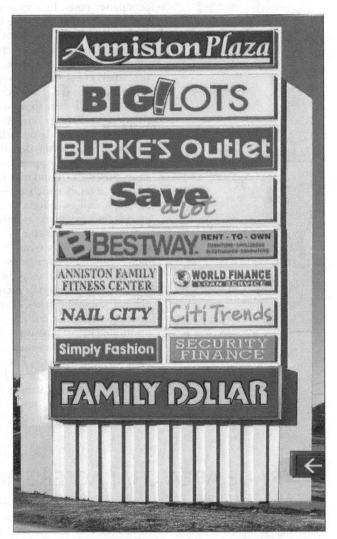

Save-A-Lot prefers locations next to Big Lots or Family Dollar because the presence of the two retailers will attract additional consumers.

on the type of tenants that are allowed in a shopping center in their lease agreement. Some of these restrictions can make the shopping center more attractive for a retailer. For example, a specialty men's apparel retailer may prefer a lease agreement that precludes other men's specialty apparel retailers from locating in the same center. A florist in a strip center may specify that if the grocery anchor tenant vacates the center, it can be released from its lease. Retailers would look unfavorably on a shopping center with a sign size restriction that prevented easy visibility of the store's name from the street. At the end of the chapter, we discuss some other restrictions and cost issues involved in negotiating a lease.

Locations within a Shopping Center

While the previous discussion focused on factors affecting the attractiveness of a shopping center location, the location within a shopping center has a significant effect on both sales and occupancy costs. The better locations have higher occupancy costs. In a strip shopping center, the locations closest to the supermarket are more expensive because they attract greater foot traffic. So a flower shop or sandwich shop that may attract impulse buyers should be close to the supermarket. But a shoe repair store, which does not cater to customers shopping on impulse, could be in a lower-traffic location farther away from the supermarket because customers in need of this service will seek out the store. In other words, it is a destination store.

The same issues apply to evaluating locations within a multilevel, enclosed shopping mall. Stores that cater to consumers engaging in comparison shopping, such as shoppers buying fashionable apparel, benefit from being in more expensive locations near the department store anchors, which are destinations for comparison apparel shoppers. As apparel shoppers enter and leave the department store, they walk by and may be attracted to neighboring specialty store retailers. In contrast, a retailer such as Foot Locker, another destination store, need not be in the most expensive location, because many of its customers know they're in the market for its type of product before they even go shopping.

Another consideration is how to locate stores that appeal to similar target markets. In essence, customers want to shop where they'll find a good assortment of merchandise. The principle of cumulative attraction applies to both stores that sell complementary merchandise and those that compete directly with one another. Consider the location of retailers in The Mall in Columbia, the centerpiece of the planned community of Columbia, Maryland. The mall's trade area includes about three-quarters of a million people, located in wealthy Howard County, which is positioned halfway between Baltimore, Maryland, and Washington, DC. Many of the tenants are positioned within the mall into category zones to better match their target markets.[10] For example, at the Mall in Columbia, retailers selling jewelry are located near each other. On the lower level are Zales Jewelers, Shaw's Jewelers, Pandora, Littman Jewelers, Monica Jewelers, and Fire and Ice. A short escalator ride to the upper level are Eastern Coral, Edward Arthur, Helzberg Diamond, Michael Kors, Reed's Jewelers, and Icing Ice.

TRADE AREA CHARACTERISTICS

LO3

Understand how retailers analyze the trade area for a site.

After identifying several sites that have acceptable traffic flow, accessibility, and other location characteristics, the next step is to collect information about the trade area that can be used to forecast sales for a store located at the site. The retailer first needs to define the trade area for the site. Once the trade area is defined, the retailer can use several different information sources to develop a detailed understanding of the nature of consumers in the site's trade area.

EXHIBIT 8–3
Zones in a Trade Area

Trade Area Definition

A **trade area** is a contiguous geographic area that accounts for the majority of a store's sales and customers. Trade areas can be divided into three zones, as shown in Exhibit 8–3. The exhibit shows the trade area zones for a shopping center located at the red square: the 5-minute drive-time zone (light brown), the 10-minute zone (blue), and the 15-minute zone (green).

The trade area zones shown in Exhibit 8–3 are not concentric circles based on distance from the store but, rather, are irregular polygons based on the location of roads, highways, and natural barriers, like rivers and valleys, that affect the driving time to the store. The location of competitive stores can also affect the actual trade area configuration.

The **primary trading area** is the geographic area from which the shopping center or store site derives 50 to 70 percent of its customers. The **secondary trading area** is the geographic area of secondary importance in terms of customer sales, generating about 20 to 30 percent of the site's customers. The **tertiary trading area** or **fringe** (the outermost area) includes the remaining customers who shop at the site but come from widely dispersed areas. These customers might travel an unusually long distance because they do not have comparable retail facilities closer to home, or they may drive near the store or center on their way to or from work.

The best way to define the three zones is based on driving time rather than distance. Thus, the primary trading area might be defined as customers within 5 minutes' driving time of the site; the secondary trading area, as customers with a 10-minute drive; and the tertiary zone, as customers more than 15 minutes away from the site by car. In bigger cities where driving times are lengthy, such as Los Angeles, the primary trading area may be 15 minutes; the secondary trading area, 40 minutes; and the tertiary trading area, more than 1 hour. However, it is much easier to collect information about the number of people and their characteristics in the different zones by geographic distance than by driving time. Thus, retailers often define the zones by distance—such as 3, 5, and 10 miles from the site—rather than driving time.

Factors Affecting the Size of the Trade Area

The actual boundaries of a trade area are determined by the store's accessibility, natural and physical barriers, level of competition, nature of the merchandise sold, the assortment offered, and the location of alternative sources for the merchandise.

A Starbucks in a central business district, for example, may have a trade area of only two or three blocks; a category specialist like Michaels may draw customers from 10 miles away; and The Container Store, which is the only store of its kind in a city, might draw customers from 30 miles away. Category specialists offer a large choice of brands and products for which customers are engaged in comparison shopping. Thus, customers generally drive some distance to shop at these stores. In general, destination stores have a large trade area—people are willing to drive farther to shop there.

Measuring the Trade Area for a Retail Site

Retailers can determine the trade area for their existing stores by customer spotting. **Customer spotting** is the process of locating the residences of customers for a store on a map and displaying their positions relative to the store location. The addresses for locating the customers' residences usually are obtained by asking the customers, recording the information from a check or Internet channel purchase, or collecting the information from customer loyalty programs. The data collected from customer spotting can be processed in two ways: manually plotting the location of each customer on a map or using a geographic information system like those described later in this chapter.

Multichannel retailers use their catalog and Internet sales data to spot customers and use that information to identify potential store locations. The number of catalog and Internet channel customers in an area can be used predict the sales of a store placed in the area.

Sources of Information about the Trade Area

To analyze the attractiveness of a potential store site, retailers use information about both the consumers and the competitors in the site's trade area. Two widely used sources of information about the nature of consumers in a trade area are (1) data published by the U.S. Census Bureau, based on the Decennial Census of the United States, and (2) data from geographic information systems, provided by several commercial firms.

REFACT

The United States was the first country to institute a periodic census.[11]

Demographic Data from U.S. Census Bureau   Every 10 years, **census** takers gather demographic information (sex, age, ethnicity, education, marital status, etc.) from every household in the United States. The decennial census is more than just a head count; it provides a snapshot of the country's demographic, social, and economic characteristics. The U.S. Census Bureau prepares periodic reports summarizing the data. There are 8 million **census blocks** in the United States, each containing the residences of about 40 people. The smallest unit of analysis is the **block group**, a collection of adjacent blocks that contain between 300 and 4,000 people.[12]

REFACT

California, Florida, and New York account for one-quarter of the U.S. population.[13]

Although the data from the U.S. Census Bureau can be used to develop a better understanding of the nature of consumers in a region or trade area, these data have several limitations. First, because they are based on information collected every 10 years, they are not very current, although the projections are reasonably accurate. Second, the data are not particularly user-friendly. It is difficult to utilize census data to examine the trade areas for various locations for specific products or services. Thus, most retailers rely on the geographic information system data offered by a number of companies to examine trade areas for potential stores.

Geographic Information System Suppliers   A **geographic information system (GIS)** is a system of hardware and software used to store, retrieve, map, and analyze geographic data; a GIS also includes the operating personnel and the data that go into the system. The key feature of GIS data is that they are identified with a coordinate system (latitude and longitude) that references a particular place on Earth. The data in the systems include spatial features such as rivers and roads,

EXHIBIT 8–4
GIS Map for the Trade
Area of a Bank

as well as descriptive information associated with the spatial features, such as the street address and the characteristics of the household at the address.

Firms such as ESRI (www.esri.com), Nielsen, which purchased Claritas (www.claritas.com/sitereports/Default.jsp), and Pitney Bowes, which purchased MapInfo (www.pbinsight.com/welcome/mapinfo/) offer services that combine updated demographic census data with data from other sources that describe consumer spending patterns and lifestyles in a geographic area. In addition, they provide a user-friendly interface so that the data can be accessed and analyzed easily. Frequently, the outputs from the system are maps that enable retailers to visualize the implications of the data quickly. For example, the map in Exhibit 8–4 shows the trade areas for three branch banks that a retailer has in an MSA and a fourth branch it is considering, as well as the residences of its customers relative to the branch at which they bank. This map suggests that people bank near their work and, thus, that the new location might cannibalize from the other branches.

Retailers interested in developing a deeper understanding of their trade areas for several sites can provide one of these firms with the street addresses for the sites under consideration. The system then provides the projected data shown in the following table for current year estimates and five-year projections pertaining to people living within a 3-, 5-, and 10-mile radius of the sites. In addition, these GIS firms can provides data on the lifestyles of consumers, consumer spending potential, and the locations of competitive retailers. An example of a report on the retail goods and services purchased by residents in a trade area is shown in Exhibit 8–5.

Gender	Occupation
Income	Travel time to work
Disposable income	Transportation mode to work
Net worth	Household composition
Education	Household expenditures by NAICS categories
Age	Geodemographic market segment
Race/ethnicity	Market potential index
Employment status	Spending potential index

220   SECTION II   Retailing Strategy

EXHIBIT 8–5   GIS Data for Retail Expenditures in a Trade Area

esri

Retail Goods and Services Expenditures
Sample Report

Proposed Location
100 S Wacker Dr, Chicago, IL 60606-4006
Ring: 1 mile radius

Latitude: 41.8805
Longitude: -87.63715

Top Tapestry Segments:		Demographic Summary	2010	2015
Metro Renters	68.4%	Population	45,534	50,151
Laptops and Lattes	23.4%	Households	24,338	26,808
City Strivers	2.7%	Families	7,223	7,843
Main Street, USA	1.8%	Median Age	35.7	35.8
Metropolitans	1.6%	Median Household Income	$81,441	$100,632

	Spending Potential Index	Average Amount Spent	Total
Apparel and Services	120	$2,873.94	$69,945,928
Men's	112	$512.65	$12,476,953
Women's	104	$861.55	$20,968,522
Children's	121	$485.96	$11,827,277
Footwear	84	$349.13	$8,497,153
Watches & Jewelry	173	$335.43	$8,163,589
Apparel Products and Services[1]	352	$329.21	$8,012,434
Computer			
Computers and Hardware for Home Use	169	$324.62	$7,900,647
Software and Accessories for Home Use	169	$48.15	$1,171,788
Entertainment & Recreation	155	$4,996.06	$121,594,105
Fees and Admissions	155	$960.54	$23,377,534
Membership Fees for Clubs[2]	155	$253.65	$6,173,216
Fees for Participant Sports, excl. Trips	145	$154.42	$3,758,358
Admission to Movie/Theatre/Opera/Ballet	172	$260.56	$6,341,578
Admission to Sporting Events, excl. Trips	149	$88.77	$2,160,410
Fees for Recreational Lessons	147	$201.16	$4,895,736
Dating Services	257	$1.98	$48,236
TV/Video/Audio	161	$2,003.60	$48,763,617
Community Antenna or Cable TV	157	$1,130.81	$27,521,629

Tapestry Segmentation   ERSI and other GIS suppliers have developed schemes for classifying geographic areas in the United States by combining census and survey data about people's lifestyles and purchasing behavior with the mapping capabilities of GIS. The analysis is based on the premise that "birds of a feather flock together." Specifically, people who live in the same neighborhoods tend to have similar lifestyles and consumer behavior patterns.

The ESRI Tapestry Segmentation system classifies all U.S. residential neighborhoods into 65 distinctive segments, based on demographic and socioeconomic characteristics. Exhibit 8–5 is a hypothetical report for the area within a 1.5-mile radius of 100 S. Wacker Drive in Chicago. Each segment provides a description of the typical person in that segment. The largest segment in the trade area report in Exhibit 8–5 is Metro Renters.[14] According to ESRI, residents of Metro Renters neighborhoods are young (approximately 30 percent are in their 20s), well-educated singles beginning their professional careers in some of the largest U.S. cities such as New York City, Los Angeles, and Chicago. The median age is 33.6 years; the median household income is $56,311. Most rent apartments in high-rise buildings, living alone or with a roommate. They travel, read two or more daily newspapers, listen to classical music and public radio, and go online. To stay fit, they work out regularly at clubs, play tennis and volleyball, practice yoga, ski, and jog. They go dancing and to the movies, attend rock concerts, visit museums, and throw frisbees. Painting and drawing are favorite hobbies. They are politically liberal. Several similar, competing segmentation systems are currently commercially available, including PRIZM (Potential Rating Index for Zip Markets), which was developed by Nielsen Claritas.

Exhibit 8–6 shows the location of customers who have the desired geodemographic profile on a trade area map for a shopping center. Note that most of the retailer's desirable customers are not even in the tertiary trade area; thus, this shopping center would not be a desirable location. (The shopping center is designated by the red star. The primary trade area is green; the secondary trade area is lavender; and the tertiary trade area is turquoise.)

Spending Potential Index   Data in ESRI's consumer spending database is reported by product or service; variables include total expenditures, average amount spent per household, and a **Spending Potential Index (SPI)**. The SPI compares the local average expenditure by product to the national average amount spent. An index of 100 is average. For example, an SPI of 120 shows that average spending by local consumers is 20 percent above the national average; an SPI of 80 means that average local spending is 20 percent below the national average. (See Exhibit 8–5.)

Competition in the Trade Area

In addition to needing information about the residents in a trade area, retailers need to know about the amount and type of competition in the trade area. Although GIS vendors provide data on the location of competitive retailers, there are also other sources for this information. For example, most retailer websites list not only all current store locations, but future sites as well. A more traditional method of accessing competitive information is to look through the Yellow Pages of the telephone book. Other sources of competitive information include directories published by trade associations, chambers of commerce, Chain Store Guide (published by CSG Information Services, www.csgis.com), and municipal and county governments.

ESTIMATING POTENTIAL SALES FOR A STORE SITE

LO4

Determine the forecasted sales for a new store location.

Three approaches for using information about the trade area to estimate the potential sales for a store at the location are (1) the Huff gravity model, (2) regression analysis, and (3) the analog method.

Huff Gravity Model

The **Huff gravity model** is used to predict the probability that a consumer will patronize a store.[15] The model specifies two factors that assess the probability: (1) the attractiveness of the store's location (larger stores and shopping centers are more attractive) and (2) the time it takes a consumer to travel to the store (stores that take more time to get to are less attractive). The mathematical formula for predicting the probability of a customer's going to a specific store location is

$$P_{ij} = \frac{S_j/T_{ij}^{\lambda}}{\Sigma S_j/T_{ij}^{\lambda}}$$

where

P_{ij} = probability that customer i shops at location j

S_j = size of the store at location j

T_{ij} = travel time for customer i to get to location j

The formula indicates that the larger the size (S_j) of the store compared with competing stores' sizes, the greater the probability that a customer will shop at the location. A larger size is generally more attractive in consumers' eyes because it means more merchandise assortment and variety. Travel time or distance (T_{ij}) has the opposite effect on the probability that a consumer will shop at a location. The greater the travel time or distance from the consumer, compared with that of competing locations, the lower the probability that the consumer will shop at the location. Generally, customers would rather shop at a close store than a distant one.

The exponent λ reflects the relative effect of travel time versus store size. When λ is equal to 1, store size and travel time have an equal but opposite effect on the probability of a consumer's shopping at a store location. When λ is greater than 1, travel time has a greater effect, and when λ is less than 1, store size has a greater effect. The value of λ is affected by the nature of the shopping trips consumers generally take when visiting the specific type of store. For instance, travel time or distance is generally more important for convenience goods than for shopping goods because people are less willing to travel a great distance for a quart of milk than they are for a new pair of shoes. Thus, a larger value for λ is assigned if the store being studied specializes in convenience shopping trips rather than comparison shopping trips. The value of λ is usually estimated statistically using data that describe shopping patterns at existing stores.

To illustrate the use of the Huff model, consider the situations shown in Exhibit 8–7. A small town has two communities, Rock Creek and Oak Hammock. The town currently has one 5,000-square-foot drugstore with annual sales of $8 million, $3 million of which come from Oak Hammock residents and $5 million from Rock Creek residents. A competitive chain is considering opening a 10,000-square-foot store. As the exhibit illustrates, the driving time for the average Rock Creek resident to the existing store is 10 minutes, but it would be only 5 minutes to the new store. In contrast, the driving time for the typical Oak Hammock resident to the existing drugstore is 5 minutes and would be 15 minutes

EXHIBIT 8–7
Application of the
Huff Gravity Model for
Estimating Store Sales

to the new store. Based on its past experience, the drugstore chain has found that λ equals 2 for its store locations. Using the Huff formula, the probability of a Rock Creek resident's shopping at the new location, P_{RC}, is

$$P_{RC} = \frac{10,000/5^2}{10,000/5^2 + 5,000/10^2} = .889$$

The probability of Oak Hammock residents shopping at the new location, P_{OH}, is

$$P_{OH} = \frac{10,000/15^2}{10,000/15^2 + 5,000/5^2} = .182$$

This simple application assumes that the market size for drugstores in the community will remain the same at $8 million with the addition of the new store. We also could have considered that two drugstores would increase the total size of the market. In addition, rather than doing the calculations for the average customer located in the middle of each community, we could have calculated the probabilities that each customer in the two communities would go to the new location.

Even though the Huff gravity model considers only two factors affecting store sales—travel time and store size—its predictions are quite accurate because these two factors typically have the greatest effect on store choice.[16] The regression approach discussed in the next section provides a way to incorporate additional factors into the sales forecast for a store under consideration.

Regression Analysis

The **regression analysis** approach is based on the assumption that factors that affect the sales of existing stores in a chain will have the same impact on stores located at new sites being considered. When using this approach, the retailer employs a technique called multiple regression to estimate a statistical model that predicts sales at existing store locations. The technique can consider the effects of the wide range of factors discussed in this chapter, including site characteristics, such as visibility and access, and characteristics of the trade area, such as demographics and lifestyle segments represented.

Consider the following example: A chain of sporting goods stores has analyzed the factors affecting sales in its existing stores and found that the following model is the best predictor of store sales (the weights for the factors, such as 275 for the number of households, are estimated using multiple regression):

Stores sales = 275 × Number of households in trade area (15-minute drive time)
+ 1,800,000 × Percentage of households in trade area with children under 15 years of age
+ 2,000,000 × Percentage of households in trade area in Tapestry segment "aspiring young"
+ 8 × Shopping center square feet
+ 250,000, if visible from street
+ 300,000, if Walmart in center

The sporting goods retailer is considering the following two locations:

Variable	Estimated Weight	Location A	Location B
Households within a 15-minute drive time of the location	275	11,000	15,000
Percentage of households with children under 15	1,800,000	70%	20%
Percentage of households in the Aspiring Young Tapestry geodemographic segment	2,000,000	60%	10%
Gross leasable square feet of shopping center	8	200,000	250,000
Visibility of store (1 = yes, 0 = no)	250,000	yes	no
Walmart store in shopping center (1 = yes, 0 = no)	300,000	yes	no

Using the regression model, the forecasted sales for location A are:

Stores sales at location A = \$7,635,000 = 275 × 11,000
+ 1,800,000 × 0.7
+ 200,000 × 0.6
+ 8 × 200,000
+ 250,000 × 1
+ 300,000 × 1

and forecasted sales for location B are:

Store sales at location B = \$6,685,000 = 275 × 15,000
+ 1,800,000 × 0.2
+ 2,000,000 × 0.1
+ 8 × 250,000
+ 250,000 × 0
+ 300,000 × 0

Note that location A has greater forecasted sales, even though it has fewer consumers in its trading area and shopping center size, because the profile of its target market fits the retailer's target market (families with children under 15 and in the Aspiring Young Tapestry segment) better.

Analog Approach

To estimate a regression model to predict sales from a site, a retailer needs data about the trade area and site characteristics from a large number of stores. Because small chains cannot use the regression approach, they use the similar but more subjective analog approach. When using the **analog approach,** the retailer simply describes the site and trade area characteristics for its most successful stores and attempts to find a site with similar characteristics. The use of this approach is described in the following illustration.

ILLUSTRATION OF SITE SELECTION: EDWARD BEINER PURVEYOR OF FINE EYEWEAR

Edward Beiner Purveyor of Fine Eyewear is an 11-store Florida retailer specializing in upper-end, high-fashion eyewear. Its store in South Miami lacks the entertainment and recreation found in shopping centers. Other problems with the location are a lack of protection against the heavy rains that characterize the area's subtropical climate, security, and parking. However, some positive features of the location are the low rent, high pedestrian traffic, few restrictions, and no other high-quality and fashion optical stores in the area, although there are other optical stores in the general area.

LO5
Illustrate the site selection process.

Edward Beiner Purveyor of Fine Eyewear wants to open a new location. Because the South Miami site is its best store, it would like to find a location whose trade area has similar characteristics. It has identified several potential locations that it is evaluating.

Using the analog approach, Edward Beiner undertakes the following steps:

1. Conduct a competitive analysis.

2. Define present trade area.

3. Analyze trade area characteristics.

4. Match characteristics of present trade area with potential sites.

Edward Beiner Purveyor of Fine Eyewear specializes in high-fashion eyewear and targets affluent customers.

EXHIBIT 8–8   Competitive Analysis of Potential Locations

(1) Trade Area	(2) Eyeglasses/ Year/ Person	(3) Trade Area Population	(4) Total Eyeglasses Potential	(5) Estimated Eyeglasses Sold	(6) Trade Area Potential Units	(7) Trade Area Potential Percentage	(8) Relative Level of Competition
South Miami	0.2	85,979	17,196	7,550	9,646	56.09%	Low
Site A	0.2	91,683	18,337	15,800	2,537	13.83	Medium
Site B	0.2	101,972	20,394	12,580	7,814	38.32	Low
Site C	0.2	60,200	12,040	11,300	740	6.15	High
Site D	0.2	81,390	16,278	13,300	2,978	18.29	Medium

Step 1: Conduct Competitive Analysis

The competitive analysis of the four potential sites being considered by Edward Beiner is shown in Exhibit 8–8. To perform the analysis, Edward Beiner first estimated the number of eyeglasses sold per year per person (column 2), obtained from industry sources. Then the area population was taken from U.S. Census data (column 3). Column 4 is an estimate of the trade area potential reached by multiplying column 2 by column 3.

The estimates of the number of eyeglasses sold in the trade areas, column 5, are based on visits to competitive stores. Column 6 represents the unit sales potential for eyeglasses in the trade areas, or column 4 minus column 5. Then the trade area potential penetration is calculated by dividing column 6 by column 4. For instance, because the total eyeglass potential for the South Miami store trade area is 17,196 pairs and an additional 9,646 pairs could be sold in that trade area, 56.1 percent of the eyeglass market in this area remains untapped. The bigger the number, the lower the competition.

Column 8, the relative level of competition, is subjectively estimated on the basis of column 7. Unlike other optical stores in the trade area, Edward Beiner carries a very exclusive merchandise selection. In general, however, the higher the trade area potential, the lower the relative competition will be.

On the basis of the information in Exhibit 8–8, Edward Beiner should locate its new store at site B. The trade area potential is high, and competition is relatively low. Of course, relative competition is only one issue to consider. Later in this section, we'll consider competition along with other issues to determine which is the best new location for Edward Beiner.

Step 2: Define Present Trade Area

On the basis of customer spotting data gathered from Beiner's data warehouse of current customers, the trade area map in Exhibit 8–9 was generated using ESRI's GIS software. The zones are based on drive times: 5 minutes for the primary trade area (red), 10 minutes for the secondary trade area (purple), and 20 minutes for the tertiary trade area (green). Note that the trade area boundaries are oblong because the major highways, especially U.S. 1, run north and south. Not only do the north–south highways bring traffic to the area, but heavy traffic often makes them difficult to cross. Biscayne Bay also limits the trade area on the east.

Edward Beiner trade area is smaller than it would be if the store were located in a regional shopping mall. However, Edward Beiner is one of several optical shops in this business district. Having similar shopping goods stores in the same vicinity expands its trade area boundaries; more people are drawn to the area to shop because of its expanded selection. In addition, Edward Beiner's trade area is limited

Trade Area for Edward Beiner Purveyor of Fine Eyewear   **EXHIBIT 8–9**

on the south by a large regional shopping center that has several stores carrying similar merchandise.

Step 3: Identify Trade Area Characteristics

Having defined its trade area, Edward Beiner reviewed a number of reports describing the characteristics of its trade area. Some of interesting findings from these reports were:

- The average household income is $92,653. In addition, 27.6 percent of the households have incomes between $75,000 and $149,000, and 13.7 percent have incomes greater than $150,000. The 3-mile ring surrounding Edward Beiner is very affluent.

- The area surrounding Edward Beiner has a population that is more than 50 percent Hispanic.

Step 4: Match Characteristics of Present Trade Area with Potential Sites

Edward Beiner believes that the profile of its current trade area is high income, predominantly white-collar occupations, a relatively large percentage of older residents, upscale geodemographic segments, and relatively low competition for expensive, high-fashion eyewear. Exhibit 8–10 compares Edward Beiner's current location with four potential locations on these five factors.

228   SECTION II   Retailing Strategy

EXHIBIT 8–10   Four Potential Locations for a New Store

Store Location	Average Household Income	White-Collar Occupations	Percentage Residents Age 45 and Over	Predominant Geodemographic Segments	Level of Competition
Edward Beiner Optical	$100,000	High	37%	Top One Percent	Low
Site A	60,000	High	25	Young Immigrant Families	Medium
Site B	70,000	Low	80	Gray Power	Low
Site C	100,000	High	30	Young Literati	High
Site D	120,000	High	50	Upper-Income Empty-Nesters	Medium

Although the potential customers of site A typically have white-collar occupations, they also have relatively low incomes and are comparatively young. Young Immigrant Families also tend to have young families, so expensive eyewear may not be a priority purchase. Finally, there's a medium level of competition in the area.

The Gray Power residents surrounding site B have moderate incomes and are mostly retired. Even though competition would be low and most residents need glasses, these customers are more interested in value than in fashion.

Site C has strong potential because the Young Literati residents in the area are young and have a strong interest in fashion. Although working, they are busy furnishing their first homes and apartments and paying off college loans. They probably would appreciate Edward Beiner's fashionable assortment, but they won't appreciate the high prices. Also, other high-end optical stores are entrenched in the area.

Site D is the best location for Edward Beiner. The residents are older professionals or early retirees with high incomes. Upper-Income Empty-Nesters are sophisticated consumers of adult luxuries like high-fashion eyewear. Importantly, this geodemographic segment is similar to a large segment in Edward Beiner's current location.

Unfortunately, finding analogous situations isn't always as easy as in this example. The weaker the analogy, the more difficult the location decision will be. When a retailer has a relatively small number of outlets (say, 20 or fewer), the analog approach is often best. As the number of stores increases, it becomes more difficult for the analyst to organize the data in a meaningful way. More analytical approaches, such as regression analysis, then are necessary.

NEGOTIATING A LEASE

Explain the different types and terms of leases.

Once a particular site is chosen, retailers still face a multitude of decisions, including the types and terms of the lease.

Types of Leases

There are two basic types of leases: percentage and fixed rate.

Percentage Leases   Although there are many combinations within each type of lease, the most common form is a **percentage lease,** in which the rent is based on a percentage of sales. In addition to the percentage of sales, retailers typically pay a common area maintenance (CAM) fee based on a percentage of their gross leasable square footage. Most malls use some form of percentage lease. Because retail leases typically run for 5 to 10 years, they appear equitable to both parties if rents go up (or down) with sales and inflation.

A **percentage lease with a specified maximum** is a lease that pays the shopping center manager a percentage of sales up to a maximum amount. This type of lease rewards good retailer performance by allowing the retailer to hold rent constant above a certain level of sales. A similar variation, the **percentage lease with a specified minimum,** specifies that the retailer must pay a minimum rent, no matter how low sales are.

Another type of percentage lease is a **sliding scale lease,** in which the percentage of sales paid as rent decreases as the sales go up. For instance, a retailer may pay 4 percent on the first $200,000 in sales and then 3 percent on sales greater than $200,000. Similar to the percentage lease with a specified maximum, the sliding scale rewards high-performing retailers.

Fixed-Rate Leases   The second basic type of lease is a **fixed-rate lease,** most commonly used by community and neighborhood centers. A retailer pays a fixed amount per month over the life of the lease. With a fixed-rate lease, the retailer and shopping center management know exactly how much will be paid in rent, but this type of lease is not as popular as the various forms of percentage leases.

A variation of the fixed-rate lease is the **graduated lease,** in which rent increases by a fixed amount over a specified period of time. For instance, rent may be $1,000 per month for the first three years and $1,250 for the next five years.

Terms of the Lease

Although leases are formal contracts, they can be changed to reflect the relative power of the retailer and shopping center management and specific needs of the retailer. In addition to the rent, some other negotiable aspects of the lease are cotenancy, prohibited-use, and exclusive-use clauses.

Cotenancy Clause   Some retail leases contain **cotenancy clauses.** These clauses may require that a certain percentage of a shopping center be leased or that specified stores be in the center. For example, if The Gap goes into a mall, it doesn't want to be by itself. In all likelihood it has a group of retailers that it views as complements. These may include Abercrombie and Fitch, Banana Republic (also owned by The Gap), Aeropostale, American Eagle Outfitters, Ann Taylor, Anthropologie, and bebe, among others. It would not be uncommon to see a lease requirement where The Gap will only sign if at least four of the seven retailers just listed are also in the development.

If these terms are violated, the retailers with the cotenancy clauses may demand rent reductions or leave altogether. Cotenancy clauses have become particularly important in the past few years because many retailers, including several large chains like Circuit City, Borders, and Linens 'N Things, have created vacancies as a result of their bankruptcies.[17]

Prohibited-Use Clause   A **prohibited-use clause** limits the shopping center management from leasing to certain kinds of tenants. Many retailers don't want the shopping center space to be leased to establishments that take up parking spaces but do not bring in shoppers, such as a bowling alley, skating rink, meeting hall, dentist, or real estate office. Retailers may also wish to restrict the use of space from those establishments that could harm the shopping center's image. Prohibited-use clauses often specify that bars, pool halls, game parlors, off-track betting establishments, massage parlors, and pornography retailers are unacceptable.

Suppose, for instance, that Tiffany & Co., the famous jeweler, has a store in a high-end shopping center that is about to sign a lease with H&M. It could envoke its lease's prohibited-use clause in a lawsuit against the shopping center management company. Specifically, the lease forbids retailers "whose merchandise and/or price points are not considered to be luxury, upscale or better by conventional retail industry standards" to use or lease certain spaces within, fronting, or adjacent to the Tiffany store.

Exclusive-Use Clause   An **exclusive-use clause** prohibits the shopping center management from leasing to retailers that sell competing products. For example, a discount store's lease may specify that the landlord cannot lease to other discount stores, variety stores, or limited-assortment value retailers.

Some retailers also are particular about how the storefront appears. For instance, a women's specialty store may specify that the storefront must have floor-to-ceiling glass to maximize window displays and improve customers' ability to see into the store. Other retailers believe it is important that nothing blocks the view of the store from the street, so they specify that the landlord cannot place any outparcels in the parking lot. An **outparcel** is a building (such as a bank or McDonald's) or kiosk (such as an automatic teller machine) that sits in the parking lot of a shopping center but is not physically attached to the center.

Common Area Maintenance Costs   In retail leases, **common area maintenance (CAM) clauses** often require the most extensive negotiations. These clauses traditionally assign responsibilities for taking care of common areas, including sidewalks or parking lots. Modern versions have extended these responsibilities such that tenants might need to agree to contribute to capital improvement projects, pay for new roofing, or participate in the purchase of adjoining land parcels. As a result of this expansion of the meaning of CAM clauses, many leases today call them simply operating costs; in some cases, these costs outpace even rents. This status helps explain why they require such extensive negotiations. Retail tenants seek to limit their responsibilities, and they ask for the right to monitor any common area costs, to confirm their portion is charged legitimately.[18]

SUMMARY

LO1 Summarize the factors considered in locating a number of stores.

Four factors that retailers consider when evaluating an area for store locations are economic conditions, competition, strategic fit, and operating costs. Areas where the population is large and growing, have limited competition, and have a profile that matches the retailer's target market are more attractive. Finally, the cost of servicing an area needs to be considered. When determining the number of stores to locate in an area, retailers need to determine the incremental sales and profits from exploiting scale economies and increasing cannibalization by adding more stores.

LO2 Review the characteristics of a particular site.

Some characteristics of a site that affect store sales and thus are considered in selecting a site are (1) the traffic flow past the site and accessibility

to the site, (2) parking, (3) visibility, (4) adjacent tenants, and (5) restrictions and costs.

LO3 Understand how retailers analyze the trade area for a site.

Trade areas are typically divided into primary, secondary, and tertiary zones. The boundaries of a trade area are determined by how accessible it is to customers, the natural and physical barriers that exist in the area, the type of shopping area in which the store is located, the type of store, and the level of competition. Two sources of information to assess the trade areas are census data and GIS.

LO4 Determine the forecasted sales for a new store location.

Once retailers have the data that describe their trade areas, they use several analytical techniques to estimate demand. The Huff gravity model predicts the probability that a customer will choose a particular store in a trade area. The model is based on the premise that customers are more likely to shop at a given store or shopping center if it is conveniently located and offers a large selection. Regression analysis is a statistically based model that estimates the effects of a variety of factors on existing store sales and uses that information to predict sales for a new site. The analog approach—one of the easiest to use—can be particularly useful for smaller retailers. Using the same logic as regression analysis, the retailer can make predictions about sales by a new store on the basis of sales in stores in similar areas.

LO5 Illustrate the site selection process.

Edward Beiner Purveyor of Fine Eyewear is used to illustrate the analysis involved in opening a new location using the analog technique. This example illustrates how to (1) conduct a competitive analysis, (2) define the present trade area, (3) analyze the trade area's characteristics, and (4) match characteristics of the present trade area with potential sites.

LO6 Explain the different types and terms of leases.

Retailers need to negotiate the terms of a lease. Although leases are formal contracts, they can be changed to reflect the relative power of the retailer and shopping center management and specific needs of the retailer. These lease terms affect the cost of the location and may restrict retailing activities. There are two basic types of leases: percentage and fixed rate. In addition to the rent, some other negotiable aspects of the lease are cotenancy, prohibited-use, and exclusive-use and common area maintenance clauses.

KEY TERMS

accessibility, *213*

analog approach, *225*

artificial barrier, *213*

block group, *218*

census, *218*

census block, *218*

common area maintenance (CAM) clause, *230*

congestion, *215*

cotenancy clause, *229*

cumulative attraction, *215*

customer spotting, *218*

exclusive-use clause, *230*

fixed-rate lease, *229*

fringe, *217*

geographic information system (GIS), *218*

graduated lease, *229*

Huff gravity model, *222*

metropolitan statistical area (MSA), *208*

micropolitan statistical area (μSA), *208*

natural barrier, *213*

outparcel, *230*

percentage lease, *228*

percentage lease with a specified maximum, *229*

percentage lease with a specified minimum, *229*

primary trading area, *217*

prohibited-use clause, *229*

regression analysis, *223*

secondary trading area, *217*

sliding scale lease, *229*

Spending Potential Index (SPI), *221*

tertiary trading area, *217*

trade area, *217*

traffic flow, *212*

visibility, *215*

GET OUT AND DO IT!

1. **CONTINUING CASE ASSIGNMENT** Evaluate the location of a store operated by the retailer you have selected for the Continuing Case. What is the size and shape of the retailer's trade area? Describe the positive and negative aspects of its location. Compare the store's location with the locations of its competitors.

2. **INTERNET EXERCISE** Go to www.esri.com/library/fliers/pdfs/tapestry_segmentation.pdf, and identify five segments that you would expect to find in your zip code. Then go to http://www.arcwebservices.com/services/servlet/EBIS_Reports?serviceName=FreeZip&errorURL=http%3A%2F%2Fbao.esri.com%2Fesribis%3Fcommand%3Dzipcodelookup&zipcode=02453&x=0&y=0, and type in your zip code. Compare the segments that are found in your zip code with your initial prediction. Are they similar or different?

3. **INTERNET EXERCISE** Go to http://www.esri.com/what-is-gis, the home page for ESRI Geographical Information Systems, and read about GIS. Afterwards, explain how retailers can make better decisions with GIS.

4. **INTERNET EXERCISE** The U.S. Census Bureau tracks key population characteristics, such as age, gender, disability, employment, income, language, poverty, and race. Go to the U.S. Census Bureau home page at http://factfinder2.census.gov/faces/nav/jsf/pages/index.xhtml, and, using the Population Finder, look up key demographic data for your state. Explain which factors would be most important for retailers considering this location to evaluate.

5. **GO SHOPPING** Go to a shopping mall. Get or draw a map of the stores. Analyze whether the stores are clustered in some logical manner. For instance, are all the high-end stores together? Is there a good mix of retailers catering to comparison shoppers near one another?

6. **GO SHOPPING** Visit a jewelry store in an enclosed mall and one in a neighborhood strip shopping center. List the pros and cons for each location. Which location is the most desirable? Why is this the case?

7. **WEB OLC EXERCISE** Go to the student side of the book's website, and click on "Location." You will see an Excel spreadsheet that contains the sales for 45 retail locations of a sporting goods retail chain, plus the characteristics of each location: number of households in trading area, percentage of households with children under 15 years old, percentage of households in appropriate Tapestry segments that the retailer is targeting, distance from a Walmart store, and distance from a Sports Authority store. Estimate a multiple regression model that predicts sales as a function of the site characteristics, and use the estimate weights to evaluate the two sites at the bottom of the spreadsheet.

DISCUSSION QUESTIONS AND PROBLEMS

1. Which factors do retailers consider when evaluating an area of the country to locate stores? How do retailers determine the trade area for a store?

2. True Value Hardware plans to open a new store. Two sites are available, both in middle-income neighborhood centers. One neighborhood is 20 years old and has been well maintained. The other was recently built in a newly planned community. Which site is preferable for True Value? Why?

3. Trade areas are often described as concentric circles emanating from the store or shopping center. Why is this practice used? Suggest an alternative method. Which would you use if you owned a store in need of a trade area analysis?

4. Under what circumstances might a retailer use the analog approach for estimating demand for a new store? What about regression analysis?

5. Retailers have a choice of locating on a mall's main floor or second or third level. Typically, the main floor offers the best, but most expensive, locations. Why would specialty stores such as Radio Shack and Foot Locker choose the second or third floor?

6. What retail locations are best for department stores, consumer electronics category killers, specialty apparel stores, and warehouse stores? Discuss your rationale.

7. If you were considering the ownership of a Taco Bell franchise, what would you want to know about the location in terms of traffic, population, income, employment, and competition? What else would you need to research about a potential location?

8. A drugstore is considering opening a new location at shopping center A, with hopes of capturing sales from a new neighborhood under construction. Two nearby shopping centers, B and C, will provide competition. Using the following information and the Huff gravity model, determine the probability that residents of the new neighborhood will shop at shopping center A:

Shopping center	Size (000's sq. ft.)	Distance from new neighborhood (miles)
A	3,500	4
B	1,500	5
C	300	3

Assume that $\lambda = 2$.

SUGGESTED READINGS

Baumgartner, H., and J. B. E. M. Steenkamp. "Retail Site Selection." In L.A.M. Moutinho and G.D. Hutcheson (Eds), *The SAGE Dictionary of Quantitative Management Research*. Thousands Oak, CA: Sage, 2011.

Can, Cui, Jiechen Wang, Yingxia Pu, Jinsong Ma, and Gang Chen, "GIS Based Method of Delimitating Trade Area for Retail Chains," *International Journal of Geographical Information Science* 26, 19 (2012), pp. 1863–1879.

Cox, Emmett. *Retail Analytics: The Secret Weapon*. Hoboken, NJ: Wiley, 2011.

Duggal, Nini. *Use of GIS in Retail Location Analysis*. Saarbrücken, Germany: VDM Verlag, 2008.

Gibbs, Robert. *Principles of Urban Retail Planning and Development*. Hoboken, NJ: Wiley, 2012.

Joseph, Lawrence, and Michael Kuby. "Gravity Modeling and Its Impacts on Location Analysis." In H. A. Eiselt (Ed), *Foundations of Location Analysis*. New York: Springer, 2011.

Ki, Yingru Li, and Lin Liu. "Assessing the Impact of Retail Location on Store Performance: A Comparison of Wal-Mart and Kmart Stores in Cincinnati." *Applied Geography* 32, no. 2 (March 2012), pp. 591–600.

Suárez-Vega, Rafael, Dolores R. Santos-Peñate, and Pablo Dorta-González. "Location Models and GIS Tools for Retail Site Location." *Applied Geography* 35, no. 1–2 (November 2012), pp. 2, 35.

Teller, Christoph, and Thomas Reutterer. "The Evolving Concept of Retail Attractiveness: What Makes Retail Agglomerations Attractive When Customers Shop at Them?" *Journal of Retailing and Consumer Services* 15, no. 3 (2008), pp. 127–143.

Tyman, Jeff, and Lewis Poi. "Retail Site Selection and Geographic Information Systems." *Journal of Applied Business Research* 11, no. 2 (2011), pp. 46–54.

Wood, Steve, and Sue Browne. "Convenience Store Location Planning and Forecasting—a Practical Research." *International Journal of Retail and Distribution Management* 35, no. 4 (2007), pp. 233–255.

Managing the Merchandise Planning Process

EXECUTIVE BRIEFING

Moussa Coulibaly, Senior Vice President, Planning and Allocation, DICK'S Sporting Goods, Inc.

I'm a numbers guy; I have always been one. I purchased one of the first IBM PCs while studying finance and accounting at Duquesne University and used it early in my career to analyze margin and inventory turnover. What I was doing back then didn't have a name, but today it's known as retail analytics.

Currently, I serve as the senior vice president of planning and allocation at DICK'S Sporting Goods. However, I began my career in merchandising at Horne's Department Store corporate headquarters in Pittsburgh, PA. This role was unique, as Horne's corporate headquarters was located in the same building as its downtown flagship store. As a result, all merchandising associates were required to work the floor every day during high-traffic lunch hours to interact with customers. Looking back, it was this hands-on experience that was one of the most valuable aspects in my career as it gave me unique insight into providing superior customer service.

On my own time, I analyzed the productivity of jewelry showcases at Horne's for different vendors. Using my IBM PC, I determined the margin and inventory turnover for each vendor's merchandise. When vendors would meet with our buyers to present their new merchandise, our buyers would use my data to show them how the performance of their

jewelry compared with other vendors. The vendors with low productivity would work to identify ways to increase their productivity, ensuring they did not lose space in the display cases.

Eventually, Horne's was merged into Lazarus department store (Macy's predecessor), and I accepted a merchandising role at Kaufmann's. During my tenure there, I held a variety of merchandising-related positions working with buyers to track inventory, place re-orders and set discounts. In addition, I also worked to develop reports to identify and address slow-moving items. I spent eight years at Kaufmann's, and served as the director of financial planning

CHAPTER 12

when the headquarters closed in 2002. When this occurred I joined DICK'S Sporting Goods.

Retailing offers many different career paths and opportunities for people with a wide variety of skills and interests. I joined DICK'S in 2002 as the director of planning, and in 2003, I was promoted to vice president, planning and allocation. After several years, I assumed the role of treasurer and vice president of strategic planning where I was involved in a broad spectrum of responsibilities, from analyzing potential acquisitions and mergers to securing a revolving credit facility. In 2012, I was promoted to my current role, senior vice president of planning and allocation, where I am responsible for both hard and soft lines. As my experience illustrates, a successful career can begin with experimenting on your personal computer and eventually lead to a leadership role within a great company.

Merchandise management activities are undertaken primarily by buyers and their superiors, divisional merchandise managers (DMMs), and general merchandise managers (GMMs). Many people view these jobs as very exciting and glamorous. They think that buyers spend most of their time trying to identify the latest fashions and trends, attending designer shows replete with celebrities in Paris and Milan, and going to rock concerts and other glamorous events to see what the trendsetters are wearing. But, in reality, the activities of retail buyers are more like those of Wall Street investment analysts than globe-trotting trend spotters.

Investment analysts manage a portfolio of stocks. They buy stocks in companies they think will increase in value and sell stocks in companies they believe do not have a promising future. They continuously monitor the performance of the stocks they own to see which are increasing in value and which are decreasing.

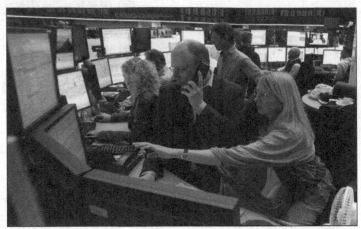

Retail inventory management is similar to managing an investment portfolio.

Sometimes, they make mistakes and invest in companies that do not perform well. So they sell their stock in these companies and lose money, but they use the money from the sold stocks to buy more attractive stocks. Other times, the stocks they buy increase dramatically in price, and they wish they had bought more shares.

Rather than managing a portfolio of stocks, retail buyers manage a portfolio of merchandise inventory. They buy merchandise they think will be popular with their customers. Like investment analysts, they use an information system to monitor the performance of their merchandise portfolio—to see what is selling and what is not. Retail buyers also make mistakes. When the merchandise they bought is not selling well, they get rid of it by putting it on sale so that they can use the money to buy better-selling merchandise. However, they also might take a chance and buy a lot of a new merchandise item and be rewarded when it sells well, while competitors, who were more conservative, don't have enough of the product.

Chris Manning, a former swimwear buyer at Macy's, draws an analogy between surfing and buying merchandise:

> My job is like surfing. Sometimes you catch a big wave (trend) and it's exhilarating, and sometimes you think you've caught a good wave and brown turns out not to be the color this season. But the real fun is getting the most out of the wave you can. Let me give you an example of how I worked a big wave. Vendors started to show tankinis— women's bathing suits with bikini bottoms and tank tops. My customers were women in their 40s that had a couple of kids. I thought they would really go for this new style because it had the advantages of a two-piece bathing suit, but wasn't much more revealing than a one-piece suit. I bought a wide color assortment—bright reds, yellows, pink, and black—and put them in our fashion-forward stores in January for a test. The initial sales were good, but our customers thought they were a little too skimpy. Then I started to work the wave. I went back to the vendor and got them to recut the top so that the suit was less revealing, and I placed a big order for the colors that were selling best. Sales were so good that the other Macy's divisions picked up on it, but we rode the wave the longest and had the best swimwear sales of all of the divisions.[1]

Merchandise management is the process by which a retailer attempts to offer the appropriate quantity of the right merchandise, in the right place and at the right time, so that it can meet the company's financial goals. Buyers need to be in touch with and anticipate what customers will want to buy, but this ability to sense market trends is just one skill needed to manage merchandise inventory effectively. Perhaps an even more important skill is the ability to analyze sales data continually and make appropriate adjustments in prices and inventory levels.

The first part of this chapter provides the background needed to understand the merchandise management process. In this introduction, we discuss how the process is organized, who makes the merchandise decisions, and how merchandise management performance is evaluated. The last part of the chapter examines the steps in the merchandise management process—forecasting sales, formulating an assortment plan, determining the appropriate inventory level, developing a merchandise management plan, allocating merchandise to stores, and monitoring performance. The appendix to this chapter provides a more detailed discussion of the steps used to develop a merchandise budget plan. The other activities involved in merchandise management reviewed in subsequent chapters are buying merchandise (Chapter 13) and pricing (Chapter 14).

MERCHANDISE MANAGEMENT OVERVIEW

This section provides an overview of the merchandise management process, including the organization of a retailer's merchandise management activities and the objectives and measures used to evaluate merchandise management performance. In the following section, we review the differences in the process for managing fashion and seasonal merchandise versus basic merchandise and each of the steps in the merchandise management process.

LO1

Explain the merchandise management organization and performance measures.

The Buying Organization

Every retailer has its own system for grouping categories of merchandise, but the basic structure of the buying organization is similar for most retailers. Exhibit 12–1 illustrates this basic structure by depicting the organization of the merchandise division for a department store chain such as Macy's, Belk, or Dillard's. Exhibit 12–1 shows the organization of buyers in the merchandise division. A similar structure for planners parallels the structure for buyers.

The highest classification level is the **merchandise group.** The organization chart shown in Exhibit 12–1 has four merchandise groups: (1) women's apparel; (2) men's, children's, and intimate apparel; (3) cosmetics, shoes, jewelry, and accessories; and (4) home and kitchen. Each of the four merchandise groups is managed

Illustration of Merchandise Classifications and Organization   **EXHIBIT 12–1**

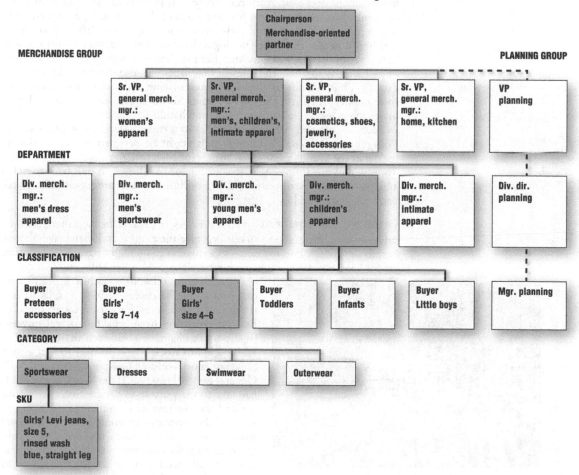

by a general merchandise manager (GMM), who is often a senior vice president in the firm. Each of the GMMs is responsible for several departments. For example, the GMM for men's, children's, and intimate apparel makes decisions about how the merchandise inventory is managed in five departments: men's dress apparel, men's sportswear, young men's apparel, children's apparel, and intimate apparel.

The second level in the merchandise classification scheme is the **department**. Departments are managed by divisional merchandise managers (DMMs). For example, the DMM highlighted in Exhibit 12–1 manages the buyers responsible for six children's apparel merchandise departments.

The **classification** is the third level for categorizing merchandise and organizing merchandise management activities. A classification is a group of items targeting the same customer type, such as girls' sizes 4 to 6. Categories are the next lower level in the classification scheme. Each buyer manages several merchandise categories. For example, the girls' sizes 4 to 6 buyer manages the sportswear, dresses, swimwear, and outerwear categories for girls who wear sizes 4 to 6.

A **stock-keeping unit (SKU)** is the smallest unit available for inventory control. In soft-goods merchandise, for instance, a SKU usually means a particular brand, size, color, and style—for example, a pair of size 5, rinsed wash, blue, straight-legged Levi jeans is a SKU.

Merchandise Category—The Planning Unit

The merchandise category is the basic unit of analysis for making merchandising management decisions. A **merchandise category** is an assortment of items that customers see as substitutes for one another. For example, a department store might offer a wide variety of girls' dresses sizes 4 to 6 in different colors, styles, and brand names. A mother buying a dress for her daughter might consider the entire set of dresses when making her purchase decision. Lowering the price on one dress may increase the sales of that dress but also decrease the sales of other dresses. Thus, the buyers' decisions about pricing and promoting specific SKUs in the category will affect the sales of other SKUs in the same category. Typically, a buyer manages several categories of merchandise.

Some retailers may define categories in terms of brands. For example, Tommy Hilfiger and Polo/Ralph Lauren each might be categories because the retailer feels that the brands are not substitutes for each other. A "Tommy" customer buys Tommy and not Ralph. Also, it is easier for one buyer to purchase merchandise and coordinate distribution and promotions for the merchandise offered by a national-brand vendor.

Category Management   While retailers, in general, manage merchandise at the category level, many supermarkets organize their merchandise management around brands or vendors. For instance, a supermarket chain might have three different buyers for breakfast cereals—one each for Kellogg's, General Mills, and General Foods.

Managing merchandise within a brand category can lead to inefficiencies because it fails to consider the interdependencies among SKUs in the category. For example, the three breakfast cereal buyers for a supermarket chain, one for each major brand, might each decide to stock a new product line of gluten-free breakfast cereals offered by Kellogg, General Mills, and General Foods. However, if the brand-organized buyers had taken a category-level perspective, they would have realized that the market for gluten-free cereals was limited and the supermarket would generate more sales by stocking one brand of gluten-free cereals and using the space set aside for the other gluten-free cereal brands to stock a locally produced cereal that has a strong following among some of its other customers.

The chilled drink department consists of several categories.

The **category management** approach to managing merchandise assigns one buyer or category manager to oversee all merchandising activities for the entire category. Managing by category can help ensure that the store's assortment includes the "best" combination of sizes and vendors—the one that will get the most profit from the allocated space.[2]

Category Captain   Some retailers select a vendor, such as General Mills or Kellogg's, to help them manage a particular category. The vendor, known as the **category captain,** works with the retailer to develop a better understanding of consumer shopping behaviors, create assortments that satisfy consumer needs, and improve the profitability of the merchandise category.

Selecting vendors as category captains has several advantages for retailers. It makes merchandise management tasks easier and can increase profits. Vendors are often in a better position to manage a category than are retailers because they have superior information about a category. The vendor's entire focus is on a specific category, while buyers are typically responsible for several categories. In addition, the insights that vendors acquire from managing the category for other retailers can be applied to a current problem.

A potential problem with establishing a vendor as a category captain is that the vendor could take advantage of its position. It is somewhat like "letting the fox into the henhouse." Suppose, for example, that Frito-Lay chose to maximize its own sales, rather than the retailer's sales, in managing the salty snack category. It could suggest an assortment plan that included most of its SKUs and exclude SKUs that are more profitable to the retailer, such as high-margin, private-label SKUs. Thus, retailers are becoming increasingly reluctant to turn over these important decisions to their vendors. They have found that working with their vendors and carefully evaluating their suggestions is a much more prudent approach. There are also antitrust considerations. The vendor category captain could collude with the retailer to fix prices. It could also block other brands, particularly smaller ones, from access to shelf space.[3]

Evaluating Merchandise Management Performance

As we discussed in Chapter 6, a good performance measure for evaluating a retail firm is ROA. Return on assets is composed of two components, asset turnover and net profit margin percentage. But ROA is not a good measure for evaluating the performance of merchandise managers because they do not have control over all of the retailer's assets or all the expenses that the retailer incurs. Merchandise managers have control only over what merchandise they buy (the retailer's merchandise inventory), the price at which the merchandise is sold, and the cost of the merchandise. Thus, buyers generally have control over the gross margin but not operating expenses, such as store operations, human resources, real estate, and logistics and information systems.

GMROI   A financial ratio that assesses a buyer's contribution to ROA is gross margin return on inventory investment (GMROI, typically pronounced "jim-roy"). It measures how many gross margin dollars are earned on every dollar of inventory investment made by the buyer. GMROI combines gross margin percentage and the sales-to-stock ratio, which is related to inventory turnover.

$$\text{GMROI} = \text{Gross margin percentage} \times \text{Sales-to-stock ratio}$$

$$= \frac{\text{Gross margin}}{\text{Net sales}} \times \frac{\text{Net sales}}{\text{Average inventory at cost}}$$

$$= \frac{\text{Gross margin}}{\text{Average inventory at cost}}$$

The reason we use the sales-to-stock ratio to calculate GMROI (instead of inventory turnover) is that GMROI is a type of return on investment measure, so the investment in inventory is expressed at cost. Inventory turnover and sales-to-stock ratios are very similar in concept, but they are calculated slightly differently.

EXHIBIT 12–2
Illustration of GMROI

		Fresh Bakery Bread	Gourmet Canned Food
	Sales	$1,000,000	200,000
	Gross margin	200,000	100,000
	Average inventory	100,000	50,000

$$\text{GMROI} = \frac{\text{Gross margin}}{\text{Net sales}} \times \frac{\text{Net sales}}{\text{Average inventory}} = \frac{\text{Gross margin}}{\text{Average inventory}}$$

Fresh Bakery Bread
$$\text{GMROI} = \frac{200,000}{1,000,000} \times \frac{1,000,000}{100,000} = \frac{200,000}{100,000}$$
$$= 20\% \times 10 = 200\%$$

Gourmet Canned Food
$$\text{GMROI} = \frac{100,000}{200,000} \times \frac{200,000}{50,000} = \frac{100,000}{50,000}$$
$$= 50\% \times 4 = 200\%$$

The difference between the sales-to-stock ratio and inventory turnover is the numerator of the equation. When you are calculating the sales-to-stock ratio, the numerator is net sales. When you are calculating inventory turnover, the numerator is the cost of goods sold. To convert the sales-to-stock ratio to inventory turnover, simply multiply the sales-to-stock ratio by (1 − Gross margin percentage). Thus, if the sales-to-stock ratio is 9.0 and the gross margin percentage is 0.40, the inventory turnover for the category is 5.4:

Inventory turnover = (1 − Gross margin percentage) × Sales-to-stock
5.4 = (1 − 0.4) × 9.0

Buyers have control over both components of GMROI. The gross margin component is affected by the prices they set and the prices they negotiate with vendors when buying merchandise. The sales-to-stock ratio is affected by the popularity of the merchandise they buy. If they buy merchandise that customers want, it sells quickly and the sales-to-stock ratio is high.

Like the profit and asset management paths to assess ROA, there are two paths to achieving high GMROI: gross margin and inventory turnover (sales-to-stock ratio). For instance, within a supermarket, some categories (e.g., wine) are high-margin–low-turnover, while other categories (e.g., milk) are low-margin–high-turnover. If the wine category's performance were compared with that of milk using inventory turnover alone, the contribution of wine to the supermarket's performance would be undervalued. In contrast, if only gross margin were used, wine's contribution would be overvalued.

Consider the situation in Exhibit 12–2, in which a supermarket wants to evaluate the performance of two categories: fresh bakery bread and gourmet canned food. If evaluated on gross margin percentage or sales alone, gourmet canned food is certainly the winner, with a 50 percent gross margin and sales of $300,000, compared with fresh bakery bread's gross margin of 1.33 percent and sales of $150,000. Yet gourmet canned food's sales-to-stock ratio is only 4, whereas fresh bakery bread has a sales-to-stock ratio of 150. Using GMROI, both categories achieve a GMROI of 200 percent and so are equal performers from an ROA perspective.

The bakery department in a supermarket typically has a high sales-to-stock ratio and a low gross margin.

Measuring Sales-to-Stock Ratio   Retailers normally express inventory turnover (sales-to-stock) ratios on an annual basis rather than for part of a year. If the sales-to-stock ratio for a three-month season equals 2.3, the annual sales-to-stock ratio will be four times that number (9.2). Thus, to convert a sales-to-stock ratio based on part of a year to an annual figure, multiply it by the number of such time periods in the year.

The most accurate way to measure average inventory is to measure the inventory level at the end of each day and divide the sum by 365. Most retailers can use their information systems to get accurate average inventory estimates by collecting and averaging the inventory in stores and distribution centers at the end of each day. Another method is to take the end-of-month (EOM) inventories for several months and divide by the number of months. For example,

Month	End-of-Month Inventory
January	$22,000
February	35,000
March	38,000
Total	$93,000
Average (Total/3)	$31,000

Improving GMROI

There are two paths that buyers can take to increase GMROI: (1) improve inventory turnover (sales-to-stock ratio) or (2) increase gross margin.

Improve Inventory Turnover (Sales-to-Stock Ratio) To improve the inventory turnover (sales-to-stock ratio), buyers can either reduce the level of inventory or increase sales. One approach that buyers take to increase inventory turnover is to reduce the number of SKUs within a category. Buyers need to provide backup stock for each SKU so that the products will be available in the sizes and colors that customers are seeking. Fewer SKUs means that less backup stock is needed. However, reducing the number of SKUs could reduce sales because customers will be less likely to find what they want. Even worse, if they continually can't find the brand or product line at all, customers might start shopping at a competitor and also urge their friends to do the same.[4]

A second approach for reducing the level of inventory is to keep the same number of SKUs but reduce the backup stock for each SKU. This approach has the same problem as reducing the number of SKUs. Less backup stock increases the chances that customers will not find the size and color they want when visiting a store or website.

A third approach for increasing inventory turnover is to buy merchandise more often but in smaller quantities because this reduces average inventory without reducing sales. But buying smaller quantities decreases the gross margin because buyers can't take advantage of quantity discounts and transportation economies of scale. It also requires the buying staff to spend more time placing orders and monitoring deliveries.

A fourth approach is to increase sales and not increase inventory proportionally. For example, buyers could increase sales by reducing prices. While inventory turnover would increase in this situation, gross margin would also decrease, which could have a negative impact on GMROI.

Increasing inventory turnover can have positive impacts on sales by attracting more customer visits, improving sales associate morale, and providing more resources to take advantage of new buying opportunities. Higher inventory turnover increases sales because new merchandise is continually available to customers. New merchandise attracts customers to visit the store more frequently because they know they will be seeing different merchandise each time they visit the store. When inventory turnover is low, the merchandise begins to look **shopworn**—slightly damaged from being displayed and handled by customers for a long time.

Salespeople are excited about and more motivated to sell the new merchandise, and thus sales increase, increasing inventory turnover even further. Finally, when inventory turnover increases, more money is available to buy new merchandise. Having money available to buy merchandise late in a fashion season can open up profit opportunities. For instance, buyers can take advantage of special prices offered by vendors that have too much inventory left over at the end of the season.

Increase Gross Margin   Three approaches to increasing the gross margins are increasing prices, reducing the cost of goods sold, or reducing customer discounts. Increasing prices increases gross margin, but it can also decrease sales and inventory turnover, because price-sensitive customers buy less. Buyers usually attempt to lower the cost of goods sold by negotiating for better prices from vendors, though they also might increase the percentage of private-label merchandise in a category's assortment, because private-label merchandise is generally less costly than similar merchandise made by national brand vendors (see Chapter 13). Finally, buyers can increase gross margins by reducing the customer discounts needed to sell unwanted merchandise or merchandise left over at the end of the season. To minimize these discounts, buyers need to do a better job of buying products that customers want and accurately forecasting sales.

In summary, when attempting to increase GMROI, buyers need to strike a balance to determine appropriate levels of inventory turnover and gross margins. Some approaches for improving inventory turnover have secondary effects that can lower GMROI by lowering sales volume or reducing gross margins. As we discussed in Chapter 10, several steps can be taken to improve supply chain efficiency, such as improved vendor relationships, VMI, and CPFR, which increase inventory turnover without negative side effects.

MERCHANDISE PLANNING PROCESSES

LO2

Contrast the merchandise management processes for staple and fashion merchandise.

As shown in Exhibit 12–3, the merchandise management process involves buyers forecasting category sales, developing an assortment plan for merchandise in the category, and determining the amount of inventory needed to support the forecasted sales and resulting assortment plan. Then buyers develop a plan outlining the sales expected for each month, the inventory needed to support the sales, and the money that can be spent on replenishing sold merchandise and buying new merchandise. Along with developing the plan, the buyers or planners decide what type and how much merchandise should be allocated to each store. Having developed the plan, the buyer negotiates with vendors and buys the merchandise. Merchandise buying activities are reviewed in Chapter 13.

Finally, buyers continually monitor the sales of merchandise in the category and make adjustments. For example, if category sales are less than forecasted in the plan and the projected GMROI for the category falls below the buyer's goal, the buyer may decide to dispose of some merchandise by putting it on sale and then use the money generated to buy merchandise with greater sales potential

EXHIBIT 12–3
Merchandise Planning Process

or to reduce the number of SKUs in the assortment to increase inventory turnover.

Although Exhibit 12–3 suggests that these decisions follow each other sequentially, in practice, some decisions may be made at the same time or in a different order. For example, a buyer might first decide on the amount of inventory to invest in the category, and this decision might determine the number of SKUs that can be offered in the category.

Types of Merchandise Management Planning Systems

Retailers use different types of merchandise planning systems for managing (1) staple and (2) fashion merchandise categories. **Staple merchandise** categories, also called **basic merchandise** categories, are those categories that are in continuous demand over an extended time period. While consumer packaged goods companies introduce many "new products" each year, the number of "new to the world" product introductions each year in staple categories is limited. Some examples of staple merchandise categories include most categories sold in supermarkets, white paint, copy paper, and basic casual apparel such as T-shirts and men's underwear.

Because sales of staple merchandise are fairly steady from week to week, it is relatively easy to forecast demand, and the consequences of making mistakes in forecasting are not great. For example, if a buyer overestimates the demand for canned soup and buys too much, the retailer will have excess inventory for a short period of time. Eventually the canned soup will be sold without having to resort to discounts or special marketing efforts.

Because the demand for staple merchandise is very predictable, merchandise planning systems for staple categories often involve **continuous replenishment.** These systems involve continuously monitoring merchandise sales and generating replacement orders, often automatically, when inventory levels drop below predetermined levels.

Fashion merchandise categories are in demand only for a relatively short period of time. New products are continually introduced into these categories, making the existing products obsolete. In some cases, the basic product does not change, but the colors and styles change to reflect what is "hot" that season. Some examples of fashion merchandise categories are athletic shoes, tablets, smartphones, and women's apparel. Retailing View 12.1 describes how Mango creates and manages its fashion merchandise assortments.

Forecasting the sales for fashion merchandise categories is much more challenging than doing so for staple categories. Buyers for fashion merchandise categories have much less flexibility in correcting forecasting errors. For example, if the tablet buyer for Best Buy purchases too many units of a particular model, the excess inventory cannot be easily sold when a new upgraded model is introduced. Due to the short selling season for most fashion merchandise, buyers often do not have a chance to reorder additional merchandise after an initial order is placed. So if buyers initially order too little fashion merchandise, the retailer may not be able to satisfy the demand for the merchandise and will develop a reputation for not having the most popular merchandise in stock. If buyers order too much fashion merchandise, they will have to put it on sale at a discount or dispose of it in some other way at the end of the season. Thus, an important objective of merchandise planning systems for fashion merchandise categories is to be as close to out of stock as possible at the same time that the SKUs move out of fashion.

Seasonal merchandise categories consist of items whose sales fluctuate dramatically depending on the time of year. Some examples of seasonal merchandise are Halloween candy, Christmas ornaments, swimwear, and snow shovels. Both

12.1 RETAILING VIEW Fast Fashion at Mango

Mango is a specialty apparel fast-fashion retailer headquartered in Barcelona, Spain, though its more than 2,500 stores spread across 107 countries. Mango places more emphasis on the "fashion" rather than the "fast" element in its "fast-fashion" retail concept—as pioneered by Spain's Zara, Sweden's H&M, and the United States' Forever 21.

Mango's Hangar Design Center, the biggest design center in Europe, spreads over more than 100,000 square feet and houses around 550 sharply dressed professionals, creating fashion garments and accessories, predominately for women. The design, purchasing, and quality departments are also located in the Hangar. More than 80 percent of the company's employees are women, with an average age of 32 years. The work environment is very casual, in that suits or ties are rare, but fashion creativity is abundant, with employees expressing themselves through the way they dress. Mango headquarters also includes 2,000 employees representing 37 nationalities, communicating in several languages.

Mango's merchandise planning cycle begins every three months, when designers meet to discuss important new trends for each of its main collections, each of which contain five or six mini-collections. Shops receive a near-constant stream of new merchandise, ranging from clingy short dresses to work wear and sparkly evening gowns. New items get sent to stores once a week, roughly six times as often as typical apparel clothing chains.

To get ideas for each collection, designers attend traditional fashion shows and trade fairs. But they also stay close to the customer. They take photos of stylish young women and note what people are wearing on the streets and in nightclubs. "To see what everyone's going to do for next season is very easy," says David Egea, Mango's merchandising director, "but that doesn't mean this is the thing that is going to catch on." Hoping to stay *au courant,* design teams meet each week to adjust to ever-changing trends.

Mango describes each of its stores and clothing designs according to a set of traits: trendy, dressy, suitable for hot weather, and so on. When collection designs are set, a proprietary computer program then matches the new products' traits with compatible stores.

In addition, Mango stores display only a limited merchandise assortment. On each rack, only one item per size hangs. This policy encourages a sense of urgency by

Mango uses celebrity models such as Miranda Kerr to emphasize its fashion orientation.

playing on customers' worst fear: Maybe your size is going to run out.

Sources: www.mango.com; Jennifer Overstreet, "Mango Executive Shares Global Expansion Insights," *NRF Blog,* January 3, 2013; Kim Bhasin, "There Has Been a Changing of the Guard at Mango," *The Guardian,* November 24, 2012; and Vertica Bhardwaj and Ann Fairhurst, "Fast Fashion: Response to Changes in the Fashion Industry," *International Review of Retail, Distribution and Consumer Research* 20 (February 2010), pp. 165–173.

DISCUSSION QUESTION

What are the benefits of fast-fashion retailing from a retailer's perspective?

fashion and more mundane merchandise can be seasonal categories. For example, swimwear is fashionable and snow shovels are more mundane.

However, from a merchandise planning perspective, retailers buy seasonal merchandise in much the same way that they buy fashion merchandise. Retailers could store unsold snow shovels at the end of the winter season and sell them the next winter, but it is typically more profitable to sell the shovels at a steep discount near the end of the season rather than incur the cost of carrying this excess inventory until the beginning of the next season. Thus, plans for seasonal merchandise, like fashion merchandise, hope to zero out inventory at the end of the season.

These two different merchandise planning systems, staple and fashion, affect the nature of the approaches used to forecast sales and manage inventory. In the following section, each of the steps in the merchandise management process for staple and fashion merchandise is described.

FORECASTING CATEGORY SALES

As indicated in Exhibit 12–3, the first step in merchandise management planning is to develop a forecast for category sales. The methods and information used for forecasting staple and fashion merchandise categories are discussed in this section.

LO3
Describe how to predict sales for merchandise categories.

Forecasting Staple Merchandise

The approach for forecasting sales of staple merchandise is to project past sales trends into the future, while making adjustments for any anticipated factors, such as promotions and weather, that may affect future sales.

Use of Historical Sales   The sales of staple merchandise are relatively constant from year to year. Thus, forecasts are typically based on extrapolating historical sales. Because there are substantial sales data available, sophisticated statistical techniques can be used to forecast future sales for each SKU.[5] However, these statistical forecasts are based on the assumption that the factors affecting item sales in the past will be the same and have the same effect in the future. Thus, even though sales for staple merchandise categories are relatively predictable, controllable and uncontrollable factors can have a significant impact on sales.

REFACT

According to the "Lipstick Index," lipstick sales increase as perceptions of economic conditions decline.[6]

Adjustments for Controllable and Uncontrollable Factors   Controllable factors include the opening and closing of stores, the price set for the merchandise in the category, special promotions for the category, the pricing and promotion of complementary categories, and the placement of the merchandise categories in the stores. Some factors beyond the retailer's control are the weather, general economic conditions, special promotions or new product introductions by vendors, and the new product, pricing, and promotional activities by competitors.[7] Thus, buyers need to adjust the forecast on the basis of statistical projections to reflect the effects of these controllable and uncontrollable factors. Retailing View 12.2 illustrates how retailers use long-range weather forecasts to improve their forecasts.

Forecasting Fashion Merchandise Categories

Forecasting sales for fashion merchandise is challenging because buyers typically need to place orders and commit to buying specific quantities between three to

12.2   RETAILING VIEW   Weather's Effects on Retail Sales

Home improvement centers know that when hurricane season comes, they need to be ready with bottled water, batteries, flashlights, plywood, and generators. However, more subtle weather conditions, like a warmer-than-normal holiday season, can have a significant impact on retail sales as well. As the weather becomes warmer in the summer, some obvious categories increase sales, such as ice, bottled water, and sports drinks. A hot summer results in consumers seeking out air-conditioned spaces. Big-box retailers and movie theatres offer a chilly respite from the sweltering heat. A warm winter stimulates sales of lawn tools, barbeques, and garden equipment in February and March rather than April, May, or June. One category that thrives during extended summer seasons is fashion. Retailers typically roll out their summer collections well before consumers can comfortably wear the clothes outside, but if the weather is already warm, it will ignite sales early. If the summer stays warmer longer, retailers can delay sales discounts, thus improving their margins.

To incorporate weather effects into their forecasts, many retailers subscribe to long-range weather forecasting services. Merchandise managers use the information provided by these services to make decisions about the timing of merchandise deliveries, promotions, and price discounts. Thus, when one year Planalytics (one of the companies offering long-range weather forecasts) informed a Canadian men's clothing retailer that the spring would be colder than normal, but the summer temperatures would be higher than normal, it made a few strategic movies. First, it delayed taking markdowns on shorts for sale. Second, it moved nearly 10,000 pairs of shorts to stores along the west coast, which was predicted to be even hotter than the east. Third, it adjusted its sales staff to match the weather-related demands. As a result, it earned an additional $250,000 in revenues, beyond its expectations.

However, clothing retailers that target younger shoppers tend to rely less on weather forecasts, because 18-to-24-year-olds buy clothes well in advance of the season they need to wear them. In contrast, retirees and older shoppers wait until it feels warm before they load up on summertime gear.

REFACT

When the temperature increases by 18 degrees, sales of barbecue meat generally triple, while demand for lettuce jumps 50 percent.[8]

REFACT

According to some estimates, approximately one-third of U.S. gross domestic product depends, directly or indirectly, on the climate.[9]

The first cold snap in the fall stimulates the sale of winter apparel.

Sources: www.planalytics.com; Catherine Valenti, "More Companies Use Weather to Forecast Sales," *ABC News*, March 12, 2013; "How Does Hot Weather Affect People's Buying Patterns?" *CBC*, July 2012; Cecilia Sze and Paul Walsh, "How Weather Influences the Economy," *ISO Review*, www.iso.com/Research-and-Analyses/ISO-Review/How-Weather-Influences-the-Economy.html.

DISCUSSION QUESTION

Why might Kohl's sales be more affected by the weather than Nordstrom's sales?

six months before the merchandise will be delivered and made available for sale.[10] In addition, for fashion items, there often is no opportunity to increase or decrease the quantity ordered before the selling season has ended. Suppliers of popular merchandise usually have orders for more merchandise than they can produce and excess inventory of unpopular items. Finally, forecasting fashion merchandise sales is particularly difficult because some or all of the items in the category are new and different from units offered in previous seasons or years. Some sources of information that retailers use to develop forecasts for fashion merchandise categories are (1) previous sales data, (2) market research, (3) fashion and trend services, and (4) vendors.

Previous Sales Data   Although items in fashion merchandise categories might be new each season, many items in a fashion category are often similar to items sold in previous years. Thus, accurate forecasts might be generated by simply projecting past sales data. For example, football video games, such as *Madden NFL*, might change from season to season with new editions, but while the SKUs are different each season, the total number of football video games sold each year might be relatively constant and predictable.

Market Research   Buyers for fashion merchandise categories undertake a variety of market research activities to help them forecast sales. These activities range from informal, qualitative research about trends affecting the category to more formal experiments and surveys.

To find out what customers are going to want in the future, buyers immerse themselves in their customers' world. For example, buyers look for information about trends by going to Internet chat rooms and blogs, attending soccer games and rock concerts, and visiting hot spots around town like restaurants and nightclubs to see what people are talking about and wearing. Buyers are information junkies and read voraciously. What movies are hits at the box office, and what are the stars wearing? Who is going to see them? What books and albums are on the top 10 lists? What magazines are consumers purchasing? Are there themes that keep popping up across these sources of information?

Social media sites are important sources of information for buyers. Buyers learn a lot about their customers' likes, dislikes, and preferences by monitoring their past purchases and by monitoring their interactions with social network sites such as Facebook, Pinterest, and Twitter. Customers appear keen to submit their opinions about their friends' purchases, interests, and blogs.

Retailers also use traditional forms of marketing research such as in-depth interviews and focus groups. The **in-depth interview** is an unstructured personal interview in which the interviewer uses extensive probing to get individual respondents to talk in detail about a subject. For example, one grocery store chain goes through the personal checks received each day to identify customers to interview. Representatives from the supermarket chain call these customers and interview them to find out what they like and don't like about the merchandise in the store.

A more informal method of interviewing customers is to require that buyers spend some time on the selling floor waiting on customers. Buying offices for Target and The Gap are in Minnesota and northern California, respectively, yet their stores are located throughout the United States. It has become increasingly hard for buyers in large chains to be attuned to local customer demand. Frequent store visits help resolve the situation. Some retailers require that their buyers spend a specified period of time, like one day a week, in a store. Lululemon, the yoga and athletic gear retailer, is one such company: Its CEO, Christine Day, spends several hours each week in one of the chain's stores, solely to listen to customers' complaints and feedback. Furthermore, the design of the stores turns each

REFACT
The top fashion blog based on an analysis of 20 factors is *CollegeFashion.net*.[11]

employee into a corporate eavesdropper. The tables at which sales clerks fold merchandise are located next to changing rooms, where shoppers tend to critique items openly. A whiteboard in the dressing room also encourages them to leave written feedback, if necessary.[12]

A **focus group** is a small group of respondents interviewed by a moderator using a loosely structured format. Participants are encouraged to express their views and comment on the views of others in the group. To keep abreast of the teen market, for instance, some stores have teen boards consisting of opinion leaders who meet to discuss merchandising and other store issues. Abercrombie & Fitch brings in groups of teenagers and has them rate their preferences for different items.

Asda, a U.K. supercenter owned by Walmart, regularly surveys its customers to forecast sales of new products. It e-mails a group of 25,000 customers, which it has termed its "Pulse of the Nation" group, sets of images and descriptions of new products. The Pulse group is asked to respond, positively or negatively, and indicate whether or not they think the new products should be carried in the stores.[13]

Finally, many retailers have a program for conducting merchandise sales experiments. For example, retailers continually run experiments to determine whether new merchandise concepts will produce adequate sales. They introduce the new merchandise into a representative sample of stores and sees what sales are generated for the items. Multichannel retailers often run similar experiments by offering new items on their websites before making a decision to stock them in their stores.

Fashion Trend Services There are many services that buyers—particularly buyers of apparel categories—can subscribe to that forecast the latest fashions, colors, and styles. For example, Doneger Creative Services offers various forecasting services, describing the color trends it anticipates for men's, women's, and children's apparel, lifestyle products, and accessories. Its color forecast service provides color direction for each season using dyed-to-specification color standards, plus suggested color combinations and applications for specific categories. Its online clipboard reports present actionable information and style news from the runways to the streets.

Vendors Vendors have proprietary information about their marketing plans, such as new product launches and special promotions that can have a significant impact on retail sales for their products and the entire merchandise category. In addition, vendors tend to be very knowledgeable about market trends for particular merchandise categories because they typically specialize in fewer merchandise categories than do retailers. Thus, information from vendors about their plans and market research about merchandise categories is very useful to buyers as they develop category sales forecasts.

Sales Forecasting for Service Retailers

Due to the perishable nature of services, service retailers face an even more extreme problem than fashion retailers. Their offering perishes at the end of the day, not at the end of the season. If there are empty seats when a plane takes off or a rock concert ends, the revenue that might have been generated from these seats is lost forever. Likewise, if more people are interested in dining at a restaurant than there are tables available, a revenue opportunity also is lost. So service retailers have devised approaches for managing demand for their offering so that it meets but does not exceed capacity.

Some service retailers attempt to match supply and demand by taking reservations or making appointments. Physicians often overbook their appointments, so many patients have to wait. They do this so that they will always fill their capacity and not have unproductive, non-revenue-generating time. Restaurants take reservations so that customers will not have to wait for a table. In addition, the reservations indicate the staffing levels needed for the shift. Another approach is to sell advance tickets for a service, such as arenas do for concerts.[14]

DEVELOPING AN ASSORTMENT PLAN

After forecasting sales for the category, the next step in the merchandise management planning process is to develop an assortment plan (see Exhibit 12–3). An **assortment plan** is the set of SKUs that a retailer will offer in a merchandise category in each of its stores and from its website.

Summarize the trade-offs for developing merchandise assortments.

Category Variety and Assortment

The assortment plan reflects the breadth and depth of merchandise that the retailer plans to offer in a merchandise category. In the context of merchandise planning, **variety,** or **breadth,** of a merchandise category is the number of different merchandising subcategories offered, and the **assortment,** or **depth,** of merchandise is the number of SKUs within a subcategory.

Determining Variety and Assortment

The process of determining the variety and assortment for a category is called **editing the assortment.** An example of an assortment plan for girls' jeans shown in Exhibit 12–4 includes 10 types or varieties (skinny or boot-cut, distressed denim or rinsed wash, and three price points reflecting different brands). For each type, there are 81 SKUs (3 colors $\times$ 9 sizes $\times$ 3 lengths). Thus, this retailer plans to offer 810 SKUs in girls' jeans.

When editing the assortment for a category like jeans, the buyer considers the following factors: (1) the firm's retail strategy, (2) the effect of assortments on

Assortment Plan for Girls' Jeans   **EXHIBIT 12–4**

Styles	Skinny	Skinny	Skinny	Skinny	Skinny	Skinny
Price levels	$20	$20	$35	$35	$45	$45
Fabric composition	Distressed	Rinsed wash	Distressed	Rinsed wash	Distressed	Rinsed wash
Colors	Light blue	Light blue	Light blue	Light blue	Light blue	Light blue
	Indigo	Indigo	Indigo	Indigo	Indigo	Indigo
	Black	Black	Black	Black	Black	Black
Styles	**Boot-Cut**	**Boot-Cut**	**Boot-Cut**	**Boot-Cut**		
Price levels	$25	$25	$45	$45		
Fabric composition	Distressed	Rinsed wash	Distressed	Rinsed wash		
Colors	Light blue	Light blue	Light blue	Light blue		
	Indigo	Indigo	Indigo	Indigo		
	Black	Black	Black	Black		

GMROI, (3) the complementarities among categories, (4) the effects of assortments on buying behavior, and (5) the physical characteristics of the store.[15]

Retail Strategy   The number of SKUs offered in a merchandise category is a strategic decision. For example, ALDI supermarkets focus on customers who are looking for low prices and do not care much about brands, so they offer very few SKUs in a category. With limited SKUs, ALDI can increase its inventory turnover, lower costs, and charge lower prices. In contrast, Best Buy's target customers are interested in comparing many alternatives, so the retailer must offer several SKUs in each consumer electronics category.

The breadth and depth of the assortment in a merchandise category can affect the retailer's brand image too. Retailers might increase the assortment in categories that are closely associated with their image. For example, Staples carries only a few SKUs of candy bars because candy is not part of the core office supply assortment for which it is known. But it carries a much broader and deeper assortment of paper products, because its customers expect to find such options when they visit the office supplier.

Assortments and GMROI   In developing the assortment plan, buyers need to be sensitive to the trade-off of increasing sales by offering greater breadth and depth but, at the same time potentially reducing inventory turnover and GMROI because of the increased inventory investment. Increasing assortment breadth and depth also can decrease gross margin. For example, the more SKUs offered, the greater the chance of **breaking sizes**—that is, stocking out of a specific size or color SKU. If a stockout occurs for a popular SKU in a fashion merchandise category and the buyer cannot reorder during the season, the buyer will typically discount the entire merchandise type, thus reducing gross margin. The buyer's objective is to remove the merchandise type from the assortment altogether so that customers will not be disappointed when they don't find the size and color they want.

Complementary Merchandise   When buyers develop assortment plans, they need to consider the degree to which categories in a department complement each other. For instance, Blu-Ray players may have a low GMROI, suggesting that the retailer carry a limited assortment. But customers who buy a Blu-Ray player might also buy complementary products and services such as accessories, cables, and warranties that have a high GMROI. Thus, the buyer may decide to carry more Blu-Ray player SKUs to increase the more profitable accessory sales.

Effects of Assortment Size on Buying Behavior   Offering large assortments provides a number of benefits to customers. First, increasing the number of SKUs that customers can consider increases the chance they will find the product that best satisfies their needs. Second, large assortments are valued by customers because they provide a more informative and stimulating shopping experience due to the complexity associated with numerous products and the novelty associated with unique items. Third, large assortments are particularly appealing to customers who seek variety—those who want to try new things. However, offering a large assortment can make the purchase decision more complex and time-consuming and potentially overwhelms the consumer, which could reduce sales.

Research indicates that customers' perceptions of assortments are not based simply on the number of SKUs offered in a product category. Instead, assortment perceptions are affected by the similarity of the SKUs in the category, the size of the category's display, and the availability of the customer's favorite SKU. Perceived assortment is greater when the items in the assortment are different, the category occupies more space, and the customer's favorite product is available. In one study, customer perception of the assortment offered by a retailer did not change when a retailer decreased the number of SKUs by 54 percent, but kept the category display size, similarity of the products, and availability of the favorite product the same. In another study, the perceived assortment actually increased by 25 percent when the actual assortment decreased but the display of the most popular brands increased because customers could more easily locate their favorite brand. Other factors affecting how customers perceive assortments are discussed in Chapter 17.[16]

Many retailers have initiated **SKU rationalization programs** in their efforts to analyze the benefits they might gain from deleting, adding, or keeping certain items in their assortments. The objective of such a program is to increase inventory turnover by reducing the number of SKUs without reducing sales. Of the 40,000 SKUs offered by a typical supermarket, the average household annually uses only 350 SKUs. Because typically 20 percent of the SKUs account for 80 percent of sales, eliminating the bottom 15 percent of the SKUs should have limited effect on sales. Retailing View 12.3 illustrates how Costco and Walmart rationalizes their assortment.

Physical Characteristics of the Store   Buyers need to consider how much space to devote to a category. More space is needed to display categories with large assortments. In addition, a lot of space is needed to display individual items in some categories, and this limits the number of SKUs that can be offered in stores. For example, furniture takes up a lot of space, and thus furniture retailers typically display one model of a chair or sofa and then have photographs and cloth swatches or a virtual display on a computer to show how the furniture would look with different upholstery.

Multichannel retailers address space limitations in stores by offering a greater assortment through their Internet and catalog channels than they do in stores. For example, Staples offers more types of laptop computers and printers on its Internet site than it stocks in its stores. If customers do not find the computer or printer they want in the store, sales associates direct them to the company's Internet site and can even order the merchandise for them on the spot from a POS terminal.

SETTING INVENTORY AND PRODUCT AVAILABILITY LEVELS

Model Stock Plan

LO5

Illustrate how to determine the appropriate inventory levels.

The **model stock plan,** illustrated in Exhibit 12–5, is the number of each SKU in the assortment plan that the buyer wants to have available for purchase in each store. For example, the model stock plan in Exhibit 12–5 includes nine units of size 1, short, which represent 2 percent of the 429 total units for girls' skinny $20 denim jeans in light blue. Note that there are more units for more popular sizes.

Retailers typically have model stock plans for the different store sizes in a chain. For example, retailers typically classify their stores as A, B, and C stores on the basis of their sales volume. The basic assortment in a category is stocked in C stores. For the larger stores, because more space is available, the number of SKUs increases. The larger A and B stores may have more brands, colors, styles, and sizes.

12.3   RETAILING VIEW   Costco and Walmart: Two Approaches to SKU Rationalization

Costco's sale items create a sense of a treasure hunt.

Costco is a master of continually editing its assortment. Costco stores feature 3,950 SKUs, compared with 5,250 at Sam's Club and 6,890 at B.J.'s. Although it collaborates with various partners to devise appealing products, new items only qualify for a 13-week run, and if they fail to perform, Costco does not hesitate to yank them from its shelves. As a result, customers constantly find a new assortment of shifting products, even if the overall number of SKUs in the store remains relatively constant. Thus, Costco's approach to SKU rationalization has a positive impact on GMROI. The sales-to-stock ratio (inventory turnover) is strong because its total number of SKUs is relatively low. Customers shop often, looking for new deals and "treasures." Its gross margin and sales are also strong because it carries high-demand items for which there is no need for significant markdowns.

Reducing the number of SKUs is not always a good strategy, however. Walmart, like many retailers, initiated a SKU rationalization program. The initiative was spurred by an industry study showing that shoppers thought Target had a larger assortment than Walmart, even though Walmart stores had more SKUs. So Walmart reduced the number of SKUs in its stores and added some SKUs that appealed to higher-income households. However, sales declined, particularly in rural areas, so Walmart reversed its decision and added back 8,000 SKUs.

Sources: "Costco Keeps It Simple," *Frozen Food and Dairy Buyer*, March 12, 2012; Warren Thayer and Miguel Bustillo, "Wal-Mart Merchandise Goes Back to Basics," *The Wall Street Journal*, April 11, 2011; and "Changes in the Wind at Wal-Mart," *RFF Retailer*, February 17, 2009.

DISCUSSION QUESTION

Why does maintaining a relatively low number of SKUs work at Costco, but not at Walmart?

EXHIBIT 12–5
Model Stock Plan
for Girls' Jeans

LENGTH		SIZE								
		1	2	4	5	6	8	10	12	14
Short	%	2	4	7	6	8	5	7	4	2
	units	9	17	30	26	34	21	30	17	9
Medium	%	2	4	7	6	8	5	7	4	2
	units	9	17	30	26	34	21	30	17	9
Long	%	0	2	2	2	3	2	2	1	0
	units	0	9	9	9	12	9	9	4	0
Total 100%										
429 units										

Product Availability

The number of units of **backup stock,** also called **buffer** or **safety stock,** in the model stock plan determines product availability. **Product availability** is defined as the percentage of the demand for a particular SKU that is satisfied. For instance, if 100 people go into a PetSmart store to purchase a small Great Choice portable kennel but only 90 people can make the purchase before the kennel stock is depleted, the product availability for that SKU is 90 percent. Product availability is also referred to as the **level of support** or **service level.**

More backup stock is needed in the model stock plan if a retailer wants to increase product availability—that is, increase the probability that customers will find the product they want when they visit the retailer's store or website. Choosing an appropriate amount of backup stock is critical to successful assortment planning. If the backup stock is too low, the retailer will lose sales and possibly customers as well when they find that the products they want are not available from the retailer. If the level is too high, scarce financial resources will be wasted on needless inventory, which lowers GMROI, rather than being more profitably invested in increasing variety or assortment.

Exhibit 12–6 shows the trade-off between inventory investment and product availability. Although the actual inventory investment varies in different situations, the general relationship shows that extremely high levels of product availability result in a prohibitively high inventory investment.

The trade-off among variety, assortment, and product availability is a crucial issue in determining a retailer's merchandising strategy. Buyers have a limited budget for the inventory investments they can make in a category. Thus, they are forced to sacrifice breadth of merchandise if they opt to increase depth, or they must reduce both depth and breadth to increase product availability.

Retailers often classify merchandise categories or individual SKUs as A, B, or C items, reflecting the product availability the retailer wants to offer. The A items are best-sellers bought by many customers. For example, white paint is an A item for Sherwin Williams, and copy paper is an A item for Office Depot. A retailer rarely wants to risk A-item stockouts because running out of these very popular SKUs would diminish the retailer's brand image and customer loyalty. On the other hand, lower product availability is acceptable for C items, which are purchased by a small number of customers and are not readily available from other retailers. The greater the fluctuations in demand, the lead time for delivery from the vendor, and the fluctuations in vendor lead time, the greater the backup stock

EXHIBIT 12–6
Inventory Investment and Product Availability

levels required to maintain a particular product availability level. However, less backup stock is needed to maintain a particular product availability level with more frequent store deliveries.

ESTABLISHING A CONTROL SYSTEM FOR MANAGING INVENTORY

LO6

Analyze merchandise control systems.

The first three steps in the merchandise planning process—forecasting SKU and category sales, determining the assortment plan, and establishing the model stock plan (see Exhibit 12–3)—quantify the buyer's sales expectations and service level. The fourth step in the merchandise management process is to establish a control system for how the orders, deliveries, inventory levels, and merchandise sales will evolve over time. The objective of this control system is to manage the flow of merchandise into the stores so that the amount of inventory in a category is minimized but the merchandise will still be available when customers want to buy it. The differences between the control systems for staple and fashion merchandise are discussed in the following sections.

Control System for Managing Inventory of Staple Merchandise

The SKUs in a staple merchandise category are sold month after month, year after year. Lowe's sales of purple paint this month will be about the same as they were during the same month a year ago. If the sales of purple paint are below forecast this month, the excess inventory of purple paint can be sold during the following month. Thus, an automated continuous replenishment control system is used to manage the flow of staple merchandise SKUs and categories. The continuous replenishment system monitors the inventory level of each SKU in a store and automatically triggers the reorder of an SKU when the inventory falls below a predetermined level.

Flow of Staple Merchandise   Exhibit 12–7 illustrates the merchandise flow in a staple merchandise management system. At the beginning of week 1, the retailer had 150 units of the SKU in inventory and the buyer or merchandise planner placed an order for 96 additional units. During the next two weeks, customers purchased 130 units, and the inventory level decreased to 20 units. At the end of week 2, the 96-unit order from the vendor arrived, and the inventory level jumped up to 116 units. The continuous replenishment system placed another order with the vendor that will arrive in two weeks, before customer sales decrease the inventory level to zero and the retailer stocks out.

Inventory for which the level goes up and down due to the replenishment process is called **cycle stock** or **base stock** (shown in gold in Exhibit 12-7). The retailer hopes to reduce the cycle stock inventory to keep its inventory investment low. One approach for reducing the cycle stock is to reorder smaller quantities more frequently. But more frequent, smaller orders and shipments increase administrative and transportation costs, and reduce quantity discounts.

Staple merchandise management systems are used for items like this rubber mat.

EXHIBIT 12–7
Merchandise Flow of a
Staple SKU

Because sales of each SKU and on-time deliveries of orders from vendors cannot be predicted with perfect accuracy, the retailer has to carry backup stock, as a cushion, so that it doesn't stock out before the next order arrives. Backup stock is shown in green in Exhibit 12–7. Backup stock is the level of inventory needed to ensure merchandise is available in light of these uncertainties.

Determining the Level of Backup Stock   Several factors determine the level of backup stock needed for an SKU. First, the level depends on the product availability the retailer wants to provide. As discussed previously, more backup stock is needed when the retailer wants to reduce the chances of a stockout and increase the availability of the SKU. Thus, if Lowe's views white paint as an A item and rarely wants to stock out of it, a higher level of backup stock is needed. However, if melon paint is a C item and 75 percent product availability is acceptable, the level of backup stock can be lowered.

Second, the greater the fluctuation in demand, the more backup stock is needed. Suppose a Lowe's store sells an average of 30 gallons of purple paint in two weeks. Yet in some weeks sales are 50 gallons, and in other weeks they are only 10 gallons. When sales are less than average, the store ends up carrying a little more merchandise than it needs. But when sales are much more than average, there must be more backup stock to ensure that the store does not stock out. Note in Exhibit 12–7 that during week 4, sales were greater than average, so the retailer had to dip into its backup stock to avoid a stockout.

Third, the amount of backup stock needed is affected by the lead time from the vendor. **Lead time** is the amount of time between the recognition that an order needs to be placed and the point at which the merchandise arrives in the store and is ready for sale. If it took two months to receive a shipment of purple paint, the possibility of running out of stock is greater than it would be if the lead time was only two weeks. The shorter lead times inherent in collaborative supply chain management systems like CPFR (described in Chapter 10) result in a lower level of backup stock required to maintain the same level of product availability.

Fourth, fluctuations in lead time also affect the amount of backup stock needed. If Lowe's knows that the lead time for purple paint is always two weeks, plus or minus one day, it can more accurately plan its inventory levels. But if the lead time is one day on one shipment and then ten days on the next shipment, the stores must carry additional backup stock to cover this uncertainty in lead time. Many retailers using collaborative supply chain management systems require that their vendors deliver merchandise within a very narrow window—sometimes two or three hours—to reduce the fluctuations in lead time and thus the amount of required backup stock.

When planning the amount of inventory to order for a staple merchandise category, such as paint, Lowe's buyers must consider current inventory, customer demand, lead time for replenishment, and backup stock needed to avoid stockouts in the department.

Fifth, the vendor's fill rate affects the retailer's backup stock requirements. The percentage of SKUs received complete on a particular order from a vendor is called the **fill rate.** For example, Lowe's can more easily plan its inventory requirements if the vendor normally ships every item that is ordered. If, however, the vendor ships only 75 percent of the ordered items, Lowe's must maintain more backup stock to be certain that the paint availability for its customers isn't adversely affected.

Automated Continuous Replenishment   Once the buyer sets the desired product availability and determines the variation in demand and the vendor's lead time and fill rate, the continuous replenishment systems for staple SKUs can operate automatically. The retailer's information system determines the inventory level at each point in time, the **perpetual inventory,** by comparing the sales made through the POS terminals with the shipments received by the store. When the perpetual inventory level falls below the predetermined level, the system sends an EDI reorder to the retailer's distribution center and the vendor. When the reordered merchandise arrives at the store, the level of inventory is adjusted up.

However, it is difficult to achieve fully automated continuous replenishment of staple merchandise because of errors in determining the actual inventory. For example, the retailer's information system might indicate that 10 Gillette Fusion razors are in the store when, in fact, 10 razors were stolen by a shoplifter and there are actually zero razors in the store. Because there are no razors in the store, there are no sales, and the automated continuous replenishment system will never reorder razors for the store. Such inaccuracies also can arise when an incorrect number of units is input into the information system about a shipment from the distribution center to the store when it is delivered. To address these problems, store employees need to periodically check the inventory recorded in the system with an actual inventory of the store by physically counting all inventory.

Inventory Management Report   The inventory management report provides information about the inventory management for a staple category. The report indicates the decision variables set by the buyer, such as product availability, the backup stock needed to provide the product availability, the order points and quantities plus performance measures such as planned and actual inventory turnover, the current sales rate or velocity, sales forecasts, inventory availability, and the amount on order. Exhibit 12–8 is an inventory management report for Rubbermaid bath mats.

EXHIBIT 12–8   Inventory Management Report for Rubbermaid SKUs

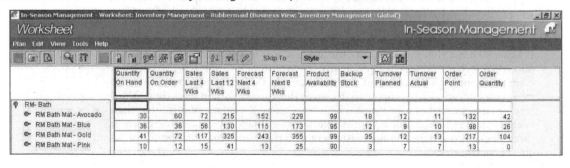

	Quantity On Hand	Quantity On Order	Sales Last 4 Wks	Sales Last 12 Wks	Forecast Next 4 Wks	Forecast Next 8 Wks	Product Availability	Backup Stock	Turnover Planned	Turnover Actual	Order Point	Order Quantity
RM- Bath												
RM Bath Mat - Avocado	30	60	72	215	152	229	99	18	12	11	132	42
RM Bath Mat - Blue	36	36	56	130	115	173	95	12	9	10	98	26
RM Bath Mat - Gold	41	72	117	325	243	355	99	35	12	13	217	104
RM Bath Mat - Pink	10	12	15	41	13	25	90	3	7	7	13	0

The first five columns of Exhibit 12–8 contain the descriptions of each item, how many items are on hand and on order, and sales for the past 4 and 12 weeks. The first-row SKU is a Rubbermaid bath mat in avocado green. There are 30 units on hand and 60 on order. Thus, the quantity available of this SKU is 90. Sales for the past 4 and 12 weeks were 72 and 215 units, respectively.

Sales forecasts for the next 4 and 8 weeks are determined by the system using a statistical model that considers the trends in past sales and the seasonal pattern for the SKU. However, in this case, the buyer made an adjustment in the forecast for the next 4 weeks to reflect an upcoming special promotion on avocado, blue, and gold bath mats.

The product availability is a decision variable that is input by the buyer. For the avocado bath mat SKU, the buyer wants 99 out of every 100 customers to find it in stock (99 percent product availability). But the buyer is less concerned about stocking out of pink bath mats and thus sets its product availability at 90 percent (on average, 90 out of 100 customers will find it in stock). The system then calculates the necessary backup stock for the avocado bath mat based on a predetermined formula—18 units. This number is determined by the system on the basis of the specified product availability, the variability in demand, the vendor delivery lead time, and the variability in the lead time.

The planned inventory turnover for the SKU, 12 times, is a decision variable also set by the buyer on the basis of the retailer's overall financial goals; it drives the inventory management system. For this SKU, the system determined that the actual turnover, based on the cost of goods sold and average inventory, is 11.

Order Point   The **order point** is the amount of inventory below which the quantity available shouldn't go or the item will be out of stock before the next order arrives. This number tells the buyer that when the inventory level drops to this point, additional merchandise should be ordered. For this SKU, the buyer needs to place an order if the quantity in inventory falls to 132 or fewer units to produce the desired product availability.

Order Quantity   When inventory reaches the order point, the buyer, or system, needs to order enough units to ensure product availability before the next order arrives. Using the avocado bath mats in Exhibit 12–8 as an example, the order quantity is 42 units.

Control System for Managing Inventory of Fashion Merchandise

The control systems for managing fashion merchandise categories are the merchandise budget plan and the open-to-buy.

Merchandise Budget Plan   The **merchandise budget plan** specifies the amount of merchandise in dollars (not units) that needs to be delivered during each month, based on the sales forecast, the planned discounts to employees and customers, and the level of inventory needed to support the sales and achieve the desired GMROI objectives.

Exhibit 12–9 shows a six-month merchandise budget plan for men's casual slacks at a national specialty store chain. Appendix 12A describes in detail how the plan is developed. Most retailers use commercially available software packages to develop merchandise budget plans.

Inventory turnover, GMROI, and the sales forecast are used for both planning and control. Buyers negotiate GMROI, inventory turnover, and sales forecast goals with their superiors, the GMMs and DMMs. Then, merchandise budgets are developed to meet these goals. Well before the season, buyers purchase the amount of merchandise specified in the last line of the merchandise budget plan to be delivered in those specific months—the monthly additions to stock.

EXHIBIT 12–9   Six-Month Merchandise Budget Plan for Mens' Casual Slacks

Worksheet	Spring	April	May	June	July	August	September
1. Sales % Distribution to Season	100.00%	21.00%	12.00%	12.00%	19.00%	21.00%	15.00%
2. Monthly Sales	$130,000	$27,300	$15,600	$15,600	$24,700	$27,300	$19,500
3. Reduc % Distribution to Season	100.00%	40.00%	14.00%	16.00%	12.00%	10.00%	8.00%
4. Monthly Reductions	$16,500	$6,600	$2,310	$2,640	$1,980	$1,650	$1,320
5. BOM Stock to Sales Ratio	4.00	3.60	4.40	4.40	4.00	3.60	4.00
6. BOM Inventory	$98,280	$98,280	$68,640	$68,640	$98,800	$98,280	$78,000
7. EOM Inventory	$65,600	$68,640	$68,640	$98,800	$98,280	$78,000	$65,600
8. Monthly Additions to Stock	$113,820	$4,260	$17,910	$48,400	$26,160	$8,670	$8,420

After the selling season, the buyer must determine how the category actually performed compared with the plan. If the actual GMROI, inventory turnover, and forecast are greater than those in the plan, performance is better than expected. However, performance evaluations should not be based solely on any one of these measures. Several additional questions should be answered to evaluate the buyer's performance: Why did the performance exceed or fall short of the plan? Was the deviation from the plan due to something under the buyer's control? For instance, was too much merchandise purchased? Did the buyer react quickly to changes in demand by either purchasing more or having a sale? Was the deviation instead due to some external factor, such as a change in the competitive level (e.g., new competitors' stores opened in the area) or economic activity (e.g., recession)? Every attempt should be made to discover answers to these questions. Later in this chapter, several additional tools used to evaluate merchandise performance will be examined.

Open-to-Buy System   After the merchandise is purchased on the basis of the merchandise budget plan, the **open-to-buy** system is used to keep track of the actual merchandise flows—what the present inventory level is, when purchased merchandise is scheduled for delivery, and how much has been sold to customers. In the same way that you must keep track of the checks you write, buyers need to keep track of the merchandise they purchase and when it is to be delivered so they don't buy more (over-bought) or less (under-bought) than they have money in their budget to spend each month. Without the open-to-buy system keeping track of merchandise flows, merchandise could be delivered when it isn't needed or be unavailable when it is needed.

The open-to-buy system compares the planned end-of-month inventory to the actual end-of-month inventory. Differences between actual and planned levels may arise because an order was shipped late or sales deviated from the forecast. When sales are greater than planned, the system determines how much merchandise to buy, in terms of dollars the buyer has available, to satisfy the increased customer demand.

ALLOCATING MERCHANDISE TO STORES

LO7

Describe how multistore retailers allocate merchandise to stores.

After developing a plan for managing merchandise inventory in a category, the next step in the merchandise management process is to allocate the merchandise purchased and received to the retailer's stores (see Exhibit 12–3). Research indicates that these allocation decisions have a much bigger impact on profitability than does the decision about the quantity of merchandise to purchase.[17] In other words, buying too little or too much merchandise has less impact on a category's profitability than does making mistakes in allocating the right amount and type of merchandise to stores. Allocating merchandise to stores involves three decisions: (1) how much merchandise to allocate to each store, (2) what type of merchandise to allocate, and (3) when to allocate the merchandise to different stores.

Amount of Merchandise Allocated

Retail chains typically classify each of their stores on the basis of annual sales. Thus, A stores would have the largest sales volume and typically receive the most inventory, while C stores would have the lowest sales volume and receive the least inventory for a category. In addition to the store's sales level, when making allocation decisions for a category, allocators consider the physical characteristics of the merchandise and the depth of assortment and level of product availability that the firm wants to portray for the specific store.

Type of Merchandise Allocated

The geodemographics of a store's trading area (discussed in Chapter 8) are considered in making allocation decisions. Consider the allocation decision of a national supermarket for its ready-to-eat cereal assortment. Some stores are located in areas dominated by segments called "Rustbelt Retirees," and other areas are dominated by the "Laptops and Lattes" segment, as described in Exhibit 12–10.

The ready-to-eat breakfast cereal planner would offer different assortments for stores in these two areas. Stores with a high proportion of Rustbelt Retirees in their trading areas would get an assortment of lower-price, well-known brands and more private-label cereals. Stores in areas dominated by the Laptops and Lattes geodemographic segment would get an assortment with higher-price brands that feature low sugar, organic ingredients, and whole wheat. Private-label cereals would be de-emphasized.

Even the sales of different apparel sizes can vary dramatically from store to store in the same chain. Exhibit 12–11 illustrates this point. Notice that store X sells significantly more large sizes and fewer small sizes than is average for the chain. If the planner allocated the same size distribution of merchandise to all stores in the chain, store X would stock out of large sizes, have an oversupply of small sizes, and be out of some sizes sooner than other stores in the chain. Retailing View 12.4 provides a glimpse of how Saks Fifth Avenue allocates merchandise to stores on the basis of customer characteristics.

REFACT

Southerners prefer white, green, and pink. Women on the East and West Coasts wear smaller sizes than their middle-American counterparts.[18]

Laptops and Lattes: The most eligible and unencumbered marketplace	Rustbelt Retirees
Laptops and Lattes are affluent, single, and still renting. They are educated, professional, and partial to city life, favoring major metropolitan areas such as New York, Boston, Chicago, Los Angeles, and San Francisco. Median household income is more than $87,000; median age is 38 years. Technologically savvy, the Laptops and Lattes segment is the top market for notebook PCs and PDAs. They use the Internet on a daily basis to trade stocks and make purchases and travel plans. They are health conscious and physically fit; they take vitamins, use organic products, and exercise in the gym. They embrace liberal philosophies and work for environmental causes.	Rustbelt Retirees can be found in older, industrial cities in the Northeast and Midwest, especially in Pennsylvania and other states surrounding the Great Lakes. Households are mainly occupied by married couples with no children and singles who live alone. The median age is 43.8 years. Although many residents are still working, labor force participation is below average. More than 40 percent of the households receive Social Security benefits. Most residents live in owned, single-family homes, with a median value of $118,500. Unlike many retirees, these residents are not inclined to move. They are proud of their homes and gardens and participate in community activities. Some are members of veterans' clubs. Leisure activities include playing bingo, gambling in Atlantic City, going to the horse races, working crossword puzzles, and playing golf.

EXHIBIT 12–10
Examples of Geodemographic Segments

342   SECTION III   Merchandise Management

EXHIBIT 12–11
Apparel Size
Differences for the
Average and Specific
Store in a Chain

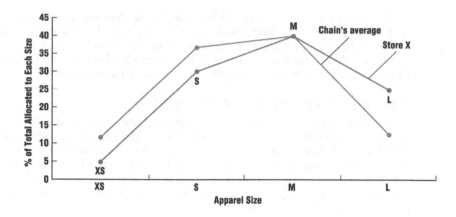

Timing of Merchandise Allocation

In addition to the need to allocate different inventory levels and types of merchandise across stores, differences in the timing of category purchases across stores need to be considered. Exhibit 12–12 illustrates these differences by plotting sales data over time for capri pants in different regions of the United States. Comparing regions shows that capri sales peak in late July in the Midwest and at the beginning of September in the West, due to seasonality

12.4   RETAILING VIEW   Customer-Centric Merchandise Allocation at Saks Fifth Avenue

Having the right merchandise in the right stores at the right time is the key to merchandising success for fashion retailers like Saks Fifth Avenue. For instance, Saks considers its core shopper at its New York flagship store in Manhattan to be a woman, between 46 and 57 years of age, with a largely "classic" style, especially when it comes to work clothes, and a taste for slightly more modern looks when she goes out with friends on weekends. But it also recognizes that the merchandise selections for stores located elsewhere needs to be less New York–centric. Even stores close to New York City attract different types of shoppers. A Greenwich, Connecticut, Saks caters to a slightly older shopper than does the Saks in Stamford, Connecticut, about five miles away. Stamford shoppers tend to be women who work in town, whereas Greenwich attracts a higher proportion of women who are at home full-time. Online Saks shoppers are seven years younger than a regular Saks customer, but they seek out specific items, whereas in-store shoppers are looking to be outfitted from head to toe during a single shopping trip.

To better match its assortments with its stores, Saks has developed a nine-box grid. On one side of the matrix are style categories: "Park Avenue," or classic; "Uptown," or modern; and "Soho," meaning trendy or contemporary. On the other axis are pricing levels, from "good" (brands such as Dana Buchman, Real Clothes [Saks's private label], and Eileen Fisher) to "better" (Piazza Sempione and Armani Collezioni) to "best" (Chanel, Gucci, and Yves

Saint Laurent). By cross-referencing the preferred styles and spending levels for each assortment at each location, the grid charts the best mix of clothes, brands, and accessories to stock at the store.

Such careful assortment planning was not quite sufficient to enable Saks to weather the recent global economic crisis, though. Assortments chosen during boom years led to massive leftover inventory during the bust times, prompting Saks to take more and deeper discounts—of up to 75 percent—than it ever had in its long history. When sales rebounded by about 15 percent with a slightly improved economy, Saks slowly eliminated its discounts and increased its inventory levels. But rather than returning to pre-recession levels, the bump in inventory was less than 3 percent overall to ensure it was never again stuck with massive overstocks.

Sources: Elizabeth Holmes, "At Saks, It's Full Price Ahead as CEO Pares Back Discounts," *The New York Times*, September 12, 2011; Stephanie Rosenbloom, "As Saks Reports a Loss, Its Chief Offers a Plan," *The New York Times*, February 26, 2009; Vanessa O'Connell, "Park Avenue Classic or Soho Trendy?" *The Wall Street Journal*, April 20, 2007, p. B1; and www.saks.com.

DISCUSSION QUESTION

What box on the grid best describes the Saks Fifth Avenue closest to where you live? Do you think it is the most appropriate box for that store's target market?

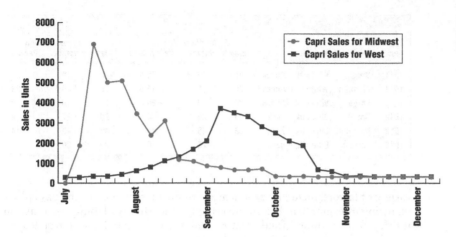

EXHIBIT 12–12
Sales of Capri Pants by Region

differences and differences in consumer demand. To increase inventory turnover in the category, buyers need to recognize these regional differences and arrange for merchandise to be shipped to the appropriate regions when customers are ready to buy.

Retailers are also considering the "paycheck cycle" when making merchandise allocation and promotion decisions, particularly in difficult economic times. Cash-strapped consumers are showing a tendency to make their largest purchases when they get their paychecks at the beginning of the month and to cut back on purchases as that money runs out toward the end of the month. As a result, some supermarket chains devote more shelf space and promote larger-package sizes at the beginning of the month and smaller sizes at the end of the month.[19]

ANALYZING MERCHANDISE MANAGEMENT PERFORMANCE

The next step in the merchandise planning process (see Exhibit 12–3) is to analyze the performance of the process and make adjustments, such as ordering more or less merchandise, lowering prices to increase sales, allocating different assortments to specific stores, or changing the assortment and model stock plans. Three types of analyses related to the monitoring and adjustment step are (1) sell-through analysis, (2) ABC analysis of assortments, and (3) multiattribute analysis of vendors. The first analysis provides an ongoing evaluation of the merchandise management plan compared with actual sales. The remaining two analyses offer approaches for evaluating and altering the assortment plan using the specific SKUs in the plan and the vendors that provide the merchandise to support the plan.

LO8

Review how retailers evaluate the performance of their merchandise management decisions.

Sell-Through Analysis: Evaluating the Merchandise Plan

A **sell-through analysis** compares actual and planned sales to determine whether more merchandise is needed to satisfy demand or whether price reductions (markdowns) are required. Exhibit 12–13 shows a sell-through analysis for blouses for the first two weeks of the season.

These blouses are high-fashion items that experience significant uncertainty in sales. Thus, after two weeks in the stores, the buyer reviews sales and determines if adjustments are needed. Buyers would use a longer review period for merchandise with an extended fashion cycle. The need to make adjustments depends on a

EXHIBIT 12–13
Example of Sell-
Through Analysis

Stock Number		Description	WEEK 1			WEEK 2		
			Plan	Actual-to-Plan		Plan	Actual-to-Plan	
				Actual	Percentage		Actual	Percentage
1011	Small	White silk V-neck	20	15	−25%	20	10	−50%
1011	Medium	White silk V-neck	30	25	−16.6	30	20	−33
1011	Large	White silk V-neck	20	16	−20	20	16	−20
1012	Small	Blue silk V-neck	25	26	4	25	27	8
1012	Medium	Blue silk V-neck	35	45	29	35	40	14
1012	Large	Blue silk V-neck	25	25	0	25	30	20

variety of factors, including experience with the merchandise in the past, plans for featuring the merchandise in advertising, and the availability of **markdown money** from vendors (funds that a vendor gives a retailer to cover lost gross margin dollars that result from markdowns).

In this case, the white blouses are selling significantly less well than planned. Therefore, the buyer makes an early price reduction to ensure that the merchandise isn't left unsold at the end of the season. The decision regarding the blue blouses isn't as clear. The small blue blouses are selling slightly ahead of the plan, and the medium blue blouses are also selling well, but the large blue blouses start selling ahead of plan only in the second week. In this case, the buyer decides to wait another week or two before taking any action. If actual sales stay significantly ahead of planned sales, a reorder might be appropriate.

Evaluating the Assortment Plan and Vendors

ABC Analysis   An **ABC analysis** identifies the performance of individual SKUs in the assortment plan. It is used to determine which SKUs should be in the plan and how much backup stock and resulting product availability are provided for each SKU in the plan. In an ABC analysis, the SKUs in a merchandise category are rank-ordered by several performance measures, such as sales, gross margin, inventory turnover, and GMROI. Typically, this rank order reveals the general 80–20 principle; namely, approximately 80 percent of a retailer's sales or profits come from 20 percent of the products. This principle suggests that retailers should concentrate on the products that provide the biggest returns.

After rank-ordering the SKUs, the next step is to classify the items. On the basis of the classification, the buyer determines whether to maintain the items in the assortment plan and, if so, what level of product availability to offer. For example, a men's dress shirt buyer might identify the A, B, C, and D SKUs by rank-ordering them by sales volume.

The A items account for only 5 percent of the SKUs in the category but represent 70 percent of sales. The buyer decides that these SKUs should never be out of stock and thus plans to maintain more backup stock for A items, such as keeping more units for each SKU of long- and short-sleeved white and blue dress shirts, than of the B and C items.

The B items represent 10 percent of the SKUs and 20 percent of sales. These items include some of the other better-selling colors and patterned shirts and contribute to the retailer's image of having fashionable merchandise. Occasionally, the retailer will run out of some SKUs in the B category because it does not carry the same amount of backup stock for B items as it does for A items.

The C items account for 65 percent of SKUs but contribute to only 10 percent of sales. The planner may plan to carry some C items only in the most popular sizes of the most basic shirts, with special orders used to satisfy customer demand.

Finally, the buyer discovers that the remaining 20 percent of the SKUs, D items, have virtually no sales until they are marked down. Not only are these items excess merchandise and an unproductive investment, but they also distract from the rest of the inventory and clutter the store shelves. The buyer decides to eliminate most of these items from the assortment plan.

Multiattribute Method for Evaluating Vendors   The **multiattribute analysis** method for evaluating vendors uses a weighted-average score for each vendor.[20] The score is based on the importance of various issues and the vendor's performance on those issues. This method is similar to the multiattribute approach that can be used to understand how customers evaluate stores and merchandise, as we discussed in Chapter 4.

To better understand the multiattribute method of evaluating vendors, either current or proposed, consider the example in Exhibit 12–14 for vendors of men's casual slacks.

A buyer can evaluate vendors using the following five steps:

1. Develop a list of issues to consider in the evaluation (column 1).

2. In conjunction with the GMM, determine the importance weights for each issue in column 1 on a 1-to-10 scale (column 2), where 1 equals not important and 10 equals very important. For instance, the buyer and the merchandise manager believe that vendor reputation should receive a 9 because it's very important to the retailer's image. Merchandise quality receives a 5 because it's moderately important. Finally, a vendor's selling history is less important, so it could be rated 3.

3. Make judgments about each individual brand's performance on each issue (remaining columns). Note that some brands have high ratings on some issues but not on others.

4. Develop an overall score by multiplying the importance of each issue by the performance of each brand or its vendor. For instance, vendor reputation importance (9) multiplied by the performance rating for brand A (5) is 45.

EXHIBIT 12–14
Multiattribute Method for Evaluating Vendors

Issues (1)	Importance Evaluation of Issues (I) (2)	PERFORMANCE EVALUATIONS OF INDIVIDUAL BRANDS ACROSS ISSUES			
		Brand A (P_a) (3)	Brand B (P_b) (4)	Brand C (P_c) (5)	Brand D (P_d) (6)
Vendor reputation	9	5	9	4	8
Service	8	6	6	4	6
Meets delivery dates	6	5	7	4	4
Merchandise quality	5	5	4	6	5
Markup opportunity	5	5	4	4	5
Country of origin	6	5	3	3	8
Product fashionability	7	6	6	3	8
Selling history	3	5	5	5	5
Promotional assistance	4	5	3	4	7
Overall evaluation a $\sum_{i=1}^{n} I_i \times P_{ij}$		280	298	212	341

$\sum_{i=1}^{n}$ = Sum of the expression.

I_i = Importance weight assigned to the ith dimension.

P_{ij} = Performance evaluation for jth brand alternative on the ith issue.

I = Not important.

10 = Very important.

Promotional assistance importance (4) multiplied by the performance rating (7) for vendor D is 28. This type of analysis illustrates an important point: It doesn't pay to perform well on issues that retailers don't believe are very important. Although vendor D performed well on promotional assistance, the buyer didn't rate this issue highly in importance, so the resulting score was still low.

5. To determine a vendor's overall rating, add the products for each brand for all issues. In Exhibit 12–14, brand D has the highest overall rating (341), so D is the preferred vendor.

SUMMARY

LO1   Explain the merchandise management organization and performance measures.

Merchandise is broken down into categories for planning purposes. Buyers and planners manage these categories, often with the help of their major vendors. The key performance measures used to assess merchandise management are GMROI and its components; sales-to-stock ratio, which is similar to inventory turnover; and gross margin. High inventory turnover is important for a retailer's financial success. But if the retailer attempts to push inventory turnover to its limit, stockouts and increased costs may result.

LO2   Contrast the merchandise management processes for staple and fashion merchandise.

Retailers use different types of merchandise planning systems for managing (1) staple and (2) fashion merchandise categories. Staple merchandise categories, also called basic merchandise categories, are categories that are in continuous demand over an extended time period. Fashion merchandise categories are in demand only for a relatively short period of time. New products are continually introduced into these categories, making the existing products obsolete. Seasonal merchandise categories consist of items whose sales fluctuate dramatically depending on the time of year.

The steps in the merchandise management planning process are (1) forecast category sales, (2) develop an assortment plan, (3) determine appropriate inventory levels and product availability, (4) develop a plan for managing inventory, (5) allocate merchandise to stores, and (6) monitor and evaluate performance and make adjustments.

LO3   Describe how to predict sales for merchandise categories.

The first step in merchandise management planning is to develop a forecast for category sales. The approach for forecasting sales of staple merchandise is to project past sales trends into the future, making adjustments for anticipated factors affecting future sales.

Forecasting sales for fashion merchandise is challenging because buyers typically need to

place orders and commit to buying specific quantities between three and six months before the merchandise will be delivered and made available for sale. Some sources of information that retailers use to develop forecasts for fashion merchandise categories are (1) previous sales data, (2) market research, (3) fashion and trend services, and (4) vendors.

LO4   Summarize the trade-offs for developing merchandise assortments.

After forecasting sales for the category, the next step in the merchandise management planning process is to develop an assortment plan. An assortment plan is the set of SKUs that a retailer will offer in a merchandise category in each of its stores and from its website. When determining the assortment for a category, buyers consider the following factors: the firm's retail strategy, the effect of assortments on GMROI, the complementarities between categories, the effects of assortments on buying behavior, and the physical characteristics of the store.

LO5   Illustrate how to determine the appropriate inventory levels.

After developing the assortment plan, the third step in the merchandise planning process is to determine the model stock plan for the category. The model stock plan is the number of units of backup stock for each SKU. Retailers typically have different model stock plans for the different store sizes in a chain.

The first three steps in the merchandise planning process—forecast SKU and category sales, determine the assortment plan, and establish the model stock plan—quantify the buyer's sales expectations and service level.

LO6   Analyze merchandise control systems.

The fourth step in the merchandise management process is to establish a control system for how the orders, deliveries, inventory levels, and merchandise sales will evolve over time. The objective of this control system is to manage the flow of merchandise into the stores so that the amount of inventory in a category is minimized but the merchandise will still be available when customers want to buy it.

Buying systems for staple merchandise are very different from those for fashion merchandise. Because staple merchandise is sold month after month and the sales levels are predictable, an automated continuous replenishment system is often used to manage staple merchandise categories. By definition, SKUs within a fashion category change rapidly, so fashion merchandise categories are managed in dollars (i.e., how much money is spent on each category), rather than in units as is staple merchandise.

LO7 **Describe how multistore retailers allocate merchandise to stores.**

Allocating merchandise to stores involves three decisions: (1) how much merchandise to allocate to each store, (2) what type of merchandise to allocate, and (3) when to allocate the merchandise to different stores. Retail chains typically classify each of their stores on the basis of annual sales. Thus, A stores would have the largest sales volume and typically receive the most inventory, while C stores would have the lowest sales volume and receive the least inventory for a category. In addition to the store's sales level, when making allocation decisions for a category, allocators consider the physical characteristics of the merchandise and the depth of assortment and level of product availability that the firm wants to portray for the specific store.

LO8 **Review how retailers evaluate the performance of their merchandise management decisions.**

Three different approaches for evaluating aspects of merchandise management and planning performance are sell-through analysis, ABC analysis, and the multiattribute model. The sell-through analysis is useful for examining the performance of individual SKUs in the merchandise plan. The buyer compares actual with planned sales to determine whether more merchandise needs to be ordered or whether the merchandise should be put on sale. In an ABC analysis, merchandise is rank-ordered from highest to lowest. The merchandising team uses this information to set inventory management policies. The multiattribute analysis method for evaluating vendors uses a weighted-average score for each vendor based on the importance of various issues and the vendor's performance on those issues. Buyers choose the vendor with the highest weighted score.

KEY TERMS

GET OUT AND DO IT!

1. **CONTINUING ASSIGNMENT** Go to a store of the retailer you selected for the continuing assignment, and and audit the variety and assortment for a specific merchandise category. Record the breadth and depth of the assortment and the level of support (average number of items for the SKUs in each category). Compare the variety, assortment, and support for the same category in a competing retail store.

Evaluate both stores' assortment on that category. Which is better?

2. **INTERNET EXERCISE** Go to the home page of Merchandise Management Company (MMC) at www.merchmanco.com. Watch the three-minute video, and read the posted information and press releases at this website. How does this service provider support vendors to manage merchandise sold at this discount department store? What is the "Store Vision" system? How is it used to measure merchandise performance?

3. **IN-STORE OR INTERNET EXERCISE** Go to the store location or home page of a craft store such as Michaels Stores, Jo-Ann Fabric and Craft Stores, or A.C. Moore Arts & Crafts (www.michaels.com, www.joann.com, or www.acmoore.com). How does this retailer organize its merchandise in terms of merchandise group, department, category, and stock-keeping unit? Select two categories of merchandise: one that you would expect to have a high inventory turnover and the other, a low inventory turnover. Explain your reasoning for each selection.

4. **GO SHOPPING** Visit a big-box office supply store and then a discount store to shop for school supplies. Contrast the variety and assortment offered at each. What are the advantages and disadvantages of breadth versus depth for each retailer? What are the advantages and disadvantages from the consumer's perspective?

5. **INTERNET EXERCISE** Go to the home page of the following three retail trade publications: *Chain Store Age* at www.chainstoreage.com, and *Retailing Today* at www.retailingtoday.com. Find an article in each that focuses on managing merchandise. How can these articles assist retailers with merchandise planning decisions?

6. **INTERNET EXERCISE** Go to http://www.sas.com/industry/retail/merchandise/index.html, the SAS Merchandise Intelligence website. How does the SAS Merchandise Intelligence product provide retailers with information to support merchandising planning, forecasting, and measurement?

7. **WEB OLC EXERCISE** The merchandise budget plan determines how much merchandise should be purchased in each month of a fashion buying season (in dollars), given the sales and reduction forecast, inventory turnover goals, and seasonal monthly fluctuations in sales. Go to the student side of the Online Learning Center, and click "Merchandise Budget Plan." The merchandise budget plan generally covers one fashion season for one merchandise category. This application presents both one-month and six-month examples. In addition, practice calculations are presented for the one-month example. Have your calculator ready! In the calculation section, you have access to an Excel-based six-month merchandise budget plan that can be used to complete Case 20 in the text.

8. **WEB OLC EXERCISE** The vendor evaluation model utilizes the multiattribute method to evaluate vendors. Go to the student side of the Online Learning Center, and click "Vendor Evaluation Model." There are two spreadsheets. Open the first spreadsheet, vendor evaluation 1.xls. This spreadsheet is the same as Exhibit 12–14. If you were selling brand A to the retailer, which numbers would change? Change the numbers in the matrix, and see the effect of that change on the overall evaluation. Go to the second spreadsheet, evaluation 2.xls. This spreadsheet can be used to evaluate brands or merchandise you might stock in your store. Assume you own a bicycle shop. List the brands you might consider stocking and the issues you would consider in selecting the brands to stock. Fill in the importance of the issues (10 = very important, 1 = not very important) and the evaluation of each brand on each characteristic (10 = excellent, 1 = poor). Determine which is the best brand for your store.

DISCUSSION QUESTIONS AND PROBLEMS

1. How and why would you expect variety and assortment to differ between JCPenney's store and Internet channel?

2. Simply speaking, increasing inventory turnover is an important goal for a retail manager. What are the consequences of turnover that's too low? Too high?

3. Assume you are the grocery buyer for canned fruits and vegetables at a five-store supermarket chain. Del Monte has told you and your boss that it would be responsible for making all inventory decisions for those merchandise categories. Del Monte will now determine how much to order and when shipments should be made. It promises a 10 percent increase in gross margin dollars in the coming year. Would you take Del Monte up on its offer? Justify your answer.

4. A buyer at Old Navy has received a number of customer complaints that he has been out of stock on some sizes of men's T-shirts. The buyer subsequently decides to increase this category's product availability from 80 percent to 90 percent. What will be the impact on backup stock and inventory turnover? Would your answer be the same if the product category were men's fleece sweatshirts?

5. Variety, assortment, and product availability are the cornerstones of the merchandise planning process.

Provide examples of retailers that have done an outstanding job of positioning their stores on the basis of one or more of these issues.

6. The fine jewelry department in a department store has the same GMROI as the small appliances department, even though characteristics of the merchandise are quite different. Explain this situation.

7. Calculate the GMROI and inventory turnover given annual sales of $20,000, average inventory (at cost) of $4,000, and a gross margin of 45 percent.

8. As the athletic shoe buyer for Sports Authority, how would you go about forecasting sales for a new Nike running shoe?

9. Using the 80–20 principle, how can a retailer make certain that it has enough inventory of fast-selling merchandise and a minimal amount of slow-selling merchandise?

10. A buyer at a sporting goods store in Denver receives a shipment of 400 ski parkas on October 1 and expects to sell out by January 31. On November 1, the buyer still has 350 parkas left. What issues should the buyer consider in evaluating the selling season's progress?

11. A buyer is trying to decide from which vendor to buy a certain item. Using the information in the accompanying table, determine from which vendor the buyer should buy.

	VENDOR PERFORMANCE		
	Importance Weight	Vendor A	Vendor B
Reputation for collaboration	8	9	8
Service	7	8	7
Meets delivery dates	9	7	8
Merchandise quality	7	8	4
Gross margin	6	4	8
Brand name recognition	5	7	5
Promotional assistance	3	8	8

SUGGESTED READINGS

Broniarczyk, Susan, and Wayne Hoyer. "Retail Assortment: More ≠ Better." In M. Kraft and M. Mantrala (Eds.), *Retailing in the 21st Century*, 2nd ed. New York: Fairchild Books, 2010, pp. 271–284.

Connell, Dana. *A Buyer's Life: A Concise Guide to Retail Planning and Forecasting.* New York: Fairchild, 2010.

Donnellan, John Do. *Buying and Management*, 4th ed. New York: Fairchild, 2013.

Fowler, Deborah, and Ben Goh. *Retail Category Management.* Englewood Cliffs, NJ: Prentice Hall, 2011.

Heller, Al. *Consumer-Centric Category Management: How to Increase Profits by Managing Categories Based on Consumer Needs.* New York: Wiley, 2012.

Kok, A. Gorhan, Marshall Fisher, and Ramnath Vaidyanathan. "Assortment Planning: Review of Literature and Industry Practice." In Narendra Agrawal and Stephen A. Smith (Eds.),

Retail Supply Chain Management: Quantitative Models and Empirical Studies. New York: Springer, 2009, pp. 99–150.

Murtulus, Mumin, and L. Berl Toktay. "Category Captaincy in the Retail Industry," in Narendra Agrawal and Stephen A. Smith (Eds.), *Retail Supply Chain Management: Quantitative Models and Empirical Studies.* New York: Springer, 2008, pp. 79–99.

Mantrala, Murali, Michael Levy, Barbara Kahn, Edward Fox, Peter Gaidarev, Bill Dankworth, and Denish Shahg. "Why Is Assortment Planning So Difficult for Retailers? A Framework and Research Agenda." *Journal of Retailing* 85, no. 1, pp. 71–83.

Zinn, Walter and Peter Liu. "A Comparison of Actual and Intended Consumer Behavior in Response to Retail Stockouts." *Journal of Business Logistics* 29, no. 2 (2008), pp. 141–159.

APPENDIX 12A   Merchandise Budget Report and Open-to-Buy System for a Fashion Merchandise Category

MERCHANDISE BUDGET PLAN

In this appendix, we describe the steps in developing the merchandise budget plan for a fashion merchandise category. These steps are taken to develop the bottom line—line 8, "Monthly Additions to Stock"—in Exhibit 12–15. The figures on this line tell the buyer how much merchandise in retail dollars he or she needs to have, on average, at the beginning of each month for the retailer's financial goals to be met. Note that Exhibit 12–15 is the same as Exhibit 12–9 in the chapter.

350　SECTION III　Merchandise Management

EXHIBIT 12–15　Six-Month Merchandise Budget Plan for Men's Casual Slacks

Worksheet							Financial Planning
Plan Edit View Tools Help							
	Spring						
		April	May	June	July	August	September
1. Sales % Distribution to Season	100.00%	21.00%	12.00%	12.00%	19.00%	21.00%	15.00%
2. Monthly Sales	$130,000	$27,300	$15,600	$15,600	$24,700	$27,300	$19,500
3. Reduc % Distribution to Season	100.00%	40.00%	14.00%	16.00%	12.00%	10.00%	8.00%
4. Monthly Reductions	$16,500	$6,600	$2,310	$2,640	$1,980	$1,650	$1,320
5. BOM Stock to Sales Ratio	4.00	3.60	4.40	4.40	4.00	3.60	4.00
6. BOM Inventory	$98,280	$98,280	$68,640	$68,640	$98,800	$98,280	$78,000
7. EOM Inventory	$65,600	$68,640	$68,640	$98,800	$98,280	$78,000	$65,600
8. Monthly Additions to Stock	$113,820	$4,260	$17,910	$48,400	$26,160	$8,670	$8,420

Monthly Sales Percentage Distribution to Season (Line 1)

Line 1 of the plan projects what percentage of the total sales is expected to be sold in each month. In Exhibit 12–15, 21 percent of the six-month sales are expected to occur in April.

		SPRING			SUMMER		
	Six-Month Data	April	May	June	July	August	September
Sales % distribution to 1 Month	100.00%	21.00%	12.00%	12.00%	19.00%	21.00%	15.00%

Historical sales data provide the starting point for determining the percentage distribution of sales by month. The percentage of total category sales that occurs in a particular month doesn't vary much from year to year. However, the buyer might adjust the historical percentages to reflect changes in buying patterns and special promotions. For instance, the buyer might feel that the autumn selling season for men's casual slacks continues to be pushed further back into summer and thus increase the percentages for July and decrease the percentages for August and September. The buyer might also decide to hold a special Easter sale promotion, increasing the April percentage and decreasing the other percentages.

Monthly Sales (Line 2)

Monthly sales are the forecasted total sales for the six-month period in the first column ($130,000) multiplied by each monthly sales percentage (line 1). In Exhibit 12–15, monthly sales for April = $130,000 × 21 percent = $27,300.

		SPRING			SUMMER		
	Six-Month Data	April	May	June	July	August	September
Sales % distribution to 1 Month	100.00%	21.00%	12.00%	12.00%	19.00%	21.00%	15.00%
2 Monthly sales	$130,000	$27,300	$15,600	$15,600	$24,700	$27,300	$19,500

Monthly Reductions Percentage Distribution to Season (Line 3)

To have enough merchandise every month to support the monthly sales forecast, the buyer needs to consider other factors that reduce the inventory level in addition to sales made to customers. Although sales are the primary reduction, the value of the inventory is also reduced by markdowns (sales discounts), shrinkage, and discounts to employees. The merchandise budget planning process builds these additional reductions into the planned purchases. If these reductions were not considered, the category would always be understocked. Note that in Exhibit 12–15, 40 percent of the season's total reductions occur in April as a result of price discounts (markdowns) during end-of-season sales as well.

Markdowns also can be forecasted from historical records. However, changes in markdown strategies—or changes in the environment, such as competition or general economic activity—must be taken into consideration when forecasting markdowns as well.

Discounts to employees are like markdowns, except that they are given to employees rather than to customers. The level of the employee discount is tied fairly closely to the sales level and number of employees. Thus, employee discounts also can be forecasted from historical records.

Shrinkage refers to inventory losses caused by shoplifting, employee theft, merchandise being misplaced or damaged, and poor bookkeeping. Retailers measure shrinkage by taking the difference between (1) the inventory's recorded value based on merchandise bought and received and (2) the physical inventory actually in stores and distribution centers. Shrinkage varies by department and season, but typically it varies directly with sales as well. So if sales of men's casual pants increase by 10 percent, then the buyer can expect a 10 percent increase in shrinkage.

		SPRING			SUMMER		
	Six-Month Data	April	May	June	July	August	September
3 Reduction % distribution to season	100.00%	40.00%	14.00%	16.00%	12.00%	10.00%	8.00%

Monthly Reductions (Line 4)

Monthly reductions are calculated by multiplying the total reductions by each percentage in line 3. The total reductions for this example are based on historical data. In Exhibit 12–15, April reductions = $16,500 × 40 percent = $6,600.

		SPRING			SUMMER		
	Six-Month Data	April	May	June	July	August	September
3 Reduction % distribution to season	100.00%	40.00%	14.00%	16.00%	12.00%	10.00%	8.00%
4 Monthly reductions	$16,500	$6,600	$2,310	$2,640	$1,980	$1,650	$1,320

BOM (Beginning-of-Month) Stock-to-Sales Ratio (Line 5)

The **stock-to-sales ratio,** listed in line 5, specifies the amount of inventory that should be on hand at the beginning of the month to support the sales forecast and maintain the inventory turnover objective for the category. Thus, a stock-to-sales ratio of 2 means that the retailer plans to have twice as much inventory on hand at the beginning of the month as there are forecasted sales for the month. Both the BOM stock and forecasted sales for the month are expressed in retail sales dollars.

		SPRING			SUMMER		
	Six-Month Data	April	May	June	July	August	September
5 BOM stock-to-sales ratio	4.0	3.6	4.4	4.4	4.0	3.6	4.0

Rather than specifying the stock-to-sales ratio, many retailers specify a related measure, weeks of inventory. A stock-to-sales ratio of 4 means there are 16 weeks of inventory, or approximately 112 days, on hand at the beginning of the month. A stock-to-sales ratio of 1/2 indicates a two-week supply of merchandise, or enough for approximately 14 days. The stock-to-sales ratio is determined so the merchandise category achieves its targeted performance—its planned GMROI and inventory turnover. The steps in determining the stock-to-sales ratio for the category are shown next.

Step 1: Calculate Sales-to-Stock Ratio   The GMROI is equal to the gross margin percentage times the sales-to-stock ratio. The sales-to-stock ratio is conceptually similar to inventory turnover except the denominator in the stock-to-sales ratio is expressed in retail sales dollars, whereas the denominator in inventory turnover is the cost of goods sold (sales at cost). The buyer's target GMROI for the category is 123 percent, and the buyer feels the category will produce a gross margin of 45 percent. Thus,

GMROI = Gross margin percent × Sales-to-stock ratio

Sales-to-stock ratio = GMROI/Gross margin percent = 123/45 = 2.73

Because this illustration of a merchandise budget plan is for a six-month period rather than a year, the sales-to-stock ratio is based on six months rather than annual sales. So for this six-month period, sales must be 2.73 times the inventory cost to meet the targeted GMROI.

Step 2: Convert the Sales-to-Stock Ratio to Inventory Turnover Inventory turnover is

$$\begin{aligned} \text{Inventory turnover} &= \text{Sales-to-stock ratio} \times (1.00 - \text{Gross margin \%}/100) \\ &= \quad 2.73 \quad \times (1.00 - 45/100) \\ 1.50 &= \quad 2.73 \quad \times .55 \end{aligned}$$

This adjustment is necessary because the sales-to-stock ratio defines sales at retail and inventory at cost, whereas inventory turnover defines both sales and inventory at cost. Like the sales-to-stock ratio, this inventory turnover is based on a six-month period.

Step 3: Calculate Average Stock-to-Sales Ratio The average stock-to-sales ratio is

$$\text{Average stock-to-sales ratio} = 6 \text{ months/Inventory turnover}$$
$$4 = 6/1.5$$

If preparing a 12-month plan, the buyer divides 12 by the annual inventory turnover. Because the merchandise budget plan in Exhibit 12–15 is based on retail dollars, it's easiest to think of the numerator as BOM retail inventory and the denominator as sales for that month. Thus, to achieve a six-month inventory turnover of 1.5, on average, the buyer must plan to have a BOM inventory that equals four times the amount of sales for a given month, which is equivalent to four months, or 16 weeks of supply.

One needs to be careful when thinking about the average *stock-to-sales ratio*, which can be easily confused with the *sales-to-stock ratio*. These ratios are not the inverse of each other. Sales are the same in both ratios, but stock in the sales-to-stock ratio is the average inventory at cost over all days in the period, whereas stock in the stock-to-sales ratio is the average BOM inventory at retail. Also, the BOM stock-to-sales ratio is an average for all months. Adjustments are made to this average in line 5 to account for seasonal variation in sales.

Step 4: Calculate Monthly Stock-to-Sales Ratios The monthly stock-to-sales ratios in line 5 must average the stock-to-sales ratio calculated previously to achieve the planned inventory turnover. Generally, monthly stock-to-sales ratios vary in the opposite direction of sales. That is, in months when sales are larger, stock-to-sales ratios are smaller, and vice versa.

To make this adjustment, the buyer needs to consider the seasonal pattern for men's casual slacks in determining the monthly stock-to-sales ratios. In the ideal situation, men's casual slacks would arrive in the store the same day and in the same quantity that customers demand them. Unfortunately, the real-life retailing world isn't this simple. Note in Exhibit 12–15 (line 8) that men's casual slacks for the spring season start arriving slowly in April ($4,260 for the month), yet demand lags behind these arrivals until the weather starts getting warmer. Monthly sales then jump from 12 percent of annual sales in May and June to 19 percent in July (line 1). But the stock-to-sales ratio (line 5) decreased from 4.4 in May and June to 4.0 in July. Thus, in months when sales increase (e.g., July), the BOM inventory also increases (line 6) but at a slower rate, which causes the stock-to-sales ratios to decrease. Likewise, in months when sales decrease dramatically, like in May (line 2), inventory also decreases (line 6), again at a slower rate, causing the stock-to-sales ratios to increase (line 5).

When creating a merchandise budget plan for a category such as men's casual slacks with a sales history, the buyer also examines previous years' stock-to-sales ratios. To judge how adequate these past ratios were, the buyer determines if inventory levels were exceedingly high or low in any months. Then the buyer makes minor corrections to adjust for a previous imbalance in inventory levels, as well as for changes in the current environment. For instance, assume the buyer is planning a promotion for Memorial Day. This promotion has never been done before, so the stock-to-sales ratio for the month of May should be adjusted downward to allow for the expected increase in sales. Note that monthly stock-to-sales ratios don't change by the same percentage that the percentage distribution of sales by month is changing. In months when sales increase, stock-to-sales ratios decrease but at a slower rate. Because there is no exact method of making these adjustments, the buyer must make some subjective judgments.

BOM Stock (Line 6)

The amount of inventory planned for the beginning-of-the-month (BOM) inventory for April equals

BOM inventory = Monthly sales (line 2) × BOM stock-to-sales ratio (line 5)
$98,280   = $27,300   × 3.6

		SPRING			SUMMER		
	Six-Month Data	April	May	June	July	August	September
6 BOM inventory	$98,280	$98,280	$68,640	$68,640	$98,800	$98,280	$78,000

EOM (End-of-Month) Stock (Line 7)

The BOM stock for the current month is the same as the EOM (end-of-month) stock in the previous month. That is, BOM stock in line 6 is simply EOM inventory in line 7 from the previous month. Thus, in Exhibit 12–15, the EOM stock for April is the same as the BOM stock for May, $68,640. Forecasting the ending inventory for the last month in the plan is the next step in the merchandise budget plan. Note that EOM inventory for June is high, which indicates planning for a substantial sales increase in July.

		SPRING			SUMMER		
	Six-Month Data	April	May	June	July	August	September
7 EOM inventory	$65,600	$68,640	$68,640	$98,800	$98,280	$78,000	$65,600

Monthly Additions to Stock (Line 8)

The monthly additions to stock needed is the amount to be ordered for delivery in each month to meet the inventory turnover and sales objectives.

Additions to stock = Sales (line 2) + Reductions (line 4) + EOM inventory (line 7)
                − BOM inventory (line 6)
Additions to stock (April) = $27,300 + 6,600 + 68,640 − 98,280 = $4,260

At the beginning of the month, the inventory level equals BOM stock. During the month, merchandise is sold, and various inventory reductions affecting the retail sales level occur, such as markdowns and theft. So the BOM stock minus monthly sales minus reductions equals the EOM stock if nothing is purchased. But something must be purchased to get back up to the forecast EOM stock. The difference between EOM stock if nothing is purchased (BOM stock − sales − reductions) and the forecast EOM stock is the additions to stock.

		SPRING			SUMMER		
	Six-Month Data	April	May	June	July	August	September
8 Monthly additions to stock	$113,820	$4,260	$17,920	$48,400	$26,160	$8,670	$8,420

OPEN-TO-BUY SYSTEM

The open-to-buy system is used after the merchandise is purchased and is based on the merchandise budget plan or staple merchandise management system. The merchandise management systems discussed previously provide buyers with a plan for purchasing merchandise. The **open-to-buy** system keeps track of merchandise flows while they are occurring. It keeps a record of how much is actually spent purchasing merchandise each month and how much is left to spend.

Open-to-buy is like the buyer's checkbook. It keeps track of how much money has been spent and how much money is left to spend.

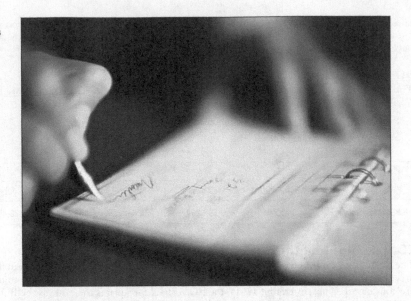

In the same way that you must keep track of the checks you write, buyers need to keep track of the merchandise they purchase and when it is to be delivered. Without the open-to-buy system keeping track of merchandise flows, buyers might buy too much or too little. Merchandise could be delivered when it isn't needed and be unavailable when it is needed. Thus, sales and inventory turnover would suffer. For consistency, we will continue with our example of an open-to-buy system using the merchandise budget plan previously discussed. The open-to-buy system is also applicable to staple goods merchandise management systems.

To make the merchandise budget plan successful (i.e., meet the sales, inventory turnover, and GMROI goals for a category), the buyer attempts to buy merchandise in quantities with delivery dates such that the actual EOM stock for a month will be the same as the forecasted EOM stock. For example, at the end of September, which is the end of the spring/summer season, the buyer would like to be completely sold out of spring/summer men's casual slacks so there will be room for the fall styles. Thus, the buyer would want the projected EOM stock and the actual EOM stock for this fashion and/or seasonal merchandise to both equal zero.

Calculating Open-to-Buy for the Current Period

Buyers develop plans indicating how much inventory for the merchandise category will be available at the end of the month. However, these plans might be inaccurate. Shipments might not arrive on time, sales might be greater than expected, and/or reductions (price discounts due to sales) might be less than expected.

The open-to-buy is the difference between the planned EOM inventory and the projected EOM. Thus, open-to-buy for a month is:

Open-to-buy = Planned EOM inventory − Projected EOM inventory

If open-to-buy is positive, then the buyer still has money in the budget to purchase merchandise for that month. If the open-to-buy is negative, then the buyer has overbought, meaning he or she has spent more than was in the budget.

The planned EOM inventory is taken from the merchandise budget plan, and the projected EOM inventory is calculated as follows:

Projected EOM inventory = Actual BOM inventory
+ Monthly additions actual (received new merchandise)
+ On order (merchandise to be delivered)
− Sales plan (merchandise sold)
− Monthly reductions plan

Six-Month Open-to-Buy System Report   **EXHIBIT 12–16**

Loc - 10	Spring					
Merch - Aged Soft ...	April	May	June	July	August	September
EOM Stock Plan	$68,640	$68,640	$98,800	$98,280	$78,000	$65,800
EOM Actuals	$69,950					
BOM Stock Plan	$98,280	$68,640	$68,640	$98,800	$98,280	$78,000
BOM Stock Actual	$95,000	$59,500				
Monthly Additions Plan	$4,260	$17,910	$48,400	$26,160	$8,670	$8,420
Monthly Additions Actuals	$3,500	$7,000				
OnOrder	$45,000	$18,000	$48,400			
Sales Plan	$27,300	$15,600	$15,600	$24,700	$27,300	$19,500
Sales Actuals	$26,900					
Monthly Reductions Plan	$6,600	$2,310	$2,640	$1,960	$1,650	$1,320
Monthly Reductions Actuals	$1,650					
Projected EOM Stock Plan	$59,500	$66,590	$96,750	$70,070	$41,120	$20,300
Projected BOM Stock Plan	$24,570	$59,500	$66,500	$96,760	$70,070	$41,120
OTB	$0.00	$2,050	$2,050	$26,210	$36,880	$45,300

Exhibit 12–16 presents the six-month open-to-buy for the same category of men's casual slacks discussed in the fashion merchandise planning section of this chapter. Consider May as the current month. The BOM stock (inventory) actual level is $59,500, but there is no EOM actual inventory yet because the month hasn't finished. When calculating the open-to-buy for the current month, the projected EOM stock plan comes into play. Think of the projected EOM stock plan as a new and improved estimate of the planned EOM stock from the merchandise budget plan. This new and improved version takes information into account that wasn't available when the merchandise budget plan was made. The formula for projected EOM inventory for the category is

$$
\begin{aligned}
\text{Projected EOM inventory} = \text{Actual BOM inventory} &\quad \$59,500 \\
+ \text{Monthly additions actual} &\quad 7,000 \\
+ \text{On order} &\quad 18,000 \\
- \text{Sales plan} &\quad 15,600 \\
- \text{Monthly reductions plan} &\quad \underline{2,310} \\
= &\quad \$66,590
\end{aligned}
$$

The open-to-buy for the current month is:

$$
\begin{array}{ccccc}
\text{Open-to-buy plan} & = & \text{EOM inventory planned} & - & \text{Projected EOM inventory} \\
\$2,050 & = & \$68,640 & - & \$66,590
\end{array}
$$

Therefore, the buyer has $2,050 left to spend in May to reach the planned EOM stock of $68,640. This is a relatively small amount, so we can conclude that the buyer's plan is right on target. But if the open-to-buy for May were $20,000, the buyer could then go back into the market and look for some great buys. If one of the vendors had too much stock of men's casual slacks, the buyer might be able to use the $20,000 to pick up some bargains that could be passed on to customers.

If, however, the open-to-buy was a negative $20,000, the buyer would have overspent the budget. Similar to overspending your checkbook, the buyer would have to cut back on spending in future months so the total purchases would be within the merchandise budget. Alternatively, if the buyer believed that the overspending was justified because of changes in the marketplace, a negotiation could take place between the buyer and the divisional merchandise manager to get more open-to-buy.

Buying Merchandise

EXECUTIVE BRIEFING

Audrey Schwarz, Director of Merchandising, Chico's Brand

I have been fortunate to work for Chico's FAS (comprised of four brands: Chico's, White House/Black Market, Soma, and Boston Proper) for five years and be a part of a team that is committed to putting our customers first. What makes the Chico's brand unique is that almost all of the merchandise we sell in our 600+ Chico's boutiques and through our Internet and mobile channels is private label. What that means is our teams collaborate on strategies, design the merchandise, and have it manufactured to our exact specifications—from every detail (thread color, zippers, buttons, etc.) to the type of fabric and the fit. My responsibility within the organization is to help lead our cross-functional team to deliver a merchandise assortment that our customers will love and purchase and achieve our financial objectives. The teams consist of many individuals partnering together with the objective of providing an amazing product that will delight our customers—merchandising, planning, allocation, design, product development, sourcing, technical design, visual merchandising, and marketing.

In today's environment, fast fashion retailers like Forever 21, Zara, and H&M are getting a lot of attention for their "speed to market" ability and being ahead of the trends. Chico's also has the ability to quickly react to fashion trends and respond to our customers' needs based on our strategic initiatives and innovative processes. Our competitive advantage is that we focus on quality as well as fashion to provide great value in our product. Our customers want to be stylish and see the versatility in our pieces to help them create many fabulous looks. They trust us to be the fashion experts and look to us to give them many outfitting options to fit into their busy lifestyles.

To be a successful merchant in the specialty retail sector, you have to (1) be aware of who your target customer is, (2) know what they are looking for, (3) know what they don't have yet, (4) know how to attract a new customer, and (5) know how to emotionally connect with them as you innovate the product. You need to be a student and learn from as many resources as possible, such as fashion magazines and runway shows on the Internet, and study aspirational brands as well as your direct competition. You need to be able to identify the trends and understand how to interpret them for your customer. In addition, many valuable insights come from observing what people are wearing everyday—whether

CHAPTER 13

LEARNING OBJECTIVES

LO1 Identify the branding options available to retailers.

LO2 Describe how retailers buy national brands.

LO3 List the issues retailers consider when developing and sourcing store-branded merchandise internationally.

LO4 Understand how retailers prepare for and conduct negotiations with their vendors.

LO5 Determine why retailers build strategic relationships with their vendors.

LO6 Indicate the legal, ethical, and social responsibility issues involved in buying merchandise.

it's on the streets or on TV/Internet, you can see trends change. My husband claims that when we are out at a restaurant, shopping, or basically anywhere, I spend more time looking at what everyone is wearing than talking with him. I like to think that my anthropology undergraduate degree has paid off as it reflects my interest in observing people, what they wear, and how they behave.

One of the most rewarding aspects of my job is seeing how the apparel we develop and sell can actually change the way our customers look and feel about themselves. You just know when someone feels good about how they look and what they are wearing as they have an undeniable confidence. Clothing has the ability to transform a person, and I love being a little part of making a difference in people's lives.

The preceding chapter outlined the merchandise management process and the steps in the process that buyers go through to determine what and how much merchandise to buy. After creating an assortment plan for the category, forecasting sales, and developing a plan outlining the flow of merchandise (how much merchandise needs to be ordered and when it needs to be delivered), the next step in the merchandise management process is to acquire the merchandise.

Buying merchandise isn't easy. At a grocery chain like Kroger, for instance, the soup category manager must decide on the mix between purchasing well-known national brands like Campbell or Progresso or developing store brands like Wholesome@Home. Whether offering national or store brands, the category manager negotiates many issues, such as prices, delivery dates, payment terms, and financial support for advertising and markdowns. The buying process for store brands is often more complex than for national brands because the store takes an active role in developing the products.

This chapter begins with a description of the different merchandise branding alternatives. Then we review the issues involved in buying national and store brands, including negotiating with vendors. Next, the development of strategic partnering relationships between retailers and their suppliers is discussed. The chapter concludes with an examination of the legal, ethical, and social responsibility issues surrounding the buying of merchandise.

BRAND ALTERNATIVES

LO1

Identify the branding options available to retailers.

REFACT

Private-label sales in grocery stores, drugstores, and discount department stores in the United States have been growing at more than 7 percent each year, such that they now amount to $86 billion annually, including sales by Walmart. In contrast, sales of national brands have been declining by approximately 3 percent each year.[1]

REFACT

The five most valuable world brands are Coca-Cola, Apple, IBM, Google, and Microsoft. The value of each of these brands is more than $50 billion.[2]

REFACT

Macy's was among the first department stores to pioneer the concept of private-label brands for fashion goods. In the 1890s, its "Macy's" and "Red Star" brands were the rage in New York.[3]

REFACT

In Europe, consumers buy store brands just as much as they do national brands; in many countries, they view the store brands as equally good, if not better in quality, as national brands. Store brands have a 30 percent market share on average.[4]

Retailers and their buyers face a strategic decision about the mix of national brands and private-label brands offered in a category. Three types of brands discussed in this section are national, store, and generic brands.

National Brands

National brands, also known as **manufacturer's brands,** are products designed, produced, and marketed by a vendor and sold to many different retailers. The vendor is responsible for developing the merchandise, producing it with consistent quality, and undertaking a marketing program to establish an appealing brand image. Examples of national brands are Tide detergent, Ralph Lauren polo shirts, and Hewlett-Packard printers.

In some cases, vendors use an **umbrella** or **family brand** associated with their company and a **subbrand** associated with the product, such as Kellogg's (family brand) Frosted Flakes (subbrand) or Ford (family brand) F-series trucks (subbrand). In other cases, vendors use individual brand names for different product categories and do not associate the brands with their companies. For example, most consumers probably don't know that Procter & Gamble makes Iams pet food, Crest toothpaste, Ivory soap, Vick's NyQuil, Hugo by Hugo Boss cologne, and Swiffer.

Some retailers organize their buying activities around national-brand vendors that cut across merchandise categories. Thus, buyers in department stores may be responsible for all cosmetic brands offered by Estée Lauder (Estée Lauder, Origins, Clinique, and Prescriptives) rather than for a product category (such as skin care or eye makeup). Managing merchandise by vendor rather than by category gives retailers more clout when dealing with vendors. However, as indicated in Chapter 12, there are inefficiencies associated with managing merchandise at the brand or vendor level rather than the category level.

Store Brands

Store brands, also called **private-label brands**, **house brands**, or **own brands**, are products developed by retailers. In many cases, retailers develop the design and specifications for their store-brand products, then contract with manufacturers to produce those products. In other cases, national-brand vendors work with a retailer to develop a special version of its standard merchandise offering to be sold exclusively by the retailer. In these cases, the national-brand vendor or manufacturer is responsible for the production of the merchandise.

In the past, sales of store brands were limited. National brands had the resources to develop customer loyalty toward their brands through aggressive marketing. It was difficult for smaller local and regional retailers to gain the economies of scale in design, production, and promotion that were needed to develop well-known brands. In recent years, though, as the size of retail firms has increased, more retailers have obtained sufficient scale economies to develop store brands and use this merchandise to establish a distinctive identity. Now, retailers offer a broad spectrum of store brands ranging from lower price/lower quality products, to those with superior quality and performance to national brands. Three examples of store brands are premium store brands, exclusive brands, and copycat brands.

Premium Store Brands **Premium store brands** offer the consumer a product that is comparable to a manufacturer's brand quality, sometimes with modest price savings. Examples of premium store brands include Kroger's Private Selection, Tesco Finest (UK), "The Men's Collection" at Saks Fifth Avenue, and Bloomingdale's Aqua.[5] Safeway, a leading grocery chain, earns a substantial portion of its $45 billion in sales from its premium store brands. Not only is its main store brand, Safeway Select, recognized for its high quality, but it also stocks various other strong store brands, such as Signature Café (fresh food), Primo Taglio (premium cheese and cold cuts), Eating Right (healthy foods), Snack Artist (nuts and snacks), and Open Nature (natural foods).[6]

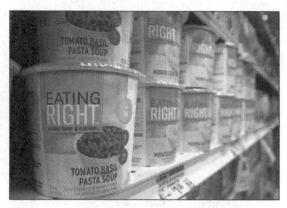

Safeway's customers increasingly are drawn to strong store brands.

Exclusive Brands An **exclusive brand** is a brand that is developed by a national-brand vendor, often in conjunction with a retailer, and sold exclusively by the retailer. The simplest form of an exclusive brand occurs when a national-brand manufacturer assigns different model numbers and has different exterior features for the same basic product sold by different retailers, but the product is still marketed under the manufacturer's brand. For example, a Canon digital camera sold at Best Buy might have a different model number than a Canon digital camera with similar features available at Walmart. These exclusive models make it difficult for consumers to compare prices for virtually the same camera sold by different retailers.

A more sophisticated form of exclusive branding occurs when a manufacturer develops an exclusive product or product category for a retailer and markets it under a brand name that is exclusive to the retailer. For example, cosmetics powerhouse Estée Lauder sells two brands of cosmetics and skin care products—American Beauty and Flirt—exclusively at Kohl's. The products are priced between mass-market brands such as Cover Girl or Maybelline (sold mainly in drugstores, discount stores, and supermarkets) and Lauder's higher-end brands (sold primarily in more fashion-forward department stores such as Macy's and Dillard's). Levi Strauss has also developed its Signature brand jeans for sale at Walmart.

Exclusive branding with manufacturers or designers is effectively applied by HSN. Rather than creating entirely new private-label products, this retailer "invests in partners that help it develop products, such as a jewelry line with R. J. Graziano or Tori Spelling . . . handbags from Chi by Falchi, Serious Skin Care and Beauty from Jennifer Stallone."[8] Some of these designers, such as R. J. Graziano, sell separate lines in other outlets. Others, including Paula Abdul, are totally exclusive to HSN. In differentiating itself, whether in terms of an individual line of products or the entire collection associated with a designer, HSN promises customers that they can find items here that they find nowhere else.

The highest level of differentiation takes place when a retailer develops a store brand with its own unique identity. At Macy's, for example, customers do not often realize that the brands they purchase are its store brands. Thus, its American Rag brand has reached a significant market share in the young men's category, without ever communicating to this brand-conscious customer segment that the brand is produced by Macy's. In this case, it becomes difficult to distinguish Macy's brands, such as American Rag and INC, from national brands such as Levi's—except that consumers can find American Rag and INC only in Macy's stores.

Several well-known examples of exclusive store brands appear in Exhibit 13–1.

Copycat Brands **Copycat brands** imitate the manufacturer's brand in appearance and packaging, generally are perceived as lower-quality, and are offered at lower prices. Copycat brands abound in drugstores and grocery stores. For

REFACT

Exclusive and limited distribution brands from Martha Stewart, Donald Trump, and Tommy Hilfiger account for approximately 43 percent of merchandise and 20 percent of sales at Macy's.[7]

EXHIBIT 13–1   Exclusive Store Brands

Retailer	Manufacturer/Designer	Product Category	Product Name
Kohl's	Estée Lauder	Cosmetics	American Beauty, Flirt, and Good Skin
Walmart	Mary Kate and Ashley Olsen	Apparel and accessories	Mary Kate and Ashley
HSN	Chris Lu, R. J. Graziano Tory Spelling, Paula Abdul, Iman, Serena Williams (jewelry); Chi by Falchi (handbags); Jennifer Stallone (skin care)	Jewelry, handbags, skin care	
Macy's	Martha Stewart	Soft home (sheets, towels)	Martha Stewart Collection
Macy's	Jones Apparel Group (Rachel Roy)	Apparel and accessories	Rachel by Rachel Roy
Macy's	Karl Lagerfeld	Apparel and accessories	Karl Lagerfeld Capsule Collection
McDonald's	Newman's Own Organic	Coffee	Newman's Own Organic
JCPenney	Ralph Lauren	Home goods, apparel, and accessories	American Living
Target	Gwen Stefani	Children's apparel	Harajuku Mini

instance, CVS or Walgreens brands are placed next to the manufacturer's brands and often look like them.

Generic Brands

In a sense, a generic brand isn't actually a brand at all and, as such, is neither a store nor a national brand. **Generic brands** are labeled with the name of the commodity and thus actually have no brand name distinguishing them. These products target a price-sensitive segment by offering a no-frills product at a discount price. They are used typically for prescription drugs and commodities like milk or eggs. Except for prescription drugs, where the use of generics has increased significantly over the last few decades, the sales of generics have declined significantly.

National Brands or Store Brands?

When determining the mix between national versus store brands, retailers consider the effect on their overall assortment, profitability, and flexibility.

Store Brands Enhance and Expand Assortments   Retailers examine their assortments to make sure they are providing what their customers want. They may introduce an innovative new store-branded product that isn't being offered by their national brand vendors or a product that can be offered at a better value—or both. Staples, for example, carries a large number of shredders, produced by many different manufacturers. But the company's market researchers found that people tend to sort through their mail in their kitchens. Thus, it produces, under its store brand, the MailMate, a small shredder that fits on a kitchen counter and is less expensive than the national-brand options. Thus, Staples filled a key gap in its assortment by producing an innovative, yet value-oriented product for families tired of stacks of junk mail but also worried about their privacy.

Many categories contain a market-leading national brand, such as Tide or All in the laundry detergent category. There may be opportunities for store brands in these categories, but the greatest potential appears in categories where there is no national-brand domination, such as with organic products in grocery stores. Whole Foods largely pioneered the concept in grocery retailing, but competitors such as Supervalu (which owns the Shaw's and Albertsons chains) have rapidly increased the number of products offered under its organic labels, such as Wild Harvest. At the wholesale club retailer BJ's, shoppers choose between the basic Elias store-brand frozen pizza and the premium organic store-brand Earth's Pride.

Many store brands today extend assortments by creating multiple price tiers, often referred to as low cost, value, and premium. The low-cost and value tiers have long been in place; the premium option is relatively newer. Such premium options offer consumers quality that is comparable to that of national brands, sometimes (but not always) at a modest price savings. Retailing View 13.1 examines how Kroger uses price tiers in its store brands to enhance and expand its assortments.

Profitability   Stocking national brands is a double-edged sword for retailers. Many customers have developed loyalty to specific national brands. They only patronize retailers selling these national-brand merchandise. This loyalty toward the national brand develops because customers know what to expect from the products and like them. They trust the brand to deliver consistent quality. Every bottle of Chanel No. 5 will have the same fragrance, and every pair of Levi's 501 jeans will have the same fit. In addition, the availability of national brands can affect customer's image of the retailer. For example, the fashion image of JCPenney increased when it added Liz Claiborne and Sephora to its assortment. If a retailer

REFACT
Store brands sales are worth almost $100 billion and account for more than 17 percent of total retail food and beverage sales.[9]

RETAILING VIEW   Kroger's Store Brands Have It All   13.1

Kroger runs its own store brands as if they were separate vendors, demanding high-quality standards and price competitiveness. The grocer even demands that its store brands earn 50 percent higher rankings than national brands in taste tests. In response, customers express their loyalty to the store brands, which means they are loyal to the store. The retailer can even brag that among the customers it cares most about, "99.5 percent of our loyal and our premium loyal customer segments are buying our corporate brands."

Yet Kroger also takes a broad perspective on its use of store brands. It acknowledges that "our stores would go away if we didn't have national brands. And our stores would go away if we didn't have our own brand. And there is a lot of upside for both of them."

Kroger's vision for its store brands is to build loyalty among customers, with strong store brands that are exclusive to the retailer. It pursues a multiple-tier store brand strategy to provide Kroger products to all customer segments. In the ice cream category, for instance, it offers the "Value" brand for its price-sensitive customers, with "adequate" packaging and quality. In the middle is the "Banner Brand," which is geared to the customer who wants ice cream comparable to Breyers. At the higher end is the "Private Selection" brand, which competes with Dove and Häagen Dazs. Developing products for all these customer segments means that Kroger closes any gaps in the ability of its current assortment to meet customers' needs.

Not all three tiers appear in every product category, though. For commodities with minimal differentiation (sugar is sugar), it limits the assortment to two store brands, Value and Banner—although it recently has added a specialty line of organic sugar, "Private Selection Organic." The flower selection in stores consists of only the "Private Selection" label. Figuring that flowers must

be alive and attractive if they are to sell, Kroger assumes it can target mainly upscale or aspirational customers willing to spend money simply to make their homes more beautiful. Similarly, homemade breads, pies, and cookies are branded by "Private Selection," whereas in the bread aisle, packaged bread carries the Banner and Value brand labels.

Coordinating store brands within and across categories is difficult. At Kroger, in the past, the category managers had control of the store brands within their category. For example, the category manager for canned soup bought national brands like Campbell's and Progresso and managed the store brands. The category manager would control the store brand's packaging, pricing, promotion, and even the brand's name. Because of this relative autonomy, Kroger had more than 40 store-brand names. Because there was little synergy between the brands, each brand had relatively low customer recognition. Through an extensive editing process, Kroger developed a structure that stresses a consistent vision for each brand. Customers have come to recognize and demand these store brands, resulting in synergies across categories. So, if a customer likes Kroger's "Private Selections" ice cream, they will likely be drawn to its "Private Selections" angus beef or artisan breads.

Source: Personal Communication with Linda Severin, Kroger.

DISCUSSION QUESTION

When you buy store brands, what is the primary reason: price, quality, or value?

does not offer the national brands, customers might view its assortment as lower in quality, with a resulting loss of profits.

On the other hand, the consistency of national brands means that it is easy to compare the retailer's prices for national brands. Thus, the same national brands offered by competing retailers can only be differentiated on price, which means retailers often have to offer significant discounts on some national brands to attract customers to their stores, further reducing their profitability.

While store brands offer an opportunity for retailers to differentiate their products and reduce price competition, the retailer incurs additional costs designing and marketing store brands, which reduces its profitability. In addition, the retailers assume the risk associated with uncertain sales. If, for instance, a product doesn't sell, the retailer can negotiate to either send the merchandise back to the vendor, have the vendor pay for the difference in lost gross margin if the merchandise has to be marked down, or sell the inventory to an off-price retailer. Retailers have no such cushions for their store brands. Because private-label products are specific to the store, there are few alternative options for getting rid of excess inventory.

The potential profitability for exclusive store brands is stronger, however. Customers can't compare prices for these products because they are, in fact, exclusive to one retailer. Because the retailers are less likely to compete on price when selling exclusive brands, the profitability potential for exclusive store brands is higher, and they are motivated to devote more resources toward selling them than they would for similar national brands.[11]

Flexibility   National brands can limit a retailer's flexibility. Vendors of strong brands can dictate how their products are displayed, advertised, and priced. Ralph Lauren, for instance, tells retailers exactly when and how its products should be advertised.

REFACT

Although on average, store brands cost 29 percent less than national versions, their prices are rising by 5.3 percent annually, whereas the industry average is only 1.9 percent. In some categories, store brands are the most expensive choices.[10]

BUYING NATIONAL-BRAND MERCHANDISE

LO2

Describe how retailers buy national brands.

In this section, we review how retail buyers of national brands meet with vendors, review the merchandise they have to offer at wholesale markets, and place orders.

Meeting National-Brand Vendors

A **wholesale market** for retail buyers is a concentration of vendors within a specific geographic location, perhaps even under one roof or over the Internet. Wholesale markets may be permanent wholesale market centers, annual trade shows, or trade fairs. Retailers also interact with vendors at their corporate headquarters. News about various tradeshows is readily available on the Trade Show News network (www.tsnn.com). Its database features more than 25,000 tradeshows and 100,000 registered users.[12]

Wholesale Market Centers   For many types of merchandise, particularly fashion apparel and accessories, buyers regularly visit with vendors in established market centers. Wholesale market centers have permanent vendor showrooms that retailers can visit throughout the year. At specific times during the year, these wholesale centers host **market weeks,** during which buyers make appointments to visit the various vendor showrooms. Vendors that do not have permanent showrooms at the market center lease temporary space to participate in market weeks.

Probably the world's most well-known wholesale market center for many merchandise categories is in New York City. The Fashion Center, also known as the Garment District, is located from Fifth to Ninth Avenues and from 34th to 41st Streets. Thousands of apparel buyers visit every year for five market weeks and numerous annual trade shows. The Garment District hosts thousands of show-rooms and factories.[13] There are also major wholesale market centers in London, Milan, Paris, and Tokyo. The United States also has various regional wholesale market centers—like the Dallas Market Center (positioned as the world's most complete wholesaler) or the Atlanta Merchandise Mart—that smaller retailers rely on to view and purchase merchandise.

REFACT
Wholesale transactions amounting to more than $8 billion are conducted within the Dallas Market Center complex annually.[14]

Trade Shows   **Trade shows** provide another opportunity for buyers to see the latest products and styles and interact with vendors. Vendors display their merchandise in designated areas and have sales representatives, company executives, and sometime seven celebrities available to talk with buyers as they walk through the exhibit area. For example, consumer electronics buyers always make sure that they attend the annual International Consumer Electronics Show (CES) in Las Vegas, the world's largest trade show for consumer technology (www.cesweb.org). The most recent show was attended by 153,000 people (including more than 34,000 international attendees), such as vendors, developers, and suppliers of consumer technology hardware, content, technology delivery systems, and related products and services. Nearly 3,100 vendor exhibits take up 1.861 million net square feet of exhibit space, showcasing the very latest products and services. Vendors often use CES to introduce new products, including the first camcorder (1981), high-definition television (HDTV, 1998), and Internet protocol television (IPTV, 2005). More than 20,000 new products were launched at the 2012 conference alone.[15]

Trade shows are typically staged at convention centers not associated with wholesale market centers. McCormick Place in Chicago (the nation's largest convention complex, with more than 2.7 million square feet) hosts more than 65 meetings and trade shows a year, including the National Hardware Show and National Houseware Manufacturers Association International Exposition.[16]

Vendors from outside the United States and store-brand manufacturers attend trade shows to learn about the market and pick up on trend information. Some store-brand manufacturers attend and display at trade shows, but most participants are national-brand vendors.

The International Consumer Electronics Show (CES) in Las Vegas is the world's largest trade show for consumer technology.

National-Brand Buying Process

When attending market weeks or trade shows, buyers and their supervisors typically make a series of appointments with key vendors. During these meetings, the buyers discuss the performance of the vendor's merchandise during the previous season, review the vendor's offerings for the coming season, and possibly place orders for the coming season. These meetings take place in conference rooms in the vendors' showrooms at wholesale market centers. During trade shows, these meetings typically are less formal. The meetings during market weeks offer an opportunity for an in-depth discussion, whereas trade shows provide the opportunity for buyers to see a broader array of merchandise in one location and gauge reactions to the merchandise by observing the level of activity in the vendor's display area.

Often, buyers do not negotiate with vendors or place orders during the market week or trade show. They typically want to see what merchandise and prices are available from all the potential vendors before deciding what items to buy. So, after attending a market week or trade show, buyers return to their offices, review requested samples of merchandise sent to them by vendors, meet with their supervisors to review the available merchandise, make decisions about which items are most attractive, and then negotiate with the vendors before placing an order. The issues involved in negotiating the purchase of national-brand merchandise are discussed later in this chapter.

DEVELOPING AND SOURCING STORE-BRAND MERCHANDISE

LO3

List the issues retailers consider when developing and sourcing store-branded merchandise internationally.

Retailers use a variety of different processes to develop and buy store brands.

Developing Store Brands

Larger retailers that offer a significant amount of store-brand merchandise, such as J.Crew, Macy's, The Gap, and American Eagle Outfitters, have large divisions with people devoted to the development of their store-brand merchandise. Employees in these divisions specialize in identifying trends, designing and specifying products, selecting manufacturers to make the products, maintaining a worldwide staff to monitor the conditions in which the products are made, and managing facilities to test the quality of the manufactured products. For example, MAST Global Fashion lives up to its name by maintaining joint ventures and manufacturing operations in dozens of countries, where it fulfills contracts for manufacturing, importing, and distributing various products. In addition to being the major store-brand supplier of Limited Brands (Victoria's Secret and Bath & Body Works), it provides store-brand merchandise for Express, Chico's, and Betsey Johnson. However, most retailers do not own and operate or have ownership stakes in manufacturing facilities.[17]

Smaller retail chains can offer store brands without making a significant investment in the supporting infrastructure. Smaller retailers often ask national-brand or store-brand suppliers to make minor changes to products they offer and then provide the merchandise with the store's brand name or a special label copyrighted by the national brand. Alternatively, store-brand manufacturers can sell to them from a predetermined stock selection. Hollander thus makes more than 30 million pillows, for companies such as Laura Ashley, Karen Neuberger, and Simmons. It also makes store-brand versions for various retailers (e.g., Walmart, JCPenney).[18] Retailing View 13.2 describes how the Chinese government has helped create specialized apparel cities with economies of scale so great that they dominate apparel manufacturing in the world.

Sourcing Store-Brand Merchandise

Once the decision has been made about which and how much store-brand merchandise will be acquired, the designers develop a complete specification plan and work with the sourcing department to find a manufacturer for the merchandise. For example, JCPenney has sourcing and quality assurance offices in 19 countries. These offices take the specification developed by the designer, negotiate a contract to produce the item with manufacturers, and monitor the production

RETAILING VIEW   Chinese Government Creates Specialized Apparel Cities   **13.2**

As a result of government and private investment, China has become the leading manufacturer of apparel.

In the 1970s, the residents of Datang, China, grew rice; for extra income, they also stitched socks to sell to travelers passing through. Noting these tendencies, China's central government designated Datang a sock-production village. Today, it has been informally renamed "Sock City" because it is the source of approximately one-third of the world's supply, making two pairs for every person in the world every year.

Other specialized production sites focus on everything from underwear to neckties to sweaters to children's clothing. As a result, Chinese development zones achieve impressive economies of scale and other competitive benefits that enable them to outperform decentralized manufacturing firms in other countries. Industrial parks planned by the state enjoy tax breaks, as well as partnerships with logistics providers and other firms that provide the necessary input to support their own output. Furthermore, the rapid development of China's infrastructure has helped these firms move their

products into global markets quickly and efficiently. In turn, with the support of the central government, these private companies host massive dormitory complexes for their workers, providing shelter, food, basic necessities, and health care.

Sources: Tania Branigan, "Sock City's Decline May Reveal an Unravelling in China's Economy," *The Observer*, September 8, 2012; "Datang Socks It to the Financial Crisis," *Xie Frang (China Daily)*, March 4, 2009; and Geoffrey Colvin, "Saving America's Socks—but Killing Free Trade," *Fortune*, August 22, 2005, p. 38.

DISCUSSION QUESTION

From a retail buyer's perspective, what are the opportunities and threats associated with buying from vendors located in one of China's specialized production sites?

The rise of the value of the U.S. dollar against the euro and other important world currencies in recent years has made imports to the United States less expensive and exports from the United States more expensive.

process.[19] As barriers to international trade continue to fall, retailers can consider more sources for merchandise, anywhere in the world. In this section, we examine the cost factors and managerial issues that influence global sourcing.

Costs Associated with Global Sourcing Decisions

Retailers use production facilities located in developing economies for much of their private-label merchandise because of the very low labor costs in these countries. To counterbalance the lower acquisition costs, however, there are other expenses that can increase the costs of sourcing private-label merchandise from other countries. These costs include the relative value of foreign currencies, tariffs, longer lead times, and increased transportation costs.[20]

Retailers can hedge against short-term foreign currency fluctuations by buying contracts that lock the retailer into a set price, regardless of how the currency fluctuates. But in the longer term, the relative value of foreign currencies can have a strong influence on the cost of imported merchandise. For example, if the Indian rupee has a sustained a significant increase relative to the U.S. dollar, the cost of store-brand merchandise produced in India and imported for sale into the United States will increase. **Tariffs,** also known as **duties,** are taxes collected by a government on imports. Import tariffs have been used to shield domestic manufacturers from foreign competition. Inventory turnover also is likely to be lower when purchasing from foreign suppliers. Because lead times are longer and more uncertain, retailers using foreign sources must maintain larger inventories to ensure that the merchandise is available when the customer wants it. Larger inventories mean larger inventory carrying costs. Finally, transportation costs are higher when merchandise is produced in foreign countries.

Managerial Issues Associated with Global Sourcing Decisions

Whereas the cost factors associated with global sourcing are easy to quantify, some more subjective issues include quality control, time to market, and social/political risks. When sourcing globally, it is harder to maintain consistent quality standards than it is when sourcing domestically. Quality control problems can cause delays in shipment and adversely affect a retailer's image.

The collaborative supply chain management approaches described in Chapter 10 are more difficult to implement when sourcing globally. Collaborative systems are based on short and consistent lead times. Vendors provide frequent deliveries of smaller quantities. For a collaborative system to work properly, there must be a strong alliance between the vendor and the retailer that is based on trust and shared information. These activities are more difficult to perform globally than domestically.

Another issue related to global sourcing is the problem of policing potential violations of human rights and child labor laws. Many retailers have had to publicly defend themselves against allegations of human rights, child labor, or other abuses involving the factories and countries in which their goods are made. Due to the efforts of U.S. retailers and nonprofit organizations, fewer imported goods are produced in sweatshop conditions today. Some retailers are quite proactive in enforcing the labor practices of their suppliers. Limited Brands, for instance, was one of the first U.S. apparel manufacturers to develop and implement policies requiring that vendors and their subcontractors and suppliers observe core labor standards as a condition of doing business. Among other things, this requirement ensures that each supplier pays minimum wages and benefits; limits overtime to local industry standards; does not use prisoners, forced labor, or child labor; and provides a healthy and safe environment.[21] Other companies that rely on firms in low-wage countries for their production also pursue self-policing to avoid unpleasant surprises and reputational risks. Retailing View 13.3 examines how Walmart is pushing its vendors to be environmentally responsible.

Resident Buying Offices   Many retailers purchasing private-label merchandise use **resident buying offices,** which are organizations located in major market centers that provide services to help retailers buy merchandise. As retailers have become larger and more sophisticated, these third-party, independent resident buying offices have become less important. Now, many large retailers have their own buying offices in other countries.

RETAILING VIEW   It Isn't Easy to Sell to Walmart   13.3

Walmart is known for its low prices—and for driving its vendors to tears to get them. Now it is pressuring its vendors to also supply it with environmentally friendly merchandise, with labels to prove it. In the future, merchandise sold at Walmart will have the environmental equivalent of nutritional labels, providing information on the product's carbon footprint, the amount of water and air pollution used to produce it, and other environmental issues. To measure how a vendor's products are doing, Walmart has developed a sustainability index that simultaneously takes several issues into consideration.

REFACT

Walmart buys from more than 100,000 vendors, from all over the globe.[22]

Walmart has laid out three goals that it aspires to achieve: to use 100 percent renewable energy, to reduce its waste production to zero, and to market products that will sustain both customers and the environment. These are very lofty aspirations that have resulted in multiple, concrete goals.

Walmart is also requiring that its top 200 factories become 20 percent more energy efficient by 2012, a feat that many experts believe may be impossible, even with Walmart's help. Initial results are promising, though. For example, Jiangsu Redbud Dyeing Technology in China has cut its coal consumption by one-tenth and is attempting to cut its toxic emissions to zero.

Walmart hasn't always been touted as such a good corporate citizen, though. In the 1990s, it came to light that workers at some factories producing clothing for Walmart were subjected to inhumane conditions. More recently, two government organizations accused Walmart of buying from 15 factories that engage in abuse and labor violations, including child labor, 19-hour shifts, and below-subsistence wages. Walmart and other companies have also been accused of dumping hazardous waste in Oklahoma City.

Some wonder why Walmart is attempting to position itself as the retail industry's sustainability leader. Certainly, initiatives that show that it is a good corporate citizen enhance its image. But Walmart expects that these initiatives will be good for business as well. Its customers, especially those born between 1980 and 2000, are increasingly concerned about how the products they use affect the environment and the people who produce them. Also, Walmart believes that many of these initiatives will help streamline supply chain processes and, therefore, provide additional financial benefits to its suppliers and customers.

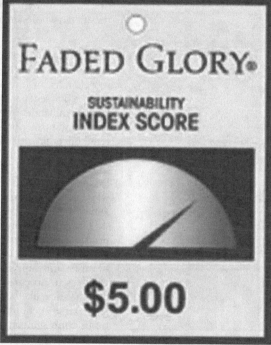

Faded Glory products score well on Walmart's sustainability index.

Sources: "Beyond 50 Years: Building a Sustainable Future," Walmart 2012 Global Responsibility Report; http://sustainabilitycases.kenexcloud.org/about; http://corporate.walmart.com/global-responsibility/environment-sustainability/sustainability-index; Stephanie Rosenbloom, "At Wal-Mart, Labeling to Reflect Green Intent," *The New York Times,* July 16, 2009; Stephanie Rosenbloom, "Wal-Mart to Toughen Standards," *The New York Times,* October 22, 2008; and Adam Aston, "Wal-Mart: Making Its Suppliers Go Green," *BusinessWeek,* May 18, 2009.

DISCUSSION QUESTION

Is Walmart trying to be a good corporate citizen with its sustainability initiatives, or is it doing these things just because it is good business?

To illustrate how buying offices operate, consider how David Smith of Pockets Men's Store in Dallas uses his when he goes to market in Milan. Smith meets with market representative Alain Bordat of the Doneger Group. Bordat, an English-speaking Italian, knows Smith's store and his upscale customers, so before Smith's visit, he sets up appointments with Italian vendors that he believes will fit Pockets' image.

When Smith is in Italy, Bordat accompanies him to the appointments and acts as a translator, negotiator, and accountant. Bordat informs Smith of the cost of importing the merchandise into the United States, taking into account duty, freight, insurance, processing costs, and so forth.

Once the orders are placed, Bordat writes the contracts and follows up on delivery and quality control. The Doneger Group also acts as a home base for buyers like Smith, providing office space and services, travel advisers, and emergency aid. Bordat and his association continue to keep Smith abreast of what's happening on the Italian fashion scene through reports and constant communication. Without the help of a resident buying office, it would be difficult, if not impossible, for Smith to access the Italian wholesale market.

Reverse Auctions   Rather than negotiating with a specific manufacturer to produce the merchandise, some retailers use reverse auctions to get quality private-label merchandise at low prices.[23] In traditional auctions like those conducted on eBay, there is one seller and many buyers. Auctions conducted by retailer buyers of private-label merchandise are called **reverse auctions** because there is one buyer (the retailer) and many potential sellers (the manufacturing firms). In a reverse auction, the retail buyer provides a specification for what it wants to a group of potential vendors. The competing vendors then bid on the price at which they are willing to sell until the auction is over. However, the retailer is not required to place an order with the lowest bidder. The retailer can choose to place an order at the offered price from whichever vendor the retailer feels will provide the merchandise in a timely manner and with the specified quality.

The most common use of reverse auctions is to buy the products and services used in retail operations rather than merchandise for resale. Some operating materials that are frequently bought through reverse auctions are store carpeting, fixtures, and supplies. However, reverse auctions also are being used by several retailers to procure store-brand merchandise, such as commodities and seasonal merchandise like lawn furniture.

Reverse auctions are not popular with vendors. Few vendors want to be anonymous contestants in bidding wars where price alone, not service or quality, seems to be the sole basis for winning the business. Strategic relationships are also difficult to nurture when the primary interactions with vendors are through electronic auctions.

NEGOTIATING WITH VENDORS

LO4

Understand how retailers prepare for and conduct negotiations with their vendors.

When buying national brands or sourcing private-label merchandise, buyers and firm employees responsible for sourcing typically enter into negotiations with suppliers. To understand how buyers negotiate with vendors, consider a hypothetical situation in which Carolyn Swigler, women's jeans buyer at Bloomingdale's, is preparing to meet with Dario Carvel, the salesperson from Juicy Couture, in his office in New York City. Swigler, after reviewing the merchandise during the women's wear market week in New York, is ready to buy Juicy Couture's spring line, but she has some merchandising problems that have yet to be resolved from last season.

Knowledge Is Power

The more Carolyn Swigler knows about her situation and Juicy Couture's, as well as the trends in the marketplace, the more effective she will be during the negotiations. First, Swigler assesses the relationship she has with the vendor. Although Swigler and Carvel have met only a few times in the past, their companies have had a long, profitable relationship. A sense of trust and mutual respect has been established, which Swigler feels will lead to a productive meeting.

Although Juicy Couture jeans have been profitable for Bloomingdale's in the past, three styles sold poorly last season. Swigler plans to ask Carvel to let her return some merchandise. Swigler knows from past experience that Juicy Couture normally doesn't allow merchandise to be returned but does provide **markdown money**—funds vendors give retailers to cover lost gross margin dollars due to the markdowns needed to sell unpopular merchandise.

Vendors and their representatives are excellent sources of market information. They generally know what is and isn't selling. Providing good, timely information about the market is an indispensable and inexpensive marketing research tool. So Swigler plans to spend at least part of the meeting talking to Carvel about market trends.

Just as Carvel can provide market information to Swigler, she can provide information to him. For example, on one of her buying trips to Japan, she found jeans in a great new wash made by a small Japanese firm on old selvage looms. She bought a pair and gave them to Carvel, who passed it along to Juicy Couture's designers. They used the jeans to develop a new wash that was a big success.

When negotiating with a vendor, the more knowledge that is available about the vendor, the market, and the products, the more successful the negotiation will be.

Swigler also knows that Carvel will want her to buy some of the newest and most avant-garde designs in Juicy Couture's spring product line. Carvel knows that many U.S. buyers go to market in New York and that most stop at Bloomingdale's to see what's new, what's selling, and how it's displayed. Thus, Carvel wants to make sure that Juicy Couture is well represented at Bloomingdale's.

Negotiation Issues

In addition to taking care of last season's leftover merchandise, Swigler is prepared to discuss six issues during the upcoming meeting: (1) prices and gross margin, (2) additional markup opportunities, (3) terms of purchase, (4) exclusivity, (5) advertising allowances, and (6) transportation.

Price and Gross Margin   Of course, Swigler wants to buy the merchandise at a low price so that she will have a high gross margin. In contrast, Carvel wants to sell the jeans at a higher price because he is concerned about Juicy Couture's own margins. Two factors that affect the price and gross margin are margin guarantees and slotting allowances.

Margin Guarantees by Providing Markdown Money   Swigler, like most buyers, has a gross margin goal for each merchandise category that is quantified in her merchandise budget plans (Chapter Appendix 12A). The wholesale price Swigler negotiates for the Juicy Couture merchandise might enable her to achieve her gross margin goal. However, if the merchandise does not sell as expected, Swigler might have to put the items on sale, and she will not make her margin goal. Faced with this uncertainty, Swigler, and other buyers, may seek a commitment from Juicy Couture to "guarantee" that she will realize her gross margin goal on marked-down merchandise by providing Bloomingdale's with markdown money to make up the lost margin due to the markdown.

Carvel, like many vendors, might be willing to provide this gross margin guarantee. However, Carvel is concerned that Swigler might not aggressively promote Juicy Couture's merchandise if she knows that her gross margin is guaranteed. Thus, Carvel will offer the guarantee only in exchange for a commitment from Swigler that she will feature Juicy Couture merchandise in the store and advertise the product line.

Slotting Fees   In addition to negotiating the wholesale price, supermarket buyers often negotiate slotting fees. **Slotting fees,** or **slotting allowances,** are charges imposed by a retailer to stock a new item. When a vendor agrees to pay that fee, the retailer will stock the product for a period of time, assess its sales and margin, and, if it is successful, continue to offer the product after the trial period. For example, when Kraft wants to introduce a new product, supermarket chains might charge between $1 million and $2 million for a national rollout to stock the product. The fee varies, depending on the nature of the product and the relative power of the retailer. Products with low brand loyalty pay the highest slotting allowances. Likewise, large supermarket chains can demand higher slotting allowances than can small, independent retailers.

Vendors may view slotting allowances as extortion, and small vendors believe these fees preclude their access to retail stores. However, retailers and most economists argue that slotting allowances are a useful method for retailers to determine which new products merit inclusion in their assortment. The vendor has more information than the retailer about the quality of its new product. Thus, the slotting fee is a method for getting the vendor to reveal this private information. If the new product is good, the vendor will be willing to pay the fee because the vendor knows that the product will sell and generate adequate margins during the trial period. However, a vendor promoting a poor product will be reluctant to pay the fee.[24]

Additional Markup Opportunities   At times in the past, Juicy Couture has offered Swigler discounted prices to take excess merchandise. The excessive merchandise arises from order cancellations, returned merchandise from other retailers, or simply an overly optimistic sales forecast. Although Swigler can realize higher-than-normal gross margins on this merchandise or put the merchandise on sale and pass the savings on to customers, Bloomingdale's has to preserve its image as a fashion leader, and thus Swigler is not very interested in any excess inventory that Juicy Couture has to offer.

Terms of Purchase   Swigler would like to negotiate for a long period in which to pay for merchandise. A long payment period improves Bloomingdale's cash flow, lowers its liabilities (accounts payable), and can reduce its interest expense if it is borrowing money from financial institutions to pay for its inventory. But Juicy Couture also has its own financial objectives it wants to accomplish and thus would like to be paid soon after it delivers the merchandise.

Exclusivity   Retailers often negotiate with vendors for an exclusive arrangement so that no other retailer can sell the same item or brand. Through an exclusive arrangement, the retailer can differentiate itself from competitors and realize higher margins due to reduced price competition. In some cases, vendors also benefit by making sure that the image of retailers selling their merchandise is consistent with their brand image. For example, Prada might want to give exclusive rights for its apparel to only one store in a major market, such as Neiman Marcus. In addition, an exclusive arrangement offers a monopoly to the retailer and thus a strong incentive to promote the item.

In fashion merchandise categories, being the first retailer in a market to carry certain products helps that retailer hold a fashion-leader image and achieve a differential advantage. Swigler wants her shipment of the new spring line to arrive as early in the season as possible and would like to have some jeans styles and washes that won't be sold to competing retailers. In contrast, Juicy Couture wants to have its products sold by many different retailers to maximize its sales.

Advertising Allowances   Retailers often share the cost of advertising through a cooperative arrangement with vendors known as **co-op (cooperative) advertising**—a program undertaken by a vendor in which the vendor agrees to pay for all or part of a pricing promotion. As a fashion leader, Bloomingdale's advertises heavily. Swigler would like Juicy Couture to support an advertising program with a generous advertising allowance.

Transportation   Transportation costs can be substantial, though this concern is less prominent for Juicy Couture jeans because its merchandise has a high unit price and low weight. Nonetheless, the question of who pays to ship merchandise from the vendor to the retailer remains a significant negotiating point.

Now that some of the issues involved in the negotiation between Juicy Couture and Bloomingdale's are on the table, the next section presents some tips for effective negotiations.

Tips for Effective Negotiating[25]

Have at Least as Many Negotiators as the Vendor   Retailers have a psychological advantage at the negotiating table if the vendor is outnumbered. At the very least, retailers want the negotiating teams to be the same size. Swigler plans to invite her divisional merchandise manager (DMM) to the discussion if Carvel comes with his sales manager.

Choose a Good Place to Negotiate   Swigler may have an advantage in the upcoming meeting because it will be in her office. She'll have ready access to information, plus secretarial and supervisory assistance. From a psychological perspective, people generally feel more comfortable and confident in familiar surroundings. However, Swigler also might get more out of the negotiation if Carvel feels comfortable. In the end, selecting the location for a negotiation is an important decision.

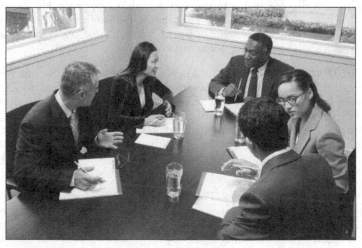

In a negotiation, have at least as many negotiators as the vendor.

Be Aware of Real Deadlines   Swigler recognizes that Carvel must go back to his office with an order in hand because he has a quota to meet by the end of the month. She also knows that she must get markdown money or permission to return the unsold jeans by the end of the week or she won't have sufficient open-to-buy funds to cover the orders she wishes to place. Recognizing these deadlines will help Swigler come to closure quickly in the upcoming negotiation.

Separate the People from the Problem   Suppose Swigler starts the meeting with, "Dario, you know we've been friends for a long time. I have a personal favor to ask. Would you mind taking back $10,000 in shirts?" This personal plea puts Carvel in an uncomfortable situation. Swigler's personal relationship with Carvel isn't the issue here and shouldn't become part of the negotiation. An equally detrimental scenario would be for Swigler to say, "Dario, your line is terrible. I can hardly give the stuff away. I want you to take back $10,000 in jeans. After all, you're dealing with Bloomingdale's. If you don't take this junk back, you can forget about ever doing business with us again." Threats usually don't work in negotiations. They put the other party on the defensive. Threats may actually cause negotiations to break down, in which case no one wins.

Insist on Objective Information   The best way to separate the people from the business issues is to rely on objective information. Swigler must know exactly how many jeans need to be returned to Juicy Couture or how much markdown money is necessary to maintain her gross margin. If Carvel argues from an emotional perspective, Swigler will stick to the numbers. For instance, suppose that after Swigler presents her position, Carvel says that he'll get into trouble if he takes back the merchandise or provides markdown money. With the knowledge that Juicy Couture has provided relief in similar situations in the past, Swigler should ask what Juicy Couture's policy is regarding customer overstock problems. She should also show Carvel a summary of Bloomingdale's buying activity with Juicy Couture over the past few seasons. Using this approach, Swigler forces Carvel to acknowledge that providing assistance in this overstock situation—especially if it has been done in the past—is a small price to pay for a long-term profitable relationship.

Invent Options for Mutual Gain   Inventing multiple options is part of the planning process, but knowing when and how much to give, or give up, requires quick thinking at the bargaining table, and, as such, should be decided in advance, whenever possible. Consider Swigler's overstock problem. Her objective is to get the merchandise out of her inventory without significantly hurting her gross margin. Carvel's objective is to maintain a healthy, yet profitable, relationship with Bloomingdale's. Thus, Swigler must invent options that could satisfy both parties, such as offering to buy some of Juicy Couture's most avant-garde jeans in return for markdown money for her excess inventory.

Let Them Do the Talking   There's a natural tendency for one person to continue to talk if the other person involved in the conversation doesn't respond. If used properly, this phenomenon can work to the negotiator's advantage. Suppose Swigler asks Carvel for special financial support for Bloomingdale's Christmas catalog. Carvel begins with a qualified no and cites all the reasons he can't cooperate. But Swigler doesn't say a word. Although Carvel appears nervous, he continues to talk. Eventually, he comes around to a yes. In negotiations, those who break the silence first lose.

Know How Far to Go   There's a fine line between negotiating too hard and walking away from the table without an agreement. If Swigler negotiates too aggressively for the markdown money, better terms of purchase, and a strong advertising allowance, the management of Juicy Couture may decide that other retailers are more worthy of early deliveries and the best styles. Carvel may not be afraid to say no if Swigler pushes him beyond a legal, ethical, profitable relationship.

Don't Burn Bridges   Even if Swigler gets few additional concessions from Carvel, she shouldn't be abusive or resort to threats. Bloomingdale's may not want to stop doing business with Juicy Couture on the basis of this one encounter. From a personal perspective, the world of retailing is relatively small. Swigler and Carvel may meet at the negotiating table again, possibly both working for different companies. Neither can afford to be known in the trade as unfair, rude, or worse.

Don't Assume   Many issues are raised and resolved in any negotiating session. To be certain there are no misunderstandings, participants should orally review the outcomes at the end of the session. Swigler and Carvel should both summarize the session in writing as soon as possible after the meeting.

STRATEGIC RELATIONSHIPS

Chapter 5 emphasized that maintaining strong vendor relationships is an important way to develop a sustainable competitive advantage. Chapters 10 and 12 discussed some of the ways partnering relationships can improve information exchange, planning, and the management of supply chains. For example, a vendor-managed inventory system cannot operate effectively without the vendor and retailer making a commitment to work together and invest in the relationship.[26] In this section, we examine how retailers develop strategic relationships and the characteristics of successful long-term relationships.

LO5

Determine why retailers build strategic relationships with their vendors.

Defining Strategic Relationships

Traditionally, relationships between retailers and vendors have focused on haggling over how to split up a profit pie.[27] The relationships were basically win–lose encounters because when one party got a larger portion of the pie, the other party got a smaller portion. Both parties were interested exclusively in their own profits and unconcerned about the other party's welfare. These relationships continue to be common, especially when the products being bought are commodities and have limited impact on the retailers' performance. In these situations, there is no benefit to the retailer from entering into a strategic relationship.

A **strategic relationship**, also called a **partnering relationship**, emerges when a retailer and vendor are committed to maintaining the relationship over the long term and investing in opportunities that are mutually beneficial to both parties. In this relationship, it is important for the partners to take risks to expand the profit pie to give the relationship a strategic advantage over other companies. In addition, the parties have a long-term perspective: They are willing to make short-term sacrifices because they know that they will get their fair share in the long run.[28]

Strategic relationships are win–win relationships. Both parties benefit because the size of the profit pie increases. Both the retailer and the vendor increase their sales and profits, because the parties in strategic relationships work together to develop and exploit joint opportunities. They depend on and trust each other heavily. They share goals and agree on how to accomplish those goals, and they thus reduce the risks of investing in the relationship and sharing confidential information. Even as the power in supply chains has shifted from large manufacturers to large retailers such as Walmart and Target, the relationships are generally not adversarial. Instead, these supply chain partners share point-of-sale data and collaborate and cooperate on issues such as which items to buy, how much, and when. As a result of these collaborative efforts, financial performance throughout the supply chain has been enhanced.[29]

For example, when Karl Lagerfeld, designer of brands such as Chanel and Fendi, embarked on an exclusive branding program with Macy's, he worked together with its merchandising team to determine their customers' needs, likes, and dislikes.[30] Then they jointly developed an assortment and pricing strategy that has proved to be much more successful than would have been possible if the two sides had worked separately and just negotiated a quantity and price. To sustain their successful momentum, they share trends in the market and agree to respond quickly when a change occurs or when a product should be produced in a short time.

A strategic relationship is like a marriage. When businesses enter strategic relationships, they're wedded to their partners for better or worse. For example, Spain-based fast-fashion retailer Zara manufactures about 40 percent of its finished garments with the help of about 450 independently owned workshops located near the corporate headquarters that sew pre-cut fabric into finished garments.[31] Most of these relatively small workshops have had long-term relationships with Zara. Zara provides them with technology, logistics, and financial support, as well as other types of assistance. In return, the workshops support Zara's mission of being able to quickly provide women and men in 73 countries with relatively inexpensive fashion apparel. Like any supplier, these small workshops sometimes miss a deadline or make a mistake on a garment. But as in a marriage, Zara doesn't dump them and move on to someone else. It works with them to make things work. Another company that works closely with its vendors, Zappos, is discussed in Retailing View 13.4.

Building Partnering Relationships

Although not all retailer–vendor relationships should or do become strategic partnerships, the development of strategic partnerships tends to go through a series of phases characterized by increasing levels of involvement: (1) awareness, (2) exploration, (3) expansion, and (4) commitment.

Awareness In the awareness stage, no transactions have taken place. This phase might begin with the buyer seeing some interesting merchandise at a retail market or an ad in a trade magazine. The reputation and image of the vendor can play an important role in determining if the buyer moves to the next stage.

Exploration During the exploration phase, the buyer and vendor begin to explore the potential benefits and costs of a partnership. At this point, the buyer may make a small purchase and try to test the demand for the merchandise in several stores. In addition, the buyer will get information about how easy it is to work with the vendor.

Expansion Eventually, the buyer has collected enough information about the vendor to consider developing a longer-term relationship. The buyer and the vendor determine if there is the potential for a win–win relationship. They begin to work on joint promotional programs, and the amount of merchandise sold increases.

Commitment If both parties continue to find the relationship mutually beneficial, it moves to the commitment stage and becomes a strategic relationship. The buyer and vendor then make significant investments in the relationship and develop a long-term perspective toward it.

It is difficult for retailer–vendor relationships to be as committed as some supplier–manufacturer relationships. Manufacturers can enter into monogamous (sole-source) relationships with other manufacturers. However, an important function of retailers is to provide an assortment of merchandise for

RETAILING VIEW   Zappos Values Relationships with Its Vendors, the Merchandise Experts   **13.4**

High efficiency light-emitting diode (LED) lights are featured at Home Depot. Most screw-in incandescent light bulbs have been phased out because they use too much energy.

Founded in 1999, Zappos is best known as an online shoe retailer. Through its emphasis on customer service, it has grown into the largest shoe retailer in the world. Acquired by Amazon in July 2009, Zappos was recently valued at more than $1.6 billion. It may sell shoes, clothing, and more, but the "secret sauce" that has led to its blockbuster success has less to do with the products Zappos sells and more to do with the relationships it builds—with customers, employees, and every supplier with which it deals. Its customer service and resulting customer satisfaction are legendary. For employees, its emphasis on relationships is evidenced by Zappos' consistent rating as one of the best companies to work for, buoyed by its offerings of benefits such as onsite "laughter yoga" classes and opportunities for every employee to pitch new business ideas.

But with a portfolio of more 50 brands, strong vendor relations may be even more key to the success of Zappos. Vendors feel valued, respected, and appreciated in all aspects of the business relationship. When vendors come to visit, a Zappos representative picks them up at the airport using the corporate shuttle and snacks and drinks await them when they arrive. New vendors receive a tour of the facilities. If a vendor contacts Zappos, the company either calls back the same day or responds to e-mails within a few hours. When they dine out together, Zappos always picks up the bill. Its signals of appreciation don't stop with one-on-one visits; Zappos hosts appreciation events for its vendors year-round. The last Friday of every month, Zappos hosts a golf tournament for vendors, and once a year, it hosts a lavish vendor appreciation party.

Cleary, Zappos is interested in strong vendor relationships. But what exactly does the company get out of it?

What's the return on its investment? Normally, retailers seek to beat vendors in negotiations, to get the lowest prices and best terms. Zappos believes, instead, that strong relationships lead to better partnerships. Instead of adversarial negotiations, it embraces transparency. Vendors gain access to information on Zappos' inventory, sales, and profitability. With these collaborative efforts, it seeks to encourage shared risks and rewards, and thus shared goals. With shared goals also come greater accountability and, at the end of the day, more committed vendors.

In a time when most retailers are trying to reduce their costs by cutting back on employee and vendor benefits, Zappos has taken the opposite strategy. As a top online retailer, its emphasis on building strong relationships with its vendors has resulted in a unique competitive advantage. Instead of buyers needing to wrestle with more than 50 vendors, Zappos has converted them into advocates for the company.

Sources: Tom Ryan, "Zappos Makes Nice with Vendors," *Retail Wire*, March 2, 2011; Tony Hisch, "A Lesson from Zappos: Follow the Golden Rule," *HBR Blog*, June 4, 2010; "About Us," Zappos, about.zappos.com; and Aida Ahmed, "Zappos Ranks No. 11 on List of Best Companies to Work For," *VegasInc*, January 19, 2012.

DISCUSSION QUESTIONS

Why do Zappos' vendors love them? Why are these relationships good for Zappos?

their customers. Thus, they must always deal with multiple, sometimes competing suppliers.

Regardless of which partner-building phase a retailer is in with a supplier, the retailer is constantly involved in the give-and-take process of negotiations. The next section looks at some of the legal and ethical issues that arise when buying merchandise.

Maintaining Strategic Relationships

The four foundations of successful strategic relationships are: (1) mutual trust, (2) common goals, (3) open communication, and (4) credible commitments.

Mutual Trust   The glue in a strategic relationship is trust. **Trust** is a belief that a partner is honest (reliable and stands by its word) and benevolent (concerned about the other party's welfare).[33] When vendors and buyers trust each other, they are more willing to share relevant ideas, clarify goals and problems, and communicate efficiently. Information shared between the parties becomes increasingly comprehensive, accurate, and timely. There is less need for the vendor and buyer to constantly monitor and check up on each other's actions, because each believes the other will not take advantage, even when given the opportunity.[34] If Walmart's sustainability initiatives described previously in Retailing View 13.3 are to be achieved, it is important for Walmart to trust its vendors, and vice versa.

Common Goals   Vendors and buyers must have common goals for a successful relationship to develop.[35] Shared goals give both members of the relationship an incentive to pool their strengths and abilities and exploit potential opportunities between them. They also create an assurance that the other partner will not do anything to hinder goal achievement within the relationship.

For example, Walmart and its vendors have recognized that it was in their common interest to develop and sell products that have a positive impact on the environment. Walmart cannot demand that its vendors take on sustainability programs that are so expensive that they won't make money, and its vendors must try to accommodate the demands of its biggest customer. With a common goal, Walmart and its suppliers have an incentive to cooperate because they know that by doing so, both can achieve their common sustainability goals and still make profits.

Common goals also help sustain the relationship when goals are not realized according to plan. If, for instance, a vendor fails to reach an acceptable score on Walmart's sustainability index but has made significant progress, Walmart won't suddenly call off the whole arrangement. Instead, Walmart is likely to work harder to help the vendor raise its score and remain in the relationship because Walmart knows that it and the vendor are committed to the same goals in the long run.

Open Communication   To share information, develop sales forecasts together, coordinate deliveries, and achieve their sustainability common goals, Walmart and its vendors must have open and honest communication. This requirement may sound easy in principle, but most businesses don't like to share information with their business partners. They believe it is none of the other's business. But open, honest communication is a key to developing successful and profitable relationships.[36] Buyers and vendors in a relationship need to understand what is driving each other's business, their roles in the relationship, each firm's strategies, and any problems that arise over the course of the relationship.

Credible Commitments   Successful relationships develop because both parties make credible commitments. Credible commitments are tangible investments in the relationship. They go beyond just making the hollow statement, "I want to be your partner." Credible commitments involve spending money to improve

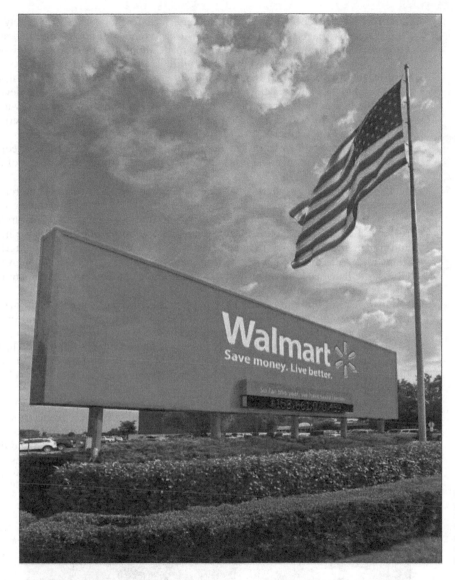

Walmart builds strategic relationships with its vendors by fostering mutual trust, having open communications and common goals, and making credible commitments.

products or services and, in the case of Walmart and its vendors, taking mutual steps to improve the sustainability index. For example, the goal of reducing Jiangsu Redbud Dyeing Technology's toxic emissions in China is a joint effort and investment by Walmart and Jiangsu.

LEGAL, ETHICAL, AND SOCIAL RESPONSIBILITY ISSUES FOR BUYING MERCHANDISE

Legal and Ethical Issues

Given the many negotiations and interactions between retail buyers and vendors, ethical and legal issues are bound to arise. This section reviews some practices that arise in buyer–vendor negotiations that may have legal and/or ethical implications, and it looks at some ways that retailers are becoming more socially responsible in their buying practices.

LO6

Indicate the legal, ethical, and social responsibility issues involved in buying merchandise.

Counterfeit Merchandise   Selling counterfeit merchandise can negatively affect a retailer's image and its relationship with the vendor of the legitimate brand. **Counterfeit merchandise** includes goods made and sold without the permission of the owner of a trademark or copyright. Trademarks and copyrights are **intellectual property,** that is, intangible and created by intellectual (mental) effort as opposed to physical effort. A **trademark** is any mark, word, picture, device, or nonfunctional design associated with certain merchandise (e.g., the crown on a Rolex watch, the red Levi's tag on the back pocket of a pair of jeans). A **copyright** protects the original work of authors, painters, sculptors, musicians, and others who produce works of artistic or intellectual merit. This book is copyrighted, so these sentences cannot be used by anyone without the consent of the copyright owners.

The nature of counterfeiting has changed during the past decade. Counterfeit name-brand merchandise, such as women's handbags or dresses, has improved in quality, making these items more expensive and difficult to distinguish from the real merchandise. In response, Chanel made the bold move of filing a cyberpiracy and trademark infringement lawsuit, accusing 399 websites of selling counterfeit items under the Chanel name.[37] Chanel believes that these websites operate in China, the Bahamas, and other overseas areas, where trademark infringement law often is not strictly enforced.

Historically, high-end brands have focused their battle tactics on minimizing the sales of street corner knock-offs. Chanel's lawsuit transforms this fight into a larger war by seeking to seize or permanently disable websites from selling any counterfeit merchandise, from T-shirts to expensive jewelry, bearing the Chanel name. Tiffany filed a similar suit targeting 223 unnamed websites: Louis Vuitton filed a suit against 182 websites. Each of these lawsuits includes several website operators that are also named in the Chanel case.

Also, there is a thriving business in counterfeit information products such as music, software, and Blu-Rays. This type of merchandise is attractive to counterfeiters because it has a relatively high unit value, is easy to duplicate and transport, and prompts high consumer demand. The ease of illegally downloading and distributing music means that neither the record label nor the artist receives any money for their investment, work, or talent, and thus both may be less motivated to develop and produce music.

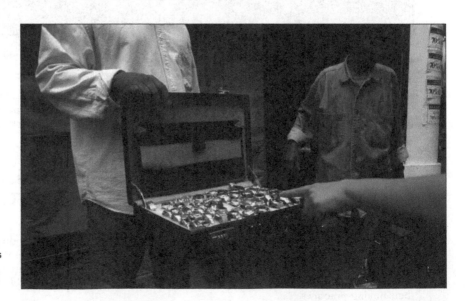

It is illegal for this "street retailer" to sell counterfeit watches because it violates the watch manufacturers' rights to control the use of their trademarks.

Gray-Market, Diverted, and Black-Market Merchandise   **Gray-market goods,** also known as **parallel imports,** involve the flow of merchandise through distribution channels, usually across international borders, other than those authorized or intended by the manufacturer or producer. For example, to increase its profits, McGraw-Hill, the publisher of this textbook, charges a higher wholesale price for this textbook in the United States than in other countries. An importer could buy textbooks at a low price in other countries, import them into the United States, and sell them at a price lower than that in U.S. bookstores.

Diverted merchandise is similar to gray-market merchandise except there need not be distribution across international borders. Suppose, for instance, that the fragrance manufacturer Givenchy grants an exclusive scent to Saks Fifth Avenue. The Saks buyer has excess inventory and sells it at a low price to a discount retailer in the United States, such as an off-price retailer. In this case, the merchandise has been diverted from its legitimate channel of distribution, and Saks would be referred to as the diverter.

A **black market,** on the other hand, occurs when consumer goods are scarce, such as water or gasoline after a natural disaster; heavily taxed, such as cigarettes or alcohol; or illegal, such as drugs or arms. We rarely see black-market merchandise sold through legitimate channels in the United States.

While Saks may benefit from diverting its excess inventory to an off-price retailer, the fragrance manufacturer is concerned about gray markets and diversions. Making the product available at discount stores at low prices may reduce the vendor's brand image and the service normally provided with the brand. So, though such practices are usually legal, vendors seek to minimize gray-market and diverted merchandise.

In a recent U.S. Supreme Court case, Omega SA, a subsidiary of Swatch Group Ltd., alleged that Costco violated U.S. copyright law by selling watches it had obtained from a third party at a significantly lower price than was suggested by Omega.[38] Costco argued that Omega could not impose limits on how its watches were imported and resold, once the watchmaker made its first sale of the goods abroad. The Court was deadlocked with a 4–4 vote, which means that a lower-court ruling against Costco was upheld, though the decision failed to set any precedent because of the tie vote.

Vendors engage in other activities to avoid gray-market/diversion problems, though. They require that all of their retail and wholesale customers sign a contract stipulating that they will not engage in gray marketing. If a retailer is found in violation of the agreement, the vendor will refuse to deal with it in the future. Another strategy is to produce different versions of products for different markets. For instance, McGraw-Hill sells a different version of this textbook in India than it sells in the United States.

Terms and Conditions of Purchase   The Robinson-Patman Act, passed by the U.S. Congress in 1936, potentially restricts the prices and terms that vendors can offer to retailers. The act makes it illegal for vendors to offer different terms and conditions to different retailers for the same merchandise and quantity. Sometimes called the Anti-Chain-Store Act, it was passed to protect independent retailers from chain-store competition. Thus, if a vendor negotiates a good deal on the issues discussed in the previous section (price, advertising allowance, markdown money, transportation), the Robinson-Patman Act requires that the vendor offer the same terms and conditions to other retailers.

However, vendors can offer different terms to retailers for the same merchandise and quantities if the costs of manufacturing, selling, or delivery are different. The cost of manufacturing is usually the same, but selling and delivery could be more expensive for some retailers. For example, vendors may incur larger transportation expenses due to smaller shipments to independent retailers.

Different prices can also be offered if the retailers are providing different functions. For example, a large retailer can get a lower price if its distribution centers store the merchandise or its stores provide different services valued by customers. In addition, lower prices can be offered to meet competition and dispose of perishable merchandise.[39]

Commercial Bribery   **Commercial bribery** occurs when a vendor or its agent offers or a buyer asks for "something of value" to influence purchase decisions. Say a salesperson for a ski manufacturer takes a sporting goods retail buyer to lunch at a fancy private club and then proposes a ski weekend in Vail. These gifts could be construed as bribes or kickbacks, which are illegal unless the buyer's manager is informed of them. To avoid such problems, many retailers forbid employees to accept any gifts from vendors. Other retailers have a policy that it is fine to accept limited entertainment or token gifts, such as flowers or wine for the holidays. As we discussed in Retailing View 13.4, Zappos stops potential commercial bribery in its tracks by bestowing free lunches and other favors on its vendors, rather than accepting anything from vendors. In any case, retailers want their buyers to decide on purchases solely on the basis of what is best for the retailer.

Chargebacks   A **chargeback** is a practice used by retailers in which they deduct money from the amount they owe a vendor. Retailers often use a chargeback when a vendor did not meet the agreed-on terms, for example, if it improperly applied labels to shipping containers or merchandise or sent shipments that had missing items or were late. Chargebacks are especially difficult for vendors because once the money is deducted from an invoice and the invoice is marked "paid," it is difficult to dispute the claim and get the amount back. Vendors sometimes feel that the chargebacks retailers take are not justifiable and thus are unethical.

Buybacks   Similar to slotting allowances, **buybacks**, also known as **stocklifts** or **lift-outs,** are activities engaged in by vendors and retailers to get old products out of retail stores and new products in their place. Specifically, in a buyback situation, either a retailer allows a vendor to create space for its merchandise by "buying back" a competitor's inventory and removing it from the retailer's system, or the retailer forces a vendor to buy back slow-moving merchandise. A vendor with significant market power can violate federal antitrust laws if it stocklifts from a competitor so often that it shuts the competitor out of a market, but such cases are difficult to prove.

Exclusive Dealing Agreements   **Exclusive dealing agreements** occur when a vendor restricts a retailer to carrying only its products and nothing from competing vendors. For example, Ford may require that its dealers sell only Ford cars and no cars made by General Motors. The effect of such arrangements on competition is determined by the market power of the vendor. For example, it may be illegal for a market leader like Coca-Cola to sell its products to a small supermarket chain only if the chain agrees not to sell a less popular cola product like RC Cola.

Tying Contract   A **tying contract** exists when a vendor requires that a retailer take a product it doesn't necessarily desire (the tied product) to ensure that it can buy a product it does desire (the tying product). Tying contracts are illegal if they substantially lessen competition or tend to create a monopoly. But the complaining party has the burden of proof. Thus, it is typically legal for a vendor to require that a buyer buy all items in its product line. For example, if a gift store sued a postcard manufacturer for requiring that it purchase as many "local view" postcards (the tied product) as it did licensed Disney character postcards (the tying product), the court would probably dismiss the case because the retailer would be unable to prove a substantial lessening of competition.

Refusal to Deal   The practice of refusing to deal (buy or sell to) can be viewed from both vendors' and retailers' perspectives. Generally, both vendors and retailers have the right to deal or refuse to deal with anyone they choose. But there are exceptions to this general rule when there's evidence of anticompetitive conduct by one or more firms that wield market power. A vendor may refuse to sell to a particular retailer, but it cannot do so for the sole purpose of benefiting a competing retailer. For example, Mattel decided not to offer certain popular Barbie packages to wholesale clubs. This action in itself would not have been illegal. However, it was determined that Mattel agreed to do so as part of a conspiracy among 10 toy manufacturers orchestrated by Toys "R" Us to prevent wholesale clubs from underselling the same toy packages that Toys "R" Us sold. The refusal to deal then became an illegal group boycott.[40]

Corporate Social Responsibility

Corporate social responsibility describes the voluntary actions taken by a company to address the ethical, social, and environmental impacts of its business operations. Retailers act socially responsible in many ways, from giving to charity to donating time to philanthropic community activities. Recently, however, retailers have been increasing their efforts to buy merchandise in a socially responsible way.

Whole Foods considers local to be anything produced within seven hours or fewer from one of its stores. It requires that all its stores buy from at least four local farmers. It gives $10 million a year in low-interest loans to help small, local farmers and producers of grass-fed and humanely raised meat, poultry, and dairy animals.[41]

Some retailers are getting involved in **fair trade**, a socially responsible movement that ensures that producers receive fair prices for their products. The coffee retailers Starbucks and Peet's offer some, but not all, blends that use fair trade coffee.[43] Walmart is investing heavily in fair trade coffee, partially in response to a new corporate philosophy that goes beyond "everyday low prices" to "doing well by doing good." Bono, the U2 lead singer and an activist, is selling his high-priced fair trade apparel line, Edun, to stores such as Saks Fifth Avenue and Nordstrom.

Home Depot is encouraging its suppliers to include their products in its Eco Options marketing campaign. Some products are obviously attractive to green customers, such as organic gardening products and high-efficiency light bulbs. But a number of less obvious products are also good for the environment. Home Depot also has introduced some new environmentally sensitive products into its assortment, including solar-powered landscape

REFACT

A *locavore* is a person whose primary source of food is from his or her local foodshed or areas within a relatively modest radius.[42]

How green are these solar-powered landscape lights?

lighting, biodegradable peat pots, and paints that discharge fewer pollutants. Home Depot encourages its vendors to use recyclable plastic or cardboard packaging.[44] While these are examples of what retailers are doing to change their green orientation, Retailing View 13.5 discusses how one retailer seized the opportunity to sell eco-friendly products.

Other retailers are demanding smaller, eco-friendly packages from their suppliers. Smaller packages save not only materials but also energy. Because more packages can be transported on a truck, the transportation cost per unit goes down. Several other manufacturers (Patagonia and Timberland), retailers (e.g., Walmart, JCPenney, H&M), and organizations involved in the supply chain (e.g., Environmental Protection Agency, Environmental Defense Fund) have recently cooperated to create the Sustainable Apparel Coalition. One of the Coalition's key objectives is to create a database that summarizes the environmental issues associated with each manufacturer and its processes, such that ultimately the Coalition can provide a score or ranking for each garment that consumers may consider.[45]

These initiatives and many others suggest a complicated business model. Are socially responsible activities good for business? Some are more expensive than traditional products and initiatives. Are consumers interested in or willing to pay the higher prices? Are firms really interested in improving the environment, or are they **greenwashing** (doing a green whitewash) or practicing **green sheen**, which is the disingenuous practice of marketing products or services as being environmentally friendly with the purpose of gaining public approval and sales rather than actually improving the environment. Consumers should question whether a firm is spending significantly more money or time advertising that it is **green** or that it operates with consideration for the environment rather than spending resources on environmentally sound practices.

13.5 RETAILING VIEW Buying Green on an Amazon-Owned Site

Over the past decade, consumers have become increasingly environmentally conscious, or "green." For example, for the end-of-year holidays, some consumers are choosing to either forgo purchasing new items and regift or purchase eco-friendly products. Some forward-thinking retailers are cashing in on this trend.

One of these retailers is Amazon. Working with Quidsi, a company that Amazon acquired in 2010, the retailing giant launched Vine.com. Similar to other Amazon-owned companies like Zappos and Woot, Vine does not carry the Amazon brand name. The company sells a great variety of products—everything from household paper products to groceries, to beauty supplies, to pet food. Exercise enthusiast and environmentally conscious? Vine.com has just the thing for you. How about a Kulae Organic Yoga Mat Cleaner ($14.84) or a Mountainsmith Recycled Series Vibe TS R Backpack ($27.99)?

Vine.com appeals to a very specific market segment, the environmentally conscious, and as such, lays out specific guidelines for all of the products it carries. To be sold at Vine, a product must be energy efficient, natural, organic, powered by renewable energy, reusable, designed to remove toxins, made of sustainable materials, or water efficient. Not all of its products have all of these attributes, but each has at least one. Because bamboo is a sustainable material, bamboo cutting boards are sold. Similarly, low-flow shower heads conserve water, and cloth diapers can be washed and reused. To further ensure they are carrying "green" products, Vine requires vendors to certify that their products meet Vine's standards and do not contain substances banned by Vine. These rigorous standards led Seventh Generation to be the official launch sponsor of Vine.com, further adding to its credibility. By paying attention to emerging trends, retailers such as Vine can offer innovative products that attract segments of consumers that have previously been underserved.

Sources: Justin Gillis, "An Odometer Moment on a Warming Planet," *The New York Times*, December 17, 2012; "Green," *The New York Times Environment Blog*, Claire Cain Miller, "Amazon Starts a Shopping Site for the Environmental Crowd," *The New York Times: Bits*, September 26, 2012; John Cook, "Amazon Unveils Eco-Friendly Products Site Vine.com," *Geek Wire*, September 26, 2012; and "About Us," *Vine.com*.

DISCUSSION QUESTIONS

Would you shop at Vine.com? Does it help or hurt to know it is owned by Amazon.com?

SUMMARY

LO1 **Identify the branding options available to retailers.**

Retailers can purchase either national brands or store (or private-label) brands. Each type has its own relative advantages. Choosing appropriate brands and a branding strategy is an integral component of a firm's merchandise and assortment planning process.

LO2 **Describe how retailers buy national brands.**

Buyers of manufacturer's brands attend trade shows and wholesale market centers to meet with vendors, view new merchandise, and place orders. Virtually every merchandise category has at least one annual trade show at which retailers and vendors meet.

LO3 **List the issues retailers consider when developing and sourcing store-branded merchandise internationally.**

Buying merchandise sometimes is facilitated by resident buying offices. Market representatives of the resident buying offices facilitate merchandising purchases in foreign markets. The process for buying store brands or private-label merchandise can be more complicated than that for buying national brands because the retailer takes on some of the responsibilities that a national-brand manufacturer normally would have, such as designing and specifying products and selecting manufacturers to make the products. A large percentage of private-label merchandise is manufactured outside the United States. The cost, managerial, and ethical issues surrounding global sourcing decisions must be considered.

LO4 **Understand how retailers prepare for and conduct negotiations with their vendors.**

Buyers of both national brands and store brands engage in negotiating a series of issues with their vendors, including markdown money, slotting fees, advertising allowances, terms of purchase, exclusivity, and transportation costs. Successful vendor relationships depend on planning for and being adept at negotiations.

LO5 **Determine why retailers build strategic relationships with their vendors.**

Retailers that can successfully team up with their vendors can achieve a sustainable competitive advantage. There needs to be more than just a promise to buy and sell on a regular basis. Strategic relationships require trust, shared goals, strong communications, and a financial commitment.

LO6 **Indicate the legal, ethical, and social responsibility issues involved in buying merchandise.**

Buyers need to be aware of ethical and legal issues that can guide them in their negotiations and purchase decisions. There are also problems associated with counterfeit and gray-market merchandise and issues that vendors face when selling to retailers, such as exclusive territories and tying contracts. Care should be taken by vendors when placing restrictions on which retailers they will sell to, what merchandise, how much, and at what price. Some retailers are taking giant steps toward being more socially responsible.

KEY TERMS

black market, *379*
buybacks, *380*
chargeback, *380*
commercial bribery, *380*
co-op (cooperative)
    advertising, *371*
copycat brands, *359*
copyright, *378*
corporate social responsibility, *381*
counterfeit merchandise, *378*
diverted merchandise, *379*
duties, *366*
exclusive brands, *359*
exclusive dealing agreements, *380*
fair trade, *381*
family brand, *358*

generic brands, *360*
gray-market goods, *379*
green, *382*
green sheen, *382*
greenwashing, *382*
house brands, *358*
intellectual property, *378*
lift-outs, *380*
manufacturer's brands, *358*
markdown money, *369*
market weeks, *362*
national brands, *358*
own brands, *358*
parallel imports, *379*
partnering relationship, *373*
premium store brands, *359*

private-label brands, *358*
resident buying offices, *367*
reverse auctions, *368*
slotting allowances, *370*
slotting fees, *370*
stocklifts, *380*
store brands, *358*
strategic relationship, *373*
subbrand, *358*
tariffs, *366*
trademark, *378*
trade shows, *363*
trust, *376*
tying contract, *380*
umbrella brand, *358*
wholesale market, *362*

GET OUT AND DO IT!

1. **CONTINUING ASSIGNMENT** Go visit the retailer you have selected for the continuing assignment and perform an audit of its manufacturer's and store brands. Ask the manager to comment on the store's philosophy toward manufacturer's versus store brands. Why does it use store brands? Does it offer different store brands to appeal to different customer segments? Select three different merchandise categories. Compare the price of the same item for store versus the manufacturer brand. Has the percentage of store brands increased or decreased during the past five years? On the basis of what you see and hear, assess its branding strategy.

2. Read articles about the NBA warning fans about counterfeit merchandise. Go to the home page for the

Coalition to Advance the Protection of Sports Logos (CAPS) at www.capsinfo.com, and read "About CAPS." What are college and professional sports teams doing to prevent the sale of counterfeit merchandise? Will these measures be effective? Explain why or why not.

3. Go to the home page for the Private Label Manufacturers Association (PLMA), and read the "What are Store Brands?" page, which can be found at http://plma.com/storeBrands/facts13.html. What are store-brand products? Who purchases store brands? Who makes store brands? What store brands are you purchasing on a regular basis?

DISCUSSION QUESTIONS AND PROBLEMS

1. Assume you have been hired to consult with Forever 21 on sourcing decisions for sportswear. What issues would you consider when deciding whether you should buy from Mexico or China or find a source within the United States?

2. What are the differences among counterfeit, gray-market, and black-market merchandise? Is the selling of this type of merchandise legal? Do you believe that selling these types of merchandise should be allowed? Provide a rationale for your position. Would you purchase a counterfeit wallet? What about a counterfeit car part or prescription medication?

3. What are the advantages and disadvantages of manufacturer's brands versus store brands? Consider both the retailer's and customer's perspectives.

4. Does your favorite clothing store have a store-brand strategy? If yes, how does it build store loyalty? If no, how could a store brand create loyalty?

5. Explain why a grocery store, such as Kroger, offers more than one tier of store brands within a particular product category.

6. Why have retailers found exclusive store brands to be an appealing branding option? Choose a department store, a discount store, and a grocery store. What exclusive store brands do they offer? How are they positioned in relation to their national brand counterparts?

7. When you go shopping, in which product categories do you prefer store brands or national brands? Explain your preference.

8. What are retailers doing to be more socially responsible in buying merchandise? Why are they becoming more socially responsible? Do you buy products that you believe were produced in a socially responsible manner, even if they cost more?

9. You have decided that you don't want to take the final in this class. Explain how you would negotiate this request with the instructor. Consider place, deadlines, past relationship, possible objections, options for mutual gain, and how to maintain a professional relationship.

SUGGESTED READINGS

Boyle, Peter J., and E. Scott Lathrop. "The Value of Private Label Brands to U.S. Consumers: An Objective and Subjective Assessment," *Journal of Retailing and Consumer Services* 20 (January 2013), pp. 80–86.

Deepak, Malhotra, and Max Bazerman. *Negotiation Genius: How to Overcome Obstacles and Achieve Brilliant Results at the Bargaining Table and Beyond.* New York: Bantam, 2008.

Diamond, Jay. *Retail Buying*, 9th ed. Upper Saddle River, NJ: Pearson, 2012.

Donaldson, Bill, and Tom O'Toole. *Strategic Market Relationships: From Strategy to Implementation*, 2nd ed. Indianapolis: Wiley, 2007.

Fisher, Roger, William L. Ury, and Bruce Patton. *Getting to Yes: Negotiating Agreement Without Giving In.* New York: Penguin Books, 2011.

Foros, Oystein, Hans Jarle Kind, and Jan Yngve Sand. "Slotting Allowances and Manufacturers' Retail Sales Effort." *Southern Economic Journal* 76, no. 1 (2009), pp. 266–282.

Johnston, Robert, and Roy Staughton. "Establishing and Developing Strategic Relationships: The Role for Operations Managers." *International Journal of Operations & Production Management* 29, no. 6 (2009), pp. 564–590.

Kennedy, Gavin. *Negotiation: An A–Z Guide (Economist A–Z Guide)*. London: Economist Books, 2009.

Kumar, Nirmalya, and Jan-Benedict E. M. Steenkamp. *Private Label Strategy: How to Meet the Store Brand Challenge*. Boston: Harvard Business Press, 2007.

Lamey, L., B. Deleersnyder, Jan-Benedict E. M. Steenkamp, and Marnik G. Dekimpe. "Effect of Business Cycle Fluctuations on Private-Label Share: What Has Marketing Conduct Got to Do with It?" *Journal of Marketing* 76 (January 2012), pp. 1–19.

Lincoln, Keith, and Lars Thomassen. *Private Label: Turning the Retail Brand Threat into Your Biggest Opportunity*. London: Kogan, 2009.

Quelch, John A. "Brands vs. Private Labels: Fighting to Win." *Harvard Business Review*, March 3, 2009.

Sugden, David R. *Gray Markets: Prevention, Detection and Litigation*. New York: Oxford University Press, 2009.

Retail Pricing

EXECUTIVE BRIEFING

Debbie Harvey, President and Chief Operating Officer, Ron Jon Surf Shop

I am proud to be the president of Ron Jon Surf Shop, one of the most recognized names in surfing. Ron Jon started on the New Jersey Shore in 1959 when the founder, Ron DiMenna, sold his first surfboard. Two years later he opened a tiny oceanside shop in Long Beach Island, New Jersey. A much larger "original" store is still located in Ship Bottom, New Jersey. Our flagship store located in Cocoa Beach, Florida, was opened in 1963 and has grown over the years to be known as the world's largest surf shop. The 52,000-square-foot store is open 24 hours a day, 365 days a year and welcomes about two million visitors annually. Ron Jon has expanded over the last couple of years and now owns and operates 11 stores at coastal locations in Florida, South Carolina, Maryland, and New Jersey. We also have licensees that operate airport locations, Caribbean locations, and a Ron Jon resort.

Ron Jon's targets families with active lifestyles who are looking for entertaining and fun experiences. Our customers typically visit us while on vacation or during a visit to the beach. Our marketing goal is to continue to build the Ron Jon brand and experience rather than focus our customers on price or a particular product. Our extensive billboard program has made us familiar to millions of visitors to our market areas. Every customer in our stores receives a free sticker for his or her car. We promote the surfing lifestyle by sponsoring surf teams and contests. In addition we use the Internet, not only for a shopping site, but also to promote our brand through social media.

In setting our prices, we do not use a specific pricing formula. We price our products at the final price we feel our customers will pay; and we try to keep the prices on our exclusive Ron Jon merchandise at or below the prices of similar brands. We do not run regular sales events, we typically only markdown or promote slow-selling merchandise. We want our customers to feel our prices are price neutral: both fair and that they are getting a good value when they buy our merchandise. Our prices are the same across all of our locations and channels.

CHAPTER 14

LEARNING OBJECTIVES

LO1 Explain the difference between a high/low pricing strategy and an everyday low-pricing strategy.

LO2 Identify the factors retailers consider when pricing their merchandise.

LO3 Describe how retailers set prices.

LO4 Examine how and why retailers take markdowns.

LO5 Identify the pricing techniques retailers use to increase sales and profits.

LO6 Describe how the Internet and social and mobile channels are used to make pricing decisions.

LO7 Indicate the legal and ethical issues retailers should consider when setting prices.

Frequently when families visit our stores, the parents give the children a "budget" they can spend during the visit. For example, the children are told they can spend $10 or $25. Keeping this in mind, we develop merchandise assortments that accommodate different budgets. We have the inexpensive souvenir for the customer on a budget as well as products that would appeal more to the high-end shopper. We strive to have deep assortments in the categories we carry and offer products at a variety of price points.

I graduated from the University of Florida with a BSBA in marketing on a Friday and started working for Maas Brothers (now part of Macy's) on the following Monday. I have been working in the retail industry ever since. My first position was as a manager of the women's department. After about a year of working in the stores, I was promoted to a position in the buying office and eventually held senior merchandising leadership positions at Maas Brothers, Bealls Florida, HSN, and Goody's before joining Ron Jon.

I was attracted to retail because of family friends who were in the retail business. They both had worked for several large retailers, working their way up the ladder before starting their own businesses. After years in the business they still looked forward to the diversity and challenges that each new day presented. This has also been my experience. I truly look forward to coming to work each day. While each company I have worked for had a different culture and customer profile, the basics of retailing are the same: you have to serve your customers' needs.

Retailing is an industry that offers many daily challenges. Our business is not static and is constantly evolving and changing. For me that is what makes it fun and rewarding. We have to figure out what merchandise the customers want, manage the logistics of the merchandise flow, have efficient operations, provide outstanding customer service, and provide an exciting shopping environment for our customers.

The decisions examined in this textbook are directed toward facilitating exchanges between retailers and their customers. As discussed in Chapter 1, retailers offer a number of benefits to their customers, including making merchandise available to customers when they want it, at a convenient location, and in the quantities they want. In addition, retailers provide services, such as the opportunity for customers to see and try out merchandise before buying it. In exchange for these benefits, customers pay money for the merchandise and services provided by retailers.

The importance of pricing decisions is growing because today's customers have more alternatives to choose from and are better informed about the alternatives available in the marketplace. Thus, they are in a better position to seek a good value when they buy merchandise and services. **Value** is the ratio of what customers receive (the perceived benefit of the products and services offered by the retailer) to what they have to pay for it:

$$Value = \frac{Perceived\ benefits}{Price}$$

Retailers can increase value and stimulate more sales (exchanges) by either increasing the perceived benefits offered or reducing the price. To some customers, a good value means simply paying the lowest price because other benefits offered by retailers are not important to them. Others are willing to pay extra for additional benefits as long as they believe they're getting their money's worth in terms of product quality or service.

If retailers set prices higher than the benefits they provide, sales and profits will decrease. In contrast, if retailers set prices too low, their sales might increase but profits might decrease because of the lower profit margin. In addition to offering an attractive value to customers, retailers need to consider the value proposition offered by their competitors and legal restrictions related to pricing. Thus, setting the right price can be challenging.

The first section of this chapter examines two very different pricing strategies used by retailers. The factors retailers consider in setting retail prices are then reviewed. Then the actual process that retailers use to determine prices is described. The next section examines the reasons retailers reduce their prices when taking markdowns. The pricing techniques retailers use for increasing sales and profits are then examined. How the Internet and social and mobile channels have changed the way retailers price merchandise and communicate price to customers is then described. The chapter concludes with a discussion of the legal and ethical issues retailers should consider when making pricing decisions.

PRICING STRATEGIES

LO1

Explain the difference between a high/low pricing strategy and an everyday low-pricing strategy.

Retailers use two basic retail pricing strategies: high/low pricing and everyday low pricing. Each of these strategies and its advantages and disadvantages is discussed in this section.

High/Low Pricing

Retailers using a **high/low pricing strategy** frequently—often weekly—discount the initial prices for merchandise through sales promotions. However, some customers learn to expect frequent sales and simply wait until the merchandise they want goes on sale and then stock up at the low prices.

Everyday Low Pricing

Many retailers, particularly supermarkets, home improvement centers, and discount stores, have adopted an **everyday low-pricing (EDLP) strategy.** This strategy emphasizes the continuity of retail prices at a level somewhere between

The retailer on the left is using a high/low pricing strategy, whereas the one on the right is using an everyday low pricing strategy.

the regular nonsale price and the deep-discount sale price of high/low retailers. Although EDLP retailers embrace their consistent pricing strategy, they occasionally have sales, just not as frequently as their high/low competitors.

The term *everyday low pricing* is somewhat misleading because low doesn't mean "lowest." Although retailers using EDLP strive for low prices, they aren't always the lowest prices in the market. At any given time, a sale price at a high/low retailer may be the lowest price available in a market. Retailing View 14.1 highlights how a number of retailers have experimented with EDLP but have reversed their

RETAILING VIEW   Does Everyone Love an Everyday Low Price?   14.1

In light of the number of retail sales, many consumers are concerned that they are paying too much when they buy merchandise at full price. Thus, they wait for products to go on sale before they buy them. JCPenney's announcement that it would offer "fair and square pricing," issued through an extensive advertising campaign, reflects its attempt to revamp its image among consumers. It also hopes that by issuing straightforward prices, it can prevent or reverse the trend in which shoppers always wait for a sale before they buy. As part of this strategy, JCPenney is trying to eliminate coupons and reduce the number of annual sales from 600 to a more manageable number. By doing so, JCPenney is trying to emulate Walmart's longstanding everyday low-price strategy. However, JCPenney has realized that changing customer behaviors is difficult. As a result of the difficulties inherent in an implementing an EDLP strategy, especially after years of using a high/low strategy, JCPenney found it necessary to bring back sales events and highlight reference prices, such as Penney's everyday price, manufacturer's suggested list price, and prices elsewhere.

Lowe's built its business around EDLP but started offering more sales when the housing market began to sour. Recently, Lowe's has been dramatically cutting prices to compete with Home Depot. Lowe's is struggling to find the right balance between everyday low pricing and temporary promotional discounts. SteinMart similarly is cutting back on the number of coupons it offers, by 50 percent, while also lowering its regular prices. The Mango chain is simply dropping all prices by 20 percent. And both American Eagle Outfitters and Urban Outfitters are overhauling their pricing systems to get away from the glut of promotions they had been running.

Yet these retailers might want to examine their industries' recent history. Several years ago, when Macy's decided to slash the number of coupons it offered, customers revolted. Angered by the disappearance of their coveted clearance promotions, customers demanded their return, and within six months, Macy's relented. The same reaction might be in the works for these current price cutters.

EDLP is a hard sell for many customers. For example, America's Research Group found that almost 75 percent of consumers surveyed said it would take discounts of more than half-off to persuade them to purchase a product. Some retail experts say that retailers have to take responsibility for their customers' reluctance to give up their bargains. After all, the retailers started the vicious sale and promotion cycle, not their customers. Their customers will expect a lot in return—top-notch service or access to exclusive merchandise.

Sources: Anne D'Innocenzio, "Penney Brings Back the Big Discounts It Ditched Last Year in a Bid to Woo Back Shoppers," *Associated Press*, January 28, 2013; Anne D'Innocenzio, "Deal Junkies Hurt Stores' Profits," *Associated Press*, September 2, 2012; and Stephanie Clifford, "Knowing Cost, the Customer Sets the Price," *The New York Times*, March 27, 2012.

DISCUSSION QUESTION

Why might customers prefer EDLP pricing in one situation but like coupons and promotions in another?

strategies because of its implementation difficulties. To reinforce their EDLP strategy, many retailers have adopted a **low-price guarantee policy** that guarantees customers that the retailer will have the lowest price in a market for products it sells. The guarantee usually promises to match or beat any lower price found in the market and might include a provision to refund the difference between the seller's offer price and the lower price.

Advantages of the Pricing Strategies

The high/low pricing strategy has the following advantages:

- *Increases profits.* High/low pricing allows retailers to charge higher prices to customers who are not price-sensitive and will pay the "high" price and to charge lower prices to price-sensitive customers who will wait for the "low" sale price.
- *Creates excitement.* A "get them while they last" atmosphere often occurs during a sale. Sales draw a lot of customers, and a lot of customers create excitement. Some retailers augment low prices and advertising with special in-store activities, such as product demonstrations, giveaways, and celebrity appearances.
- *Sells slow moving merchandise.* Sales allow retailers to get rid of slow-selling merchandise by discounting the price.

The EDLP approach has its own advantages, as follows:

- *Assures customers of low prices.* Many customers are skeptical about initial retail prices. They have become conditioned to buying only on sale—the main characteristic of a high/low pricing strategy. The EDLP strategy lets customers know that they will get the same low prices every time they patronize the EDLP retailer. Customers do not have to read the ads and wait for items they want to go on sale.
- *Reduces advertising and operating expenses.* The stable prices caused by EDLP limit the need for the weekly-sale advertising used in the high/low strategy. In addition, EDLP retailers do not have to incur the labor costs of changing price tags and signs and putting up sale signs.
- *Reduces stockouts and improves inventory management.* The EDLP approach reduces the large variations in demand caused by frequent sales with large markdowns. As a result, retailers can manage their inventories with more certainty. Fewer stockouts mean more satisfied customers, resulting in higher sales. In addition, a more predictable customer demand pattern enables the retailer to improve inventory turnover by reducing the average inventory needed for special promotions and backup stock.

CONSIDERATIONS IN SETTING RETAIL PRICES

LO2

Identify the factors retailers consider when pricing their merchandise.

Four factors retailers consider in setting retail prices are: (1) the price sensitivity of consumers, (2) the cost of the merchandise, (3) competition, and (4) legal constraints. Legal constraints are discussed at the end of the chapter. The other considerations occur when setting prices for services and are discussed in this section.

Customer Price Sensitivity and Cost

Generally, as the price of a product increases, the sales for the product will decrease because fewer and fewer customers feel the product is a good value. The price sensitivity of customers determines how many units will be sold at different price levels. If customers in the target market are very price-sensitive, sales will decrease significantly when prices increase. If customers are not very price-sensitive, sales will not decrease significantly if the prices are increased.

One approach that can be used to measure the price sensitivity of customers is a price experiment. Consider the following situation: A restaurant chain wants to determine the best price for a new item, a riblet basket. It selects restaurants in the chain with very similar trade areas and sets prices at different levels in each of the restaurants for a week. Assume that the variable cost of the riblets is $5 per plate and the fixed cost of operating the restaurant for a week, the cost for rent, labor and energy, is $8,000.

The results of this experiment are shown in Exhibit 14–1. Notice in Exhibit 14–1a that as prices increase, the fixed costs remain the same, sales and variable costs both decrease, but sales decrease at a faster rate than variable costs (Exhibit 14–1b). So the

To determine the most profitable price for a riblet basket, a restaurant chain may set different prices at different locations.

Price Experiment   EXHIBIT 14–1

(a) Data from Price Experiment   EXHIBIT 14–1a

(1) Theater	(2) Price	(3) Quantity Sold	(4) Column (2) × Column (3) = Revenue	(5) Column (3) × $5 Variable Cost per Riblet Basket = Variable Cost	(6) Fixed Cost	(7) Column (4) − Column (5) − Column (6) = Contribution to Profit
1	$6.00	9,502	$57,012	$47,510	$8,000	$1,502
2	6.50	6,429	41,789	32,145	8,000	1,644
3	7.00	5,350	37,450	26,750	8,000	2,700
4	7.50	4,051	30,383	20,255	8,000	2,128
5	8.00	2,873	22,984	14,365	8,000	619
6	8.50	2,121	18,029	10,605	8,000	−577

EXHIBIT 14–1b
(b) Quantity Sold at Different Prices

EXHIBIT 14–1c
(c) Profit at Different Prices

highest profit level occurs at a $7 price (Exhibit 14–1c). If the restaurant considers only customers' price sensitivity and cost in setting prices, it would set the price for the riblet basket with these demand characteristics at $7 to maximize profits. Retailing View 14.2 highlights how showrooming and mobile apps are increasing consumers' price sensitivity.

14.2   RETAILING VIEW   Turning Showrooming on Its Head

The costs of maintaining a well-staffed, effectively inventoried, nicely decorated store are much higher than the costs of hosting a website. Accordingly, many retailers offer lower prices online than in stores, which leaves them at the mercy of a rapidly increasing trend: showrooming. **Showrooming** customers visit stores to touch and feel the available products or receive advice from expert salespeople, then purchase their preferred item from the firm's website, at a price lower than the store would charge, or even worse, from a competitor's website.

Amazon has embraced and encouraged this practice, naturally. Its price check app allows customers to scan bar codes in competing stores, and then provides them with Amazon's price for the same item. Best Buy has grown so frustrated with such efforts that it stopped posting manufacturers' bar codes on its shelf labels. But even without such an app, the ubiquity of smartphones makes it easy for customers to search for lower-priced alternatives for national-brand products online, at the very moment they are holding the product in their hand.

The solutions for retailers operating a store channel are varied. Some commentators suggest that multichannel retailers should embrace the trend and truly turn their stores into showrooms, encouraging buyers to use their websites to purchase. Retailers such as Walmart and The Container Store have expanded their offerings to appeal to potential showroomers, such as providing free shipping for items purchased in store or allowing customers to order online and then pay and pick up the items in stores. The latter option is particularly appealing for customers without credit or debit cards who need to pay cash for their purchases.

For retailers determined to fight the trend, the options focus mainly on branding and pricing choices. Showrooming can be reduced by placing more emphasis on store brands. Store brands are more difficult to compare on price because the exact same brand is not available from a competing retailer.

If the retailer can match prices in stores and online, it is less likely to lose price-sensitive customers. At the very least, stores must make sure their in-store prices are aligned with online competitors' price offerings. Alternatively, some stores seek to stock more unique merchandise that simply is not subject to price comparisons.

Finally, some stores have chosen to exploit the presence of mobile phones in other ways. By requiring customers to check-in at a store before they receive exclusive coupons, retailers draw coupon-loving shoppers into their locations. The same deals are not available

Amazon's price check app allows customers to scan bar codes in stores and then provides them with Amazon's price for the same item.

online, which means the store can circumvent the appeal of showrooming.

Sources: Suzy Sandberg, "4 Ways Retailers Can Fight Showrooming," *Mobile Commerce Daily*, March 15, 2012; Chantal Tode, "How to Leverage Mobile to Combat Showrooming," *Mobile Commerce Daily*, May 31, 2012; and Stephanie Clifford, "Luring Online Shoppers Offline," *The New York Times*, July 4, 2012.

DISCUSSION QUESTION

Which of the activities mentioned would be most effective to prevent you from showrooming?

Price Elasticity   A commonly used measure of price sensitivity is **price elasticity**, or the percentage change in quantity sold divided by the percentage change in price:

$$\text{Elasticity} = \frac{\text{Percentage change in quantity sold}}{\text{Percentage change in price}}$$

Assume that a retailer originally priced a private-label DVD player at $90 and then raised the price to $100. Before raising the price, the retailer was selling 1,500 units a week. When the price increased, sales dropped to 1,100 units per week. The calculation of the price elasticity is as follows:

$$\begin{aligned}
\text{Elasticity} &= \frac{\text{Percentage change in quantity sold}}{\text{Percentage change in price}} \\
&= \frac{(\text{New quantity sold} - \text{Old quantity sold}) \div (\text{Old quantity sold})}{(\text{New price} - \text{Old price}) \div (\text{Old price})} \\
&= \frac{(1100 - 1500)/1500}{(10 - 9)/9} = \frac{-0.2667}{.1111} = -2.4005
\end{aligned}$$

Because the quantity sold usually decreases when prices increase, price elasticity is a negative number.

The target market for a product is generally viewed to be price-insensitive (referred to as **inelastic**) when its price elasticity is more positive than -1.0 (e.g., -0.50)—that is, when a 1 percent decrease in price results in a 1/2 percent increase in quantity sold. The target market for a product is price-sensitive (referred to as **elastic**) when the price elasticity is more negative than -1 (e.g., -2.0), that is, when a 1 percent decrease in price produces a 2 percent increase in quantity sold. The price elasticity for a product can be estimated by conducting an experiment as described previously or by using statistical techniques to analyze how sales have changed in the past when prices changed.

Various factors affect the price sensitivity for a product. First, the more substitutes a product or service has, the more likely it is to be price-elastic (sensitive). For example, there are many alternatives for a riblet basket at a restaurant like Applebee's, and thus fast-food prices are typically price-elastic, but branded luxury goods have almost no substitutes and are price-inelastic (insensitive). Second, products and services that are necessities are price-inelastic. Thus, medical care is price-inelastic, whereas airline tickets for a vacation are price-elastic. Third, products that are expensive relative to a consumer's income are price-elastic. Thus, cars are price-elastic, and books and movie tickets tend to be price-inelastic. The estimated elasticities for some commonly purchased items are shown in the following table.[1]

	PRICE ELASTICITY	
Product Class	Short Run	Long Run
Clothing	-0.90	-2.90
Wine	-0.88	-1.17
Jewelry and watches	-0.44	-0.67
Gasoline	-0.20	-0.60

On the basis of these estimates, a 1 percent decrease in the price of clothing would result in only a 0.9 percent increase in the quantity sold in the short run but a 2.9 percent increase in the long run. So, if you must have that new sweater today, you are much less responsive to a low price than you would be if you could wait for the sweater to be on sale three months from now. In contrast, Americans aren't going to change their gasoline purchases much in the short or long run, regardless of slight price decreases or increases. However, these elasticity estimates are based on relatively small changes in prices and might be different for large price changes.

For products with price elasticities less than 1, the price that maximizes profits can be determined by the following formula:

$$\text{Profit-maximizing price} = \frac{\text{Price elasticity} \times \text{Cost}}{\text{Price elasticity} + 1}$$

So, if the private-label DVD player described in the preceding example costs $50, the profit-maximizing price would be:

$$\text{Profit-maximizing price} = \frac{\text{Price elasticity} \times \text{Cost}}{\text{Price elasticity} + 1}$$

$$= \frac{-2.4005 \times \$50}{-2.4005 + 1} = \$85.70$$

Competition

Consumers have lots of choices for goods and services, and they typically search for the best value. Retailers therefore need to consider competitors' prices when setting their own. The previous discussion about setting price on the basis of customer price sensitivity (elasticity) ignores the effects of competitors' prices. For example, assume the restaurant chain that conducted the experiment had a $7.50 price for the riblet basket and, following the results of its experiment, dropped its price to $7 to increase sales and profits. If the increased sales occurred, other restaurant chains would see a decline in their sales and react by dropping their prices to $7, and the experimenting restaurant chain might not realize the sales and profit increases it anticipated. Retailing View 14.3 examines the impact of intense price competition among the big discounters.

Retailers can price above, below, or at parity with the competition. The chosen pricing policy must be consistent with the retailer's overall strategy and its relative market position. Consider, for instance, Walmart and Tiffany and Co. Walmart tries to price the products it sells below its competition. Tiffany, in contrast, offers significant benefits to its customers beyond just the merchandise. Its brand name and customer service assure customers that they will be satisfied with the jewelry they purchase. Due to the unique nature of its offering, Tiffany is able to set its prices higher than those of competitors.

Collecting and Using Competitive Price Data   Most retailers routinely collect price data about their competitors to see if they need to adjust their prices to remain competitive. Competitive price data are typically collected using store personnel, but pricing data also are available from business service providers such as The Nielsen Company and SymphonyIRI.

Pricing Strategies Used by Services Retailers

Additional issues that need to be considered when pricing services are (1) the need to match supply and demand and (2) the difficulties customers have in determining service quality.[2]

Matching Supply and Demand   Services are intangible and thus cannot be inventoried. When retailers are selling products, if the products don't sell one day, they can be stored and sold the next day. However, when a plane departs with empty seats or a play is performed without a full house, the potential revenue from the unused capacity is lost forever. In addition, most services have limited capacity. For example,

Airlines use yield management to adjust prices in response to demand.

RETAILING VIEW   The Big Discounters' Pure Price Competition   14.3

Although Target might try to tempt customers with designer-named brands, and Walmart might promise green practices, when it comes down to consumer choice between these two discount store giants, the store that offers the lowest prices will probably win in the long run. In this battle, Walmart has won the price competition battle most of the time. As the self-professed leader of everyday low pricing, Walmart has tended to beat Target's price on a typical basket of 150 similar goods.

But a recent comparison showed that Target was victorious—it was 0.46 percentage point less expensive. That is, had the basket cost $100, Target shoppers would have saved 46 cents over Walmart shoppers. This cost margin also was the widest one found in nearly two years. Considering such incredibly slim margins, does the comparison really matter?

Because of the stores' promises to customers, it does. Discounters struggle to attract price-conscious customers while also protecting their market from increasing competition from online retailers such as Amazon. Both Target and Walmart claim in their well-known slogans that customers can "Expect More. Pay Less" or "Save Money. Live Better." The one that gets to show that it really does live up to this slogan better than the other is likely to be the one customers prefer.

At the same time, another study suggested that for parents seeking back-to-school supplies for their children, the best prices were neither at Walmart nor Target. For that type of merchandise, they would have to visit a store that isn't even a discounter: Office Depot.

Target is reinforcing its low prices by highlighting its price match guarantee.

Sources: Matt Townsend and David Welch, "Target Cheaper Than Wal-Mart as Gap Widest in Two Years," *Bloomberg News*, August 23, 2012; Brad Tuttle, "Target Battles Walmart for Low-Price Supremacy," *Time*, August 27, 2012; and David Welch, "Target Undercuts Wal-Mart on Price," *Star Tribune*, August 23, 2012.

DISCUSSION QUESTIONS

Which retailer do you prefer—Walmart, Target, or Amazon? Do you shop there because you think it has the lowest prices?

restaurants are limited in the number of customers that can be seated. Due to capacity constraints, services retailers might encounter situations in which they cannot realize as many sales as they could make.

To maximize sales and profits, many services retailers engage in yield management.[3] **Yield management** is the practice of adjusting prices up or down in response to demand to control the sales generated. Airlines are masters at yield management. Using sophisticated computer programs, they monitor the reservations and ticket sales for each flight and adjust prices according to capacity utilization. Prices are lowered on flights when sales are below forecasts and there is significant excess capacity. As ticket sales approach capacity, prices are increased.

Other services retailers use less sophisticated approaches to match supply and demand. For example, more people want to go to a restaurant for dinner or see a movie at 7 p.m. than at 5 p.m. Restaurants and movie theaters thus might not be able to satisfy the demand for their services at 7 p.m. but have excess capacity at 5 p.m. Therefore, restaurants and movie theaters often price their services lower for customers who use them at 5 p.m. rather than 7 p.m. in an effort to shift demand from 7 p.m. to 5 p.m.

Theaters use a variety of strategies to try to ensure that the seats are sold and that they are sold at prices equivalent to what customers are willing to pay.

Targeted direct mail coupons are often used when a play opens, and two-for-one tickets are introduced about halfway through the run. In some cities, like New York and Boston, theaters partner with half-price ticket brokers, which sell unsold tickets for 50 percent off the ticket price but only for performances on the same day.

Determining Service Quality   Due to the intangibility of services, it is often difficult for customers to assess service quality, especially when other information is not available.[4] Thus, if consumers are unfamiliar with a service or service provider, they may use price to make quality judgments. For example, most consumers have limited information about lawyers and the quality of legal advice they offer. They may, therefore, base their assessment of the quality of legal services offered on the fees they charge. They may also use other nondiagnostic cues to assess quality, such as the size and décor of the lawyer's office.

Another factor that increases the dependence on price as a quality indicator is the risk associated with a service purchase. Higher-risk situations tend to arise in relation to credence services—legal or medical services, even hair salons—for which the customer may need price to provide a surrogate for quality.

Because customers depend on price as a cue of quality and because price creates expectations of quality, service prices must be determined carefully. In addition to being chosen to manage capacity, prices must be set to convey the appropriate quality signal. Pricing too low can lead to inaccurate inferences about the quality of the service. Pricing too high can set expectations that may be difficult to match in service delivery.

SETTING RETAIL PRICES

LO3

Describe how retailers set prices.

As described in the previous section, theoretically, retailers maximize their profits by setting prices on the basis of the price sensitivity of customers and the cost of merchandise. One limitation of just using price sensitivity and cost for setting prices is that doing so fails to consider the prices being charged by competitors. Another problem is that implementing this approach requires knowledge of the price sensitivity (price elasticity) of each item. Many retailers have to set prices for more than 50,000 SKUs and make thousands of pricing decisions each month. From a practical perspective, they cannot conduct experiments or do statistical analyses to determine the price sensitivity for each item.

Setting Prices Based on Costs

Most retailers set price by marking up the item's cost to yield a profitable gross margin. Then, this initial price is adjusted on the basis of insights about customer price sensitivity and competitive pricing. The following section describes how retailers typically set prices solely on the basis of merchandise cost.

Retail Price and Markup   When setting prices on the basis of merchandise cost, retailers start with the following equation:

Retail price = Cost of merchandise + Markup

The **markup** is the difference between the retail price and the cost of an item. Thus, if a sporting goods retailer buys a tennis racket for $75 and sets the retail price at $125, the markup is $50. The appropriate markup is the amount that covers all of the retailer's operating expenses (labor costs, rent, utilities, advertising, etc.) incurred to sell the merchandise and produces a profit for the retailer.

The **markup percentage** is the markup as a percentage of the retail price:

$$\text{Markup percentage} = \frac{\text{Retail price} - \text{Cost of merchandise}}{\text{Retail price}}$$

Thus, the markup percentage for the tennis racket is:

$$\text{Markup percentage} = \frac{\$125 - \$75}{\$125} = 40\%$$

The retail price based on the cost and markup percentage is:

$$\begin{aligned}
\text{Retail price} &= \text{Cost of merchandise} + \text{Markup} \\
&= \text{Cost of merchandise} + \text{Retail price} \times \text{Markup percentage} \\
&= \frac{\text{Cost of merchandise}}{1 - \text{Markup percentage (as a fraction)}}
\end{aligned}$$

Thus, if a buyer for an office supply category specialist purchases calculators at $14 and needs a 30 percent markup to meet the financial goals for the category, the retail price needs to be:

$$\text{Retail price} = \frac{\text{Cost}}{1 - \text{Markup percentage}} = \frac{\$14.00}{1 - 0.30} = \$20$$

For instance, if an apparel retailer used a 50 percent markup, an approach referred to as **keystoning,** the retail price would be double the cost.

Initial Markup and Maintained Markup   The previous discussion is based on the assumption that the retailer sells all items at an initially set price. However, retailers rarely sell all items at the initial price. They frequently reduce the price of items for special promotions or to get rid of excess inventory at the end of a season. In addition, discounts are given to employees, and some merchandise is lost to theft and accounting errors (**inventory shrinkage**). These factors that reduce the actual selling price from the initial sales price are called **reductions.** Thus, there is a difference between the initial markup and the maintained markup.

The **initial markup** is the retail selling price initially set for the merchandise minus the cost of the merchandise. The **maintained markup** is the actual sales realized for the merchandise minus its costs. It is the amount of profit realized from merchandising decisions.

Thus, the maintained markup is conceptually similar to the gross margin, but slightly different. Some retailers have workroom costs, such as alterations of a suit or assembly of a bicycle, that would reduce the maintained markup compared with the gross margin. Retailers often receive cash discounts from vendors for paying invoices early, which increase the maintained markup compared with the gross margin. Because workroom costs and cash discounts are not typically under the buyer's control, they are accounted for separately. To summarize:

$$\text{Gross margin percentage} = \frac{\text{Maintained markup} - \text{Workroom costs} + \text{Cash discounts}}{\text{Net sales}}$$

The difference between the initial and maintained markups is illustrated in Exhibit 14–2. The item illustrated costs $0.60, and the initial price for the item is $1.00, so the initial markup is $0.40 and the initial markup percentage is 40 percent. However, the average actual sale price for the item is $0.90. The reductions are $0.10, so the maintained markup is $0.30 and the maintained markup percentage is 33 percent (0.30/0.90).

The relationship between the initial and maintained markup percentages is:

$$\text{Initial markup percentage} = \frac{\begin{array}{c}\text{Maintained markup percentage} \\ \text{(as a percentage of planned} \\ \text{actual sales)}\end{array} + \begin{array}{c}\text{Percent reductions} \\ \text{(as a percentage of planned} \\ \text{actual sales)}\end{array}}{100\% + \begin{array}{c}\text{Percent reductions} \\ \text{(as a percentage of planned} \\ \text{actual sales)}\end{array}}$$

EXHIBIT 14–2
Difference between
Initial Markup and
Maintained Markup

Thus, if the buyer setting the price for the item shown in Exhibit 14–2 planned on reductions of 10 percent of actual sales and wanted a maintained markup of 33 percent, the initial markup should be:

$$\text{Initial markup percentage} = \frac{33\% + (\$0.10/\$0.90 = 11.111\%)}{100\% + 11.111\%} = 40\%$$

and the initial retail price should be:

$$\text{Initial retail price} = \frac{\text{Cost}}{1 - \text{Initial markup percentage}} = \frac{\$0.60}{1 - 0.40} = \$1.00$$

Pricing Optimization Software

Setting prices by simply marking up the merchandise cost neglects a number of other factors that retailers need to consider, such as price sensitivities, competition, and the sales of complementary products. Since the early 2000s, many retailers have taken a comprehensive approach to setting prices that uses **pricing optimization software.** The software programs use a set of algorithms that analyze past and current merchandise sales and prices, as well as competitors' prices; estimate the relationship between prices and sales generated; and then determine the optimal (most profitable) initial price for the merchandise and the appropriate size and timing of markdowns. Optimization can be accomplished at the store level and even sometimes at the individual customer level, which is very useful for creating loyalty and behavioral intentions.

To set initial prices, the software uses historical sales data from its own and competitors' stores. It determines the price–sales relationship of complementary items—those that have a similar sales pattern, such as Pepsi and Lays Potato Chips. Thus, not only can the software tell buyers the best price for Pepsi, but it also suggests a price for the chips. Buyers can also determine how much Pepsi they will sell at a given price if they lower the price of Coke or their private-label (or store) brand. The software can incorporate other factors, such as the store's image (e.g., cheap or premium price), where the nearest rival is located, seasonal factors (e.g., soft drinks sell better in the summer than in the winter), or whether an item is featured in coupons.[5] It can set decision rules, such as optimizing the regular price to never be more than a nickel above a competitor's price. Or the software might suggest offering a very competitive price on products for which customers are very sensitive, such as milk or diapers, but take a larger margin on less price-sensitive items, such as baby accessories and store brands.[6] Merchandising optimization software can be expensive, but its use can have an impressive impact on bottom-line profitability. For instance, the Walgreens-owned and New York City–based Duane Reade pharmacy chain used merchandising optimization software to boost its sales of diapers.[7] The chain had tried discounts and coupons, but the category was losing ground to the competition. The software indicated that the markup should be a function of the age of the child for whom parents were buying diapers. For newborn sizes, Duane Reade raised prices, but once the child got to the training pants stage, it offered lower unit prices. A year later, Duane Reade's revenues in the baby care category had jumped 27 percent, with gross margin increases of 2 percent. With a traditional analysis, the chain was unlikely to ever guess that brand-new parents exhibit little price sensitivity, compared with parents who have been at it a while.

Profit Impact of Setting a Retail Price: The Use of Break-Even Analysis

Retailers often want to know the number of units they need sell to begin making a profit. For example, a retailer might want to know:

- Break-even sales to generate a target profit.
- Break-even volume and dollars to justify introducing a new product, product line, or department.
- Break-even sales change needed to cover a price change.

A useful analytical tool for making these assessments is **break-even analysis**, which determines, on the basis of fixed and variable costs, how much merchandise needs to be sold to achieve a break-even (zero) profit.

The **break-even point quantity** is the quantity at which total revenue equals total cost, and then profit occurs for additional sales.

The formula for calculating the sales quantity needed to break even is:

$$\text{Break-even quantity} = \frac{\text{Total fixed costs}}{\text{Actual unit sales price} - \text{Unit variable cost}}$$

The following examples illustrate the use of this formula in determining the break-even volume of a new private-label product and the break-even change in volume needed to cover a price change.

Calculating Break-Even for a New Product   Hypothetically, PetSmart is considering an introduction of a new private-label, dry dog food targeting owners of older dogs. The cost of developing this dog food is $700,000, including salaries for the design team and costs of testing the product. Because these costs do not change with the quantity of product produced and sold, they're known as **fixed costs.** PetSmart plans to sell the dog food for $12 a bag—the unit price. The **variable cost** is the retailer's expenses that vary directly with the quantity of product produced and sold. Variable costs often include direct labor and materials used in producing the product. PetSmart will be purchasing the product from a private-label manufacturer. Thus, the only variable cost is the dog food's cost, $5, from the private-label manufacturer.

$$\text{Break-even quantity} = \frac{\text{Fixed costs}}{\text{Actual unit sales price} - \text{Unit variable cost}}$$

$$= \frac{\$700,000}{\$12 - \$5} = 100,000 \text{ bags}$$

Thus, PetSmart needs to sell 100,000 bags of dog food to break even, or make zero profit, and for every additional bag sold, it will make $7 profit.

Now assume that PetSmart wants to make $100,000 profit from the new product line. The break-even quantity now becomes:

$$\text{Break-even quantity} = \frac{\text{Fixed cost}}{\text{Actual unit sales price} - \text{Unit variable cost}}$$

$$= \frac{\$700,000 + \$100,000}{\$12 - \$5} = 114,286 \text{ bags}$$

Calculating Break-Even Sales An issue closely related to the calculation of a break-even point is determining how much unit sales would have to increase to make a profit from a price cut or how much sales would have to decline to make a price increase unprofitable. Continuing with the PetSmart example, assume the break-even quantity is 114,286 units, based on the $700,000 fixed cost, the $100,000 profit, a selling price of $12, and a cost of $5. Now PetSmart is considering lowering the price of a bag of dog food to $10. How many units must it sell to break even if it lowers its selling price by 16.67 percent, to $10? Using the formula,

$$\text{Break-even quantity} = \frac{\text{Fixed cost}}{\text{Actual unit sales price} - \text{Unit variable cost}}$$

$$= \frac{\$700,000 + \$100,000}{\$10 - \$5} = 160,000 \text{ bags}$$

So, if PetSmart decreases its price by 16.67 percent, from $12 to $10, unit sales must increase by 40 percent: $(160,000 - 114,286) \div 114,286$.

MARKDOWNS

LO4

Examine how and why retailers take markdowns.

REFACT

During difficult economic times, if a brand lowers its prices, 70 percent of consumers believe "the brand is normally overpriced," and 62 percent think "the product is old, about to expire or about to be updated, and the company is trying to get rid of it to make room for the new stuff." When a brand does not lower its prices during tough times, 64 percent believe "the product is extremely popular," and another 64 percent assume "the product is already a good value."[8]

REFACT

Some vendors, such as Gucci, Cartier, and Christian Louboutin, have become so concerned with protecting their images that they require that some of their retailers exclude their products from certain markdown sales events.[9]

The preceding section reviewed how retailers initially set prices on the basis of the merchandise cost and desired maintained margin. However, retailers also take **markdowns** by reducing the initial retail price. This section examines why retailers take markdowns, how they optimize markdown decisions, how they reduce the amount of markdowns, and how they liquidate markdown merchandise.

Reasons for Taking Markdowns

Retailers' reasons for taking markdowns can be classified as either clearance (to dispose of merchandise) or promotional (to generate sales). Clearance markdowns are examined in this section, while promotional markdowns are discussed later in this chapter as a method of increasing sales and profits.

When merchandise is selling at a slower rate than planned and will become obsolete at the end of its season, or is priced higher than competitors' goods, buyers generally mark it down for clearance purposes. As discussed in Chapter 12, slow-selling merchandise decreases inventory turnover; prevents buyers from acquiring new, better-selling merchandise; and can diminish the retailer's image for selling the most current styles and trends.

Markdowns are part of the cost of doing business, and thus buyers plan for them. They tend to order more fashion merchandise than they forecast actually selling because they are more concerned about under-ordering and stocking out of a popular item before the end of the season than about over-ordering and having to discount excess merchandise at the end of the season. Stocking out of popular merchandise can have a detrimental effect on a fashion retailer's image, whereas discounting merchandise at the end of the season just reduces maintained markup.

Thus, a buyer's objective isn't to minimize markdowns. If markdowns are too low, the buyer is probably pricing the merchandise too low, not purchasing enough merchandise, or not taking enough risks with the merchandise being purchased. Thus, buyers set the initial markup price high enough that even after markdowns and other reductions have been taken, the planned maintained markup is still achieved.

Optimizing Markdown Decisions Retailers have traditionally created a set of arbitrary rules for taking markdowns to dispose of unwanted merchandise. One retailer, for instance, identifies markdown candidates when its weekly sell-through percentages fall below a certain level. Another retailer cuts prices on the basis of

The output from the Oracle Retail markdown model indicates that the model's recommended markdown of $18.95 will result in more than $5,000 greater profit than the buyer's planned markdown of $22.95.

how long the merchandise has been in the store—marking products down by 20 percent after 8 weeks, then by 30 percent after 12 weeks, and finally by 50 percent after 16 weeks. Such a rule-based approach, however, is limiting because it does not consider the demand for the merchandise at different price points or in different locations and thus produces less-than-optimal profits.

The optimization software described previously in this chapter, used to set initial retail prices, can also indicate when to take markdowns and how much they should be in different locations.[10] It works by continually updating its pricing forecasts on the basis of actual sales throughout the season and factoring in differences in price sensitivities. For example, the software recognizes that in early November, a winter item's sales are better than expected in Colorado, so it delays taking a markdown that had been planned but takes the markdown in New England. Each week, as new sales data become available, it readjusts the forecasts to include the latest information. It computes literally thousands of scenarios for each item—a process that is too complicated and time-consuming for buyers to do on their own. It then evaluates the outcomes on the basis of expected profits and other factors and selects the action that produces the best results across all regions.

Reducing the Amount of Markdowns

Retailers have several options for reducing the amount of markdowns. They can work closely with vendors to choose merchandise and coordinate deliveries to help reduce the financial burden of taking markdowns. They can also buy smaller quantities to make it easier to forecast demand for a shorter time period and create a feeling of scarcity. Finally, retailers can strive to offer a good value.

Vendors have a partnering relationship with their retailers and thus a vested interest in their success. Vendors that are knowledgeable about the

Pricing optimization software recognizes when sales for winter coats are slower than expected and suggests both the timing and amount of markdowns.

market and competition can help with stock selections. Of course, a retailer must also trust its own taste and intuition; otherwise, its store will have the same merchandise as all other stores. As discussed in Chapter 13, buyers can often obtain markdown money—funds a vendor gives the retailer to cover lost gross margin dollars that result from markdowns and other merchandising issues.

Another method of reducing markdowns is to buy smaller quantities.[11] By adopting a just-in-time inventory policy, in which small amounts of merchandise arrive just in time to be sold, customers perceive a scarcity and purchase at full price. (See Chapter 13 for more on this strategy.) Creating a feeling of scarcity among customers is an excellent method of reducing markdowns. Even if there are adequate quantities of merchandise available in the stockroom or in a distribution center, displaying just a few items on the sales floor sends a signal to the customer to "buy them now, while they last!" If retailers simply change their displays frequently, customers will perceive that the merchandise is new and available in limited quantities.

When customers believe that a particular retailer offers them a good value, they will be less likely to wait for markdowns. An everyday low-price strategy implies that a retailer's products are already at low prices and therefore will not be further discounted. Zara and H&M don't need to advertise their low prices. Loyal customers return time after time to look for low-priced treasures. A few retailers, like Apple, focus on quality and image and therefore simply don't have sales! It is an enviable position, to which most retailers can only aspire.

Liquidating Markdown Merchandise   Even with the best planning, some merchandise may remain unsold at the end of a season. Retailers use one of six strategies to liquidate this unsold merchandise.

Sell to Another Retailer   Selling the unsold merchandise to another retailer is a very popular strategy among retailers. For instance, off-price retailers such as TJX Corporation (owners of TJ Maxx and Marshalls) and Bluefly.com purchase end-of-season merchandise from other retailers and sell it at deep discounts. However, this approach for liquidating unsold merchandise only enables retailers to recoup a small percentage of the merchandise's cost—often a mere 10 percent.

Consolidate Unsold Merchandise   Markdown merchandise can be consolidated in a number of ways. First, the consolidation can be made into one or a few of the retailer's regular locations. Second, markdown merchandise can be consolidated into another retail chain or an outlet store under the same ownership. Saks Fifth Avenue OFF Fifth, Nordstrom Rack, and Neiman Marcus Last Call Clearance Center each use this approach. Third, unsold merchandise can be shipped to a distribution center or a rented space such as a convention center for final sale. However, consolidation sales can be complex and expensive due to the extra transportation and record keeping involved.

Sell at Internet Auction   The Internet is increasingly useful for liquidating unsold merchandise. For example, an electronics store might utilize eBay to sell goods it has received from trade-ins. Many retailers have separate areas of their websites for clearance merchandise.

Return to Vendor   Some large retailers have enough clout to negotiate an agreement that some merchandise be returned to vendors. Although an outstanding option, it is not generally viable unless the balance of power rests solidly with the retailer.

Donate to Charity   Donating clearance merchandise to charities is a common practice. Charitable giving is always a good corporate practice. It is a way of giving back to the community and has strong public relations benefits. Also, the cost value of the merchandise can be deducted from income, thus reducing the firm's tax liability.

Carry the Merchandise Over to the Next Season   The final liquidation approach—to carry merchandise over to the next season—is used with relatively high-priced nonfashion merchandise, such as traditional men's clothing and furniture. Generally, however, it is not profitable to carry over merchandise because of excessive inventory carrying costs and the potential of having the merchandise look "shopworn" or outdated.

PRICING TECHNIQUES FOR INCREASING SALES AND PROFITS

This section reviews several techniques used by retailers to increase sales and profits. The first is variable pricing, in which retailers charge different prices to different customers. The other techniques—dealing with perceptions of fairness, leader pricing, price lining, and odd pricing—take advantage of the way customers process information. The section concludes with a discussion of how the Internet has changed the way retailers and their customers make pricing decisions.

LO5

Identify the pricing techniques retailers use to increase sales and profits.

Variable Pricing and Price Discrimination

Retailers use a variety of techniques to maximize profits by charging different prices to different customers.

Individualized Variable Pricing   Ideally, retailers could maximize their profits if they charged each customer as much as the customer was willing to pay. For instance, if a wealthy, price-insensitive customer wants to buy a new car battery, AutoZone would like to price the battery at $200 but then price the same battery at $125 to make a sale to a more price-sensitive, lower-income customer. Charging each individual customer a different price based on their willingness to pay is called **first-degree price discrimination**.[12]

REFACT

The most expensive charity auction ever on eBay was for a lunch with Warren Buffett, the CEO of investment company Berkshire Hathaway. The anonymous winner paid $2.6 million.[13]

Pricing merchandise through auction bidding is an example of first-degree price discrimination. A retailer offering a Rolls Royce on eBay Motors maximizes its profits because the customer with the highest willingness to pay bids and pays the highest price.

Although individualized variable pricing is legal and widely used in some retail sectors, such as automobile and antique dealers, it is not very practical in most retail stores. First, it is difficult to assess each customer's willingness to pay; second, retailers cannot change the posted prices in stores as customers with different willingness to pay enter the store. In addition, customers might feel they are being

By selling on eBay Motors' online auction, this seller is using first-degree price discrimination to get the highest price for this Rolls Royce.

treated unfairly if they realize that they are being charged a higher price than other customers. Staples, however, uses individualized variable pricing at the point-of-sale as a strategic differentiator. The best loyalty program customers receive different (lower) prices than "regular" customers. When these loyal customers swipe their cards, the point-of-sale system automatically re-prices the items in that shopper's basket. No one other than Staples and the customer knows—certainly not the next person in line or the competition.[14]

Now, more and more retailers have started to use sophisticated models that allow them to increase the frequency of updating their prices and the ability to implement the price changes throughout the chain. The prices are driven by changes in demand and supply and price elasticities and takes into account localized market issues. A limitation of these models tends to be the fact that the input is historical data, which may reduce their predictive ability.[15]

Retailers have increased their use of dynamic pricing techniques due to the information that is available from point-of-sale data collected on Internet purchases and in stores. **Dynamic pricing,** also known as **individualized pricing,** refers to the process of charging different prices for goods or services based on the type of customer, time of the day, week, or even season, and level of demand. Retailers may also charge customers different prices based on their loyalty status derived from their CRM systems—that is, platinum customers receive lower prices than silver ones. Early adopters of dynamic pricing techniques were service retailers, such as airlines, hotels, and cruises lines. It is quite common for passengers on the same plane to have paid different fares depending on when they bought their ticket. The ease of using dynamic pricing when selling merchandise on the Internet is much greater than in a store because only one person sees the price. Retailing View 14.4 highlights how some retailers are using dynamic pricing.

14.4 RETAILING VIEW Just What Makes Dynamic Pricing So Appealing?

Today, it is easier for retailers using an Internet channel to change their online prices than the prices in their physical stores. These retailers are using software that allows them to adjust prices the moment it finds a competitor selling the same item for a lower (or higher) price. As an example, in one day Amazon changed the price of a single microwave oven nine times. If buyers happened to be shopping at the right time or had the right characteristics, they might have gotten a lower price. Those shopping an hour later or having different characteristics probably paid a higher price.

Such price shifts are familiar to travelers: Buying an airline ticket on a Tuesday is often cheaper than buying the exact same flight on a Saturday. Consumers' sense that such tactics are unfair led to the unique selling proposition of Orbitz, which promises that if another customer books the same flight for less, it will refund a higher-price-point customer the difference.

In some cases, online retailers are less interested in the actual price than in what the lowest price does for them. By ensuring they have a lower price than any other competitor—even if just by a cent or two—a retailer earns the top rank in a price comparison search engine. Also, if they find that all their competitors are charging higher prices, retailers learn that they can bump up their own

price and margins, without losing customers. Thus the increasing use of dynamic prices appears largely driven by the upside profit potential—being higher in the online search ranking enables them to sell more and charge higher prices.

Customers may not embrace retailers that use dynamic pricing. Charging different prices according to the time of day or the identity of the shopper is not illegal, but a survey showed that 87 percent of people thought it should be. If consumers find these changing rules, prices, and methods irritating, tiresome, or unfair, they may choose to avoid retailers that engage in dynamic pricing.

Sources: Julia Angwin and Dana Mattioli, "Coming Soon: Toilet Paper Priced Like Airline Tickets," *The Wall Street Journal,* September 5, 2012; Gilon Miller, "How Online Dynamic Pricing Can Hurt Retailers and Consumers," *UpsteamCommerce.com,* September 11, 2012; Laura Gunderson, "Amazon's 'Dynamic' Prices Get Some Static," *The Oregonian,* May 5, 2012; and Susan Reda, "Pricing Transparency," *Stores,* February 2012.

DISCUSSION QUESTION

Would you patronize a retailer that used dynamic pricing?

Self-Selected Variable Pricing   An alternative approach for dynamic pricing is to offer the same multiple-price schedule to all customers, which encourages price-sensitive customers to take advantage of the lower price. This approach is referred to as **second-degree price discrimination.** Retailers use second-degree price discrimination when they offer promotional and clearance markdowns, coupons, price bundling, and multi-unit pricing.

Promotional Markdowns   Retailers employ promotional markdowns to promote merchandise and increase sales. Markdowns can increase customer traffic flow. Retailers plan promotions in which they take markdowns for holidays, for special events, and as part of their overall promotional program. Retailers hope that customers will purchase other products at regular prices while they're in the store. Another opportunity created by promotional markdowns is to increase the sale of complementary products. For example, a supermarket's markdown on hot-dog buns may be offset by increased demand for hotdogs, mustard, and relish—all sold at regular prices.

Clearance Markdowns for Fashion Merchandise   While the discussion of clearance markdowns earlier in the chapter focused primarily on how retailers get rid of unwanted merchandise, this merchandise can also be used to attract different market segments based on their degree of price sensitivity. Fashion-conscious customers who have a high willingness to pay because they want to be the first to wear the latest fashions self-select to pay higher prices. More price-sensitive customers wait to buy the merchandise at the end of the season when prices are lower.

Coupons   **Coupons** offer a discount on the price of specific items when they're purchased. Coupons are issued by manufacturers and retailers in newspapers, on products, on the shelf, at the cash register, over the Internet and mobile devices, and through the mail. Retailers use coupons because they are thought to induce customers to try products for the first time, convert first-time users to regular users, encourage large purchases, increase usage, instill loyalty, and protect market share against the competition. Coupons are an attractive way to target price-sensitive customers because they will likely expend the extra effort to collect and redeem coupons, whereas price-insensitive customers will not. Retailers are increasingly concerned about the growth of extreme couponing (see Retailing View 14.5).

Price Bundling   **Price bundling** is the practice of offering two or more different products or services for sale at one price.[17] For instance, McDonald's offers a bundle of a sandwich, French fries, and a soft drink in a Value Meal at a discount compared with buying the items individually. Price bundling increases both unit and dollar sales by increasing the amount of merchandise bought during a store visit. The practice is an example of second-degree price discrimination because it offers more price-sensitive customers a lower-priced alternative.

Multiple-Unit Pricing   The term **multiple-unit pricing,** or **quantity discounts,** refers to the practice of offering two or more similar products or services for sale at one lower total price. For example, a convenience store may sell three one-liter bottles of soda for $2.39 when the price for a single one-liter bottle is 99 cents—a saving of 58 cents. Like price bundling, this variable-pricing approach is used to increase sales

McDonald's uses price bundling when it combines a sandwich, French fries, and a soft drink in a Value Meal.

14.5   RETAILING VIEW   Moving Beyond Extreme Couponing

Initially presented as a somewhat odd and possibly compulsive behavior on TV shows such as *Extreme Couponing*, the practice of relying heavily on coupons for a household's grocery purchases has gone mainstream. Increasing rates of heavy use of coupons by customers challenges retailers, especially in their supply chains. If a single extreme couponer buys out all of the store's stock on a particular SKU, other customers are bound to be frustrated.

In response, several grocers and drugstore chains have implemented limits on coupon redemptions. Rite Aid limits the number of coupons any one customer may use in one trip. Kroger has banned stacking, which is when a customer combines paper and online coupons for a given item. Walmart rings up multiple coupon purchases separately, creating more inconvenience for extreme couponers.

Yet as these brick-and-mortar stores work to mitigate the impacts of coupon use, online merchants are ramping up their offers. Foursquare introduced a targeted couponing extension to its service. With it, businesses can offer impressive coupons, but only to those Foursquare users who check in to their location. As Amazon continues its efforts to provide virtually everything a household might need, it has added manufacturers' coupons to its site. Thus, if a shopper is willing to buy diapers from Amazon, he or she can "clip" a coupon by simply clicking on it through the site. Amazon promises that by using its electronic coupons, shoppers can stop worrying, because they will "never leave the coupon book at home or walk out of the store without redeeming your discounts again."

For traditional retailers, extreme couponers disrupt their long-standing tactics to attract shoppers to their stores. For online retailers, this situation may be just the thing to encourage more consumers to buy their products online, where no one will tell them how to coupon.

Extreme couponing causes havock on a retailer's supply chain when one customer buys all of a store's stock of a single SKU.

Sources: E. J. Schultz, "Retailers Start to Suffer Super-Couponer Fatigue," *Advertising Age*, July 11, 2011; Martha C. White, "Stores Confront Extreme Couponers' Tactics with Policy Changes," *Time*, February 29, 2012; Amanda Fortini, "Honey, I Got a Year's Worth of Tuna Fish: Coupon Clipping as the Key to Economic Rebirth," *The New York Times*, May 3, 2012; Spencer E. Ante, "Foursquare Joins the Coupon Craze," *The Wall Street Journal*, May 8, 2012; and "Amazon Coupons," *Amazon.com*, www.amazon.com/Coupons/b?ie=UTF8&node=2231352011.

DISCUSSION QUESTION

Is extreme couponing worth the trouble to you? What about your parents?

volume. Depending on the type of product, however, customers may stockpile the items for use at a later time, thus having no impact on sales over time. Multi-unit pricing is an example of second-degree price discrimination because customers who buy and consume more of a product are presumably more price-sensitive and thus attracted by the lower prices if they buy more units.

Offering two or more similar products or services for sale at one lower price is called multiple-unit pricing.

Variable Pricing by Market Segment   Retailers often charge different prices to different demographic market segments, a practice referred to as **third-degree price discrimination.** For example, movie theaters have lower ticket prices for seniors and college students, presumably because these segments are more price-sensitive than other customers. This practice is generally legal, although gender-based pricing, in which men and women are charged different prices for the same service, has come into question, and it is not always clear whether this type of pricing is legal. For instance, New York salons were issued numerous gender-pricing violations. Salons routinely charge men and women different prices for things such as haircuts and waxing. Salon owners argue that men should get lower prices for haircuts because they are generally less work and they come in more often, sometimes as much as twice a month; they also argue that men should be charged more for waxing as a man's back is generally much more labor-intensive. The city views these pricing policies as discrimination.[18]

Another example is women have always paid more to have their shirts laundered, and that tradition continues to endure. Dry cleaners argue that women's shirts don't fit properly on the industrial presses, so they have to be done by hand. Some dry cleaners have taken a rational and presumably fairer approach. Shirts that can be pressed on the shirt-pressing machines get one price, while hand-pressed shirts get another, higher price. All dry-cleaned shirts are charged the same price.[19]

Another example of third-degree price discrimination is zone pricing. **Zone pricing** is the practice of charging different prices in different stores, markets, regions, or zones. Retailers generally use zone pricing to address different competitive situations in their various markets. For example, some multichannel retailers implement zone pricing by asking customers to enter their zip code if they want a price quote. A single city might comprise five or so pricing zones, categorized by their proximity to a Walmart versus a less economical regional grocery chain, for example. Although widely considered unethical, many retailers have charged higher prices in stores located in lower-income or urban areas because these customers, including elderly retirees, have less access to alternatives. Furthermore, the cost of operating businesses in those areas can be more expensive than in others. Thus, such third-degree price discrimination, when used in this manner to discriminate on the basis of income and age, is considered an unethical practice by many.

Dealing with Perceptions of Fairness　Setting different prices for similar products or services, such as a shirt sold at the manufacturer's suggested retail price versus discounted at the end of the season, or a seat on an airplane discounted on the day of the flight, may seem unfair to customers. To lessen this feeling, retailers can offer additional benefits, such as an unlimited return policy or customization, with the higher-priced products or services, whereas they place more restrictions on the less-expensive items.[20]

Beyond encouraging consumers to recognize the greater value of a higher-priced option, stores can engage in tactics to reduce the sense of unfairness overall. By providing more information, such as where a product was made or what sorts of tools a service provider needs, the customer can more effectively decide whether the price is fair. That is, a consumer who regards the prices for a bunch of carrots unfairly high might revise his or her perception upon learning that the carrots were grown in organic soil by a local farmer who uses no chemical pesticides. These attributes imply the higher quality of the product and the high costs of production, which should help the buyer recognize the justification for the higher price.

To lessen the impacts of a perceived unfair price, retailers also can draw the customer's attention to particular attributes that add perceived value to the product or service, such as handwork on apparel or friendly cancellation policies at a hotel.

Leader Pricing

Leader pricing is the practice of pricing certain items lower than normal to increase customers' traffic flow or boost sales of complementary products. Some retailers call these products **loss leaders.** In a strict sense, loss leaders are sold below cost and would therefore be considered predatory pricing, which is discussed in the next section. But a product doesn't have to be sold below cost for the retailer to use a leader-pricing strategy.

The best items for leader pricing are frequently purchased products like white bread, milk, and eggs or well-known brand names like Coca-Cola and Kellogg's Corn Flakes. Customers take note of ads for these products because they're purchased weekly. The retailer hopes consumers will also purchase their entire weekly grocery list while buying the loss leaders.

When retailers like Kroger offer three SKUs for ice cream that reflect good, better, and best quality at three different price points, they are using a price lining technique.

One problem with leader pricing is that it might attract shoppers referred to as **cherry pickers,** who go from one store to another, buying only items that are on special. These shoppers are clearly unprofitable for retailers.[21]

Price Lining

Retailers frequently offer a limited number of predetermined price points within a merchandise category, a practice known as **price lining.** For instance, because Kroger's vision for its store brands is to build loyalty among customers, with strong store brands that are exclusive to the retailer, it pursues a price lining store brand strategy to provide Kroger products to all customer segments. As discussed in Chapter 13, in the ice cream category, for instance, it offers the "Value" brand for its price-sensitive customers, with "adequate" packaging and quality. In the middle is the "Banner Brand," which is geared to the customer that wants ice cream comparable to Breyers. At the higher end is the "Private Selection" brand, which competes with Dove and Häagen Dazs. Developing products for all these customer segments means that Kroger closes any gaps in the ability of its current assortment to meet customers' needs. Other reasons customers and retailers benefit from price lining are:

- Confusion that often arises from multiple-price choices is essentially eliminated. The customer can choose the ice cream with the low, medium, or high price.
- From the retailer's perspective, the merchandising task is simplified. That is, all products within a certain price line are merchandised together. Furthermore, when going to market, the firm's buyers can select their purchases with the predetermined price lines in mind.
- Price lining can also give buyers greater flexibility. If a strict formula is used to establish the initial retail price (initial markup), there could be numerous price points. But with a price-lining strategy, some merchandise may be bought a little below or above the expected cost for a price line. Of course, price lining can also limit retail buyers' flexibility. They may be forced to pass up potentially profitable merchandise because it doesn't fit into a price line.

Although many manufacturers and retailers are simplifying their product offerings to save distribution and inventory costs and make the choice simpler for consumers, price lining can be used to get customers to "trade up" to a more expensive model.

Odd Pricing

Odd pricing refers to the practice of using a price that ends in an odd number, typically a 9. Odd pricing has a long history in retailing. In the nineteenth and early twentieth centuries, odd pricing was used to reduce losses due to employee theft. Because merchandise had an odd price, salespeople typically had to go to the cash register to give the customer change and record the sale, making it more difficult for salespeople to keep the customer's money. Odd pricing was also used to keep track of how many times an item had been marked down. After an initial price of $20, the first markdown would be $17.99, the second markdown $15.98, and so on.

The results of empirical studies in this area are mixed;[23] however, many retailers believe that odd pricing can increase profits. The theory behind odd pricing is the

REFACT

Apple Computer may have saved the music industry from oblivion by pricing songs on iTunes at 99 cents in 2003. At the time, no one was sure that anyone would pay for online music when people could steal it from several peer-to-peer networks.[22]

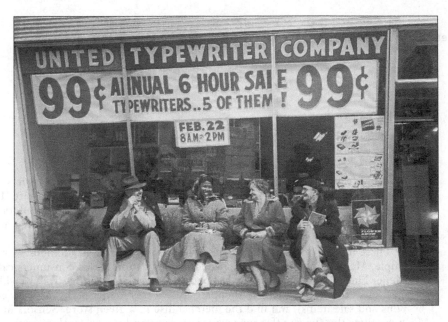

The practice of offering odd prices—a price that ends in an odd number, typically a 9—is more than 100 years old. Although empirical studies have mixed results, many retailers believe that the practice can increase profits.

assumption that shoppers don't notice the last digit or digits of a price, so that a price of $2.99 is perceived as $2. An alternative theory is that "9" endings signal low prices. Thus, for products that are believed to be sensitive to price, many retailers will round the price down to the nearest 9 to create a positive price image. If, for example, the price would normally be $3.09, many retailers will lower the price to $2.99.

Research results suggest the following guidelines for making price-ending decisions:

- When the price sensitivity of the market is high, it is likely to be advantageous to raise or lower prices so that they end in high numbers such as 9.

- When the price sensitivity of the market is not especially high, the risks to the retailer's image of using "9" endings are likely to outweigh the benefits. In such cases, the use of even dollar prices and round-number endings would be more appropriate.

- Many upscale retailers appeal to price-sensitive segments of the market through periodic discounting, which suggests the value of a combination strategy: Only break from a standard policy of round-number endings to use "9" endings when communicating discounts and special offers.

Using the Internet and Social and Mobile Channels to Make Pricing Decisions

The growth of the electronic channel, the popularity of social media and the adoption of smartphones has greatly changed the way consumers get and use information to make purchasing decisions based on price. Traditionally, price competition between store-based retailers offering the same merchandise was reduced by geography because consumers typically shop at the stores and malls closest to where they live and work. However, Internet sites such as Shopzilla, RedLaser, TheFind, ShopStyle, and PriceGrabber allow customers to compare prices across a range of retailers. As discussed earlier in this chapter, showrooming enables customers with mobile devices to check prices in stores and purchase online, ostensibly at a lower price.

Today, growing numbers of consumers are opting into services provided by various mobile firms and their applications (e.g., Foursquare, LocalResponse) to receive mobile offers (see Exhibit 14–3). The latest generation of price promotional offers takes into account the consumers' geographical location that is

LO6

Describe how the Internet and social and mobile channels are used to make pricing decisions.

REFACT

In 2011, consumers redeemed more than 3 billion coupons using their mobile devices.[24]

EXHIBIT 14–3
How Consumers Get
Mobile Coupons

accessed from their phone location or locational coding via certain sites and offers them localized promotions for retailers who are in close proximity. This concept is called **geofencing.** As a consequence, these coupons and offers are increasingly relevant, and the redemption of online coupons is growing at an astronomical rate.

These mobile offers can be delivered by a host of different methods. For example, Meijer supermarkets has created an application for its consumers called Meijer Find-it.[25] This application has a host of interesting features from providing customers the ability to create shopping lists, access Meijer perks (Mperks coupons and sale items), and find the merchandise in a given store. Sensors in the store allow the app to offer appropriate coupons and to constantly organize the list by the user's location in the store.[26]

Although consumers shopping electronically can collect price information with little effort, they also can get a lot of other information about the quality and performance of products, thus making them less sensitive to price. For instance, an Internet site that offers custom-made Oriental rugs can clearly show real differences in the patterns and materials used for construction. Electronic grocery services offered by Safeway allow customers to sort cereals by nutritional content, thus making it easier to use that attribute in their decision making. If a customer wants to make an egg dish for breakfast, the site can also recommend numerous recipes that include eggs, as well as providing the nutritional information. The additional information about product quality might lead customers to pay more for high-quality products, thus decreasing the importance of price.

The classic response to the question "What are the three most important things in retailing?" used to be "location, location, location." In the new world of social, mobile, and online, the answer will be "information, information, information."

LEGAL AND ETHICAL PRICING ISSUES

LO7

Indicate the legal and ethical issues retailers should consider when setting prices.

Retailers consider certain legal and ethical issues when setting prices. Some of the legal and ethical pricing issues are predatory pricing, resale price maintenance, horizontal price fixing, bait-and-switch tactics, scanned versus posted prices, and deceptive reference prices.

Predatory Pricing

Predatory pricing arises when a dominant retailer sets prices below its costs to drive competitive retailers out of business. Eventually, the predator hopes to raise prices when the competition is eliminated and earn back enough profits to compensate for its losses. For instance, independent booksellers accuse Walmart, Target, and Amazon of pricing best-selling books below their cost, such as Walter

Isaacson's biography of Steve Jobs, for as low as $8.95 when the cover price is $35. The American Booksellers Association has complained to the Department of Justice, claiming that these retailers are engaging in illegal predatory pricing, which is damaging to the book industry and harmful to consumers.[27] They have also complained about Amazon's e-book low-pricing strategy. The latest court ruling allows Amazon to continue to offer low prices on its Kindle books based on how difficult it is to prove whether e-book retailers will really drive the competition out of business and then raise the prices.[28] It appears that lower prices for e-books are here to stay. Some states have old statutes that declare it illegal to sell goods at unreasonably low prices, usually below their cost. However, a retailer generally may sell merchandise at any price as long as the motive isn't to eliminate competition.

Independent booksellers accuse Walmart, Target, and Amazon of predatory pricing when they sell best-selling books below their cost, such as Walter Isaacson's biography of Steve Jobs.

Resale Price Maintenance

As discussed in Chapter 13, vendors often encourage retailers to sell their merchandise at a specific price, known as the manufacturer's suggested retail price (MSRP). Vendors set MSRPs to reduce retail price competition among retailers and stimulate retailers to provide complementary services. Vendors enforce MSRPs by withholding benefits such as cooperative advertising or even refusing to deliver merchandise to noncomplying retailers. The latest U.S. Supreme Court ruling suggests that the ability of a vendor to require that retailers sell merchandise at MSRPs would be decided on a case-by-case basis, depending on the individual circumstances.[29]

Horizontal Price Fixing

Horizontal price fixing involves agreements between retailers that are in direct competition with each other to set the same prices. This practice clearly reduces competition and is illegal. As a general rule of thumb, retailers should refrain from discussing prices or terms and conditions of sale with competitors. If buyers or store managers want to know competitors' prices, they can look at a competitor's advertisements, its websites, or check out its stores.

Bait-and-Switch Tactics

A **bait and switch** is an unlawful, deceptive practice that lures customers into a store by advertising a product at a lower-than-normal price (the bait) and then, once they are in the store, induces them to purchase a higher-priced model (the switch). Bait and switch usually involves the store either having inadequate inventory for the advertised product or pushing salespeople to disparage the quality of the advertised model and emphasize the superior performance of a higher-priced model. To avoid disappointing customers and risking problems with the Federal Trade Commission (FTC), the retailer should have sufficient inventory of advertised items and offer customers rain checks if stockouts occur. A **rain check** is a promise to customers to sell currently out-of-stock merchandise at the advertised price when it arrives.

Scanned versus Posted Prices

Although customers and regulators are concerned about price-scanning accuracy, studies usually find a high level of accuracy. In general, retailers lose money from scanning errors because the scanned price is below the posted price.[30] However, consumer groups and states' attorneys general do find and pursue price discrepancies in retailers' favor. Periodic price audits are an essential component of good pricing practices. Price audits of a random sample of items should be done periodically to identify the extent and cause of scanning errors and develop procedures to minimize errors.

Deceptive Reference Prices

A **reference price** is the price against which buyers compare the actual selling price of the product, and thus it facilitates their evaluation process. Typically, the retailer labels the reference price as the "regular price" or "original price." When consumers view the "sale price" and compare it with the provided reference price, their perceptions of the value of the product or service will likely increase.[31]

If the reference price is bona fide, the advertisement is informative. If the reference price has been inflated or is just plain fictitious, however, the advertisement is deceptive and may cause harm to consumers. But it is not easy to determine whether a reference price is bona fide. What standard should be used? If an advertisement specifies a "regular price," just what qualifies as regular? How many units must the store sell at this price for it to be a bona fide regular price—half the stock? A few? Just one? Finally, what if the store offers the item for sale at the regular price but customers do not buy any? Can it still be considered a regular price? In general, if a seller is going to label a price as a regular price, the Better Business Bureau suggests that at least 50 percent of the sales should have occurred at that price.[32] Retailing View 14.6 highlights the ethical issues associated with advertised discounts.

14.6   RETAILING VIEW   Is It Really 45 Percent Off?

For the truly fashionable—or at least those who consider themselves as members of that group—the trade-off between luxury and affordability can be a tricky one. You want the newest, hottest fashion, but trying to keep up can be exhausting on your wallet. What's a maven to do?

Private-sale online sites such as Gilt, RueLaLa, and HauteLook promise a solution. They host limited-time sales of products from high-end fashion brands. A sale starts at a specified time and lasts for 48 hours, or until the sale is sold out. So, if you must have the Nova Armored Baby Beaton handbag from Burberry, you can have it for 45 percent off the list price, or $877 instead of $1,595, as long as you are on HauteLook.com when the sale starts. Brick-and-mortar retailers are following suit with "flash sales," such as when Banana Republic offers 40 percent off its full-priced sweaters but only between 11:00 a.m. and 2:00 p.m. on specific days.

But is it really 40 or 45 percent off—and 45 percent off what? A reference price like $1,595 gives consumers a clue as to what that specific handbag should be worth. Research shows that the greater the difference between a suggested retail and a sale price, the greater the perceived value. When customers see Sears offering a refrigerator for $1,300 off its original price, that huge number is nearly impossible to ignore. The better the deal, the more consumers will be attracted to buy. But if the retailer inflates the suggested or original price, the percentage discount and dollars off seem much better than they actually are.

When the private sale sites have been caught inflating the suggested retail prices to show a greater percentage discount, they generally claim that the original prices they list are accurate and come from the manufacturer. Any errors, they argue, are because the manufacturer gave them the wrong price, or else it might be due to employee error. For example, if the suggested retail price of the Burberry bag was actually only $1,100 instead of $1,595, then the bag was only discounted 20 percent. A customer in the heat of the moment may buy the bag because it is reported to be 45 percent off; were it only 20 percent off, she might not have purchased.

In some cases, the complicated coupon, discount, and flash pricing offers make it nearly impossible to determine the extent of the deal without a calculator. Because consumers rarely have the time or energy to calculate exactly what kind of discount they are getting, retailers can play on their excitement when it seems like a great deal.

Sources: Carl Bialik, Elizabeth Holmes, and Ray A. Smith, "Many Discounts, Few Deals," *The Wall Street Journal*, December 15, 2010; Vanessa O'Connell, "It's 50% Off . . . Well, Maybe 35%. How Good Are Deals on Members'-Only Web Sites?" *The Wall Street Journal*, January 16, 2010; www.hautelook.com; and www.gilt.com.

DISCUSSION QUESTIONS

Should private-sale sites and in-store retailers be required to substantiate their reference prices? Which price should they use as the reference price?

SUMMARY

LO1 Explain the difference between a high/low pricing strategy and an everyday low-pricing strategy.

Setting prices is a critical decision in implementing a retail strategy because price is a critical component in customers' perceived value. Retailers use two basic retail pricing strategies: everyday low pricing (EDLP) and high/low pricing. Each of these strategies has its advantages and disadvantages. The high/low strategy increases profits through price discrimination, creates excitement, and provides an opportunity to sell slow-moving merchandise. The EDLP approach assures customers of low prices, reduces advertising and operating expenses, reduces stockouts, and improves supply chain management.

LO2 Identify the factors retailers consider when pricing their merchandise.

In setting prices, retailers consider the price sensitivity of customers in their target market, the cost of the merchandise and services offered, competitive prices, and legal and ethical restrictions. Theoretically, retailers maximize their profits by setting prices on the basis of the price sensitivity of customers and the cost of merchandise. However, this approach does not consider the prices being charged by competitors. Another problem with attempting to set prices on the basis of customer price sensitivity is the implementation challenges associated with the large number of pricing decisions a retailer must make. Additional challenges arise when pricing services, due to the need to match supply and demand and the difficulties customers have in determining service quality. Retailers use yield management techniques to match supply and demand for services.

LO3 Describe how retailers set prices.

Most retailers set price by marking up the item's cost to yield a profitable gross margin. Then this initial price is adjusted on the basis of insights about customer price sensitivity and competitive pricing. To determine the initial retail price, retailers apply a markup as a percentage of the retail price. Retailers often do not sell merchandise at the initial retail price. The average initial price is reduced by markdowns, discounts given to employees, and theft.

Planning for these so-called reductions is important when determining the initial retail price so that the planned profit for the merchandise is obtained. Pricing optimization software can be used to determine the most profitable initial retail price and the appropriate size and timing of markdowns. Break-even analysis is also useful for determining how much a retailer needs to sell to begin making a profit.

LO4 Examine how and why retailers take markdowns.

Initial prices are adjusted over time using markdowns and for different market segments using variable-pricing strategies. Retailers take markdowns to either dispose of merchandise or generate sales. Markdowns are part of the cost of doing business, and thus buyers plan for them.

LO5 Identify the pricing techniques retailers use to increase sales and profits.

Retailers use a variety of techniques to maximize sales and profits by charging different prices to different customers. These techniques include setting different prices for individual customers, providing an offering that enables customers to self-select the price they are willing to pay, and setting different prices according to customer demographics. Retailers also use price lining, leader pricing, and odd pricing to stimulate sales.

LO6 Describe how the Internet and social and mobile channels are used to make pricing decisions.

The increased access to the Internet and the use of social media and smartphones has resulted in consumers having greater access to product and price information as they go about making purchasing decisions. It has also resulted in a growth in dynamic price promotions.

LO7 Indicate the legal and ethical issues retailers should consider when setting prices.

There are several legal and ethical issues retailers consider when setting prices. These include predatory pricing, resale price maintenance, horizontal price fixing, bait-and-switch tactics, scanned versus posted prices, and deceptive reference prices.

KEY TERMS

bait and switch, *411*
break-even analysis, *399*
break-even point quantity, *399*
cherry picker, *408*
coupons, *405*
dynamic pricing, *404*
elastic, *393*

everyday low pricing (EDLP) strategy, *388*
first-degree price discrimination, *403*
fixed cost, *399*
geofencing, *410*
high/low pricing strategy, *388*

horizontal price fixing, *411*
individualized pricing, *404*
inelastic, *393*
initial markup, *397*
inventory shrinkage, *397*
keystoning, *397*
leader pricing, *407*

GET OUT AND DO IT!

1. **CONTINUING ASSIGNMENT** Go shopping at the retailer you have selected for the continuing assignment. Does the retailer use high/low pricing or an EDLP strategy? Ask the store manager how markdown decisions are made and how the store decides how much a markdown should be. What rule-based approaches are used to make markdowns, or does the retailer use markdown optimization software? Does the retailer use techniques for stimulating sales such as price lining, leader pricing, bundling, or multi-unit and odd pricing? Are the prices on its website the same as those in the store? Evaluate your findings. Do you believe the retailer is using the best pricing strategies and tactics for its type of store? What, if anything, could it do to improve?

2. Go to the web page of Overstock.com, and look at its top-selling merchandise. Select a few key items, and compare the price of each product at other online retail sites, such as Target.com, Amazon.com, Sears.com, and Macys.com. How do the prices at this Internet outlet compare to those at a discount store, online retailer, and department store? Are the results what you expected, or were you surprised? Explain your reaction.

3. Go to the website of Sandals (www.sandals.com), and see what you can get for an all-inclusive price. Describe how bundling services and products provides vacationers with value. Find an example of price bundling outside the travel industry. Which method, bundling or nonbundling, do you believe provides the customer with the best value? Which makes the retailer or service provider more profits?

4. Go to your favorite food store and your local Walmart to find their prices for the market basket of goods listed in the accompanying table. What was the total cost of the market basket at each store? How did the prices compare? Did Walmart live up to its slogan of "Always lower prices"?

Competitive Pricing: Grocery Store vs. Walmart

Item	Size	Brand	Grocery	Walmart	Price Difference	Percent Savings
Grocery						
Ground coffee	11.5 oz can	Folgers				
Raisin Bran	25.5 oz box	Kellogg's				
Pet Supplies						
Puppy Chow	4.4 lb bag	Purina				
Cleaning						
Liquid laundry detergent	100 oz bottle	All				
Dryer sheets	80 count	Bounce				
Liquid dish detergent	25 oz bottle	Palmolive				
Health and beauty						
Shampoo	12 oz bottle	Dove				
Toothpaste	4.2 oz tube	Colgate Total				
Total cost of the market basket of goods						

DISCUSSION QUESTIONS AND PROBLEMS

1. What types of retailers often use a high/low pricing strategy? What types of retailers generally use an everyday low-pricing strategy? How would customers likely react if a retailer switched its pricing strategy from one to the other? Explain your response.

2. Why would sewing pattern manufacturers such as Simplicity, Butterick, and McCall's print a price of $12.95 (or more) on each pattern and then two times a year offer patterns for sale at $1.99 each? How could this markdown influence demand, sales, and profits?

3. Reread Retailing View 14.1. Will an EDLP strategy work for JCPenney? Explain your answer.

4. Reread Retailing View 14.5. What are your thoughts about extreme couponing? Should retailers take steps to restrict it?

5. What is the difference between bundled pricing and multiunit pricing?

Note: **For questions 6–10, you may use the Online Learning Center. Click on "pricing."**

6. A department store's maintained markup is 38 percent, reductions are $560, and net sales are $28,000. What's the initial markup percentage?

7. Maintained markup is 39 percent, net sales are $52,000, and reductions are $2,500. What are the gross margin in dollars and the initial markup as a percentage? Explain why initial markup is greater than maintained markup.

8. The cost of a product is $150, markup is 50 percent, and markdown is 30 percent. What's the final selling price?

9. Men's Wearhouse purchased black leather belts for $15.99 each and priced them to sell for $29.99 each. What was the markup on the belts?

10. Answer the following questions:
    (a) The Limited is planning a new line of jackets for fall. It plans to sell the jackets for $100. It is having the jackets produced in the Dominican Republic. Although The Limited does not own the factory, its product development and design costs are $400,000. The total cost of the jacket, including transportation to the stores, is $45. For this line to be successful, The Limited needs to make $900,000 profit. What is its break-even point in units and dollars?
    (b) The buyer has just found out that The Gap, one of The Limited's major competitors, is bringing out a similar jacket that will retail for $90. If The Limited wants to match The Gap's price, how many units will it have to sell?

SUGGESTED READINGS

Ashworth, Lawrence, and Lindsay McShane. "Why Do We Care What Others Pay? The Role of Other Consumers' Prices in Inferences of Seller Respect." *Journal of Retailing* 88, no. 1 (2012), pp. 145–155.

Bambauer-Sachse, Silke, and Dhruv Grewal, "Temporal Price Reframing: When Is It Beneficial?" *Journal of Retailing* 87, no. 2 (2011), pp. 156–165.

Dutta, Sujay, Abhijit Biswas, and Dhruv Grewal. "Regret from Post-Purchase Discovery of Lower Market Prices: Do Price Refunds Help?" *Journal of Marketing* 75 (November 2011), pp. 124–138.

Grewal, Dhruv, Kusum Ailawadi, Dinesh Gauri, Kevin Hall, Praveen Kopalle, and Jane Robertson, "Innovation in Pricing and Promotion Strategies," *Journal of Retailing* 87S, no. 1 (2011), pp. S43–S52.

Ho, Hillbun (Dixon), Shankar Ganesan, and Hermann Oppewal. "The Impact of Store-Price Signals on Consumer Search and Store Evaluation." *Journal of Retailing* 87, no. 2 (2011), pp. 127–141.

Kopalle, Praveen, P. K. Kannan, Lin Bao Boldt, and Neeraj Arora. "The Impact of Household Level Heterogeneity in Reference Price Effects on Optimal Retailer Pricing Policies." *Journal of Retailing* 88, no. 1 (2012), pp. 102–114.

Maxwell, Sarah. *The Price Is Wrong: Understanding What Makes a Price Seem Fair and the True Cost of Unfair Pricing.* New York: Wiley, 2008.

Nagle, Thomas T., John E. Hogan, and Joseph Zale. *The Strategy and Tactics of Pricing: A Guide to Growing More Profitably,* 5th ed. Upper Saddle River, NJ: Prentice Hall, 2010.

Spann, Martin, Gerald Haubl, Bernd Skiera, and Martin Bernhardt. "Bid-Elicitation Interfaces and Bidding Behavior in Retail Interactive Pricing." *Journal of Retailing* 88, no. 1 (2012), pp. 131–144.

Suri, Rajneesh, Jane Zen Cai, Kent Monroe, and Mrugank V. Thakor. "Retailers' Merchandise Organization and Price Perceptions," *Journal of Retailing* 88, no. 1 (2012), pp. 168–179.

Theotokis, Aris, Katerina Pramatari, and Michael Tsiros. "Effects of Expiration Date-Based Pricing on Brand Image Perceptions." *Journal of Retailing* 88, no. 1 (2012), pp. 72–87.

Managing the Store

EXECUTIVE BRIEFING
Tara Carroll, Store Manager, Kohl's

When I was attending the University of Florida, I really didn't know what I wanted to do when I graduated. As a classics major, I hoped to work in a museum or take the graduate school route, but I was ready to stop taking classes. Upon graduation and a brief hiatus overseas, I began my career with Kohl's as an assistant store manager. As is often the case in retail, mobility facilitates promotions; unfortunately for me, my mobility was somewhat limited due to my husband's job, so after only five years and two moves I was happily promoted to store manager.

I love my job, and I love working for Kohl's. My store near Amelia Island, Florida, is only one year old and is in a smaller building than your typical Kohl's. Our sales neared $8 million last year, and I have about 75 associates on my team. To me, those 75 associates are the heartbeat of the building, and it's my job as a store manager to make them feel valued and appreciated. I truly believe a happy associate makes for a happy customer. Although managing goals and workload can be challenging and stressful, I've instituted "Thank you Thursdays" in the building, which can be anything from Oreos and milk to popcorn and a movie. These events are meant to show my appreciation and, I hope, to make what might seem to some a boring, minimum-wage job into a fun and motivating career. From Good Fortune Fridays with Chinese food and fortune cookies to cupcake bake-off wars, my main roles in the building are cheerleader, coach, and party planner.

Kohl's values the manager-on-duty program highly and refers to it as "E3," for "Every Customer, Every Time, Every Store." With this mantra in mind, I go about my day with a strong customer focus and model the behavior I expect from my team. I have created games and contests to help them meet and exceed store-specific goals and have been known to use crowns, scepters, hats, and bling to keep the fun and positive atmosphere new and exciting. This type of atmosphere not only makes our customers laugh, it piques their interest, and they often want to know what we are celebrating. This results in consistently high customer service scores, which we are always proud to boast about!

CHAPTER 16

LEARNING OBJECTIVES

LO1 Describe how to improve the ability of workers through efficient recruiting, socializing, and training.

LO2 Examine how to improve the effort of workers through proper motivation, evaluation, rewards, and compensation.

LO3 Illustrate effective leadership strategies of a store manager.

LO4 Explore the various strategies a store manager can undertake to control costs.

Finding a job that pays six figures and is wholly fulfilling right out of college is an improbability. I recommend that you find a career that allows you to use your skills in a way that positively affects those around you; when you do, you'll find not only success, but happiness as well.

Store managers play an important role in formulating and executing retail strategies. Due to their frequent contacts with customers, they have the best knowledge of local customer needs and competitive activity. They also provide the shopping experience that plays a major role in building customer loyalty. Buyers can develop exciting merchandise assortments and procure them at low cost, but retailers realize the benefits of the buyers' efforts only when the merchandise is sold. Good merchandise doesn't sell itself. Store managers make sure that the merchandise is presented effectively, and sales associates offer services that stimulate and facilitate customer buying decisions.

Some store managers are responsible for $150 million in annual sales and manage more than 1,000 employees. Even in national chains, store managers are treated as relatively independent managers of a business within the corporation. For example, James Nordstrom, former CEO of Nordstrom, told his store managers, "This is your business. Do your own thing. Don't listen to us in Seattle, listen to your customers. We give you permission to take care of your customers."

Store managers are responsible for the productivity of two of the retailer's most important assets: the firm's investments in its employees and its real estate. Most of this chapter is devoted to increasing labor productivity—the sales generated by each store employee. Three critical drivers of labor productivity and performance

EXHIBIT 16–1
Drivers of Employee Performance

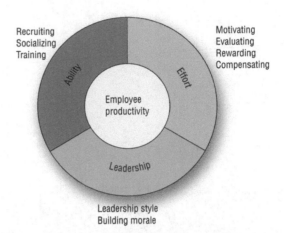

Recruiting
Socializing
Training

Ability

Employee
productivity

Effort

Motivating
Evaluating
Rewarding
Compensating

Leadership

Leadership style
Building morale

of store employees, and employees in general, are ability, effort, and leadership. *Ability* is the skills that employees possess to do their job; *effort* is how hard they work; and *leadership* is the degree to which store managers influence employees to engage in behaviors consistent with firms' objectives.[1] In the next three sections, we examine management practices that affect each of these performance drivers as shown in Exhibit 16–1.

In addition to increasing labor productivity, store managers affect their stores' profits by controlling costs. The major costs are employee compensation and benefits. Efficiently scheduling labor offers another opportunity for store managers to control labor costs. In addition, they are responsible for costs associated with operating and maintaining their buildings and reducing inventory shrinkage resulting from shoplifting and employee theft. These cost-control issues are discussed at the end of the chapter.

The first portion of this chapter focuses on the management of store employees and complements the strategic human resource management issues discussed in Chapter 9. Chapter 9 examined the organization of the tasks performed by retail managers and the general approaches for motivating retail employees and building their engagement with the firm. This chapter discusses how store managers implement the retailer's human resource strategy.

RECRUITING, SOCIALIZATION, AND TRAINING OF STORE EMPLOYEES

LO1

Describe how to improve the ability of workers through efficient recruiting, socializing, and training.

This section examines how store managers can improve the abilities of their employees through effective recruiting, socializing, and training.

Recruiting Employees

To recruit skillful, or potentially skillful, employees, store managers prepare a job description, find potential applicants with the desired capabilities, and screen the best candidates to interview.[2] These steps in the recruiting process are described in this section. (Appendix 1A of Chapter 1 describes the recruiting and selection process from the perspective of people interested in pursuing retail careers and applying for management trainee positions.)

Developing the Job Description   The **job description** identifies essential activities to be undertaken and is used to determine the qualifications of potential employees. It includes specific activities the employee needs to perform and the

- How many salespeople will be working in the department at the same time?
- Do the salespeople have to work together in dealing with customers?
- How many customers will the salesperson have to work with at one time?
- Will the salesperson be selling on an open floor or working behind the counter?
- How much and what type of product knowledge does the salesperson need?
- Does the salesperson need to sell the merchandise or just ring up the orders and provide information?
- Is the salesperson required to make appointments with customers and develop a loyal customer base?
- Does the salesperson have the authority to negotiate price or terms of the sale?
- Does the salesperson need to demonstrate the merchandise?
- Will the salesperson be expected to make add-on sales?
- Is the salesperson's appearance important? How should an effective salesperson look?
- Will the salesperson be required to perform merchandising activities such as stocking shelves and setting up displays?
- Whom will the salesperson report to?
- What compensation plan will the salesperson be working under?

EXHIBIT 16–2
Questions for
Undertaking a Job
Description

performance expectations expressed in quantitative terms. The job description is a guideline for recruiting, selecting, training, and eventually evaluating employees. Retail salespeople's responsibilities vary from company to company and department to department within a store. Retail employees in self-service stores such as supermarkets and full-line discount stores typically help customers find merchandise, bring out and display merchandise, and ring up sales. In contrast, employees who work in jewelry stores, high-end apparel department stores, or furniture stores typically get involved in a more extensive selling process that begins with determining the customer's needs, then proposing solutions, overcoming objections, closing the sale, and providing after-sale support.[3] The skill level required for employees engaged in selling high-involvement merchandise such as jewelry or home entertainment systems are much greater than the skills needed for employees who have limited interactions with customers. Exhibit 16–2 lists some questions that managers use when undertaking a job description of store employees.

Locating Prospective Employees   Some creative approaches being used by retailers to recruit applicants, in addition to placing ads on Craigslist and posting job openings on websites such as LinkedIn and TweetMyJobs, are working with

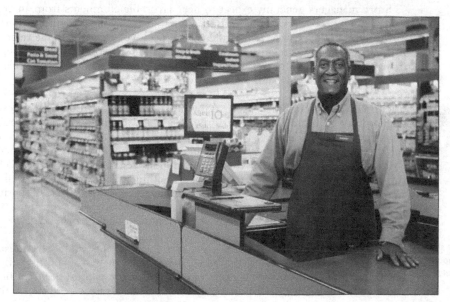

Many retailers find that the productivity and engagement of older employees is greater than younger employees.

the American Association of Retired Persons (AARP) to match seniors with job openings at their companies. Other options include partnering with government agencies to recruit the unemployed, veterans, and former welfare recipients, or using employees as talent scouts. That is, retailers often ask their own employees if they know someone the company could hire.[4] When Starbucks store managers receive exceptional service from other providers, they give the associate a business card, inviting him or her to drop into Starbucks, have a free latte, and discuss employment opportunities. Some employers provide employees rewards, such as $500 for every full-time hire and $200 for every part-timer.

Screening Applicants to Interview The screening process matches applicants' qualifications with the job description. Many retailers use automated prescreening programs as a low-cost method of identifying qualified candidates. Applicants initially apply in the store using a traditional paper application or through a web-enabled store kiosk. They can also apply online or call a toll-free telephone number.

Application Forms **Job application forms** contain information about the applicant's employment history, previous compensation, reasons for leaving his or her previous employment, education and training, and references. This information enables the manager to determine whether the applicant has the minimum qualifications, and it also provides information that is useful when the manager interviews the applicant. Today, many large retailers have found that having a nationwide centralized recruiting process reduces costs considerably and improves the quality of candidates that are eventually hired. Retailing View 16.1 describes the benefits Home Depot realizes by centralizing its recruitment processes.

References and Online Checks Most retailers verify the information given on an application form by contacting the applicant's references and doing an online search. Because people are more likely to be honest in conversations, managers often talk to the references, rather than relying on written opinions. Due to potential legal problems, however, many companies have a policy of not commenting on prior employees. A Google search can also be useful for finding out information that may not appear on the job application or emerge through contacts with references.

Store managers generally expect to hear favorable comments from an applicant's references or previous supervisors, even if they may not have thought highly of the applicant. One approach to reduce this positive bias is to ask the reference to rank the applicant relative to others in the same position. For example, the manager might ask, "How would you rate Pat's customer service skills in relation to other retail sales associates you have worked with?"

Social Media Social media such as Twitter, Facebook, and LinkedIn are excellent sources of information on prospective employees. These sites often reveal more about the person than a face-to-face interview. While social media platforms can provide employers with a wealth of information about job candidates, there is a risk of relying too heavily on this information for selecting employees. Much of the information on social media sites—such as ethnicity, age, religion, marital status, and sexual orientation, is sensitive and protected by law. The use of sensitive, protected information could expose an employer to discrimination claims, especially if it is not relevant for the employee's eventual job performance.[6]

Testing Some retailers use intelligence, ability, personality, and interest tests to gain insights about candidates. Tests also can be used to match applicants with job openings and to develop training programs. However, tests must be scientifically and legally valid. They can be used only when the scores have been shown to be related to job performance. It is illegal to use tests that assess factors that are not job-related or discriminate against specific groups.

Due to potential losses from theft, many retailers require that applicants take drug tests. Some retailers also use tests to assess applicants' honesty and ethics. Paper-and-pencil honesty tests include questions designed to find out if an applicant has ever thought about stealing and if he or she believes other people steal ("What percentage of people take more than $1 from their employer?").

Realistic Job Preview   Turnover declines when applicants understand both the attractive and unattractive aspects of the job.[9] For example, PetSmart, a pet supply category specialist, shows each applicant a 10-minute video that begins with the advantages of being a company employee and continues with scenes of employees dealing with irate customers and cleaning up animal droppings. Using job previews like this typically screens out many applicants who would most likely have quit due to the job requirements within three months if hired.

Selecting Applicants   After screening applicants, the selection process typically involves a personal interview. Because the interview is usually the critical factor in the hiring decision, the store manager needs to be well prepared and have complete control over the interview.

Preparation for the Interview   The objective of the interview is to gather relevant information, not simply to ask a lot of questions. The most widely used

REFACT

Of retailers, 71 percent check references as part of the selection process, 54 percent do drug screening, and 43 percent use paper-and-pencil honesty tests.[8]

RETAILING VIEW   Home Depot Centralizes Its Recruitment Processes   16.1

Before Home Depot centralized its recruitment process, the management in its 2,200 U.S. stores wasted a lot of time interviewing applicants who were not qualified or interested when they found out what the job entailed. So Home Depot decided to centralize its recruitment process—a decision that reduced costs and increased the quality of the more than 200,000 sales associates hired each year. Today, most of the recruitment process is done by 450 people in Home Depot's human resource department at its corporate headquarters in Atlanta.

The process begins with a candidate submitting an application using a kiosk located in every store. When a store has an opening, the HR department goes to its applicant pool and identifies 10 or more potential candidates. Then each candidate is interviewed by telephone twice. During the interviews, candidates are told about the job, the responsibilities, and the pay. If speaking Spanish is required for the position, interviewers fluent in Spanish talk with the candidates to assess their language skills. The phone interviews enable the screeners to assess the enthusiasm and energy level of

Home Depot attracts and does an initial screening of prospective employees using web-enabled kiosks in their stores.

the candidates—characteristics that are important to Home Depot but not easily assessed from an application form. Then the store managers interview the four or five best candidates and select one.

Due to the centralized process, the number of candidates store managers need to interview is dramatically reduced, leaving the store managers with more time to spend on improving the customer's shopping experience. Because the corporate screeners have more experience in screening candidates than the store managers, the quality of the new hires has increased, and the legal violations have decreased.

Sources: www.homedepot.com; and Arielle Kass, "Home Depot Centralizes In-store Hiring Process," *The Atlanta Journal-Constitution*, March 13, 2011.

DISCUSSION QUESTION

How has centralized recruiting improved the candidate pool at Home Depot?

interview technique, called the **behavioral interview,** asks candidates how they have handled actual situations they have encountered in the past, especially situations requiring the skills outlined in the job description. For example, applicants applying for a job requiring that they handle customer complaints would be asked to describe a situation in which they were confronted by someone who was angry about something they had done. Candidates might be asked to describe the situation, what they did, and the outcomes of their actions. These situations also can be used to interview references for the applicants. Exhibit 16–3 lists some questions that manager might ask. Here are some suggestions for questioning the applicant during the interview:

- Encourage long responses by asking questions like "What do you know about our company?" rather than "How familiar are you with our company?"

- Avoid asking questions that have multiple parts.

- Avoid asking leading questions like "Are you prepared to provide good customer service?"

- Be an active listener. Evaluate the information being presented and sort out the important comments from the unimportant ones. Some techniques for active listening include repeating or rephrasing information, summarizing the conversation, and tolerating silences.

EXHIBIT 16–3 Interviewing Questions

EDUCATION	PREVIOUS EXPERIENCE	QUESTIONS THAT SHOULD NOT BE ASKED PER EQUAL EMPLOYMENT OPPORTUNITY GUIDELINES
What were your most and least favorite subjects in college? Why?	What's your description of the ideal manager? Subordinate? Coworker?	Do you have plans for having children/a family?
What types of extracurricular activities did you participate in? Why did you select those activities?	What did you like most/least about your last job?	What are your marriage plans?
If you had the opportunity to attend school all over again, what, if anything, would you do differently? Why?	What kind of people do you find it difficult/easy to work with? Why?	What does your husband/wife do?
How did you spend the summers during college?	What has been your greatest accomplishment during your career to date?	What happens if your husband/wife gets transferred or needs to relocate?
Did you have any part-time jobs? Which of your part-time jobs did you find most interesting? What did you find most difficult about working and attending college at the same time? What advice would you give to someone who wanted to work and attend college at the same time?	Describe a situation at your last job involving pressure. How did you handle it?	Who will take care of your children while you're at work?
What accomplishments are you most proud of?	What were some duties on your last job that you found difficult?	(Asked of men) How would you feel about working for a woman?
	Of all the jobs you've had, which did you find the most/least rewarding?	How old are you?
	What is the most frustrating situation you've encountered in your career?	What is your date of birth?
	Why do you want to leave your present job?	How would you feel working for a person younger than you?
	What would you do if . . . ?	Where were you born?
	How would you handle . . . ?	Where were your parents born?
	What would you like to avoid in future jobs?	Do you have any handicaps?
	What do you consider your greatest strength/weakness?	As a handicapped person, what help are you going to need to do your work?
	What are your responsibilities in your present job?	How severe is your handicap?
	Tell me about the people you hired on your last job. How did they work out? What about the people you fired?	What's your religion?
	What risks did you take in your last job, and what were the results of those risks?	What church do you attend?
	Where do you see yourself in three years?	Do you hold religious beliefs that would prevent you from working on certain days of the week?
	What kind of references will your previous employer give?	Do you feel that your race/color will be a problem in your performing the job?
	What do you do when you have trouble solving a problem?	Are you of _____ heritage/race?

Legal Considerations in Selecting and Hiring Store Employees   Heightened social awareness and government regulations emphasize the need to avoid discriminating against hiring people with disabilities, women, minorities, and older workers.[10] Title VII of the Civil Rights Act prohibits discrimination on the basis of race, national origin, gender, or religion in company personnel practices. Discrimination is specifically prohibited in the following human resource decisions: recruitment, hiring, firing, layoffs, discipline, promotion, compensation, and access to training. The expansion of this Act in 1972 led to the creation of the **Equal Employment Opportunity Commission (EEOC),** which allows employees to sue employers that violate the law. Several major retailers have been successfully sued because they discriminated in hiring and promoting minorities and women.

Discrimination arises when a member of a **protected class** (women, minorities, etc.) is treated differently from nonmembers of that class (**disparate treatment**) or when an apparently neutral rule has an unjustified discriminatory effect (**disparate impact).** An example of disparate treatment occurs when a qualified woman does not receive a promotion, which instead goes to a less qualified man. Disparate impact occurs, for instance, when a retailer requires a college degree for all its employees, thereby excluding a larger proportion of disadvantaged minorities, when at least some of the jobs (e.g., store maintenance) could be performed just as well by people who did not graduate from high school. In such cases, the retailer is required to prove that the imposed qualification is actually needed to be able to perform the job. The **Age Discrimination in Employment Act** makes it illegal to discriminate in hiring and terminating people over the age of 40 years.

Finally, the **Americans with Disabilities Act (ADA)** opens up job opportunities for disabled individuals by requiring that employers provide accommodating work environments. A **disability** is any physical or mental impairment that substantially limits a person's major life activities or any condition that is regarded as being such an impairment. Although being HIV-positive does not limit any life activities, it may be perceived as doing so and is therefore protected as a disability under the ADA.

Socialization of New Store Employees

Having hired employees with the required skills or potential to develop these skills, retailers need to introduce the new employees to the firm and its policies, values, and strategies. This **socialization process** affects the degree to which newcomers become involved, engaged contributors to the firm's successful performance. In addition, socialization helps newly hired employees learn about their job responsibilities and the company they've decided to join.

Orientation Programs   Orientation programs are critical in socializing new employees.[11] For example, overcoming the shock of starting a new job can be a problem for even the most knowledgeable and mature new employees. College students who accept management trainee positions often find significant differences between their role as students and employees. Retailing View 16.2 describes some of these differences.

The orientation and training program for new store employees might be limited to several hours during which the new employee learns the retailer's policies and procedures and how to use the point-of-sale (POS) terminal. Other retailers, like The Container Store, have a much more intensive training program. Selected by *Fortune* magazine as one of the best places to work, new The Container Store employees go through a program called Foundation Week.[12] Before employment really begins, they receive a handbook and assignments to complete. The first day of Foundation Week begins with the company philosophy and a visit from store managers. Employees immediately see this introduction as different from the traditional first day, which typically entails completing forms and learning where to park. Days 2 through 5 continue with hands-on, on-the-floor training, including

16.2 RETAILING VIEW   Transition from Student to Management Trainee

Many students have some difficulty adjusting to the demands of their first full-time job because student life and professional life are very different. Students typically "report" to three or four supervisors (professors) and they select new "supervisors" every three or four months. In contrast, management trainees have limited involvement, if any, in selecting the one supervisor they'll report to, and they often report to the supervisor for several years.

Student life has fixed time cycles—one- to two-hour classes with a well-defined beginning and end. Retail managers, however, are involved in a variety of activities with varied time horizons, ranging from having a five-minute interaction with a customer to implementing a six-month plan to develop a sales associate into an assistant manager.

The decisions students encounter differ dramatically from the decisions retailers make as well. For example, business students might make several major decisions in a day when they discuss cases in class. These decisions are made and implemented in one class period, and then a new set of decisions is made and implemented in the next class. In a retail environment, however, strategic decisions evolve over a longer time period. Most decisions, such as those regarding merchandise buying and pricing, are made with incomplete information. Store managers in real life often lack the extensive information provided in many business cases studied in class. Finally, there are long periods of time when store managers undertake mundane tasks associated with implementing decisions and no major issues are being considered. Students typically don't have these mundane tasks to perform in their classes.

Source: Professor Daniel Feldman, University of Georgia.

DISCUSSION QUESTION

How can universities improve the socialization process for college students entering their first jobs?

---

interaction with and instruction about various positions in the store. The culmination of Foundation Week is a ceremony during which the new employees finally receive their aprons, signifying their membership in this elite organization. The orientation process also continues past Foundation Week. Customer service is the company's core competency, so every first-year, full-time salesperson receives about 263 hours of training, compared with 8 hours in the retail industry, on average. Training continues throughout an employee's career.[13]

The orientation program is just one element in the overall training program. It needs to be accompanied by a systematic follow-up to ensure that any problems and concerns arising after the initial period also are considered.

In this structured training program, newly hired Men's Wearhouse sales associates learn about the merchandise they will be selling.

Training Store Employees

To be effective, new employee training should feature both structured and more informal, on-the-job lessons.[14]

Structured Program   A **structured training program** helps new employees acquire basic skills and knowledge, which they need to be able to do their jobs. For example, sales associates learn what the company policies are, how to use the POS terminal, and basic selling skills. Stockroom employees learn procedures for receiving merchandise.

Some retailers find that providing structured training over the

Internet offers benefits compared to the on-the-job training. There is greater consistency, because the same material is presented rather than having material presented by different trainers or supervisors. Costs are lower; once the system is set up, there is no need for instructors or travel, and employees can undertake the training whenever they want.

JCPenney has used an e-training system that combines one-way video with two-way audio and data exchange capability, which allows instructors to chat on-line with students during training programs. Along with the presentations from the instructors, the training includes pre-class and post-class testing to measure comprehension levels. Instructors also break students into groups in which they are given case studies and asked to make recommendations.

On-the-Job Training Structured training programs also need to be combined with **on-the-job training** in which new employees work in specific jobs under the direct supervision of their managers. New employees can learn about company policies and skills needed to perform their jobs through structured programs, but they must be able to apply the information they have learned from training programs on the job. The best way to learn is to practice what is being taught. New employees learn by engaging in activities, making mistakes, and then learning how not to make those mistakes again.

The outdoor equipment retailer Recreational Equipment Inc. (REI), for instance, spends hours helping new salespeople spot the difference between transactional customers, who want a specific product, and consultative customers, who want to chat about choices.[15] This knowledge helps salespeople engage in productive selling interactions and provides a pleasant experience for customers. It would be difficult to teach this type of skill using a structured program.

Blended Approach Because of the relative advantages of structured and on-the-job training, many firms use a blended approach. Teams of Best Buy associates attend monthly, nearly three-hour long training sessions led by qualified instructors. As a result, Best Buy often is ranked among the top 30 firms for employee training.[16] The after-hours training sessions focus on new products, service updates, or concerns related to their departments. Furthermore, the employees role-play to practice customer interactions. In online training sessions, available through the retailer's proprietary learning management system, associates complete courses that enable them to use virtual versions of the products they sell or play interactive video games to practice challenging interactions with virtual customers.

Analyzing Successes and Failures
Every new employee makes mistakes. Effective store managers provide an atmosphere in which sales associates can try out different approaches for providing customer service and selling merchandise. Store managers need to recognize that some of these new approaches are going to fail, and when they do, effective managers do not criticize the individual sales associate. Instead, they talk about the situation, analyze why the approach didn't work,

Best Buy employees receive a lot of training about the latest products and services.

and discuss how the sales associate could avoid the problem in the future. Managers also work with employees to help them understand and learn from their successes. For example, salespeople shouldn't consider a large, multiple-item sale to occur simply due to luck. They should be encouraged to reflect on the sale, identify their key behaviors that facilitated the sale, and then remember these sales behaviors for future use.

It's important to help sales associates assign the right kinds of reasons for their performance. For example, some sales associates take credit for successes and blame the company, the buyers, or the merchandise for their failures. This tendency to avoid taking responsibility for failures doesn't encourage learning. When sales associates adopt this reasoning pattern, they aren't motivated to change their sales behavior because they don't take personal responsibility for losing a sale.

Managers can help sales associates constructively analyze their successes and failures by asking "why" questions that force them to analyze the reasons for effective and ineffective performance. To encourage learning, managers get salespeople to recognize that they could have satisfied the customer if they had used a different approach or been more persistent. When sales associates accept such responsibility, they'll be motivated to search for ways to improve their sales skills.[17]

MOTIVATING, EVALUATING, REWARDING, AND COMPENSATING STORE EMPLOYEES

LO2

Examine how to improve the effort of workers through proper motivation, evaluation, rewards, and compensation.

The second performance driver is effort (see Exhibit 16–1). High-performance store employees work hard, and the activities they work on should be consistent with the retailer's strategy and goals. Motivating employees to perform up to their potential may be store managers' most important and challenging task. The implementation of the retailer's evaluation, rewards, and compensation schemes, discussed in this section, together affect the motivation of store employees and the effort they expend. We use the following hypothetical situation to illustrate some issues pertaining to employee motivation.

After getting an associate's degree at a local community college, Jim Taylor was hired for a sales position at a department store in San Jose's Eastridge Mall. The position offered firsthand knowledge of the firm's customers, managers, and policies. Taylor was told that if he did well in this assignment, he could become a management trainee.

After observing Taylor on the sales floor, his manager, Jennifer Chen, evaluated Taylor's performance as average. She felt he was only effective when interacting with customers like himself: young, career-oriented men and women. To encourage Taylor to sell to other types of customers, Chen reviewed Taylor's performance goals with him. She reduced the portion of his compensation composed of a fixed salary and increased his commission rate. Taylor now feels a lot of pressure to increase his sales level. He's beginning to dread coming to work in the morning and is thinking about getting out of retailing and working for a bank.

In this hypothetical situation, Chen focused on increasing Taylor's motivation by providing some feedback and more incentive-based compensation. In discussing this illustration, we'll examine the appropriateness of this approach versus other approaches for improving Taylor's performance.

Setting Goals to Motivate Employees

To effectively motivate employees, store managers need to set goals for their employees and provide feedback on the employees' performance relative to those goals.

Employee performance improves when employees feel that (1) their efforts will enable them to achieve the goals set for them by their managers and (2) they'll receive rewards they value if they achieve their goals. Thus, managers can motivate employees by setting realistic goals and offering rewards that employees want.[18]

For example, Jennifer Chen set specific selling goals for Jim Taylor when he started to work in her department. Taylor, like other store sales associates, has goals in five selling areas: sales per hour, average amount per transaction (size of average sale), percentage multiple transactions (percentage of sales with add-on items), number of preferred customers, and number of preferred customer appointments made. This retailer defines preferred clients as customers who have a high CLV (see Chapter 11). In addition to being evaluated on their selling goals, sales associates like Taylor are often evaluated on the overall department inventory loss due to stolen merchandise (departmental shrinkage), the errors they make in using the POS terminal (system errors), and their contribution to maintaining the department's appearance (merchandise presentation). In addition to the evaluation, Chen also designed a program for Taylor's development as a sales associate. The activities she outlined over the next six months required Taylor to attend in-house classes to improve his selling skills.

Chen needs to be careful in setting goals for Taylor. If she sets the goals too high, he might become discouraged, feel the goals are unattainable, and thus not be motivated to work harder. However, if she sets the goals too low, Taylor can achieve them easily and won't be motivated to work to his full potential.

Goals are most effective at motivating employees when they're based on the employee's experience and confidence. Experienced salespeople have confidence in their abilities and should have "stretch" goals (high goals that will make them work harder). New salespeople need lower goals that they have a good chance of achieving. The initial good experience of achieving and surpassing goals builds new salespeople's confidence and motivates them to improve their skills. The use of rewards to motivate employees is discussed later in this chapter.

Evaluating Store Employees and Providing Feedback

The objective of the evaluation process is to identify the employees who are performing well and those who aren't. On the basis of the evaluation, high-performing employees should be rewarded and considered for positions with greater responsibility. Plans need to be developed to increase the productivity of employees performing below expectations. Should poor performers be terminated? Do they need additional training? If yes, what kind of training do they need?[19]

Who Should Do the Evaluation?   In large retail firms, the evaluation system is usually designed by the human resource department. But the evaluation itself is done by the employee's immediate supervisor—the manager who works most closely with the employee. For example, in a discount store, the department manager is in the best position to observe a sales associate in action and understand the reasons for the sales associate's performance. The department manager also oversees the recommendations that come out of the evaluation process. Inexperienced supervisors are often assisted by a senior manager in evaluating employees.

How Often Should Evaluations Be Made?   Most retailers evaluate employees annually or semiannually. Feedback from evaluations is the most effective method for improving employee skills. Thus, evaluations should be done more frequently when managers are developing inexperienced employees. However, frequent formal evaluations are time-consuming for managers and may not give employees enough time to respond to suggestions before the next evaluation. Effective managers supplement formal evaluations with frequent informal ones. For example, Jennifer Chen should work with Jim Taylor informally and not wait for the formal six-month evaluation. The best time for Chen to provide this informal feedback is immediately after she has obtained, through observations or reports, positive or negative information about Taylor's performance.

464   SECTION IV   Store Management

EXHIBIT 16–4   Factors Used to Evaluate Sales Associates at a Specialty Store

50%
SALES/CUSTOMER RELATIONS

1. Greeting. Approaches customers within 1 to 2 minutes with a smile and friendly manner. Uses open-ended questions.

2. Product knowledge. Demonstrates knowledge of product, fit, shrinkage, and price and can relay this information to the customer.

3. Suggests additional merchandise. Approaches customers at fitting room and cash/wrap areas.

4. Asks customers to buy and reinforces decisions. Lets customers know they've made a wise choice and thanks them.

25%
OPERATIONS

1. Store appearance. Demonstrates an eye for detail (color and finesse) in the areas of display, coordination of merchandise on tables, floor fixtures, and wall faceouts. Takes initiative in maintaining store presentation standards.

2. Loss prevention. Actively follows all loss prevention procedures.

3. Merchandise control and handling. Consistently achieves established requirements in price change activity, shipment processing, and inventory control.

4. Cash/wrap procedures. Accurately and efficiently follows all register policies and cash/wrap procedures.

25%
COMPLIANCE

1. Dress code and appearance. Complies with dress code. Appears neat and well groomed. Projects current fashionable store image.

2. Flexibility. Able to switch from one assignment to another, open to schedule adjustments. Shows initiative, awareness of store priorities and needs.

3. Working relations. Cooperates with other employees, willingly accepts direction and guidance from management. Communicates to management.

Format for Evaluations   Evaluations are only meaningful if employees know what they're required to do, the expected level of performance, and how they'll be evaluated. Exhibit 16–4 shows a specialty retailer's criteria for evaluating sales associates.

In this case, the employee's overall evaluation is based on subjective evaluations made by the store manager and assistant managers. It places equal weight on individual sales/customer relations activities and activities associated with overall store performance. By emphasizing overall store operations and performance, the assessment criteria motivate sales associates to work together as a team.

The criteria used at the department store to evaluate Jim Taylor are objective sales measures based on point-of-sale data, not subjective measures like those used by the specialty store. Exhibit 16–5 summarizes Taylor's formal six-month evaluation. The evaluation form lists results for various factors in terms of both what's considered average performance for company salespeople and Taylor's actual

EXHIBIT 16–5
Summary of Jim Taylor's Six-Month Evaluation

	Average Performance for Sales Associates in Department	Actual Performance for Jim Taylor
Sales per hour	$75	$65
Average amount per transaction	$45	$35
Percentage multiple transactions	55%	55%
Number of preferred customers	115	125
Number of preferred customer appointments	95	120
Departmental shrinkage	2.00%	1.80%
Systems errors	10	2
Merchandise presentation (10-point scale)	5	8

performance. His department has done better than average on shrinkage control, and he has done well on system errors and merchandise presentation. However, his sales performance is below average even though he made more than the average number of presentations to preferred customers. These results suggest that Taylor's effort is good but his selling skills may need improvement.

Evaluation Errors   Managers can make evaluation errors when they first form an overall opinion of the employee's performance and then allow this opinion to influence their ratings of each performance factor. For example, a store manager might feel that a salesperson's overall performance is below average and then rate the salesperson as below average on selling skills, punctuality, appearance, and stocking. When an overall evaluation casts such a negative halo on multiple aspects of a salesperson's performance, the evaluation is no longer useful for identifying specific areas that need improvement.

In making evaluations, managers are often unduly influenced by recent events and their evaluations of other salespeople. For example, a manager might remember a salesperson's poor performance with a customer the day before and forget the salesperson's outstanding performance over the past three months. Similarly, a manager might be unduly harsh in evaluating an average salesperson just after completing an evaluation of an outstanding salesperson. Finally, managers have a natural tendency to attribute performance (particularly poor performance) to the salesperson and not to the environment in which the salesperson is working. When making evaluations, managers tend to underemphasize effects of external factors on the department, such as merchandise and competitors' actions.

The department store's approach for evaluating sales associates avoids many of these potential biases because most of the ratings are based on objective data. In contrast, the specialty store's evaluation approach (Exhibit 16–4) considers a wider range of activities but uses more subjective performance measures. Because subjective information about specific skills, attitudes about the store and customers, interactions with coworkers, enthusiasm, and appearance aren't used in the department store's evaluation, performance on these factors might not have been explicitly communicated to Jim Taylor. The subjective characteristics in the specialty store evaluation are more prone to bias, but they also might be more helpful to salespeople as they try to improve their performance. To avoid bias when making subjective ratings, managers need to observe performance regularly, record their observations, avoid evaluating many salespeople at one time, and remain conscious of the various potential biases.

Rewarding Store Employees

Store employees receive two types of rewards from their job: extrinsic and intrinsic.

Extrinsic Rewards   **Extrinsic rewards** are rewards provided by either the employee's manager or the firm, such as compensation, promotion, and recognition.[20] Managers can offer a variety of extrinsic rewards, such as compensation, as discussed in the next section, to motivate employees.[21] However, store employees don't all seek the same rewards. For example, some salespeople want more compensation; others strive for a promotion in the company or public recognition of their performance. Jim Taylor wants a favorable evaluation from his manager so that he can enter the management training program.

Because of these different employee needs, managers may not be able to use the same rewards to motivate all employees. However, it is hard to develop unique reward programs for each individual, as some (especially part-time employees) are more motivated by nonmonetary compensations such as time off and store discounts. One response is to offer **à la carte plans** that give effective employees a choice of rewards for their good performance. For example, salespeople who achieve their goals could choose a cash bonus, extra days off, or a better discount on merchandise sold in the store. This type of compensation plan enables employees to select the rewards they want and thus will be the strongest individual motivators.

Recognition is another important nonmonetary extrinsic reward for many employees. Although telling employees they've done a job well is appreciated, it's typically more rewarding for them when their good performance is recognized publicly. In addition, public recognition can motivate all store employees, not just the star performers, because it demonstrates management's interest in rewarding employees.

Benefits, another extrinsic reward, are often more important to employees than financial compensation. For example, an employee survey conducted by a quick-service restaurant chain revealed that the top concern of the chain's employees was affordable health care. The chain invested approximately $1.5 million to offer an affordable health care plan, such that any employee who worked at least 20 hours a week and had been there for at least six months could pay a $30 monthly fee ($150 for family coverage) and receive health coverage. Before the restaurant implemented the plan, turnover rates hovered around 125 percent. One year after the new initiative went into effect, turnover dropped to 54 percent and stayed there. The reduced turnover rates allowed the company to save approximately $500,000 in training and recruitment costs annually. In addition, both productivity and employee confidence jumped, while absenteeism fell drastically.

Intrinsic Rewards   **Intrinsic rewards** are rewards employees get personally from doing their job well. For example, salespeople often like to sell because they think it's challenging and fun. Of course, they want to be paid, but they also find it rewarding to help customers and make sales.[22] Most managers focus on extrinsic rewards to motivate employees.[23] However, an emphasis on extrinsic rewards can make employees lose sight of their job's intrinsic rewards. Employees can begin to feel that their only reason for working is to earn money and that the job isn't fun. Note that Jennifer Chen tried to motivate Jim Taylor by using extrinsic rewards when she linked more of his compensation to how much he sold. This increased emphasis on extrinsic financial rewards may be one reason Taylor now dreads coming to work in the morning. He might not think his job is fun anymore.

When employees find their jobs intrinsically rewarding, they're motivated to learn how to do their job better. This is similar to a person who runs a marathon or climbs a mountain simply for the pride and joy they get from accomplishing it. Some managerial actions that affect intrinsic rewards are contests and job enrichment.[24]

Contests   An approach to making work fun is to hold contests with relatively small prizes. Contests are most effective when everyone has a chance to win. Contests in which the best salespeople always win aren't exciting and may even be demoralizing. For example, consider a contest in which a playing card is given to salespeople for each men's suit they sell during a two-week period. At the end of two weeks, the best poker hand wins. This contest motivates all salespeople during the entire period of the contest. A salesperson who sells only four suits can win with four aces on cards they got on the last day of the contest. Contests should be used to create excitement and make selling challenging for everyone, not to pay the best salespeople more money.[25]

Job Enrichment   Experienced employees often lose interest in their jobs. Extrinsic rewards, such as pay or promotion, may not be particularly motivating because the employees might be satisfied with their present income and job responsibilities. But these employees can be motivated by intrinsic rewards presented as job enrichment. **Job enrichment** is the redesign of a job to include a greater range of tasks and responsibilities, including skill variety, task significance, autonomy, and job feedback.[26] For example, an experienced sales associate who has lost some interest in his or her job could be given responsibility for merchandising a particular area, training new salespeople, or planning and managing a special event.

Compensation Programs

The objectives of a compensation program are to attract and keep good employees, motivate them to undertake activities consistent with the retailer's strategy, and strike a balance between controlling labor costs and providing enough compensation to keep high-quality employees.

A compensation plan is most effective for motivating and retaining employees when the employees feel that the plan is fair and that their compensation is related to their efforts. In general, simple plans are preferred to complex plans because they are easier to administer and employees have no trouble understanding them.

Types of Compensation Plans   Retail firms typically use one or more of the following compensation plans: straight salary, straight commission, salary plus commission, and quota-bonus.

With **straight salary compensation,** salespeople receive a fixed amount of compensation for each hour or week they work. For example, a salesperson might be paid $12 an hour or a department manager $1,000 a week. This plan is easy for the employee to understand and for the store to administer. Under a straight salary plan, the retailer has flexibility in assigning salespeople to different activities and sales areas. For example, salaried salespeople will undertake nonselling activities, such as stocking shelves, and won't be upset if they're transferred from a high-sales-volume department to a low-sales-volume department.

The major disadvantage of the straight salary plan is employees' lack of immediate incentives to improve their productivity. They know their compensation won't change in the short run, regardless of whether they work hard or slack off. Another disadvantage for the retailer is that a straight salary becomes a fixed cost that the firm incurs even if sales decline, which means a greater loss of profits during hard economic times.

Incentive compensation plans reward employees on the basis of their productivity. Many retailers use monetary incentives to motivate greater sales productivity by their employees.[27] With some incentive plans, a salesperson's income is based entirely on commission—called a **straight commission.** For example, a salesperson might be paid a commission based on a percentage of sales made minus merchandise returned. Normally, the percentage is the same for all merchandise sold (such as 7 percent of sales). But some retailers use different percentages for different categories of merchandise (such as 4 percent for low-margin items and 10 percent for high-margin items). Different percentages provide additional incentives for salespeople to sell specific items. Typically, the compensation of salespeople selling high-priced items such as men's suits, cars, furniture, and appliances is based largely on their commissions.

Incentive plans also may include a fixed salary plus a commission on total sales or a commission on sales over quota. For example, a salesperson might receive a salary of $200 per week plus a commission of 2 percent on all sales over a quota of $50 per hour.

Incentive compensation plans are a powerful motivator for salespeople to sell merchandise, but they have a number of disadvantages. For example, it's hard to get salespeople who are compensated totally by commission to perform nonselling activities. They're reluctant to spend time stocking shelves when they could be making money by selling. Also, salespeople will concentrate on the more expensive, fast-moving merchandise and neglect other merchandise. Sales incentives can also discourage salespeople from providing good customer service. Finally, salespeople compensated primarily by incentives don't develop loyalty to their employer. The employer doesn't guarantee them an income, so they feel no obligation to the firm.

Under a straight commission plan, salespeople's incomes can fluctuate from week to week, depending on their sales. Because retail sales are seasonal, salespeople might earn most of their incentive income during the Christmas season but much less during the summer months. To provide a more steady income for salespeople who are paid by high-incentive plans, some retailers offer a drawing account. With a **drawing account,** salespeople receive a weekly check based on their estimated annual income, and commissions earned are credited against the weekly payments. Periodically, the weekly draw is compared with the commissions earned. If the draw exceeds the earned commissions, the salespeople return the excess money they've been paid, and their weekly draw is reduced. If the earned commissions exceed the draw, salespeople are paid the difference.

Quotas are often used with compensation plans. A **quota** is a target level used to motivate and evaluate performance. Examples might include sales per hour for salespeople or maintained margin and inventory turnover for buyers. For department store salespeople, selling quotas vary across departments due to differences in sales productivity levels.

A **quota-bonus plan** provides sales associates with a bonus when their performance exceeds their quota. A quota-bonus plan's effectiveness depends on setting reasonable, fair quotas, but this can be hard to do. Usually, quotas are set at the same level for everyone in a department, yet salespeople in the same department may have different abilities or face different selling environments. For example, in the men's department, salespeople in the suit area have much greater sales potential than salespeople in the accessories area. Newly hired salespeople might have a harder time achieving a quota than more experienced salespeople. Thus, a quota based on average productivity may be too high to motivate the new salesperson and too low to motivate experienced salespeople. Thus quotas should be developed for each salesperson based on their experience and abilities.

To encourage employees in a department or store to work together, some retailers provide additional **team incentives** based on the performance of the department or store as a whole. For example, salespeople might be paid a commission based on their individual sales and then receive additional compensation according to the amount of sales generated by all salespeople in the department. The group incentive encourages salespeople to work together in their nonselling activities and while handling customers so that the department sales target will be achieved.[28]

Designing the Compensation Program   A compensation program's two elements are the total amount of compensation and the percentage of compensation based on incentives. Typically, market conditions determine the amount of compensation. When economic conditions are good and labor is scarce, retailers pay higher wages. Retailers that hire inexperienced salespeople pay lower wages than those that recruit experienced salespeople who are motivated and have good skills and abilities.

Incentive compensation is most effective when a salesperson's performance can be measured easily and precisely. It's difficult to measure individual performance when salespeople work in teams or must perform a lot of nonselling activities. Retailers can easily measure a salesperson's actual sales, but it's hard to measure her or his customer service or merchandising performance.

When the salesperson's activities have a great impact on sales, incentives can provide additional motivation. For example, salespeople who are simply cashiers have little effect on sales and thus are not typically compensated with incentives. However, incentives are appropriate for salespeople who provide a lot of information and assistance to customers about complex products, such as designer dresses or automobiles. Incentives are less effective with inexperienced salespeople, who are less confident in their skills, because they inhibit learning and thereby can cause excessive stress.

Finally, compensation plans in which too much of the incentive is based on sales may not promote good customer service. Salespeople on commission become interested in selling anything they can to customers, and they aren't willing to spend time helping customers buy the merchandise they need. They tend to stay close to the cash register or the dressing room exits so that they can ring up a sale for customers who are ready to buy.

Setting the Commission Percentage   Assume that a specialty store manager wants to hire experienced salespeople. To get the type of people she wants, she feels she must pay $12 an hour, and her selling costs are budgeted at 8 percent of sales. With compensation of $12 an hour, salespeople each need to sell $150 worth of merchandise every hour ($12 divided by 8 percent) for the store to keep within its sales cost budget. The manager believes the best compensation would be two-thirds salary and one-third commission, so she decides to offer a compensation plan consisting of an $8-an-hour salary (66 percent of $12) and a 2.66 percent commission on sales. If salespeople sell $150 worth of merchandise an hour, they'll earn $12 an hour ($8 an hour in salary plus $150 multiplied by 2.66 percent, which equals $4 an hour in commission).

Legal Compensation Issues

The **Fair Labor Standards Act** of 1938 set minimum wages, maximum hours, child labor standards, and overtime-pay provisions. Enforcement of this law is particularly important to retailers because they hire many low-wage employees and teenagers and ask their employees to work long hours.

The **Equal Pay Act**, now enforced by the EEOC (Equal Employment Opportunity Commission), prohibits unequal pay for men and women who perform equal work or work of comparable worth. Equal work means that the jobs require the same skills, effort, and responsibility and are performed in the same working environment. Comparable worth implies that men and women who perform different jobs of equal worth should be compensated the same. Differences in compensation are legal when compensation is determined by a seniority system, an incentive compensation plan, or market demand.

LEADERSHIP

LO3

Illustrate effective leadership strategies of a store manager.

The third driver of employee performance is leadership (see Exhibit 16–1). **Leadership** is the process by which a person attempts to influence others to accomplish a common goal or task. Store managers are leaders of their group of employees. They use a variety of motivational techniques to increase productivity by helping employees achieve professional goals consistent with their firm's objectives.[29]

Types of Leader Behavior

Leaders engage in task performance and group maintenance behaviors. **Task performance behaviors** are the store manager's efforts to plan, organize, motivate, evaluate, and coordinate store employees' activities. **Group maintenance behaviors** are the activities store managers undertake to make sure that employees are satisfied and work well together. These activities include considering employees' needs, showing concern for their well-being, and creating a pleasant work environment.

Leader Decision Making Style

Store managers vary in how much they involve employees in making decisions. **Autocratic leaders** make all decisions on their own and then announce them to employees. They use the authority of their position to tell employees what to do.

470   SECTION IV   Store Management

Great leaders know when to use democratic and autocratic styles to produce happy, motivated employees.

For example, an autocratic store manager determines who will work in each area of the store, when they'll take breaks, and what days they'll have off.

In contrast, **democratic leaders** seek information and opinions from employees and base their decisions on this information. Democratic store managers share their power and information with their employees. They ask employees where and when they want to work and make schedules to accommodate those employee desires as much as possible.

There is no one best leadership style. Effective store managers use all styles, selecting the style most appropriate for each situation. For example, a store manager might be autocratic with an insecure new trainee but democratic with an effective, experienced employee.

The best store managers (leaders) go beyond influencing employee behaviors. **Transformational leaders** get people to transcend their personal needs for the sake of the group or organization. They are engaged and generate excitement. They revitalize organizations. Transformational store managers create this enthusiasm in their employees through their personal charisma. They are self-confident and have a clear vision that grabs employees' attention. They communicate this vision through words and symbols. Finally, transformational leaders delegate challenging work to subordinates, have free and open communication with them, and provide personal mentoring to develop subordinates.

Maintaining Morale

Store managers play an important role in improving the work atmosphere and its effect on the performance of store employees. Typically, morale goes up when things are going well and employees are highly motivated. But when sales aren't

Apple Store managers build morale and motivate their sales associates by holding "morning meetings" before the store opens.

going well, morale tends to decrease and employee motivation declines. Effective managers build morale by doing small but meaningful things for employees like throwing a party when goals are met or dividing the charity budget by the number of employees and inviting them to suggest how their "share" should be used. One store manager used real-time sales data collected in her firm's information system (see Chapter 10) to build excitement among her employees. On the first day of the Christmas season, she wrote $4,159 on a white board in the store. That was the store's sales during the first day of the Christmas season last year. She told her sales associates that beating that number was not enough; she wanted to see a 25 percent increase, the same sales increase the store achieved over the previous Christmas season. By setting financial objectives and keeping sales associates informed of up-to-the-minute results, managers can convert an eight-hour shift of clock watchers into an excited team of racers. All day, as customers come and go, sales associates take turns consulting the backroom computer that records sales from the store's POS terminals.

Sexual Harassment

Sexual harassment is an important issue affecting the productivity of the work environment. Managers must avoid, and make sure that store employees avoid, any actions that are, or can be interpreted as, sexual harassment. Otherwise, the retailer and the manager may be held liable for the harassment. The EEOC guidelines define **sexual harassment** as a form of gender discrimination, as follows:

> Unwelcome sexual advances, requests for sexual favors, and other verbal or physical conduct of a sexual nature constitutes sexual harassment when . . . submission to or rejection of such conduct by an individual is used as a basis for employment decisions affecting such individual, or . . . such conduct has the purpose or effect of unreasonably interfering with an individual's work performance or creating an intimidating, hostile, or offensive working environment.

An appropriate procedure for dealing with a sexual harassment allegation involves establishing and posting an anti-sexual harassment policy including a complaint procedure, treating complaints seriously, creating a safe environment for individuals to make complaints without retaliation, getting information from the alleged victim, document the meeting with the alleged victim, and informing the human resource department or the next-higher level of company management of the complaint and of the meeting with the alleged victim.[30]

CONTROLLING COSTS

Labor scheduling, store maintenance, and inventory shrinkage offer three opportunities to reduce store operating expenses. Retailing View 16.3 describes how a convenience store chain reengineered its operations to reduce costs and increase customer service.

LO4

Explore the various strategies a store manager can undertake to control costs.

Labor Scheduling

Using store employees efficiently is an important and challenging problem. Although store employees provide important customer service and merchandising functions that can increase sales, they also are the store's largest operating expense. **Labor scheduling** (determining the employees assigned to each area of the store

472   SECTION IV   Store Management

16.3   RETAILING VIEW   Sheetz Increases Operating Efficiency

Sheetz, a Pennsylvania-based convenience store chain, reengineered its operations to reduce costs and increase customer service.

Sheetz, a convenience store chain with 441 stores based in Altoona, Pennsylvania, started a series of detailed studies to determine how store-level tasks could be performed more efficiently. The research considered everything, from how employees emptied trash to how managers closed out at the end of each day. In the latter case, it found that managers were required to complete information sheets that took up 40 different computer screens. Such demands meant that they needed up to four hours to close out an eight-hour workday.

Furthermore, the time spent to close stores was affecting customer service. Managers would do the paperwork during the morning of the following day, the busiest traffic time, when they should have been out in the stores managing. When Sheetz reexamined these practices, it eliminated more than 160,000 hours annually of time the store managers were spending on nonproductive administrative tasks.

Sheetz also found that a lot of the information being sent to store managers was of questionable value. There were too many redundant reports. Thus, the 204 reports that had been available on the store managers' computers were reduced to 23.

Then, Sheetz saved 55 employee-hours per week per store by reexamining its labor scheduling. Before the study, staffing for stores was based on sales. But this universal approach ignored differences among stores. For example, some stores generated most of their sales through food service, which demanded substantial labor. Others earned most of their revenue from gasoline sales, which required minimal employee effort (i.e., *outside sales* in convenience store lingo).

As the company has added distribution centers and its own bakery, managers have gained greater control over product delivery timing and levels as well. The distribution center and Sheetz Bros. Kitchen provide personalized deliveries to approximately 350 stores. By coordinating these deliveries with their staffing levels, store managers also ensure they have enough staff to restock shelves, usually during customer downtimes.

In addition, some in-store tasks were eliminated. In particular, noting that it made minimal margins on newspaper sales, Sheetz stopped tracking its newspaper sales at the individual level. By eliminating this task for store employees, it made sure it continued to earn at least some money on each paper it sells.

As a result of these changes and implemented recommendations, within two years, Sheetz had saved $5.1 million, just in payroll costs. These savings, together with increased efficiency achieved through a chainwide switch to more efficient LED lighting in stores, suggest great promise for the future of the convenient store chain.

Sources: Walt Frank, "From Dairy Store to Convenience Restaurants, Sheetz Empire Now Spans Six States," *Altoona Mirror*, November 18, 2012; "LED Lighting Improves Sheetz Convenience Restaurants," *Restaurant Facilities Business*, November 28, 2012; "Sheetz Hits the Mark," *Retail Merchandiser*, September–October 2007, pp. 28–31; and Neil Stern, "Convenience Reborn," *Chain Store Age*, May 2007, pp. 34–39.

DISCUSSION QUESTION

What types of data would Sheetz need to have collected to implement all of these changes?

Labor scheduling software assures that there are enough associates to take care of customers when it is busy (left), but not so many that the associates have little to do when business is slow (right).

during each hour) is difficult because customer traffic varies greatly during the day and the week. In addition, multiple shifts are required to staff stores up to 24 hours a day, seven days a week. Poor labor scheduling can result in long checkout lines, sales associates with nothing to do, and lower labor productivity. For example, if 6 percent of a store's sales volume and 9 percent of the total labor-hours occur between 2 and 3 p.m., the store might be overstaffed during this time period and understaffed in others.

Many retailers utilize computer software to deal with the complexities of labor scheduling. By analyzing sales, transactions, and customer traffic for each time period, the software determines the appropriate number of employees to have in each area of the store during each time period and develops a work schedule for each employee.[31]

Although these scheduling systems benefit both retailers and customers, they can have an adverse impact on employees. The schedules suggested by this software often recommend the use of part-time workers and irregular work hours. Sales associates can be burdened with unpredictable schedules, including requirements that they remain "on call" on their days off. While some employees prefer part-time work because it fits in with their lifestyle, many others prefer to work full-time.[32]

Store Maintenance

Store maintenance entails the activities involved with managing the exterior and interior physical facilities associated with the store. The exterior facilities include the parking lot, entrances to the store, and signs on the outside of the store. The interior facilities include the walls, flooring, ceiling, bathrooms, HVAC systems, and displays and signs. Store maintenance affects both the sales generated in the store and the cost of running the store. A store's cleanliness and neatness affect consumer perceptions of the quality of its merchandise, but this maintenance is costly. For instance, floor maintenance for a 40,000-square-foot home center runs about $10,000 a year. Poor maintenance shortens the useful life of air-conditioning units, floors, and fixtures.

Inventory Shrinkage

Shrinkage is the inventory loss due to employee theft, shoplifting, mistakes, inaccurate records, and vendor errors. It is the difference between the recorded value of inventory (at retail prices) based on merchandise bought and received and the value of the actual inventory (at retail prices) in stores and distribution centers, divided by retail sales during the period. For example, if accounting records indicate that inventory should be $1,500,000, the actual count of the inventory reveals $1,236,000, and sales were $4,225,000, the shrinkage is 6.2 percent [($1,500,000 − $1,236,000) ÷ $4,225,000].

Reducing shrinkage is an important store management issue because retailers' annual loss from shrinkage averages about 1.5 percent of total sales.[33] Worldwide, retail theft costs retailers more than $107 billion annually. In the United States alone, retailers lost nearly $3 billion to theft, which is equivalent to costing each U.S. family $422.68 each year.[34]

Although shoplifting receives the most publicity, employee theft accounts for more inventory loss. A recent survey attributes 44 percent of inventory shrinkage to employee theft, 36 percent to shoplifting, 15 percent to mistakes and inaccurate records, and 3 percent to vendor fraud, with an unaccounted for 2 percent.[35] Examples of employee mistakes are failing to ring up an item when it's sold and miscounting merchandise when it's received or during physical inventories. Inventory shrinkage due to vendor mistakes arises when vendor shipments contain less than the amount indicated on the packing slip and the retailer fails to recognize this error. The remainder of this section focuses on losses due to shoplifting and employee theft.

Shoplifting

REFACT

Shoplifting is at least 400 years old. In 1591, Robert Greene, wrote a pamphlet providing advice for shoplifters. One of his recommendations was to be "attired in the form of a civil country gentleman."[36]

To develop a loss prevention program to reduce shoplifting, retailers confront a trade-off between providing shopping convenience on the one hand, and preventing losses due to shoplifting on the other. The key to an effective loss prevention program is determining the most effective way to protect merchandise while preserving an open, attractive store atmosphere and a feeling among employees that they are trusted. Loss prevention requires coordination among store management, visual merchandising, and store design.

In response to the high rates of theft, retailers spent $28.3 billion on security measures in 2011.[37] Losses due to shoplifting can be reduced by store design, security measures, and personnel policies.

Store Design   The following store design choices may help deter shoplifting:

- Do not place expensive or small merchandise near an entrance.
- Put easily stolen merchandise near POS terminals because there typically is an employee near the terminal.
- Keep the height of fixtures low so employees can see customers in the store and have an open line-of-sight to the dressing rooms and exits.
- Use mirrors.
- Alternate clothing hanger directions so professional shoplifters cannot easily grab a lot of apparel at once.
- Lock up all items that are easily stolen.

Security Measures   The following security measures may help deter shoplifting:

- Use closed-circuit TV cameras.
- Include some nonoperating equipment that looks like a TV camera to provide a psychological deterrent to shoplifters and save costs.
- Use **electronic article surveillance (EAS)** and **radio-frequency identification (RFID) systems.** These special tags are placed on merchandise. When the merchandise is purchased, the tags are deactivated by the point-of-sale (POS) scanner.
- Have an employee stationed at the door to check receipts.

Personnel Policies   The following personnel policies may help deter shoplifting:

- Use mystery and honesty shoppers to watch for employee and customer theft.
- Have store employees monitor fitting rooms.
- Store employees should be trained to be aware, visible, and alert to potential shoplifting situations.
- Provide attentive customer service.

Exhibit 16–6 outlines some rules for spotting shoplifters. Perhaps the best deterrent to shoplifting is an alert employee who is very visible.

Prosecution   Many retailers have a policy of prosecuting all shoplifters. They feel a strictly enforced prosecution policy deters shoplifters. Some retailers also sue shoplifters in civil proceedings for restitution of the stolen merchandise and the time spent in the prosecution.

Although many of these measures reduce shoplifting, they can also make the shopping experience more unpleasant for honest customers. The atmosphere of an apparel store, for example, is diminished when guards, mirrors, and TV cameras are highly visible. Customers may find it hard to try on clothing secured with a lock and chain or an electronic tag. They can also be uncomfortable trying on clothing if they think they're secretly being watched via a surveillance monitor. Thus, when evaluating security measures, retailers need to balance the benefits of reducing shoplifting with the potential losses in sales.

Using Technology   Retailers are turning to technology to help stop shoplifting. Some stores have installed systems that use computer software to analyze

Retailers use EAS tags to reduce shoplifting. The tags contain a device that is deactivated when the merchandise is purchased. If a customer has not purchased the merchandise, an alarm is triggered when the stolen merchandise passes through sensor gates at the store's exit.

DON'T ASSUME THAT ALL SHOPLIFTERS ARE POORLY DRESSED
To avoid detection, professional shoplifters dress in the same manner as customers patronizing the store. Over 90 percent of all amateur shoplifters arrested have the cash, checks, or credit to purchase the merchandise they stole.

SPOT LOITERERS
Amateur shoplifters frequently loiter in areas as they build up the nerve to steal something. Professionals also spend time waiting for the right opportunity but less conspicuously than amateurs.

LOOK FOR GROUPS
Teenagers planning to shoplift often travel in groups. Some members of the group divert employees' attention while others take the merchandise. Professional shoplifters often work in pairs. One person takes the merchandise and passes it to a partner in the store's restroom, phone booths, or restaurant.

LOOK FOR PEOPLE WITH LOOSE CLOTHING
Shoplifters frequently hide stolen merchandise under loose-fitting clothing or in large shopping bags. People wearing a winter coat in the summer or a raincoat on a sunny day may be potential shoplifters.

WATCH THE EYES, HANDS, AND BODY
Professional shoplifters avoid looking at merchandise and concentrate on searching for store employees who might observe their activities. Shoplifters' movements might be unusual as they try to conceal merchandise.

EXHIBIT 16–6
Spotting Shoplifters

shoppers' movements captured by TV cameras. When the system recognizes unusual activity, such as when dozens of items get moved off the shelf or a locked case is opened, it sets off an alarm for security guards. If someone enters the store at an unauthorized time, the system takes a picture of the entrant, as well as of the people who entered before and after.[38]

Because some shoplifters are less subtle—they simply load a lot of stuff into a cart and run—stores have started adding RFID chips to the carts themselves. If a cart with unpaid for merchandise approaches the sensor-equipped doors, its wheels simply lock, such that it stops moving easily. In addition, new cameras mounted to the bottom of checkout stations check to make sure thieves have not stuck stolen items underneath their carts, in the hope that no one will notice that they never paid for them. Such technologies enable immediate, unobtrusive identification of theft, using signals that can be sent to security guards' handheld devices.[39]

Customers continue to steal merchandise using conventional methods that haven't changed for thousands of years. They hide it under their clothing or at the bottom of their shopping carts, attempt to divert store employees, or simply walk out of the store quickly in the hope that they won't be noticed. Like retailing itself, shoplifting has become sophisticated, as described in Retailing View 16.4.

Reducing Employee Theft   Like shoplifting, employee theft has become a more sophisticated, high-tech activity. The increasing use of gift cards has created new opportunities for employee theft. In collaboration with criminal accomplices, retail employees accept fake merchandise returns and put the "refund" onto gift cards. The employee might use the card him- or herself or hand it to the accomplice. Later, they redeem the card at another store or sell it online. The Internet makes it easy to convert such gift cards into cash. In response, many retailers have hired loss prevention specialists who spend most of their time searching auction sites for suspicious gift card offerings, such as those for much below face value or sales of dozens of cards from the same retailer.[40] Similarly, a great deal of credit card sales information is entered manually. Multiple returns, or multiple returns of the same item, suggest that the employee at that register is acting illegally, whether stealing from the store or from the customer. Retailers are utilizing software that monitors abnormal sales at the POS. Video technology complements this software, allowing managers to see exactly what cashiers are doing when the irregular patterns of activity occur.[41]

The most effective approach for reducing employee theft and shoplifting is to create a trusting, supportive work environment. When employees feel they're respected members of a team, they identify their goals with the retailer's goals. Stealing from their employer thus becomes equivalent to stealing from themselves or their family, and they go out of their way to prevent others from stealing from the "family." Thus, retailers with a highly committed workforce and low turnover typically have low inventory shrinkage. Additional approaches for reducing employee theft are carefully screening employees, creating an atmosphere that encourages honesty and integrity, and establishing security policies and control systems.

Other approaches for reducing employee theft are discussed in the following sections.

Screening Prospective Employees   As mentioned previously, many retailers use paper-and-pencil honesty tests and undertake extensive reference checks to screen out potential employees with theft problems. A major problem related to employee theft is drug use. Some retailers now require that prospective employees submit to drug tests as a condition of employment. Employees

RETAILING VIEW   Using Technology to Steal Merchandise   16.4

Although shoplifting, in which customers steal merchandise from retailers, is an age-old problem, thieves have become more high tech and often work in gangs. One popular scam used by thieves is to create counterfeit bar codes at lower prices. For example, a thief created $19 bar codes for $100 Lego sets and got away with sets worth approximately $600,000. Bar-code thieves are hard to catch, because when an alert cashier notices the mispriced item, the thief can either pay the difference or just walk out the door. A similar technique is to create fake receipts. A thief in New Mexico simply created Sam's Club receipts for electronic products, which he used to walk out of the store with merchandise that he never paid for, even though his fake receipt indicated that he had. This criminal stole more than $25,000 in electronics from his local warehouse club before being caught and arrested.

Another technology-based scam is tampering with gift cards by professional and amateur shoplifters and employees. The thieves may create duplicate gift cards that can be used by the thief or resold online, or they may use active gift card account information to create duplicate cards or make web purchases. Thieves also have been known to steal merchandise and then return it to the store for credit in the form of gift cards, which they can then sell online, often at less than face value.

Furthermore, 96 percent of retailers recently surveyed indicated that they had been victims of organized retail theft. Gangs of professional thieves concentrate in over-the-counter medications, infant formula, health and beauty aids, electronics, and specialty clothing. Internet sales, especially through auctions, have provided a ready outlet to sell this merchandise. Some gangs of thieves are using store credits to steal. In one case, a gang took a valid $500 store credit receipt, digitally altered it to read $1,200, printed multiple copies that it distributed to gang members across the country, and then sent the members out to 16 stores in 12 states to get their refunds—all within the same hour.

Another gang-related high-tech method of shoplifting known as **flash robs,** is when groups plot via social media and text messages to arrive suddenly at retail stores and wreak havoc, usually by stealing large amounts of merchandise. A Sears store in Philadelphia experienced a flash rob when about 40 boys flooded the store and stole thousands of dollars in merchandise. Chicago's Magnificent Mile was less than magnificent when teens ran into Armani Exchange and The North Face stores screaming,

Professional shoplifters are developing new approaches to stealing that include flash robs.

knocking over displays and merchandise, and fleeing with expensive jeans and other merchandise. A survey by National Retail Federation (NRF) found that 10 percent of the retailers surveyed had experienced a flash rob.

Sources: Liz Parks, "Allied Against ORC," *Stores Magazine*, August 2012; Chris Morran, "Man Scores 100% Discount on Electronics by Making Fake Receipts at Home," *Consumerist*, January 25, 2011; Michael Hartnett, "Remaining Vigilant," *Stores Magazine*, December 2011; Ann Zimmerman and Miguel Bustillo, "'Flash Robs' Vex Retailers," *The Wall Street Journal*, October 21, 2011; and Ann Zimmerman, "As Shoplifters Use High-Tech Scams, Retail Losses Rise," *The Wall Street Journal*, October 25, 2006, p. A1.

DISCUSSION QUESTION

What should retailers do to address new forms of high-tech shoplifting?

with documented performance problems, an unusual number of accidents, or erratic time and attendance records are also tested. Unless involved in selling drugs, employees who test positive are often offered an opportunity to complete a company-paid drug program, submit to random testing in the future, and remain with the firm.

Establishing Security Policies and Control Systems   To control employee theft, retailers need to adopt policies related to certain activities that may facilitate theft. Some of the most prevalent policies are:

- Randomly search containers, such as trash bins, where stolen merchandise can be stored.
- Require that store employees enter and leave the store through designated entrances.
- Assign salespeople to specific POS terminals, and require that all transactions be handled through those terminals.
- Restrict employee purchases to working hours.
- Provide customer receipts for all transactions.
- Have all refunds, returns, and discounts cosigned by a department or store manager.
- Change locks periodically, and issue keys to authorized personnel only.
- Provide a locker room where all employees' handbags, purses, packages, and coats must be checked before the employees leave.
- Maintain rotating employee assignments. Team different employees together.

In the end, it is important that employees do not feel that management is overly suspicious of their actions or that they are treated with disrespect, as this sense will erode morale.

SUMMARY

LO1 Describe how to improve the ability of workers through efficient recruiting, socializing, and training.

Store managers can improve the abilities of their employees through effective recruiting, socializing, and training. To recruit skillful, or potentially skillful, employees, store managers prepare a job description, find potential applicants with the desired capabilities, and screen the best candidates to interview. Having hired employees with the required skills or potential to develop these skills, retailers need to introduce the new employees to the firm and its policies, values, and strategies. This socialization process affects the degree to which newcomers become involved, engaged contributors to the firm's successful performance. In addition, socialization helps newly hired employees learn about their job responsibilities and the company they've decided to join. Effective training for new store employees includes both structured and on-the-job learning experiences.

LO2 Examine how to improve the effort of workers through proper motivation, evaluation, rewards, and compensation.

High-performance store employees work hard, and the activities they work on are consistent with the retailer's strategy and goals. Motivating employees to perform up to their potential may be store managers' most important and challenging task. To effectively motivate employees, store managers need to set goals for the employees and provide feedback on the employee's performance relative to these goals. Store employees receive two types of rewards from their job: extrinsic and intrinsic. Extrinsic rewards are rewards provided by either the employee's manager or the firm, such as compensation, promotion, and recognition. Intrinsic rewards are rewards employees get personally from doing their job well. For example, salespeople often like to sell because they think it's challenging and fun. The compensation program is the strongest motivator. It attracts and keeps good employees, motivates them to undertake activities consistent with the retailer's strategy, and strikes a balance between controlling labor costs and providing enough compensation to keep high-quality employees.

LO3 **Illustrate effective leadership strategies of a store manager.**

Leadership is the process by which a person attempts to influence others to accomplish a common goal or task. Store managers are leaders. The best store managers (leaders) go beyond influencing employee behaviors. There is no one best leadership style. Effective store managers use all styles, selecting the style most appropriate for each situation. Transformational leaders get people to transcend their personal needs for the sake of the group or organization so they are engaged and excited about their job.

LO4 **Explore the various strategies a store manager can undertake to control costs.**

Labor scheduling, store maintenance, and inventory shrinkage offer three opportunities to reduce store operating expenses. Using store employees efficiently is an important and challenging problem. Although store employees provide important customer service and merchandising functions that can increase sales, they also are the store's largest operating expense. An important issue facing store management is reducing inventory losses due to employee theft, shoplifting, mistakes, inaccurate records, and vendor errors. In developing a loss prevention program, retailers confront a trade-off between providing shopping convenience and a pleasant work environment on the one hand, and preventing losses due to shoplifting and employee theft on the other. The key to an effective loss prevention program is determining the most effective way to protect merchandise while preserving an open, attractive store atmosphere and a feeling among employees that they are trusted. Loss prevention requires coordination among store management, visual merchandising, and store design.

KEY TERMS

GET OUT AND DO IT!

1. **CONTINUING CASE ASSIGNMENT** Go to the store you have selected for the continuing case assignment, and meet with the person responsible for personnel scheduling. Report on the following:

- Who is responsible for employee scheduling?
- How far in advance is the schedule made?
- How are breaks and lunch periods planned?
- How are overtime hours determined?
- On what is the total number of budgeted employee hours for each department based?

- How is flexibility introduced into the schedule?
- How are special requests for days off handled?
- How are peak periods (hours, days, or seasons) planned for?
- What happens when an employee calls in sick at the last minute?
- What are the strengths and weaknesses of the personnel scheduling system from the manager's and employees' perspectives?

2. **CONTINUING CASE ASSIGNMENT** Go to the store you have selected for the continuing case assignment, and talk to the person responsible for human resource management to find out how sales associates are compensated and evaluated for job performance.

- How are sales associates trained? What are the criteria for evaluation?
- How often are they evaluated?
- Do salespeople have quotas? If they do, how are they set? What are the rewards of exceeding quotas? What are the consequences of not meeting these objectives?
- Can sales associates make a commission? If yes, how does the commission system work? What are the advantages of a commission system? What are the disadvantages?
- If there is no commission system, are any incentive programs offered? Give an example of a specific program or project used by the store to boost employee morale and productivity.

Evaluate each of the answers to these questions, and make recommendations for improvement where appropriate.

3. **GO SHOPPING** Go to a store, observe the security measures in the store, and talk with a manager about the store's loss prevention program.

- Are there surveillance cameras? Where are they located? Are the cameras monitored, or are they just there to thwart shoplifting?
- What is the store's policy against shoplifters?
- What are the procedures for approaching a suspected shoplifter?

- What roles do sales associates and executives play in the security programs?
- Is employee theft a problem? Elaborate.
- How is employee theft prevented in the store?
- How is customer service related to loss prevention in the store?
- What is this retailer doing well in terms of security and loss prevention, and in which areas should it improve its policies and procedures?

4. **INTERNET EXERCISE** Go online and research the shoplifting laws implemented by the state where you live or attend school. What are the fines, jail time, community service, or punishments for perpetrators in your local jurisdiction? What factors are weighed and evaluated in shoplifting cases? Are the laws in your state a deterrent to shoplifting? Please explain.

5. **LIBRARY EXERCISE** Go to one of your library's business databases and find an article that describes a case of a retailer violating Title VII in either its hiring or promotion practices. Summarize the case and court decision. What should this retailer do differently in the future to improve its employment policies?

6. **INTERNET EXERCISE** Go to the home page for Greening Retail (www.greeningretail.ca), and examine the company's research and programs that help retailers implement environmental best practices. Select a company in the "Featured Retailer Archive" (www.greeningretail.ca/featured/archive.dot) as a case example, and briefly describe what this retailer is doing to be a more sustainable company.

DISCUSSION QUESTIONS AND PROBLEMS

1. How do on-the-job training, Internet training, and classroom training differ? What are the benefits and limitations of each approach?

2. Give examples of a situation in which a manager of a McDonald's fast-food restaurant should utilize different leadership styles.

3. Using the interview questions in Exhibit 16–3, role-play with another student in the class as both the interviewer and the applicant for an assistant store manager position at a store of your choice.

4. Name some laws and regulations that affect the employee management process. Which do you believe are the easiest for retailers to adhere to? Which are violated the most often?

5. What's the difference between extrinsic and intrinsic rewards? What are the effects of these rewards on the behavior of retail employees? Under what conditions would you recommend that a retailer emphasize intrinsic rewards over extrinsic rewards?

6. Many large department and specialty stores are changing their salespeople's reward system from a

salary to a commission-based system. What problems can commission-based systems cause? How can department managers avoid these problems?

7. When evaluating retail employees, some stores use a quantitative approach that relies on checklists and numerical scores similar to the form in Exhibit 16–5. Other stores use a more qualitative approach, whereby less time is spent checking and adding and more time is devoted to discussing strengths and weaknesses in written form. What are the advantages and disadvantages of quantitative versus qualitative evaluation systems?

8. Some staff pharmacists working for retail chains refuse to dispense the Plan B "morning after" contraceptive pill because of their religious beliefs. In another situation, Muslims and Jewish checkout clerks working for supermarket chains refused to touch, scan, or bag products that contained any pork because of their religious beliefs. Do managers have the right to force employees to take actions that are contrary to their beliefs? Should customers be unable to buy products they want because of an employee's beliefs?

Should employee be required to ignore their religious beliefs? What would you do if you were faced with these or similar ethically sensitive situations?

9. Discuss how retailers can reduce shrinkage from shoplifting and employee theft.

10. Drugstore retailers such as CVS place diabetic test strips and perfume behind locked glass cabinets and nearly all over-the-counter medicines behind Plexiglas panels. What are the pros and cons of these locked glass cabinets from the retailer's perspective? From the customer's perspective?

SUGGESTED READINGS

Arthur, Diane. *Recruiting, Interviewing, Selecting & Orienting New Employees*, 5th ed. New York: AMACOM, 2012.

Bell, Simon, Bülent Mengüç, and Robert E. Widing II. "Salesperson Learning, Organizational Learning, and Retail Store Performance." *Journal of the Academy of Marketing Science* 38, no. 2 (2010), pp. 187–201.

Bernardin, H. John. *Human Resource Management: An Experiential Approach*, 5th ed. Burr Ridge, IL: McGraw-Hill, 2010.

Carmel-Gilfilen, Candy. "Advancing Retail Security Design: Uncovering Shoplifter Perceptions of the Physical Environment." *Journal of Interior Design* 36, no. 2 (2011), pp. 21–38.

Hollinger, Richard, and Amanda Adams. *2011 Annual Retail Security Survey*. Gainesville, FL: Security Research Project, University of Florida, 2012.

Ng, Eddy, Sean Lyons, and Linda Schweitzer. *Managing the New Workforce: International Perspectives on the Millennial Generation*. Northampton, MA: Edward Elgar Publishing, 2012.

Purpura, Philip. *Security and Loss Prevention*, 6th ed. New York: Butterworth-Heinemann, 2013.

Phillips, Jack J. *Handbook of Training Evaluation and Measurement Methods*. New York: Routledge, 2012.

Rothstein, Mark, and Lance Leibman. *Employment Law*, 7th ed. St. Paul, MN: Thomson/West, 2012.

U.S. Equal Employment Opportunity Commission. "Sexual Harassment." Washington, DC: 2011.

Store Layout, Design, and Visual Merchandising

EXECUTIVE BRIEFING
Fredrik Holmvik, Head of Media,
ICA Sweden

ICA is a leading Nordic retailer with more than 2,100 retailer- and company-owned stores. The company is owned by the ICA Group. ICA operates in Sweden, Norway, and the Baltic countries. It operates four store formats: ICA Nära (ICA Nearby—convenience store), ICA Supermarket, ICA Kvantum (superstore), and Maxi ICA Hypermarket (which has approximately 1,300 stores in Sweden). ICA is the largest supermarket chain in Sweden and serves more than 10 million customers per week. ICA's mission is to be the leading retailer focused on food and meals. In Sweden, ICA stores are owned by independent retailers. However, ICA (the parent organization) handles the centralized operations such as purchasing, communications, and logistics.

I am currently the head of ICA media. I have been actively working with ICA for many years, first as a consultant and now as an employee. Prior to this, I was the CEO of QB Food Tech Ltd. I have also worked as a consultant for Accenture and at Unilever in a variety of roles.

ICA has historically used a variety of traditional media (e.g., TV commercials, home flyers) and in-store paper signage to provide our customers relevant information, ranging from prices to campaigns to cooking tips. Some years ago, we introduced

digital screens and signage (what we call ICA's in-store media channel) to augment the traditional media. These screens allow us to provide relevant content, such as ICA campaigns, cooking tips, as well as vendor commercials and point-of-purchase promotions.

Our goals for these digital displays include increasing sales, improving campaign reach and effectiveness, and creating a more up-to-date image and feel for our stores. In a short time frame, we have introduced digital signage in 350 stores, covering a reach of more than 55 percent of our weekly customers. Price deals that have been advertised using our digital screens have seen sales go up by almost 100 percent. Traditional vendor advertisements drive sales as well as brand awareness. These digital displays attract consumer attention and increase their likelihood of purchasing the products being displayed. Our research shows that digital displays with moving images or films, compared to ordinary displays, double customer attention.

CHAPTER 17

LEARNING OBJECTIVES

LO1 Identify the critical issues retailers need to consider when designing a store.

LO2 List the advantages and disadvantages of alternative store layouts.

LO3 Describe how to assign store floor space to merchandise departments and categories.

LO4 Illustrate the best techniques for merchandise presentation.

LO5 Understand how retailers can create a more appealing shopping experience.

These insights have important implications for the design of stores, such as where to locate digital displays, what type of displays to use, and most importantly, what to communicate In certain departments/areas of the store. For instance, displays in the fruit and vegetable section focus on relevant communication in that area, just as displays in the bread section focus within its relevant communication range. The effectiveness of these displays varies as a function of their location in the store and the type of store. For instance, our research has shown that these digital signs can increase sales by as much as 5 percent in hypermarkets. In smaller stores, sales are also affected, and the most interesting finding here is the actual effect on being more up-to-date. The customer actually experiences a more "modern" store environment, which contributes to the overall perception of the store in a favorable way.

These digital screens also provide cost efficiencies through lower costs associated with production, printing, and getting the traditional printed material to the stores, as well as better coordination of promotions between our vendors and stores.

The environment in a store, the design of the store, and the presentation and location of merchandise in the store have significant impacts on shopping behavior. The design of a store or website attracts customers to visit the location, increases the time they spend in the store or on the site, and increases the amount of merchandise they purchase. Store design also has long-term effects on building customer loyalty toward the retailer by enhancing the retailer's brand image and providing rewarding shopping experiences that encourage repeat visits.

This chapter is part of the Store Management section because store managers are responsible for implementing the design and visual merchandising developed by specialists at the retailer's corporate headquarters. They adapt the prototype plans to the unique characteristics of their stores, then make sure the image and experience provided by the design are consistent over time. However, as discussed in this chapter, store design and visual merchandising are also elements of a retailer's communication mix and play an important role in creating and reinforcing a retailer's brand image.

The chapter begins with a discussion of store design objectives. Next, the elements of store design are discussed. The decisions about how much space to allocate to different merchandise categories and departments and where they should be located in the store are reviewed. The chapter concludes with an examination of how retailers use store design elements, such as color, lighting, and music, to enhance the customer's shopping experience.

STORE DESIGN OBJECTIVES

LO1

Identify the critical issues retailers need to consider while designing a store.

Some store design objectives are to (1) implement the retailer's strategy, (2) build loyalty by providing a rewarding shopping experience, (3) increase sales on a visit, (4) control costs, and (5) meet legal requirements.

Implement the Retail Strategy

The primary objective for store design is to implement the retailer's strategy. The design must be consistent with and reinforce the retailer's strategy by meeting the needs of the target market and building a sustainable competitive advantage. Starbucks' store designs are inspired by the Italian coffee bars that not only have great coffee, but also serve as a place to meet friends, socialize, and relax. Soft lighting, wood tables, comfortable seating, free wi-fi, and clean bathrooms make Starbucks a place where people just want to hang out and have a good cup of coffee. Retailing View 17.1 details how another innovative retailer, Apple, makes store design decisions to reinforce its overall strategy.

Build Loyalty

When customers consistently have rewarding experiences when patronizing a retailer's store and/or website, they are motivated to visit repeatedly and develop loyalty toward the retailer. Store design plays an important role in making shopping experiences rewarding. Customers seek two types of benefits when shopping— utilitarian and hedonic benefits.[1]

Store design provides **utilitarian benefits** when it enables customers to locate and purchase products in an efficient and timely manner with minimum hassle. Such utilitarian benefits are becoming increasingly important in today's time-poor society. Therefore, drugstore retailers such as CVS and Walgreens have designed their stores to include drive-through pharmacies and have invested in various technologies to augment customer convenience associated with these store design elements. They have developed mobile apps to help people refill their prescriptions; they then pick them up through the drive-through. These design elements and connected apps are further speeding up customers' shopping trips.[2]

Store design provides **hedonic benefits** by offering customers an entertaining and enjoyable shopping experience. They then want to spend more time in the store or on the website because the visit itself is rewarding. For example, Cabela's, a chain of stores catering to outdoor enthusiasts, provides an educational and entertaining experience that mixes museum-quality dioramas of wildlife on display, massive huge aquariums featuring native fish, a restaurant where diners can order wild-game sandwiches, and a shooting gallery that teaches basic shooting and

RETAILING VIEW   The Innovator Designs a Space, By and For the Geniuses   **17.1**

The glass cube that sits on Fifth Avenue has become nearly legendary at this point—just one more example of how Apple continually seeks new ideas to appeal to people's aesthetic and tactile senses. The cube and other visually remarkable glass entryways tell consumers that they have arrived at an Apple destination. Once they enter the light-filled spaces, Apple applies its design genius to keep them shopping happily.

Consider, for example, the Shanghai store. A glass cylinder (Apple had already done the cube in New York) rises up, seemingly from the ground. In the Hamburg, Germany, stores, the stairs to move between floors are all glass and are attached only at the top and bottom, creating a sense as if they are hanging in the air. As the architect hired to conceive of these ideas noted, "Steve [Jobs] wanted us to push the edge of technology, but it had to be comfortable for people. . . . It's an interesting challenge, how to marry the two."

Not all stores can afford a glass entryway, though. For more traditional retail spaces, such as in malls, Apple instead focuses on drawing people in by creating high ceilings, using bright but soft lighting, and placing its offerings on warm wood tables. The physical retail atmosphere helps build the communal sense initiated by its products. It also encourages and enables consumers to interact with Apple's technologically sophisticated products in a safe, inviting setting.

The layout of the stores and the products they feature also draw people further into the stores. To get to the Genius bar, they have to traverse all the way to the back of the store, walking past appealingly designed products as they do so. Even the displays of the computers are tilted at just the right angle to draw their eye.

Overall though, Apple stores reinforce the image of Apple as an innovation master. By adding unique and

The unique design of the Apple store in New York City reinforces the company's image of developing and retailing products with innovative design features.

unseen architectural elements to its flagship stores and ensuring all its stores are appealing, Apple shows just how cutting edge it remains. As the architect for the stores further noted, in lamenting Jobs's death, "Steve was a great client. . . . He would not discourage innovation that was within his vision of what Apple is or he is."

Sources: James B. Stewart, "A Genius of the Storefront, Too," *The New York Times,* October 15, 2011; Matthew Carroll, "How Retailers Can Replicate the Magic of the Apple Store . . . Online," *Forbes,* June 26, 2010; and Apple Store, www.apple.com/cn/retail/pudong/.

DISCUSSION QUESTION

How has Apple's innovative store design reinforced its innovative image?

safety lessons while also providing a fun experience. These shopping and tourism destinations draw customers from the local area certainly, but they also can attract travelers from hundreds of miles away.

Of course, few retailers can offer only utilitarian or hedonic benefits. Most need to use both routes to ensure customer loyalty. Thus, in the face of the global economic downturn, Wegmans has applied a more utilitarian look and feel in some sections, to welcome price-sensitive customers and reassure its existing shoppers that it recognizes their economic constraints.[3] The Wegmans supermarket chain explicitly designs its stores to make the chore of grocery shopping more fun: Instead of linoleum floors, harsh fluorescent lights, and narrow aisles, shoppers experience the feel of an open air market. Wegmans also offers various eat-in options, an exotic tea bar, a trail mix bar, and gourmet chef-prepared meals to take

To enhance the shopping experience, Wegmans offers gourmet chef-prepared meals to take home.

home. This unique experience for customers has helped Wegmans' 77 stores earn nearly $6 billion in sales annually.[4]

Increase Sales on Visits

A third design objective is to increase the sales made to customers on any particular visit. Store design has a substantial effect on which products customers buy, how long they stay in the store, and how much they spend during a visit. Because most consumers spend very little time and thought on shopping and selecting items in supermarkets, these purchase decisions are greatly influenced by what products customers see during their visit. What they see in turn is affected by the store layout and how the merchandise is presented. Thus, retailers attempt to design their stores in a manner that motivates unplanned purchases. As discussed later in this chapter, retailers use the cash wrap area, where people pay for merchandise, to display and therefore stimulate the sale of impulse items such as candy at a supermarket check-out terminal or jewelry at a women's apparel store.

Control Costs to Increase Profits

The fourth design objective is to control the cost of implementing the store design and maintaining the store's appearance. Although the types of lighting that Neiman Marcus shines on its expensive jewelry and crystal use more electricity and are less ecologically friendly than rows of bare fluorescent bulbs, the retailer considers such costs necessary to highlight these high-ticket items. In contrast, other retailers have embraced the notion of gaining efficiency in their energy use, as Retailing View 17.2 details.

Store designs can also affect labor costs and inventory shrinkage. Some stores are organized into isolated departments, which provides an intimate, comfortable shopping experience that can result in more sales. However, the design prevents sales associates from observing and covering adjacent departments, which makes it necessary to have at least one sales associate permanently stationed in each department to provide customer service and prevent shoplifting.

Another design consideration related to controlling cost is flexibility. Retailing is a very dynamic business. Competitors enter a market and cause existing retailers to change the mix of merchandise offered. As the merchandise mix changes, so

RETAILING VIEW   Walmart Goes Green and Lowers Its Energy Costs   17.2

In an initiative begun several years ago, Walmart continues to design new stores and retrofit older stores to ensure their energy efficiency. These stores are among the "greenest" in the world. The three main design objectives for these stores are reducing the amount of energy and other natural resources required for store operations, minimizing the raw materials used to construct each facility, and using renewable materials whenever possible.

These design elements reflect Walmart's three broad environmental goals: (1) to be supplied 100 percent by renewable energy, (2) to create zero waste, and (3) to sell products that sustain the world's resources and environment. Although such design features reduce the stores' impact on the environment, they also are expensive to build. Initial projections call for the energy used at these new stores to be 25 to 30 percent less than older stores that have not been retrofitted, reducing a store's energy costs by $500,000 annually. Such savings could increase if energy costs continue to climb.

Some of the sustainable features that have passed these steps or are currently being tested are as follows:

- A wind turbine on top of a store that produces sufficient energy to offset 5 percent of each store's electricity consumption.

- A system to collect and treat rainwater, which in turn can provide nearly all of the water required for irrigation and thus will reduce demands placed on local stormwater systems.

- The use of grass for landscaping that does not need irrigation or mowing.

- LEDs, instead of fluorescent lighting, in refrigerated cases. In cold temperatures, fluorescent lights lose life expectancy every time they are switched on and off; LEDs do not suffer from this limitation. The lights stay off until the customer opens the case. In addition to saving energy, the lights add a theatrical appeal for customers.

- A system that captures the heat generated by each building's refrigeration system, then redirects that heat to warm the water in restroom sinks or support new radiant, floor-heating systems located beneath the entries and other areas.

Although many of these changes have been made globally, Walmart also customizes some green design choices by region:

- Brazil: Stores employ smart lights that dim when natural sunlight is available.

- Mexico: Walmart invested 640 million pesos (US$57 million) to convert a 25-acre, 50-foot deep dump into a green mall, which created 1,500 jobs. The trash produced energy through a bio-gas burning process. The green mall is now home to a Walmart supercenter, Sam's Club, Vips, and El Porton restaurants.

- Central America: 70 percent of stores have installed skylights to reduce lighting costs, covering approximately 15 percent of the roof space of each store.

- China: Walmart has begun to switch over to LED lighting throughout stores and integrated lighting controls to reduce energy usage by a target amount of 30 percent in existing stores and 40 percent in prototype stores.

- Japan: Prototype stores use a desiccant temperature and humidity system to reduce energy costs and CO_2 emissions.

Sources: "Taking Sustainability to New Heights," www.walmartgreeenroom/com, October 15, 2012; "No Matter the Season, Our Energy Commitment Is Always On," www.walmartgreenroonm.com, September 28, 2012; Michelle Moran, "Seeing Green," *Progressive Grocer*, March 2010, pp. 16–31; Cathy Jett, "New Design's Goal: To Cut the Clutter," *McClatchy-Tribune Business News*, October 14, 2009; and Aaron Besecker, "Walmart Store Gets Green Light," *McClatchy-Tribune Business News*, August 31, 2009.

DISCUSSION QUESTION

Are green store designs worth their cost? Why or why not?

must the space allocated to merchandise categories and the layout of the store. Thus, store designers attempt to design stores with maximum flexibility.

Flexibility is an important design consideration for college bookstores because they need to expand and contract their spaces to accommodate the large seasonal fluctuations inherent in the college-bookstore business. At the beginning of a semester, considerable space needs to be allocated to textbooks. But after the first week of the semester, the demand for textbooks decreases quickly, and space allocated to textbooks needs to be reallocated to apparel and consumer electronics. The key to providing this flexibility often lies in innovative fixture and wall systems that portion off the textbook area. **Fixtures** refer to the equipment used to display merchandise.

Legal Considerations—Americans with Disabilities Act

All store design and redesign decisions must comply with the 1990 Americans with Disabilities Act (ADA) and its 2008 amendments.[5] This law protects people with disabilities from discrimination in employment, transportation, public

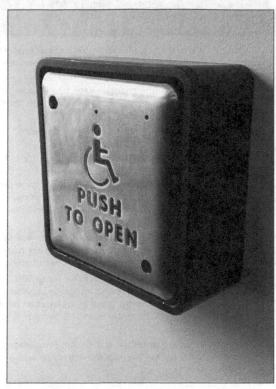

The ADA has made stores more accessible for disabled consumers.

accommodations, telecommunications, and activities of state and local governments. It affects store design because the act calls for "reasonable access" to merchandise and services in retail stores built before 1993; stores built after 1993 must be fully accessible.

The act also states that retailers should not have to incur "undue burdens" to comply with ADA requirements. Although retailers are concerned about the needs of their disabled customers, they are also worried that making merchandise completely accessible to people in a wheelchair or a motorized cart will result in less space available to display merchandise and thus will reduce sales. However, providing for wider aisles and more space around fixtures can result in a more pleasant shopping experience for able-bodied as well as disabled customers.

The ADA does not clearly define critical terms such as "reasonable access," "fully accessible," or "undue burden." So the actual ADA requirements are being defined through a series of court cases in which disabled plaintiffs have filed class-action suits against retailers.[6] On the basis of these court cases, retailers are typically required to (1) provide 32-inch-wide pathways in the main aisle, to bathrooms, dressing rooms, and elevators, and around most fixtures; (2) lower most cash wraps (checkout stations) and fixtures so that they can be reached by a person in a wheelchair; (3) create disability-accessible checkout aisles; (4) provide bathrooms with handrails or grab bars; and (5) make dressing rooms fully accessible. Nor does the ADA stop at the store exit. Very clear guidelines establish the number of handicapped accessible parking spaces that stores must provide.[7] Some of these accessibility requirements are somewhat relaxed for retailers in very small spaces and during peak sales periods such as the Christmas holidays.

Design Trade-Offs

Few store designs can achieve all of these objectives, so any store design involves trade-offs among the objectives. Home Depot's traditional warehouse design can efficiently store and display a lot of merchandise with long rows of floor-to-ceiling racks, but this design is not conducive for a pleasant shopping experience.

Retailers often make trade-offs between stimulating impulse purchases and making it easy to buy products. For example, supermarkets place milk, a commonly purchased item, at the back of the store to make customers walk through the entire store, thus stimulating more impulse purchases. Realizing that some customers may want to buy only milk, Walgreens places its milk at the front of the store, enabling it to compete head-to-head with convenience stores.

The trade-off between making it easy to find merchandise and providing an interesting shopping experience is determined by the customer's shopping needs. For example, supermarket and drugstore shoppers typically focus on utilitarian benefits and want to minimize the time they spend shopping, so the design of supermarkets emphasizes the ease of locating merchandise (there are exceptions, such as Wegmans). In contrast, customers shopping for specialty goods like a computer, a home entertainment center, or furniture are more likely to spend time in the store browsing, comparing, and talking with the salesperson. Thus, specialty store retailers that offer this type of merchandise place more emphasis on providing hedonic benefits and encouraging exploration than on making it easy to find merchandise.

Another trade-off is the balance between giving customers adequate space in which to shop and productively using this scarce resource for merchandise. Customers are attracted to stores with wide aisles and fixtures whose primary purpose is to display rather than hold the merchandise. Also, shoppers do not like it when a store is so cramped that they touch one another, a phenomenon known as the "butt-brush effect."[8] However, a spacious design reduces the amount of merchandise that can be available to buy and thus may also reduce impulse purchases and the customers' chances of finding what they are looking for. But too many racks and displays in a store can cause customers to feel uncomfortable and even confused. There must be a compromise between been having a store that is too spacious and one that is overcrowded.

This section examined the various objectives retailers seek to satisfy when designing their stores. In the next section, important elements of design are explored.

STORE DESIGN ELEMENTS

Three elements in the design of stores are the (1) layout, (2) signage, and (3) feature areas. Each of these elements is discussed in this section.

LO2
List the advantages and disadvantages of alternative store layouts.

Layouts

Retailers use three general types of store layout design: grid, racetrack, and free form. Each of these layouts has advantages and disadvantages.

Grid Layout   The **grid layout**, illustrated in Exhibit 17–1, has parallel aisles with merchandise on shelves on both sides of the aisles. Cash registers are located at the entrances/exits of the stores.

The grid layout is well suited for customers who are primarily interested in the utilitarian benefits offered by the store. They are not interested in the hedonic

EXHIBIT 17–1
Grid Store Layout

benefits provided by a visually exciting design. They want to easily locate products they want to buy, and they make their purchases as quickly as possible. Most supermarkets and full-line discount stores use the grid layout, because this design enables their customers to easily find the product they are looking for and minimize the time spent on a shopping task that most don't enjoy.

The grid layout is also cost-efficient. There's less wasted space with the grid layout than with other layouts because the aisles are all the same width and designed to be just wide enough to accommodate shoppers and their carts. The use of high shelves for merchandise enables more merchandise to be on the sales floor compared with other layouts. Finally, because the fixtures are generally standardized, the cost of the fixtures is low.

One limitation of the grid layout, from the retailer's perspective, is that customers typically aren't exposed to all the merchandise in the store because, due to the height of the shelves, they see only products displayed in the aisle they are in. Thus the layout does not encourage unplanned purchases. Supermarket retailers overcome this limitation, to some extent, by complementing the packaged goods in the center-store grid with a racetrack of fresh, perishable merchandise categories (meat, seafood, dairy, poultry, baked goods, and produce) around the periphery of the store. Unplanned purchases are also stimulated by special displays, which are discussed later in the chapter.

In the past, supermarket retailers and consumer packaged goods manufacturers did not feel this limitation was very important. They believed that customers would be exposed to all the merchandise in the store because they would walk up and down each aisle, pushing their shopping carts. However, researchers have equipped carts with GPS locators and found that most supermarket customers enter a supermarket, turn right, go along the periphery of the store looking down the aisles, and occasionally walk down an aisle with their carts or leave the cart at the end of the aisle and walk down the aisle to select a specific item and return to the cart. A path taken by a typical customer is shown in Exhibit 17–2.[9]

Supermarket retailers and consumer packaged goods companies now recognize this problem of decreased traffic in the center core of supermarkets. Whereas the outer circumference of the store has seen some exciting improvements, such that "store perimeters have become warm, inviting, exciting, genuine and diverse," according to David Milka, director of consumer insight for S.C. Johnson, the center of the store has remained "cold, obscure, boring and non-differentiated."[10]

The answer is to get customers to spend more time in the center store. Recent research shows that the more time customers spend in stores in general, the more unplanned purchases they make.[11] One way to extend their shopping time is to make their shopping path less efficient. Thus, to expose customers to more

EXHIBIT 17–2
Example of a Traffic Pattern in a Grid Layout Supermarket

merchandise and increase their unplanned purchases in the core, supermarket retailers need to get customers to walk down more aisles. One potential approach for increasing traffic in the core would alter the straight aisles to form a zig-zag pattern. As discussed in Retailing View 17.3, IKEA uses a similar method. Another approach locates power brands—those with high awareness and market share such as Coca-Cola and Tide—and eye-attracting displays in the middle of the aisle rather than at the ends. The power brands appear from the top to the bottom, creating a swath of color that captures the attention of customers as they peek down the aisle.

RETAILING VIEW   A Hedonic Maze Filled with Utilitarian Products   **17.3**

IKEA stores are designed to inspire customers to weave their way through the store.

At its largest North American store in Montreal, IKEA offers 464,694 feet of functional, reasonably priced furniture, décor, and housewares. It contains various settings that showcase its products, including three full homes and approximately 50 "inspirational room settings," as well as a market hall and a restaurant that can seat 600. If you walked the entire store, you'd have completed a nearly one-mile hike.

Of course, few shoppers want to cover all that ground. Visitors looking for a new ottoman for their living room have little reason to swing through the bedroom sets. And yet, somehow, most of them wind up doing just that.

The reason is likely IKEA's distinctive, maze-like layout for its stores. Once customers enter the maze, it is difficult for them to find a specific department, or even the exit, unless they follow the path laid out for them. According to IKEA, this layout benefits customers by giving them inspiration and decorating ideas. But still the notion seems contradictory. Shouldn't a retailer make it easier for customers to find what they want?

Instead, IKEA's store flows create disorientation and directional confusion to push customers through each department. That means they spend more time in the stores and may consider more purchases. They might have stopped for an ottoman, but the bedside lamp they see in

an inspirational bedroom setting might be just the thing. In addition, customers are more likely to place appealing items in their carts for fear that they will be unable to find it again if they leave it behind. Finally, the length of time customers spend in the store makes them feel committed to the visit. If they don't pick up a few items, all that expenditure of time might seem wasted.

According to various observers, the effect is either brilliant or underhanded—or both. No one seems to leave IKEA without buying more than he or she had planned. This near-inability to stick to a shopping list seems a direct result of the carefully designed layout that causes customers to buy a number of uplanned items.

Sources: Elizabeth Tyler, "How IKEA Seduces Its Customers: By Trapping Them," *Time*, January 28, 2011; and Kathryn Blaze Carlson, "Enter the Maze: IKEA, Costco, Other Retailers Know How to Get You to Buy More," *National Post*, June 1, 2012.

DISCUSSION QUESTION

What features of IKEA and its strategy make its unique store layout appropriate for it, but not for other types of retailers?

Retailers are experimenting with creative promotional approaches to keep people shopping. For example, LocalResponse allows retailers to know what merchandise customers are talking about using social media (e.g., a tweet, Facebook update, photo on Instagram, or check-in using Foursquare) while in the store. Consequently, retailers can use the latest advances in technology to offer customers instant coupons on their mobile phones for merchandise adjacent to where they are physically located, which might entice them to find the product and buy it. Additionally, giving them an electronic coupon for merchandise located at another, potentially distant, location in the store, along with a map of where it is located, may lure them to meander through the store with the possibility that they will purchase other items along the way.

Racetrack Layout   The **racetrack layout,** also known as a **loop,** is a store layout that provides a major aisle that loops around the store to guide customer traffic around different departments within the store. Point-of-sale terminals are typically located in each department bordering the racetrack.

The racetrack layout facilitates the goal of getting customers to see the merchandise available in multiple departments and thus encourages unplanned purchasing. As customers go around the racetrack, their eyes are forced to take different viewing angles rather than looking down one aisle, as in the grid design. Low fixtures are used so that customers can see merchandise beyond the products displayed on the racetrack.

Exhibit 17–3 shows the layout of a department store. Because the store has multiple entrances, the racetrack layout places all departments on the main aisle by drawing customers through the store in a series of major and minor loops. To entice customers through the various departments, the design places some of the more

EXHIBIT 17–3   Racetrack Layout

EXHIBIT 17–4
Free-Form Store
Layout

popular departments, like juniors, toward the rear of the store. The newest items also are featured on the aisles to draw customers into departments and around the loop.

The racetrack usually is wider than other aisles and defined by a change in flooring surface or color. For instance, the aisle flooring might be marblelike tile, whereas the department floors vary in material, texture, and color, depending on the desired ambience.

Free-Form Layout A **free-form layout**, also known as **boutique layout**, arranges fixtures and aisles in an asymmetric pattern (Exhibit 17–4). It provides an intimate, relaxing environment that facilitates shopping and browsing. It appears most commonly in specialty stores or as departments within department stores. However, creating this pleasing shopping environment is costly. Because there is no well-defined traffic pattern, as there is in the racetrack and grid layouts, customers aren't naturally drawn around the store or department, and personal selling becomes more important to encourage customers to explore merchandise offered in the store. In addition, the layout reduces the amount of merchandise that can be displayed.

Signage and Graphics

Signage and graphics help customers locate specific products and departments, provide product information, and suggest items or special purchases. Graphics, such as photo panels, can reinforce a store's image. Signage is used to identify the location of merchandise categories within a store and the types of products offered in the category. The signs are hung typically from the ceiling to enhance their visibility. Frequently, icons rather than words are used to facilitate communication with customers speaking different languages. For example, a red and yellow circus tent icon identifies the area for children's toys more effectively than a black and white, worded rectangular sign. Smaller signs are used to identify sale items and provide more information about specific products. Finally, retailers may use images, such as pictures of people and places, to create moods that encourage customers to buy products. Some different types of signs are:

- **Call-to-action signage.** Placed in strategic locations in the store can convey how, where, and why to engage with the retailer via QR codes on customers' cellphones, via e-mail, short-message services, Facebook, or other digital channels.

- **Category signage.** Used within a particular department or sector of the store to identify types of products offered. They are usually located near the goods to which they refer.

- **Promotional signage.** Describes special offers and found within the store or displayed in windows to entice the customer into the store. For instance, value apparel stores for young women often display large posters in their windows of models wearing new or sale items.

- **Point-of-sale signage.** Point-of-sale signs are placed near the merchandise they refer to so that customers know its price and other detailed information. Some of this information may already be on product labels or packaging. However, point-of-sale signage can quickly identify for the customer those aspects likely to be of greater interest, such as whether the product is on sale. Walmart uses this sort of signage effectively to show customers when the price of an item has been "rolled back."

Digital Signage   Many retailers are replacing traditional signage with digital signage systems.[12] **Digital signage** includes signs whose visual content is delivered electronically through a centrally managed and controlled network, distributed to servers in stores, and displayed on flat-panel screens. The content delivered can range from entertaining video clips to simple price displays.

Digital signage provides a number of benefits over traditional static-print signage. Due to their dynamic nature, digital signs are more effective in attracting the attention of customers and helping them recall the messages displayed. Digital signage also offers the opportunity to enhance a store's environment by displaying complex graphics and videos to provide an atmosphere that customers find appealing.[13] Because the content is delivered digitally, it can easily be tailored to a store's market and remain consistent in every store, displayed at the right time and right place. Furthermore, by overcoming the time-to-message hurdle associated with traditional print signage, digital signage enables the content to be varied within and across stores at different times of the day or days of the week—without incurring the expense of printing, distributing, and installing new static signs or hiring labor to post them. If the temperatures rise, digital in-store signage might automatically advertise cold drinks; if the forecast continues to be warm and sunny, it might promote sunscreen. Of course, there is a drawback too. The initial

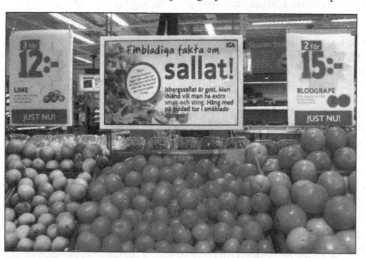

In-store digital displays highlight key product features and experiential elements at the point of purchase.

cost of the display devices and the system that supports the delivery of signage can be quite high.

Recent research shows customers spend $1.52 more, per trip, at grocery stores when digital displays are used. Less than $2 might not seem like that much, but the overall effect is huge in the grocery sector, with its tight margins and high volume of shoppers.[14] The effect of digital signage on sales is not limited to grocers. Lord & Taylor has added digital signage to its flagship store in Manhattan and plans to expand its use. The store reports the addition of digital signage in its fragrance department paid for itself in less than a year, and digital technology in the men's suit department led to double-digit sales increases.[15]

Feature Areas

In addition to using layout and signage, retailers can guide customers through stores and influence buying behavior through the placement of feature areas. **Feature areas** are the areas within a store that are designed to get customers' attention. They include windows, entrances, freestanding displays, mannequins, end caps, promotional aisles or areas, walls, dressing rooms, and cash wraps.

Windows   Window displays draw customers into the store and provide a visual message about the type of merchandise offered in the store and the type of image the store wants to portray. Research suggests that storefront window displays are an effective tool for building the store image, particularly with new customers who are unfamiliar with the store.[17]

Effective window displays are not easy to achieve, however, and they often demand the collaboration of a large team of designers. At The Limited, an extensive design team, led by the senior vice president of visual merchandising and store design and construction, takes several weeks, or even months, to find just the right combination of women's fashions that will attract mall shoppers strolling by the stores. Only after extensive analysis does the design team introduce their display to the stores throughout the nation.[18]

Entrances   The first impression caused by the entry area affects the customer's image of the store. Department stores typically have the cosmetics and fragrance categories at the main entrance, while grocery stores have fresh produce because these categories are visually appealing and create a sense of excitement. Whole Foods places cut flowers near the entrance to connote freshness.[19]

While the entry area plays a prominent role in creating an image, the first 10 feet of the store are often referred to as the "decompression zone," because customers are making an adjustment to the new environment: escaping from the noisy street or mall, taking off their sunglasses, closing their umbrellas, and developing a visual impression of the entire store. Customers are not prepared to evaluate merchandise or make purchase decisions in the decompression zone, so retailers try to keep this area free of merchandise, displays, and signage.[20]

Freestanding Displays   **Freestanding displays** are fixtures that are located on aisles and designed primarily to attract customers' attention and bring them into a department. These fixtures often display and store the newest, most exciting merchandise in the particular department.

Window displays need to catch the attention of the shopper and draw them into the store.

Whimsical mannequins attract the attention of children in Disney stores.

REFACT

An international survey
of supermarket shoppers
found that end caps are
noticed by more than
three-quarters of shoppers
and could influence
60 percent to make a
purchase.[22]

Mannequins   A **mannequin** is a life-size representation of the human body, used for displaying apparel. In the past, mannequins were often plain and boring. Twenty-first-century retailers have begun to realize that mannequins don't need to be hairless, feature-less, blindingly white, skinny space holders. They can help personify a brand, push customers to enter their stores, and perhaps even offer an ideal image that encourages shoppers to buy a little something extra that looks great on display. At the Disney Store, children are enchanted as whimsical mannequins swoop down from the ceiling or execute a perfect princess curtsy. The stylish customers moving through Ralph Lauren stores instead perceive a sense of style and sophistication, conveyed through the mannequin with a recreated face of British model Yasmin Le Bon.[21]

End Caps   **End caps** are displays located at the end of an aisle in stores using a grid lay-out. Due to the high visibility of end caps, sales of a product increase dramatically when that merchandise is featured on an end cap. Thus, retailers use end caps for higher-margin, impulse, and sale merchandise. In the supermarket industry, vendors often negotiate for their products to be on end-cap displays when they are offering special promotional prices.

Promotional Aisle or Area   A **promotional aisle** or **promotional area** is a space used to display merchandise that is being promoted. Drugstores, for instance, use promotional aisles to sell seasonal merchandise, such as lawn and garden products in the summer and Christmas decorations in the fall. Specialty stores and department stores tend to locate a promotional area at the back of the store or department. To get to the items on sale, customers must pass through all the full-price merchandise, which makes it more likely that something will catch their eye.

The arrangement of merchandise helps tells the story.

Walls   Because retail floor space is often limited, many retailers increase their ability to store extra stock, display merchandise, and creatively present a message by utilizing wall space. Merchandise can be stored on shelving and racks and coordinated with displays, photographs, or graphics featuring the merchandise. At the French clothier Lacoste, for instance, merchandise is displayed in bold color swaths relatively high on the wall. Not only does this allow the merchandise to "tell a story," but it also helps customers feel more comfortable because they aren't crowded by racks or by other people, and they can get a perspective on the merchandise by viewing it from a distance.

Dressing Rooms   Dressing rooms are critical spaces, where customers often decide whether to purchase an item. Large, clean, and comfortable dressing rooms put customers in the mood to buy. In recent years, retailers have even begun to compete aggressively on the basis of the quality of their dressing rooms. Old Navy has moved dressing rooms to the front of stores, so they no longer feel like "dungeons." To achieve a more refined, upscale feel, Ann Taylor stores feature chandeliers and attractive color accents in fitting rooms. Recognizing that many shoppers make trying on clothes a social event, Anthropologie has expanded the size of dressing rooms to make it easier for women to bring friends in with them. And to make the experience of waiting for a spouse trying on clothes more enjoyable, Macy's has added couches and flat-screen televisions outside dressing rooms.[23]

 Virtual dressing rooms are becoming more important and interesting to online shoppers. People cannot try on clothes displayed on a website, but the spread of webcams embedded in laptops, tablets, and desktop computers is making it possible for programmers to create "virtual dressing rooms" that could permit Internet customers to "try on" clothing and accessories, simply by standing in front of their webcams.[24]

Although technology and decor can enhance the experience of trying on clothing, some retailers are cautious about the extent to which they will use technology. The personal attention provided by sales associates remains the most effective agent for providing customer service.

Cash Wraps   **Cash wraps**, also known as **point-of-purchase (POP) counters** or **checkout areas**, are places in the store where customers can purchase merchandise. Because many customers go to these areas and wait in line to make a purchase, retailers often use them to display impulse purchase items. For example, in supermarkets, batteries, candy, gum, and magazines are often shelved at the checkout counter.

REFACT

Dressing rooms help retailers sell merchandise. Customers who try on clothes in dressing rooms have a 67 percent conversion rate (i.e., two-thirds of customers buy something that they try on), compared with a 10 percent conversion rate for customers who do not try on clothes.[25]

SPACE MANAGEMENT

LO3

Describe how to assign store floor space to merchandise departments and categories.

The space within stores and on the stores' shelves and fixtures is a scarce resource. Space management involves key resource decisions: (1) the allocation of store space to merchandise categories and brands,[26] (2) the location of departments or merchandise categories in the store, and (3) the size of the store.

Space Allocated to Merchandise Categories

Some factors that retailers consider when deciding how much floor or shelf space to allocate to merchandise categories and brands are (1) the productivity of the allocated space, (2) the merchandise's inventory turnover, (3) the impact on overall store sales, and (4) the display needs for the merchandise.

Space Productivity   A simple rule of thumb for allocating space is to allocate on the basis of the merchandise's sales. For example, if artificial plants represent 15 percent of the total expected sales for a hobby and craft retailer such as Michaels, then 15 percent of the store's space is allocated to artificial plants.

But as the discussion of marginal analysis for advertising allocations in Chapter 15 indicated, retailers really should allocate space to a merchandise category on the basis of its effect on the profitability of the entire store. In practice, this recommendation means that Michaels should add more space to the artificial plant section as long as the profitability of the additional space is greater that the profitability of the category from which space was taken away. In this condition, the additional space for artificial plants will increase the profitability of the entire store. However, at some point, it will be more profitable to not take away space from other categories.

Two commonly used measures of space productivity are **sales per square foot** and **sales per linear foot.** Apparel retailers that display most of their merchandise on freestanding fixtures typically measure space productivity as sales per square foot. In supermarkets, most merchandise is displayed on shelves. Because the shelves have approximately the same width, only the length, or the linear dimension sales per linear foot, is used to assess space productivity.

A more appropriate productivity measure, such as gross margin per square foot, would consider the contribution generated by the merchandise, not just the sales. Thus, if salty snacks generate $400 in gross margin per linear foot and canned soup generates only $300 per linear foot, more space should be allocated to salty snacks. However, factors other than marginal productivity need to be considered when making space allocation decisions. These factors are discussed in the next section.

In addition, retailers need to allocate space to maximize the profitability of the store, not just a particular merchandise category or department. Supermarkets often "overallocate" space to some low-profitability categories such as milk because an extensive assortment in these categories attracts customers to the store and positively affects the sales of other categories. Retailers might also overallocate space to categories purchased by their platinum customers—that is, those customers with the highest lifetime value.

Inventory Turnover   Inventory turnover affects space allocations in two ways. First, as discussed in Chapter 12, both inventory turnover and gross margin contribute to GMROI—a measure of the retailer's return on its merchandise inventory investment. Thus, merchandise categories with higher inventory turnover merit more space than merchandise categories with lower inventory turnover. Second, merchandise displayed on the shelf is depleted more quickly for items with high inventory turnover. Thus, more space needs to be allocated to this fast-selling merchandise to minimize the need to restock the shelf frequently and reduce stockouts. Many retailers, however, compensate for high inventory turnover items by assigning them more frequent deliveries so they don't take up so much space.

Display Considerations   The physical limitations of the store and its fixtures affect space allocation. Of course, store planners must provide enough merchandise to fill an entire fixture dedicated to a particular item. But in addition, a retailer might decide it wants to use a merchandise display to enhance its image. For Target to set itself apart as a source of high-quality home goods, it makes its display of private-label organic cotton sheets attractive and expansive. To really emphasize this offering, it even might overallocate space for the sheets and present a wide range of colors.

Location of Merchandise Categories and Design Elements

As discussed previously, the store layout, signage, and feature areas can guide customers through the store. The location of merchandise categories also plays a role in how customers navigate the store. By strategically placing impulse and demand/destination merchandise throughout the store, retailers increase the chances that customers will shop the entire store and that their attention will be focused on the merchandise that the retailer is most interested in selling—merchandise with a high GMROI. **Demand/destination merchandise** refers to products that customers have decided to buy before entering the store.

As customers enter the store and pass through the decompression zone, they are welcomed with introductory displays, including graphics. Once through the decompression zone, they often turn right (in Western cultures) and observe the prices and quality of the first items they encounter. This area, referred to as the "strike zone," is critical, because it creates the customer's first impression of the store's offering. Thus, retailers display some of their most compelling merchandise in the strike zone.

After passing through the strike zone, the most heavily trafficked and viewed area is the right-hand side of the store because most people turn right when come into a store. By this point in their journey through the store, customers have become accustomed to the environment, have developed a first impression, and are ready to make purchase decisions. Thus the right-hand side is a prime area for displaying high GMROI merchandise. For example, supermarkets typically locate the produce section in this area because produce appeals to the shoppers' senses. The visual/color appeal of all the different produce—bright oranges, deep reds of tomatoes and peppers, rich greens of zucchini and kale—gets a shopper's mouth watering, and the best grocery store customer is a hungry one.

Impulse Merchandise The prime store locations for selling merchandise are heavily trafficked areas such as 10 feet beyond the entrance on the right side of the store and areas near escalators and cash wraps. In multilevel stores, a space's value decreases the farther it is from the entry-level floor. Thus, **impulse products,** or products that are purchased without planning, such as fragrances and cosmetics in department stores and magazines in supermarkets, are almost always located near the front of the store, where they're seen by everyone and may actually draw people into the store.

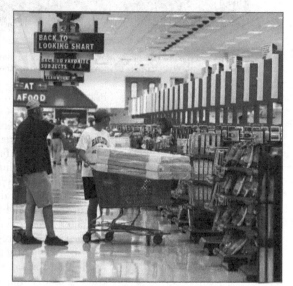

The checkout counter at a supermarket is an ideal place to display merchandise typically bought on impulse.

Demand and Promotional Merchandise Demand merchandise and promotional merchandise are often placed in the back left-hand corner of the store. Placing high-demand merchandise in this location pulls customers through the store, increasing the visibility of other products along the way. So supermarkets typically put items almost everyone buys— milk, eggs, butter, and bread—in the back left-hand corner. In department stores, children's merchandise and furniture, as well as customer service areas like beauty salons, credit offices, and photography studios, are demand or destination areas and thus located in lightly trafficked areas of the store.

Special Merchandise Some merchandise categories involve a buying process that is best accomplished in a lightly trafficked area. For example, women's lingerie is typically located in a remote area to offer a more private shopping experience. Categories that require large amounts of floor space, like furniture, are often located in less desirable locations. Some categories, like curtains, need significant wall space, whereas others, like shoes, require easily accessible storage rooms.

Category Adjacencies Retailers often put complementary categories next to each other to encourage unplanned purchases. Thus at the end of the cereal aisle, grocery shoppers often find an end cap filled with fresh bananas, and audio cables tend to hang on a display near the section featuring sound systems in an electronics store. Such displays help encourage cross-selling, as discussed in Chapter 5.

Another option is to contradict traditional placement schemes to surprise and excite shoppers. A well-known example places beer next to diapers, based on the observation that fathers making an emergency diaper run often late at night buy themselves a treat during the same trip. Consumer goods companies also hope to exploit a "halo effect" created by the fresh produce aisle in supermarkets.[27] If their

500   **SECTION IV**   Store Management

Retailers often place complementary products, such as chips and salsa, next to each other to increase unplanned purchases.

REFACT

Whereas 65 percent of men's toiletries are purchased by women, men are highly apprehensive of women's products and more likely to purchase products that are farther away from feminine-themed products.[28]

packaged goods appear next to healthy, fresh vegetables and fruit, consumers are more likely to associate those appealing traits with the manufacturers' products. But supermarkets are cautious about such moves, because the quality of the fresh produce section is a real competitive advantage. These critical trade-offs remain a constant challenge for grocers.

Location of Merchandise within a Category   As discussed in Chapter 4, most purchases in food, discount, drug, and many category specialists are either based on limited problem solving or habitual decision making. As such, retailers have a very short time, often a matter of a few seconds, to get their attention and induce them to grab an item for purchase. Retailers use a variety of rules to locate specific SKUs within a category.[29] For instance, supermarkets and drugstores typically place private-label brands to the right of national brands. Because Western consumers read from left to right, they will see the higher-priced national brand first and then see and possibly purchase the lower-priced, higher-margin private-label item on the right that looks similar to the national brand. Produce departments in grocery stores are arranged so that apples are the first item most customers see because apples are a very popular produce item and thus can best initiate a buying pattern.

Supermarkets typically display merchandise on four shelves, with the most profitable merchandise on the third shelf from the floor. The third shelf attracts the most attention because it is at eye level for adults. Merchandise that appeals to a smaller group of customers is often displayed on the top shelf because reaching for the items requires significant effort. Heavy, bulky items are stocked on the bottom shelf for safety reasons.

However, when purchase decisions are influenced by shorter consumers, positioning merchandise on the lower shelves might be more effective. For example, children may influence breakfast cereal purchases when accompanying their parents to the supermarket. Thus, the second shelf from the floor might be a prime location for the most profitable cereal brands.

Exhibit 17–5 illustrates some innovative merchandise placement options with which some grocery stores are experimenting. Specifically,

1. Place the dairy section near the front of the store so it is associated with fresh produce.

2. Place other premium products in the produce section since it makes them sell better.

3. Redesign carts to have a second shelf for fragile items and have holders for flowers and coffee.

4. Have a small milk refrigerator near the front door to better compete with convenience stores.

5. Use wood and other natural materials to induce a "farm-fresh" image.

6. Group ingredients necessary for a particular recipe, such as tomatoes, basil, and mozzarella cheese.

7. Place some organic products together and others throughout the produce section to experiment with how they sell best.

8. Bananas should go at the back of the produce department to get customers to walk through the entire department.

9. To simulate farmers' markets, add some low shelves so customers can see through the department and locate various-colored items adjacent to each other for visual appeal.

EXHIBIT 17–5
Grocery stores are experimenting in their produce departments with unconventional product placements.

Some tools that retailers use to make decisions on the positioning of items in a category are planograms, virtual-store software, and videotapes of consumers as they move through the store.

Planograms A **planogram** is a diagram that shows how and where specific SKUs should be placed on retail shelves or displays to increase customer purchases. The locations can be illustrated using photographs, computer output, or artists' renderings. In developing the planogram, the retailer needs to make the category visually appealing, consider the manner in which customers shop (or the manner in which it would like customers to shop), and work to achieve its strategic and financial objectives. Planograms are also useful for merchandise that doesn't fit nicely on shelves in supermarkets or discount stores. Most specialty apparel retailers provide their managers with photographs and diagrams of how merchandise should be displayed. Retailing View 17.4 describes how the SAS planogramming system automated Marks & Spencer's food business.

Virtual-Store Simulation Virtual-store simulations are another tool used to determine the effects of placing merchandise in different areas of a store and evaluating the profit potential for new items.[30] In these simulations, customers sit in front of computer screens that depict a store aisle. Retina-tracking devices record the eye movements of the customers. When the customers push forward on a handle, similar to the handle on a shopping cart, they progress down the simulated aisle. Customers can virtually reach forward, pick an item off the shelf, look at the packaging, and

Kimberly-Clark is using virtual-store software that uses a retina-tracking device to record a customer's glances. The information obtained from the software enables the retailer to get a fast read on new-product designs and displays without having to conduct real-life tests in the early stages of product development.

then place the item in the virtual cart. These virtual shopping trips allow retailers and their suppliers to develop a better understanding of how customers will respond to different planograms.

Videotaping Consumers Another research method used to assess customer reactions to planograms involves tracking customers in actual store environments. Traditionally, retailers would videotape customers' movements, but Microsoft's Kinect sensors are providing a less intrusive option. Discretely embedded in aisles, the sensors provide three-dimensional spatial recognition.

17.4   RETAILING VIEW   Marks & Spencer Automates with Planograms

Marks & Spencer is a large retailer of clothing, home goods, and high-quality food products in the United Kingdom. Its food business, specializing in high-quality convenience and fresh foods, such as sandwiches and take-home dinners, occupies a prominent position in the U.K. food retailing sector.

The retailer is continuously updating its product range with new products. That process was incredibly labor-intensive: Adjusting 50 displays in 50 stores required 2,500 new, individual planograms. It took 80 to 100 full-time planogrammers to implement weekly changes in its approximately 300 stores. So, the $8.6 billion retailer worked with SAS to develop an automated planogramming system that could optimize weekly fresh-food assortments to individual stores, as well as improve product layout and customer satisfaction.

The Marks & Spencer SAS system calculates an optimal layout by determining how many shelf facings are needed for each SKU in each store. At the same time, the system maintains a consistent look but considers specific fixtures and store layouts.

By implementing automated space planning, Marks & Spencer has greatly increased the productivity of its space-planning team and gained control over store layout and product presentation. It can now do weekly plans with 20 planogrammers—and it does a much better job than before. Product placement is more efficient and uniform throughout the chain, and customers can more easily find specific products.

Such successes have driven other grocers to follow this lead. In Finland, the SOK supermarket chain is using SAS analytics to shift from 1,500 cut-and-paste planograms to store-specific versions, or around 100,000 plans to meet the needs of its 800 stores. As a further step, SOK integrates customer data gathered through its loyalty card program into the planograms. It also shares the resulting information with its suppliers to improve efficiency and supply chain planning.

Marks & Spencer in the United Kingdom uses a planogram system developed by SAS to develop a layout that maximizes space productivity.

DISCUSSION QUESTION

Why are planograms particularly helpful for grocery retailers?

Sources: Communication with SAS; and Joanna Perry, "SOK: Using Store-Specific Plans," *RetailWeek*, November 20, 2009.

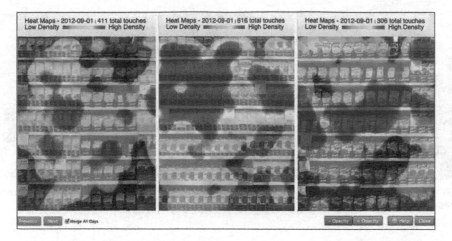

Using Microsoft Kinect sensors, firms like Shopperception create heatmaps of shopper interactions with the products (touches, pickups, and returns). The red represents the hot zones where shoppers touch the most, yellow less, and blue not at all.

Thus, retailers can unobtrusively track the amount of time people spend in front of a shelf, which products they touch or pick up, the products they return to shelves, and finally what they add to their carts to purchase.[31] The data gathered can be used to improve layouts and planograms because they can identify causes of slow-selling merchandise, such as poor shelf placement. By studying customers' movements, retailers can also learn where customers pause or move quickly or where there is congestion. This information can help them decide if the layout and merchandise placement is operating as expected, such as whether new or promoted merchandise is getting the attention it deserves.

Determining Store Size

A key space management decision is deciding how big the store should be. With the rise of online shopping and the recent recession, retailers are coming to find that bigger is not always better. Improvements in supply chain management enable stores to decrease their size but still provide sufficient inventory levels. Thus, some big-box stores are reducing their inventory on hand while also looking for other creative ways to increase their revenue. However, some of these tactics appear contradictory with the recommendations for creating an inviting atmosphere.

Stores such as Walmart and Anchor Blue simply reduced their inventory; Anchor Blue actually erected temporary walls to reduce available floor space and stopped carrying unpopular styles and sizes. Other chains, including Kmart and Home Depot, leased their unused space to other retailers, such as related small business owners and fast-food restaurants. In the longer term, most large retailers also are looking for ways to reduce store footprints. Smaller stores mean fewer SKUs available, but they also can be erected in new markets that could never support a supercenter. Small-format "Walmart Express" stores target urban markets with shops that are approximately one-third the square footage of a regular Walmart location. Staples and Office Depot similarly are opening smaller formats, between 5,000 and 8,000 square feet, to service smaller and urban trade areas.[32]

Such changes do not come easy, nor without cost. There are potentially significant benefits to retailers, though. With their smaller spaces, they likely pay less rent, can hire fewer employees and thus reduce their payroll costs, minimize inventory costs by reducing the number of SKUs, and gain access to new

Small-format "Walmart Express" stores (left) target urban markets with shops that are approximately one-third the square footage of a regular Walmart location (right).

markets. There are also negative effects of the change, and most of those focus on the customer. Customers face reduced selection, decreased comfort, and little entertainment. Smaller formats mean there is no room for communal dressing rooms, entertaining digital displays, or wide aisles that facilitate browsing. The potential outcomes suggest a broader question: Are modern consumers—time-pressured, price-sensitive, and computer-savvy—likely to embrace these new, smaller-format stores that cannot offer one-stop shopping or a seemingly unlimited selection? The promise is great for retailers that hope to entice new segments of customers, but their offer might not be enough for the average consumer.

While this section explored how retailers manage the precious and scarce resource of space in their stores, the next section looks at the "softer side" of managing a store's interior—visual merchandising.

VISUAL MERCHANDISING

LO4

Illustrate the best techniques for merchandise presentation.

Visual merchandising is the presentation of a store and its merchandise in ways that will attract the attention of potential customers. This section examines issues related to the presentation of merchandise, and the following section explores more sensory aspects of the store's environment. This section begins with a review of the fixtures used to display merchandise and then discusses some merchandise presentation techniques.

Fixtures

The primary purposes of fixtures are to efficiently hold and display merchandise. At the same time, they define areas of a store and direct traffic flow. Fixtures work in concert with other design elements, such as floor coverings and lighting, as well as the overall image of the store. For instance, in stores designed to convey a sense of tradition or history, customers automatically expect to see lots of wood rather than plastic or metal fixtures. Wood mixed with metal, acrylic, or stone changes the traditional orientation. Apparel retailers utilize the straight-rack, rounder, and four-way fixtures, while the principle fixture for most other retailers is the gondola.

The **straight rack** consists of a long pipe balanced between supports in the floor or attached to a wall (Exhibit 17–6A). Although the straight rack can hold a lot of apparel, it cannot effectively feature specific styles or colors. All the customer can see is a sleeve or a pant leg. As a result, straight racks are often found in discount and off-price apparel stores.

EXHIBIT 17–6
Types of Fixtures

(A) Straight rack

(B) Rounder

(C) Four-way

(D) Gondola

A **rounder,** also known as a **bulk fixture** or **capacity fixture,** is a round fixture that sits on a pedestal (Exhibit 17–6B). Although smaller than the straight rack, it's designed to hold a maximum amount of merchandise. Because they are easy to move and efficiently store apparel, rounders are found in most types of apparel stores. But, as with the straight rack, customers can't get a frontal view of the merchandise.

A **four-way fixture,** also known as a **feature fixture,** has two crossbars that sit perpendicularly on a pedestal (Exhibit 17–6C). This fixture holds a large amount of merchandise and allows the customer to view the entire garment. The four-way is harder to maintain properly than is the rounder or straight rack, however. All merchandise on an arm must be of a similar style and color, or the customer may become confused. Due to their superior display properties, four-way fixtures are commonly utilized by fashion-oriented apparel retailers.

A **gondola** is an island type of self-service counter with tiers of shelves, bins, or pegs. (Exhibit 17–6D). Because they are extremely versatile, they are used extensively, but not exclusively, in grocery and discount stores to display everything from canned foods to baseball gloves. Gondolas are also found displaying towels, sheets, and housewares in department stores. Folded apparel can be efficiently displayed on gondolas as well, but because the items are folded, it's even harder for customers to view apparel on gondolas than it is on straight racks.

Presentation Techniques

Some presentation techniques are idea-oriented, item and size, color, price lining, vertical merchandising, tonnage merchandising, and frontage presentation.

Idea-Oriented Presentation   Some retailers use an **idea-oriented presentation**—a method of presenting merchandise based on a specific idea or the image of the store. Individual items are grouped to show customers how the items could be used and combined. Women's blouses are often displayed with skirts and accessories to present an overall image or idea. Also, furniture stores display a combination of furniture in room settings to give customers an idea of how it would look in their homes. This approach encourages the customer to make multiple complementary purchases.

Item and Size Presentation   Probably the most common technique of organizing stock is by style or item. Discount stores, grocery stores, hardware stores, and drugstores employ this method for nearly every category of merchandise, as do many apparel retailers. When customers look for a particular type of merchandise, such as breakfast cereals, they expect to find all items in the same location. Arranging items by size is a common method of organizing many types of merchandise, from nuts and bolts to apparel. Because the customer usually knows the desired size, it's easy to locate items organized in this manner.

Color Presentation   A bold merchandising technique is organizing by color. For instance, Ralph Lauren stores often have entire collections in one color hue, all merchandised together. White House/Black Market women's apparel stores take color presentation to an extreme—most of its merchandise is black, white, or a combination of the two.

Price Lining   **Price lining** occurs when retailers offer a limited number of predetermined price points and/or price categories within another classification that are merchandised together. This approach helps customers easily find merchandise at the price they wish to pay. For instance, men's dress shirts may be organized into three groups selling for $49, $69, and $99 (see Chapter 14).

Vertical Merchandising   Another common way of organizing merchandise is **vertical merchandising.** In this approach, merchandise is presented vertically using walls and high gondolas. Customers shop much as they read a newspaper—from left to right, going down each column, top to bottom. Stores can effectively organize merchandise to follow the eye's natural movement. Retailers take advantage of this tendency in several ways. Many grocery stores put national brands at eye level and store brands on lower shelves because customers scan from eye level down. In addition, retailers often display merchandise in bold vertical bands of an item. For instance, you might see vertical columns of towels of the same color displayed in a department store or a vertical band of yellow and orange boxes of Tide detergent followed by a band of blue Cheer boxes in a supermarket.

Tonnage Merchandising   As the name implies, **tonnage merchandising** is a display technique in which large quantities of merchandise are displayed together. Customers have come to equate tonnage with low price, following the retail adage "Stock it high and let it fly." Tonnage merchandising is therefore used to enhance and reinforce a store's price image. Using this display concept, the merchandise itself is the display. The retailer hopes customers will notice the merchandise and be drawn to it. For instance, grocery stores often use an entire end of a gondola (i.e., an end cap) to display six-packs of Pepsi.

Frontal Presentation   Often, it's not possible to create effective displays and efficiently store items at the same time. But it's important to show as much of the merchandise as possible. One solution to this dilemma is the **frontal presentation,** a method of displaying merchandise in which the retailer exposes as much of the product as possible to catch the customer's eye. Book manufacturers, for instance, make great efforts to create eye-catching covers. But bookstores usually display books exposing only the spine. To create an effective display and break the monotony, book retailers often face an occasional cover out like a billboard to catch the customer's attention. A similar frontal presentation can be achieved on a rack of apparel by simply turning one item out to show the merchandise.

CREATING AN APPEALING STORE ATMOSPHERE

To provide a rewarding shopping experience, retailers go beyond presenting appealing merchandise. **Atmospherics** refers to the design of an environment by stimulation of the five senses.[33] Many retailers have discovered the subtle benefits of developing atmospherics that complement other aspects of the store design and the merchandise. Therefore, they use lighting, colors, music, scent, and even flavors to stimulate customers' perceptual and emotional responses and ultimately affect their purchase behavior. Research has shown that it is important for the atmospheric elements to work together—for example, the right music with the right scent.[34]

LO5

Understand how retailers can create a more appealing shopping experience.

Lighting

Good lighting in a store involves more than simply illuminating space. Lighting can highlight merchandise and capture a mood or feeling that enhances the store's image. Retailers also are exploring ways to save energy with technologically advanced lighting. Having the appropriate lighting positively influences customer shopping behavior.[35]

Highlighting Merchandise   A good lighting system helps create a sense of excitement in the store. At the same time, lighting must provide an accurate color rendition of the merchandise. It also allows the retailer to focus spotlights on special featured areas and items. The key determinant appears to be achieving an appropriate level of contrast, which helps attract visual attention.[36] Using lighting to focus on strategic pockets of merchandise trains shoppers' eyes on the merchandise and draws customers strategically through the store. Nike, for example, uses a lot of contrast and shadows, highlighting the merchandise but not necessarily the architecture.

Mood Creation   Retailers use lighting to set the mood for their customers. Ralph Lauren stores and boutiques in department stores use low levels of light to coordinate with their overall ambience of resembling a townhouse. Abercrombie & Fitch keeps stores purposefully dark, discouraging too many parents from entering. With their lesser concern about atmospherics, full-line discount stores, food retailers, and category specialists tend to brighter and less-expensive fluorescent lighting.

Energy-Efficient Lighting   As the price of energy soars and retailers and their customers become more energy-conscious, retailers are looking for ways to cut their energy costs and be more ecologically friendly. One obvious source of energy consumption is the lighting in a store, which makes up approximately one-third of a large store's energy costs. Light-emitting diode (LED) lighting is replacing fluorescent lighting in many stores because it reduce these costs by up to 75 percent, and they last 10 times longer than standard bulbs. Yet LEDs are more expensive initially than traditional lighting.[37]

Color

The creative use of color can enhance a retailer's image and help create a mood. Warm colors (red, gold, and yellow) produce emotional, vibrant, hot, and active responses. Thus, for sellers using online auction sites like eBay, it may be a good

Abercrombie & Fitch creates a dark environment targeted at the younger consumer.

idea to use red tones, because bidders instinctively respond with higher bids in the online auction, compared with a sale page dominated by blue hues.[38] Cool colors (white, blue, and green) have a peaceful, gentle, calming effect and appear to induce abstract thinking, leading customers to view products more favorably. Thus brick-and-mortar stores may want to use these more relaxing colors of the spectrum.[39] Although these trends are common, colors can have differential impacts, depending on various consumer traits, such as their culture (e.g., in the East, white is a color of mourning, whereas in the West, it often implies purity), their age, and their gender.

Music

Music can either add to or detract from a retailer's total atmospheric package. Most shoppers notice music playing in stores, and nearly half of them say they will leave if they do not like the selections being played.[40]

Fortunately, unlike other atmospheric elements though, music can be easily changed. For example, one retailer has a system that allows different types of music to be played at certain times of the day. It can play jazzy music in the morning when its customer base is older and adult contemporary in the afternoon for a 35-to-40-year age range customer. For its West Coast stores, it wants modern rock in the morning and Caribbean beats in the afternoon. And in Texas, it's country music all day, every day. The retailer also can "zone" music by demographics, playing more Latin music in stores that attract a higher Hispanic population.

Retailers also can use music to affect customers' behavior. Music can control the pace of store traffic, create an image, and attract or direct consumers' attention. For instance, one U.K. toy store switched from children's songs like "Baa Baa Black Sheep" to relaxed classical music and watched sales jump by 10 percent.[41] Managers realized that though children are the consumers of their products, adults are the customers. In general, slow is good. A mix of classical or otherwise soothing music encourages shoppers to slow down, relax, and take a good look at the merchandise.

Scent

Smell has a large impact on a customer's mood and emotions. In conjunction with music, it can increase customers' excitement and satisfaction with the shopping experience.[42] Customers in scented stores think they spent less time in the store than do those in unscented stores. Scents thus can improve customers' subjective shopping experience by making them feel that they are spending less time examining merchandise, waiting for sales help, or checking out.

Retailers also use different essences in different departments: baby powder in the baby store; suntan lotion in the bathing suit area; lilacs in lingerie; and cinnamon and pine scents during the holiday season.[43] Some high-end retailers, such as Saks Fifth Avenue, utilize their own unique scents, and mall shoppers can sniff out an Abercrombie & Fitch store yards away. Yet these apparel retailers are not the only ones to use this atmospheric tool. Goodwill Stores now disperse the scent of honeysuckle and sweet orange in an attempt to make its retail sites more appealing. According to a Goodwill spokesperson, "Even if the recession weren't happening, we'd be doing everything we can to create a great shopping experience. We've already taken the approach of trying to have better lighting, [a] great layout . . . this is just one more thing that we hope will help enhance the shopping environment."[44]

When New Balance spread into China, it aimed for a (Western) nostalgic sensory experience to introduce the U.S. brand. Thus, not only did the stores feature wooden floors and 1950s pop music, but they also smelled like wood and leather. Even pop singers get in on this scent action. During her California Dreaming tour, Katy Perry appealed to young fans by spreading the scent of cotton candy throughout the stadiums she played.[45]

Taste

It is a little more difficult to appeal subtly to consumers' taste buds. However, many department stores are reintroducing an old-fashioned offering to appeal to shoppers: the store restaurant. The option to grab a bite without leaving the store encourages customers to linger longer and enjoy their shopping experience more. Café SFA at Saks Fifth Avenue offers a stellar view of Rockefeller Center, while Bergdorf Goodman's BG Restaurant shows off Central Park. And for those shoppers who must have a $36 lobster club sandwich to complete their shopping expedition, Fred's at Barney's New York is the place to go.[46]

Just How Exciting Should a Store Be?

Retailers such as Cabela's, REI, Bass Pro Shops, and Barnes & Noble attempt to create an entertaining shopping environment by viewing their stores as theatrical scenes: The floor and walls constitute the stage and scenery; the lighting, fixtures, and displays are the props; and the merchandise represents the performance. This

Customers enjoying a bite between their purchases stimulates longer stays and more purchases.

creation of a theatrical experience in stores has resulted in the combination of retailing and entertainment. In contrast, retail chains such as Costco and Home Depot successfully use minimalist, warehouse-style shopping environments, but create excitement in other ways, such as giving away food samples and hosting do-it-yourself classes.

Does providing an exciting, entertaining store environment lead customers to patronize a store more frequently and spend more time and money during each visit? The answer to this question is: It depends.[47]

The impact of the store's environment depends on the customer's shopping goals. The two basic shopping goals are task completion (utilitarian), such as buying a new suit for a job interview, and recreation (hedonic), such as spending a Saturday afternoon with a friend wandering through a mall. When customers are shopping to complete a task that they view as inherently unrewarding, they prefer to be in a soothing, calming environment—a simple atmosphere with slow music, dimmer lighting, calming scents, and blue-green colors. However, when customers go shopping for fun, an inherently rewarding activity, they want to be in an exciting atmosphere—a complex environment with invigorating smells, fast tempo music, bright lighting, and red-yellow colors.

What does this mean for retailers? They must consider the typical shopping goals for their customers when designing their store environments. Grocery shopping is typically viewed as an unpleasant task, and thus supermarkets should be designed in soothing colors and use slow background music. In contrast, shopping for fashion apparel is typically viewed as fun, so an arousing environment in apparel retail outlets will have a positive impact on the shopping behavior of their customers.

The level of excitement caused by the environment might vary across the store. A consumer electronics retailer might create a low-arousal environment in the accessories area to accommodate customers who typically are task oriented when shopping for print cartridges and batteries, and it might create a high-arousal environment in the home-entertainment centers that are typically visited by more pleasure-seeking shopping customers.

Finally, retailers might vary the nature of their websites for customers depending on their shopping goals. For example, research suggests that Amazon should serve up complex, high-arousal websites with rich media to customers who indicate they are browsing but provide simpler, low-arousal sites to customers looking for a specific book.[48]

SUMMARY

LO1 Identify the critical issues retailers need to consider when designing a store.

To design a store, retailers must consider their main objectives: (1) implement their strategy, (2) influence customer buying behavior, (3) provide flexibility, (4) control design and maintenance costs, and (5) meet legal requirements. Because few store designs can achieve all of these objectives, managers make trade-offs among objectives, such as providing convenience rather than encouraging exploration or vice versa.

LO2 List the advantages and disadvantages of alternative store layouts.

Regardless of the type used, a good store layout helps customers find and purchase merchandise.

The grid design is best for stores in which customers are likely to explore the entire store, such as grocery stores and drugstores. Racetrack designs are more common in large upscale stores, such as department stores. Free-form designs are usually found in small specialty stores and within the departments at department stores.

LO3 Describe how to assign store floor space to merchandise departments and categories.

Space management involves three decisions: (1) allocating store space to merchandise categories and brands, (2) locating departments or merchandise categories in the store, and (3) determining the appropriate store size. To determine how much floor or shelf space to allocate to merchandise categories, retailers might consider the productivity of the allocated space (e.g., using sales per square foot or sales per linear foot), the merchandise's inventory turnover, its impact on store sales, and display needs. In addition, by strategically placing impulse and demand/destination merchandise throughout the store, retailers can encourage customers to shop the entire store and focus their attention on merchandise that the retailer wants to sell most.

LO4 **Illustrate the best techniques for merchandise presentation.**

Signage and graphics help customers locate specific products and departments, provide product information, and suggest items or special purchases. Digital signage has several advantages over traditional printed signage, but the initial fixed costs

have made its adoption slow. Feature areas are designed to get customers' attention. They include windows, entrances, freestanding displays, mannequins, end caps, promotional aisles or areas, walls, dressing rooms, and cash wraps. Finally, various types of display racks and shelving are more or less appropriate for different types of merchandise.

LO5 **Understand how retailers can create a more appealing shopping experience.**

Retailers employ various forms of atmospherics—lighting, colors, music, scent, and even taste—to influence shopping behaviors. The use of these atmospherics can create a calming environment for task-oriented shoppers or an exciting environment for recreational shoppers.

KEY TERMS

GET OUT AND DO IT!

1. **CONTINUING ASSIGNMENT** Go into the physical store location of the retailer you have chosen for the continuing assignment, and evaluate the store layout, design, and visual merchandising techniques employed. Explain your answers to the following questions:

    (a) In general, are the store layout, design, and visual merchandising techniques consistent with the exterior of the store and its location?

    (b) Is the store's ambience consistent with the merchandise presented and the customer's expectations?

    (c) How do the store's layout, design, and visual merchandising support the following objectives: (1) implements the retailer's strategy, (2) builds

loyalty, (3) increases sales, (4) controls costs, and (5) meets legal requirements?

    (d) To what extent are the store's layout, design, and merchandising techniques flexible?

    (e) How does the store utilize atmospheric elements such as color, lighting, music, and scent? Are these uses appropriate given the store's merchandise and target market?

    (f) Is the store's design environmentally friendly? If yes, please describe. If no, how could it become more "green"?

    (g) Are the fixtures consistent with the merchandise and the overall ambience of the store? Are they flexible?

(h) Evaluate the store's signage. Does it do an effective job of selling merchandise?

(i) Has the retailer used any theatrical effects to help sell merchandise?

(j) Does the store layout help draw people through the store?

(k) Has the retailer taken advantage of the opportunity to sell merchandise in feature areas?

(l) Does the store make creative use of wall space?

(m) What type of layout does the store use? Is it appropriate for the type of store? Would another type of layout be better?

(n) Ask the store manager how the profitability of space is evaluated (e.g., profit per square foot). Is there a better approach?

(o) Ask the store manager how space is assigned to merchandise. Critically evaluate the answer.

(p) Ask the store manager if planograms are used. If so, try to determine what factors are considered when putting together a planogram.

(q) Are departments in the most appropriate locations? Would you move any departments?

(r) What method(s) has the retailer used to organize merchandise? Is this the best way? Suggest any appropriate changes.

2. **INTERNET EXERCISE** Go to the home page of CoolHunters (www.thecoolhunter.net). Look at examples posted in their retail subpage. How can this information of latest trends assist with store layout, design, and visual merchandising?

3. **INTERNET EXERCISE** VMSD is the leading resource for retail designers and store display professionals, serving the retail industry since 1869 (then called Display World). Go to its web page at http://vmsd.com, and develop a list of three or four items that describe the latest trends in visual merchandising.

4. **INTERNET EXERCISE** Go to the home page of Envirosell (www.envirosell.com). How does this marketing research consulting firm support retailers by collecting consumer information to assist with store layout, design, and visual merchandising?

DISCUSSION QUESTIONS AND PROBLEMS

1. One of the fastest-growing sectors of the population is the over-60 age group. Customers in this group may have limitations in their vision, hearing, and movement. How can retailers develop store designs with this population's needs in mind?

2. Assume you have been hired as a consultant to assess a local discount store's floor plan and space productivity. Look back at Chapter 6 and decide which analytical tools and ratios you would use to assess the situation.

3. What are the different types of design that can be used in a store layout? How does the layout impact the types of fixtures used to display merchandise? Describe why some stores are more suited for a particular type of layout than others.

4. A department store is building an addition. The merchandise manager for furniture is trying to convince the vice president to allot this new space to the furniture department. The merchandise manager for men's clothing is also trying to gain the space. What points should each manager use when presenting his or her rationale?

5. As an architect for retail space, you are responsible for Americans with Disabilities Act compliance. How would you make sure that a store's retail layout both meets accessibility requirements and enables the company to reach profitability objectives?

6. What are the advantages and disadvantages of offering virtual dressing rooms from the retailers' perspective?

7. Complete the following table by briefly describing how the different retail formats could use each of the areas listed to enhance the store's image and atmosphere.

Area	Drugstore	Clothing Store	Music Store	Restaurant
Entrance				
Walls				
Windows				
Merchandise displays				
Cash wrap				

8. Reread Retailing View 17.2, "Walmart Goes Green and Lowers Its Energy Costs." Which of the environmental practices discussed do you think will be implemented by other retailers? Explain your response.

9. Reread Retailing View 17.3, "A Hedonic Maze Filled with Utilitarian Products." What do you think about IKEA's layout? Does it provide them with a competitive edge? Explain your response.

10. How can signage and graphics help both customers and retailers? Consider the following types of retail formats that you likely have visited in the past: discount store, department store, office superstore, and card and gift store. Describe which retail formats have implemented the best practices for coordinating signs and graphics with each store's image and which formats should improve this aspect of their store layout, design, and visual merchandising.

SUGGESTED READINGS

Krishna, Aradhna (Ed.). *Sensory Marketing: Research on the Sensuality of Consumers.* New York: Routledge, 2009.

Bell, Judy, and Kate Ternus. *Silent Selling: Best Practices and Effective Strategies In Visual Merchandising*, 4th ed. New York: Fairchild Publication, 2011.

Law, Derry, Christina Wong, and Joanne Yip, "How Does Visual Merchandising Affect Consumer Affective Response?: An Intimate Apparel Experience." *European Journal of Marketing*, 46 no. 1/2 (2012), pp. 112–133.

Manganari, Emmanouela E., George J. Siomkos, and Adam P. Vrechopoulos. "Store Atmosphere in Web Retailing." *European Journal of Marketing* 43 (September 2010), pp. 1140–1153.

Nordfalt, Jens. *In-Store Marketing*, 2nd ed. Sweden: Forma Magazine, 2011.

Ortinau, David J., Barry J. Babin, and Jean-Charles Chebat. "Development of New Empirical Insights in Consumer–Retailer Relationships within Online and Offline Retail Environments: Introduction to the Special Issue." *Journal of Business Research*, available electronically 2011.

Pegler, Martin. *Store Presentation and Design*, 3rd ed. New York: RSD, 2010.

Pegler, Martin. *Visual Merchandising and Display*, 6th ed. New York: Fairchild Publication, 2012.

Sorensen, Herb. *Inside the Mind of the Shopper*. Upper Saddle River, NJ: Pearson Education, 2009.

Underhill, Paco. *Why We Buy: The Science of Shopping*, 3rd ed. New York: Simon and Schuster, 2009.

Valenzuela, Ana, Priya Raghubir, and Chrissy Mitakaki. "A Shelf Space Schemas: Myth or Reality?" *Journal of Business Research*, available online, 11 January 11, 2012.

Wang, Yong Jian, Michael S. Minor, and Jie Wei. "Aesthetics and the Online Shopping Environment: Understanding Consumer Responses." *Journal of Retailing*, 87 (March 2011), pp. 46–58.

Case Studies

CASE 1   Tractor Supply Company Targets the Part-Time Rancher

Tractor Supply Company (TSC), a large and fast-growing retailer with more than $4 billion in annual sales and more than 100 stores in 44 states, was the inventor of the "do-it-yourself" (DIY) trend. Its origins date to 1938, when Charles E. Schmidt Sr. established a mail-order tractor parts business. After the success of his first retail store in Minot, North Dakota, he opened additional stores to serve the needs of local farmers. But eventually TSC's sales stagnated because small farms and ranches were being acquired by large farming and ranching corporations. These large agricultural firms buy supplies and equipment directly from manufacturers rather than through local farm supply stores like TSC.

TARGET MARKET

Since the early 1990s, TSC has targeted a growing group of people interested in recreational farming and ranching. Called "sundowners," "U-turners," "hobby farmers," "ruralpolitans," "micropolitans," "gentlemen farmers," and "ex-urbanites," these people have turned to farming to escape the hubbub of urban and suburban life. They are drawn to what they believe is a more private, simple, and stress-free lifestyle. They typically live on 5 to 20 acres in a rural community outside a metropolitan area, where they work at a full-time profession, and use some of their earnings to keep their farms in operation. Many of them are the sons and daughters of traditional production farmers and inherited the family farm and decided to keep it running. Today less than 10 percent of TSC's customers classify themselves as full-time farmers or ranchers, and many of its customers do not farm at all.

RETAIL OFFERING

The typical TSC store has 15,000 to 24,000 square feet of inside selling space and a similar amount of outside space used to display agricultural fencing, livestock equipment, and horse stalls. The company tries to locate stores in the prime retail corridor of rural communities, two or three counties away from major metropolitan areas. Fifty percent of its stores are in previously occupied buildings.

The typical store stocks about 15,000 SKUs, using a combination of national and private-label brands. TSC constantly tests new merchandise programs in its stores. For instance, based on a successful test of expanded clothing and footwear categories, TSC doubled the size of these areas of the store and added more lifestyle clothes and workwear for both men and women.

TSC stores are designed to make shopping an enjoyable experience and, at the same time, maximize sales and

EXHIBIT 1
TSC's Mission and
Value Statements

operating efficiencies. Their environment allows plenty of space for individual departments and visual displays. Informative signs assist customers with purchasing decisions by delineating "good, better, best" qualities, pointing out their "everyday low-pricing" policy, and providing useful information regarding product benefits and suggestions for appropriate accessories.

TSC emphasizes customer service. The company tries to hire store employees who have farming and ranching backgrounds. Its training programs include (1) a full management training program, which covers all aspects of its operations; (2) product knowledge modules produced in conjunction with key vendors; (3) frequent management skills training classes; (4) semiannual store managers' meetings, with vendor product presentations; (5) vendor-sponsored in-store training programs; and (6) ongoing product information updates at its management headquarters. This extensive training, coupled with a management philosophy that stresses empowerment, enables store employees to assist customers in making their purchase decisions and solve customer problems as they arise. Store employees wear highly visible red vests, aprons, or smocks and nametags. TSC uses a variety of incentive programs that provide the opportunity for store employees to receive additional compensation based on their team, store, and/or company performance.

While TSC creates a "hometown farmer" shopping experience for customers, there is nothing "small-town" or "laid back" about its operations and use of technology. Its management information and control systems include a point-of-sale system, a supply chain management and replenishment system, a radio-frequency picking system in the distribution centers, a vendor purchase order control system, and a merchandise presentation system. These systems work together to track merchandise from the initial order through to the ultimate sale.

TSC has a centralized supply chain management team that focuses on replenishment and forecasting and a buying team that selects merchandise, develops assortments, and evaluates new products and programs. Almost all purchase orders and vendor invoices are transmitted through an electronic data interchange (EDI) system.

MISSION AND VALUES

Despite changes to TSC's retail strategy in the past 70 years, its mission and values have remained constant. The company's mission and value statements appear on its website (Exhibit 1), on cards handed out to all employees, and on the walls of every store. According to TSC management, the first discussion with new employees centers on the firm's values and mission because the firm steadfastly maintains that "being a great place to work enables the company to be a great place to shop and invest."

Sources: Tractor Supply Co., Annual Report 2011; www.tractorsupply.com.

This case was written by Barton Weitz, University of Florida.

DISCUSSION QUESTIONS

1. What is Tractor Supply Company's growth strategy? What retail mix does TSC provide?

2. Why and how has TSC's target customer changed over time?

3. How does TSC's retail mix provide the benefits sought by its target market?

4. How vulnerable is TSC to competition? Why is this the case?

5. Why does TSC place so much emphasis on training employees?

CASE 2   Build-A-Bear Workshop: Where Best Friends Are Made

Modern consumers want good value, low prices, and convenience, but they also appreciate a great shopping experience. Build-A-Bear Workshop usually locates its more than 425 stores in malls worldwide. It generates more than $390 million in annual sales by offering customers the opportunity to make their own stuffed animals, complete with clothing and accessories.

In 1997, Maxine Clark came up with the idea for Build-A-Bear Workshop and opened a storefront in St. Louis. She had plenty of experience in the corporate side of retailing, having worked for Payless ShoeSource and May Department Stores. Clark left corporate America on a mission to bring the fun back to retailing. Currently, the company has sold more than 70 million furry friends.

The bear-making process consists of eight steps, Choose Me, Hear Me, Stuff Me, Stitch Me, Fluff Me, Dress Me, Name Me, and Take Me Home. The stores mirror the chain's name: Customers, or builders, choose an unstuffed animal and, working with the retailer's staff, move through eight "creation stations" to build their own bear (or other animal). At the first station, the Stuffiteria, children can pick fluff from bins marked "Love," "Hugs and Kisses," "Friendship," and "Kindness." The stuffing is sent through a long, clear tube and into a stuffing machine. A sales associate holds the bear to a small tube while the builder pumps a foot peddle. In seconds, the bear takes its form. Before the stitching, builders must insert a heart. The builders follow the sales associates' instructions and rub the heart between their hands to make it warm. They then close their eyes, make a wish, and kiss the heart before putting it inside the bear. After selecting a name and having it stitched on their animal, builders take their bears to the Fluff Me station, where they brush their bears on a "bathtub" that features spigots blowing air. Finally, they move to a computer station to create a birth certificate.

Bears go home in Cub Condo carrying cases, which act as mini-houses complete with windows and doors. In addition to serving as playhouses, the boxes advertise Build-A-Bear Workshop to the child's friends. "[You] could buy a bear anywhere," says Clark, Chief Executive Bear. "It's the experience that customers are looking for." The experience isn't limited to the stores themselves. The retailer's website, buildabear.com, embraces the same theme. Build-A-Bearville (buildabearville.com) is its online virtual world where users can play with each other and play games. The bears that they bought at the store have a unique code that allows the user to redeem gifts while playing games in Build-A-Bearville.

Customers pay about $25 for the basic bear, but they can also buy music, clothing, and accessories. To keep the experience fresh, Build-A-Bear Workshop regularly introduces new and limited-edition animals. Clothes and accessories are also updated to reflect current fashion trends. Outfits for the bears complement the owner's interests and personalities with themes such as sports, colleges, hobbies, and careers. Some children and their parents hold in-store birthday parties, with music playing from the store's official CD. To ensure customers enjoy a great experience every time they visit, all sales associates attend a three-week training program at "Bear University," and the firm offers incentive programs and bonuses. The inventory in the stores changes frequently, with different bear styles arriving weekly. Build-A-Bear Workshops also feature limited-edition and seasonal merchandise, such as a Beary Businesslike Curly Teddy for Father's Day; mummy, wizard, and witch bears for Halloween; and a Sweet Hugs & Kisses Teddy for Valentine's Day.

In 2013, responding to the changing interests of children, Build-A-Bear announced a sweeping upgrade to its retail stores. Clark noted that developments in digital technology have changed how kids play: "[In 1997] children were playing board games. Now they're playing games online . . . Kids are being bombarded with the next new shiny objects. But they've always loved teddy bears and that's not going to change."[1]

Because the stores are a mix between the product (the teddy bear) and the experience of creating the teddy bear, the new design incorporates several digital upgrades. To help determine appropriate changes, the company enlisted several children, termed "Cub Advisors," and their moms for advice on the changes they would like to see in the stores.

Based on this research and advice, the stores are undergoing a massive redesign. Starting at the storefront, signage has been incorporated with Microsoft Kinect technology that enables kids to play with the signage before entering. The use of digital signage allows stores to highlight sales and new products, as well as several holiday themes. The revamped "Love Me" station allows kids to give their stuffed animals personalities at an interactive table using emoticons, which are pictorial representations of a facial expression like a happy face. The "Hear Me" station has a touchscreen that allows customers to choose and load prerecorded music and animal noises, or record their own voice. The "Stuff Me" station offers the option to add custom scents such as bubble gum, cotton candy, and chocolate chip. Finally, kids can wash their bears in a digital bathtub at the "Fluff Me" station. In an effort at contingency planning, "low-tech" options are being designed that can be put over the digital stations if computers act up.

REFACT

The teddy bear came into being in 1903, when President Teddy Roosevelt refused to shoot a cub while bear hunting. The spared animal was thereafter referred to as the Teddy Bear.

[1] Sandy Smith, "Integration Specialists," *Stores*, January 2013.

Sources: www.buildabear.com; www.buildabearville.com; Sandy Smith, "Integration Specialists," *Stores*, January 2013; Tom Ryan, "Build-A-Bear Workshop Goes High-Tech," *Retail Wire*, October 8, 2012.

This case was written by Barton Weitz, University of Florida; and Scott Motyka, Babson College.

DISCUSSION QUESTIONS

1. Is the Build-A-Bear Workshop concept a fad, or does it have staying power?

2. Describe the target customer for this retailer.

3. What can Build-A-Bear Workshop do to generate repeat visits to the store?

CASE 8   Diamonds from Mine to Market

According to the American Museum of Natural History, a diamond is carbon in its most concentrated form. Because of their chemical makeup and crystalline structure, diamonds possess unique characteristics. They are the hardest known natural substance. These traits determine their status as the "king of gems," a reference to their vast popularity as jewelry and decoration.

The diamond supply chain consists of six steps: exploration, mining, sorting, cutting and polishing, jewelry design and production, and retail display. According to the website for De Beers, the producer of approximately 40 percent of the world's supply of rough or uncut diamonds, members of this extensive supply chain include geologists, engineers, environmentalists, miners, sorters, distributors,

cutters, polishers, traders, manufacturers, exporters, and salespeople, who in turn employ vast technology, artistic, and skill-related resources to discover, produce, and distribute jewelry-quality diamonds.

The jewelry-quality designation refers to a particular rating according to four key elements of a diamond, better known as the 4Cs: cut, carat, color, and clarity. The De Beers Corporation introduced these criteria in 1939 to provide consumers with a reference for evaluating diamonds, as Exhibit 1 summarizes.

Before they reach showrooms to be evaluated on these criteria, diamonds have endured approximately 3 billion years of hot temperatures and intense pressures under the Earth's surface. Production estimates from the World

EXHIBIT 1

De Beers' Description of the Four Cs for Diamond Quality

Cut	Cut refers to the angles and proportions a skilled craftsperson creates in transforming a rough diamond into a polished diamond.
	A well-cut diamond will reflect light internally from one mirrorlike facet to another, dispersing it through the top of the stone.
	To cut a diamond perfectly, a craftsperson will often need to cut away more than 50 percent of the rough diamond.
	Cut also refers to the shape of a diamond: round, emerald, heart, marquise, or pear.
Carat weight	Carat is often confused with size, even though it is actually a measure of weight. The cut of a diamond can make it appear much larger or smaller than its actual weight.
	One carat is the equivalent of 200 milligrams. One carat can also be divided into 100 "points." A .75-carat diamond is the same as a 75-point- or a three-quarter-carat diamond.
Color	Most diamonds appear icy white, but many have tiny hints of color. Diamonds are graded on a color scale established by the Gemological Institute of America (GIA), ranging from D (colorless) to Z.
	Colorless diamonds are extremely rare and therefore very valuable.
	Diamonds are also sometimes found in "fancy" colors: pink, blue, green, yellow, brown, orange, and, very rarely, red. These diamonds, called "fancies," are incredibly rare and valuable. These colors extend beyond the GIA color grading system.
Clarity	Diamonds, like people, have natural blemishes in their makeup. Minerals or fractures form these tiny faults, or inclusions, while the diamond is forming in the earth.
	When light enters a diamond, it is reflected and refracted. If anything disrupts the flow of light in the diamond, such as an inclusion, a proportion of the light reflected will be lost.
	Most inclusions are not visible to the naked eye unless magnified.
	To view inclusions, trained gemologists use a magnifying loupe. This tool allows experts to see a diamond at 10 times its actual size. Even with a loupe, the birthmarks in the VVS (Very, Very Slightly Included) to VS (Very Slightly Included) range can be extremely difficult to find. It is only when a diamond is graded "I" that it is possible to see the birthmarks with the naked eye.

Diamond Council indicate diamond mining operations are in more than 20 countries, including Russia, Botswana, the Democratic Republic of the Congo, Australia, South Africa, Canada, Angola, Namibia, Ghana, Brazil, and Sierra Leone.

The world diamond supply is dominated by African countries, which generate between 60 and 65 percent (by weight) of current diamond production. Other key sources for diamonds span the globe, for example, the remote northern regions of Western Australia, which produce roughly 30 million carats (20 percent of global production) each year from both open pit and underground operations. These diamonds are known for the range of colors, especially pink stones.

Diamonds prompt significant competition, as depicted in the movie *Blood Diamond*, which portrays the gruesome conflict and violence in Sierra Leone over diamonds. In many countries, profits from diamonds go to fund civil wars that take millions of lives. To prevent such abuses, the Kimberly Process, an international diamond certification scheme, was established to abolish trade in diamonds that fund conflict. Since its launch in 2003, the Kimberly Process has become law in 75 countries and received backing from the United Nations. It requires that governments of diamond-producing nations certify that shipments of rough diamonds are not funding violence.

Even with a certification process though, some diamonds continue to be smuggled out of African countries. Violent groups find ways to exploit the Kimberley Process to traffic in illicit diamonds. "Conflict diamonds continue to be certified in countries that are members of the Kimberley Process, legitimized by the very scheme which was designed to eradicate them." A contrasting report from the World Diamond Council claims that "because of the Kimberly Process, more than 99% of the world's diamond supply is from sources free from conflict."

When the international diamond industry agreed to implement a voluntary system of warranties, it promised consumers it could track diamond jewelry up to the point of sale. Invoices for the sale of conflict-free diamond jewelry must include a written guarantee of that status. To ensure the diamonds they purchase for their spouses, fiancées, or themselves are indeed sourced appropriately, consumers are expected to take some responsibility, such as asking a series of questions of the jeweler from which they are purchasing:

- What is the country of origin for the diamonds in your jewelry?
- Can I see a copy of your company's policy on conflict-free diamonds?
- Can you show me a copy of the written warranty from your diamond supplier stating that your diamonds are conflict-free?

Sources: "Blood Diamonds Are Still a Reality," Amnesty International, http://web.amnesty.org/pages/ec-230107-feature-eng; "Combating Conflict Diamonds," Global Witness, www.globalwitness.org/pages/en/conflict_diamonds.html; "Conflict Free Diamond Jewelry," Brilliant Earth, www.brilliantearth.com/conflict-free-diamond-definition; "Diamond Pipe," Antwerp Diamond Centre, www.awdc.be/diamond-pipeline; "Forever Diamonds," Gemnation, www.gemnation.com/base?processor=getPage'pageName=forever_diamonds_1; "Kimberley Process," www.kimberleyprocess.com/home/index_en.html; "The Argyle Diamond Mine," Argyle Diamonds, www.argylediamonds.com.au/index_whoweare.html; "The Four Cs," DeBeers, www.debeers.com/page/guidance&layout=popups#author2.

This case was written by Hope Bober Corrigan, Loyola University, Maryland.

DISCUSSION QUESTIONS

1. How important is it for consumers to buy conflict-free diamonds? Why?

2. What should the jewelry industry do to inform diamond customers about buying conflict-free gems and about the Kimberley Process?

3. Select a retail jewelry store in your area to visit. Is its policy on conflict diamonds posted anywhere, such as in the store or on the company's website? Ask store personnel the three questions posed at the end of the case. What did you learn from the web page and store visit?

564   SECTION V   Cases

CASE 10   Walmart: Pioneer in Supply Chain Management

Walmart dominates the retailing industry in terms of its sales revenue, its customer base, and its ability to drive down costs and deliver good value to its customers. After all, the world's largest corporation takes pride in having received numerous accolades for its ability to continuously improve efficiency in the supply chain while meeting its corporate mandate of offering customers everyday low prices.

Tight inventory management is legendary at Walmart through its just-in-time techniques that allow the firm to boast one of the best supply chains in the world. Walmart has not only transformed its own supply chain but influenced how vendors throughout the world operate because the company has the economic clout to request changes from its vendor partners and to receive them. Recognized for its ability to obtain merchandise from global sources, Walmart also pioneered the strategy of achieving high levels of growth and profitability through its precision control of manufacturing, inventory, and distribution. Although the company is not unique in this regard, it is by far the most successful and most influential corporation of its kind and has put into practice various innovative techniques.

And when Walmart does something, it does it on a massive scale. Walmart's computer system, for example, is second only to that of the Pentagon in storage capacity. Its information systems analyze more than 10 million daily transactions from point-of-sale data and distribute their analysis in real time both internally to its managers and externally via a satellite network to Walmart's many suppliers, who use the information for their production planning and order shipment.

Much of the popularity of supply chain management has been attributed to the success of Walmart's partnership with Procter & Gamble. During the 1980s, the two collaborated in building one of the first collaborative planning, forecasting, and replenishment (CPFR) systems, a software system that linked P&G to Walmart's distribution centers, taking advantage of advances in the world's telecommunications infrastructure. When a Walmart store sold a particular P&G item, the information flowed directly to P&G's planning and control systems. When the inventory level of P&G's products at Walmart's distribution center got to the point where it needed to reorder, the system automatically alerted P&G to ship more products. This information helped P&G plan its production. Walmart was also able to track when a P&G shipment arrived at one of its distribution warehouses, which enabled it to coordinate its own outbound shipments to stores. Both Walmart and P&G realized savings from the better inventory management and order processing, savings that in turn were passed on to Walmart's consumers through its everyday low prices.

A history of success doesn't mean Walmart executives can rest. Changes in social values, economic fluctuations, technology advances, and other marketplace factors demand that Walmart continue its search for innovative ways to keep consumer prices down.

WALMART'S INNOVATIONS

Walmart has pioneered many innovations in the purchase and distribution processes of the products it sells. More than 20 years ago, Walmart drove the adoption of UPC bar codes throughout the retail industry; it also pioneered the use of electronic data interchange (EDI) for computerized ordering from vendors. Its hub-and-spoke distribution network ensures goods are brought to distribution centers around the country and then directed outward to thousands of stores, each of which is within a day's travel. Through the use of cross-docking, one of its best-known innovations, half the goods trucked to a distribution center from suppliers ship to stores within 24 hours. The other half, called "pull stock" is stored at the distribution center until needed at stores. In addition, Walmart uses a dedicated fleet of trucks to ship goods from warehouses to stores in less than 48 hours, as well as to replenish store inventories about twice a week. Thus, with flow-through logistics, the company speeds the movement of goods from its distribution centers to its retail stores around the world.

Today, the retail giant continues to push the supply chain toward greater and greater efficiency, prioritizing customer needs while employing new technologies and greener practices. One of the early adopters of RFID technology to increase efficiency in its supply chain, Walmart discovered the value of balancing vision with technology maturity levels after mandating that its suppliers apply RFID tags to crates and pallets bound for its stores. Some companies thrived using the new technology. Others, including Walmart itself, ran into trouble. At the time of the mandate, RFID technology was in its infancy, and costs for planning, hardware, software, and training were prohibitive for many suppliers. Additionally the technology was new enough that the industry lacked best practices for implementation. Indeed, it lacked any examples that might help newcomers avoid pitfalls. Walmart repealed its edict, but continues to probe the usefulness of the technology. Today, Walmart is slowly testing the usefulness of RFID tags with apparel.

In response to criticism from consumer groups, Walmart tackled environmental sustainability in its supply chain and, as is frequently the case because of the company's size, became a trendsetter for other retailers. After vowing to reduce its greenhouse gas emissions by the equivalent of taking nearly 4 million cars off the roads for a year, Walmart directed its suppliers to think green throughout the full product lifecycle. Suppliers are required to pay for sustainability efforts—a price most accept willingly to retain their relationship with Walmart. Many also recognize that reducing energy use will benefit them as energy costs rise. Harnessing energy, increasing recycling, reducing waste, and minimizing packaging and transportation all reduce cost in the supply chain in addition to appealing to today's eco-conscious consumers and preserving global resources.

In a third innovation, Walmart is consolidating its global sourcing. The new model focuses on increasing the percentage of products purchased directly from suppliers and buying from global merchandising centers rather than through individual countries. Third-party procurement providers, who previously enjoyed a substantial business from the retail giant, will find themselves increasingly bypassed in the supply chain. In addition to eliminating the cost of a middle party, this effort may give Walmart increased control over inbound freight. Better control, in turn, can lower inventory costs. Thus, Walmart's continuous use of innovations leads to lower inventory and operating costs, which enables Walmart to keep its lean costs.

Following the fire in a Bangladesh factory that supplied clothing to Walmart in November of 2012 that killed 112 workers, Walmart has further tightened its control over its supply chain. The clothing being made and supplied to Walmart in this factory was done without Walmart's knowledge; it was an unapproved subcontract by one of its vendors. As a result, Walmart has moved to a "zero tolerance" policy on suppliers subcontracting without Walmart's knowledge and approval.

Finally, responding to growing criticism that Walmart purchases too many products from foreign countries and does not do enough to support the American economy, it has announced a new initiative to hire 100,000 veterans and source more products from the United States. As of March 1, 2013, any honorably discharged veteran who applies for a job with Walmart will be given one. The plan is to reach its goal of 100,000 veteran hires in five years. Additionally, over the next 10 years, Walmart plans to purchase an additional $50 billion in U.S.-made goods, increasing its already large share of U.S.-made products. Currently, approximately 55 percent of Walmart's U.S. sales come from items such as groceries, health and beauty products, household goods, and pet supplies, most of which are sourced in the United States.

Walmart continues to hone its management of the flow of products and information among its suppliers, distribution centers, and individual stores through technology to increase its control of logistics and inventory. Thoughtful use of innovation has put Walmart at the top of the retailing game. Not all organizations can pull this approach off as well. Walmart is a unique case in which a single, very powerful firm took primary responsibility for improving performance across its own supply chain. By developing a superior supply chain management system, it has reaped the rewards of higher levels of customer service and satisfaction, lower production and transportation costs, and more productive use of its retail store space. Fundamentally, it boils down to Walmart's ability to link together suppliers, distribution centers, retail outlets, and, ultimately, customers, regardless of their location. Although operational innovation isn't the only ingredient in Walmart's success, it has been a crucial building block for its strong competitive position.

Sources: Mike Troy, "Wal-Mart's Inventory Equation," *Retailing Today*, September 11, 2006; "Financial Outlook: Restoring the Productivity Loop," *Retailing Today*, June 26, 2006; Sharon Gaudin, "Some Suppliers Gain From Failed Wal-Mart RFID Edict," *Computer World*, April 28, 2008; "RFID News: JC Penney CEO Says Retailer Going All in on RFID, Perhaps with Significant Impact on the Industry," *Supply Chain Digest*, August 15, 2012; William B. Cassidy, "Wal-Mart Tightens the Chain," *Journal of Commerce*, January 18, 2010; "Wal-Mart Tightens Rules for Suppliers," *CBC News*, January 22, 2013; "Walmart Announces $50 Billion Buy American Campaign," *Huffington Post*, January 15, 2013.

This case was written by Jeanne L. Munger, University of Southern Maine; Kate Woodworth; and Dhruv Grewal, Michael Levy, and Scott Motyka, all of Babson College.

DISCUSSION QUESTIONS

1. How does an individual firm like Walmart manage a supply chain, particularly considering that supply chains include multiple firms with potentially conflicting objectives? Describe some of the conflicts that could arise in such a circumstance.

2. What are some of the ways that Walmart's supply chain management system has provided it the benefits of higher levels of product availability and lower merchandise acquisition and transportation costs? Provide specific examples of each benefit.

CASE 12   Choosing a Store Location for a Boutique

Stephanie Wilson must decide where to open a ready-to-wear boutique she's been contemplating for several years. Now in her late 30s, she's been working in municipal government ever since leaving college, where she majored in fine arts. She's divorced with two children (ages 5 and 8) and wants her own business, at least partly to be able to spend more time with her children. She loves fashion, feels she has a flair for it, and has taken evening courses in fashion design and retail management. Recently, she heard about a plan to rehabilitate an old arcade building in the downtown section of her midwestern city. This news crystallized her resolve to move now. She's considering three locations.

THE DOWNTOWN ARCADE

The city's central business district has been ailing for some time. The proposed arcade renovation is part of a master redevelopment plan, with a new department store and several office buildings already operating. Completion of the entire master plan is expected to take another six years.

Dating from 1912, the arcade building was once the center of downtown trade, but it's been vacant for the past 15 years. The proposed renovation includes a three-level shopping facility, low-rate garage with validated parking, and convention center complex. Forty shops are planned for the first (ground) floor, 28 more on the second, and a series of restaurants on the third.

The location Stephanie is considering is 900 square feet and situated near the main ground-floor entrance. Rent is $20 per square foot, for an annual total of $18,000. If sales exceed $225,000, rent will be calculated at 8 percent of sales. She'll have to sign a three-year lease.

TENDERLOIN VILLAGE

The gentrified urban area of the city where Stephanie lives is called Tenderloin Village because of its lurid past. Today, however, the neat, well-kept brownstones and comfortable neighborhood make it feel like a trendy enclave. Many residents have done the remodeling work themselves and take great pride in their neighborhood.

About 20 small retailers are now in an area of the village adjacent to the convention center complex, along with some vegetarian and nouveau cuisine restaurants. There are also three small women's specialty clothing stores.

The site available to Stephanie is on the village's main street on the ground floor of an old house. Its space is also about 900 square feet. Rent is $15,000 annually, with no extra charge based on the level of sales. The landlord knows Stephanie and will require a two-year lease.

APPLETREE MALL

This suburban mall has been open for eight years. A successful regional center, it has three department stores and 100 smaller shops just off a major interstate highway about 8 miles from downtown. Of its nine women's clothing retailers, three are in a price category considerably higher than what Stephanie has in mind.

Appletree has captured the retail business in the city's southwest quadrant, although growth in that sector has slowed in the past year. Nevertheless, mall sales are still running 12 percent ahead of the previous year. Stephanie learned of plans to develop a second shopping center east of town, which would be about the same size and character as Appletree Mall. But groundbreaking is still 18 months away, and no renting agent has begun to enlist tenants.

The location available to Stephanie in Appletree is two doors from the local department store chain. At 1,200 square feet, it's slightly larger than the other two possibilities. But it's long and narrow—24 feet in front by 50 feet deep. Rent is $24 per square foot ($28,800 annually). In addition, on sales that exceed $411,500, rent is 8 percent of sales. There's an additional charge of 1 percent of sales to cover common-area maintenance and mall promotions. The mall's five-year lease includes an escape clause if sales don't reach $411,500 after two years.

This case was prepared by Professor David Ehrlich, Marymount University.

DISCUSSION QUESTIONS

1. List the pluses and minuses of each location.
2. What type of store would be most appropriate for each location?
3. If you were Stephanie, which location would you choose? Why?

CASE 15   Sephora Loyalty Programs: A Comparison between France and the United States

Sephora is a beauty products retail chain founded in France by Dominique Mandonnaud in 1970 and owned today by Louis Vuitton Moet Hennessy (LVMH), the world's leading luxury goods group. Sephora's self-service environment carries classic and emerging brands as well as Sephora's own private label across a broad range of product categories, including skin care, color, fragrance, body, and hair care.

Sephora has a strong presence in several countries around the world. It operates approximately 1,300 stores in 27 countries worldwide, with more than 300 stores in North America. It opened its first U.S. store in New York in 1998. Since 2006, Sephora stores are also found inside some JCPenney stores. These stores, smaller than normal with approximately 1,500 square feet, feature the signature Sephora look and an edited assortment. The company launched its Internet retail store in the United States in 1999 and Canada in 2003, which is Sephora's largest North American store in terms of sales and selection of products and brands.

U.S. LOYALTY PROGRAM: SEPHORA BEAUTY INSIDER

In 2007, Sephora launched a customer loyalty program in the United Stated called "Sephora Beauty Insider." When customers sign up for the program, they become a Beauty Insider and receive a loyalty card. Beauty Insiders earn Perk points for purchases, both in-store and online. For every one dollar spent, one Point is added to the customer's Beauty Insider balance. The rewards for these points are given at two levels: 100 and 500. Insiders don't have to use their points once they hit 100. Instead, they can choose to accumulate points for the 500-point Perk. At the 100-point level, the reward is a sample-sized product. The 500-point level reward is a limited-edition, full-sized product offered exclusively to Beauty Insiders. Sephora typically displays three frequently changing rewards at the point of sale. These rewards are not available at Sephora inside JCPenney stores, even if customers accumulate their points there. Beauty Insiders also receive invitations to Beauty Insider-only events. On Sephora's Insiders account on the Internet, customers also receive special offers on products not available to the general public. Finally, every Insider receives a free birthday gift each year. Last year's gift was a bottle of Philosophy's shampoo,

custom-designed to wish customers a happy birthday. Insiders can get the birthday gift either by visiting a store or by ordering online within 14 days of their birth date.

In 2009, Sephora launched V.I.B. [Very Important Beauty Insider], a premium level for its U.S. Beauty Insiders. V.I.B. status is conferred on customers who spend at least $350 per year at U.S. and Canadian Sephora stores (including Sephora.com and Sephora inside JCPenney locations). The benefits for V.I.B.s, in addition to the regular Beauty Insider benefits, include deluxe samples, exclusive monthly perks and gifts, access to prereleased products, event invitations, a 10 percent savings welcome offer, and special discounts (They recently offered a weeklong 15 percent discount.). V.I.B.s are required to requalify each year by purchasing at least $350 worth of products.

FRENCH LOYALTY PROGRAM

Sephora is the leading perfume and cosmetic chain in France, despite fierce competition. Sephora's French loyalty program, launched in 2003, offers special products, exclusive information, and an all-access pass to personalized beauty products available in Sephora stores nationwide and on its website. It consists of three levels—White, Black, and Gold—and has 8 million members in Europe.

In an attempt to start a relationship with its customers, the White card is offered to anyone who asks for it in the store or applies on the Internet website. It is the first level of the customer relationship. After four purchases on the Internet website or in a store, a 10 percent discount coupon is given for the customer's next purchase.

When customers have at least four purchases during a year, or spend a minimum of 150€ a year, they automatically receive the Sephora Black card, which is the middle-level program. Sephora Black customers get a 10 percent discount coupon either after four purchases or with every 150 points earned (1point earned for 1 euro spent). They also have access to specific and personalized rewards, such as invitations to special Sephora events, a sample-sized birthday surprise, private sales with a 20 percent discount, special discounts on customers' favorite brands, special gifts, updated information on the latest in beauty innovation, and personalized offers based on customers' skin type or makeup style.

574   SECTION V   Cases

The Gold Card, which is the premium-level program, is dedicated to customers who purchase a minimum of 1500€ a year. In addition to the Black Card benefits, Sephora Gold customers get access to exclusive private sales, a full-sized birthday gift of the customer's choice either in-store or online, free shipping on Sephora's website, free access to the Sephora's in-store Beauty Bar once a month (customers get made-up and advised by Sephora's specially trained salespeople), an e-newsletter with exclusive beauty news, a special telephone line, a dedicated in-store salesperson or personal shopper, and access to the Sephora Gold boutique, where they can choose among several limited-edition Sephora Gold gifts in exchange for 1000 points. Since 2012, Gold Card holders must purchase a minimum of 700€ to re-qualify. If they drop below 700€, they receive the Black Card instead.

Sources: http://hittingpan.tumblr.com/post/4962507405/7-reasons-for-joining-sephoras-beauty-insider; http://savingslifestyle.com/2010/08/sephora-beauty-insider-rewards/; www.sephora.fr; www.sephora.com; Astrid de Montbeillard, "Sephora," *Relation Customer Magazine* 86 (April 1, 2010), www.relationcustomermag.fr/Relation-Customer-Magazine/Article/SEPHORA-37070-1.htm.

This case was written by Sandrine Heitz-Spahn, ICN Business School, and Nancy France and Michael Levy, Babson College.

DISCUSSION QUESTIONS

1. Identify the benefits for a company to implement a loyalty program.

2. What are the design characteristics of an effective loyalty program?

3. What are the benefits of having a tiered loyalty program such as Sephora's?

4. Describe Sephora's loyalty program design characteristics in both countries. What are the main differences? Which loyalty program is most effective at developing customer loyalty? Why?

5. Are both Sephora's French and American premium programs worth what they spend to reward customers? Why do both programs have a limited time validity and a specific requirement regarding the amount spent per year?

6. Could the premium loyalty program implemented in France be adapted to the U.S. market? Explain.

The country's second-largest retailer, Minneapolis-based Target, has been an innovator in structuring retail partnerships that offer customers something special: fashion-forward housewares and apparel at prices they can afford. In addition to its Target.com website, the company operates nearly 1,800 stores in 49 states, along with 37 distribution centers nationally and a separate headquarters location in India. Apparel and accessories account for approximately 20 percent of Target's annual sales.

Similar to its more standardized rivals Walmart and Kmart, Target offers the vast breadth of a full-line discount store, featuring everything from cosmetics to baby clothes, housewares to electronics. But Target also has uniquely positioned itself through a series of exclusive partnerships with top designers, such as Michael Graves and Isaac Mizrahi, who have collaborated with the retailer to offer limited-edition, distinctive products. Although other retailers also have developed relationships with designers to create exclusive brands—such as

Kohl's Simply Vera line from designer Vera Wang, which accounted for 50 percent of its apparel sales in 2010—those competitors have struggled to maintain their lower prices.

Thus, though it is not alone in partnering with designers, Target appears to be the best practitioner of this strategy. The company launched its first retail partnership in 1999 with renowned architect Michael Graves, whose teakettles and toasters were hailed for having brought the word "design" back to the housewares category. Since then, the company has worked with more than 80 design partners who have generally welcomed the chance to reach a mass market with their exclusive labels.

Most of the partnerships have been limited to a specific time, which also has built a sense of urgency and exclusivity around the offers. Target's 2011 holiday offerings featured a number of designer labels: Harajuku Mini kids' clothing from designer Gwen Stefani, hats from Albertuse Swanepoel, and a jewelry line featuring designs by Dana Kellin. Whether time-limited or longer term, such partnerships have consistently offered high-profile labels at moderate prices, helping the retailer boost its bottom line.

Target's collaboration with Missoni made a splash. The fashion world was stunned when the Italian fashion house agreed to create a collection for Target. The big American retail store is the diametric opposite of the high-end shops that have typically carried Missoni's expensive knitwear and apparel. Target's announcement through Facebook, other social media sites, and a Manhattan pop-up shop for fashion editors, celebrities, and other Missoni clientele helped stoke public excitement.

Of course, such excitement can cause problems as well. Target's website crashed just moments after the Missoni launch, as customers clicked in droves to buy up the designer duds. Although the site remained up when Jason Wu (the designer of Michelle Obama's famous 2010 inaugural gown) released his line, many stores reported nearly immediate stockouts. Customers in a Miami store watched in shock and dismay as one couple swooped in and purchased the entire selection that was on the retail floor.

Although Target learned from its Missoni mistakes, it encountered a new set of problems in 2012. Collaborating with Neiman Marcus, both stores simultaneously introduced several lines of products for the 2012 holiday season. The collection included items from designers such as Marc Jacobs, Oscar de la Renta, and Diane Von Furstenberg. Although it expected popularity similar to its Missoni products, the opposite actually occurred, with prices needing to be marked down as much as 70 percent to get rid of the merchandise. What were the problems? The designers, perhaps trying to protect the image of their brand, released products that were not what they were known for; Tory Burch made thermoses and Diane von Furstenberg made yoga mats. Also, Target may have overpriced its market, offering scarves for as much as $70. Taken together, Target lost sight of its mass-market appeal.

Now, Target has created a new model for retail partnerships as a way to offer its shoppers something different. Through a store-inside-a-store initiative that it has dubbed The Shops at Target, the retailer is partnering directly with small specialty shops and boutiques to offer their limited-edition merchandise, from dog biscuits to vintage furniture, at prices ranging from $1.99 to $159.99.

The store-within-a-store, with dedicated space branded by the designer, has already proven a successful strategy elsewhere. Macy's has Ralph Lauren boutiques; Bloomingdale's has Chanel boutiques; JCPenney, a close Target competitor, also hosts Sephora boutiques and other designer brands.

The Shops at Target collaboration is being rolled out as a series of six-week partnerships. For its first round, which was launched in 2012, the retailer chose five independently owned specialty shops—The Candy Store; the Cos Bar cosmetic shop; Polka Dog Bakery; the Privet House home accessories shop; and The Webster, a high-end Miami clothing store—all getting their first crack at a national market through Target's nearly 1,800 locations, not to mention its website. Target plans to repeat the program subsequently with new sets of boutiques, but the initial group alone will add nearly 400 new and exclusive products to Target's online and store inventories.

Target shoppers thus have come to expect a steady stream of exclusive new designer brands, along with the constant possibility of finding something unique, even unpredictable, in the next aisle over. Now the big merchandiser is hoping to keep that excitement going with its new specialty-shop partnerships. The question going forward will be whether Target—the store loyal customers have dubbed "Tarzhay" for its supply of "cheap chic"—can keep its steady customers coming back, while attracting more shoppers with new rounds of boutique surprises.

This case was written by Laurie Covens, Michael Levy, Dhruv Grewal, and Scott Motyka, all of Babson College.

Sources; Target.com, "Corporate Overview," http://pressroom.target.com/pr/news/corporate-overview.aspx; Jessica Wohl, "Target Hopes Exclusive Designer Deals Boost Sales," *Reuters*, August 2, 2011; Mary Catherine O'Connor, "Target Shoppers: Say Goodbye to Michael Graves' Budget-Friendly Design," *smartplanet*, February 16, 2012; Target.com, "Target Unveils New Design Partnership Program," January 13, 2012; Emanualla Grinberg, "'Missoni for Target' Line Crashes Site," *CNN.com*, September 13, 2011; "Jason Wu for Target Apparel Sells Out in Hours," *ABCNews.com*, February 6, 2012; Ashley Lutz, "Why Target's Neiman Marcus Collaboration was a Horrible Flop," *Business Insider*, January 3, 2013.

DISCUSSION QUESTIONS

1. Assess the role of consumer expectations in Target's success as a major discount retailer.

2. What differentiates Target's new retail partnership model from its longstanding partnerships with top designers? What are the relative strengths of each?

3. What explains Target's ability to attract top designers and high-end specialty shops as retail partners?

CASE 23   American Furniture Warehouse Sources Globally

The year 1975 saw the tail end of a recession that came on the heels of the 1973 Arab oil embargo, the fall of Saigon, and the resignation of Richard Nixon. That same year, Jake Jabs took over the American Furniture Company in Denver, Colorado, renamed it American Furniture Warehouse (AFW), and started turning it into a high-volume discount home furnishings retailer. Jabs responded to concerns that resonated with consumers in a tough economy: tighter pocketbooks, job insecurity, rising energy costs, a growing number of households as baby boomers branched out, and greater receptivity to generic products. Jabs was an experienced furniture retailer and had operated his own furniture manufacturing concern. Unbeknownst to Jabs at the time, global sourcing would become a more prominent way for his company to stock its showrooms.

Fast-forward to the present. Consumers' tastes change at a faster clip. They have higher standards than ever, and they demand bargains. As an inherently frugal man, Jake Jabs loves to give the public good value while keeping overhead low.

Jabs is the CEO, but he employs no executives. No titles of vice president or executive vice president are anywhere in sight. The company is family-owned and is not beholden to stockholders demanding that high profit margins or quarterly objectives be met. Without pressure from such entities, AFW has continued to grow and thrive. Jake Jabs obsessively trolls for ideas on how to keep prices low, quality high, and merchandise current.

People from all over the western United States visit AFW's megastores. They are intrigued with the values and constantly ask that AFW open a showroom near them. To date, AFW has preferred to remain a regional player. Its buys are based on the preferences and trends of Colorado customers.

Some of the many tenets to which AFW subscribes include striving to offer the lowest prices and the best guarantee, employing a no-pressure sales staff, having the best displays and selection, employing a careful delivery staff that works seven days a week, providing outstanding product information and customer service, and repairing merchandise on site rather than shipping anything back to the manufacturer.

In the 38 years AFW has been operating, it has forged strong vendor relationships worldwide. In fact, AFW sources goods from 30 different countries. Its major trading partners include Malaysia, Indonesia, China, Vietnam, and Mexico. It has a buying office in Asia. Its reputation has matured to the point where vendors travel up to 250 miles to bring samples to a foreign AFW buying office. AFW's small buying staff maximizes its time by having vendors come to buyers at specified dates and times; buyers no longer have to make arduous trips through countries such as China. Instead, they spend their time efficiently visiting stateside wholesale market centers and trade shows and working out of the AFW buying offices the majority of the time.

One of the dilemmas AFW has been grappling with centers around setting guidelines under which it will make time to see a new vendor. AFW's reputation is well known, and vendors clamor to get appointments with Jabs and his team on their limited market and trade show visits.

Many factories in developing countries have lower cost structures than those closer to home, often due to less stringent government regulations, lower pay, and fewer benefits for workers. Foreign factories often specialize in manufacturing one or two items well rather than constantly changing what product is on the assembly line, as is often the case in the United States. The one- or two-line process is less flexible but more cost-effective.

Because AFW sells so much, it is able to buy in volume. It directly imports full containers of merchandise. Its buying staff travel the world looking for the best deals. As a result, buyers are often able to negotiate prices 30 to

60 percent less than competitors' prices for comparable merchandise. This is due in part to the size of the order and the manner in which it is shipped. AFW sometimes pays in advance to get a better price, and it has a policy of always paying on time—a value factories respect and reward. Jake Jabs is exploring other ways in which AFW can differentiate itself in the buying process.

An example of how AFW has applied creative problem solving to reduce cost unfolds through its decision to build its own chairs, saving dramatically on freight costs. A garden-variety hardwood dinette chair can be manufactured abroad and the pieces assembled at AFW for much less than the cost if it were shipped already assembled. Typically, 1000 assembled dinette chairs fit in a standard-size container. AFW buys 4000 identical chairs in pieces and fits them in that same container. It pays its domestic workers roughly $2 per chair to assemble them and can sell each chair at retail for less than what other retailers pay for the same chair at wholesale.

Yet another manifestation of its creative solutions to cost-reduction: AFW takes delivery on blanket-wrapped merchandise rather than carton-wrapped. Not only are the blankets reusable, but not putting the merchandise in cartons in the first place can save as much as 5 percent on the total purchase price. Once merchandise arrives at one of two distribution centers, it is placed into storage and samples are immediately shipped to the showrooms.

AFW makes it a policy not to return merchandise to a factory. If something is broken, its staff of 120 trained service technicians can repair just about any furniture problem they may encounter, often for pennies. Because of its no-return policy, if it makes a buying error, AFW will mark down the item and not repurchase it. With no returns to process, vendors sell to AFW for up to 15 percent less than to other retailers for that reason alone.

Artisans in Mexico make and sell accessories to AFW by the truckload. Recently, the accessories buyer was in Mexico at the invitation of the Mexican government. She was advising a group of artisans on what to create to appeal to the Colorado market. Because AFW buys items in bulk, it saves up to 50 percent over what competitors pay for similar items. Jake Jabs would like to replicate this sort of activity in other product categories in other countries. He is pondering the best way to do this.

AFW takes chances on new, upstart vendors that other retailers may not have discovered. There are risks and rewards to this strategy, but AFW has found the rewards outweigh the risks, on balance.

Sources: Jake Jabs, *An American Tiger: An Autobiography* (Denver, CO: 2000); conversation with Jake Jabs, October 9, 2009, in Parker, CO.

This case was written by Lexi Hutto, The Metropolitan State College of Denver.

DISCUSSION QUESTIONS

1. Factories in many developing nations have lower cost structures, but that is often attributable to fewer benefits and lower wages for workers. What are the ethical trade-offs for retailers and shoppers when merchandise is sourced from countries where

labor practices fall short of standards Americans deem acceptable? Do shoppers really care about workers halfway across the globe, or are they more concerned about how many dollars are flowing out of their own pockets?

2. The world is our marketplace. AFW employs global sourcing, uses many negotiating tactics and shifts channel tasks to keep its costs as low as possible.

Enumerate the tactics AFW uses to keep its prices low. What other strategies and tactics could a furniture retailer use to hold the line on retail prices?

3. What criteria should AFW use when deciding whether to see a new vendor? How might it apply some of its best practices with its biggest vendors to new, smaller vendors? What strategies or innovations could it employ to stretch the productivity of its buying staff?

CASE 24   Are Customers Addicted to Sales at JCPenney?

BRIEF HISTORY OF JCPENNEY

JCPenney (JCP), is a mid-market department store that sells men's, women's, and children's clothing along with home furnishings. Founded by James Cash Penney in the early 1900s in Kemmerer, Wyoming, JCPenney was originally called the Golden Rule store. The bedrock of Mr. Penney's business philosophy was to treat customers fairly and honestly by following the Golden Rule: Do unto others as you would have them do unto you.

Penney's philosophy and innovative merchandising practices quickly led to success. By 1971, JCPenney operated more than 2,000 stores throughout the United States and had annual revenues in excess of $5 billion. JCPenney was a pioneer in developing store-branded merchandise. Store brands grew to include Towncraft, a men's sportswear line; St. John's Bay, a line of casual men's and women's clothing; as well as Worthington, a line of women's dress shoes.

CHANGING RETAIL LANDSCAPE

By the 1990s, however, several competitors had encroached on JCPenney's mid-market position, including Macy's, Kohl's, Target, and Walmart. Target had successfully pursued the young adult market with its cheap but chic positioning, and Kohl's had positioned itself as the affordable alternative to upscale department stores by offering name-brand merchandise at reasonable prices. Competitors' success took a heavy toll on JCPenney's sales, and by 2012, the number of JCPenney stores had been pared to 1100.

The Great Recession that began in 2007 also bruised JCPenney. Annual revenue dropped from $19.9 billion in 2007 to $17.3 billion in 2011. During the same four-year span, earnings dropped from $1.1 billion to a net loss of $152 million. These losses caused JCPenney's stock to slide and facilitated the shuttering of its catalog channel.

NEW MANAGEMENT, DRASTIC CHANGES

In June 2011, because of lackluster sales, JCPenney's board of directors fired CEO Myron Ullman III and replaced him with Ron Johnson, a former Apple executive, who had also served as the head of merchandising for Target. Johnson assumed office in November 2011.

Upon analyzing JCPenney's operations, Johnson uncovered some very sobering facts: Close to three-quarters of JCPenney's merchandise was sold at a discount of 50 percent or more. Johnson's team also discovered that JCPenney had run more than 590 sales in 2011, significantly driving up operating expenses and eroding maintain markup. Yet, these deep discounts and heavy promotions were not yielding strong customer loyalty. Johnson analyzed the data, which revealed that the average JCPenney customer made only four purchases a year, which clearly indicated Penney's hi-low pricing was not delivering a high frequency yield among its customers. The second quarter 2011 sales and margins numbers were showing tepid growth at best, or trending negatively. Second quarter 2011 comparable stores sales increased a mere 1.5 percent over second quarter 2010 sales. Penney's gross margin trend painted a very distressing picture, decreasing from 32.4 percent in second quarter 2010 to 31.8 percent in 2011. In contrast, during the same second quarter 2011, Kohl's comparable store sales rose 1.9 percent. More importantly, Kohl's second quarter 2011 gross margin rose to 40.7 percent. In a nutshell, Penney's business model was failing because customers were purchasing relatively infrequently; and when they did purchase, the merchandise was heavily discounted.

To assist him in turning JCPenney's operations around, Johnson hired Michael Francis, the chief marketing officer for Target, to be JCPenney's president. Francis was viewed as one of the architects of Target's popular, hip image.

On January 5, 2012, Johnson and Frances announced their blueprint for turning JCPenney's operations around. At the core of their new strategy was a radical departure from JCPenney's previous practice of heavy discounting and special event pricing. Instead, sales would be replaced with "Fair and Square" pricing that revolved around three core tactics: one "fair" price that would reflect a minimum 40 percent discount from the previous, nondiscounted price; a month-long "value" price, where selected merchandise would be discounted up to 30 percent for an entire month; and lastly, a final "best" price that would be available on the first and third Friday of every month that reflected a discount of up to 40 percent on the "fair" price.

In addition to the radical change in JCPenney's pricing strategy, Johnson and Francis unveiled new merchandising and store layout plans to be implemented in JCPenney stores over the next four years. Basically, the stores would be redesigned around the "Town Square" theme, where each store would have a centralized Town Square

Courtesy of JCPenney.

reminiscent of the Apple Stores' "Genius" bars where customers learn about new products. Also, stores would be remodeled into the store-in-store layout, where different brand shops, like Liz Claiborne, would have dedicated space within the store. A new red-square logo with the letters JCP in the upper-left-hand corner was unveiled to emphasize the "fair and square" pricing theme. Johnson saw JCPenney's new positioning as a return to Mr. Penney's original emphasis on treating customers fairly and following the Golden Rule.

FALL OUT AND BACKPEDALING

Despite an initial jump in JCPenney stock upon hearing the shift in pricing strategy, the numbers quickly told another story: The new strategy did not resonate with consumers. Not only did the "Fair and Square Deal" approach appear to be failing, but it seemed to be driving JCPenney's customers into the competition's stores (see Exhibit 1).

EXHIBIT 1

Q1 Performance for JCPenney and Its Major Competitors (February to April 2012)

	Net Sales (in billions)	Percentage Change versus Q1 2011	Comparable Sales Percentage versus Q1 2011
JCPenney	$3.15	−20.1%	−18.9%
Kohl's	$4.2	1.9	0.2
Target	$16.87	5.9	5.3
Macy's	$6.14	4.3	4.4
TJ Maxx	$5.8	11	8

Data Source: "J.C Penney: Reinventing Fair and Square Deals," Darden Business Publishing.

EXHIBIT 2

Q2 Performance for JCPenney and Its Major Competitors (May to July 2012)

	Net Sales (in billions)	Percentage Change versus Q2 2011	Comparable Sales Percentage versus Q2 2011
JCPenney	$3.02	−22.6%	−21.7%
Kohl's	$4.2	−1	−2.7
Target	$16.45	3.5	3.1
Macy's	$6.11	3	3

Data Sources: Company profile data and SEC filings.

JCPenney's second quarter 2012 financial performance was even poorer with weaker overall and comparable store sales, while its competitors, with the exception of Kohl's, seem to be faring much better (see Exhibit 2).

One casualty of the initially weak performance of the "Fair and Square" concept was Michael Francis, who abruptly resigned from his position in June 2012. Despite the rocky start of "Fair and Square," Johnson sent an e-mail to JCPenney customers in August 2012 that basically reiterated the positives of the "Fair and Square" model and indicated that there would be no shift in strategy.

As 2012 progressed, it became apparent that "Fair and Square" in its original version was no longer a viable pricing strategy. Third quarter 2012 sales results resulted in even more losses for JCPenney, falling an alarming $1.1 billion versus third quarter 2011, from $4.0 billion to $2.9 billion. This resulted in a net loss of $203 million for third quarter 2012 versus net earnings of $38 million in third quarter 2011. Analysts were not optimistic about fourth quarter 2012 sales either, predicting that for 2012, annual sales would have dropped a total of $4 billion, or nearly 23 percent.

In August, 2012, six months after the initial "Fair and Square" launch, the month-long price reduction initiative was terminated with Johnson claiming it was too confusing for shoppers. However, the real reversal of "Fair and Square" began in earnest in January 2013, when JCPenney announced that it was going to commence running sales again. Although claiming sales would be far less frequent than prior to the launch of "Fair and Square," Johnson, citing competitive reasons, did not reveal how many sales would be run. Johnson refused to label this shift in strategy as a retreat from "Fair and Square" but described it as an "evolution." At the same time, Johnson restated that JCPenney would not resume the practice of distributing coupons.

Concurrent with the decision to reinstate sales, JCPenney management decided to implement reference pricing by adding new MSRP price tags to more than half its merchandise. Designed to reinforce savings and perceived value to the customer, reference pricing has long been a staple in deep discount chains, such as TJ Maxx and Marshall's.

So are customers addicted to sales? JCPenney would say that they definitely are. In an unfortunate conclusion to the "fair and square" pricing experiment, JCPenney's stock price dropped 44% in 2012, and as a result, Johnson stepped down as CEO in April 2013. His replacement? Former CEO Mike Ullman.

Sources: Paul Farris and Sylvie Thompson, "J.C. Penney: Reinventing Fair and Square Deals", Case Study, Darden Business Publishing, July 20, 2012; http://xfinity.comcast.net/slideshow/finance-companiesneverrecover/10/; Oliver St. John, "Ron Johnson Steps Down as CEO of Troubled J.C. Penney," *USA Today*, April 10, 2013; Meredith Galante, "How Ron Johnson Plans to Transform JC Penney into 'America's Favorite Store,'" *Businessinsider.com*, January 26, 2012; http://biz.yahoo.com/e/11097/jcp10-q.html; http://finance.yahoo.com/news/Kohls-Earnings-Cheat-Sheet-wscheats-1451845985.html; Farris and Thompson, "J.C. Penney: Reinventing Fair and Square Deals"; Ibid; JCPenney, "A Letter from our CEO" (e-mail), August 6, 2012; Loeb, Walter, "J.C, Penney—Ugly Results Leave More Doubt for 2013", www.forbes.com/sites/walterloeb/2012/11/09 (accessed February 11, 2013); "J.C. Penney Sales Are Back," www.cbsnews.com, January 28, 2013 (accessed February 11, 2013); Ibid.

This case was written by Virginia Weiler, University of Southern Indiana.

DISCUSSION QUESTIONS

1. What environmental factors contributed to JCPenney's "Fair and Square" launch?

2. What were some alternative pricing strategies that Johnson might have considered besides "Fair and Square"?

3. Why did "Fair and Square" fail to connect with JCPenney's existing customers? Why have many retailers retreated from EDLP?

4. Was JCPenney attempting to attract a new customer? If so, describe.

5. What steps could JCPenney have taken, if any, to have increased the chances of success for "Fair and Square"?

CASE 32   Zipcar: Delivering Only as Much Driving as You Want

The expectation that your car will be waiting at the curb every morning got hard-wired into many Americans, with the growth of the auto industry. But that expectation has gone haywire for many city dwellers, who have been frustrated by the soaring costs and parking pressures that confront modern drivers. For them, Zipcar, the world's leading car-sharing company, offers the pleasure of driving without the hassles of ownership.

The Cambridge, Massachusetts–based company rents self-service vehicles by the hour or day to urban residents who prefer to pay for just as much driving as they abso-

lutely need. Car sharing eliminates issues related to parking shortages; overnight parking restrictions; or soaring gas, insurance, and tax bills. That promise resonates well with consumer expectations on many fronts, especially among Zipcar's primary urban customers, the large segments of college students who also enjoy the service, and even suburbanites who just work in the city.

Still the company's biggest growth obstacle may be Americans' inability to envision life without a car. To push an attitude shift, Zipcar makes the car-sharing experience as easy as possible, with just four simple steps:

1. Join the network.
2. Reserve your car online or from your smartphone.
3. Unlock the car with your Zipcard.
4. Drive away.

Today the car-sharing network offers more than 30 makes and models of cars, and has more than 767,000 members and 10,000 vehicles in major metropolitan areas and college campuses throughout the United States, Canada, United Kingdom, Spain, and Austria. With so many locations, the company could bring convenient car sharing to a far larger market; it estimates that 10 million residents, business commuters, and university students now live or work just a short walk away from an available Zipcar.

Zipcar also is banking on more than shifting attitudes. Emerging trends due to the economic downturn and changing buying habits have helped spur growth. On average, automobiles consume 19 percent of household incomes, yet many cars stand idle for 90 percent of each day. Drivers seeking a less expensive and less wasteful alternative thus might save up to 70 percent on their transportation costs, because an annual Zipcar membership costs just $60, and the average member spends $428 a year.

Zipcar's service model also fits in with the emergence of on-demand, pay-per-use options, such as Netflix for movies, iTunes for music, and e-readers for books. Moreover, the popularity of mobile shopping and the growing expectation that they can order anything, anywhere, anytime from their smartphone have made urban young adults and college students two of Zipcar's most fervent member groups. For these "Zipsters," ordering up a set of wheels on the go is far more appealing than being saddled with car payments.

A strong urban public transportation system also helps make car sharing more attractive. That's why Zipcar started off in high-density urban areas such as Boston, New York, and Washington, DC, with their great public transportation systems already in place. Wherever subways and buses work, car sharing can extend the transit system's reach. By locating cars near transit route endpoints, travelers gain an easy extension on subway or bus schedules to their final destinations.

Finally, the logic of car sharing works well in settings marked by increased urbanization. According to the United Nations, cities will contain 59 percent of the world's population by 2030. Many of these areas already face congestion, space demands, and environmental threats from crowding too many gas-driven vehicles into a small, population-dense space. Zipcar CEO Scott Griffith estimates that every Zipcar would replace 15 to 20 personal cars. Thus, some cities even work with Zipcar to identify and secure parking spaces close to subway stops and rail stations. New York and Chicago also rent Zipcars for municipal workers so they can shuttle more efficiently across city locations during their workday. Zipcar also provides fleet management services to local, state, and federal agencies.

Car sharing could translate into a $10 billion market globally. Cities in Europe and Asia are well primed for car sharing by virtue of their strong rail systems, heavy reliance on public transit, and widespread adoption of mobile and wireless technologies. A deal with Spain's largest car-sharing company, Avancar, is a first venture in Zipcar's planned global expansion.

Such growth requires strong logistics, and Zipcar is backed by a corps of fleet managers and vehicle coordinators who track, schedule, and oversee vehicle maintenance; proprietary hardware and software technology that helps it communicate with drivers and track vehicles; and a large fleet that includes hybrid vehicles for fuel efficiency, as well as minivans to appeal to families who want to take a trip to the beach. Zipcar estimates that it processes 2.6 million reservations per year, and its reservation system has almost never failed.

These behind-the-scenes moves aim to make Zipcar's service simple, convenient, and reliable. But failures are inevitable, as one customer's experience showed. The customer went to pick up his designated vehicle at the time and place reserved for him, but he discovered no car there. The Zipcar representative told him that it might be out, being serviced or cleaned, or it could have been delayed by another driver running late. But such excuses did little to alleviate the frustration of being stuck with no transportation.

Learning of his predicament, Zipcar tried but was unable to find another car in close proximity. Therefore, it quickly authorized the customer to take a taxi and promised to reimburse him up to $100. Although the "free ride" did not altogether mitigate the stress and inconvenience of the service failure, Zipcar's response showed him that the company was committed to doing right by him, even if that meant sending business to a competitor, the taxi company.

The considerable dimensions of a global car-sharing market are already emerging. Zipcar's 10-year experience and first-mover position in the market positions it well to compete. But the race to dominate is sure to intensify, especially as traditional car rental companies with great name recognition, such as Hertz and Enterprise, move into the marketplace. Whether Zipcar can maintain its space in this market depends mostly on its ability to meet its own standards for customer service—simplicity, convenience, and reliability—consistently and effectively.

This case was written by Laurie Covens, Dhruv Grewal and Michael Levy, both at Babson College.

Sources: www.zipcar.com; April Kilcrease, "A Conversation with Zipcar's CEO Scott Griffith," *GigaOM*, December 5, 2011, U.S. Securities and Exchange Commission, "Zipcar S-1 Filing," June 1, 2010; JP Morgan SMid Cap Conference, December 11, 2011; Courtney Rubin, "How Will the IPO Market Treat Zipcar?" *Inc.com*, June 2, 2010.

DISCUSSION QUESTIONS

1. Using the five dimensions of service quality (reliability, assurance, tangibility, empathy, and responsiveness), evaluate Zipcar.

2. Compare Zipcar's service quality performance with that of the most recent car rental service (e.g., Avis, Hertz) that you may have used.

3. How well has Zipcar handled service failure situations? What could it do to improve recovery efforts?

CASE 33 Building the Apple Store

Founded in 1976 by the late Steve Jobs and Steve Wozniak, Apple has become an innovative leader in the consumer electronics industry. In addition to offering traditional desktop and laptop computers, Apple essentially founded the digital music player market when it introduced the iPod and online music store markets with iTunes; launched easy-to-use iPhones and iPads with increasingly more features; and introduced online movie/TV services through AppleTV and publishing and multimedia software.

BEFORE APPLE RETAIL STORES

During the early 1990s, Apple struggled as computer sales began shifting from specialized computer stores to mainstream retail stores. Big-box retailers such as Best Buy and Circuit City could offer a wider selection of computers at lower prices, although they lacked adequate customer service and support. These big-box retailers and specialized stores faced even more competition in the form of mail-order outlets, including CompuAdd, Gateway, and Dell.

Beginning in 1990, Dell shifted from selling its computers in warehouse and specialized computer stores to operating as an online direct mail-order company. Dell facilitated its online operations with an efficient online store that could handle high-volume sales. The online Dell store (dell.com) represented a new strategy for manufacturing: Computers were built as they were ordered. In turn, Dell could reduce inventory because it no longer produced computers in mass quantities and then pushed inventory through the channel to resellers.

While establishing its online store, Apple needed to balance its direct orders with the sales initiated by its channel partners, mail-order resellers, independent dealers, and CompUSA, with which it initiated a "stores within stores" strategy to focus on Apple's products. Apple's partnership with CompUSA paid off. When the San Francisco CompUSA store was equipped with Macs, Apple's sales jumped from 15 to 35 percent of overall store sales.

Apple also put its own employees to work in various retail outlets to help inform and educate customers, as well as ensure its products were being displayed in working order. The company estimated it spent between $25,000 and $75,000 per month on this initiative. Apple executives soon realized they could not compete with PC brands by selling just laptops and desktops in big-box retail stores because retailers could earn greater profits by selling lower-quality PC models. They had little to no incentive to sell Macs. Without its own retail store, Apple would always be at the mercy of the independent dealers and partners that operated with different strategic goals.

DESIGNING THE APPLE STORE

To compete with the PCs sold by big-box retailers, Apple needed to shift from selling its electronics through intermediaries to offering products directly through Apple stores. This shift would not come easily. Steve Jobs, Apple's dynamic founder, first looked to bring in new executives. Mickey Drexler, former CEO of The Gap and now CEO of J.Crew, was hired in 1999 as part of Apple's board of directors. Next, Jobs brought in Ron Johnson, who had been a merchandising executive with Target, to run Apple's retail division as vice president of retail operations.

Instead of launching stores from the start, Drexler suggested that Jobs rent a warehouse and build a prototype store, coined Apple Store Version 0.0. Apple executives then continuously redesigned the store until they achieved a layout that would entice shoppers to not only enter, but make purchases. The first store prototype was configured by product category, with hardware laid out according to the internal organization of the company rather than by how customers logically shop. Executives quickly decided to redesign the store to match customer interests better. Although the redesign cost Apple more than six months, the executives believed this time investment was necessary to achieve a successful store that could compete with well-established electronics retailers and remain consistent with the Apple brand. Its first store opened in Tyson's Corner, Virginia, in May 2001.

THE APPLE STORE LAYOUT

When considering a site for a retail store, Apple uses its customer base to forecast visitor volume and revenues. Most Apple stores locate within existing shopping malls or lifestyle centers, where retail traffic is already present. There are two types of full-size stores: a street-facing building or an in-mall store. The stores range from 3,600 to 20,000 square feet, although most fall in the 3,000- to 6,000-square-feet range. Storefronts are typically all glass with a backlit Apple logo, and the front display windows change occasionally to focus on the newest marketing campaign. Apple's internal team designs the window displays, often using slot and cable systems to suspend design elements within the window. In some cases, the swinging entrance doors are in the middle, but in other stores, a logo wall appears in the middle with two doors located on either side. Store interiors feature only three materials: glass, stainless steel, and wood.

In addition to the retail floor, Apple stores have backroom areas that sometimes include a public restroom, offices, and the inventory area. At some sites that lack sufficient space, inventory storage is located at a separate facility, always within walking distance.

The store layout changes multiple times throughout the year. Apple executives organize planograms to coincide with the introduction of new products or heavily marketed merchandise. The layouts depend on the size of the store. A typical in-mall store locates merchandise in the front half of the store and customer service and support areas in the rear. Apple stores carry fewer than 20 products, and every display piece is available for hands-on use so that customers can get an accurate feel for the available hardware and software.

On tables along the right wall, iPhones and iPods take up the front half of the store. Along the left wall, tables hold various models of general and high-end desktop and laptop computers. These displays give way to The Studio, a newer section hosted by experts who will answer application-oriented, creative questions. Two to three island tables in the front center display software on Apple computers; additional island tables exhibit peripherals such as iPod docking stations and printers. A small children's area houses Apple computers running children's software. The Genius Bar takes up the back wall, with stools before a counter staffed with Apple experts for repairs and consultations. Larger stores also have a theater area in the back, featuring a rear-projection screen with an audience area of either U-shaped wooden benches or full theater seats in rows. This store layout is typical for a store located in a super-regional mall.

Apple stores thus follow a free-form layout, which allows customers to browse the store according to their own interests. Signage hanging from the ceiling, for greater visibility, directs customers to specific areas within the store. Bright lighting draws attention to merchandise and creates a sense of excitement. Highlighted merchandise also helps draw customers strategically through the store. As customers browse the products, employees wearing Apple T-shirts and lanyards make themselves available to answer any questions.

Through its intensive development efforts, Apple has created a unique, customer service–oriented shopping experience. Customers can schedule face-to-face appointments at an Apple store to test-drive products. One-to-one personal training sessions help customers become familiar with the array of Apple products. The company also offers free one-hour instructional or informational workshops every day for iPod, iPhone, and Mac owners. It also offers support for business customers by providing insight and advice about how to create a presentation from start to finish using Apple products.

Sources: Philip Elmer-Dewitt, "Apple Ranks No. 4 in E-Retailing Survey," *Fortune*, May 5, 2010; Daniel Eran, "Apple's Retail Challenge," *RDM*, November 8, 2006; "The Stores," *IfoAppleStore.com*; Jerry Useem, "Apple: America's Best Retailer," *Fortune*, March 8, 2007.

This case was written by Brienne Curley, while an MBA student at Loyola College in Maryland, under the supervision of Hope Corrigan.

DISCUSSION QUESTIONS

1. Have you ever visited an Apple store? If yes, did you make a purchase? Why or why not?

2. Why are Apple's store layout and atmosphere important?

3. Is Apple America's best retailer?

4. Visit your local Apple store. Does the layout of the store help to provide you with an excellent customer experience? Explain.

CASE 34   Generating Advertising Revenue from a Digital Screen Network at Harrods of London

Retailers have slowly been implementing digital screen networks. In most instances, the messages are focused on branding and affecting the customer shopping experience. Very few networks, like Walmart's SMART Network and, to a lesser extent, Target's Channel Red, have also been able to generate a stream of advertising revenue. In the department store category, Harrods is the only high-end luxury store to successfully sell advertising on its in-store digital signage network. Factors such as a solid and consistent customer base and the store's unique environment have contributed to the success of the signage.

It is difficult to imagine any retail environment as unique as Harrods. It is a key destination for millions of visitors who come to the United Kingdom every year (it is the UK's third-largest tourist attraction). It houses the world's finest luxury brands across a million square feet of retail space. It has a history dating back to 1849 and can count the rich and famous from all corners of the globe as its customers. The brand is synonymous with luxury, the "finer things in life," and a range of merchandise unequaled under one roof. Average daily traffic is 45,000 customers (occasionally rising to 100,000 on special days). Many of them are high-net-worth individuals, including royalty from around the world, as well as celebrities and billionaires.

Advertisements on the network are sold to premium brands, such as Armani and Cartier. The medium is often sold as part of an integrated marketing campaign, which often includes other media such as posters, lift-wraps (signage on elevator doors), windows, and even pages in the Harrods magazine. Combined with other in-store media, screens are an integral part of the campaign providing impact, awareness, and, often, directional signage leading customers to the "heart of the promotion"—the place where the product and the customer meet.

The specific location of each screen was carefully considered so that each customer would have a multiscreen sight line. In most cases, customers see more than one screen within their view. The same content appears simultaneously on each screen in the network, so the advertisers have high impact with their ads appearing several times at once.

In most cases, screens are positioned on the sides of escalators in the store. Unlike the case at many transport hubs, most customers in Harrods stand still on the moving steps. As they glide up to the next floor, they take in the view, which includes the digital screens. Each advertiser has a 15-second slot.

Harrods' digital screen network is managed all in-house. There is a dedicated ad sales team, an operations team, and a technical and creative team—all of whom are committed Harrods employees who live and breathe the brand. These employees believe in and are included in how and what is being marketed. They sit in the building and pass by the media that they are selling and marketing 20 times a day. They also see with their own eyes the audience that they are selling to the advertisers. They see the clothes they are wearing, the limos that deliver them to the store, and the number of Harrods' famous green bags they are carrying. They can see the impact that the screens can have on a consumer purchasing decision, or even simply see customers watching content through their Dior sunglasses as they glide up an escalator.

Network staff also have relationships with the brands and the advertisers. They have a relationship that has been nurtured and developed so that they are working "alongside" a brand to find marketing solutions to drive brand sales and awareness, which in turn benefits not only the brand, but also Harrods as a store.

The store is continuously changing, and as part of that development, additional digital screens are introduced as part of new departments and remodels. When Harrods first introduced its digital signage network, it realized that it had to do something special to integrate the screens into the environment. It didn't want screens hanging from ceilings above walkways that looked tacky, amateur, and cheap. It invested heavily in each screen installation, with customized reinforced glass, polished steel bezels, additional cooling fans, and color schemes that are consistent with the store's decor. This gave the screens a look of luxury. A lot of care, thought, and attention have been invested in each location to give the advertiser the optimum in presentation.

Harrods monitors the effectiveness of a campaign via sales data. It has some impressive results from advertisers that have enjoyed double-digit sales increases during and following a digital campaign in the store. So, the natural question is, "Well, why isn't everyone advertising on the screens?" The answer to this question involves many factors including, among other things, the following:

- The medium is new and many vendors are unfamiliar with its benefits.
- Vendors are not always sure about where the funding of digital screen ads should come from. That is, is it a marketing/advertising expenditure or an in-store promotional expenditure?

- There are creative challenges associated with messages. For instance, is the message capturing the attention of the customers? Does it have a call to action or an offer?

If there is one way to deter advertisers, then it's to have blank, malfunctioning screens. It seems obvious, but so many networks in retail lumber on with as many as 25 percent of the screens nonoperational. No wonder they find selling ads a struggle! Harrods has a "zero tolerance" strategy within the operations team, resulting in the team's touring the store every morning before the store opens checking that all is as it should be. As well, it has invested heavily in preventive maintenance contracts and has a backup stock of spare screens available should a screen die and require replacement.

Digital networks can make money for a retailer. Harrods has realized both ad sales revenue and increased sales of advertised products. However, such results take significant investments in time, resources, and money. The future success for generating advertising sales is dependent on improvements in technical reliability of the hardware and software, combined with more investment in content and creativity. Interactivity via mobile/cell phones is clearly part of the future. Harrods is investing in the latest technology, implementing new and unique content that captures people's imagination, and working alongside brands that are prepared to invest to realize the benefits.

This case was written by Steven Keith Platt, Platt Retail Institute, and Guy Cheston, Director of Advertising Sales and Sponsorship, Harrods.

DISCUSSION QUESTIONS

1. What are the reasons that Harrods has been successful at selling advertising on its digital signage network and other retailers have not? Why would consumer product manufacturers be interested in advertising on Harrods' network?

2. What are the pluses and minuses for a retailer offering a digital network in its stores?

CASE 36 PetSmart: Where Pets Are Family

PetSmart Inc. is the largest specialty pet retailer with more than 1160 brick-and-mortar pet stores in the United States and Canada. This retailer also sells products through its PetSmart website. Each store offers 10,000 products, which are sold under national brands and PetSmart's own private labels. While 89 percent of PetSmart's sales come from pet food and supplies, the service side (grooming, obedience training, boarding, etc.) of its business has been growing. Veterinary services are available in more than 750 locations. PetSmart's key competitors include Petco, Target, and Walmart.

RECENT TRENDS

In the animal-loving society of the United States, 62 percent of households, or 71.4 million homes, own pets. The resulting pet retail industry has benefited from pet owners' tendency to humanize and treat their pets like family members, which has increased industry revenues rapidly. Pet industry expenditures have almost tripled since 1994, making pet care the second fastest growing retail category, with an average annual growth rate of 9 percent. Today, U.S. pet industry expenditures are expected to exceed $47 billion.

An industry once dominated by bland pet food and basic supplies has transformed into a highly differentiated market with diverse and creative offerings, including pet fashions and accessories, gourmet pet cuisine, and even pet massages. The ever-expanding composition of the pet industry spending includes the sale of pet food, supplies, veterinary care, medicine, animal purchases, and pet services such as grooming and boarding.

PETSMART CAPITALIZES ON INDUSTRY TRENDS

A survey conducted by the Washington-based Pew Research Center found that 85 percent of pet owners called their dogs members of the family, as do 78 percent of those with cats. The study also noted that 80 percent of the owners buy holiday and birthday gifts for their pets, and nearly half of the female respondents said that they relied more on their pet's affection than on their spouse's or children's. Pet owners have become emotionally tied to their pets and, in turn, treat their pets like humans by dressing them in the latest fashions, prolonging their lives through expensive medical treatments, and buckling them into specially designed car seats.

PetSmart has taken advantage of pet humanization trends and increased revenues and profitability. Three key features mark the expanded pet retail industry: (1) increased merchandise offerings, (2) more licensing agreements for pet products, and (3) innovative pet services.

Pet ownership drives demand, and retailer profitability depends on the ability to generate store traffic. PetSmart has expanded its store offerings to include a wider range of merchandise and services to meet growing demand. A typical PetSmart store stocks 10,000 in-store products and offers an even larger variety of products online. In addition, this retailer has increased its assortment within each product category. PetSmart presently stocks a deep selection of pet foods from a large array of suppliers, including low-cost, all natural, breed-specific, preservative-free, diet, organic, and premium foods with real meats and vegetables. The company introduced a wide range of private-label brands, positioned as low-cost alternatives to national brands to provide total solutions to its customers. According to the Private Label Manufacturers Association, store brands account for 11 percent of cat food, 12 percent of dog food, 13 percent of pet supplies, and 21 percent of cat litter sales.

Consumers interested in spoiling their pet often walk into a pet store to buy and coordinate outfits for their cat or dog, with choices ranging from personalized T-shirts to dresses to water-activated cooling bandanas. Through partnerships with PetSmart, renowned companies are leveraging their own brands within the pet sector. Store aisles are lined with toys, clothing, accessories, bedding, and aquariums displaying popular cartoon characters such as SpongeBob SquarePants, Clifford the Big Red Dog, Barbie, Blues Clues, Disney, and Peanuts. In an exclusive manufacturing and marketing deal with Martha Stewart Pets, PetSmart is now offering a new line of pet apparel, bedding, grooming, and bath supplies. In addition, companies from a diverse collection of industries—such as Paul Mitchell, Polo Ralph Lauren, Harley Davidson, and Old Navy—have developed their own pet product lines. Even Jeep has released its own line of branded strollers and pet ramps for cars and trucks to attempt to profit from the endless licensing opportunities within the pet retailing industry.

In the past, pet retailers provided just the most basic products. Today, they aim to create lasting relationships with customers. The service sector of the pet retail industry has higher profit margins, so PetSmart is incorporating various service offerings into its business model, including in-store grooming, six- to eight-week obedience training sessions, and doggie day care and "Pet Hotel" boarding facilities with cozy beds and televisions airing Animal Planet programming. As a result, PetSmart's business services represents about 11 percent of its annual sales revenue. Pet service industry competitors similarly attempt to position themselves to reach a portion of the market. Doggie spas, for example, offer high-end services such as massage therapy and pedicures, while pet walking and waste pick-up services enjoy greater success within the industry.

HUMAN RESOURCES AS A BRAND STRATEGY

Through various employee development programs, PetSmart trains its employees to reinforce the firm's brand image. It hires people who love pets and thus helps provide customers with value, quality, and service. PetSmart administers a 120-hour educational program for its trainers, a six-month instructional program for its groomers, and 16 hours of role-play training before any store opens to the public. As a result, the cheerful demeanor of PetSmart employees remains consistent across the country. PetSmart's staff passionately converses with customers, asks pet-related questions, and gives recommendations. This sense of helpfulness and friendliness aligns the service staff with the company's overall brand strategy and creates an emotional connection to the brand. Well-behaved pets are allowed to shop with their owners, which creates a pleasant, comfortable, animal-loving store atmosphere that further supports brand equity.

PetSmart regularly displays highly visible corporate charity and donation-related signs for animal-related causes (spay/neuter initiatives, pet adoption programs, food for pet shelters, etc.) at its checkout counters to reinforce the company's animal-loving culture. The business made a conscious decision to encourage adoption from shelters instead of selling cats and dogs, even though sales of cats and dogs would generate higher annual revenues. The decision to encourage and facilitate adoptions is decreasing euthanization of abandoned animals. PetSmart CEO Philip Francis notes, "by the time you factor in the bed, food, a collar, a leash, a training program, a bath, and a vet appointment, this adopted dog or cat could be a $300 to $400 event for us, and could be the opportunity for a lifetime relationship with that pet and that pet parent."

This case was written by James Pope, while an MBA student at Loyola University, Maryland, and Hope Corrigan, Loyola University, Maryland.

DISCUSSION QUESTIONS

1. Using Excel, create a column graph for U.S. pet industry expenditures over time. The y-axis will be sales in billions of dollars and the x-axis will be years. Go to the American Pet Products Association Inc. for the industry statistics and trends at: http://americanpetproducts.org/press_industrytrends.asp.

2. Using Excel, create a pie graph for the most recent year of estimated U.S. pet expenditures by category. Be sure to label each pie wedge with the category name and percent value. Go to the American Pet Products Association Inc. for the industry statistics and trends at http://americanpetproducts.org/press_industrytrends.asp.

3. How can PetSmart recruit, hire, and retain the best employees to support its brand strategy, meet customer expectations, and reach sales objectives?

4. What else could PetSmart do to increase store traffic, revenues, and profitability?

5. Consider other retailers that might begin to sell a larger assortment of pet products and services. How will this competition affect PetSmart?